The Devil and the *Dolce Vita*

THE DEVIL AND THE DOLCE VITA

Catholic Attempts to Save Italy's Soul, 1948–1974

ROY DOMENICO

The Catholic University of America Press • Washington, D.C.

The paper used in this publication meets the minimum requirements of American National Standards for Information Science—Permanence of Paper for Printed Library Materials, ANSI Z39.48-1984.
∞
Cataloging-in-Publication Data available from the Library of Congress
ISBN 978-0-8132-3433-5

Contents

Acknowledgments

I have presented some of this work at various conferences in Rome, Milan, Castellammare di Stabia, Prato's Monash University campus, New York, Notre Dame, Indiana, and Chapel Hill, North Carolina. I am indebted to Margherita Repetto-Alaia, Paola Gaiotti-Biase, Guido Convents, Francesco Malgeri, Mario Casella, Peter Kent, Silvia Gavuzzo Stewart, Steven White, Giovanni Sale, SJ, Father Peter Malone, Jim Fisher, Jonathan Nashel, George Sirgiovanni, Helen Holmes, Andrew Fear, Eliana Versace, Norman Holub, and three gentlemen of recent demise who are sorely missed—Sal Rotella, David Pike, and John Naylon for conversations, correspondence, and support. Tante grazie to Mario Di Napoli, Giuliana Previti, and all of the generous souls at the Mazzini Society in Rome. In the early stages of this project, we lost the great Lamberto Mercuri, who, with his dear Vera, will always occupy a very special place in my heart.

At Scranton, students Trish Ross, Vhalla Otarod, Muzio Pierotti, Anthony Molina, and Kayla Moschetti, and our History Department administrative assistants Rosemarie Pryle, Jane Wesloski, and Jenn Kretsch provided essential help throughout the project. While I researched and wrote, colleagues in the History Department helped in a million ways, particularly three chairs who guided it and made it a great place to work: Mike DeMichele, Willis Conover, and Dave Dzurec. A thousand thanks to colleagues in our Weinberg Memorial Library, especially those in the Inter-library Loan Office—Sheila Ferraro, Magdalene Ristuccia, and Kevin Kocur. In Scranton and beyond, Lynn Berrettoni, Anthony Smith, Kelly Boyd, Robert Shaffern, Adam Pratt, Eliana Versace, and Trish Ross kindly gave of themselves to read and critique parts of this work.

University of Scranton provosts Hal Baillie and Joe Dreisbach and Dean Brian Conniff rendered persistent and much appreciated support. The University of Scranton supplied essential summer research funding, while a Senior Research Fulbright Award in 2005 and a University sabbatical in 2015 saved the day, enabling me to work in Italy for extended periods. In the United States, I had the great pleasure of collaborating with wonderful folks at the National Archives in College Park, Maryland, the Library of Congress in Washington, D.C., and libraries at Yale University, Columbia University, Rutgers University, and Seton Hall University. In Rome, I worked with very talented and helpful people at the Archivio Centrale dello Stato, the Biblioteca di storia moderna e contemporanea, the Biblioteca nazionale, the Ente dello Spettacolo's library, and the Biblioteca Fondazione Lelio e Lisli Basso; in Milan at the Archivio storico diocesano and the seminary library; and in Casale Monferrato at the Archivio Storico. I am especially grateful to Concetta Argiolas and Michela Ghera at Rome's Istituto Luigi Sturzo; Marcello Menni and Michelangelo Prena at the Fondazione Vittorino Colombo in Milan; and to Ernesto Preziosi at the Istituto Paolo VI in Rome. Special thanks also for the great people at the Catholic University of America Press—Trevor Lipscombe, Theresa Walker, Aldene Fredenburg, and Tanjam Jacobson.

As always, first and last, for inspiration and love—my wife, Robin, and our brood—Katie, John, Matt, and Clare.

Abbreviations

AC	Azione cattolica italiana
ACEC	Associazione cattolica esercenti cinema
ACLI	Associazioni cristiani dei lavoratori italiani
ACS	Archivio Centrale dello Stato, Rome
ANICA	Associazione nazionale industrie cinematografiche e affini
API	Associazioni pionieri d'Italia
AS	Archivio storico, Casale Monferrato
ASDM	Archivio storico diocesano di Milano
b	busta
CCC	Centro cattolico cinematografico
CCR	Centro cattolico radiofonico
CCT	Centro cattolico teatrale
CEI	Conferenza episcopale italiano
CIF	Centro Italiano femminile
CLN	Comitato di liberazione nazionale
CONI	Comitato olimpico nazionale italiano
CSI	Centro sportivo italiano
DC	Democrazia Cristiana
DL	Decreto legislativo/legge
DLL	Decreto legislativo luogotenenziale
EIAR	Ente italiano per le audizioni radiofoniche
f	fascicolo

FUCI	Federazione universitaria cattolica italiana
FVC	Fondazione Vittorino Colombo, Milan
GF	Gioventù femminile
GIAC	Gioventù italiana di Azione Cattolica
IPVI	Istituto Paolo VI, Rome
IS	Istituto Luigi Sturzo, Rome
M	Mazzo
MSI	Movimento sociale italiano
MTS	Ministero del Turismo e dello Spettacolo
OCIC	Office catholique internationale du cinema
ONMI	Opera nazionale maternità e infanzia
OR	*Osservatore Romano*
PCI	Partito comunista italiano
PCM	Presidenza del consiglio dei ministri
Pg	Presidenza Generale
PLI	Partito liberale italiano
PPI	Partito popolare italiano
PRI	Partito repubblicano italiano
PSI	Partito socialista italiano
PSDI	Partito socialdemocratico italiano
PWB	Psychological Warfare Branch
RAI	Radio Audizioni Italiane
RDL	Regio decreto-legge
RSI	Repubblica sociale italiano
s	sottofascicolo
sc	scatola
Sg	Segreteria generale
UCIC	Ufficio cattolico internazionale di cinema
UDACI	Unione Donne di Azione Cattolica Italiana

The Devil and the *Dolce Vita*

Introduction

Federico Fellini's iconic film *La dolce vita* concludes one early morning on a beach near Rome. The central figure, Marcello, played by Marcello Mastroianni, sits in the sand, his head muddled after an evening's debauched revels. He looks up when he hears someone calling to him from across a rivulet. It is Paolina, played by Valeria Ciangottini, an innocent and pretty teenager who works at a seaside bar recently visited by Marcello. In a modest black dress with a dainty lace collar, she can be read as a nostalgic metaphor of a fading Italy, a land of honest, generous, and devout people, the salt of the earth. In his jazzy get-up, Marcello represents the modern, self-absorbed, and cold Italy; and he fails to understand Paolina. The two cannot connect, although she tries and tries until the sad truth becomes apparent. On his side of the beach, another party-goer calls Marcello; it's time to go. He nods, gives Paolina one last look, turns, delivers a limp wave, and lumbers off. Fellini then focuses on Paolina's sad smile and follows her face as it turns from looking at Marcello until she finally gazes into the camera and at the audience, who watch for a final, painful moment before the film fades to black. Upon its release in 1960, *La dolce vita* seized the imagination of Italy and the world, not only as a brilliant work of art, but as something of a warning. Paolina's world and the souls of the good people that inhabited it were in danger.

This work discusses the cultural politics of Italian Catholics during the roughly thirty years after the Second World War. It deals with those who understood and perhaps identified with Paolina; it explores their sentiments and their efforts to renew what they saw as a traditional Catholic ethos. For much of the century and a half that preceded Fellini's film, this spirit had suffered significant challenges from an expanding "lay," or secular, culture represented across the political spectrum, from liberals and Masons to Marxists and Fascists. Much of what follows is roughly chronological, although chapters 2 and 3 offer examinations of two of the most important and closely linked battlefields of the Italian Catholic culture wars—namely, the media and family matters. This study casts light on attempts to influence or censor the media based on Catholic morality and to exalt and protect traditional familial and sexual relationships. Catholics' use of such terms as *buon costume* (proper comportment) or *pudore* (shame) revealed their attitude toward conduct at home and on the street. They took cues mostly from three leads: the church itself, the chief Catholic party, the Christian Democracy (Democrazia Cristiana, or DC), and the laymen's association, Italian Catholic Action (Azione Cattolica italiana, or AC). All three presented a vision of a revitalized Christian culture—one of proper comportment and sexual ethics—that revealed what one historian termed Italy's "strange rapport with moralism."[1]

Italian Catholics were not alone. Europe's most determined postwar effort to temper politics with religion probably occurred during Francisco Franco's dictatorship in Spain, when the church strove "to create a fortress of faith and virtue isolated from a corrupt secular world."[2] The war, of course, dampened authoritarianism and strengthened more democratic impulses in Western Europe. Among Europe's free nations, therefore, Italy tried as much as or more than any other to protect its Catholic identity, efforts made more striking in that they took place in the land of an ancient and extremely powerful church and the capital of Catholicism. West Germany, particularly under Konrad Adenauer's Christian Democratic governments from 1949 until 1963, offers the clearest analogies. Heide Fehrenbach, for instance, showed how German Catholics and the Christian Democrats labored to infuse motion pictures with their vision. Women maintained a special place in that vision, with strong echoes in the Italian case.[3] In France, the Jesuit Emmanuel Flipo's campaign to ensure a Catholic presence in film production and criticism met with failure, mostly because he enjoyed little backing from the church or from Catholic organizations. Compared to Italy, his looked like a lonely crusade.[4] Among the smaller nations, Ire-

1. Saverio Vertone, ed., *La Cultura degli italiani* (Bologna: Il Mulino, 1994), 14–15. All translations in this book are mine, unless otherwise stated.

2. William J. Callahan, *The Catholic Church in Spain, 1875–1998* (Washington, D.C.: The Catholic University of America Press, 2000), 488–89.

3. Heide Fehrenbach, *Cinema in Democratizing Germany: Reconstructing National Identity after Hitler* (Chapel Hill: University of North Carolina Press, 1995), particularly chapters 3 and 4, 92–147.

4. Mélisande Leventopoulos, "An Alternative Way of Moralizing Cinema: Father Flipo's Remedy for the Catholic Church's Propaganda Failure in France (1945–1962)," in *Moralizing Cinema: Film*

land's traditionalist Catholics put up the greatest fight against the forces of secularization, much of which backfired and fizzled in the new millennium. In non-Catholic Europe, Britain sometimes looked similar to Italy. The Church of England and government officials, like the home secretary William Joynson-Hicks in the 1920s, struggled on behalf of traditional culture, although he often stood alone among his cabinet colleagues. A few decades earlier, in the United States, Anthony Comstock, a postal inspector, led a famous campaign against obscenity.[5]

Italy's postwar politics also offered special opportunities to wage a culture war on a large scale. This work begins on April 18, 1948, when Christian Democracy scored a major electoral victory that established what some critics derided as a "clerical regime" and allowed it to dominate Italian politics. It ends with the Referendum of May 1974, which confirmed the legality of divorce and dealt the Catholic agenda a devastating and irreparable blow.[6] From then on, the faithful witnessed a decade-long unraveling of their hopes, so that by 1985 the historian Pietro Scoppola, among the most prescient observers of Catholic struggles, acknowledged "a profound and radical devastation of all traditional cultures and preexisting collective identities." He concluded that, indeed, "postwar Italy did not witness the birth of a 'New Christianity,' but a secularized society."[7]

Few European countries can identify as fully as Italy does with the Catholic Church and its culture. Indeed, the Bible's Gospel of St. Matthew reveals how God's plan for his church placed it in the Eternal City, when Christ entrusted the building of his Earth-bound community to his disciple, Simon Peter. The apostle made his way from the Holy Land to

Catholicism and Power, ed. Daniela Treveri Gennari and Daniel Biltereyst (New York: Routledge, 2014), 100–113.

5. On Joynson-Hicks, see W. Sydney Robinson, *The Last Victorians: A Daring Reassessment of Four Twentieth-Century Eccentrics—Sir William Joynson Hicks; Dean Inge; Lord Reith; and Sir Arthur Bryant* (London: Robson, 2014); on Comstock, see Amy Werbel, *Lust on Trial: Censorship and the Rise of American Obscenity in the Age of Anthony Comstock* (New York: Columbia University Press, 2018); and Anna Bates, *Weeder in the Garden of the Lord: Anthony Comstock's Life and Career* (Lanham, Md.: University Press of America, 1995).

6. On the Christian Democratic "clerical regime," see Marco Barbanti, "La classe dirigente cattolica e la 'battaglia per la moralità,' 1948–1960: Appunti sul 'regime clericale,'" *Italia contemporanea*, no. 189 (December 1992): 606–7. The historian Arturo Carlo Jemolo coined the term. In the aforementioned article and in his "Cultura Cattolica: Lotta anticomunista a moralità pubblica (1948–60)," *Rivista di storia contemporanea* 1 (1992), Barbanti provided a valuable scholarly introduction to this subject.

7. Pietro Scoppola, *La Nuova cristianità perduta* (Rome: Studium, 1986), 141; Agostino Giovagnoli, *Chiesa e democrazia: La lezione di Pietro Scoppola* (Bologna: Il Mulino, 2011), 189–95. See also a review of Giovagnoli's book in the newspaper *La Repubblica*: "La rivoluzione morale di Pietro Scoppola," February 18, 2011, at http://ricerca.repubblica.it/repubblica/archivio/repubblica/2011/02/18/la-rivoluzione-morale-di-pietro-scoppola.html (accessed October 23, 2019).

Italy and to the great city of Rome, the *caput mundi*, capital of the world, as Romans still sometimes say, where his evangelization complemented that of St. Paul.[8] At first, most skeptical and conservative Romans resisted the gospel; but by the 300s and 400s A.D., significant elements of the city and of the whole Italian peninsula accepted the new faith. In the ancient tradition, then, throne married altar in 380 when Emperor Theodosius confirmed Christianity as the imperial creed. Consequently, Peter's successors as bishops of Rome emerged to lead Latin Christianity, anchoring the papacy, the Holy See, in Italy, where it remains today. Over the centuries, the Catholic Church cobbled together a diocesan network, monasteries, convents, confraternities, and parishes, hospitals, schools, and orphanages in a system that would facilitate Catholic political efforts in the twentieth century. A ready-made base mobilized for Mass every Sunday morning in the local parish. Along with the obvious holidays such as Christmas and Easter, the Catholic calendar reminded everyone throughout the year of the next solemnity, festival, or procession. The veneration of saints also helped Italians identify with their church, sharing in the tradition of the *onomastico*, a kind of alternate birthday to celebrate the saint for whom one is named. Furthermore, every profession and condition has historically had its patron saint. Fishermen looked to St. Peter; expectant mothers identified with Margaret; those inflicted with cancer asked for Peregrine's help; and a Christian with a bad tooth might pray to St. Apollonia. Each city enjoyed the patronage of its special saint and celebrated his or her feast day. Rome's historic and popular character is bound with Sts. Peter and Paul, Milan's with Ambrose, Venice's with Mark, Florence's with John the Baptist, Bologna's with Petronius, and Catania's with Agatha. At the top, Sts. Francis and Catherine of Siena share the patronage of the whole nation, and the list continues one way or another down through every village. Even today, "*un buon Cristiano*" can be heard to convey the highest compliment.

Three factors, however, hampered efforts toward a more Christian society—the process of secularization, the actions of secularists, and the deeds of the Catholics themselves. The greatest danger was the apolitical but relentless march of secularization, revealed in phenomena

8. Mt 16:18–19: "So now I say to you: You are Peter and on this rock I will build my community. And the gates of the underworld can never overpower it. I will give you the keys of the kingdom of Heaven: whatever you bind on earth will be bound in heaven; whatever you loose on earth will be loosed in heaven." Unless stated otherwise, all biblical quotations come from *The New Jerusalem Bible* (New York: Doubleday, 1985).

such as leisure time or in innocuous gadgets like motor scooters, refrigerators, radios, and televisions. Most of the era treated here was one of impressive economic growth, particularly the golden years from about 1958 until 1963, often identified as *il boom* or the *dolce vita*, that coincided with greater access to such consumer goods.[9]

One obstacle to our understanding of secularization, one scholar noted, is that "it is not a universally applicable law, but a description and an explanation." And, to complicate matters, secularization is an apolitical and, some believe, an inevitable process with many appearances like consumerization, Americanization, and modernity.[10] Modernity had a lot going for it over the old traditional ways. It tantalized with an easier life, one sexier and more fun. Why attend Mass, for example, when a new car can provide a day at the beach or in the country? The Austrian historian Reinhold Wagnleitner saw this and coined the "Marilyn Monroe" doctrine to describe that ever-successful scourge of Catholics—the seductive "gospel of consumerism and hedonism."[11] Secularization enables abominations condemned by the church, like murder or adultery, to penetrate homes via television screens. It erodes not only the church's political strength but even religious practice—it gets to the core of the faith. Questions of belief, however, must be treated with caution, especially when trying to track them over time. Public declarations of devotion cannot always indicate the depth of a person's faith. "Who knows," queried Graham Greene, "what [the pope] thinks at night in his bed when he has said his prayers?"[12] This has characterized faith since the start and has always been a problem for historians of religion. Recent investigations of the Middle Ages, the Christian Age of Faith if ever there was one, question the totality of its religious sincerity. Obeisance to church laws is one thing; authentic fidelity is another.[13]

9. Silvio Lanaro, *Storia dell'Italia repubblicana: L'economia, la politica, la cultura, la società, dal dopoguerra agli anni '90* (Venice: Marsilio, 1992), 223.

10. Steve Bruce, "Secularization and the Impotence of Individualized Religion," *Hedgehog Review* 8, nos. 1 and 2 (Spring–Summer 2006): 35–45. Discussing Scoppola, Giovagnoli recognized the "dramatic rapport between the Church and the modern world"; Giovagnoli, *Chiesa e democrazia*, 53.

11. Reinhold Wagnleitner, "The Marilyn Monroe Doctrine, or the Promise of the Democracy of Plenty," unpublished paper, 1994, quoted in Carl Strikwerda, "Parties, Populists and Pressure Groups: Christian Democracy in Comparative Perspective," in *European Christian Democracy: Historical Legacies and Comparative Perspectives*, ed. Thomas Kselman and Joseph A. Buttigieg (Notre Dame, Ind.: University of Notre Dame Press, 2003), 285. In his *Coca-Colonization and the Cold War: The Cultural Mission of the United States in Austria after the Second World War* (Chapel Hill: University of North Carolina Press, 1994). Wagnleitner expanded on this, describing the Cold War as a "total war of consumption" (xiv).

12. Graham Greene, *Monsignor Quixote* (New York: Simon and Schuster, 1982), 32.

13. William H. Swatos and Daniel V. A. Olson, eds., *The Secularization Debate* (Lanham, Md.: Rowman and Littlefield, 2000). Among the essays in this collection, see particularly Swatos and Kevin

Secularization and secularism—known in Italy as laicism (*laicismo*)—are tricky terms that have rightly been contested—a debate complicated by the fact that the two often travel together.[14] Of the two, *laicismo* is the easier to identify. It is not a process like anonymous secularization but an ideology with a self-conscious agenda. It is a cause to which women and men dedicate themselves; its goal is the decline of the church, or Christianity, or religious influence in the state and public life. Here the enemies of Catholicism assembled—the heritage of the Reformation, the Scientific Revolution and the Enlightenment, the materialism of the modern age.[15] Postwar Italian Catholics confronted tangible foes—active agents of secularism arrayed in the Marxist and "lay" political parties. After World War II, Communist, Socialist, Liberal, Republican, Social Democrat, Radical, and Protestant *laicisti* sooner or later battled Catholics on the cultural front. Some ex-Fascists even burrowed into Christian Democracy's own bureaucracy and played a role in both the application and sabotage of the Catholic cultural program. All told, here was a roster of enemies across the political spectrum that the reactionary Joseph DeMaistre might have called *le secte* and that, according to Isaiah Berlin, included "those who throw dust in the eyes of the people or seek to subvert the appointed order . . . [*le secte*] never sleeps, it is forever boring from within."[16] In 1950, this *secte* prompted don Giovanni Calabria to ask, "How many energies, how much effort to de-Christianize the world?"[17]

Catholics sensed that these assaults from faceless secularization

---

Christiano, "Secularization Theory: The Course of a Concept," 11–12, and Rodney Stark, "Secularization, R.I.P."

14. Surveys of secularization/secularism literature include Kevin M. Schultz, "Secularization: A Bibliographic Essay," *Hedgehog Review* 8, nos. 1 and 2 (Spring–Summer 2006): 170–77, and J. C. D. Clark, "Secularization and Modernization: The Failure of a 'Grand Narrative,'" *Historical Journal* 55, no. 1 (2012): 161–94. Terms here can sometimes be confusing. In discussions outside the church, "lay" normally is associated with "secular," although it can also denote the nonclerical faithful—laymen and laywomen. Within the Catholic Church, moreover, secularization might also refer to a suspension of obligation to Holy orders or the surrender of property to lay authorities.

15. In the popular newsmagazine *L'Europeo*, Sandro Dini wrote that the era's ills sprouted from a modern "cataclysm" that began "when cars replaced carriages, phones replaced notes, I.O.U.s replaced words of honor and family authority was replaced by easy-going chumminess [*promiscuo cameratismo*—although *cameratismo* also holds a Fascist connotation]"; Dini, "Siamo in pericolo a causa della nostra frenesia," *L'Europeo*, January 2, 1955.

16. Isaiah Berlin, "Joseph De Maistre and the Origins of Fascism," in *The Crooked Timber of Humanity: Chapters in the History of Ideas*, ed. Henry Hardy (New York: Knopf, 1991), 119. Recalling the Saracen king in Ariosto's Renaissance poem, one Catholic priest labeled the secular enemy as "Agramante"; Istituto Paolo VI (henceforth IPVI), p. XII, b. 31; Ferdinando Prosperini / Federico Alessandrini, November 4, 1948.

17. Giovanni Calabria, "Un problema urgente, Viribus unitus," *Rivista del clero italiano*, March 1950, 93.

and *laicismo*—both blaring or cunning—aimed to push Italy toward a less godly and more secular place, drives that Max Weber identified as "the fate of our times ... characterized by rationalization and intellectualization and, above all, by the 'disenchantment of the world.'"[18] In a 1955 article, the Vatican's newspaper, the *Osservatore Romano*, already recognized that "the deficiency of contemporary culture is in the lack of a sense of transcendence."[19] Many Catholics considered *laicismo* as a wickedness that must be met head on. Moralists argued that if left unchecked, current trends prepared the landscape for a secular, hedonist, and narcissistic evil that one cleric condemned as a "Satanic mania to enjoy ... anything that satisfies ... bestial appetites."[20] In October 1952, for example, Pope Pius XII cautioned a throng of 30,000 men to guard against threats "not only [to] Rome and Italy, but the entire world." Determined to crush Christianity, he said, secularists held a diabolical vision of "nature without grace, reason without faith, freedom without authority and sometimes authority without freedom." Bit by bit they would destroy the Holy Faith—first "Christ yes, Church no. Then: God yes, Christ no. Finally their unholy cry, God is dead, or rather, there never was a God." They labored to subtract God from everything—from the economy to the schools, from the family to the courts; and their tools included "media and entertainments that kill the sense of shame among youth and little ones and destroy love between spouses."[21]

While they appreciated the challenges posed by secularization and secularism, Catholics constituted the third obstacle to their own agenda. Obviously, they were more united than not; and most of them, at least until the divorce catastrophe of the early 1970s, closed ranks easily on fundamental cultural certainties of sexual and familial morality and comportment where the faith provided clear guidelines. Who among them could question scriptural teachings on love or sin, shame and modest comportment, or the divine commandments on adultery and

18. Max Weber, "Science as a Vocation," in *From Max Weber: Essays in Sociology*, ed. H. H. Gerth and C. Wright Mills (New York: Oxford University Press, 1946), 155. See also Patrick Sherry, "Disenchantment, Re-enchantment and Enchantment," *Modern Theology* 25, no. 3 (July 2009), and Michael Saler, "Modernity and Enchantment: A Historiographic Review," *American Historical Review* 111, no. 3 (June 2006): 692–716. In his preface to Sabino Acquaviva's *The Decline of the Sacred in Industrial Society*, trans. Patricia Lipscomb (New York: Harper and Row, 1979), vii, Gabriel Le Bras understands the development as "the world's conversion to the profane."

19. "La deficienza della cultura contemporanea è nella mancanza del senso della trascendenza," *Osservatore Romano* (henceforth OR), September 4, 1955.

20. Alfredo Ottaviani, *Il Baluardo* (Rome: Edizioni Ares, 1961), 45.

21. "Il memorando allo Discorso del Sommo Pontefice Pio XII nel XXX della Unione Uomini di Azione Cattolica Italiana," OR, Oct 13–14, 1952.

obeying parents? St. Peter's admonition of lust's war on the soul was only one of many biblical proscriptions of libertine sexual conduct and the desires of the flesh.[22] Therefore, despite political squabbles over taxes or employment, and although turf battles and arguments over emphasis sometimes nuanced the issue, everyone from the pope to DC and Catholic Action leaders could display unity on proper comportment among the faithful. Theirs was an image of the traditional family and marriage, a merger of man and woman blessed by God and his church that produced progeny and formed the social bedrock. Love between spouses brought them to a closer understanding of Christ and his church, and the fruits of their union were children who should be properly reared so that, as one publication put it in 1955, they would "know and love [the Church] as a second home, and respect the priest as Jesus' representative on Earth."[23]

This unity, however, was severely tested as *Catholics* ceaselessly squabbled among themselves for myriad reasons. The DC's inclination to internecine personality and turf battles sometimes harmed its greater vision. Catholic Action, furthermore, usually exhibited more of a zeal than the DC did, and its members famously considered themselves, often with good reason, as militants closer to the pope than the wayward or lax Christian Democrats, often led astray in their willingness to compromise with lay factions. Clergy often jumped into these often debilitating quarrels, choosing one side over the other.[24]

The Catholic cultural mission, furthermore, suffered from an intellectual inferiority complex. Nineteenth- and twentieth-century Catholics battled a lay mentality that they felt rarely and only reluctantly conceded anything of value in their culture, a dilemma aggravated by the fact that the elite institutes were largely secular, as were most artists, critics, and arbiters of taste. Catholics' answers could be combative or defensive. One of the faithful regarded as absurd such accusations that Catholicism could not appreciate beauty, insisting that an entrance ticket to the Vatican Museums would enable the doubter to see the error of such charges.[25] In another case, however, commenting on morality and

22. 1 Pt 2:11: "I urge you, my dear friends, as *strangers and nomads*, to keep yourselves free from the disordered natural inclinations that attack the soul."

23. Carlo Carbone, "Famiglia e vita sociale," *Noi uomini*, September 30, 1955. See also Carbone, "Vita religiosa della famiglia," *Noi uomini*, August 15–31, 1956.

24. Mario Casella, "Azione Cattolica e Democrazia Cristiana negli anni del passagio dal Fascismo alla Repubblica (1943–1948)," *Archivio Storico Italiano*, April–September 1997; repr. in Casella, ed., *L'Azione Cattolica del Novecento: Aspetti, momenti, interpretazioni, personaggi* (Rome: Ave, 2003), 25–64.

25. IPVI, Pg XII, b. 18, *Gavuzzo Circular*, June 15, 1956.

cinema, a leading clerical critic admitted, "Film lacks a Christian face ... why are the Catholics absent?"[26]

Writing for the Catholic Action press in 1950, Giampietro Dore wrestled with the familiar argument that modern Catholicism had no art. He directed his fire at the writer Corrado Alvaro, who claimed in the militantly secularist journal *Il Mondo* that the church's cultural retreat since the Counter Reformation effectively handed the art world over to the laity.[27] Reaction to *Il Mondo*'s and still other secularist attacks came ten years later. In 1960 the Catholic poet Carlo Betocchi admitted in the DC's *Il Popolo* that the sting hurt when secularists belittled Catholic intellectuals because at a certain level the snipes were warranted. But deep down (*in fondo*), he felt, the secularists were wrong.[28]

Catholics eager to combat *laicismo* located historical precedent for their works in the sixteenth-century Council of Trent, which predicted some of the same fervor and many of the same doubts of the 1950s and 1960s. While the Reformation spread through Germany and Switzerland, the Farnese Pope Paul III declared that heresy had even begun to infect Italy and called for a general council at Trent. The delegates faced a wide-ranging task—to deal with the Protestants, to reform the church, and to extend its influence into the lives of the faithful. The pope sanctioned the Jesuits to deal with many of the frontline issues. Education of the clergy became a central mission; the Council strengthened the identity of the parish, and it expanded the church's role in marriage.[29] A militant moralism emerged in the fight against heretics; but Catholics weren't alone on this. Their Tridentine efforts resembled, some might say paled in comparison to, those in the Protestant north. Calvinist Geneva, for instance, famously concerned itself with reformist standards, where Jean Calvin "saw danger lurking behind the trivial." Even in Tudor England, Archbishop Cranmer issued a "model ecclesiastical law of 1552" that declared "fornication and unbridled lusts of every kind are to be checked with great severity of punishment, so that they may eventually be uprooted from the kingdom."[30]

26. Albino Galletto, "I giudizi morali sui film," *Rivista del cinematografo*, February 1950.

27. Dore, "L'Arte e i cattolici," *Il Quotidiano*, April 2, 1950.

28. Betocchi, "I polli di Renzo Tramaglino," *Il Popolo*, February 20, 1960.

29. Christopher F. Black, *Church, Religion and Society in Early Modern Italy* (New York: Palgrave, 2004), 86–87, 93–96, regarding the parish, and 27–28 regarding marriage.

30. Owen Chadwick, *The Reformation* (New York: Penguin, 1985), 85; Faramerz Dabhoiwala, *The Origins of Sex: A History of the First Sexual Revolution* (Oxford: Oxford University Press, 2012), 40.

Like Calvin and Cranmer, the Tridentine church wanted, as one historian wrote, to fashion new men and women.[31] Central to that task was Paul III's bull *Licet ab initio* of 1542, which created the "Holy Office," a Supreme Congregation to establish the Inquisition in Rome under the Theatine zealot Gian Pietro Caraffa, the future Pope Paul IV.[32] His successor, Pius IV, chose as one of his chief advisors his nephew, the "austere, dedicated, humorless, and uncompromising" Carlo Borromeo. Borromeo epitomized "the 'Counter Reformation,' for his intransigence against heresy . . . [his] puritanism, dictatorial controls, as well as his implementation of Trent recommended institutions and procedures." He "essentially operated a moral police force, and imposed public penance and humiliations on the immoral, as well as fines (which helped poor communities)." Later canonized, he fought to sanctify Sundays and Feast Days in faithful hearts and campaigned against dancing in or anywhere near a church. In his inability "to overlook the smallest transgressions," however, the cardinal set a problematic precedent for Italy's moralist reformers.[33]

The Tridentine crackdowns may have given Italy's twentieth-century moral reformers a few lessons in what *not* to do. Some found the Inquisition and Borromeo's prosecutorial fervor unsettling and hardly compatible with Christian mercy and compassion. They could point to the church's teachings as a brake on Tridentine zealotry in the war against immorality. Along with Christ's declaration that he who is without sin should cast the first stone, Thomas Aquinas claimed in his *Super Matthaeum* that mercy "does not destroy justice, but is a certain kind of fulfillment of justice. . . . Mercy without justice is the mother of dissolution; [and] justice without mercy is cruelty." The historian Christopher Black has shown, furthermore, that many Italians second-guessed the Inquisition as excessive and foreign, with a particular Spanish and Dominican

31. Anne Jacobson Schutte, "Religion, Spirituality and the Post-Tridentine Church," in *Early Modern Italy, 1550–1796*, ed. John A. Marino (New York: Oxford University Press, 2002), 125–26.

32. Black, *Church, Religion and Society*, 51–54. On the Italian Inquisition, see also Jane K. Wickersham, *Rituals of Prosecution: The Roman Inquisition and the Prosecution of Philo-Protestants in Sixteenth-Century Italy* (Toronto: University of Toronto Press, 2012).

33. John B. Tomaro, "San Carlo Borromeo and the Implementation of the Council of Trent," in *San Carlo Borromeo: Catholic Reform and Ecclesiastical Politics in the Second Half of the Sixteenth Century*, ed. John M. Headley and John B. Tomaro (Cranbury, N.J.: Associated University Presses, 1988), 67–83; Black, *Church, Religion and Society*, 69, 97. Borromeo came to Milan as archbishop after a period of over eighty years in which Milan had no sitting bishop. During that time, the civil authorities enacted a number of measures dealing with morality, a corpus that the new archbishop was determined to revise to suit the church. His zeal prompted a backlash in 1579 from secular leaders who protested to Pope Gregory XIII. Black concludes that Borromeo's morality campaign "seems to have petered out."

stamp. Prison security was often lax, and lucky heretics enjoyed the largesse of "accommodating" jailers who permitted escapes "out of sympathy or for money." Elsewhere, Black cites an incident in Como where a friar who "tried to read out a declaration of the Inquisition against heretics was drowned out by bells and driven from the Cathedral."[34] Jane Wickersham's work on the same subject further illustrates tendencies toward mercy. With a "time of grace" wherein the Inquisitors allowed the accused to confess and repent, she points out that a magnanimous bent—a "guaranteed leniency"—had been built into the system.[35]

To fight heresy, the Tridentine church also tried censorship, with spotty success. Pens and scissors had long been weapons in the arsenal of throne and altar, and the church had a history of using them to meet the challenges of competing religions and Christian heresies, from Islam and Zoroastrianism, from Arianism and Donatism, to paganism and dualism. As part of Trent's reforms Paul IV issued a list of proscribed books that his successor, Pius IV, institutionalized as the Congregation for the Index in 1571.[36] Yet Pius softened his predecessor's harsh intentions and, in one of the first instances of backtracking that distinguished the history of the Index, rehabilitated some of Erasmus's works. Historians have also noted the confusion and sloppiness of the Index (or Indices). One noted that "the brilliance of the virtuoso, the originality of the pioneer, the penetration of the sage were not required for the Congregation for the Index of Prohibited Books.... The Church's task of surveillance, poorly defined and worse executed, demanded above all the capacity to establish order from mess. That capacity was rare." While their immediate aim was to expose heresy, censors muddied the water by expanding their aim to pornography and bawdy stories. One instruction of 1576, for instance, bade Bologna's Inquisitor to keep an eye peeled for "comic stories or other vulgar books or ones about love." Censors, furthermore, rarely reached beyond Italian-language editions,

34. Christopher F. Black, *The Italian Inquisition* (New Haven, Conn.: Yale University Press, 2009), 60, 109.

35. Wickersham, *Rituals of Prosecution*, particularly chapter 4, "The Mercy of the Court." On the plight of heretics (or lack thereof) in Tridentine Venice, see John Martin, *Venice's Hidden Enemies: Italian Heretics in a Renaissance City* (Berkeley: University of California Press, 1993), particularly chapter 5, "Hiding."

36. On the birth of the Index, see Vittorio Frajese, *Nascita dell'Indice: La censura ecclesiastica dal Rinascimento alla Controriforma* (Brescia: Morcelliana, 2006). On censorship more generally, see Paul F. Grendler, *Culture and Censorship in Late Renaissance Italy and France* (London: Variorum, 1981); and Cristina Stagno, ed., *Censura ecclesiastica e cultura politica in Italia tra cinquecento e seicento* (Florence: Leo S. Olschki editore, 2001).

and lazy Inquisitors who shied from reading all of an author's oeuvre frequently conflated it without identifying specific works that stank of heresy. In any case, the church often failed to alert the faithful of its decisions. Condemnations simply gathered dust, and few, if anyone, kept track of all of the works placed on the Index.[37]

In the centuries after Trent, challenges to the church became more complicated. The Scientific Revolution and the frequently anticlerical, Masonic, and sometimes godless Enlightenment pushed the church into defensive positions. In the 1950s, the conservative Cardinal Alfredo Ottaviani stated that Luther's "betrayals" of God continued through "the Enlightenment, rationalism, humanism and now *laicismo*."[38] Seventeenth- and eighteenth-century thinkers such as the skeptic Pierre Bayle, the atheist Baron d'Holbach, and the libertine Marquis de Sade joined others to prepare the way for modern Europe's secular and lay traditions.[39] Fueled by a well-educated elite from Giambattista Vico to Cesare Beccaria, the eighteenth-century Italian states had already experienced a home-grown Enlightenment, although spottier and more modest than France's. Enlightened Italians bred a new national culture expressed, as the historian Lucy Riall has written, "in their language, literature, music and visual arts, and it was further shaped by the presence of the Catholic Church and by opposition to it."[40] The French invasion of 1796–97 then brought revolution and ushered an era of violent and unprecedented secularism. Establishing republics (and later kingdoms) on the wreck of the ancient regime, much of the assault turned into an attack on a church that Napoleon Bonaparte and his revolutionaries considered the source of "corruption and depravity." The conquered principalities were all rotten, they acknowledged, but Rome had a particularly wick-

37. Peter Godman, *The Saint as Censor: Robert Bellarmine between Inquisition and Index* (Leiden: Brill, 2000), 207; Black, *Italian Inquisition*, 158–75; Chadwick, *The Popes and European Revolution* (New York: Oxford University Press, 1981), 325. In his discussion of the eighteenth-century church, Chadwick found "no pattern or reason about the selection of books banned" and that many "consultors" of the Inquisition were not "as literate as they should have been." See also John Jeffries Martin, "Religion, Renewal and Reform in the Sixteenth Century," in Marino, *Early Modern Italy*, who dismissed the Index as "an authoritative but hardly enforceable list" (42).

38. Ottaviani, *Il Baluardo*, 40.

39. On Enlightenment criticisms of the Catholic Church and of Christianity, see Jean Delumeau, *Catholicism between Luther and Voltaire: A New View of the Counter-Reformation* (London: Burns and Oates, 1977), 203–31; and Richard H. Popkin, *The History of Scepticism from Erasmus to Descartes* (Assen, Netherlands: Royal Van Gorcum, 1964). On the Tridentine church before the French Revolution, see Robert Bireley, *The Refashioning of Catholicism, 1450–1700: A Reassessment of the Counter Reformation* (Washington, D.C.: The Catholic University of America Press, 1999); and Gerald R. Cragg, *The Church and the Age of Reason, 1648–1789* (New York: Penguin, 1985).

40. Lucy Riall, *Risorgimento: The History of Italy from Napoleon to Nation State* (London and New York: Palgrave Macmillan, 2009), 122.

ed status as "the breeder of corruption" and "the root of all evil." The French considered strange Italy's "cheek by-jowl existence of piety and promiscuity" and blamed the Tridentine church for producing a nation of "effeminate mothers' boys and sluttish, coldly calculating women, bereft of personal happiness."[41] As expected, Napoleon's administration confiscated church properties and abolished religious orders; but it also attacked popular Catholicism through such pettiness as allowing work on Sundays and attempting to replace local and traditional festivals with the Feast of St. Napoleon. After the French took Rome and arrested Pope Pius VI—he died in captivity—"they sought to weaken the hold of religion in the hearts of the common people." Among other outrages, they defaced the statue of St. Michael atop the Castel Sant'Angelo with coats of revolutionary red, white, and blue paint, and they "suppressed twenty feasts and abolished the legal obligation to be present at Mass."[42] The French also maligned the goals of Trent by introducing civil marriage and divorce, wildly detested measures. In Naples, Napoleon's brother Joseph refused even to publish the announcements out of fear of an uprising, and, in the end, only a handful of divorces took place across the peninsula, while some rebellious priests risked French wrath and performed church marriages in advance of civil ones, ensuring the primacy of the Holy rites.[43] One unanticipated result of French secularist oppression was the intensification of Italian devotion to the Mother of God, leading to the attribution of miracles to her and the explosion of "Marian" revolts in 1799—uprisings that persisted through Napoleon's second occupation until his final defeats.[44]

After the French occupations and through the long nineteenth century, at one time or another, nationalists, Masons, capitalists, liberals, and Marxists joined lay ranks across Europe in culture wars against the church, allowing it no place in the public square unless it played a cynical role in keeping the masses in a docile stupor. "This bourgeois, secular public sphere," Riall contended, "which developed rapidly in the 1830s and 1840s, revolved around clubs, cafés, theatres and the press, rather than around the family, community and the church." From wea-

41. Michael Broers, *The Politics of Religion in Napoleonic Italy: The War against God, 1801–1814* (New York: Routledge, 2002), 24–25.

42. Chadwick, *Popes and European Revolution*, 462–71. The French renamed the Castel Sant'Angelo the "Castle of Genius."

43. Broers, *Politics of Religion in Napoleonic Italy*, 48, 52–54. On the other hand, Broers noted that the French code gave more power to the parents of the betrothed than had existed in the Tridentine system.

44. Broers, *Politics of Religion in Napoleonic Italy*, 54–66.

ry and disoriented factory workers, moreover, to Friedrich Nietzsche's critiques of Christianity, religion suffered attacks and defeats through the nineteenth century until, with the Great War on the horizon, the French prime minister, René Viviani, prematurely voiced the lay triumph that "we have extinguished in the firmament lights that will never be rekindled."[45]

Catholics retaliated. After the collapse of Napoleonic Italy, for example, a backlash Zelanti faction controlled the papal court, ostracizing the moderate Cardinal Ercole Consalvi and electing of one of their own in 1823 as Pope Leo XII. First considered restrained, the new pope turned to a revitalization of morals. His policies soon revealed themselves, wrote Nicholas Atkin and Frank Tallett, as

> a grotesque caricature of tyranny. Imprisonment was ordered for those caught playing games on Sundays or feast days; a similar punishment befell those who walked too closely behind women, the latter being forbidden to wear tight-fitting dresses; the waltz was banned as provocative; works of art featuring nudes were removed from public view; encores and ovations were banned in the theater lest they provided an opportunity for seditious comment and for the same reason actors were not allowed to ad lib; press censorship which was already rigorous, was strengthened still further; police visits to brothels were discontinued in case this lent a legitimacy to the prostitutes' activities, though one result was a rapid rise in venereal disease; most unpopular of all was the closure of bars in Rome so that alcohol could be purchased only at grilles in the street—a procedure that led to unprecedented levels of drunkenness.[46]

Nineteenth-century *laicisti* targeted the Catholic Church as Italy's enemy of freedom and nationhood; and they defeated it in the battle of national Unification, the *Risorgimento*. Influenced by such figures as Giuseppe Mazzini and (later) Giuseppe Garibaldi and peppered with *carbonaro* and Masonic thought, it acquired a deeply anticlerical disposition, viewing the church as a source of obscurantism, superstition, and

45. Riall, *Risorgimento*, 81; the Viviani quote can be found in Stephen Schloesser, *Jazz Age Catholicism: Mystic Modernism in Postwar Paris 1919–1933* (Toronto: University of Toronto Press, 2005), 45. The literature on nineteenth-century secularization, Christianity, and the Catholic Church is enormous. See, for example, E. E. Y. Hales, *Revolution and the Papacy, 1769–1846* (Notre Dame, Ind.: University of Notre Dame Press, 1966); Charles Taylor, *A Secular Age* (Cambridge, Mass.: Harvard University Press, 2007); Christopher Clark and Wolfram Kaiser, eds., *Culture Wars: Secular-Catholic Conflict in Nineteenth-Century Europe* (Cambridge: Cambridge University Press, 2003); Chadwick, *The Secularization of the European Mind in the 19th Century* (Cambridge: Cambridge University Press, 1975), and Michael Burleigh, *Earthly Powers: The Clash of Religion and Politics in Europe, from the French Revolution to the Great War* (New York: Harper Collins, 2007).

46. Nicholas Atkin and Frank Tallett, *Priests, Prelates and People: A History of European Catholicism since 1750* (New York: Oxford University Press, 2003), 103. See also Chadwick, *Popes and European Revolution*, 567–69.

oppression.[47] To their war cries, Camillo Benso di Cavour, Italy's first prime minister, added what was probably the most sacred lay mantra, a "free church in a free state." Until the rise of Christian Democracy after the Second World War, lay agendas held sway in Europe, whether on the left where it was more comfortable or the right in its most notorious twentieth-century guise—fascism.

With its nationalist goals and usually at odds with the pontiff, the *Risorgimento* failed to attract many notable Catholics. Some, like Cesare Balbo, Vincenzo Gioberti, Alessandro Manzoni, Antonio Rosmini, and a few others, stood out; but they found little support from the church. None of the nineteenth-century popes embraced the new liberal world of the Unification. Rather, they condemned it. According to George Mosse, Pope Gregory XVI's reactionary denunciation of liberal thought, *Mirari vos* of 1832, "was to dominate the Church's policy during the century," leading to the historian's perhaps facile conclusion that Italian Catholicism was "intellectually sterile."[48] Gregory's successor, Pius IX, continued the fight. The historian E. E. Y. Hales wrote that this would be a struggle not in the traditional sense in that earlier pontiffs had generally met foreign challenges—by calling for crusades against the Muslims in far-off Jerusalem, for example—but remaining far from the fighting. Instead, the nineteenth-century popes, especially Pius IX, "experienced and suffered the impact in his person." Forced to flee revolutionary Rome in 1849 and restored only with the aid of French cannons, Pius later grieved the loss of the Papal States in two stages: 1859–61 and 1870. In 1864 he provided the reactionaries with their manifesto, the "Syllabus of Errors," "a gesture of defiance hurled by an outraged pope against the nineteenth century." Issued as an addendum to his encyclical *Quanta cura*, Pius condemned almost every modern development. His succinct eightieth "error" placed all the cards on the table: "The Roman Pontiff can, and ought to, reconcile himself, and come to terms with progress, liberalism and modern civilization."[49]

47. Guido Verucci, "Le due Italie: Il giudizio sul cattolicesimo italiano nella cultura laica," in *La Chiesa e l'Italia: Per una storia dei loro rapporti negli ultimi due secoli*, ed. Antonio Acerbi (Milan: Vita e pensiero, 2003), 153–93. Garibaldi was notoriously anticlerical and vowed to wrest the Eternal City from the "vampire of the Vatican." See also Francesco Traniello, *Città dell'Uomo: Cattolici, partito e stato nella storia d'Italia* (Bologna: Il Mulino, 1990).

48. George Mosse, *The Culture of Western Europe: The Nineteenth and Twentieth Centuries* (Boulder, Colo.: Westview, 1988), 131. John Pollard, nonetheless, attributes some level of *Risorgimento* "ideas and opinion" to the Catholics; Pollard, *Catholicism in Modern Italy: Religion, Society and Politics since 1861* (New York: Routledge, 2008), 17–19.

49. Hales, *Pio Nono: A Study in European Politics and Religion in the Nineteenth Century* (London: Eyre and Spottiswoode, 1954), 255–76. Hales wrote that "seen in its wider aspect, then, the Syllabus was a

The young Italian Kingdom dealt the Papal States their deathblow in 1870. Pius's champion, Emperor Louis Napoleon, went to war with Prussia, withdrawing his troops from the Eternal City and leaving it defenseless. Then on September 20, Italian guns fired on the old Aurelian walls near the Porta Pia and blew open a hole that allowed soldiers to enter. They raced down the via del Quirinale to the papal palace, and the Rome of the popes surrendered. The royal forces stayed out of the Vatican area on that first day, but the papal government quickly asked for intervention for security reasons. King Victor Emmanuel II moved into the Quirinale Palace, and Rome became Italy's capital the following July. Under the new regime the via del Quirinale became the via 20 Settembre, and the state proclaimed that date as a national holiday. It also expropriated many monastic and other church properties while taking over or disbanding the old charitable organizations, the *opere pie*.

A disgusted Pius retreated into the Vatican that, he proclaimed, had become his prison. Victor Emmanuel permitted him unrestricted freedom of movement with complete access to St. Peter's, Rome's Cathedral of St. John Lateran, and the summer residence at Castel Gandolfo. Italy had also offered the pope a Law of Guarantees that included financial compensation, which Pius rejected as an insult, while he condemned the obnoxious "subalpine government." His *non expedit* of 1868 had already forbidden Italians from voting and participation in the state, and it was immediately clear that a cold war existed between the Holy See and Italy, a tension soon labeled the "Roman question."[50]

In the church-state divorce, few Italian political leaders before the end of World War II were sincere or even baptized Catholics, and most still breathed the *Risorgimento*'s liberal and Masonic air. Men like Ernesto Nathan, a Jew and leading Mason who served as Rome's mayor from 1907 until 1913, distinguished the new Kingdom.[51] At the apex of po-

reply—an interim reply—to the eighteenth century 'enlightenment' incarnate in the French revolution and the *risorgimento*; what people like Prince Napoleon boasted of as 'Modern Civilization'" (275). On the Syllabus, see also Frank J. Coppa, *Pope Pius IX: Crusader in a Secular Age* (Boston: Twayne, 1979), 140–53. The Syllabus can be found on many websites, for example, http://www.papalencyclicals.net/Pius09/p9syll.htm (accessed October 21, 2019).

50. On the conquest of Rome, see Hales, *Pio Nono*, 313–18; Coppa, *Pope Pius IX*, 169–80.

51. On Italian Masons, see Anna Maria Isastia and Alessandro Visani, *L'Idea laica tra Chiesa e massoneria: La questione della scuola* (Rome: Atanòr, 2008); Guglielmo Adilardi, *Chiesa cattolica e massoneria: Antiche lotte—Nuovi orizzonti* (Foggia: Bastogi, 2009); Rosario F. Esposito, SSP, *La Massoneria e L'Italia dal 1800 ai nostri giorni* (Rome: Paoline, 1979); and José Ferrer Benimeli and Giovanni Caprile, *Massoneria e Chiesa Cattolica: Ieri, oggi e domani* (Rome: Edizioni Paoline, 1979). The church had banned membership in Masonic lodges from the eighteenth century, and Canon 2335 of the 1917 Code of Canon Law subjected Masons to immediate excommunication. In his study of Liberal Italy, R. J. B. Bosworth

litical life, prime ministers included the Sicilian *mangiaprete* (or "priest-eater") and Mason Francesco Crispi, who was raised Greek Orthodox. The Romagnole Alessandro Fortis and the Venetian Luigi Luzzatti were Jews, and Benito Mussolini's Catholicism, while he finally married his common-law wife in a church, was entirely fraudulent. Neither did King Victor Emmanuel III, who ruled from 1900 until 1946, harbor much sympathy for the church. With an eye on the pontiff across the Tiber as a possible rival, the famously petty king preferred the services of English Protestant nannies for his children.[52]

As much as possible, the new state purged education, welfare, and marital law of church influence. It reduced the status of religious lessons in state primary schools from obligatory to optional, then replaced them with civics, while it abolished chairs of theology at all state universities; an attempt to end religious instruction in secondary schools failed.[53] Although the nation remained firm in its denial of divorce, obligatory civil marriages took precedence over optional religious ones in the 1865 Civil Code. The state also paid some of its debt to the *Risorgimento*'s heroes by erecting monuments to them—most famously, the equestrian statue of Garibaldi on the Janiculum hill, at the approximate site of the general's command during the 1849 defense of the Roman Republic. Prime Minister Crispi dedicated this secularist shrine, fittingly, on September 20, 1895, the twenty-fifth anniversary of Italy's conquest of the papal city. In 1889, he had unveiled in the Campo dei fiori another statue laden with anticlerical messages, that of the heretic Giordano Bruno, who in 1600 died at the stake on the same spot.[54]

After the Unification, disoriented Catholics tried to regroup and mo-

---

wrote that "anti-clericalism (and Masonry) had been the touchstone of Italian Liberalism," although that bond weakened in the years before the First World War. He also quoted the Communist leader Palmiro Togliatti, who claimed, "The Italian bourgeoisie did have one unified political organization, . . . Freemasonry"; Bosworth, *Italy, Least of the Great Powers: Italian Foreign Policy before the First World War* (London: Cambridge University Press, 1979), 31–32.

52. Arturo Carlo Jemolo recounted that the king stayed away from churches and only tolerated episcopal presence at formal occasions where the bishop might recall the piety of his ancestors, particularly that of his mother, Queen Margherita. Victor Emmanuel participated only once in the inauguration of a religious structure in Rome, the Jewish Synagogue; Jemolo, *Church and State in Italy*, trans. David Moore (Philadelphia: Dufour, 1961), 102–6.

53. S. William Halperin, "Italian Anticlercalism, 1871–1914," *Journal of Modern History*, no.1 (March 1947): 23; Giovanni Spadolini, *L'Opposizione cattolica da Porta Pia al '98* (Milan: Mondadori, 1994), 127.

54. Bosworth, *Whispering City: Rome and Its Histories* (New Haven, Conn.: Yale University Press, 2011), 83–90, regarding Garibaldi and a second statue to his wife, Anita, dedicated in 1932. See also Bosworth, *Whispering City*, 107–11, and Halperin, "Italian Anticlericalism," 27, regarding the statue of Bruno. Halperin saw the event as "the climactic stroke of the anticlerical offensive." In 1885, on the floor of the chamber, Crispi declared his esteem for the separation of church and state found in the United States; Jemolo, *Church and State in Italy*, 70.

bilize. One important option came in Christian Democracy, promoted by Giambattista Valente and Father Romolo Murri. The two suffered defeat, ironically not at the hands of the secular state but at those of Pope Leo XIII, who condemned the movement in his 1901 encyclical *Graves de communi*. While the faithful could and should engage in social work, wrote Leo, they must nevertheless refrain from political organization. In giving Christian Democracy a political meaning, the pontiff lumped it together with other errors such as Christian socialism and social democracy, noting that it stripped the faith down to a mere political act. One year later the patriarch of Venice, Giuseppi Sarto, denounced Murri as guilty of "black ingratitude." Sarto soon moved to Rome as Pope Pius X and excommunicated the broken priest in 1909.[55]

More successful were less overtly political organizations. Catholic Action was born from *Risorgimento* challenges to the church. The "most solid of all the Italian Catholic organizations," according to Giorgio Candeloro, it was founded in 1867 by Count Mario Fani-Ciotti of Viterbo and the Bolognese lawyer Giovanni Acquaderni as the Italian Catholic Youth Society (Società della gioventù cattolica italiana) with a four-point program of devotion to the Holy See, religious study, living the Christian life, and charity.[56] Marco Impagliazzo wrote that "since the beginning of the twentieth century, the Catholic movement has been structurally associated with Catholic Action," and the tone for such lay activity as outlined in Pius X's 1905 encyclical *Fermo proposito* was to be "obedient, docile and submissive to the teachings of the Church."[57] Giovanni Spadolini wrote that its members were "true *camelots du roi* of militant Catholicism, unresponsive to the seductions of liberalism, impermeable to lay temptations, imbued with a discipline and devotion that gave no

55. Cesare Balbo's dream of a Catholic political party never bore fruit after the trauma of the *Risorgimento*. Others, such as Enrico Cenni and the Jesuit Carlo Maria Curci, who founded the Civiltà Cattolica but then left the order, and later figures such as the beatified economist Giuseppe Toniolo and don Davide Abertario, worked toward the idea of Catholic politics, something that found expression in the rather progressive *Rassegna nazionale*. For the period between 1870 and 1914, see Richard Webster, *Christian Democracy in Italy, 1860–1960* (London: Hollis and Carter, 1961), 3–37; Traniello, *Città dell'uomo*, 65–97; Gabriele De Rosa, *Il movimento cattolico in Italia dalla restaurazione all'età giolittiana* (Rome and Bari: Laterza, 1988). On Curci, who struggled with the idea of political action for Catholics and later left the Jesuits, see De Rosa, *Il movimento cattolico in Italia*, 45–53. Murri subsequently married the daughter of the president of the Norwegian Senate but was received back into the Church shortly before his death in 1944.

56. Giorgio Candeloro, *Il movimento cattolico in Italia* (Rome: Editori Riuniti, 1982), 120; De Rosa, *Il movimento cattolico in Italia*, 39–42; Giacomo de Antonellis, *Storia dell'Azione cattolica dal 1867 a oggi* (Milan: Rizzoli, 1987), 46–52.

57. Marco Impagliazzo, "Movimenti e nuove comunità," in *La Nazione cattolica: Chiesa e società in Italia, 1958–oggi*, ed. Marco Impagliazzo (Milan: Guerini, 2004), 254.

countenance to anxieties of study or flights of fantasy."[58] *Fermo proposito* reorganized the association as Catholic Action, while new statutes in 1922 restructured it into four sections—a Men's Federation, a Women's Union, the Italian Catholic University Federation, and the Italian Catholic Youth Society, which in 1931 became the Society of Italian Catholic Youth.

Even with Catholic Action's appeal, and despite papal efforts at suppression, political Catholicism did not die, and the First World War era witnessed its resurgence. Along with its other provisions, Pius X's *Fermo proposito* also ended the *non expedit*, and Catholics began to resurface on the political waters. The Great War, moreover, served to link church and state together when the embattled soldiers' spiritual hunger demanded a role for religion at the front. At the start of the conflict, the Italian army had no chaplains. Twenty-four thousand priests were drafted, with two thousand entering the ranks as "medical orderlies." These last became the initial core group of military chaplains.[59] In an effort to form a war cabinet representative of the whole nation, additionally, in 1916 Prime Minister Paolo Boselli chose Filippo Meda, the first Catholic in the Italian government who was chosen *as* a Catholic, as finance minister.

Momentum continued after the war when the Sicilian don Luigi Sturzo founded the Italian Popular Party (Partito popolare italiano, PPI), which quickly occupied middle ground between left and right. In October of 1922, the PPI participated in Mussolini's first government coalition and contributed two cabinet ministers, an arrangement described by the historian Gabriele De Rosa as "a difficult collaboration." That same year, Achille Ratti succeeded Benedict XV as Pope Pius XI. His first encyclical, *Ubi arcano Dei consilio*, proclaimed a Christian reconquest of the world, where the faith would revive in all sectors of life, from politics to personal conduct. He identified Catholic Action, in Italy and elsewhere, as a force in the struggle of Christian revival. Pius's 1925 encyclical *Quas primas* sanctioned the feast of Christ the King, a criticism of modern politics and probably a slap at Mussolini, with a call to arms against "the plague of our age . . . so-called laicism with its errors and Godless aims."[60]

58. Spadolini, *L'Opposizione cattolica da Porta Pia al '98*, 52–56.

59. Pollard, *Catholicism in Modern Italy*, 72–74.

60. Atkin and Tallett, *Priests, Prelates and People*, 234; Gabriele De Rosa, *Il Partito Popolare Italiano* (Rome and Bari: Laterza, 1974), chapter 8; Daniela Saresella, *Cattolici a sinistra: Dal modernismo ai giorni nostri* (Rome and Bari: Laterza, 2011), 43.

On the other hand, Pius hinted at a fresh willingness to resolve the Roman Question, something indicated in February of 1922 when he announced his pontificate. For the first time since the Italian conquest of 1870, Pius blessed the faithful in St. Peter's Square directly from the outer portico and not from inside the basilica. He began to see Mussolini as the man who could not only deal with the Roman Question, but return the church to its rightful place in Italian society, helping along the way to vanquish its Masonic, Protestant, Socialist, and Communist enemies. For his part, and beyond the obvious political capital gained by reconciliation, Mussolini wanted the pontiff to rein in the new PPI. By the end of 1922 and the start of 1923, his "religious package" sent a clear message that included an expanded program of military chaplains, increased salaries for priests, and the placement of crucifixes in public buildings, as well as his bail-out of the troubled papal Banco di Roma. The government, moreover, proceeded to restrict the Masons and Protestants, particularly the more evangelical branches such as the YMCA. Other symbolic acts followed—the designation in 1925 of October 4, the Feast of St. Francis, as a national holiday and the cancellation of the September 20 holiday that recalled the 1870 conquest. To fulfill his end of the bargain, Pius, who had never been an enthusiastic supporter, took aim at the PPI, and on July 10, 1923, Sturzo submitted to an order to resign as secretary-general. By 1926, the PPI disbanded, the last non-Fascist party to do so, and Sturzo left Italy for two decades of exile.[61]

This cooperation bore fruit in the Lateran Pacts, signed by Italy and the Holy See on February 11, 1929, resolving the Roman Question and affirming Catholicism as "the sole religion of the state."[62] Although Pius still had to contend with Mussolini, Richard Webster had a point when he wrote, "Much of the work of the *Risorgimento* was undone in 1929, and the papacy returned as a great force, at least indirectly, in the political

61. Pollard, *The Vatican and Italian Fascism, 1929–1932: A Study in Conflict* (New York: Cambridge University Press, 1985), 27–37; Jemolo, *Church and State in Italy*, 168; Alberto Guasco, *Cattolici e fascisti: La Santa sede e la politica italiana all'alba del regime (1919–1925)* (Bologna: Il Mulino, 2013), 175, 196–205. Regarding the crackdowns on Masons and Protestants, see Giorgio Rochat, *Regime fascista e Chiese evangeliche* (Turin: Claudiana, 1990), and David I. Kertzer, *The Pope and Mussolini: The Secret History of Pius XI and the Rise of Fascism in Europe* (New York: Random House, 2014), 181–98.

62. On the Lateran Pacts, see Frank Coppa, ed., *Controversial Concordats: The Vatican's Relations with Napoleon, Mussolini and Hitler* (Washington, D.C.: The Catholic University of America Press, 1999), 81–119; Kertzer, *Pope and Mussolini*, 98–113; Pollard, *Vatican and Italian Fascism*, 42–47; and Renzo De Felice, *Mussolini il fascista: L'organizazzione dello Stato fascista 1925–1929* (Turin: Einaudi, 1995), 383–436. The chief Vatican negotiators were Father Pietro Tacchi Venturi and Francesco Pacelli, the brother of Eugenio, the future Pope Pius XII. The text can be found at the Vatican website: http://www.vatican.va/roman_curia/secretariat_state/archivio/documents/rc_seg-st_19290211_patti-lateranensi_it.html#CONCORDATO_FRA_LA_SANTA_SEDE_E_LITALIA (accessed October 24, 2019).

affairs of the Italian peninsula."[63] The pacts consisted of three parts. First, a political treaty created the Vatican City state and gave it jurisdiction over basilicas and other church buildings in Rome, such as the old Chancellery. The pacts also contained a financial agreement and, finally, a Concordat that sanctioned a renewed Catholic presence in Italian society and culture. Catholic weddings, for instance, now received equal footing with civil ones; a church marriage no longer needed a civil ceremony for validation, and a Catholic diploma equaled one from a state school. Article 2 of the Concordat stated that, "like the Holy See, so the bishops can freely publish ... instructions, ordinances, pastoral letters, parish bulletins, and other acts regarding the spiritual realm [*governo spirituale*] of the faithful." It allowed for Catholic journals and reviews, all of which had already been circulating, from the Holy See's *Osservatore Romano* and the Jesuit *Civiltà Cattolica* to myriad Catholic Action magazines and down to the approximately 5,000 parish bulletins. Article 43, furthermore, permitted the existence of Italian Catholic Action, something that did not sit well with many anticlerical Fascists, who considered it a rival to the dictatorship's youth organizations. The pacts also charged the Italian state with maintaining the sacred nature of the Eternal City, making offenses and insults (*vilipendio*) against the pontiff crimes. In the spirit of the agreements, moreover, the Fascists supported or joined the church in campaigns against blasphemy in schools and public places, as well as against beach and dance hall immodesty and birth control.[64] The anti-Fascist Max Ascoli concluded that "for the first time the Italian state and the Catholic Church faced each other without hiding behind veils."[65] Ascoli's judgment, intended as a criticism, nevertheless expressed a relief in other quarters that, indeed, the veil *had* dropped, and the barque of St. Peter finally emerged from a darkness imposed by the lay world.

The Lateran Pacts triggered deep misgivings among many Catholic intellectuals, particularly exiled *popolari*, starting with don Sturzo and those of a Christian Democratic mind, many of whom reacted to this

63. Webster, *Christian Democracy in Italy, 1860–1960*, 110.

64. Francesco Malgeri, *Chiesa, cattolici e democrazia da don Sturzo a De Gasperi* (Brescia: Morcelliana, 1990), 35–82. The 5,000 figure and others came from a Vatican survey of 1936, which also concluded that 937 religious reviews operated in Italy (46–47). Regarding Catholic culture under the Fascists, see Stefano Pivato, *Clericalismo e laicismo nella cultura popolare italiana* (Milan: Franco Angeli, 1990), particularly chapter 3, "Il regime clericale di massa," 121–261. See also Lucia Ceci, *L'interesse superiore: Il Vaticano e l'Italia di Mussolini* (Rome and Bari: Laterza, 2013), 114–15.

65. Max Ascoli, "The Roman Church and Political Action," *Foreign Affairs* 13, no. 3 (April 1935): 447.

"trauma" by reaching out to kindred spirits of lay anti-Fascism.[66] At home, however, the pacts enjoyed genuine and widespread popularity among both faithful and clergy. Across Italy, church bells celebrated the end of the Roman Question, and the pontiff hailed the *Duce* as "the man of providence" who gave God back to Italy and Italy back to God. The pacts marked the high point of relations between the church and the regime, although the cooperation of the twenties did not persist through the more turbulent thirties, which began with Blackshirt violence against Catholic Action, assaults that Pius condemned in his 1931 encyclical *Non abbiamo bisogno*.[67] Catholic Action remained an issue of contention through the end of the decade—and the pope's last days—although the *Duce*'s anti-Semitic measures made relations worse.[68]

On February 10, 1939, one day short of the tenth anniversary of the Lateran Pacts, Pius XI died. Eugenio Pacelli succeeded him on March 3 and honored his mentor by choosing the name of Pius XII.[69] Tall, thin, and rather aloof, Pacelli and his personality did not recall that of his sturdier and more combative predecessor. But he shared Ratti's goal of increasing Catholicism's presence in the modern world. Pius's first encyclical, *Summi pontificatus*, issued during the early weeks of World War II, identified the "alpha and omega" of his hopes as the "spread of the Kingdom of Christ." He warned of the exclusion of "Christ from modern life, especially from public life," which led to "ever clearer, ever more distinct, ever more distressing . . . signs of a corrupt and corrupting paganism."[70] The pontiff elaborated his vision of a robust Christianity in later communications such as his 1942 Christmas message. This called for a "social crusade" and a "new order" based on five points: the dignity and rights of the human person, the defense of social unity, particularly that of the family, recognition of the dignity and rights of labor, restoration of the rule of law, and the conception of the state according to the Christian spirit.[71] Toward that end, Pius considered the faithful as

66. Malgeri, *Chiesa, cattolici e democrazia*, 17–30.

67. On tensions between Catholic Action and the regime during this period, see Renzo De Felice, *Mussolini il duce: Gli anni del consenso 1929–1936* (Turin: Einaudi, 1996), 248–79, and Pollard, *Vatican and Italian Fascism*, 103–66. Pollard wrote that "relations between the Church and the Regime were ultimately determined by one central problem—Catholic Action and its youth organizations" (103).

68. Kertzer, *Pope and Mussolini*, 291–301.

69. Robert Ventresca, *Soldier of Christ: The Life of Pope Pius XII* (Cambridge, Mass.: Harvard University Press, 2013), 132–38.

70. The encyclical can be found at http://w2.vatican.va/content/pius-xii/en/encyclicals/documents/hf_p-xii_enc_20101939_summi-pontificatus.html (accessed October 28, 2019).

71. Mario Casella, *L'Azione cattolica alla caduta del fascismo: Attività e progetti per il dopoguerra (1942–'45)* (Rome: Studium, 1984), 33–44. Casella recorded that, from the Catholic University in Milan, Agostino

the church's first line in, what one historian wrote, was "the defense of the faith and in the construction of the new Christian order, assuming a defensive position in the face of the modern world and its culture."[72]

The Second World War brought disaster to Fascist Italy. After three years of defeat and humiliation, in 1943 state institutions and the government appeared bankrupt. Fascism had become an embarrassing and spent force that reached its end when Allied forces, led by the Anglo-Americans, landed in Sicily on July 10–11, 1943. On the nineteenth, while the *Duce* conferred with Adolf Hitler in northern Italy, the American Air Force struck Rome, employing five hundred bombers in a daylight raid.[73] The capital had largely escaped war damage up until that point, and news of the attack stunned not only the city but the entire nation. Pope Pius watched the bombardment from his window and called for a car to take him to the main site of the damage, the working-class San Lorenzo neighborhood between the Tiburtina and Termini train stations. Almost 1,500 people lost their lives there, and much of the ancient basilica of San Lorenzo-beyond-the-Walls lay ruined. Accompanied by Monsignor Giovanni Battista Montini, Pius reached the scene and, without police protection, mingled for three hours among the victims and frightened crowd, delivering aid and kneeling to pray with them in the still-smoldering ruins of shops and apartments, his garments stained with debris and blood.[74] The papal visit to San Lorenzo contrasted dramatically with the experience of King Victor Emmanuel III, whose separate tour of the damage met with "icy silence" and hostile jeers, an incident that traumatized him and galvanized his decision to get rid of Mussolini. The end came on the night of July 24–25, when the Fascist Grand Council delivered a vote of no confidence. The king arrested the *Duce* the next day.[75]

While the regime tottered, Catholics offered alternatives. Despite the destruction of Sturzo's Popular Party in the 1920s, fresh Catholic po-

---

Gemelli specifically asked the pontiff whether the 1942 message was a religious or a political one. See also Andrea Tornielli, *Pio XII: Eugenio Pacelli, Un uomo sul trono di Pietro* (Milan: Mondadori, 2007, 367–372.

72. Malgeri, "Gli anni di transizione: Da Fanfani a Moro (1954–1962)," in *Storia della democrazia cristiana*, ed. Francesco Malgeri (Rome: Cinque Lune, 1988), 3:173.

73. Regarding the meeting at Feltre, see Renzo De Felice, *Mussolini l'alleato: I. L'Italia in Guerra, 1940–1943*, vol. 2, *Crisi e agonia del regime* (Turin: Einaudi, 1990–96), 1325–36.

74. Tornielli, *Pio XII*, 402–4. See also Ventresca, *Soldier of Christ*, 191–92, and Bosworth, *Whispering City*, 213–15.

75. Denis Mack Smith, *Italy and Its Monarchy* (New Haven, Conn.: Yale University Press, 1989), 304–6; De Felice, *Mussolini l'alleato*, 2:1240.

litical energies emerged during the war. In September 1942, for instance, the Florentine professor Giorgio La Pira organized "Study and Prayer Days," where he spoke "on the need for Christ in the current crisis." By that time, a clandestine and progressive "Guelph" faction developed in Milan, and a separate Christian Democratic underground formed in Rome under Alcide De Gasperi. De Gasperi was close to don Sturzo and served as the last secretary of the PPI until it disbanded in November 1926. Subsequently he spent time in a Fascist jail before gaining Vatican protection as a librarian. De Gasperi became the first secretary of the new Christian Democracy in 1944 and, one year later, took the reins as Italy's first DC prime minister.[76]

King Victor Emmanuel replaced the deposed Mussolini with Marshal Pietro Badoglio, a Piedmontese career military officer who had served the Fascists as a soldier and a diplomat. Upon taking the reins that summer, the so-called Forty-five Days, he secretly negotiated with the Allies while declaring that the war continued, bestowing a Kerensky-like pall on his new government. During those uncertain weeks, on August 19, frustrated by Badoglio's foot-dragging, the Allies bombed Rome again, and Pius resurfaced, this time at the Cathedral of St. John Lateran in an electric moment just as memorable as the one at San Lorenzo. One of the most remarkable Italian photos of the war captured the occasion, with the consoling Pius, arms outstretched, tightly surrounded by a crowd of anxious, worried Romans. Taken together, the San Lorenzo and St. John Lateran visits added to a growing personality cult of Pius, cementing an image of him as the shepherd, the protector of his beloved city and its people.[77]

In the meantime, Badoglio's regime, frozen between combat and surrender, collapsed along with the entire nation over the dramatic night of September 8–9, 1943. As the Allies landed at Salerno, the king and the prime minister abandoned their posts and fled to the South, behind Anglo-American lines, while the Germans occupied the Eternal City and the rest of central and northern Italy. Real power slipped into foreign hands, and in the weeks that followed two governments surfaced on the peninsula, both propped up and controlled by outsiders. In the liberated South, the shreds of the Royal-Badoglio state, known

76. Gianni Baget Bozzo, *Il Partito cristiano al potere: La Dc di DeGasperi e di Dossetti, 1945–1954* (Florence: Vallechi, 1974), 46–47, 79.

77. Oliver Logan, "Pius XII: Romanità, Prophesy and Charisma," *Modern Italy* 3, no, 2 (1998): 237–47; see especially 240–41.

as the Kingdom of the South (*Regno del sud*), emerged under Anglo-American tutelage and would extend itself northward behind the victorious Allied march, while in the North, the Fascists' so-called Salò Regime (or RSI—the Repubblica Sociale Italiana) suffered a slow death under the Nazi thumb. Although the church's relations with the "Kingdom of the South" may not have been ideal, it clearly rejected the RSI. Mussolini's army chief, Rodolfo Graziani, labored vainly for recognition, including an attempt to enroll Blackshirts in the Palatine Guard, but to no avail. Germany's ambassador to the Holy See, Ernst von Weizsäcker, complained of church support for anti-Fascist partisans in the North, while the diehard Fascist and rabid anticleric Roberto Farinacci groaned about all the *Te Deums*, bell-ringing, and clerical applause in the liberated zones.[78]

In Nazi-occupied Rome, from September 1943 until June 1944, esteem for Pius and his church grew even more. The Vatican, Castel Gandolfo, and other Catholic properties provided safe havens for Jews and resisters on the run. Consequently, in March the *Osservatore Romano* argued that Pius, "like Gregory the Great," had earned the title *Defensor Civitatis*. The historian Federico Chabod concurred that the pope's conduct in Hitler's Rome contributed to Gregory's ancient mantle, the legacy of those late imperial popes who shielded the Eternal City from the barbarian hoards. Rome's liberation also yielded another moment that affirmed Pius's almost visceral popularity. On June 6, 1944, the day after General Mark Clark and the troops of America's Fifth Army entered the capital, a mammoth and jubilant crowd spontaneously rushed into St. Peter's Square to celebrate the day with the pontiff and Allied soldiers.[79]

In the liberated areas and soon in the North, Italians could take some solace in the obvious—Mussolini's dictatorship was gone, and after two decades in a muzzle, free politics resumed. The war and the Resistance united Catholics and most anti-Fascists in a "Committee of National Liberation" (Comitato di liberazione nazionale, or CLN), an alliance

78. Malgeri, *Chiesa, cattolici e democrazia*, 145–75. In the most dramatic example, the episcopal conference of the Trevenezie in northeastern Italy issued a public call, read at Mass on May 21, 1944, for liberation. The following October, Pope Pius authorized Milan's Cardinal Ildefonso Schuster to provide spiritual aid to the partisans. One remarkable exception to the icy relations between the church and the RSI was don Tullio Calcagno, a protege of Farinacci, who published a pro-Fascist weekly, *Crociata italica*. In April 1944, the Veneto Episcopal Conference condemned his work, significantly, *before* the Liberation; Jemolo, *Church and State in Italy*, 266; Claudio Pavone, *Una guerra civile: Saggio storico sulla moralità nella Resistenza* (Turin: Bollati Boringhieri, 1994), 280–303; Ceci, *L'interesse superiore*, 303–12.

79. Agostino Giovagnoli, *Il Partito italiano: La Democrazia cristiana dal 1942 al 1994* (Rome and Bari: Laterza, 1996), 27–28; "Voci ed echi," *OR*, June 3, 1950. See also Tornielli, *Pio XII*, 404–5.

of Communists, Socialists, Christian Democrats, Liberals, Azionisti, and some minor groups. Despite its singular place on the ideological spectrum, as its only religiously oriented party, Christian Democracy emerged as the CLN's largest faction. On the left, Marxists gathered in the Italian Communist Party (Partito comunista italiano, or PCI) and the Italian Socialist Party (Partito socialista italiano, or PSI).[80] Next, gravitating toward the center, Christian Democrats and the lay factions included the Liberal Party (Partito liberale italiano, or PLI) and the moderately left Action Party (Partito d'azione, or Pd'A).[81]

By almost any measure, the most conservative lay faction within the CLN coalition was the Liberal Party, led by the internationally honored philosopher Benedetto Croce until his death in 1952. Yet even the Liberals suffered religious opprobrium, as in a 1950 article in the Catholic Action press, "Not Just Communism Is Atheist." Beyond the obvious Marxist challenge, wrote the author, Luigi Bellofiore, the church confronted a "Western ill" of "skeptical and atheist rationalism" that was "no less dangerous." It formed part of the Liberal ideology, articulated by Croce, whose ideas, according to the Catholics, were "not just anti-Christian but truly and substantially atheist," as witnessed in a 1926 speech where he proclaimed the "liquidation" of transcendent and theological philosophy.[82]

When the Allies liberated Rome in June 1944, Badoglio resigned as prime minister, and the anti-Fascist CLN coalition formed its first government under Ivanoe Bonomi, a compromise candidate from the tiny Labor Democratic Party, in which three Christian Democrats, De Gasperi, Umberto Tupini, and Giovanni Gronchi, assumed ministerial rank. The CLN coalition held for a while after the Axis collapse, first under the *azionista* prime minister Ferruccio Parri, who replaced Bonomi in June 1945, then during the early tenure of De Gasperi, who served as prime minister from December 1945 until August 1953. But the arrangement soon crumbled. The Action Party fell first, and by the summer of 1947, its adherents scattered—mostly to Ugo La Malfa and his Republicans or to the Socialists; and what came to be known as the Social Democrats

80. Until the January 1947 split with the Social Democrats, the Socialist Party held the formal name "Italian Socialist Party of Proletarian Unity" (Partito socialista italiano dell'unità proletaria, or PSIUP). They resurrected the name during a brief (1963–68) reunion with the Social Democrats, although, for the sake of simplicity, I shall maintain the PSI label throughout this work.

81. On the lay factions, see Massimo Teodori, *Storia dei laici nell'Italia clericale e comunista* (Venice: Marsilio, 2008).

82. Luigi Bellofiore, "Non solo il comunismo è ateo," *Noi uomini*, May 30, 1950.

(Partito socialdemocratico italiano, or PSDI), which split off from the Socialists in January 1946.[83]

In 1945 Italy emerged, "ruined and sobered" from five catastrophic years of war. Catholics recognized the conflict as a moral catastrophe. Alliance with Hitler, defeat, and national collapse shocked the nation, and this military and political chaos mirrored personal tragedies and ethical challenges. Aerial bombardments killed tens of thousands and smashed large swaths of industrial and urban centers. The Allied decision to invade the nation from Sicily and march up the boot to the Alps, furthermore, meant that no region would escape. About 400,000 died, at least as many civilians as soldiers, and the number climbs to half a million if one includes death from starvation. Italy's industrial production in 1945 sank to 29 percent of its 1938 level. Agriculture stood at 63 percent. Transportation, housing, and power were all in shambles. Cultural treasures from Renaissance art to Milan's La Scala opera house were lost or destroyed. The Black Market flourished, food was scarce, and its distribution was poorly managed; shortages of everything from electricity to paper and glass would persist into the end of the 1940s.[84] Alberto Moravia portrayed this mess of despair in his best-selling novel *Two Women* (*La ciociara*), the story of Cesira and her daughter, Rosetta, that takes place from the summer of 1943 until the summer of 1944. Cesira protects her angelic and devout daughter and seeks refuge along the battlefront between Rome and Naples, but a vicious gang-rape of Rosetta by French Moroccan troops changes the girl forever. Cesira sadly reconciles herself to the physical and moral disaster that, in her eyes, turned her daughter into a whore. At one point after the rape, one of Rosetta's new "boyfriends," Rosario, reproaches the mother for getting so upset over her daughter's fate. "You, Cesira, you're a pre-war woman," he scolds; "*we* all belong to *after* the war.... Everything's changed, the old days are gone, and you've got to get used to the idea." Later, when Cesira confronts Rosetta over Rosario, the daughter lashes back: "I want

83. The Social Democrats first called themselves the Socialist Party of Italian Workers (Partito socialista dei lavoratori italiani). In 1952, they changed their name to the Italian Social Democrat Party (Partito socialdemocratico italiano, or PSDI). After their reunion with the PSI (cited earlier), they reverted to the PSDI. I will henceforth refer to them as the Social Democrats or the PSDI.

84. The description of Italy "ruined and sobered" comes from the anti-Fascist Max Ascoli's introduction to Benito Mussolini's memoir *My Rise and Fall*, vol. 2, *History of a Year* (New York: Da Capo Press, 1998), 71; Giorgio Candeloro, *Storia dell'Italia moderna*, vol. 11, *La Fondazione della Repubblica e la ricostruzione: Considerazioni finali* (Milan: Feltrinelli, 1986), 15–23, 82–91; and Lanaro, *Storia dell'Italia repubblicana*. Victoria C. Belco examined the situation at a local Tuscan level in her *War, Massacre and Recovery in Central Italy, 1943–1948* (Toronto: Toronto University Press, 2010), particularly chapters 3 and 5, and 225–31.

to make love because it's the only thing I feel like doing. And from now on it's always going to be like that."[85]

Caught in a cauldron of doubt, anger, fear, and shame, many like Cesira turned to the church. Moravia's story concludes when mother and daughter return to the newly freed Rome, their home, and Cesira expresses her joy as St. Peter's dome first appears to her on the horizon. "God knows," she muses, "how earnestly I had hoped throughout the whole of the past year to see that beloved dome.... That dome, for me, was not merely Rome, it was my life in Rome ... after so many changes and tragedies, the old life would take up its course again." Her sentiment was certainly widespread and worked to favor the idea of a return to a traditional and Christian Italy. In contrast to one vision, mainly lay and Marxist, that saw Fascism's end as an opportunity for progressive change, Cesira stood with those who, as one historian wrote, "desperately wanted to 'return to normal life.'"[86]

85. Albert Moravia, *Two Women*, trans. Angus Dawson (New York: Farrar, Straus and Cudahy, 1958), 320, 326. In 1960, Vittorio De Sica issued his film version of *Two Women*, for which Sophia Loren as Cesira earned the 1961 Academy Award for best actress.

86. Moravia, *Two Women*, 338; Belco, *War, Massacre and Recovery in Central Italy*, 5. A recent expression of these feelings came from Molly Tambor's book on postwar Italian women activists. "Most ordinary Italians," she wrote, "simply craved a return to 'normalcy' ... best symbolized by family: a stable harmonious family with a working father, a nurturing mother, and children who would be well-fed, well-dressed, and, above all, safe"; Tambor, *The Lost Wave: Women and Democracy in Postwar Italy* (Oxford: Oxford University Press, 2014), 15.

Chapter 1

The "Clerical State" and Its Critics

Dramatis Personae

The Church

The Second World War's physical devastation did not spare the Italian Catholic Church. Over seven hundred clergy died, and structures across the peninsula endured severe damage—from small chapels to lofty basilicas like Rome's San Lorenzo-beyond-the-Walls and Milan's Sant'Ambrogio. Naples's Santa Chiara and the great Benedictine abbey of Monte Cassino, high on the German Gustav Line, both suffered obliteration; and in February 1944, an accidental bombardment even hit the papal retreat at Castel Gandolfo, ending five hundred lives. Beyond the churches, parishioners anguished over destroyed homes and workplaces and the deaths of neighbors and loved ones with whom they had recently shared Holy Communion. One example of the challenges faced by the survivors came from a 1950 Catholic Action (Azione Cattolica, or AC) report out of the diocese of Isernia/Venafro, a battle-scarred zone not far from Naples. There, don Antonio Broggiato despaired that the war destroyed 70 percent of his Isernia and left four thousand dead. Two-thirds of the diocesan clergy, furthermore, were over sixty-five years old, and some parishes lacked pastors. Money and supplies were scarce, but church aid, a vital chapter of Catholic Action, and a Fraternal Christian Aid society (Fraterno Aiuto Cristiano) gave cause to hope. The bishop, moreover, chipped in with the use of his car, and an optimistic don Broggiato announced with certainty, "God helps us!"[1]

1. On wartime clerical deaths, see Mario Casella, *Clero e politica in Italia* (1942–1948) (Galatina:

Italy's postwar Christian Democratic governments proved essential in the reconstruction. In 1952, the archconservative Egilberto Martire, in the *Osservatore Romano*, acknowledged this when he praised the work of the Education Ministry's General Directorate of Fine Arts and various Public Works departments that had rendered so much aid in rebuilding war-damaged churches and other religious structures. Such work, he proclaimed, would lead to a "renaissance of churches in Italy."[2] Thanks in no small measure to state help, the postwar era was, indeed, one of growth for many urban dioceses, and the number of Italian parishes expanded, from 22,412 in 1924 to 24,552 in 1951 and 27,399 in 1966.[3] Rome and northern cities where an influx of southern migrants began to make itself felt saw much of the action. In 1953 the Cardinal Vicar of Rome, for instance, tallied many achievements in his diocese, citing the construction of churches in eight new parishes, while eleven Catholic sports complexes opened in the city, with nine more in suburban parishes and the rural *Agro romano*.[4]

Moral recovery would take time. Fully ten years after the Axis surrender, the bishop of Parma still lamented the damage wrought by the conflict on the Italian family. Gone were the days, he wrote, when smiles graced the faces of suffering peasants or when that spirit formed a halo over the head of the Mamma who endured in silence "for the peace of the family."[5] Beyond war damage, deeper and older problems of secularization persisted, as reflected in lower Mass attendance. A study in the area around Mantua, the Mantovano, for example, found that Easter observance had dropped from 75–82.3 percent (depending on the zone) in 1885 to 51–69 percent in 1948.[6] Elsewhere, in 1953, Rome's Cardinal Vicar expected "very low, even discouraging" numbers at Mass, citing a survey of twenty parishes that found that only 40 percent of the faithful attended on Sundays.[7] The clergy presented more of a mixed story. While the number of diocesan priests declined—from 83,834 in 1881 to 51,364 in 1931 and 47,117 in 1951—membership in religious orders mostly

Congedo, 1999), 24–26, and f. 66; IPVI, Sg VI, b. 19, f. 5; Delegazione Interdiocesana (Isernia) report, April 30, 1950.

2. Egilberto Martire, "La rinascita delle chiese in Italia," *Osservatore Romano* (henceforth *OR*), April 6, 1952.

3. Franco Bolgiani, "La Chiesa Cattolica," in *Guida all'Italia contemporanea, 1861–1997*, ed. Augusto Cherchi (Milan: Garzanti, 1998), 93.

4. "Nell'anniversario della esortazione pontificia," *OR*, February 15, 1953.

5. Evasio Colli, "Diritti e doveri nella famiglia," *Iniziativa*, April 1955.

6. Carlo Falconi, "La Crisi della parrocchia in Italia," *Nuovi argomenti*, July–August 1953.

7. "Nell'anniversario della esortazione pontificia."

expanded, from 7,191 in 1881 to 10,819 in 1951. It would more than double to 22,464 by 1971.[8]

Father Roberto Perenna discussed some of these issues in his 1950 edited work *Innovations or Renovation of the Parish?* He pointed to "indifferentism," a dilemma that had spread over the past two generations and led to an "absence of God in the contemporary world."[9] One essay by Paolo Vigorelli identified a "mass apostasy ... [and] the weakening of sacramental life and charity in human relations." The culture was battered by "illustrated reviews, novels, films," and by a "relativism ... [that] insinuates itself," particularly into a generic religion in which everything is equally "good." Finally, Vigorelli saw lay forces chipping away at society's Christian bonds and replacing them with materialist ones. Technology assisted this assault, not only facilitating access to secularist propaganda, but making people more mobile and contributing to "the need to escape the city at the end of the week" that jeopardized the sanctity of Sundays. Those engaged in weekend fun often forgot Holy obligations. The effects were real enough, according to Vigorelli, who compared two Milanese parishes, called XX and YY. XX was "one of the best in the diocese," and YY was one of the most densely populated. In 1938, XX saw forty Holy Communions per capita, while YY's figure was closer to seven or eight. In 1948, those numbers fell drastically to, respectively, twenty and between three and four.[10]

Beyond such tales of secularization, Perenna located Catholicism's chief "external" enemies among the lay, the *laicisti*—Marxists, followed by those with a liberal mindset, Masons, followers of "insidious" Protestantism, and practitioners of "the pseudo-religious idea of the Mazzinian stripe and deviations caused by [philosophical historicism associated with Benedetto Croce] wherein God is a principle, an entity [*ente*], an abstract thing." Elsewhere, in 1954, Bologna's Cardinal Giacomo Lercaro identified the Communist menace in his archdiocese, the heart of Italy's

8. Giuseppe Brunetta, "Il Clero in Italia dal 1888 al 1989," *Polis*, December 1991, 436.

9. Roberto Perenna, ed., *Innovazioni o rinnovamento della Parrocchia? Ragioni di allarme, Motivi di speranza, Impegni di responsabilità* (Como: Cavalleri, 1950), 70–75. Perenna derived much of his discussion of the absence of God from the work of the archbishop of Paris, Cardinal Emmanuel Suhard. The French fortnightly *Documentation catholique* published an extensive denunciation of the Masons in 1953, much of which the *Osservatore Romano* reprinted for its July 22 edition as "Piani e programmi del Grande Oriente per la laicizzazione della Francia." In a March 29, 1957, editorial from Giovanni Lupo, "Il Costume del privilegio," *Il Popolo* attacked the Masons as selfish members of the bourgeoisie, jealous of their status, whose professions of egalitarianism rang phony.

10. Paolo Vigorelli, "La Parrocchia di fronte alle esigenze del mondo moderno," in Perenna, *Innovazioni o rinnovamento della Parrocchia?*, 11–19. Another study in the volume discussed the Catholic Church in the United States, where the parish was vibrant and wealthy, and "the sanctification [of Sundays was] true and real" (27).

"Red Belt." To a British journalist he reported that the PCI dominated fifty-three out of sixty communes there.[11] From Isernia, on the other hand, don Broggiato fought back with an ambitious program of conferences for men, "mothers," boys, and girls, distinguished by "a remarkable number of souls thirsty for Christ" and littered with "ripped-up Communist Party cards."[12]

For these battles the church employed its extensive media, much of which predated Fascism and then functioned under the regime, thanks to the 1929 Lateran Pacts. Along with Vatican Radio, inaugurated in 1931, stood the venerable and official newspaper the *Osservatore Romano*. Not far behind came the Jesuit review *Civiltà cattolica*. The list continued with such titles as the *Rivista del clero italiano*, intended for the nation's diocesan priests. Some cities issued their own Catholic newspapers, like the *Eco di Bergamo*, Milan's *Italia*, and the *Avvenire d'Italia* from Bologna. In addition, religious orders often produced their own magazines and other works. Founded in 1930 by the Paulist Leonardo Zega, *Famiglia cristiana* enjoyed the greatest circulation of any Catholic publication, linked in a "Pauline empire" that would later include the monthly *Famiglia Mese*, the review *Jesus*, and a television and radio network.[13] Beyond its media, the church expected and received support from Italian Catholic Action and the new power of Italian politics, Christian Democracy (Democrazia Cristiana, or DC).

Italian Catholic Action

In the early 1960s, Joseph LaPalombara discovered that four-fifths of Italian political leaders considered Italian Catholic Action to constitute "a class by itself" and "the single most powerful interest group operating in the political system."[14] Unlike Christian Democracy, however, Catholic Action was not a political party. To please the Fascists, the Lateran Pacts specified this. It was, instead, a parish-based organization of

11. Philip Merrifield (pseudonym for a British writer in Italy), "Conversation with Cardinal Lercaro," *Commonweal*, December 24, 1954.

12. IPVI, Sg VI, b. 19, f. 5; Delegazione Interdiocesana (Isernia) report, April 30, 1950.

13. On the history of the Catholic press, see Angelo Majo, *Storia della stampa cattolica in Italia: Con orientamenti bibliografiche* (Milan: NED, 1987); Mario Marazziti, *I Papi di carta: Nascita e svolta dell'informazione religiosa da Pio XII a Giovanni XXIII* (Genoa: Marietti, 1990); and Casella, *Giornali cattolici e società italiana: Religione politica democratica nelle pagine de "L'Osservatore Romano" e de "Il Quotidiano" (1944–1950)* (Naples: Edizioni scientifiche italiane, 1994).

14. Joseph LaPalombara, *Interest Groups in Italian Politics* (Princeton, N.J.: Princeton University Press, 1964), 349; cited in William Troy McCraw, "Political Sponsorship of the Arts: Subsidization and Censorship of Motion Pictures and the Performing Arts by the Italian National Government, 1943–1962" (Ph.D. diss., Stanford University, 1966), 192.

the laity that consisted of loose branches, primarily "Unions" for Men (Unione Uomini), and Women (Unione Donne di Azione Cattolica Italiana, or UDACI), male youth (Gioventù Italiana di Azione Cattolica, or GIAC), and female youth (Gioventù femminile, or GF). Other wings enrolled university students (Federazione Universitaria Cattolica Italiana, or FUCI), graduates in the Movimento Laureati, and schoolteachers in the Movimento Maestri. Members tended to identify with these smaller entities, observed the sociologist Gianfranco Poggi, "rather than with the AC, whose components [were] merely groups of leaders." Membership overall was predominantly female and young. Catholic Action women and girls outnumbered men and boys by at least two to one, and over half of Catholic Action ranks, which crested above three million in the 1950s, consisted of children and adolescents. Poggi concluded that the youngsters' ranks thinned as they grew into adulthood, leaving a smaller, harder, and more devoted core in the upper reaches of the GIAC and the GF and then in the Men's and Women's Unions.[15] Here dwelt the avant-garde militant (*militante*—a frequent term), and lay apostle. "This person," wrote Poggi, "wears his [or her] lapel button at all times, receives communion every time he attends Mass (two to five times a week), has a 'spiritual director' in the person of a priest, besides going to a weekly confession. He does not dance, even if he is in his late teens or early twenties, nor does he attend films judged unbecoming by ecclesiastical authorities. He reads the Catholic newspaper, and at election time is an active propagandist for the Catholic party . . . does not tolerate blasphemy . . . [and spends leisure time] within the framework of the parish and the [AC] local."[16]

Catholic Action was closer to the church than was Christian Democracy. During the war the church hierarchy even took direct control of it until new statutes in October of 1946 reinstituted lay leadership under Vittorino Veronese, who functioned as president along with his clerical counterpart, the *assistente ecclesiastico* (ecclesiastic assistant) Bishop Giovanni Urbani, who served from 1946 to 1955. Each lay officer in the organization had his or her *assistente ecclesiastico*, a euphemism in that each represented clerical authority, making sure its "prescriptions and directive norms [were] faithfully observed."[17]

15. Gianfranco Poggi, *Catholic Action in Italy: The Sociology of a Sponsored Organizaton* (Stanford, Calif.: Stanford University Press, 1967), 31–33. In 1957 membership figures of the four largest groups were: Unione Uomini 309,000; UDACI 630,000; GIAC 583,000; and GF 1,241,000.

16. Poggi, *Catholic Action in Italy*, 41–42.

17. Poggi, *Catholic Action in Italy*, 98.

Much depended on personality; the AC's emerging figure was Luigi Gedda. From the war years until the new Pope John replaced him in 1959, Gedda's was the face of Catholic Action. Born to a comfortable bourgeois life in Venice in 1902, he grew up in France, Turin, and Milan. In 1927, after studies at Pavia and Milan, he graduated from the University of Turin in medicine and devoted much of his academic life to the study of twins, publishing a massive tome on that subject in 1951.[18] By 1934, he had acquired a reputation as a Catholic Action militant, and Pius XI called him to Rome to head the GIAC. There, the tireless Gedda expanded his tasks to include the AC's film office, the Centro cinematografico cattolico (CCC), which had a weekly film guide and a review, the *Rivista del cinematografo*. In that capacity, he was the force behind the 1942 movie *Pastor Angelicus*, a paean to Pius XII and an immense success in Catholic circles, directed by Romolo Marcellini.[19] After the war, Gedda advanced in 1946 from head of the GIAC to the leadership of the Unione Uomini. In 1949, he became a vice president of AC, and in January 1952 he succeeded Veronese at the top. Gedda nurtured and benefitted from a relationship with Pope Pius XII about as close as any layman could boast, strengthening the ties between Catholic Action and the church. That claim did not impress the lay and Marxist camps, which directed incessant fire on Catholic Action and Gedda, with his "Mussolinian" brow and eyes, and who, one critic charged, possessed a "hormonal" tendency toward dictatorship, also comparing him to the Portuguese strongman Antonio Salazar.[20] Gedda pushed to give the organization a more conservative and political role, leading to confrontations with Veronese and others, all of whom suffered defeat at his hands. The most open of these battles pit him against the youth leader Mario Rossi, who submitted to Gedda's authority in April 1954.[21] At times, Gedda's am-

18. Luigi Gedda, *Studio dei gemelli* (Rome: Edizioni orrizonte medico, 1951).

19. The Catholics also produced Marcellini's *Guerra alla Guerra*, released in 1946; Carlo Falconi, *La Chiesa e le organizzazioni cattoliche in Italia 1945–55* (Turin: Giulio Einaudi, 1956), 265–68. On Gedda, see Poggi, *Catholic Action in Italy*, 190–98, and Falconi, *Gedda e L'azione cattolica* (Florence: Parenti editore, 1958). See also Federico Ruozzi, "Pius XII as Actor and Subject," in *Moralizing Cinema: Film Catholicism and Power*, ed. Daniela Treveri Gennari and Daniel Biltereyst (New York: Routledge, 2014), 158–72; Stefano Pivato, *Clericalismo e laicismo nella cultura popolare italiana* (Milan: Franco Angeli, 1990), 183; Roy Domenico, "Gedda, il laicato e la cultura cattolica negli anni Cinquanta," in *Luigi Gedda nella storia della Chiesa e del Paese*, ed. Ernesto Preziosi (Rome: AVE, 2013), 309–22. John Pollard belives that *Pastor Angelicus* helped to make Pius the most popular man in Italy at the end of the war. It only showed for a few days in 1942, and the Fascists shut it down, probably for that reason; Pollard, *The Papacy in the Age of Totalitarianism, 1914–1958* (Oxford: Oxford University Press, 2014), 352–53.

20. Falconi, *Gedda e L'azione cattolica*, 162–82 and 236–38.

21. Giacomo de Antonellis, *Storia dell'Azione Cattolica dal 1867 a oggi* (Milan: Rizzoli, 1987), 263–71; Falconi, *Gedda e L'azione cattolica*, 198–227; Maria Cristina Giuntella, "Cristiani nella storia: Il 'caso Rossi'

bition could try even the pope, to whom he once impetuously asked whether he "still enjoyed [his] enlightened benevolence." A somewhat rattled Pius replied, "Yes, but don't abuse it" (*Si—ma non ne abusi*).[22]

Myriad ancillary, satellite, or subordinate organizations—from political activists in Gedda's 30,000-strong Civic Committees (*Comitati civici*) to the Family Front, the National Agency [*Ente*] for the Moral Protection of Children, and leagues devoted to "Large Families," to combating blasphemy, and to "Keeping Sundays Sacred"—all committed themselves to cultivating a nation of good Christian comportment (*buon costume*). That so many wanted to get in on the act worried Veronese, who, in 1946, confessed his anxiety in a letter to an activist. He wrote that the mission of the Family Front (Fronte della famiglia), to promote the health of the institution, campaign for a national holiday, and fight attempts to legalize divorce, overlapped with perhaps six other groups.[23]

One ingredient in this Catholic stew was the Opera nazionale per la santificazione della festa, founded in December 1945 and blessed by the pope in February 1948. Aimed at keeping Sundays holy, it enjoyed the patronage of the archbishop of Florence and the bishop of Assisi, but its spirit came from a Capuchin, Father Bernardino. He and his associates launched a newsletter, the *Sunday Crusade* (*Crociata festiva*) to confront "the enemies of God [who] have forever stated: We must ban the Lord's day from the face of the Earth! We defenders of God's cause will be like the heralds of old and we will repeat to everyone with words and deeds the Holy commandment: 'Remember the Sabbath Day and keep it Holy.'"[24] Here, the DC government could provide real assistance. On May 6, 1953, the Rome prefecture ordered all food stores to close on Sundays, and the following November, the DC-controled City Council extended the order to clothing stores. Merchants and local farmers associations grumbled so much, however, that the directives were soon rescinded.[25] This issue

e i suoi riflessi nelle organizzazioni cattoliche di massa," in *Pio XII*, ed. Andrea Riccardi (Rome and Bari: Laterza, 1984), 347–77.

22. Benny Lai, "La presidenza di Gedda è forse in pericolo," *L'Europeo*, May 15, 1955.

23. Ernesto Preziosi, "Il Fronte della famiglia," in *Democrazia e coscienza religiosa nella storia del Novecento: Studi in onore di Francesco Malgeri*, ed. Augusto D'Angelo, Paolo Trionfini, and Roberto P. Violi (Rome: Ave, 2010), 88–89. Veronese's letter of May 28, 1946, was sent to Urbano Cioccetti at Catholic Action's Men's Union. During the Holy Year Pius's words to the Fronte della famiglia were collected in a book, *La Famiglia*; A. De Micheli, "L'Insegnamento di Pio XII sulla famiglia in una recente raccolta," *OR*, October 8, 1950. See also "Inaugurato il Convegno del Fronte della Famiglia" and "Concluso ieri il Convegno del Fronte della Famiglia," *Il Popolo*, November 18 and 20, 1956.

24. IPVI, Sg VII, b. 29.

25. N.A., "Il problema del riposo festive," *OR*, November 29, 1953. The report noted that the Sunday sale of milk would not pose a problem in that the product could be located easily in bars and caffès, which did not operate under the rules for food and clothing stores.

never really died, however, and four years later the DC review, *Discussione*, urged more respect for Sundays. The crisis was real, it insisted in March 1957, particularly among the young, and it cited a Catholic Youth poll showing that, indeed, 50 percent of young apprentices and laborers worked on the Lord's day. At fault were insensitive bosses whose greed challenged "a way of life, a mentality." The weary Christian worker, concluded the review, needed that special day for "leisure, rest, dedication to spirit and, above all, strengthening family life."[26]

Perusing the calendar, Catholics also identified an attack on Christmas. Godless Communists provided plenty of examples, such as when the *Osservatore Romano* recorded how East Germany wanted to replace the feast of the birth of Christ with Stalin's birthday. Freedom of religion behind the Iron Curtain, announced the journal, only meant "the freedom to suffer and die" for the faith.[27] But seductive lay challenges could prove more insidious than the brutal Communist iron fist. Catholic Action's mens' review, *Noi uomini*, criticized the proliferation in Italy of *Babbo Natale* (or "Christmas Daddy," a secular St. Nicholas), which it saw as an American import and derided as a materialist "Ice Daddy" (*Babbo Gelo*). Catholics, rather, might better rediscover their "sacred tradition of the Creche [*presepe*]."[28]

Another very visible agency was the National *Buon Costume* Association headed by Carlo Costantini; its task was to assist the government and "urge all citizens to collaborate with [it] in observance of the laws protecting *buon costume*." While insisting that it was "independent of any party," its goals were identical to Catholic Action's. In January 1951, Costantini compiled statistics on the work of his association since its birth in 1946, listing wide-ranging aims, from the elimination of disreputable movie posters to cooperating with Rome's mayor in removing "very filthy" (*sudicissimi*) graffiti in the washrooms of the city's principal cemetery, the Verano. The association also targeted and succeeded in getting the police to close a number of clandestine houses of prostitution, including one particularly vile place frequented by "perverts" who preyed on schoolchildren; and, with the help of the mobile *buon costume* (or vice) police squads, cleaned out a Roman bathing establishment on the banks of the Tiber.[29]

26. Roberto Bencivenga Jr., "Di Domenica gli italiani non riposano," *Discussione*, March 24, 1957.

27. "Voci ed echi" column, OR, December 20, 1950.

28. On *Babbo Natale*, see "Punte Secche," *Noi uomini*, January 19, 1958.

29. IPVI, Pg XII, b. 32, "Associazione nazionale per il buon costume—Relazione all'assemblea dei soci sull'attività svolta dall'associazione nel quinquennio 1946–1950," January 7, 1951.

The *Rivista del clero italiano* emphasized that women, as mothers and wives, held a special place in the fight. At the local level and under the tutelage of parish priests, the Women's Union (UDACI) worked toward "religious action: for the spread of truth and of the Christian life." This included assistance in catechism classes, helping the infirm, and bringing the word of God to traveling artists and circus folk. Beyond religious work, the union engaged in "action for the defense, the moralization and the sanctification of the family"; "educative action," wherein mothers collaborated with schools; "social action," such as assisting various social organizations like the St. Vincent De Paul Society or Catholic labor unions; and "moral action" that placed the woman in the public square to fight secularizing tendencies. Among her duties was to monitor newsstands that stood near schools and to check on morality at vacation sites.[30]

The Unione Donne found a natural ally in the six-million-member Italian Womens' Center. Established in 1944, the Centro italiano femminile (or CIF) acted as an umbrella federation of twenty-six women's groups dedicated to leading a war-wracked society "on its path of orderliness and Christian peace."[31] One found CIF footprints in many fields of women's and family activity, including the establishment of children's tuberculosis centers across Italy. Its official status as beyond clerical control was something of a fiction, with an *assistente ecclesiastico* for each CIF branch. Its leaders were DC and Catholic Action notables, like its first president, Maria Federici, and memberships dovetailed with the two groups. A seamstress from Ravenna even recalled that "once during a meeting of Catholic Action it was said that we were all passing into membership in the CIF."[32]

AC women also promoted agencies devoted to offspring. A December 1950 Catholic Action report applauded the National Campaign for the Salvation of Children (Campagna Nazionale per la Salvezza dell'Infanzia), which helped those still reeling from the "profound repercussions of the war and its difficult aftermath," their physical health and

30. Various authors, "L'Ora delle donne cattoliche," *Rivista del clero italiano*, January 1956.

31. Ambrogio Aldè, "Il Centro italiano femminile," *Rivista del clero italiano*, September 1954. See also Wendy Pojmann, *Italian Women and International Cold War Politics, 1944–1968* (New York: Fordham University Press, 2013); Perry Willson, *Women in Twentieth-Century Italy* (New York: Palgrave Macmillan, 2010), 141–42; and Molly Tambor, *The Lost Wave: Women and Democracy in Postwar Italy* (Oxford: Oxford University Press, 2014), 39–46. Tambor recognizes the CIF's "conflicted" connection to the DC, although that relationship yielded it hundreds of millions of lire in state subsidies, while the Union of Italian Women, linked, also ambiguously, to the Communist Party, received nothing.

32. Pojmann, *Italian Women and International Cold War Politics*, 27, 41–42, 54.

their "moral integrity," a crisis reflected in the "growing seriousness and frequency of juvenile delinquency." Such tasks meant confronting the "diabolically savvy," especially Communist, "seduction and corruption of childhood." Catholic Action dedicated the month of May to childhood and targeted the twenty-first for "Parish Congresses" on the subject. Furthermore, the National Campaign launched summertime activities for youth and, in the autumn, combined parish celebrations of Guardian Angels Day (Festa degli angeli custodi) and Parents and Families Day (Festa dei genitori e delle famiglie). The special day began with a Mass, followed by a children's breakfast, then parents' tours intended to explain parish action, and a sports event organized by Catholic Action's Centro sportivo italiano (Italian Sports Center, CSI). After lunch, the young ones put on shows for their mothers and fathers in a *Festa dei Fanciulli*.[33]

Central to Catholic Action's campaign for *buon costume* was its Morality Secretariat, reorganized under Lamberto Vignoli in 1937 from an earlier incarnation. Under a Catholic Action secretary and an ecclesiastical assistant in Rome, throughout its life the office maintained one or two bookkeeping employees, although it relied on diocesan chapters across Italy, staffed by local AC and clerical representatives. A postwar Catholic Action report listed the four principal duties of this office. First, to document "as thoroughly and as accurately as possible the moral conditions in all sectors of public life." Second, to study "the best ways to remove or at least attenuate serious public scandal." Third, the office would act on the public "to promote the good and reprimand the bad," and on the authorities to "ensure the proper application of current laws and to protect public morality." This required keeping an eye on any new legislation that would affect decency "and religious sentiment." The office's fourth purpose was to keep the church hierarchy informed, enabling prompt action on its part. An internal circular from 1953 simplified the objectives as "the moralization of comportment in three sectors: dress, entertainment, and the press."[34]

33. IPVI, Pg VI, b. 11, f. 5; Azione cattolica report, "Sviluppi della Crociata del Grande Ritorno: La Campagna nazionale per la Salvezza della Infanzia," 1950. See also, in the same folder, Gedda circular of September 14, 1950, in which he directed that Parents' Day merge with Guardian Angels Day as a "new and important goal to challenge the Communist trick [*insidia*] against childhood." See also I.P., "Festa dei genitori e delle famiglie," *Iniziativa*, August–September 1950.

34. The Secretariat for Morality was created in 1923; IPVI, Sg VI, b. 1, f. 3; "Relazione sulla attività degli uffici, segretariati ed enti della presidenza generale dell'ACI Novembre 1946–Ottobre 1947"; IPVI, Sg XII, b. 5, Morality circular no. 84, November 14, 1953. See also Gavuzzo report, "Il Segretariato per la moralità," n.d. (probably 1969), IPVI, Pg XII, b. 22.

In 1949, the lawyer Gino Gavuzzo, who succeeded Vignoli, published a *Guide for the Defense of Morality*, one of the key texts in the campaign for Christian *buon costume*. He revised it in 1952 and expanded it by about 150 pages.[35] For that edition, Gavuzzo and Monsignor Ferdinando Prosperini, the ecclesiastic assistant, explained and promoted its value to Catholic Action functionaries at the parish and diocesan levels. Its utility, they wrote, extended beyond AC officials to anyone interested in "this sector of the apostolate," as well as "to judges and police functionaries." To facilitate circulation, each diocesan morality office reduced the cost of the Guide from the 450 lire retail price to 300 for militants.[36]

Bishop Urbani began his guest preface to the 1952 *Guida* with an admonition from the Gospel of Matthew that whoever would cause the downfall of a little believer would have a millstone put around his neck and be thrown into the sea.[37] How current were these words, asked Urbani, in an Italy where hedonism yanked the "salutary yoke of moral law" and the corruption of conduct (*costume*) pervaded the cities, the neighborhoods, and even "the sanctuary of the family"? Faced with this deplorable state, what course should be taken by "the good, the honest, the Christians, not just those in name and tradition, but of faith and works"? Gavuzzo provided concrete answers to forge "the Christian principles of our Constitution" into effective and applicable laws and actions. "There is no doubt," wrote Urbani, "that one cannot base a firm and strong national reconstruction on the shifting sand of bad conduct [*malcostume*], but only on the rock of Christian morals."[38]

Building on Urbani's sentiments, Gavuzzo's *Guida* identified two charges, one positive and the other negative. First, as with all of Catholic Action, the Morality Office promoted the commonweal through propaganda and "moral works" (*opere moralizzatrici*), while on the other hand it labored to "eliminate the causes and occasions or moral disorder, that is, to fight evil."[39] Gavuzzo outlined a command structure that placed

35. Gino Gavuzzo, *Guida per la difesa della moralità: Indicazioni, legislazione, giurisprudenza* (Rome: Segretariato centrale per la moralità, 1952). Unless indicated, all references to the *Guida* derive from this edition. Born in Rome in 1904 but from an old Piedmontese family, Gavuzzo studied law at the University of Rome. He and his wife produced six children. He died in 1983; Alexander Donald Stewart and Silvia Gavuzzo Stewart, *Gavuzzo and Gavuzzi: The History of a Piedmontese Family from the Middle Ages to the Twentieth Century* (Amelia, Italy: n.p.), 2010.

36. IPVI, Sg XII, b. 5. Gavuzzo/Prosperini circular no. 38, February 27, 1952. Prosperini came to the Morality Office after he had been the ecclesiastic assistant to the AC's *Ente dello spettacolo*.

37. Mt 18:6–7.

38. Gavuzzo, *Guida*, 1–4 (Urbani introduction).

39. Gavuzzo, *Guida*, 18–19.

great emphasis on the diocesan secretary, the "meeting point" for everyone concerned with the moral apostolate. The diocesan secretary ran the organization, "diligently document[ing] . . . the true conditions of morality in the various sectors (press, entertainment, comportment, juvenile delinquency, fashion, etc.)," providing information to the bishop and to Gavuzzo's office for decisions on proper channels and competence. The diocesan secretary was then to work with Catholic Action to develop "an organic plan . . . to eliminate public scandal" and foster "a better moral conscience."[40]

The key to the battle, the pivot (*perno*) of the whole program, therefore, remained militant Christians, particularly those in the Morality Secretariat. They cannot be shy but, rather, loud and clear in their denunciations, which "must reach the eye and the ear" of the state. Nothing would be gained by objections whispered to well-meaning friends. Nor should one assume the mantle of the loner, grousing about the state of things; such people were soon dismissed as thin-skinned cranks, or worse. Only determined action and collective strength would bring victory in the war of *buon costume*.[41]

The *Guida*'s second part catalogued specific offenses and identified laws to employ in the battle against *malcostume*. Gavuzzo began alphabetically with "clothes and fashion" (*abbigliamento e moda*), suggesting that, in the absence of clear laws, militants lead the way as role models with their own modest attire by persuading family and friends and by avoiding noncompliant tailors.[42] Discussed next was alcoholism, "one of the worst habits," which the penal code covered in Article 686.[43] Then came dancing, a furtive amusement that "yields many dangers" and should be tightly controlled by the police, who must watch for excessive crowding, late hours, and access to minors and ensure that the dance not conflict with religious obligations.[44] Next, sanctions against blasphemy and insults "directed against God or Persons venerated in the State religion" were specified in the Lateran Pacts and incorporated into the penal code's Article 724.[45] The guide continued with juvenile delinquency

40. Gavuzzo, *Guida*, 21–25.

41. Gavuzzo, *Guida*, 28–36. Gavuzzo cited the February 2, 1950, Rome Appeals Court decision regarding the review *Otto*. Action was taken by President Costantini of the Associazione Nazionale per il Buon Costume, 133 people of Casalmonferrato, "many citizens of Rome," and others.

42. Gavuzzo, *Guida*, 55–68.

43. Gavuzzo, *Guida*, 68–88.

44. Gavuzzo, *Guida*, 89–96.

45. Gavuzzo, *Guida*, 97–113.

(*delinquenza minorile*),[46] public exhibition (*esposizione pubblica*), which dealt with store windows,[47] gambling (*giuochi d'azzardo*),[48] and incest (*incesto*).[49] Then came a grab-bag notion of "bad behavior" (*malcostume*) that Gavuzzo defined as "some acts of immorality not specifically identified in the other classifications and that relate in a broad sense to public conduct." Kissing, for example, might be *malcostume* when it crossed the line from an "expression of pure sentiment" to something lusty or carnal, and, in particular, when it might contribute to the corruption of those under seventeen years of age. He also suggested monitoring university parties and beauty contests for more evidence of *malcostume*.[50] The morality list continued with birth control (*maltusianismo*),[51] prostitution (*prostituzione*),[52] advertising (*pubblicità*),[53] and show business (*spettacolo*), which included film, variety reviews, puppet shows (and their effect on children), prose theater, radio, and other events such as the circuses or sporting contests.[54] Gavuzzo finished his list with chapters dedicated to the beach (*spiaggia*),[55] printed material (*stampa*),[56] drugs (*stupefacenti*),[57] and foul language (*turpiloquio*).[58]

Beyond the Morality Office, Catholic Action, like the church, enlisted its own media resources for the fight. In 1944, the AC's *assistente ecclesiastico*, Gilla Vincenzo Gremigni (who Urbani replaced in 1946), proposed a central press office and, to organize it, enlisted the aid of the up-and-coming FUCI and DC youth leader Giulio Andreotti, a Roman who worked closely with Prime Minister Alcide De Gasperi.[59] That same year, with papal blessing, the prolific writer Igino Giordani founded the AC's own paper, Il *Quotidiano*, taking the editorship through April of

46. Gavuzzo, *Guida*, 115–36.

47. Gavuzzo, *Guida*, 150–55.

48. Gavuzzo, *Guida*, 156–61.

49. Gavuzzo, *Guida*, 162–63.

50. Gavuzzo, *Guida*, 164–80. Gavuzzo found authorization for this in a Cassation Court verdict of March 2, 1950.

51. Gavuzzo, *Guida*, 181–86.

52. Gavuzzo, *Guida*, 188–206. Here Gavuzzo had to watch his step and needed to distinguish between "clandestine" and legal prostitution, which the state still regulated in 1952. Nevertheless, he lamented "this ignominious crime against the human personality and the dignity of women ... that unfortunately saw a rise during and after the last World War for reasons that can be guessed."

53. Gavuzzo, *Guida*, 207–25.

54. Gavuzzo, *Guida*, 226–77.

55. Gavuzzo, *Guida*, 278–84.

56. Gavuzzo, *Guida*, 285–353.

57. Gavuzzo, *Guida*, 354–68.

58. Gavuzzo, *Guida*, 369.

59. Casella, *L'Azione cattolica alla caduta del fascismo: Attività e progetti per il dopoguerra (1942–'45)* (Rome: Studium, 1984), 153–79.

1946, when he left to stand as a candidate in the Constituent elections.[60] Every branch of Catholic Action, moreover, had its own organ. *Iniziativa* was a weekly review from the president's office. In January 1947, Gedda even established his own less political and more spiritual review, *Tabor*. The Men's Union maintained *Noi uomini*, while the women published a number of overlapping *Squilli*, such as one for young working women, another for peasant women, and yet another for those in sporting organizations.

Suspicions of all this regularly surfaced in the lay and Marxist press. In 1952, an official statement from the Liberals, one of the DC's principal allies, branded the AC a threat, not only to the *Risorgimento* heritage but also to the spirit of the Lateran Pacts.[61] A series of articles in the Socialist *Avanti!* during the fall of the same year went further and targeted Catholic Action as an anti-democratic force in politics and society that, with the "cross drawn as a sword," aimed to "clericalize" Italy. This was not, it continued, merely based on nostalgic pipedreams for the defunct Papal States with its "Cardinal Legates, zouaves and Mastro Titto [the notorious papal executioner]." Rather, these reveries reached back to the medieval Pope Gregory VII, whose bull *Dictatus papae* commanded all secular princes to bow before him. Taking its orders from a reactionary and hierarchical church, the AC worked with the DC to fill, with the obedient faithful, the ranks of all the state's key functionaries. Other essays in the series focused on youth and women's organizations and the FUCI, the chief breeding ground for Christian Democratic leadership. With some notable exceptions, like Alcide De Gasperi, who came of age under the Austro-Hungarian Empire, or one of the party's chief economic thinkers, Ezio Vanoni, who started out as a Socialist, "all, we say all [of the Party heads] . . . had FUCI cards in their pockets." The AC's top-down web, moreover, hindered the growth of real Italian democracy. Always remember, *Avanti!* continued sarcastically, "that at the side (or better, above), the parish and diocesan president, stands the ecclesiastic assistant; above Gedda there is Monsignor Urbani; above Urbani is the Episcopal Commission for the Direction of Catholic Action . . . ; and above the Commission, above Monsignor Urbani and Gedda, the presidents and the assistants: He, the reigning pontiff His Holiness Pius XII

60. Casella, *L'Azione cattolica nell'Italia contemporanea (1919–1969)* (Rome: AVE, 1992), 272–91. Giordani also served as *Il Popolo*'s editor in 1946–47.

61. "La Violazione del Concordato denunciate dalla direzione del P.L.I.," *Avanti!*, February 16, 1952. Poggi (*Catholic Action in Italy*, 191) also mentions Gedda as "an Italian Salazar."

and his successors." *Avanti!* wryly concluded, "Everyone sees that [Catholic Action] is eminently democratic."[62] Such criticisms, however, could not dampen AC optimism such as that encountered in a February 1953 issue of *Iniziativa*, where Father Prosperini at the Morality Office urged one and all to keep up the fight in the face of encroaching secularism. "Let's reinforce the dikes," he wrote, "so that they hold back the sea of mud."[63]

Christian Democracy

Less tethered to the church and more independent than Catholic Action was Christian Democracy, which the 1946 referendum and the 1948 elections confirmed as Italy's dominant political party. Christian Democracy emerged during the war while Mussolini's regime tottered. As Catholics organized, a following developed around Alcide De Gasperi, a centrist who had been don Luigi Sturzo's right hand in the Italian Popular Party before the *Duce* and Pius XI liquidated it. In July 1943, De Gasperi issued his seminal "Reconstructive Ideas of Christian Democracy," the most important of the party's foundation documents. Embracing democratic and social justice principles that led De Gaspari to famously quip that his was a "centrist party that leaned left," the document also acknowledged its Catholic inspiration and aims. De Gasperi wrote, "Acknowledging that a free state will be secure if it is founded on moral values, the democratic state will protect morality, it will protect the integrity of the family and it will assist parents in their task of providing a Christian education to future generations."[64] As the war drew to a close, the DC's popularity grew, demanding attention and inviting analysis. A U.S. military intelligence report considered it "essentially a party of order with 'evolution' rather than 'revolution' as its watchword." The party's program, it continued, was religiously based and held "the family as the keystone of the social structure of the state. The family must therefore be protected against State oppression (one of the characteristics of

62. Renato Carli-Ballola wrote the articles for *Avanti!* They include "L'Azione Cattolica: Una croce impugnata come una spada," September 28, 1952; "Democratici sia pure ma attenti a non esagerare," October 1, 1952; "Un grande vivaio inesauribile per l'accaparramento delle cariche," October 3, 1952; "Preparono I sudditi del Papa e non cittadini della Repubblica," October, 7, 1952; "Un corso di preparazione anche per le fidanzate," October 9, 1952; and "Una rete per clericalizzare la scuola e la cultura italiana," October 14, 1952.

63. Ferdinando Prosperini, "È diminuita la sensibilità morale dell'uomo moderna?" *Iniziativa*, February 1953.

64. De Gasperi, *Scritti politici di Alcide De Gasperi*, ed. Pier Giorgio Zunino (Milan: Feltrinelli, 1979), 258.

Communism) and aided in every way, e.g. Education, taxation, property ownership, standard of living, etc."[65] Christian Democratic ideology intrigued and challenged other observers and scholars through the postwar era. The American Sidney Tarrow described the DC regime as one of "soft hegemony."[66] John Pollard identified it as "essentially a *parliamentary* or caucus party with little or no independent mass base at a local level." The nation's largest party, its ruling party, did not operate like other "normal" parties. Both rank and file and leaders were found in church, at Catholic Action meetings, at religious affairs, and marching in processions where they discussed issues and made decisions.[67] The historian Stephen Gundle captured the DC's leaders as "upright men who were early to bed and early to rise. They were colorless, cautious individuals who were deeply religious and personally austere. Typically, they attended mass every day."[68]

De Gasperi's tenure as party leader from 1943 and prime minister from 1945 to 1953 gained for him the reputation as "the statesman," so much so that one of the chief historians of Italian Catholicism, Gabriele De Rosa, saw the *dopoguerra* as the "De gasperian age."[69] When he surrendered the party reins in 1953, however, it became more and more apparent that an array of what were dubbed "currents"—some ideological and some personal—squabbled among themselves for a share of control. They rarely brought their differences out in the open but preferred to backstab behind closed doors.[70]

Like the church and Catholic Action, Christian Democracy had its own media. In contrast to the AC, however, whose press gladly bowed before pontifical intentions, De Gasperi's DC preferred not to be seen as a Vatican tool. Memories of Pius XI's treatment of the *Popolari* no doubt contributed to this feeling. Quashed by the Fascists in 1925, the party's newspaper, *Il Popolo*, resumed open publication in 1944 as the official

65. National Archives and Records Service (henceforth NARS) Record Group (henceforth RG) 59 865.00/2–2345, Psychological Warfare Branch report, February 15, 1945.

66. Sidney Tarrow, "Maintaining Hegemony in Italy: 'The Softer They Rise, the Slower They Fall!,'" in *Uncommon Democracies: The One-Party Dominant Regimes*, ed. T. J. Pempel (Ithaca, N.Y.: Cornell University Press, 1990), 306–32.

67. John Pollard, *Catholicism in Modern Italy: Religion, Society and Politics since 1861* (New York: Routledge, 2008), 122–23; see also Paul Furlong, "The Italian Christian Democrats: From Catholic Movement to Conservative Party," Hull Papers in Politics no. 25 (Hull: University of Hull, 1982).

68. Stephen Gundle, *Death and the Dolce Vita: The Dark Side of Rome in the 1950s* (Edinburgh: Canongate, 2011), 43.

69. Gabriele De Rosa, *Da Luigi Sturzo ad Aldo Moro* (Brescia: Morcelliana, 1988), 145.

70. The DC currents have been extensively studied and debated. See, for example, Marco Follini, *L'Arcipelago democristiano* (Rome and Bari: Laterza, 1990).

DC organ. Other postwar reviews, such as *Cronache sociali* of the so-called "little professors" (*professorini*) progressives, Giuseppe Dossetti, Giuseppe Lazzati, Amintore Fanfani, and Giorgio La Pira, *Discussione* of Giulio Andreotti, *Società nuova* of Guido Gonella, and De Gasperi's *Concretezza*, identified with certain DC leaders and their "currents" (*correnti*). The DC also established its own publishing house, Cinque Lune, and counted on other ones, Catholic Action's AVE, for example, established by Gedda before the war, and Vita e pensiero of Milan's Catholic University.[71]

Such a robust print culture could appear chaotic, competitive, and even divisive when times called for unity. A 1949 pro-memoria for the party directorate grappled with getting out the message but charged that "our press as it exists today is absolutely inadequate"; without it, the DC would be unable "to complete or even to start its transformation of the State and application of reforms (while it left) public opinion to the mercy of journals either decidedly in opposition or their allies." One solution required "the strengthening of our own media," although the dizzying jumble of Catholic press desperately begged coordination. With eight principal party organs, not counting Catholic Action publications and those in Trieste, which remained under Allied occupation until 1954, why, continued the analysis, must each maintain desks for sports or theater news? Why did at least five Italian Catholic reporters follow the last Tour de France? The expense of foreign correspondents, furthermore, disadvantaged Catholic papers and gave more weight to the argument for collaborative effort, ultimately a stillborn initiative.[72]

The report's author, Gioacchino Quarello, preferred the other option of "penetration and acquisition" of the great newspapers. One example of this concerned the influential conservative Monsignor Roberto Ronca, the Jesuit who organized the Civiltà italica movement. Skeptical of Catholic Action comptence and dissatisfied with the DC's Il *Popolo*,

71. Albertina Vittoria, "Organizzazioni e istituti della cultura," in *Storia dell'Italia repubblicana*, vol. 2, part 2, "*Istituzioni, movimenti, culture*," ed. Francesco Barbagallo et al. (Turin: Einaudi, 1995), 663–68 and 685–88. On A.V.E., see http://www.editriceave.it/un-po-di-storia (accessed December 3, 2019), and Paolo Murialdi, *La Stampa Italiana del dopoguerra*, 2 vols. (Bari and Rome: Laterza, 1978).

72. IS Seg. Pol. Taviani, Sc. 6, f. 6, "Appunti per una riorganizzazzione organizzativa e amministrativa della stampa quotidiana," n.d., n.a. (probably 1949) and, in the same folder, Gioacchino Quarello, "Pro-Memoria per la Direzione del Partito," July 16, 1949. The report listed the Rome and Milan *Popolo* and the *Sicilia del Popolo* as the three chief party organs, followed by the *Popolo Nuovo* of Turin, the *Mattino* of Florence, the *Domani d'Italia* of Naples, the *Pomeriggio* of Bologna, and Ancona's *Voce Adriatica*. Another DC report of about the same time (placed in the same archival folder), unsigned and undated, echoed many of Querelo's assertions and proposals. "In the first place," it stated that the condition of the DC press was one of "administrative chaos" (*disordine organizzativo*). Notably, it also complained of the foreign correspondent problem.

Ronca acted to extend the Catholic hand into otherwise lay territory. Toward that end, in May of 1944 he arranged with the owner of Rome's *Il Messaggero* that Catholicism inspire the paper's editorial stance.[73] Another approach was revealed in an undated note to Giorgio Tupini, the undersecretary for the press during De Gasperi's last ministry (July 1951 to July 1953). The communication dealt with gifts to journalists, 25,000 or 30,000 lire each, based on "the kindnesses that they do for us" and, in a Catholic touch, whether the recipient was a bachelor or "a father of a needy family." The list presented to Tupini, mostly of writers for Catholic publications, had a handwritten "sí" next to each of the eleven names. "For more important colleagues from other journals," concluded the note, "such as Mattei, Napolitano, Gorresio, Zatterin [and one more illegibile name] etc. we need to find something different, for example, jokingly offering them a high class pen after having it blessed.... What do you think?"[74]

The DC's reach, morerover, only began with the media. As the dominant political party, it could turn state agencies into Catholic fiefdoms, and party leaders worked diligently to control as much as possible. For example, they successfully chased Communists and other opponents from buildings that had been sequestered from the Fascists at the end of the war.[75] Elsewhere, the radio network EIAR and the giant holding company the Istituto per la ricostruzione italiana (IRI) became DC turf. Another case concerned Mussolini's National Agency for Maternity and Infancy (Opera nazionale maternità e infanzia, or ONMI), which the new republic maintained to assist pregnant women and mothers. ONMI's concern with family especially attracted a Catholic sense of proprietorship, and, much like with other old Fascist entities, the DC helped itself. When the left expressed little interest in the ONMI, in 1947 party secretary Attilio Piccioni wrote to Interior Minister Mario Scelba about the desirability of keeping it under the Catholic umbrella. The government subsequently named as ONMI's president Urbano Cioccetti, who had been close to the Vatican as a papal chamberlain. He preceded Gedda at the AC's Men's Union, was a vice president of Catholic Action, and would later succeed Salvatore Rebecchini as the DC mayor of Rome from 1958 to 1961. Cioccetti promoted ONMI's work through such events as

73. Andrea Riccardi, *Il "Partito Romano" nel secondo dopoguerra* (Brescia: Morcelliana, 1983), 20–22.

74. IS Seg. Pol. Cappi, Sc. 6, f. 6, undated note to Giorgio Tupini (Umberto's son) signed "Lino."

75. Arturo Carlo Jemolo, *Church and State in Italy, 1850–1950*, trans. David Moore (Philadelphia: Dufour Editions, 1961), 315.

the Day of the Mamma and the Day of Mother and Child, initially a Fascist holiday that, in turn, drew heavily on Christmas, for which charity packages were distributed to needy families and orphans. In acquiring OMNI, the DC also took control of over two hundred clinics, about one hundred day care centers (*asili nido*), and thousands of employees and "consultants." The *Osservatore Romano* estimated that about two million women and their offspring received OMNI aid during 1950.[76]

Concerned as they were with the proper moral development of children, the government also eyed the schools, a battlefield that must not be lost to what the patriarch of Venice considered a "petulant and fastidious" enemy. Catholic Action issued frequent calls to arms, as in a 1953 *Iniziativa* piece that decried the lay "menace" toward "religion and humanity" in its hope to separate the faith from social life and remove religious education from the curriculum. At the end of the war, lay figures led the Ministry of Public Instruction, although they respected the church's role in education. One of them, Vincenzo Arangio-Ruiz, sanctioned twenty religion lessons per year in the schools, to be conducted under the auspices of the local bishops. In July of 1946, however, the DC's Guido Gonella took the helm at the ministry and confirmed the state's intention to "guarantee religion in all teachings."[77] Informal control of a key parent-teacher organization also helped the Catholic cause. Established in December of 1946 as the Associazione Nazionale Scuola Italiana under the presidency of Vittorio Emanuele Orlando, the old World War I premier and no Catholic, most of its founders nonetheless

76. "La Giornata della Madre e del Bambino," *OR*, January 5, 1951; Maria Vittoria, "La nostra azione sociale," *A Colloquio con le dirigenti diocesani*, April 1, 1951. *Noi uomini* wrote that ONMI was necessary and "needed in a nation as poor as ours"; Armando Ravagliolo, "L'ONMI guarda all'avvenire," *Noi uomini*, March 31, 1956. See also Luigi Palma, "L'Opera Nazionale Maternità e Infanzia, campo aperto all'azione di tutti," *Iniziativa*, August–September 1950, an interview with Cioccetti after he became the ONMI president that year. See also Stefania Bernini, "Natural Mothers: Teaching Morals and Parent-Craft in Italy, 1945–1960," *Modern Italy* 9, no. 1 (May 2004); Michela Minesso, "L'ONMI nella storia dell'Italia contemporanea (1925–1975)," in *Stato e infanzia nell'Italia contemporanea: Origini, sviluppo e fine dell'Onmi 1925–1975*, ed Michela Minesso (Bologna: Il Mulino, 2007), 132 and 150–53; and Vittorio Emiliani, *L'Italia mangiata: Lo scandalo degli enti inutili* (Turin: Einaudi, 1977), 14–20. On the "Day of Mother and Child" under the Fascists, see Kate Ferris, *Everyday Life in Fascist Venice, 1929–1940* (New York: Palgrave Macmillan, 2012), 100–101.

77. Cesarina Checcaci, "La minaccia del laicismo alla religion e alla umanità," *Iniziativa*, July–August 1953. The patriarch issued his opinion in 1950; Antonio Acerbi, *Chiesa cultura società: Momenti e figure dal Vaticano I a Paolo VI* (Milan: Vita e Pensiero, 1988), 174; Tina Tomasi, *L'Idea laica nell'Italia contemporanea (1870–1970)* (Florence: La Nuova Italia Editrice, 1971), 200–201; Angelo Gaudio, *La politica scolastica dei cattolici, 1943–1953: Dai programmi all'azione di governo* (Brescia: Editrice La Scuola, 1991), 88–96. The progressive and lay Resistance leader Leo Valiani, in his study of the DC's ascension, identified Gonella as the party's representative from the "*ecclesia militans*"; Valiani, *L'avvento di De Gasperi: Tre anni di politica italiana* (Turin: F. de Silva, 1949), 80. See also "Scuole di stato e formazione cristiana," *OR*, May 11, 1950.

came from DC ranks. By its tenth anniversary in 1956, consequently, the DC's Giuseppe Caronia led the association.[78]

Cultural contest between Catholics and their adversaries reached the sports world, which early on provided some doubts.[79] After the Second World War, partly to stymie the actions of rival parties, the faithful accorded sports more status. The Communists and the Socialists had cultivated their own sporting associations—the Unione italiana sport popolare, which had ties to both parties, the PCI-aligned Red Falcons (Falchi rossi) and Pioneers, and the PSI's ASSI (Associazione sportive socialista italiana). Their wicked goal, according to one Catholic observer, was "to create an alternative recreational center outside of the parish orbit," with game times that conflicted with the Mass and where the teammates could sing, "We want Togliatti as our father—we want Stalin as our King!"[80]

Catholic sports found a friend in the pontiff himself. Pius XII enjoyed sports, and, according to the respected journalist and "Vatican watcher" Benny Lai, he received the *Gazzetta dello Sport* every day and listened to soccer on the radio.[81] When the pope died in 1958, Gedda reminded everyone that all sportsmen shared the loss. Pius had been, especially, "their" pope. Gedda fondly recalled many examples of the pontiff's keen interest in sports from his meeting with Hugo Koblet, the Protestant victor of the 1950 Giro d'Italia, to his joy in watching a basketball game

78. "Scuola e famiglia per una educazione efficace," *OR*, February 13–14, 1956.

79. The church inherited a long tradition of Catholic suspicion of athletics and an ambivalence toward sports that Stefano Pivato and others have explored. At the dawn of the twentieth century the church frowned on soccer and cycling, perhaps because of their association with Protestant and Masonic Anglo-Saxons. Later rugby and racecar driving joined boxing for low marks in the Catholic press for their violence and "recklessness." On the other hand, the church thus was not entirely against sports, and positive statements emerged here and there. Speaking to a gathering of athletes, Pius X encouraged it "because these entertainments require effort, they keep you from laziness the father of all vice."

Catholics preferred the discipline of "acrobatics" in its cultivation of a "spirit of obedience." To promote a presence in that sector, therefore, and with ecclesiastical blessing, they established a "Federation of Italian Catholic Sport Associations" (Federazione delle associazioni sportive cattoliche italiane) in 1906, partly to counter the "lay-masonic" Italian Gymnastic Federation. See, for example, C. Petino, "Fortezza o cinismo? A proposito di certi sport," *Noi uomini*, May 26, 1957; Pivato, *Il Touring Club Italiano* (Bologna: Il Mulino, 2006), 41–44. Some bishops prohibited their clergy from riding bicycles. One early Catholic sports advocate was Giuseppe Semeria, who thought that bicycles were too elitist. Rather, he preferred trekking in the tradition of St. Francis; Pivato, *Clericalismo e laicismo nella cultura popolare italiana*, 207–11. See also Paolo Andreoli, "Associazionismo sportive e ricreativo cattolico," in *Dizionario storico del movimento cattolico in Italia, 1860–1980* 1/2 I fatti e le idee, ed. Francesco Traniello and Giorgio Campanini (Turin: Marietti, 1981), 176–80. Pius X was quoted in Simon Martin, "From Cycling Priests to the 'Sportsman's Pope': Italy, Sport and the Catholic Church," *European Review*19, no. 4 (2011): 548.

80. Lorenzo Bedeschi, *Dissacrano L'infanzia! I Pionieri d'Italia* (Bologna: Editrice A.B.E.S., 1950), 28–29.

81. Lai, "Cosa legge il Papa," *L'Europeo*, November 8, 1953. Pivato noted, nonetheless, that before the war, Catholic Action sometimes portrayed Pius X as an alpinist; Pivato, *Clericalismo e laicismo nella cultura popolare italiana*, 213–14.

played on a special court constructed in St. Peter's Square.[82] Gedda was also a well-known devotee who directed some of his enormous energies toward athletics. For him, religion and sport overlapped quite nicely, as in the case of the Catholic mountaineer Pier Giorgio Frassati. The son of *La Stampa*'s liberal editor, Frassati rejected the lay vision and became a third-order Dominican and a Catholic Action activist who died prematurely from polio in 1925. Whether scaling an Alpine precipice or fighting anticlericals on Turin's streets, Frassati embodied what the French Catholic Jean Pihan described as the Christian "on the road who lives in the open air and confronts each risk with certitude."[83]

In 1944, Gedda secured the adherence of Italy's scouting network as an autonomous body to Catholic Action and founded the Centro sportivo italiano (Italian Sports Center, CSI) with the wish that it serve as a sort of "baptism of sport."[84] The CSI became Catholic Action's umbrella organization for sports and by 1955 boasted 3,000 centers across Italy and 80,000 members. Mobilized with the goal of serving as apostles on the playing field, the CSI's clerical liaison, Father Nicola Pavoni, urged each leader to launch evangelical crusades "in the gyms, on the fields, in the streets [and] in the stands." "You must act," he continued, "with prudence, with intelligence, with holiness ... but you must act!" And in 1947, after Gonella took charge of the Ministry of Public Education, the national school system favored the CSI.[85] Catholics' penetration of sports extended further when they also came to control the Comitato olimpico natzionale italiano (CONI). Although the Socialists captured the old Fascist organization in 1944, three years later its leader, Giulio Onesti, abandoned the party and joined the DC. With Gedda, he edited Catholic Action's sport review, *Stadium*.[86]

82. Gedda, "Era il Papa degli sportivi," *Il Quotidiano*, October 10, 1958.

83. Gedda, "Il suo esempio," and Ugo Sciascia, "Imparare e conoscerlo," both from *Il Quotidiano*, July 4, 1950; Jean Pihan, *Cristianesimo aperto*, cited in Maria Cristina Giuntella, "Virtù e immagine della donna nei settori femminili," in AAVV, *Chiesa e progetto educativo nell'Italia del secondo dopoguerra (1945–1958)* (Brescia: La Scuola, 1988), 287–88. Pier Giorgio Frassati was beatified in 1990. See also Maria Di Lorenzo, *Blessed Pier Giorgio Frassati: An Ordinary Christian*, trans. Robert Ventresca (Boston: Pauline Books, 2004).

84. Mario Sica, "Scautismo cattolico," in Traniello and Campanini, *Dizionario storico del movimento cattolico in Italia*, 373–79; on the prewar era and sports, particularly cycling, see Pivato, *Clericalismo e laicismo nella cultura popolare italiana*, 207–61, and Martin, "From Cycling Priests to the 'Sportsman's Pope,'" 551–52. Historical information for the Centro sportivo italiano can also be found on its website: http:://www.csi-net.it (accessed December 3, 2019). See also Gedda's 1954 speech to commemorate the CSI's tenth anniversary; Gedda, *Dieci anni al servizio dello sport* (Rome: Atena, 1954).

85. IPVI, Pg VII, b. 53, Pavoni circular, February 1, 1954. Pavoni used the term *base missionaria* for launching the crusades. The Base missionaria movement will be discussed later.

86. Fabien Archambault, "Il calcio e l'oratorio: Football, Catholic Movement and Politics in Italian

These endeavors were followed by those of the Catholic labor organization, which launched its own National ACLI Sports Union (l'Unione nazionale sportive ACLI, or UNSA) in 1950, by the DC's Libertas association, founded in 1949, and the party's Central Office on Sports Issues, launched in late 1956. With headquarters at the National Libertas Center in Rome, by 1953 ninety-two provincial branches functioned and oversaw the work of 701 local chapters, or *polisportive*. Working closely with CONI, Libertas provided DC youth with, among other activities, soccer, cycling, athletic training, basketball, water polo, skiing, swimming, baseball, equestrian sports, and even boxing. It funded other non-DC sports such as a national parachute organization and organized camping excursions and trips at home and abroad to places such as Lourdes and Villach, which, in August of 1952, hosted an "International Sport and Culture Week for Christian Democratic Youth." Finally, a 1953 report from the head of Libertas, Angelo Priore, made particular mention that, on top of all that, the dutiful Libertas provided electoral support to the Christian Democracy and that "practically all" of the *polisportive* could be found "next door to Party offices." The party's commitment to the project was such that Amintore Fanfani, who replaced De Gasperi, accorded a spot on the National Council to a delegate from Libertas.[87]

In October 1955, Pius confirmed the Catholic presence in sports. Along with seventy cardinals and Mayor Rebecchini, the pontiff greeted Gedda and 70,000 CSI athletes in St. Peter's Square and lauded their mission to keep sport "healthy" by elevating the athlete closer to God. Gedda and other Catholic Action and CSI officials entered the piazza after leading a long parade that began across town at the Esedra fountain near Termini Station. Escorted by police and Finance Guards, the colorful spectacle meandered through Rome and included five hundred flag bearers, over five thousand cyclists, fifteen thousand basketball players,

---

Post-War Society, 1944–1960," *Historical Social Research/Historische Sozialforschung* 31, no. 1 (2006): 115; Simon Martin, *Sport Italia: The Italian Love Affair with Sport* (London: I. B. Tauris, 2011), 102–5.

87. IS Sec. Pol. De Gasperi, Sc. 18, f. 5; Angelo Priore, "Relazione attività Libertas dal 1949 ad oggi," December 29, 1953. By 1955, Fanfani celebrated the inauguration of the one-thousandth *polisportiva* of the Libertas network. That year, at a competition at Rome's Baths of Caracalla, *Discussione* boasted of its "value and vitality" as a DC agency; "Un Vivaio di azzurri per la nostra atletica," *Discussione*, November 13, 1955. Libertas also promoted musical shows. See "Manifestazioni ricreative del Centro nazionale '*Libertas*,'" *Il Popolo*, May 22, 1952. On the *Libertas* representative to the DC National Council, see Francesco Malgeri, "Gli anni di transizione: Da Fanfani a Moro (1954–1962)," in *Storia della democrazia cristiana*, ed. Francesco Malgeri (Rome: Cinque Lune, 1988), 3:59. Angelo Priore was the first president of Libertas; he was soon followed by Arrigo Paganelli. On the Central Office for Sports Issues, see IS Seg. Pol. Fanfani Sc. 49, f. 64, circular dated December 27, 1956. The head (*dirigente*) of the office was Dario Antoniozzi.

and over forty-three thousand members of soccer teams. Soccer had joined cycling as one of the Catholic sports of choice, and the church's more than two thousand playing fields acted as breeding grounds for Italian teams. Nine hundred and twenty-five baseball players joined the marchers, as did a special corps of Salesian athletes. "A healthy body is not an end unto itself," Pius told the assembled throng, "but it must be directed toward the intellectual and moral perfection of the spirit."[88] Pius reminded the athletes of two frequent sports problems: the worship of heroes, often identified with America and the movie term *divismo*, and the error of *campionismo*, the hyperaggressive, win-at-all-costs mentality.[89]

Excessive enthusiasms, *campionismo*, among fans, however, gave Catholics something to ponder. An official from the Ministry of Public Instruction's Physical Education and Sports Service in 1956 proudly stated that Italians did not suffer from that problem. He nonetheless added a touch of the inferiority complex when he concluded that Italy was a second-rank sports power, forever in the shadow of America and the Communist Bloc. He envied U.S. athletic programs, anchored in the schools, where part of the day was devoted to exercise. Italy, he lamented, "nailed" its students to their benches.[90] The situation in industrial cities cultivated the wrong combination of big money and misguided fans (*tifi*), too absorbed in their passions to understand the true beauty of sport. Referring to Gedda's book on sports, which placed the *tifi* on a line that led to cocaine addiction, Ubaldo Pellegrino in the *Rivista del clero* understood that this sickness resulted from nervous tension, a false vision of sport, and a lack of true ideals.[91]

Sports stars, furthermore, arise sooner or later; and the faithful had their *divo* in the cyclist Gino Bartali, a favorite whom they hailed as a national hero. No athlete received Catholic encomiums as much as Bar-

88. "Il Papa indica agli atleti italiani i principi di una sana pratica sportiva," *Il Popolo*, October 10, 1955; "Indimenticabili giornate nel decennio del Centro sportivo," *Iniziativa*, October 1955; Gedda, "Il Centro sportivo italiano al servizio dei giovani e dello sport," *Iniziativa*, October 1955. That evening the action moved to a huge rally at the Baths of Caracalla. *Iniziativa* thought that the throng numbered 100,000. The *Osservatore Romano* recorded the event in a number of articles, such as "Il Sommo Pontefice compiendosi il primo decennio del Centro Sportivo Italiano indica le norme e le virtù per la Cristiana educazione ginnica atletica e agonistica" and "Il corteo celebrativo," both in *OR*, October 10–11, 1955. Later it noted the *L'Unità*'s resentment concerning the state's excessive presence at the affair; "Voci ed echi," *OR*, October 12, 1955; Archambault, "'Il calcio e l'oratorio': Football, Catholic Movement and Politics in Italian Post-War society, 1944–1960," *Historical Social Research* 31 (2006): 1.

89. See Cosimo Petino, "Il divismo: Frutto di stagione," *Noi uomini*, October 6, 1957.

90. "Sport ma non campionismo," *Discussione*, September 16, 1956.

91. Ubaldo Pellegrino, "Sport, tifo ed . . . antitifo," *Rivista del clero italiano*, April 1950.

tali. Dubbed Gino the Pious, the Florentine won the 1936, 1937, and 1946 Giri d'Italia and the 1938 Tour de France. In the 1948 Tour, Bartali took the lead, famously at Lourdes, and pressed on to receive another yellow jersey. In a scenario that recalled Guareschi's don Camillo stories, the Italian public developed a fondness for pitting the Catholic Bartali in a rivalry against his "Communist" nemesis, Fausto Coppi. In reality, the contest frequently turned very bitter. In Bartali's 2000 obituary, the British *Guardian* claimed that "no other sport [had] ever created such a prolonged and passionate duel." The *Rivista del clero italiano* bestowed Bartali, a devout family man and card-carrying CSI member, with a "Latin equilibrium [and] Italic good sense" as the idol of the small town and the countryside, while the atheist Coppi fooled around, was caught in a notorious scandal with the "*dama bianca*" (white lady), and suffered doping accusations. Rather, "watch your Gino Bartali," Pius exhorted to a throng in St. Peter's Square in 1947, a "member of Catholic Action." Meanwhile, Gedda's friend and Catholic Action militant Bartolo Paschetta acted as press agent and "guardian angel" for "God's cyclist."[92]

On the other hand, boxing presented challenges for Catholics. Some skepticism no doubt stemmed from memories of Fascism's glorification of boxers as embodiments of the tough and aggressive new man. Mussolini boasted, "I like the idea of a generation of such powerful fist fighters who destroy the features of the champions of other countries."[93] Most postwar Catholics preferred to take their cue from the Jesuit Alfredo Boschi, who wrote in the *Palestra del clero* that boxing looked too much like a violation of the Holy Commandment against killing, and they typically frowned upon it, as did Francesco Dorigo, who, in "Gloves on the Screen" for the *Rivista del cinematografo*, condemned the violence of boxing movies. To a 1952 gathering of athletic and health instructors, however, Pius included boxing in his list of valid sports, and the "sweet science" had enough Catholic supporters to prompt a debate in the *Rivista del clero italiano* in 1956.[94] Renato Venturini also accorded

92. Tim Hilton, "Gino Bartali," *Guardian*, May 8, 2000, which can be seen at www.guardian.co.uk/news/2000/may/09/guardianobituaries4 (accessed December 3, 2019). See also Pivato, *Clericalismo e laicismo nella cultura popolare italiana*, 221–52; Martin, *Sport Italia*, 116–28, and Daniele Marchesini, *Coppi e Bartali* (Bologna: Il Mulino, 1998). During his "*Dama bianca*" scandal, the government revoked Coppi's passport, and the "white woman," Giulia Occhini, landed in prison on adultery charges; Gundle, *Death and the Dolce Vita*, 182.

93. Silvana Patriarca, *Italian Vices: Nation and Character from the Risorgimento to the Republic* (Cambridge: Cambridge University Press, 2010), 138–39.

94. Francesco Dorigo, "Guantoni sullo schermo," *Rivista del cinematografo*, March 1957; "Il pugilato e il . . . principio di non-contraddizione," *Rivista del clero italiano*, April 1956. The "pro" article was

it some respect in a 1955 article for *Discussione*.[95] And in 1956 Benny Lai cited the Dominican Filippo Robotti's promotion of the case for good Christian boxers and added that the *papa sportivo* still had not made up his mind on it.[96]

Constructing the Clerical State

The Constitution and the Law

Along with rejecting the Savoy monarchy and its 1848 charter, the *Statuto*, Italy's referendum of June 2, 1946, established the Italian Republic and confirmed DC strength through the election of a constituent assembly, the Costituente. Christian Democracy emerged as the clear winner, with 207 Assembly seats, against 115 for the Socialists and 104 for the Communists. The Liberal-dominated National Democratic Union received 41, against 7 for the fading Action Party and 23 for the nascent Republican Party (Partito repubblicano italiano, or PRI). Of the non-CLN parties, the right-wing Uomo Qualunque received 30, and the Monarchist National Freedom Bloc took 16. The Costituente's first session took place on June 25, 1946, and it approved the charter's final draft on December 22, 1947.

The DC presented much of its cultural agenda for the upcoming assembly at its April 1946 Congress in Rome, where De Gasperi assigned Guido Gonella to deliver a key discourse toward that end. Gonella merits attention as a representative and an important figure of the DC's cultural politics. As far as those questions went, De Gasperi the statesman kept mostly to high politics—the reconstruction of the nation and securing its place in the Western alliance—and left cultural issues to others.[97] With the principal exception of the right-leaning Giulio An-

---

written by Tullo Goffi, who taught morality at the Brescia seminary, while the "con" piece came from none other than Agostino Gemelli.

95. Renato Venturini, "Il Pugilato in Italia," *Discussione*, November 27, 1955, which was mainly an interview with an important organizer for the sport, Carlo Levi della Vida, who, Venturini was sure to point out, had been brought up by his mother as a good Catholic. Benny Lai discerned the split over boxing and noted that Pius had not taken a definitive position on it; Lai, "I peccati nuovi," *L'Europeo*, February 19, 1956. See also Pivato, *Clericalismo e laicismo nella cultura popolare italiana*, 229–30.

96. Lai, "Il Domenicano che difende il pugilato," *L'Europeo*, February 1956.

97. De Gasperi could, nevertheless, strike out at the lay-left cultural assault on Catholics. Before the Constituent Assembly, for instance, he condemned "the campaign of hate against the Catholic religion which is, by God, the religion professed by the overwhelming majority of our people." To lively applause from the center and right, he went on, denouncing the "satanic campaign of defamation and hate against priests as enemies of the people and tainted by every depravity"; *Assemblea Costituente XXIX, Seduta di 14 dicembre 1946*, 995–97, also cited in Maurizio Cesari, *La censura in Italia oggi (1944–1980)* (Naples: Liguori editore, 1982), 24–25.

dreotti, who will be discussed later, most of the DC's cultural activists had more moderate reputations, like Gonella, or came from the center-left.[98] A Veronese who graduated from Milan's Catholic University in the 1920s, Gonella joined FUCI and worked for its publication, *Azione fucina*. There he befriended its ecclesiastic assistant, the future Pope Paul VI, Giovanni Battista Montini. In 1933 Montini and Giuseppe Dalla Torre persuaded Gonella to go to Rome and assume the *Osservatore Romano*'s "Acta diurna" column. From there, with "a complete panorama, rich in opinions, judgments, accounts, that no other Italian press organ could or wanted to offer," he produced some of the Vatican's boldest political commentary during the Fascist era. It was said that, through "Acta diurna," Gonella "blew smoke in Mussolini's eyes," and, in 1939, his work briefly landed him in a Fascist jail.[99] After the war Gonella served as editor of the party's *Il Popolo*, as De Gasperi's minister of public instruction from 1946 to 1951, and then as DC party secretary from 1950 to 1953. He also appeared as a frequent minister of grace and justice, starting in De Gasperi's brief last ministry in 1953 and then on and off from the late 1950s to 1973.[100]

In his address to the 1946 Party Congress, while Gonella affirmed a commitment to freedom, particularly religious liberty, he nonetheless stressed that "the Italian people are a Christian people and therefore, our country's basic political and legal principles must conform to the Christian ethic. Christianity is not only the foundation, but even the quarry [from which are taken] the stones in the construction of the new edifice." To prolonged applause, he added that "the Christian ethic, having conquered conscience and private life, must finally conquer public life." It must triumph over a "militant laicism" that permits some to call themselves Christian but refuses them the memory of their faith when they cross "the threshold of the State." The constituent assembly, he declared, must consider questions of religious and other "moral freedoms," par-

98. Massimo Scaglioni, "Cattolici e la televisione, vettore di unificazione nazionale," in *Non lamento ma azione: I cattolici e lo sviluppo italiano nei 150 anni di storia unitaria*, ed. Maria Bocci (Milan: Vita e pensiero, 2013), 128.

99. Malgeri, *Chiesa, cattolici e democracia*, 70. On Gonella and *Acta diurna*, see Malgeri, "Una voce libera negli anni di conformismo: Gli *Acta diurna*," in *Guido Gonella tra Governo, Parlamento e Partito*, ed. Giuseppe Bertagna, Alfredo Canavero, Augusto D'Angelo, and Andrea Simoncini (Rome and Soveria Mannelli: Istituto Luigi Struzo/Rubbettino Editore, 2007); Giancarlo Salemi and Gianni Martinelli, *Guido Gonella il giornalista* (Trieste: Edizioni Goliardiche, 2005), 31.

100. As party secretary, Gonella established DC schools for militants on Rome's Monte Mario and at Canazei in the Dolomites; Guido Gonella, introduction to *La Formazione politica*, by Vittorio Cervone and Giacomo Cesaro (Naples: Società Editrice Napolitana, 1980), 10.

ticularly "the freedom to form a family with the sacrament of matrimony." The Italian family faced "grave dangers" that required the state's urgent attention. Regarding the "atheist school or in the corruption of the streets," an "atomic bomb" had splintered the household; and the traditional hearth had become polluted with the radio's "numbing" sounds. The family takes care of itself as best as it can, Gonella reminded his colleagues, but it must also engage in the public square "and fight the enemy on the open field." To defeat the lay assault on the private and public levels, the state must zealously concern itself with the "moral hygiene of the people" and protect the principles of *buon costume*. The Constitution must, he declared, guarantee "freedom from vice." "Bad constitutions," he said, "are those that favor and promote vice—good constitutions hinder it and restrain it." "From the ruins of the past," he concluded, "a new Italy will finally surge, regenerated in the spirit of Christian liberty." Gonella received a standing ovation at the end of his discourse while De Gasperi embraced him on the podium.[101]

Gonella's words permeated the constituent assembly because, as the largest party there, the DC ensured a privileged Catholic place in the new charter. One of his partners toward that end was Giorgio La Pira, the devout professor of Roman law and soon-to-be mayor of Florence. Within the party, but without ever formally joining it, he belonged to the aforementioned left-leaning *professorini*. In 1945 La Pira issued *Premesse della politica*, which called for Italy's return to the fabric of a Christian society, ambitions in part realized at the *Costituente*. There were a few disappointments, and Catholics did not get everything they wanted at the assembly. Despite Gonella's support, for instance, La Pira failed to launch the charter with the words "In the name of the Lord" (*nel nome di Dio*), a gesture that "raised stupor," according to the Socialist Pietro Nenni.[102]

But Catholics won on most of the big issues, and their greatest victory was the incorporation of the Lateran Pacts into the new Constitution. They understood that, first, to get Italy back on solid Christian footing it needed the roadmap found in the Lateran Pacts and merged them into

101. Gonella, *Il Programma della democrazia cristiana per la nuova costituzione* (Rome: BUR, 1946), 18–20, 29–30, 32–33, 63–64. See also Paul Ginsborg, *A History of Contemporary Italy, Society and Politics 1943–1988* (London: Penguin, 1990), 76–77; Salemi and Martinelli, *Guido Gonella il giornalista*, 91–94.

102. Cited in Gianni Baget-Bozzo, *Il Partito cristiano al potere: La Dc di De Gasperi e di Dossetti 1945–1954* (Florence: Vallechi, 1974), 161; see also Giorgio La Pira, *Premesse della politica* (Florence: Libreria Editrice Fiorentina, 1945); Casella, *Cattolici e costituente: Orientamenti e iniziative del cattolicesimo organizzato, 1945–1947* (Perugia: Edizioni Scientifiche Italiane, 1987), 309n59. Cassella was quoting Nenni's memoirs, *Tempo di Guerra fredda: Diari 1943–1956*, ed. Giuliana Nenni and Domenico Zucàro (Milan: SugarCo, 1981), 346.

the Constitution's "Fundamental Principles." Article 7 of the Constitution put it simply: "The State and the Catholic Church are, each in its proper sphere [*ciascuno nel proprio ordine*], independent and sovereign. Relations between them are regulated in the Lateran Pacts." Article 7 obligated the Italian government to enforce respect for the church, for the pope, and for Rome as a holy place. It criminalized insult (*vilipendio*) against the man or the city. The Socialists opposed Article 7, but the Communist leader Palmiro Togliatti made it easy for the Catholics here by cooperating with the DC. For this some lay figures felt a sting of betrayal. Why did the Communists cave in on the issue?, asked a professor of medieval history and lay activist, Gabriele Pepe. Togliatti reasoned that the concession guaranteed religious peace, but in Pepe's mind Article 7 constituted a declaration of "war against non-Catholic Christians, against non-Christians [and] against anti-Catholics."[103]

An early and significant sign that the government took seriously its commitment to the Lateran measures concerned a Communist deputy, Laura Diaz. In a speech at Ortona on the Adriatic coast, Diaz declared that Pope Pius had done nothing to stop the recent Greek civil war and the conflict between the Israelis and their Arab neighbors, that his "hands dripped with the blood of [their] children," and no amount of holy water could cleanse them. These words brought charges that she had violated a law of May 27, 1947, based on the pacts, that prohibited "public offenses and insults . . . against the person of the Pontiff." It was the first time that the government brought charges against a member of Parliament for violation of the pacts. After a two-hour heated debate, the Chamber of Deputies suspended Diaz's parliamentary immunity and allowed the state to proceed against her. The trial took place in the spring of 1951, down the shore from Ortona, in Chieti. The Communist leader Fausto Gullo for the defense faced the Christian Democrat Giuseppe Togni, who reminded the court that Pius, "the pope of the white hands," was responsible for a new orphanage in Diaz's home district.

103. Baget-Bozzo, *Il Partito cristiano*, 199; Daniela Saresella, *Cattolici a sinistra: Dal modernismo ai giorni nostri* (Rome and Bari: Laterza, 2011), 67–68; Luciano Musselli, "Chiesa e stato all'Assemblea Costituente: L'Articolo 7 della Costituzione Italiana, *Il Politico* 53, no. 1 (1988); Casella, *Cattolici e costituente*, 309n59. On Gabriele Pepe's criticism, see Pepe, *La Protesta laica* (Manduria: Laicata Editore, 1949), 35–36. On La Pira, see also Gian Paolo Meucci, "La Pira e le istituzioni," *Testimonianze* 21 (April–July 1978): 198–99; and Giorgio Galli and Paolo Facchi, *La Sinistra democristiana: Storia e ideologia* (Milan: Feltrinelli, 1962), which concluded (316) that La Pira's preamble was dismissed as "too obtuse" and "too ideological." Amintore Fanfani published a collection of letters with La Pira: Fanfani, *Giorgio La Pira: Un profilo e 24 lettere inedite* (Milan: Rusconi, 1978). La Pira is also treated extensively in James Miller, *Politics in a Museum: Governing Postwar Florence* (Westport, Conn.: Praeger, 2002).

Instead of dripping blood, Togni maintained, his "holy hands" had been "raised to bless and counsel those terrified Romans" after the San Lorenzo bombardment of 1943; that Pius raised those hands "to the world in a prayer of peace." Judged guilty, Diaz received an eight-month suspended sentence.[104]

Diaz's was far from the only case. In 1951, an appellate court confirmed a one-year sentence for an assistant editor at *Avanti!* over an article that branded the pope a puppet of the large industry association *Confindustria*.[105] Another example of *vilipendio* concerned neither a parliamentary deputy nor a newspaper but a comedian in Velletri, near Rome, who had been condemned in November of 1950 for off-color references to the Catholic Mass. Although the case was subsequently appealed and dismissed, morality achieved some vengeance three years later when the Cassation court reopened the case and sent it to another tribunal, a move, wrote *Noi uomini*, that "merit[ed] the applause of all Catholics and decent people."[106]

Incorporation of the Lateran Pacts as Article 7 was not the only incidence of Catholic sentiments in the new Constitution. Above all, they surfaced in passages related to the family. In that regard, the pontiff's words might have served as a preamble when before a group of French fathers in 1951 he announced, "The family is not for the society; it is the society that is for the family." Indeed, this prompted one historian to observe that this was "not just the voice of the Church, but the interpretation of the Italian Constitution."[107] Based on the Concordat's Article 34, the Republic's Constitution's Article 29 recognized "the rights of the family as a natural society founded on matrimony. Matrimony is based on the moral and legal equality of the spouses within the limits laid down by law to guarantee the unity of the family." Scholars noted that the reference to "natural" here linked it to the Code of Canon Law (Canon 1055) and the Byzantine emperor Justinian's sixth-century code,

104. "Sarà processata l'on: Laura Diaz?," *Il Quotidiano*, March 9, 1950; "Concessa contro la on: Diaz l'autorizzazione a procedere," *Il Quotidiano*, March 10, 1950; "Scalfaro e Bettiol difendono il sentimento religioso degli italiani," *Il Popolo*, March 10, 1950; "Italy: Insult to the Pope," *Time*, April 9, 1951; "Woman Red Is Convicted of Insult to Pope Pius," *New York Times*, March 31, 1951; "Dal Tribunale di Chieti alla 'Casa' di San Pietro in Palazzi," *Noi uomini*, March 15, 1952. The deputy represented Livorno but delivered her speech in Ortona, near Chieti. Diaz was later reelected to Parliament.

105. "Diritto e storia contro la faziosità," *OR*, March 23, 1951.

106. IPVI, Sg XII, b. 6–15, Gavuzzo circulars 1950; Luigi Conti, "Il rispetto della religione cattolica," *Noi uomini*, February 28, 1953; see also IPVI, Pg XII, b. 16, Gavuzzo Circular, January 15, 1953.

107. Hervé A. Cavallera, *Storia dell'idea di famiglia in italia: Dall'avvento della Repubblica ai giorni nostri* (Brescia: Editrice La Scuola, 2006), 17–18.

the *Institutes*, which defined marriage as "the union of male and female . . . together with the procreation and upbringing of children." The Constitution's Article 31 also pledged the republic's assistance "through economic measures and other provisions [for] the formation of the family and the fulfillment of its duties, with particular consideration for large families. It protects maternity, infancy and youth, promoting the institutions necessary thereto." In one case of defeat, La Pira and Dossetti vainly fought to insert the notion of "indissolubility" into the wording on marriage. Social Democrat Umberto Grilli countered this by introducing an amendment to drop the word. His revision passed narrowly and prompted *Il Popolo* to complain that "the socialist coalition, with the support of the followers of [Giuseppe] Saragat, republicans, actionists and masons introduce[d] the threat of divorce into the Constitution."[108] Therefore, despite the spirit of the Lateran Pacts and their incorporation as Article 7, Article 29 read, "The Republic recognizes the rights of the family as a natural society founded on marriage," not "indissoluble marriage," and conceivably Parliament might *someday* permit divorce.

Elsewhere, secularist factions relied on more democratic principles found in the Constitution—values generally shared by the DC. Article 21, for example, served as an ultimate guarantee of the freedom of expression, that "all have the right to express freely their own thought by word, in writing and by all other means of communication . . . the press cannot be subjected to authorization or censorship." Nevertheless, the DC led here by Dossetti modified this sentiment in the article's last paragraph to proscribe "publications, shows and all other manifestations contrary to *buon costume*," the concept popular among Catholics but one that gave pause among the Marxists. Therefore, a Communist, Umberto Terracini, and an independent who sat with the Communists, the Arctic explorer Umberto Nobile, tried to replace terms like "manifestations contrary to *buon costume*" with "pornographic manifestations," but the effort failed.[109]

108. Thomas Glyn Watkin, *The Italian Legal Tradition* (Dartmouth: Ashgate, 1997), 157–70. Canon 1055 states that "a man and a woman establish between themselves a partnership of their whole life, and which of its own very nature is ordered to the well-being of the spouses and to the procreation and upbringing of children"; Mark Seymour, *Debating Divorce in Italy: Marriage and the Making of Modern Italians, 1860–1974* (New York: Palgrave, 2006), 166–68; and Fiamma Lussana, *L'Italia del divorzio: La battaglia fra Stato, Chiesa e gente comune; Con lettere dei 'fuorilegge del matrimonio'* (Rome: Carocci, 2014), 18–19. On La Pira's efforts and the Grilli amendment, see also Diana De Vigili, *La battaglia sul divorzio: Dalla Costituente al Referendum* (Milan: Franco Angeli, 2000), 23–27.

109. Cesari, *La censura in Italia oggi*, 31–33. During the 1920s Umberto Nobile gained international fame as a polar explorer.

Beyond the new Constitution and despite their commitment to democracy, in attempting to strengthen Italy's moral fiber Catholics sometimes took advantage of older, often Fascist acts lingering on the books. The charter called for a supreme court (*corte costituzionale*) to vet those laws, but delays in implementing that body gave the government time to annul or maintain the acts willy-nilly. Italy's 1930 Code of Criminal Procedure, for example, which Gavuzzo found so helpful in his *Guida*, dated from the Blackshirts. Known as the Rocco Code, after Mussolini's attorney general (*Guardasigilli*), Alfredo Rocco, its Title Nine concerned "Crimes against Public Morality and Decent Comportment" (*delitti contro la moralità pubblica e il buon costume*). Catholic moralists relied on a number of articles from Title Nine, including Article 519, concerning rape, and articles 527, 528, and 529 on obscenity. Article 527 called for prison sentences of from three months to three years for "obscene acts" committed in public places "or (those) open and exposed to the public." Article 528 determined the same jail time for those who "deal in or distribute or publicly display, manufacture, bring into the country, acquire, possess, export, or circulate writings, designs, images or other obscene objects of any kind." It also specified "any means of advertisement" and identified "theater or film shows, or broadcasts [*audizioni*], or 'public recitations'" as venues or vehicles for obscene material. Article 529 identified "obscene acts" as those that, "keeping with common sentiment . . . provoke indecency [or shame—*offendono pudore*]." Book Three's Article 725 on particular offenses concerning the "sale or distribution of printed matter, pictures or any other productions that offend the public decency" and 726, which specified fines for those who openly "engage in acts . . . or use language offensive to public decency," also came in handy. Beyond the Rocco Code, Catholics applied other measures, such as a 1935 Interior Ministry circular restricting the establishment of certain non-Catholic houses of worship—mostly newer pentacostal or fundamentalist sects that never received sanction from the old Liberal state.[110]

In his *Guida*, Gavuzzo still located some soft spots in the Rocco Code. He criticized articles 527 and 726 as too vague but was more generous toward Article 529, which provided some help in defining obscene acts as those that "offend decency." Definitions, however, could get slippery, particularly in judicial hands; and Gavuzzo noted one such exam-

110. On the 1935 circular, issued by Guido Buffarini Guidi, see Roy Domenico, "'For the Cause of Christ Here in Italy': Evangelical America's Holy Mission in Italy and the Cultural Ambiguities of the Cold War," *Diplomatic History* 29, no. 4 (September 2005): 630–31.

ple. A Venice Appellate ruling of October 3, 1949, found that "common sentiment" toward obscenity, gauged by the judgment of the man on the street, can change over time. Reliance on law and the courts, therefore, carried risks and was only "partly useful." Italian laws, furthermore, were not the moral laws that God gave the world and that were "retained and taught by the Catholic Church." Secular law was not necessarily interpreted "in a Catholic sense." Good Catholics needed to raise the moral level in an Italy where many had "completely lost" their sense of sin (*il senso del male*) and of the commonweal, a moral vacuum that cultivated not just immorality, but amorality, "the gravest evil."[111]

Beyond Gavuzzo in his *Guida*, other Catholics and observers of all political persuasions endlessly debated the Rocco Code's language, particularly questions of *pudore* (decency or shame), *comune sentimento* (common sentiment), and *buon costume*, key terms in the Catholic war on the devil and his earthbound troops. In his 1956 book *Obscenity and Penal Law*, the jurist Manlio Mazzanti revealed Catholic frustration when he found that, despite Rocco, filth persisted everywhere—in language, on the beach, on the stage, and in the media, infecting all levels of society and eroding "the moral sense of shame [*pudore*]."[112] Arguments arose, moreover, on the difference between obscenity and pornography, terms preferred by Marxists and secular factions, and the more nebulous *buon costume* favored by the Catholics. These critics found *buon costume* a useless term, "indeterminate and indeterminable," according to one, "abandoned to the absolute discretion of who has to judge."[113] In an important work of 1962, a jurist at the University of Turin and Catholic Action member Rodolfo Venditti expanded on these terms. A crucial determinant, he noted, was "common sentiment." But that vague term changed from time to time and from place to place. The adjective "common" might be defined as "general, diffuse, [or] equally applicable to all or to most.... A principle emerges of normality, of regularity, of universality [in the philosophical sense of the term], which is a criterion of worth [*valore*]." Venditti connected this idea of "worth" with the word "*buon*," as in "*buon costume*." At the center of his moral house stood the true standard that solved the "common sentiment" dilemma. It simply was "the sentiment of the typical man [*uomo medio*], which ... has a real and profound sense of reserve," covering even that "most private sphere of sex." The "*bo-*

111. Gavuzzo, *Guida*, 28–36.
112. Manlio Mazzanti, *L'Osceno e diritto penale* (1956; repr. Milan: Giuffrè, 1962), 383–84.
113. Giorgio Moscon, "Censura cinematografica e buon costume," *Belfagor*, May 31, 1961, 377.

nus paterfamilias" must be spared from the offenses to sexual modesty that he encounters "at every step . . . on the street, in the newspaper, at the movies, at the theater." "It's not right," Venditti concluded, "that the hypersexuals, erotic hedonists [*erotomani*], dissolute, homosexuals [*invertiti*], (or those who trade in their base passions) be allowed to impose on others their mentalities and their twisted, often pathological tastes [*gusti deteriori—non di rado patologici*] through their use of the public [media]."[114]

Another question concerned the proper method of denunciation, something that helped to teach the Catholics how to cooperate with the state in their fight against degenerates. Since clerics and AC militants had no real authority by themselves, they needed to denounce transgressors to the police or make the government aware of corrupt media in news kiosks, for example, or movie theaters. In Gavuzzo's morality guide, oddly tucked into his alphabetical roster of offenses was a "how-to" chapter on denunciation (*denuncia*)—that is, how to file complaints with the police. Here he reminded the reader that reporting crimes "against public morality and religious sentiment treated in this Guide, bar none, can be undertaken by anybody."[115] Toward that end, he had asked a colleague to fabricate a few sample denunciation forms for submission to the office of the state prosecutor (*Procuratore della Repubblica*), models that emphasized precision in describing the exact nature of the offense and suggesting where specifically the penal code might be employed in the case. The secretary always advocated close contacts with friendly DC authorities, and he was in frequent touch with sympathetic officials at the Interior Ministry, the hard-nosed Mario Scelba, or his underlings, such as Oscar Scalfaro. In a 1953 circular, Gavuzzo urged his diocesan officers to invite government authorities to Morality meetings "to solidify the best forms of collaboration."[116] Also on board was the church. In August 1951, the *Rivista del clero italiano* argued that Italy need-

114. Rodolfo Venditti, *La Tutela penale del pudore e della pubblica decenza* (Milan: Giuffrè, 1963), 23, 26–29. Transcripts of the penal code articles can be found on 235–36. See also Salvatore Messina, "La repressione dell'oscenità nell'opera cinematografica," in AAVV, *Legge penale e libertà del pensiero* (Padua: Cedam—Casa editrice dott. Antonio Milani, 1966), 104–18. On some juridical notions of *pudore*, public decency, common sentiment, obscenity, and indecency, see Camera dei deputati, Segretariato Generale, *Orientamenti giurisprudenziali in tema di buon costume* (Rome: Servizio studi legislazione e inchieste parlamentari, 1972), 504–22.

115. Gavuzzo, *Guida*, 137–45. Gavuzzo also observed that not only could anyone file a complaint, but articles 235 and 242 of the penal code allowed him or her to make a citizen's arrest. Such cases were sanctioned mostly for particularly "flagrant" offenses.

116. IPVI, PgVII, b. 20, "Appunti per un programma da svolgere nelle diocese in difesa della moralità," May 13, 1953.

ed no new laws; rather, Catholics merely needed to file denunciations, and the police needed to follow up on them. The article continued with a sample denunciation letter. Directed to the *procuratore*, it read, "The undersigned denounces to your excellency the attached publication, finding in it evidence of the crime against *buon costume* punishable by your office." In the end, however, the author still saw the state authorities as the wild cards of the operation. They are not saints, he concluded, so they need "our" help, and "right now" (*subito*).[117]

The legal footing of the Catholic morality campaign was therefore both conservative and naïve. It was conservative in the sense that Italy's return to the church would not require much new or revolutionary legislation—it was already mostly there in the new Constitution, with the Lateran Pacts woven into it, and in the Rocco Code. Only a determined application was needed. But the campaign was also naïve in the sense that Catholics expected a spirit of compliance among their rivals where little or none existed. A sword of Damocles, furthermore, hung over the whole Catholic project in its reliance on Fascist laws and decrees. Sooner or later, those tools would have to be abandoned, and, in 1956 when Italy finally inaugurated its long-delayed Constitutional Court, that process would begin.

April 18

The 1946 referendum and the Constituent Assembly determined the government of the new Italy, while the elections of April 18, 1948, settled who would rule. They determined the composition of the new republic's first legislature and provided the defining moment when the church, Catholic Action, and Christian Democracy successfully united against the Marxists and lay forces.

Before April 18, the Cold War expressed itself in DC purges of the CLN coalition. In May 1947, De Gasperi expelled from his cabinet both the PCI and its Socialist allies. Italy's subsequent administrations, all DC-controlled, never lifted the ban on Communists, a proscription that lasted until their party collapsed at the end of the 1980s. The Socialists eventually reentered the ministries with the so-called "opening to the left" in 1963. Nevertheless, as Italy's second- and third-largest parties, the PCI and PSI still participated at local and regional levels and in Par-

117. Guido Aceti, "Per una più vigile difesa del buon costume," *Rivista del clero italiano*, August 1951.

liament. The ban also provided short-term political benefits for the lay camp, particularly the Republicans, the Liberals, and the Social Democrats in that, with far fewer votes than the Marxists or the DC, they enjoyed great prestige as frequent junior partners in DC-led coalitions. Finally, prospects for the right, Uomo Qualunque, monarchists, and the neo-Fascists (eventually the Movimento sociale italiano, or MSI) were either fleeting, as in the first case, slim, or nil. In its propaganda, the DC portrayed itself as the protector of Italy and the family from both Marxist aggression and the forces of individualistic capitalism. It spoke of traditional morality in ways the other parties did not.[118]

Everybody considered the upcoming election as a contest between good and evil. Catholics worried—would April 18 determine if Italy remained a Christian land or lead it to Satanic Bolshevism—between God and the devil with all of his infernal earth-bound acolytes? Here was a clear "choice of civilizations," and references to old Christian victories over Islam at Poitiers, Lepanto, and Vienna appeared everywhere; although now, instead of the Muslim menace, the cursed Reds charged the gates. Pius condemned with regularity the Marxists in Moscow and their minions in Italy. In December of 1946, he reemphasized to the faithful in St. Peter's Square this "great spiritual battle of our time." "*For* Christ or *against* Christ," he proclaimed, "*for* His Church or *against* His Church. Awake oh Romans, the hour has sounded."[119] In February 1948, Milan's Cardinal Ildefonso Schuster famously denied absolution to a Communist, and finally, after the April election, in July 1949 the Holy Office pronounced excommunication for active Communists.[120]

A glance at Catholic propaganda posters reveals criticism, too, of the moderate lay camp, the image of a "Christian worker," for example, standing on top of capitalist and communist frogs. The most energy, however, was directed against the Marxists. One Catholic poster depicted that enemy as a fiend, wrenching children from their mothers' arms. Another portrayed a panicked little girl about to be crushed under the

118. Alessandro Brogi has highlighted a very similar emphasis on women and children in Communist propaganda—victims, for instance, of America's aggressive nuclear policies; Brogi, *Confronting America: The Cold War between the United States and the Communists in France and Italy* (Chapel Hill: University of North Carolina Press, 2011), 125–27.

119. Pius's discourse can be found on the Vatican website, https://w2.vatican.va/content/pius-xii/it/speeches/1946/documents/hf_p-xii_spe_19461222_missione-roma.html, accessed December 28, 2020.

120. Galli and Facchi, *La Sinistra democristiana*, 341–42; Owen Chadwick, *The Christian Church in the Cold War* (London: Penguin, 1993), 14–18; Robert Ventresca, *Soldier of Christ: The Life of Pope Pius XII* (Cambridge, Mass.: Harvard University Press, 2013), 243–44; Pollard, *Papacy in the Age of Totalitarianism*, 374–78.

treads of a Soviet tank. Placards depicted the DC as Italy's hope. One very famous one depicted the stern goddess "Italia" protected by a Christian Democratic shield that deflected a hammer and sickle thrown from a red hand. Still another showed a mob, glowing red as usual, storming a castle—fortress Italy—that was pulling up its DC-adorned drawbridge. One Tuscan priest expressed the widespread anxiety of Marxist victory when he wrote of April 18, "This is the day so awaited and so dreaded . . . the local Communists are already convinced of their victory. . . . It is rumored that they have drawn up lists of people to eliminate, and at the top of the lists are the priests and the nuns."[121]

Catholic mobilization for the elections, consequently, became the stuff of legend. Traditional religion weaved through politics for the showdown, revealing an enormous reserve at the DC's disposal. Front-line Christian Democrats counted on Gedda's civic committees and Monignor Ronca's Civiltà italica. To remind voters of the stakes, Catholic theaters on wheels brought them al fresco showings of *Pastor Angelicus*. Parish and diocesan networks mobilized, sure of support from the Holy See and America's efforts, both overt and covert.[122] The DC benefitted from the use of *Madonne pellegrine*, when images of the mother of Christ were displayed and received the adoration of the faithful across Italy. Pius orchestrated and launched these in 1947, and their success lasted through the following electoral season. Each Madonna was a particular statue or image held dear by local populations. The most famous was Rome's *Madonna del divino amore*, which many credited with the city's escape from Allied bombs a few years before. The pontiff brought her image from a small suburban church into the Eternal City, where it was

121. Victoria C. Belco, *War, Massacre and Recovery in Central Italy, 1943–1948* (Toronto: University of Toronto Press, 2010), 352. Regarding Lepanto, see also Andrea Mariuzzo, *Divergenze parallele: Comunismo e anticomunismo alle origini del linguaggio politico dell'Italia repubblicana (1945–1953)* (Soveria Manelli: Rubettino, 2010), 59. See also David W. Ellwood, "The 1948 Elections in Italy: A Cold War Propaganda Battle," *Historical Journal of Film, Radio and Television* 13, no. 1 (1993).

122. Massimo Teodori, *Storia dei laici nell'Italia clericale e comunista* (Venice: Marsilio, 2008), 79; Carlo Orsini, "Difesa delle conquiste della civiltà," *Noi uomini*, April 15, 1950. In his study of the elections, Robert Ventresca noted that "although their ultimate objective was the same," nevertheless, the DC and the Civic Committees "were entirely independent of each other." Catholic Action propaganda tended to stress Catholicism and Italy's religious culture more than the DC's more political message, which emphasized the depravity of communism; Ventresca, *From Fascism to Democracy: Culture and Politics in the Italian Elections of 1948* (Toronto: The University of Toronto Press, 2004), 209, 136–37. On the Civic Committees, see also Casella, *18 Aprile 1948: La mobilitazione delle organizzazioni cattoliche* (Galatina: Congedo, 1992), 77–183; and Gedda's discussion in his memoirs, *18 Aprile 1948: Memorie inedite dell'artefice della sconfitta del Fronte Popolare* (Milan: Mondadori, 1998), 114–29. On Ronca's Civiltà italica, see Giuseppe Brienza, *Identità cattolica e anticomunismo nell'Italia del dopoguerra: La figura e l'opera di mons. Roberto Ronca* (Crotone: D'Ettoris Editori, 2008); and Andrea Riccardi, *Roma "città sacra"? Dalla Conciliazione all'operazione Sturzo* (Milan: Vita e Pensiero, 1979), 306–9.

paraded up and down for months, stopping from place to place, at a church or piazza, to enormous popular acclaim. The processions and ceremonies around her clearly amounted to DC rallies. Here was an example of what John Pollard described as the Catholic preference to "fight the 'culture war' with liberal democracy on its own terrain, mobilizing the Catholic masses in great celebrations of traditional religious identity." In his study of the 1948 elections, Robert Ventresca noted as much in recalling the words of Father Umberto Terenzi, the parish priest from the Madonna's original suburban location who accompanied her on the "pilgrimage." His "description of the Marian procession through the streets of Rome in March and April 1948 reads as a metaphor for the political atmosphere in Italy on the eve of the April election."[123]

Catholics also found aid in U.S. Ambassador James Dunn, a stalwart friend who worked for months before the vote, ceremoniously greeting cargo ships from America laden with good will for Italy, riding his "Freedom Train," doling out innumerable presents along the way, and turning the embassy on the via Veneto "into a veritable election headquarters."[124] When the nascent Central Intelligence Agency used the election as its first test, Hollywood movie stars joined with Italo-Americans who wrote to their kin, imploring them to keep the nation safe from Stalin's clutches. That in February, with only weeks to go before the Italian election, Moscow's tentacles extinguished Czechoslovak freedom made the pro-West arguments all the easier.

In the end, Catholic hopes and the fear of Communism produced a DC victory, securing for it national leadership that would last almost fifty years. Legal peculiarities, furthermore, enabled the Christian Democrats, who polled just under 50 percent, to rule with an absolute majority in the Chamber of Deputies, Italy's lower house (often referred to by its location, the Montecitorio).[125] Some attributed the triumph to nothing

123. Falconi, *La Chiesa e le organizzazioni cattoliche in Italia*, 125–27; Pollard, *Catholicism in Modern Italy*, 34; Ventresca, *From Fascism to Democracy*, 108–17. The image of the *Madonna del divino amore* remains today in the Church of Sant'Ignazio di Loyola in central Rome. The number of Marian apparitions, furthermore, rose from an average of two or three per year to twenty-three in 1947 and twenty-five in 1948. They remained high through 1954, when they returned to normal; Jeff C. Pratt, *The Walled City: A Study of Social Change and Conservative Ideologies in Tuscany* (Aachen: Rader Verlag, 1986), 257n5. Pratt cites W. A. Christian's study "Religious Apparitions and the Cold War in Southern Europe," in *Religion, Power and Protest in Local Communities*, ed. E. R. Wolf (Berlin: Mouton, 1984).

124. Ventresca, *From Fascism to Democracy*, 79.

125. James Miller, *The United States and Italy, 1940–1950: The Politics and Diplomacy of Stabilization* (Chapel Hill: University of North Carolina Press, 1986); James Miller, "Taking Off the Gloves: The United States and the Italian Elections of 1948," *Diplomatic History* 9, no. 1 (Winter 1983); Ventresca, *From Fascism to Democracy*, 236–61.

less than divine intervention, while others remarked that on April 18 Italy was "saved by the *beghine*"—that is, by the pious or sanctimonious. The fifteen or so years following 1948 was the heyday of Catholic political power—when a culture took hold that extended beyond formal laws and official policies. To many, it appeared monolithic. The all-important personal factor facilitated much of this. Beyond the obvious—that virtually everyone in the DC and the AC were Catholics—a good 80 percent of DC representatives in Parliament were enrolled in Catholic Action or had been FUCI alumni. And the parish priest, as one observer noted, provided "the main organizational strength of the DC in the village."[126] Consequently, the Holy See could and did urge the Italian government to address Catholic issues. On November 20, 1955, for example, Pius held an audience with functionaries from the Interior Ministry and quite naturally urged them to aid in "expanding religious values in Italy."[127]

Witnessed on the street, one saw that a policeman would never dream of asking a mendicant brother for his *permesso*. Priests distributing propaganda could operate untouched, while similarly engaged Communists might be run into jail. Public places were constantly reserved for Catholic functions, and clerics regularly shared the podium at civic celebrations. Inauguration of a new apartment building would include a dedication to the Sacred Heart or to the Immaculate Heart of Mary.[128] The British student of Christian Democracy Michael Fogarty discerned this relationship in 1953 when he wrote, "Often the easiest way to pick out a convent in an Italian town is to see which building has the most *Democrazia Cristiana* posters plastered on its gates."[129]

In 1949, the transplanted Italian Leo Wollemborg wrote from America that "Italians must get accustomed to see Christian Democrats not only in all government posts but also at the head of banks, industries, etc."[130] In 1952, Catholics might have found satisfaction from the lay drama critic and author Vitaliano Brancati. His judgment, "the true Italy

126. Pratt, *Walled City*, 240–41, 249–50. Pratt took the 80 percent figure from F. Sartori, *Partiti e sistemi di partito* (Florence: Editrice universitaria, 1965).

127. "L'alta esortatzione di Sua Santita` agli addetti al Ministero dell'Interno," *OR*, November 21–22, 1955. The *Osservatore Romano* responded to a Communist attack on this in "Ex ore tuo," November 23, 1955.

128. Jemolo, *Church and State in Italy*, 311–24. Jemolo suspected that, underneath it all, a great deal of social conformity meant a lack of authentic religious feeling.

129. Michael Fogarty, "Christian Democracy Today," *Commonweal*, October 9, 1953. See also Fogarty, *Christian Democracy in Western Europe 1820–1953* (Notre Dame, Ind.: University of Notre Dame Press, 1957).

130. Leo Wollemborg, "Italy 1949, Still Coasting Along?," *Commonweal*, January 28, 1949.

of 1936 is Fascist Italy, and the true Italy of 1952 is Christian Democratic Italy," was more resentment than joy, but it also recognized a certain juncture reached by the Catholics. Brancati's past under the Blackshirts was not entirely clear, but his anger in 1952 was authentic, since the government refused permission to stage his play *La Governante*. Had the nation indeed become a "clerical tyranny"?, he asked. Not quite yet, but that horror was on its way. One could see it, he continued, "in the satisfying smile [*sorriso di sicurezza*] . . . of certain young ministers, the impenetrability of certain clerks, Gedda's speeches, and above all in the stiffening of censorship."[131] To an American audience, Igino Giordani added a nuance in welcoming the 1948 victory. "In Italy," he wrote, "we are not rich except in love of God and the Blessed Virgin; it is through this love that we have saved ourselves."[132] God's enemies had lost the fight, and the *Rivista del clero italiano* announced, "We have the power of God; they don't. . . . If we are united in Christ, firm in the faith, [and] enthusiastic in love, the world will be ours!"[133]

Such declarations disturbed lay and Marxist observers, who fretted that, coming on the heels of Catholic victories in the Constitution, the 1948 elections cleared the way for a clerical state or even dictatorship. To portray these critics as entirely anticlerical, however, would be a mistake. While skeptical of church politics, some, like Giovanni Spadolini, Adriano Olivetti, and Arturo Carlo Jemolo, could hardly be considered ideologues in that regard. Spadolini abandoned an early loyalty to Fascism and joined the Republican Party after the war. A respected journalist and historian, in 1981 he became the first non-Christian Democratic prime minister since Ferruccio Parri in 1945. The son of a Jewish father and Waldensian mother and heir to a business machine empire, Olivetti converted to Catholicism during the war.[134] Jemolo was a noted Florentine scholar who devoted himself to historical studies of the eighteenth- and nineteenth-century church. He concluded in a work on the rebel-

131. Vitaliano Brancati, *Ritorno alla censura* (Bari: Laterza, 1952), 42, 54. See also David Forgacs and Stephen Gundle, *Mass Culture and Italian Society: From Fascism to the Cold War* (Bloomington: Indiana University Press, 2007), 230. In "Libertà d'espressione" (*Il Popolo*, July 2, 1952), Leone Piccioni identified Brancati as "another victim, another martyr of the, 'clerical dictatorship'" and dismissed as "ridiculous" his argument. On Brancati and the Fascists, see chapter 3.

132. Igino Giordani, "Letter to an American," *Commonweal*, July 30, 1948. Giordani was responding to an earlier article by Dorothy Day that disparaged the DC's victory as inauthentic. The Italian insisted that the triumph was a true and spiritual defeat of Communism, which he called "Satan's attempt to avenge the Redemption."

133. Giovanni Calabria, "Un problema urgente: Viribus unitis," *Rivista del clero italiano*, March 1950.

134. Teodori, *Storia dei laici*, 172–81.

lious Jesuit theologian Carlo Maria Curci that "liberalism, as opposed to absolutism, is essentially Christian."[135]

Sharper anticlerical currents in the lay and Marxist camps, however, were easily located. Some critics came from beyond the pale: ex-priests—defrocked, married perhaps, or apostates. A few became Protestants. Another was "Professor" Alighiero Tondi, who turned to Communism and served the left press by undermining Vatican criticisms of oppression in the Eastern Bloc. Against his "apostate lies," the *Osservatore Romano* delivered some of its most acidic vitriol. Tondi was a "traitor to the faith ... [and] a small and vile provocateur" who had added to the chains that wrapped the church in Communist lands.[136]

Among the most notorious of the overtly anticlerical publications was *don Basilio*, which, along with other reviews, according to a U.S. Embassy report, formed part of a "campaign with pamphlets, throwaways, articles in friendly left-wing daily newspapers, speeches, demonstrations, slogans painted on buildings (including churches) and the formation of anti-clerical associations." They prompted a quick and energetic counterattack from the Holy Office, which condemned *don Basilio* in November of 1946 and excommunicated its staff, although the Americans felt this brought "only [a] slight adverse effect on the sale of this paper." It and other reviews were occasionally sequestered but then allowed to resume sales. The Action Party's journal, *L'Italia libera*, condemned this harassment as "a gross violation of the freedom of the press" and "a clear violation of Italian sovereignty." The DC's *Il Popolo* answered that unrestricted speech had limits "beyond which freedom degenerates into license." The warning approached the "threat" level when it reminded everyone of "the penal code" and of "international treaties," a clear reference to the Lateran Pacts.[137]

More serious than the sarcastic *don Basilio* were the mainline lay and Marxist political organs. The list of important newspapers started with

135. Arturo Carlo Jemolo, "Lo 'scandalo' di padre Curci," in *Scritti vari di storia religiosa e civile*, ed. Francesco Margiotta Broglio (Milan: Giuffrè, 1965), 439.

136. "Chiesa cattolica e 'democrazie popolari,'" *OR*, May 10–11, 1954; "Le menzogne dell'apostata," *OR*, May 13, 1954; "Una 'separazione' soffocatrice," *OR*, May 15, 1954; and "La verità di Barabba," *OR*, May 24–25, 1954. All four were front-page attacks on Tondi written by Federico Alessandrini, the journal's chief editor. Another disreputable figure was the defrocked Father Gaggero, who worked for the Soviet Foreign Ministry; Andrea Riccardi, *Il Vaticano e mosca* (Rome and Bari: Laterza, 1992), 201; and Falconi, *La Chiesa e le organizzazioni cattoliche in Italia*, 93.

137. National Archives and Records Service, RG59 865.404/1–647, Rome Embassy (Charge d'Affaires David McKey) / State Department, January 6, 1947; Casella, *Giornali cattolici e società italiana*, 154–58. At about the same time, a campaign by the archbishop of Bergamo and the Catholic paper *L'Eco di Bergamo* succeeded in the suppression of the anticlerical *Cittadella*, whose editor was then fired from his position as philosophy teacher in the local school system.

the Communist *L'Unità*, the Socialist *Avanti!*, the Social-Democratic *Il Tempo*, the Liberal *Risorgimento liberale*, the Republican *Voce repubblicana*, and the left-independent *Il Paese*/*Paese sera*. To this might be added vigorously independent lay reviews such as Piero Calamandrei's prestigious *Il Ponte*, Mario Pannunzio's *Il Mondo*, Ernesto Rossi's *L'Astrolabio*, and Luigi Rossi's *Belfagor*.

For *Il Ponte*, Calamandrei, who represented the Action Party at the Constituent Assembly, intended the status of the revered literary *Nuova antologia* but "livelier and more revolutionary."[138] Giuseppe Rovero wrote for the review in 1950 that the "flowering of political Catholicism" gave pause to many: the non-Catholic who feared religious intolerance, the liberal who feared "the resurgence of theocratic dreams," and the socialist who feared the exploitation of religious principles on behalf of "bourgeois interests."[139] In the same issue, Aldo Capitini delivered a back-handed attack on the church by identifying with St. Francis, the patron of Italy. Francis, he claimed, never wanted to be a priest, but rather strove inwardly to imitate Christ. The saint, Capitini implied, viewed the church as his "jailer" (*custode*).[140]

In January 1946, Russo produced the first issue of *Belfagor*, which quickly engaged the debate over church power in postwar Italy. A regular contributor to this and other anticlerical reviews was the aforementioned Gabriele Pepe, whom Catholics dismissed as a dogmatist "wrapped up in his own prejudices and in the comfort of his own reality." In the March 1947 issue, Pepe responded to a claim by Igino Giordani that Christ suffered at the hands of anticlericals. Pepe felt, in fact, that anticlericalism was an unfortunate term; indeed, he claimed that Christ's harsh reaction to the "doctrinal" Jewish hierarchy meant that the Savior himself could be considered an anticlerical. The anticlerical storm (*bufera*), wrote Pepe, gathers when religion becomes the tool of the state (*instrumentum regni*) as it had been under Mussolini and in Franco's Spain, although religious politics, theocracy, and clericalism triggered the tempest, too. The *laicisti*, he continued, offered only modest solutions. They did not seek to replace the church with another one of their own; they were not crusaders, martyrs, or saints. Rather, they sought to tame the "unruly" clerical river with a dam and channel it for the general welfare.[141]

138. Alessandro Galante Garrone, *Calamandrei* (Milan: Garzanti, 1987), 242.
139. Giuseppe Rovero, "Il problema politico dei cattolici," *Il Ponte*, June 6, 1950.
140. Aldo Capitani, "Chiesa e religione in Italia," *Il Ponte*, June 6, 1950.
141. Gabriele Pepe, "Le varie forme di protesta laica," *Belfagor* 1, no. 2 (March 15, 1947): 233–42.

The son of a Communist father and a mother from the Catholic aristocracy, and with experience at the *Risorgimento liberale* and at the news magazine *L'Europeo*, in 1949 Mario Pannunzio founded *Il Mondo*, which would rank among the most important independent lay reviews. A "counter altar" between the Catholic and Marxist worlds, it not only carried a liberal strain, but represented "the lay, *azionista* and sophisticated bourgeoisie" that vilified Pio XII as the sinister head of the clerical cabal, "obscurantist and anti-modern *par excellence*, with *flabelli* [the large, fancy, feathered fans that accompanied the pontiff while he rode on his portable throne], authoritarian reveries, [he was] above all, ignorant and démodé."[142] *Il Mondo*'s criticism extended across the Catholic movement, and the clerical regime was a frequent target, charging in 1956 that the DC occupied the "most detested and defamed" place on the political stage. Italy, it claimed, was "the most skeptical, most irreligious and most anti-Christian country that exists.... When one sees a lay Government minister kneeling before a high Church official ... no true Christian is fooled."[143]

The American hand also aligned on occasion with the more strictly secular lay factions against the Catholics. The Congress for Cultural Freedom, for example, was established in West Berlin in 1950 and secretly sponsored by the Central Intelligence Agency. The Congress assisted the secularist cause, cooperating with like-minded Italians and mobilizing such figures as the renegade socialist Ignazio Silone, who was instrumental in promoting it across the peninsula. Silone launched in 1951 an ancillary Italian Association for Cultural Freedom (Associazione italiana per la Libertà della cultura, or AILC), dedicated to the "freedom of conscience, thought and expression" toward the advancement of the "modern world." Charter members included a virtual Who's Who of *laicisti*, including Ferruccio Parri, Ernesto Rossi, Luigi Salvatorelli, Piero Calamandrei, and Leo Valiani; among its patrons stood the venerable

Pepe believed that history revealed a clerical power so out of control that certain popes, Pius IX among them, "ruled as gods!" The *Belfagor* piece came out of a speech he delivered in Rome to the "Association for the Progress of Moral and Religious Studies." He later developed his themes in his short work *La Protesta Laica*. See also Tommaso Fiore, *Gabriele Pepe e la sua protesta laica*, ed. Francesco D'Episcopo (Maduria: Laicata, 2001). The Catholic comment on Pepe came from "Gli spropositi del Prof. Pepe," *Il Quotidiano*, January 10, 1950.

142. Marazziti, *I papi di carta*, 34; Teodori, *Storia dei laici*, 170; and Teodori, *Pannunzio, Dal "Mondo" al Partito radicale: Vita di un intellettuale del Novecento* (Milan: Mondadori, 2010), 134–60. See also Antonio Cardini, *Tempo di ferro: "Il Mondo" e L'Italia del dopoguerra* (Bologna: Il Mulino, 1992). *Il Mondo* folded in 1966.

143. "Democristiani 1956," *Il Mondo*, February 14, 1956.

Benedetto Croce and Gaetano Salvemini. Six years later Silone and Nicola Chiaromonte founded *Tempo Presente* as a mouthpiece for the Congress and worked against press censorship and harassment of religious minorities.[144]

The Clerical State in Practice

The Holy Year

Few, if any, *laicisti* could have enthusiastically welcomed the Holy Year of 1950. For Catholics it seemed a natural "victory lap" after the April 18 victory, where church-AC-DC cultural cooperation was on display. The *Osservatore Romano* announced that the Jubilee reminded Italy of the totality of its Christian heritage, a patrimony that touched all aspects of life, from *costume* to art to the economy.[145] In a Holy Year pastoral letter, Genoa's young Archbishop Giuseppe Siri, from the cultural traditionalist vanguard, identified the enemy as the modern world, infatuated with novelty and presenting "distractions that overwhelm the sinner." The duty of the Christian militant was to resist "crossing the border into relaxation, into conformism, or into adaptation to the worldly spirit.... We cannot and we must not become comfortable people."[146]

On May 26, 1949, Pope Pius's bull *Jubilaeum maximum* proclaimed that 1950 offered the chance to not only atone for one's sins but to "instill the spirit and teachings of the Gospels in private and public life."[147] Italian Catholics would join their brothers and sisters from around the world in the ancient festival, the first of which Pope Boniface VIII proclaimed in 1300. A time to rejoice in the triumph of the faith and Italy's first Catholic government since 1870, when the *Risorgimento*'s lay forces thought they had entombed the *ancien regime* for good, the 1950 Holy Year provided one more way for the faithful to identify with their church, a link in the chain that started with Sunday Mass. Then attendance for holy days of obligation and for rituals such as weddings, baptisms, funerals, and parish

144. Peter Coleman, *The Liberal Conspiracy: The Congress for Cultural Freedom and the Struggle for the Mind of Postwar Europe* (New York: Free Press, 1989), 91 and 143; Teodori, *Storia dei laici*, 127–44.

145. Onorio Cairoli, "Questa Italia cristiana," OR, October 26, 1950.

146. Pius's close adviser Raimondo Spiazzi extensively quoted Siri's letter and commented on it in his article "Chiesa e modernità" (OR, June 16, 1950). He added, "Unfortunately world and Church are in conflict because the first obstinately refuses that Truth which came to redeem and elevate it."

147. "Pope Proclaims Holy Year, Asks Catholics to Visit Rome," *New York Times*, May 27, 1949. The text of the announcement can be seen at the Vatican website: http://w2.vatican.va/content/pius-xii/it/bulls/documents/hf_p-xii_bull_19490526_iubilaeum-maximum.html, accessed December 28, 2020.

activities like pilgrimages and picnics further tethered Catholics to their religious culture. As in the past, the postwar church magnified these local rituals into large-scale occasions—announcements of encyclicals, for example, or the Marian Year of 1954, or well-attended Eucharistic Congresses in Assisi (1951), Turin (1953), Catania (1959), Pisa (1965), and Udine (1972), or the 1956 Lecce congress, which saw "unforgettable" assemblies of 300,000, more than three times the city's population.[148] But until the Second Vatican Council of 1962–65, the greatest event of the postwar years was the 1950 Holy Year, the final tally for which showed that Rome hosted 1,570,000 Italian, non-Roman, pilgrims, 574,000 Europeans, 46,000 North Americans, 16,300 South Americans, 6,400 Africans, 3,460 Asians, and 1,350 pilgrims from Oceana.[149]

Pius assembled a National Holy Year Committee and placed it under Catholic Action's ecclesiastic assistant, Monsignor Urbani, who announced that the spirit of 1950 would bring an Italian "parish rebirth" in the "struggle against the spreading public immorality [that conducts] continuous and open attacks on the holiness of marriage and the family." It should also yield fruit in a return to the sacred character of Sundays and Holy Days, assistance in the Holy Mass, participation in holy prayer, and in "healthy fun" (*sano divertimento*).[150]

The Holy Year formally began with Pius's Christmas 1949 message of renewal and the Crusade of the Great Return (*Crociata del Grande Ritorno*), directed at those who strayed from the church. To lead the crusade, he chose the popular Jesuit Riccardo Lombardi.[151] He was born in Naples to a Piedmontese family in 1908; his father was a professor of electronics, and his mother was an activist in the Unione Donne. After a conversion experience triggered by a Vatican exhibit on global mission work, Lombardi was ordained in 1936 and secured a position as an editor at the *Civiltà Cattolica*.[152] There, in January 1947, he published

148. AAVV, *XV Congresso eucaristico nazionale: L'eucaristia: "Sacramentum unitatis, vinculum caritatis"* (Lecce, 1956).

149. Andrea Riccardi, *Il Potere del papa da Pio XII a Paolo VI* (Bari and Rome: Laterza, 1988), 118–19. For some variations on the figures, see Comitato Centrale Anno Santo, ed., *L'Anno santo 1950: Cronistoria del grande giubileo* (Vatican City: Tipografia poliglotta vaticana, 1952), 2:855–62.

150. Alfredo Cavagna, "Il Giubileo nella comunità parocchiale," *Rivista del clero italiano*, February 1951, 46–48.

151. Mariuzzo, *Divergenze parallele*, 60–61. On Lombardi, see Giancarlo Zizola, *Il Microfono di dio: Pio XII, Padre Lombardi e i cattolici italiani* (Milan: Mondadori, 1990), and Arnaldo Chierici, *Una Speranza per la Chiesa: Padre Lombardi ed il Movimento Mondo Migliore* (Rome: Editrice Rogate, 1984). For lay critiques of Lombardi, see Massimo Mila, "Il Ruzzolone di padre Lombardi," *Belfagor* 4, no. 1 (January 31, 1949): 91–93; or Falconi, *La Chiesa e le organizzazioni cattoliche in Italia*, particularly 91.

152. Chierici, *Una Speranza per la Chiesa*, 21–24.

what has been considered the first postwar invocation of the "great spiritual mobilization of the nation"—the reawakening of "the Italy of Saint Francis, of Saint Clare, of Saint Catherine, of Saint Bernardino, the Italy of Saint Pius V, of Saint Louis, of don Bosco, of Cottolengo, of Saint Frances Cabrini [in which] to be a good Italian [meant] to be a good Catholic; to be anti-Catholic means, for us, to be a traitor to the nation."[153] He elaborated on this theme in his book *Toward a General Mobilization of the Catholics* (*Per una mobilitazione generale dei cattolici*) in which he implored Italians not to give up on their nation. "The Fatherland is good," he wrote, "much better than what it seems today." Italians must prepare themselves, rather, for a great mission ordained by God. They must realize, he continued, that no other people on Earth have been so intimately linked to the work of Christ. At the same time, Lombardi debuted on the radio with Lenten messages, discovering another outlet for his views and becoming a fixture of Vatican propaganda over the airwaves as the "Radio Priest" or "God's Microphone." A tireless servant of the Holy See, Lombardi became a ubiquitous figure in Catholic mobilization, starting with his Goodness Crusade (*Crociata di bontà*) in 1948 and, later, in his campaign For a Better World (*Per un Mondo Migliore*) of the 1950s.[154] To a Milan assembly in 1950 Gedda pledged Catholic Action's support for Lombardi's crusade and spoke of the great work ahead, meeting the challenge "of modern ills," but particularly one of *costume* that had sunk to lower and lower standards. Italy, he continued, must revive its "living Christian conscience."[155]

The Holy Year was distinguished by papal encyclicals, most importantly, *Munificentissimus Deus* of November 1, establishing the dogma of

153. Ricardo Lombardi, "L'Ora presente in Italia," *Civiltà cattolica* 98, no. 2317 (January 4, 1947); cited in Mariuzzo, *Divergenze parallele*, 182–83.

154. On the "Goodness Crusade," see Zizola, *Il Microfono di dio*, 132–52; regarding the "Better World Movement," see 320–47; see also Falconi, *La Chiesa e le organizzazioni cattoliche in Italia*, 471–82; and Poggi, *Catholic Action in Italy*, 220–30; Riccardo Lombardi, *Per una mobilitazione generale dei cattolici* (Rome: Edizioni Civiltà Cattolica, 1948), 12, 45. See also "Duecentoquaranta Madri Superiore ai corsi per un 'mondo migliore,'" *OR*, January 5, 1956; and "Artisti ad un corso per 'un mondo migliore,'" *OR*, June 15, 1956; "L'inaugurazione del Centro Pio XII per un Mondo migliore," *OR*, December 10–11, 1956. For the following February 27 edition of the *Osservatore Romano*, the archbishop of Perugia contributed a laudatory piece on the Center and the Movement that, he wrote, were guaranteed success in that the pontiff had blessed them and in that they were planned well, not "blindly and adventurously"; Piero Parente, "Idee e movimento per un 'Mondo migliore,'" *OR*, February 27, 1957. Another promotional article came the following week: N.A., "Al Centro 'Pio XII' per un Mondo migliore," *OR*, March 2, 1957.

155. "La 'Giornata dell'Azione Cattolica' solemnemente celebrata a Milano," *OR*, February 16, 1950. Six weeks after Gedda's speech, in the *Osservatore Romano*, Bishop Carlo Rossi of Biella affirmed Catholic Action and praised its role in the fight for the Faith and the church; Carlo Rossi, "Organizzare l'Apostolato," *OR*, April 1, 1950.

Mary's assumption into Heaven. Another key document was *Humani Generis* of August 12, with its emphasis on orthodoxy and its attack on the relativism of the "new theology" that had found a foothold in France. The *Osservatore Romano* took umbrage at lay and Marxist disparagement of the encyclicals. It resented the "harshly critical" assaults, for example, on *Humani generis* and dismissed *Il Paese*'s attack on Pius's exhortation of September 23, *Menti nostrae*, on the priestly life, as "political, purely political" and *Avanti!*'s judgment that it was mere "vituperative sectarianism."[156]

As emblematic as any Holy Year event was the canonization of Maria Goretti, whose story, one of Christian bravery and nobility, touched countless Catholic hearts around the world, especially those of women and girls. Writing in 1989, an American scholar noted that "it was impossible for a girl to attend a parochial or convent school at any time in the decades prior to Vatican II and not learn about Maria Goretti, who constituted the core curriculum in moral theology for Catholic girls during this period."[157] In 1902, at a farmhouse south of Rome, the eleven-year-old Goretti refused sexual advances from a family acquaintance, Alessandro Serenelli, who then brutalized her and repeatedly stabbed her. Near death, the little girl was taken to a hospital where, after a day of excruciating pain and without anesthetic, she forgave her attacker and died. Condemned to thirty years in prison, Serenelli reported later that he saw his victim in a dream, causing him to repent and beg to be reconciled with Maria's mother. In 1935, the church launched an investigation into the girl's sanctity and beatified her in 1947. On June 24 of the Holy Year, mother and murderer joined the pontiff and about 500,000 others in St. Peter's Square to celebrate the life and martyrdom of St. Maria Goretti.

The *Osservatore Romano* linked Goretti to the Madonna and to Christ. "We invoke the woman; the pure woman, the beautiful woman who, from the beast [*drago*], from the diseased swamp dragged and abducted, raises our eye, heart, spirit toward the sublime and immaculate peak where the Lord's light, salvation and joy shine forth." The anguished world could now, continued the article, lift the "exultant shout as [did] the old scientist Archimedes's 'Eureka,' I've found it. I've found the

156. "Voci ed echi," OR, August 26 and September 27, 1950.

157. Kathleen Z. Young, "The Imperishable Virginity of Saint Maria Goretti," *Gender and Society* 3, no. 4 (December 1989): 477.

woman, my woman, Mary, the wife, the mother, the purest love of all, and the safety and the life of all."[158] Pius also famously used his discourse on Maria Goretti's canonization to warn of a communist-inspired "plot of bad behavior [*congiura del malcostume*]" dedicated, through the use of scandal and "germs of corruption," to the dechristianization of society.[159] The *Osservatore Romano* found, however, that not everyone was impressed. On August 6, the journal refuted one such doubter, Angelo Spadoni, a former cleric who called himself "God's Priest," and who let loose a barrage of scurrilous attacks on Goretti. Shortly after her canonization, Spadoni applauded her resistance to her attacker but described her struggle as "very normal" and not particularly heroic. The indignant Vatican paper responded that God urged sainthood on everyone and that action toward it does not have to be sublimely heroic.[160]

In the Goretti case and for the entire Holy Year, the Italian government stood in solidarity with the church. On December 23, 1949, President Luigi Einaudi, a Liberal, declared to Pius that "the Italian people renews with me to Your Holiness [their] most devoted sentiments" with hopes for the "solace of your paternal heart." An "Interministerial Committee for the Jubilee Year" formed under Pietro Romani, De Gasperi's tourism commissioner and brother-in-law; papal audiences for Catholic Action and Christian Democratic delegations dotted the calendar; and high-level dignitaries attended key events. Prime Minister De Gasperi went to the ceremonial opening of the Holy Door that launched the *Anno santo*, and on November 1 he attended the proclamation of the Dogma of the Assumption. Interior Minister Mario Scelba represented the government during the ceremonies for the canonization of Maria Goretti on June 24. The minister of public instruction, Guido Gonella, acted in that capacity at the closing of the Holy Door at the end of the year. Giulio Andreotti attended all four events.[161] Rome's affable mayor, Salvatore Rebecchini, pledged the whole-hearted cooperation of the DC-controlled city government. The Communal Council added to the festivities when on June 2 it unanimously changed the name of the Piazza Rusticucci to Piazza Pio XII, *Defensor Civitatis*.[162] The first in a succession of DC mayors

158. Giulio Remedi, "Il mondo cerca una donna," *OR*, July 19, 1950.

159. Marco Barbanti, "Cultura cattolica, lotta anticomunista a moralità pubblica (1948–60)," *Rivista di storia contemporanea* 1 (1992): 152; R. J. B. Bosworth, *Whispering City: Rome and Its Histories* (New Haven, Conn.: Yale University Press, 2011), 224–25.

160. "Storia e leggende," *OR*, August 6, 1950.

161. *L'Anno santo* 1950, 290–309.

162. "Voci ed echi," *OR*, June 3, 1950.

that stretched until 1976, Rebecchini turned up for key ceremonies before, during, and after the Holy Year. Among the most dramatic of such gatherings occurred on May 30, 1948, when, on the Campidoglio and accompanied by the ubiquitous Father Lombardi, the mayor pleased a crowd of nearly half a million by dedicating the city to the Immaculate Heart of Mary.[163] Three years later, before a Catholic Action congregation, Rebecchini elaborated on his vision of "The Christian City . . . the link that connects the first cell of organized social life—the family—to the body of the State; it is the most concrete and accessible entity for everybody." Just as its construction required concrete and iron, he continued, so Christianity was essential for the complete city.[164]

In Parliament, the Sicilian Christian Democrat Giuseppe Caronia proposed a suspension of home evictions throughout the Holy Year, a plan that enjoyed widespread support.[165] State railways provided 676 special trains to facilitate travel to the Eternal City, with 11,586 reserved carriages.[166] Termini Station still functioned while it underwent extensive renovations, particularly the addition of the distinctly modernist entrance hall, sometimes called the "Dinosaur." Despite the jackhammers, the structure fully reopened in December of 1950, while the faithful in search of aid could visit a "Pilgrim's House" in front of Termini and at other depots across Italy. Rome more than quadrupled its ENIT (tourist commission) budget from 190,000,000 lire in 1948–49 to 855,000,000 in 1950–51. More money came in U.S. Marshal Fund aid: 8 billion lire in ERP counterpart funds in 1948–49 and 1.8 billion in the interim aid fund were designated for low-cost accommodations during the Holy Year.[167] Among other government endeavors, the Ministry of the Interior and others arranged for special police classes at Rome's Guido Reni School

163. Vittorio Vidotto, *Roma contemporaea* (Rome and Bari: Laterza, 2001), 267–68. On the heels of the April electoral triumph, the event, it was noted, coincided with "Rome's liberation" from the Black Death in 1348.

164. IPVI, SgVI, b. 13, f. 2, Gedda/Rebecchini, April 27, 1951; Luigi Palma/Rebecchini, April 18, 1951; and "*Il comune cristiano* (*Appunti*)," n.d. The mayor added that perhaps charity was the field that best distinguished a Christian municipality from a "lay—Marxist" one.

165. Chamber of Deputies, Atti Parlamentari, Legislatura I, Disegni di Legge e Relazioni no. 1093, February 13, 1950. Caronia was joined by thirteen other sponsors, of which four were Christian Democrats (Camillo Corsanego, Igino Giordani, Stefano Reggio D'Aci, and Giorgio Tupini), three Communists (Maria Lisa Cinciari Rodano, Aldo Natoli, and Giulio Turchi), two Socialists (Oreste Lizzadri and Nicola Perrotti), two Social Democrats (Gian Matteo Matteotti and Giuseppe Saragat), and a Monarchist (Alfredo Covelli).

166. *L'Anno santo 1950*, 293. The *Osservatore Romano* also reported on April 28, 1950, that twenty-five special "white trains" would connect every region of the nation with the shrine of Loreto in the Marche.

167. NARS RG59, DF 1950–54, 865.181/3–750, Rome Embassy/State Department "Basic Report on Travel and Tourism," March 7, 1950. The report claimed that 3,980,000 "foreigners" had visited Italy in 1938, 850,000 in 1947, 1,600,000 in 1948, and 3,400,000 in 1949.

to verse officers in tourist aid and what today we might call "people skills." Similar programs were implemented across the nation.[168]

Another example of state and Catholic cooperation concerned the Foro Italico, Mussolini's sports complex on the Tiber, where statues of virile athletes ringed the track. Their Fascist audacity and pagan nakedness proved a bit too bold for pious Rome, and so the National *Buon Costume* Association partnered with the DC city administration to place seventy manufactured fig leafs over the marble genitalia. The city based its assistance on the Constitution's Article 7 provision that protected Rome's sacred and Catholic identity and that obliged Italy to "impede ... everything which could be in contrast to that character."[169] The *Voce repubblicana* mockingly linked the Foro Italico story to a trial in Florence over the obscenity of an American painting on display there. The artist's depiction of a naked and pregnant woman provoked Catholic wrath in the battle for *buon costume* and *pudore*. The Republicans considered the whole affair, like the Roman fig leaves, an absurd case of much ado about nothing.[170]

At Catholic Action, the Holy Year kept Luigi Gedda particularly busy, capturing some of the heady atmosphere in a speech to filmmakers in Rome under the auspices of the International Catholic Organization for Cinema (OCIC) and Catholic Action's CCC.[171] To the visitors, he framed the relationship of the film industry and the church in medieval terms, recalling the famous trip that Emperor Henry IV made to Canossa to implore papal forgiveness. "Cinema, this great force, this emperor," said Gedda, "has come to Rome to kneel before the majesty of the Church ... before the altar of Saint Peter as a humble pilgrim." Giulio Andreotti added his welcome as an envoy of a government that protected traditional Christian interests. In return, George Candy, the Motion Picture

168. NARS RG59, DF 1950–54, 865.181/2–1650, RomeEmbassy/State Department, February 16, 1950.

169. The second paragraph of the Concordat's Article 1 reads, "In considerazione del carattere sacro della Città Eterna, sede vescovile del Sommo Pontefice, centro del mondo cattolico e meta di pellegrinaggi, il Governo italiano avrà cura di impedire in Roma tutto ciò che possa essere in contrasto col detto carattere." See also Ermanno Graziani, *Il carattere sacro di Roma: Contributo all'interpretazione dell'art 1 Cpv., Conc* (Milan: Giuffrè, 1961).

170. "Al Tribunale di firenze il giudizio sul nudo di una donna incinta," *Voce repubblicana*, March 19, 1950. On the Foro Italico fig leaves, see IPVI, Pg XII, b. 32, Associazione nazionale per il buon costume —Relazione all'assemblea dei soci sull'attività svolta dall'associazione nel quinquennio 1946–50, January 7, 1951.

171. OCIC was founded 1928 in the Hague. It awarded prizes at a number of motion picture festivals, including Venice, Cannes, San Sabastian, and Brussels; "I 'dibattiti' cinematografici," *Iniziativa*, June 1, 1957.

Association of America's Italian agent, read letters of good wishes from Walt Disney and Irene Dunn.[172] Perhaps to their chagrin, the pilgrims were then shuttled to Cinecittà studios to meet with MGM officials, who had taken over the place to film their spectacular *Quo Vadis*. The Socialist *Avanti!* sneered that Cinecittà had become an American fortress in a "Washington-Vatican axis." It would be closed for more than seven months; three hundred Americans worked there as employees of Loew's International, and thousands of Italians took jobs on the project, thanks to Ettore Cambi, Cinecittà president and a "pupil" of Monsignor Montini at FUCI. *Avanti!*, however, failed to appreciate a certain ambiguity. The MGM production offended some Catholic sensibilities, as when Giorgio Nardoni attacked the film in the pages of *Noi uomini*. "A film that exalts our first martyrs," he wrote in a pique of thinly veiled anti-Semitism, "is made by people who are not Catholic. When will this absurdity end?"[173]

Still, the lay press remained skeptical and adopted extra vigilance to ensure that Holy Year enthusiasms did not cross the line. On guard that other cults should receive proper respect through the Jubilee, the *Voce repubblicana* located the case of Protestant evangelicals who had contracted the use of two assembly halls. At the last moment they received word that the government revoked their meeting permits, despite the Constitution's Article 8, which guaranteed freedom of worship "even," added the paper, "for heretics." Unfortunately, it continued; Catholics seemed bent on restricting that freedom during "the course of this year 1950, otherwise known as the Holy Year."[174] Some criticisms slipped into sarcasm, bringing responses from slighted Catholics. *Avanti!* scoffed at the "Holy Year Government" as myopic and full of the same tired policies; and both Marxist and lay organs charged that the DC had forgotten true Christianity. The *Voce repubblicana* mocked the conversion of the celebrated Spanish surrealist Salvador Dalí, dismissing it as phoney and lumping it with the conversions of the American poet Ezra Pound, "who is locked up in an insane ward," the "pornographer Pitigrilli," a few actors, and some "second rank ex-Communists." Despite such questions, Dalí

172. Giovanni Luccioli, "Cronaca del Congresso pellegrinaggio mondiale dei professionisti del cinema," *Rivista del cinematografo*, June 1950, 5–8; "Cineasti di ventitre paesi al pellegrinaggio-congresso dell'anno santo," *Iniziativa*, July 1950. In 2001 the OCIC merged with the international Catholic radio organization, UNDA, to form SIGNIS.

173. Luigi Cocheo, "Mobilitato per 'Quo Vadis?,' l'asse Washington-Vaticano," *Avanti!*, January 21, 1950, 3; Carlo Trabucco, "'Quo Vadis' frutterà due miliardi e mezzo," *Il Popolo*, January 29, 1950; Giorgio Nardoni, "Quattro Passi," *Noi uomini*, June 15, 1950, 3. On the production of *Quo Vadis?*, see also Forgacs and Gundle, *Mass Culture and Italian Society*, 137–39.

174. "Cronache, Articolo 8," *Voce repubblicana*, March 5, 1950.

met with the pontiff and presented to him his painting *The Madonna of Port Lligat*. Showing the Madonna's torso and head split open "like an orange," the work might have disturbed Pius; but the artist reported that "the Holy Father smiled contentedly. He understood the work's importance and said, 'I've never seen anything like this.'"[175] On another occasion, *L'Unità*'s derision of a barefoot English pilgrim who walked across the continent to Rome provoked a response from the *Osservatore Romano*. To the Communists' sardonic claim that he had hiked, Christ-like, across the waters of the English Channel, the Vatican paper retorted that *L'Unità*, "organ of the proletariat, of the humble of the simple and sincere," might have celebrated the faith of the Englishman, a waiter, rather than use the occasion to ridicule him.[176]

Base Missionaria and the Marian Year

Encouraged by the Holy Year, in 1952 the church launched the Base missionaria movement and, in 1954, the Marian Year. On February 10, 1952, the vigil of the Feast of Our Lady of Lourdes, Pius announced the Base missionaria as a "shout of reawakening" (*grido di risveglio*). He pointed with alarm to "tepid" religious feeling among Catholics, of a "low moral tone in public and private life" that threatened to reduce the Holy Year into "a splendid but fleeting comet." Starting in Rome, all the faithful, "clergy and people, authorities, families, groups, every single soul" must direct energies toward "regeneration and salvation." The DC pledged its immediate support, and Mayor Rebecchini expressed civic pride that the pontiff had chosen the Eternal City from which to unveil his ambitions. The party paper *Il Popolo* also endorsed the papal initiative and the need for such an activist surge to fight the "atheism, hate and the war on God" that brought mankind to the precipice of destruction. The journal insisted that every Christian know his or her place and embrace the task at hand.[177]

Catholic Action played a central role, designating core groups of parish militants, or "propagandists" (*propagandisti*), and assigning them the

175. "Il surrealista del Papa," *Voce repubblicana*, January 6, 1950. The audience took place on November 29, 1949, and lasted ten minutes. See also Ian Gibson, *The Shameful Life of Salvador Dalí* (New York: W. W. Norton, 1998), 507–8. The *Civiltà Cattolica* ran a series of articles on conversions of artists; Falconi, *La Chiesa e le organizzazioni cattoliche in Italia*, 137. "Pitigrilli" was the pen name for Dino Segre.

176. "Voci ed echi," *OR*, January 7–8, 1950.

177. Rodolfo Arata, "Integralismo cristiano," *Il Popolo*, February 10, 1952. See also the Catholic Action guide, n.a., *La base missionaria* (Rome: Ediroma, 1952); and Falconi, *Gedda e L'azione cattolica*, 192–96.

job of grassroots evangelization among families and neighbors.[178] Pius elaborated on those objectives on March 8 and at his Easter message in St. Peter's Square. The *propagandisti* would constitute "Missionary Bases," each of which would concern itself with the needs of about sixty families. With proper "silence and humility," every *propagandista* compiled a list of resident families and outsiders—landlords, merchants, or workers with interests in the community—and examined the "spiritual state" of his or her charges.

Then the real work began. The men and women of Catholic Action aided distressed households while drawing them into the arms of the church. One form of assistance was spiritual, such as a time of prayer or religious discussion shared by the *propagandista* and the wayward soul. A second form was "cultural," which included the supply of good reading material "for the poor boy" or "shorthand and language lessons for the young ladies of the neighborhood." A third form was "material" help that enlisted myriad organizations, both public and private, such as the state's ONMI, or the resources of the St. Vincent DePaul Society. One *propagandista*, for instance, undertook to aid a family with an unemployed father and two sons who attended neither school nor catechism classes. The *propagandista* placed the father in contact with an employer, while a woman and a Catholic Action youth member helped to redirect the boys along the right road. Another case concerned a nineteen-year-old who had never made his first communion. To remedy this, the *propagandista* arranged permission from the young man's boss to leave work one-half hour early to attend classes.[179] When in December 1953 the pope met with Base missionaria personnel, he listened to a woman convey her joy on hearing a papal radio message for Catholic Action. Pius's face brightened as he raised his hand and assured her that the message had been meant "for everybody: for you [*voi*]," and that "for you ... there is no time to lose!"[180]

Lay and Marxist factions maintained dismissive opinions toward the Base missionaria. The Social Democrat Giuseppe Saragat derided the program as "reactionary," one based on the premise that all progress ended with the Holy Roman Empire. *Base* orders, he claimed, emanated from Father Lombardi, who was nothing more than "a mediocre

178. "Il Santo Padre auspica una vasta azione rigeneratrice per la completa restaurazione dello spirito evangelico," *Il Popolo*, February 10, 1952.

179. Z.N., "Primi passi di una B.M.," *Iniziativa* supplement, January–February 1954. See also "Il grande appello di Pio XII per un mondo migliore," *OR*, April 8, 1954.

180. Tommaso Bistoncini, "Non c'è tempo da perdere," *Iniziativa*, December 1953. See also IPVI, PgVII, b. 53, undated report "Idee sulla Base Missionaria."

Fascist."[181] Catholics felt that such criticisms failed to appreciate the authentic popularity of the Base missionaria, which extended beyond the church into daily life. The GIAC chief Mario Rossi happily witnessed everywhere a new activism—at a meeting, in a book, an hour of adoration, among friends, and, he wrote, in "coordinated action." By stressing "Christian comportment" (*costume cristiano*), the movement aimed to vanquish narcissism and provide "a new horizon . . . for the construction of a Christian civilization that must permeate all categories and all reaches without defensive fears, with so much courage of conquest." In the summer of 1955 Gedda hoped that Base missionaria watchdogs, woven ever more thoroughly into the social fabric, could work closely with diocesan morality offices.[182]

To educate the *Base* activists, Catholic Action created "Propaganda Courses." One memorandum announced two such courses scheduled in Rome for November and December, probably in 1953. The earlier of the two was for 360 southern militants, of which, the report was careful to spotlight, 150 were women. The second class was for 350 northerners, of which 145 were women. Broken into small units of twelve to fifteen persons, each course lasted from Monday to Saturday. Mass launched each day, followed by sessions on the nature of the lay apostolate, parish communities, and church and Catholic Action organizations. Group discussions and meditations dotted the busy agenda.[183] Elsewhere, at the CSI, Father Pavoni urged each leader to form a Base missionaria "in the gyms, on the fields, in the streets (and) in the stands"; and, he continued, they must get going—"You must act, with prudence, with intelligence, with holiness . . . but you must act!"[184]

While the operation appeared formidable on paper, flaws appeared quickly. In 1950 Monsignor Prosperini, for example, confessed to the Catholic Action review, *Iniziativa*, that his Morality Secretariat was not entirely prepared to undertake its mission, a situation that caused the waste of valuable time. If a diocese still had no morality office, "organize

181. "La 'crociata' reazionaria si è mossa rispolverando la rettorica littoria," *Avanti!*, February 12, 1952.

182. Mario Rossi, "L'Apostolato di ambiente nella Base Missionaria," *Iniziativa*, March 1953. On the "missionary sense of Christianity," see Monsignor Luigi Cardini, "Il mistero del Regno," *Iniziativa* supplement, January–February 1954. Regarding "Costume cristiano," see Giovanni Urbani, "Per un costume cristiano," *Iniziativa*, May 1953, and "Per salvaguardare il costume cristiano," *Iniziativa*, July–August, 1955; and Barbanti "Cultura cattolica, lotta anticomunista a moralità pubblica (1948–60)," 609.

183. Fondazione Vittorino Colombo (henceforth, FVC) Fondo Gedda B. 332, unsigned promemoria, "Corsi propagandisti della B.M.," n.d.; Catholic Action pamphlet, "Corso propagandisti Base missionaria, n.d.

184. IPVI, Pg VII, b. 53, Pavoni circular, February 1, 1954.

one today without waiting for tomorrow [and], where they sleep, rouse them from their lethargy." The first task was to locate and document the problem spots, the *case malfamate*, the "ambiguous meeting places, dance halls (or schools), the public places, or those exposed to the public, where libertine couples gather."[185] Still, almost four years later, a Morality Office circular noted a subdued response at the local level, and an *Iniziativa* report found that "in many Italian parishes, AC juntas still [did] not exist." Even more broadly, an internal memorandum of 1954 lamented that the Marian Year's theme on "Christian comportment" might fizzle without any Catholic Action mobilization.[186]

The Base found some footing in events like the Marian Year, which Pius announced in his encyclical *Fulgens corona* of September 8, 1953, the Feast of the Nativity of the Blessed Mother and the tenth anniversary of Italy's collapse in World War II. That declaration deplored anti-Christian and secularist challenges from those who tried "to root out the Christian Faith from their souls, either by cunning and secret snares or else through open and arrogant preaching of their errors . . . as if they were to be considered the glory of this progressive and enlightened age."[187] Three months later, on December 8, the Feast of the Immaculate Conception, Pius opened the Marian Year, appropriately, at Rome's basilica of Santa Maria Maggiore. After the ceremony, the pontiff returned to the Vatican and delivered a radio message honoring Catholic Action's eighty-fifth anniversary. Drawing the two events together, he remarked that AC militants bore in their hearts Mary's "superhuman beauty" and urged them to use that special gift to influence others in the fight against the hateful "enemy of God and man." "Where there is Mary," he said, "there is no Satan; where there is the Sun, there is no power of the shadows."[188] His words touched a Catholic Action anxious and ready to comply.

Monsignor Urbani announced that the AC theme for the Marian Year would be "Toward a Christian Conduct" (*Per un costume cristiano*), the start of a three-year campaign against secularist individualism and hedonism.[189] Consequently, *Noi uomini* devoted a series of special Mar-

185. Ferdinando Prosperini, "Per la difesa del costume," *Iniziativa*, April 1950.

186. IPVI, Sg XII, b. 5, Morality circular N. 84, November 14, 1953; N.A., "Necessità della giunta parrocchiale," *Iniziativa* supplement, January–February 1954.

187. *Fulgens Corona* can be read on the Vatican website: http://www.vatican.va/content/pius-xii/en/encyclicals/documents/hf_p-xii_enc_08091953_fulgens-corona.html (accessed December 3, 2019).

188. "Il Sommo Pontefice Pio XII apre solennemente l'anno mariano" and "Il radiomessaggio all'Azione Cattolica Italiana," both in *OR*, December 9–10, 1953. What Pius called "the first root of the robust trunk of Catholic Action" was the work of Mario Fani after a night of prayer in Viterbo in 1868.

189. Urbani, "Per un costume cristiano." See also his "L'Anno Mariano in parrocchia," *Rivista del clero italiano*, January 1954.

ian Year articles, "Toward a Christian Comportment in the Family," beginning with an attack on laicism and relativism in "The Moral Life." The second piece in the series was more to the point, echoing Gavuzzo's criticisms of cheating, cursing, lying, public displays of kissing and other shows of affection, and merrymaking in the middle of the night. Other articles in this series extended into 1955.[190]

However, suspicions prompted Catholic Action to survey each diocese at the end of October 1954. The results illustrated spotty compliance with the Base missionaria and the campaign for a Christian comportment. Some places displayed enthusiasm and real accomplishment, particularly in the broader Catholic Action endeavors such as blood drives, charity work, and sports. In Genoa, Archbishop Siri noted the "magnificent occasion" of the Marian Year; but a Base coordinator had only "made contact" with a few parishes. Genoa's Morality Office, on the other hand, had been very energetic in the sequestration of "about one hundred" offensive publications, thirty-seven "photos, statuettes, etc.," and in filing charges regarding twenty-eight indecent acts. La Pira's Florence found that Catholic Action did not even exist in 50 percent of the parishes, and, of those, clerical indifference often acted as a drag. Nevertheless, the local Morality Office was "in the process of reconstitution," and Catholic Action actively promoted parish cinemas, opened a children's theater, and made "notable (progress) especially in the cinema sector."[191] Another report from 1955 confirmed a persistent unevenness regarding the Base's reception. While some more "efficient" chapters displayed a dynamic "new spirit," lethargic or "passive" attitudes and a "lack of seriousness" acted as brakes elsewhere.[192]

Early Complications

Scandal

Since Catholics considered themselves Italy's moral guideposts and arbiters, they were particularly alert about avoiding shame. Their lay and

190. The first title in the *Noi uomini* series on "Towards a Christian Comportment" was "La vita morale" of May 15, 1954. On May 31, the second bore the title "Moda—linguaggio—tratto" (Fashion—Language—Traits).

191. One can locate these reports in IPVI, Pg XII, b. 104. *Iniziativa* cited Genoa as a showcase for *Base* success in "Il profile cristiano di una città" from January 15, 1957.

192. IPVI, Pg XII, b. 54, Catholic Action memorandum "Note sullo sviluppo dell'azione missionaria in Italia," n.d. (c. May 1955).

Marxist enemies would happily use any whiff of scandal as ammunition in their portrayal of the devout as holier-than-thou hypocrites. Scandals, of course, plagued all shades of Italian politics throughout the period. At the start of the 1960s, for example, the Republican Randolfo Pacciardi was linked to a major imbroglio over the construction of Fiumicino airport near Rome, and tongues wagged for years over the open liaison between the married Palmiro Togliatti and his comrade, Nildc Iotti.[193] Because they governed the country, and certainly due to their claim of moral leadership, however, the DC and the Catholics attracted more than their share of controversy. Among the party's principal lightening rods, Mario Scelba drew suspicions linked to his Sicilian roots, particularly allegations of Mafia ties. Many suspected implication in the shady 1947 death of the rebel Salvatore Giuliano, even though Scelba posted a fifty-million lire reward to solve the case. Ambassador Clare Boothe Luce assumed Scelba was a drug kingpin.[194]

As might be expected, however, in an Italy that had become a battleground for *buon costume*, sexual scandals might hit moralists with a special sting. In 1959 and 1960, a spicy rumor of sexual impropriety even swirled around Scelba. It concerned a dalliance with a young married Sicilian noblewoman, presenting a wonderful opportunity for the neo-Fascist press, which always took aim at him. In 1960, Scelba's wife, Nerina, "exploded" and caused the then interior minister to appear at the Viminale Palace with, it was said, a Band-Aid on his bald head. Even here, however, political factors other than the lay press's delight in soiling Scelba's good name might have been involved. The respected journalist Giorgio Galli later wondered that something else might have been at work. The press slurs could have been linked to Pacciardi's aforementioned Fiumicino trouble in that both he and Scelba had been among the most vocal critics of the "opening to the left," and for that reason, a Machiavellian cabal anchored in the DC left targeted them.[195]

Scandals concerning financial improprieties never seemed to end;

193. Giorgio Galli, *L'Italia sottoterranea: Storia, politica e scandali* (Rome and Bari: Laterza, 1983), 81–85.

194. On the Giuliano case, for an interpretation focused on Scelba, see Onello Onelli, *Mario Scelba oltre il socialismo e il capitalismo* (Rome: Al pescatore di luna, 1955), 53–57. A scholarly discussion of the affair can be found in Francesco Malgeri, "Mario Scelba e l'ordine pubblico nell'Italia del dopoguerra," in *Mario Scelba: Contributi per una biografia*, ed. Pier Luigi Ballini (Soveria Manelli: Istituto Luigi Sturzo, Rubbettino, 2006), 130–41.

195. Galli, *L'Italia sottoterranea*, 78–90. Galli recorded that the attack might have also come from elements that advocated the DC's "opening to the left." Randolfo Pacciardi's aforementioned Fiumicino trouble could have been linked to the "opening," in that both he and Scelba were among its most vocal critics.

yet they failed to register much with the public. The DC elder Giuseppe Spataro was accused in 1950 of channeling public funds to a private distillery at Vasto, while another controversy concerned a banker, Giambattista Giuffrè, who managed, with questionable methods, a number of monastic accounts. The Giuffrè affair of the mid-1950s was spiced for the new *cronache nere* scandal sheets by a sexy girlfriend; but it was essentially a financial imbroglio complicated by Social Democratic and Republican accusations of collusion with Catholic Action, the head of GIAC, Enrico Vinci, and the DC's Giulio Andreotti. After a tense moment, when it looked like the DC might sacrifice him, Andreotti rallied, and the allegations collapsed.[196]

A few scandals even tarnished the church. One celebrated case dealt with a priest in the Vatican bureaucracy, Father Edoardo Prettner-Cippico, whose "pinwheel of scams" included theft and bank fraud. The Holy See opted to take matters into its own hands and locked the priest in a tower behind St. Peter's. He escaped, but Italian police captured him and placed him in the State's Regina Coeli prison. The court condemned Prettner-Cippico in 1952, although his penalty was later reduced and then canceled.[197] Other problems emerged in 1948 over a swindle among some discalced Augustinians in Rome, and, in 1962, news emerged of a criminal ring operating out of a Franciscan house in Messina. After a sensational trial, the state found lay associates guilty but absolved the brothers of charges that included extortion and murder.[198] Nuns also received criticism. In charge of a virtual welfare empire

196. Galli, *L'Italia sottoterranea*, 20–22 regarding Spataro; 42–50 regarding Giuffrè; Galli, *Mezzo secolo di DC* (Milan: Rizzoli, 1993), 152; and Guido Crainz, *Storia del miracolo italiano: Cultura identità, trasformazioni fra anni cinquanta e sessanta* (Rome: Donzelli, 1998), 79. See also Nerio Minuzzo, "La Marcia su Piaza del Gesù," and Vittorio Zincone, "Finanza nera," both in *L'Europeo*, September 7, 1958; and Giorgio Bocca, "La Doccia scozzese di Giuffrè," *L'Europeo*, September 21, 1958. A parliamentary inquest into the Giuffrè affair absolved Andreotti, although by the slimmest of votes, 279–78, and despite the defection of at least eleven DC deputies. The affair also prompted a newspaper battle between the *Osservatore Romano* and *L'Unità*; see in *Osservatore Romano*, "Dove vai? Scappo," of September 8–9, 1958; "Contro ogni ritengo," September 20, 1958; and "Grotteschi," in the "Voci ed echi" column, October 3, 1958.

197. Mariuzzo, *Divergenze parallele*, 77–80; Onelli, *Mario Scelba*, 57–59; "La Segreteria di Stato Vaticana al centro d'un colossale traffico di valuta" and "Cippico ed altri," both in *L'Unità*, March 8, 1948; "Lo Scandalo Cippico ritorna alla ribalta," *L'Unità*, April 4, 1954; "Ridotta interamente condonata la pena all'ex Monsignor Cippico," *L'Unità*, April 7, 1954; "Le truffe di don Cippico," *La Repubblica.it*, March 27, 1998.

198. On the Augustinians, see "Il Card. Lavitrano e i mons. Roberti e Parisella implicate in un nuovo grosso scandalo valutario," *L'Unità*, April 16, 1948. On the Franciscans, see "Schermaglie d'assaggio della difesa per portare i monaci fuori dei guai," *L'Unità*, March 13, 1962, and "In trionfo i quattro frati dopo la vittoria mafiosa," *L'Unità*, June 23, 1962. During the Holy Year, the Vatican dismissed as preposterous any suggestion that the clergy engaged in criminality on a level higher than did those of other professions. To emphasize this, the *Osservatore Romano* quoted a "Polemikon" poll that showed that transgressions committed by the clergy ranked at the bottom of the list, below "merchants, tradesmen and tramps"; "Storia e leggende," OR, October 20, 1950.

controlling 10,000 orphanages and maternity schools in 1957 and running 1,850 clinics, the nuns saw their robust business get out of hand when, on a few occasions between 1952 and 1957, news surfaced that they had directed some of their concerns to turn a profit. This led Pope Pius to admonish over two thousand sisters for their excessively entrepreneurial spirit.[199] In 1958 Prince Filippo Orsini of the papal household triggered another press flap when he tried to kill himself over his adulterous affair with the British actress Belinda Lee.[200]

Italy's most celebrated scandal, and one of potentially great embarrassment to the Christian Democracy, concerned the death of Wilma Montesi. Nothing else in the tabloids could approach it. "Behind the façade of the capital of Christendom," wrote one author, "unveiled an abyss of luxury and decadence." Rome had become a "city of perdition (under) Ministers who declared themselves observant Catholics."[201] In 1953, the corpse of the twenty-one-year-old Montesi was discovered on a beach near Rome and a short walk from Capocotta, a government-owned hunting lodge. Along with a state investigation, the press ran its own inquest, and the *cronache nere* led the pack. In October Silvano Muto and his racy right-wing tabloid *Attualità* captured the momentum when he published "The Truth about the Death of Wilma Montesi," for which he was taken to court.[202] Two culprits in Montesi's death were soon identified as Ugo Montagna and Piero Piccioni. The manager of the Capocotta estate, Montagna was a slippery figure who used the place for drug-fueled orgies. Piccioni was a musician who wrote film scores. He was also the son

199. Roberto Morozzo della Rocca, "Le Chiese parallele: I religiosi," in *Le Chiese di Pio XII*, ed. Andrea Riccardi (Bari and Rome: Laterza, 1986), 124, 129.

200. Pollard, *Papacy in the Age of Totalitarianism*, 445.

201. Francesco Grignetti, *Il caso Montesi: Sesso, potere e morte nell'Italia degli anni '50* (Venice: Marsiglio, 2006), 70. The Montesi case triggered a number of journalistic accounts. Some of the earlier attempts in English include Melton S. Davis, *All Rome Trembled* (New York: G. P. Putnam's Sons, 1957), and Wayland Young, *The Montesi Scandal* (New York: Doubleday, 1958). A more scholarly recent work, although somewhat idiosyncratic, is Karen Pinkus's *The Montesi Scandal: The Death of Wilma Montesi and the Birth of the Paparazzi in Fellini's Rome* (Chicago: University of Chicago Press, 2003). See also her essay "Chi l'ha vista? Reflections on the Montesi Case," in *Assassinations and Murder in Modern Italy: Transformations in Society and Culture*, ed. Stephen Gundle and Lucia Rinaldi (New York: Palgrave, 2007); see also Roy Domenico, "Sex, Scandal and Catholic Politics during Italy's Dolce Vita," in *Scandal! An Interdisciplinary Approach to the Consequences, Outcomes, and Significance of Political Scandals*, ed. Alison Dagnes and Mark Sachleben (New York: Bloomsbury Press, 2014). Along with the Grignetti book, Italian treatments include Massimo Polidoro, *Cronaca nera: Indagini sui delitti che hanno sconvolto l'Italia* (Farigliano: Edizioni Piemme, 2005), 141–80; Gundle's *Death and the Dolce Vita* is the definitive text on the Montesi case. A young Gabriel García Márquez, fresh from South America, cut his journalist's teeth on the Montesi affair. His essays on it are contained in *The Scandal of the Century and Other Writings*, ed. Cristóbal Pera, trans. Anne McLean (New York: Alfred A. Knopf, 2019).

202. Murialdi, *La Stampa Italiana del dopoguerra*, 260–79. Muto had ties to the neo-Fascist *Movimento sociale italiano*. Another key right-wing figure who called attention to the case was Achille Lauro, the Neapolitan shipping magnate and Monarchist Party boss.

of Attilio Piccioni, De Gasperi's foreign minister and a DC leader who became a figure of pathos, resigning his high positions to defend his son. The ecstatic lay and Marxist press hung on every development of the case, and Pietro Nenni famously declared, referring to Italy's catastrophic defeat in World War I, that Capocotta had become the DC's Caporetto. But the judgments came too fast. Neither Montagna nor Piccioni really had anything to do with the Catholic movement, least of all its morality campaign. Finally, four years after the discovery of poor Wilma Montesi's body, the public prosecutor stood up in a Venice courtroom in May 1957 and halted the proceedings. Not one shred of evidence, he declared, pointed to manslaughter. In fact, he continued, no hard evidence existed that Piccioni had ever even *met* the victim. If the DC's enemies sensed that *l'affare Montesi* might disgrace the party and bring about the end of the "clerical regime," they were mistaken.

Electoral Problems—1952 and 1953

Despite optimism for the Catholic agenda, fissures within the Catholic camp revealed themselves. As early as 1946, the DC leadership's support for the republic, for instance, countered (largely tacit) papal support for the monarchy. De Gasperi's abilities to compromise and work with lay and Marxist parties, moreover, failed to impress some clerics. One of the doubters was Palermo's notoriously conservative Archbishop Ernesto Ruffini. DC support for what he considered too-progressive land reforms and its alliance with "the revolutionary and anti-clerical Left" led Ruffini to distance himself from the party and reach out to the right-wing Uomo Qualunque and the monarchists. Others like Cardinal Alfredo Ottaviani, certain Jesuits associated with the *Civiltà Cattolica*, and the so-called Roman Party could be counted on to criticize De Gasperi's independent policies that they felt made the DC the chain's weak link.[203] Cognizant of this, the party press never lost the opportunity to stress its shoulder-to-shoulder commitment with all Catholics. In 1952, for instance, *Il Popolo* took to task a liberal journalist, Panfilo Gentile, who optimistically suggested that the DC's cooperation with lay factions might transform it into a "truly modern party," one that could secularize Catholics and stand in contrast to the hierarchy's and Catholic Action's "retrograde integralism." The DC paper's retort came,

203. Baget-Bozzo, *Il Partito cristiano*, 39; Casella, *18 Aprile 1948: La mobilitazione delle organizzazioni cattoliche* (Galatina: Congedo, 1992), 6–18; Francesco Michele Stabile, "Palermo, La Chiesa baluardo del Card. Ruffini (1946–1948)," in Riccardi, *Le Chiese di Pio XII*, 373–77.

interestingly, from a Catholic Action activist and Dominican father, Enrico di Rovasenda, who affirmed the party's Catholicism as real and strong, concluding that "spiritual plebeians" in their "lay diversions" failed to understand "the need for spirituality in all structures and activities of the contemporary world." It was a ploy to force a lay wedge into the movement, one that depicted the hierarchy as reactionary, Catholic Action as totalitarian, and the DC as a debilitated and spiritless third sibling. Christian Democracy's lay roots, he insisted, in no way infringed on its Catholic essence.[204]

Suspicions, mostly over De Gasperi, came to a head during the local elections of 1952 and the national ones of 1953. In 1952, Catholic Action rang the alarm in its review for young working women, the *Squilli lavoratrici*. Get yourself and everyone you know to the polls, it urged: "family members, relatives, girl friends, workmates, everyone included in your circle." Take the old lady to the polls and show her how to vote; then bring her over to the Civic Committee headquarters. Next, it's over to "Rosa's," where you can babysit her child and enable *her* to get to the polls. Don't make the mistake, as some did in 1948, of putting the sign of the cross over the ballot's PCI box to indicate Christianity's triumph over Communism. Finally, and above all, pray. Pray the Rosary and to the Mother of God; and remember that, as the Christians stopped the Turks at Lepanto, so too would they vanquish "the Communist heresy and the violence and aberrations of other totalitarianisms and anti-Christian ideologies."[205]

Alarmed that the upcoming local vote might yield a leftist regime in Rome, some conservative elements looked for inspiration from the tough anticommunism of Francisco Franco's and Antonio Salazar's dictatorships, an Iberian temptation that frequently surfaced from the subtext of postwar Italian Catholicism. One of the Vatican's key men, Cardinal Ottaviani of the Holy Office, for example, used Spain as a "traditionalist" model at a Lateran conference. The pope's secretary of state consequently assured the alarmed French ambassador that the cardinal had only expressed his personal opinion. Within the Vatican, however, an alternative, more democratic current challenged Ottaviani—one more favorable to the DC that included Monsignor Giovanni Battista Montini and Cardinal Domenico Tardini, who considered the party es-

204. Enrico Di Rovasenda, "Diversivi laicisti," *Il Popolo*, March 14, 1952.
205. N.A., "ALT! 25 Maggio," *Squilli lavoratrici*, May 18, 1952.

sential for Italian democracy and frequently lobbied on De Gasperi's behalf.[206]

As the 1952 election drew near, Gedda, Father Ronca, and Father Lombardi, all sympathetic to the Iberian model and convinced of the pontiff's blessings, plotted in the so-called Operation Sturzo to outflank De Gasperi and form a Catholic, monarchist, and neo-Fascist alliance led by the head of the defunct PPI. Although some Christian Democrats like Gonella showed interest in the Sturzo gambit, De Gasperi and others like Andreotti followed Montini's lead and fought back. In the end, Operation Sturzo collapsed in embarrassment, and the vindicated DC retained control of the Eternal City, enjoying a plurality of 41.9 percent against the left's 34.3 and the far right's 22.6.[207] DC success only illustrated the bad blood between the pontiff and the prime minister, to Gedda's advantage. Pius clearly preferred him and Catholic Action to De Gasperi and the DC, eventually granting Gedda sixty-five audiences, while De Gasperi enjoyed that honor only twice. Shortly after Operation Sturzo failed to supplant De Gasperi, moreover, Pius, in "nothing more than a deliberate snub," refused the prime minister's request for a blessing on his thirtieth wedding anniversary.[208] Feeling betrayed, an angry Pius also slighted Montini, exiling him as an archbishop to the diocese of Milan.[209]

In June 1953, the republic braced for its first national election since 1948. As before, Gedda's Civic Committees mobilized for Catholic victory, and the church reminded the faithful of their responsibilities, leading to lay and Marxist accusations of clerical meddling. Starting with charges against the archbishop of Ancona, the bishop of Montefiascone,

206. Regarding Vatican softness for the Franco regime, see Pollard, *Papacy in the Age of Totalitarianism*, 384–86.

207. On Operation Sturzo, see Malgeri, *La Stagione del centrismo: Politica e società nell'Italia del secondo dopoguerra (1945–1960)* (Soveria Mannelli: Rubbettino, 2002), 117–30; Sandro Magister, *La politica vaticana e l'Italia 1943–1978* (Rome: Editori Riuniti, 1979), 162–76; Eliana Versace, *Montini e l'aperatura a sinistra: Il falso mito del "vescovo progressista"* (Milan: Guerini, 2007), 25–44; Augusto D'Angelo, *De Gasperi, Le destre e L' "Operazione Sturzo": Voto amministrativo del 1952 e progetti do riforma elettorale* (Rome: Edizioni Studium, 2002); Riccardi, *Il Potere del papa da Pio XII a Paolo VI*, 29, 51–52, 62–64; Riccardi, *Il "Partito Romano" nel secondo dopoguerra*, 155–76; Piero Craveri, *De Gasperi* (Bologna: il Mulino, 2006), 366 and 533–51.

208. Steven F. White, "Christian Democracy or Pacellian Populism? Rival Forms of Postwar Italian Catholicism," in *European Christian Democracy: Historical Legacies and Comparative Perspectives*, ed. Thomas Kselman and Joseph A. Buttigieg (Notre Dame, Ind.: University of Notre Dame Press, 2003), 207; Ventresca, *Soldier of Christ*, 248. Baget-Bozzo believed that Pius considered turning Catholic Action into a bona fide political party; Baget-Bozzo, *Il Partito cristiano*, 80–82. Pius apparently had second thoughts toward De Gasperi. According to the caretaker of Castel Gandolfo, Emilio Bonomelli, upon learning of the statesman's death in August 1954, the pope said, "A saint has died. . . . He was a good Christian, a great man"; D'Angelo, *De Gasperi, Le destre e L'"Operazione Sturzo,"* 109.

209. Pollard, *Papacy in the Age of Totalitarianism*, 396.

and Genoa's Archbishop Siri, they charged ecclesiastics of electoral violations, particularly threats of excommunication for supporting Communists. Dismissing the attacks as "ridiculous," *Noi uomini* declared that bishops who instructed their flock against Marxist candidates simply exercised their rights and duties found in canon law and protected in the Constitution's Article 2 on free speech. The courts agreed and rejected all of the left's claims.[210] Although no case went to trial, Riccardo Lombardi embarked on a national speaking tour on behalf of the defamed.[211] And from Rome, the DC justice minister Adone Zoli considered the rebukes as the usual electoral rubbish to be "thrown into the garbage can."[212]

While no bishop received sanctions during the flap over clerical interference, events sometimes played differently at the lower parish level. In one of the era's more notorious cases, Paduan authorities brought charges against don Luigi Sola, who, in May 1951, printed in his parish bulletin that voting was a duty and an obligation and urged that Catholics remember the July 1949 excommunication. Don Sola in 1952 received a four-month sentence and a small fine, although the Appellate Court later absolved him. The trial ignited a controversy from the pulpits to the national press. The *Osservatore Romano* wondered why, in the Trentino town of Rovereto, a priest charged with the same thing was exonerated. Padua's fiery bishop Girolamo Bortignon defended his priest and announced in the Basilica of Santa Giustina that "to say and to write that an action is bad according to Christian morals is not an offense, it is a duty." The Jesuit Salvatore Lener published an extensive defense of Sola in the *Civiltà cattolica*, and the lay and Marxist press took up the cudgels in response.[213]

210. Luigi Bellofiore, "La Magistratura rispinge le denuncie socialcomuniste," *Noi uomini*, May 30, 1953.

211. Four Communist deputies and *L'Unità* charged that the bishops of Asti, San Miniato, and Mondovì had all violated electoral laws; "Voci ed echi elettorali," *OR*, May 8, 9 and 11–12, 1953. In the May 13 "Voci ed echi elettorali" column, the *Osservatore Romano* reported that the Communists had not only accused the archbishop of Trent, but the entire Episcopal body of Apulia of infractions. Another article ("Decisioni della magistrature," *OR*, May 25–26, 1953) chronicled the denunciations brought against Genoa's Archbishop Siri and the bishops of Ancona, Montefiacone, Novara, and Viterbo. Regarding accusations against Emilian bishops, see "Voci ed echi elettorali," *OR*, May 27, 1953. On the "lively and resolute" Catholic press reaction, see "Voci ed echi elettorali," *OR*, May 17, 1953. On Lombardi, see "Discorsi di Padre Lombardi dopo le denuncie dei Vescovi," *OR*, May 23, 1953.

212. "Decisioni della magistrature," *OR*, May 25–26, 1953. The charges of interference resurfaced again and again in later elections. Regarding 1957 see, all in *OR*, "Un episodio mortificante" of April 12, 1957, and the "Voci ed echi" columns of April 15–16 and April 21, 1957. All concerned Liberal and Republican accusations that, while hearing their confessions, a priest in Benevento pressured two women to vote DC. When they could not promise this, he withheld absolution.

213. Alessandro Naccarato, *Angeli o demoni i nostri bimbi? Storia di una montatura anticomunista; Il processo ai pionieri di Pozzonovo* (Verona: Cierre edizioni, 2011), 23–25. Lener's *Civiltà Cattolica* article was reprinted in the *Osservatore Romano* (January 17, 1953) as "Una inutile enormità: La sentenza." See also

Catholics hoped that the 1953 national elections would repeat the 1948 victory, but events proved them wrong. Arnaldo Forlani later mused in *Discussione* that the DC fought 1948 with polemics, presenting a "dramatic" choice of "totalitarianism or freedom, Christianity or communism." But in 1953 it stood as the government party, assuming an "apologetic" role.[214] Along with the drumbeats against the clerical state, other factors—Operation Sturzo, the "Swindle Law" controversy in which the DC unsuccessfully attempted to twist electoral rules to their advantage, Stalin's death and a corresponding lightening of Cold War tensions—hurt the Catholic cause.

The year 1953 ended the DC's absolute majority in the Chamber of Deputies and signaled the beginning of the end for De Gasperi. The party's vote fell from 48.5 to 40.1 percent, a share that remained fairly constant—between about 38 and 42 percent—for the next twenty-five years. The far right made the most significant gains in 1953, probably since some who rallied to the DC against the PCI in 1948 could now return to their more natural homes among the monarchists and the neo-Fascists.[215] The 1953 election showed that, while the DC had become the essential party, the "Partito italiano," it still needed partners. For a while it held out with some stop-gap *monocolore* governments, first and very briefly De Gasperi's, followed after two months by Giuseppe Pella's and then Amintore Fanfani's (his first). Finally, in February 1954 Mario Scelba extended a hand to Liberals and Social Democrats in his so-called "iron centrism" cabinet. Rejecting any national alliances with the monarchists and neo-Fascists, the DC turned instead more to its centrist lay rivals who, for their part, reluctantly accepted the prospects of junior partnerships as a case of the "awful" being superior to the Marxist "worse than awful." Even Gaetano Salvemini urged his lay colleagues to "hold their noses" and go along with it.[216]

---

the paper's "voci ed echi" columns for January 10 and 21, 1953. The Sola case prompted a discussion on the Senate floor from the Communist Umberto Terracini, who, according to the Catholics, failed to understand "that nothing—neither the threat of sanctions nor prison—could impede the clergy from fulfilling their duty to God and the Church"; N.A., "I sofismi del sen. Terracini," *OR*, February 14, 1953. The "Voci ed echi elettorali" column of May 11–12, 1953, recognized the Communists' use of the Sola case in order to strengthen their claims regarding the bishops' violations of electoral law. On the Rovereto case, see "Voci ed echi elettorali," *OR*, May 20, 1953.

214. Arnaldo Forlani, "La Propaganda democratica cristiana," *Discussione*, October 16, 1955.

215. Giovagnoli, *Il Partito italiano*, 61–64; Paul Ginsborg, *A History of Italy: Society and Politics 1943–1988* (London: Penguin, 1990), 143–45. The 1956 communal and provincial elections later added to the anxiety when the DC fell to 38.9 percent against 35.2 percent for the Communist/Socialist alliance. On the 1953 election and its impact on De Gasperi, see Craveri, *De Gasperi*, 601–15.

216. Teodori, *Storia dei laici*, 257–58. Teodori claimed that the Salvemini quote was incorrectly attributed to the conservative journalist Indro Montanelli.

At the DC's June 1954 Congress in Naples, and with only weeks to live, the ailing De Gasperi formally surrendered control of the party to the pugnacious Amintore Fanfani. The statesman stayed on as prime minister until August 17, just two days before his death, when Giuseppe Pella succeeded him. Pella served in that capacity until January of 1954, when party chief Fanfani launched a short term of less than one month.[217] Fanfani stood a bit to left of the more centrist De Gasperi and established in 1951 the *Iniziativa democratica* current in Christian Democracy. With Fanfani at the helm, the American student of Italian politics Norman Kogan discerned a more aggressive party.[218] In their study of Italy's "difficult democracy," Frederic Spotts and Theodore Weiser also identified 1953 as a turning point when the Christian Democrats started to break from their dependence on big business, and "under Fanfani's guidance they conceived the idea of constructing a power base outside the government." For this, Fanfani emphasized "public enterprises and other agencies." But this activist turn reached further, and the party would bear a greater burden—what became known as the "heavy party," guiding Italian democracy via a broader and deeper Catholic penetration into culture and society. "With the passion of youth," he announced, "with the wisdom of age, we embrace [the cross] not only as a sign of common redemption, but today, in politics, as the guarantee of freedom."[219]

Amintore Fanfani's ascendancy beckoned a new, muscular phase for the DC.[220] Born in 1908 in Pieve Santo Stefano, not far from Arezzo, and twenty-seven years after De Gasperi, Fanfani represented Christian Democracy's second generation. His father had been one of eighteen children in a family, traditionally of carpenters, who had left for the university and became a lawyer and a noted *popolare* activist. He sent young

217. *Avanti!* claimed that the 1954 Naples Congress began a turn, or involution, in the DC that abandoned any hope of attracting Socialists and Communists and moved to the political center to lure Fascists. Regarding economic issues, the Socialists were wrong. The DC did not lurch to the right. But if one thinks of cultural issues as conservative, perhaps they had a point. "La libertà di stampa, baluardo della democrazia," *Avanti!*, February 3, 1955.

218. Norman Kogan, *A Political History of Italy: The Postwar Years* (New York: Praeger, 1966), 59. Kogan felt that the statesman was partly to blame in his neglect of the grassroots organization and reliance on the parish network to handle things below.

219. Frederic Spotts and Theodor Wieser, *Italy: A Difficult Democracy* (New York: Cambridge University Press, 1986), 141; Giovagnoli, *Il Partito italiano*, 69–73, and his "Dal Partito del 18 Aprile 1948 al 'partito pesante': La Democrazia cristiana nel 1951," *Italia contemporanea*, no. 227 (June 2002); Malgeri, *La Stagione del centrismo*, 173.

220. Giovagnoli, *Il Partito italiano*, 69. See also Pietro Scoppola, *La "Nuova Cristianità" perduta* (Rome: Studium 1986), 93–94.

Amintore to the Catholic University in Milan.[221] Intensely competitive and sure of himself, Amintore earned a doctorate in economics. However, Mussolini's regime intruded and stained Fanfani's career. Attracted by corporatist arguments that owed something to Catholic thought, he joined the Fascist Party, partly, as one biographer explained, to dispel police suspicions about his *popolare* background while he applied for a docent position at the Catholic University.[222] In 1938, he took an extra step and put his signature to the notorious Fascist Racial Manifesto. Still, the war soured Fanfani, and he took the church's road to distance himself from the regime. Joining a clandestine Milanese Christian Democratic group, he fled to Switzerland in September 1943. After the conflict, in September 1945 De Gasperi called him to Rome, starting a close relationship that led to participation at the Constituent Assembly, a seat on the DC directorate, and cabinet positions, most notably as minister of labor, where he launched the gigantic low-cost public housing project Ina-Casa.[223] Finally, he served five times as Italy's prime minister, from his brief term in 1954 until his last in 1987.

Powered by enormous drive, Fanfani had "a political staying power without equal anywhere," according to one observer. Yet thanks as much to his black-and-white personality as to his policies, he became one of the most detested figures in Italian politics. The Social Democrat Giuseppe Saragat remarked of him, "Wherever he lays his hands, he creates confusion." In 1956 *Il Mondo* reported that Fanfani harbored a dark streak and that his friends described him as "desperate, a prisoner of an inextricable situation." Among his DC colleagues Andreotti was reported to have said, "There are two things you just can't do in Italian politics, live with Fanfani, and live without him," while, when Mariano Rumor supposedly asked him, "Amintore, where are you going?," Fanfani's face darkened, and he smiled a smile that appeared more like a sneer (*ghigno*).[224]

221. Both of Fanfani's parents were devout Catholics, and Giuseppe stood for election as a Popular Party candidate in 1921. Fanfani discussed his roots in *Una pieve in Italia* (Milan: Mondadori, 1964); his diaries were published in 2012: Fanfani, *Diari*, 4 vols. (Soveria Mannelli: Rubbettino, 2012).

222. Vincenzo La Russa, *Amintore Fanfani* (Soveria Mannelli: Rubbettino, 2006), 25–27.

223. On Ina-Casa, see La Russa, *Amintore Fanfani*, 121–28; Gabriele De Rosa et al., *Fanfani e la casa: Gli anni Cinquanta e il modello italiano di welfare state; Il piano INA-Casa* (Rome and Soveria Mannelli: Istituto Luigi Sturzo-Rubbettino, 2002); and Paola Di Biagi, "La 'città pubblica' e L'Ina-Casa," and Paolo Nicoloso, "Genealogie del piano Fanfani," both in *La grande ricostruzione: Il piano Ina-Casa e l'Italia degli anni '50*, ed. Paola Di Biagi (Rome: Donzelli Editore, 2001). Giorgio Galli called the Ina-Casa the most successful of the DC's reforms; Galli, *Fanfani* (Milan: Feltrinelli, 1975), 42.

224. Spotts and Wieser, *Italy*, 29; Paolo Pavolini, "Democristiani 1956," *Il Mondo*, February 14, 1956; "Obituary: Amintore Fanfani," *Independent* (UK), November 22, 1999.

However, Fanfani did not invent the DC's new cultural mission entirely on his own. Gonella and Andreotti, for instance, had broken ground for it under De Gasperi. Another figure was Mario Scelba, who expanded his role as a prominent DC culture warrior in the days of the "Heavy Party." Scelba had long been close to the center of Catholic political power. After World War I, the young Sicilian arrived at the University of Rome, the Sapienza, to work toward a law degree. While there, Scelba joined the nascent Partito Popolare and worked with don Luigi Sturzo—a bond cemented in that the two shared the same hometown of Caltagirone. Scelba became the priest's private secretary, feeding rumors on the left that they were father and son. When the Fascists forced Sturzo into exile, Scelba naturally gravitated to the De Gasperi circle. A tough and blunt man who received some of the left's greatest vitriol, after the war Scelba served as minister of the Interior from 1947 to 1953. From February 1954 to July 1955, he assumed two chairs, as prime minister and interior minister. His biographer wrote that while Scelba considered himself part of the DC, he was always confused as to what his "side" wanted.[225]

Scelba was convinced that Italy's moral health was integral to its stability. In a 1950 Interior Ministry circular, he wrote, "The defense of public order must not limit itself to the repression of violent protests, but must also face, and actively, certain sources of moral infection."[226] A bête noir for the left, he banned Communist reporters from his offices and government ministries. This pleased his supporters at the *Osservatore Romano*, who lauded him as "Banquo's ghost" to the Socialist Macbeth. "More than a name," wrote *Avanti!*, "he [was] a symbol" who ruled "the most glittering, the noisiest" office in the Christian Democratic government. His lightning *celere* police squads charged into demonstrations and fired on protesters, most notably in January of 1950 at Modena, where six died and fifty-one suffered wounds.[227] Detested by the "left press," which, as Robert Ventresca said, "decried Scelba as a goon," many bourgeois Italians also shunned him.[228] The lay press derided his

225. La Russa, *Scelba* (Soveria Manelli: Rubattino, 2002).

226. IPVI, Sg XII, b. 5, Gavuzzo/Prosperini circular, April 19, 1950. Scelba's circular was transcribed in this report, a frequent practice.

227. Corrado Pizzinelli, *Scelba* (Milan: Longanesi 1982), 112; "Presentiamo il governo dell'anno santo," *Avanti!*, January 28, 1950. *Avanti!* portrayed Scelba as the plume on the Fascist helmet; and "everybody remembers '*culturame*'"; "Voci ed echi," *OR*, June 30–July 1, 1956; Joseph Calderon, "Scelba and the Communists," *Commonweal*, May 21, 1954; Giuseppe Carlo Marino, *La Repubblica della forza: Mario Scelba e le passioni del suo tempo* (Milan: Francoangeli, 1995), 51–57, 149–51.

228. Pizzinelli, *Scelba*, 85, 113; Ventresca, *From Fascism to Democracy*, 217.

awkward use of a slang term, *culturame*, that he let slip at the 1949 party congress at Venice. A challenge to translators, the word alludes to what Scelba considered a culture of garbage that had invaded Italy. Luigi Russo depicted him in *Belfagor* as a boorish fieldhand (*campiere*), a *sicilianuzzo*, a fraud from top to bottom, and, worst of all, a phony Catholic with a medieval "nostalgia for the stake."[229] *Avanti!* depicted a fictional "museum of oppression" that included ropes, chains, whips, and Scelba's photo. *Il Mondo* loathed him and claimed that few deputies liked Scelba, who acted as if the electoral setback of June 1953 had never happened. Reasonable Italians, it continued, dismissed him as an *antipasto* before the more substantial fare to come.[230]

Along with figures like Andreotti, Gonella, and Scelba, even before De Gasperi's retirement, other voices inside the DC called for more cultural politics. At a meeting of April 29, 1950, the National Directorate took note of telegrams from Emilia protesting the lack of cultural organization and policy. A week later this junta agreed to a modest option of turning the party's Office for Artistic Activity into an Office for Intellectual Activity, subdivided into three divisions dedicated rather vaguely to artistic, scholastic, and cultural realms under the leadership of Giovanni Elkan. Entrusted with a "systematic penetration in the Italian cultural and artistic environment, utilizing men of art and culture who adhere to or sympathize with the DC," by October Elkan reported that he had met "DC representatives from culture and art" to plan a series of conferences "of a strictly literary, scientific artistic character" with some youth-directed propaganda energies mixed in. Still, the old doubts persisted. "There is widespread confusion [*perplessità*]," he wrote, "in the cultural world regarding our capacity and the possibility of satisfying its needs."[231]

Gonella's reputation was such that in 1950, at the party journal, *Il Popolo*, editor Leone Piccioni (Pietro's brother) courted him to help pre-

229. Luigi Russo, "'Culturalume' e 'culturame,'" *Belfagor* 4, no. 4 (July 31, 1949): 462–64; Pizzinelli, *Scelba*, 112; Marino, *La Repubblica della forza*, 274–77. Stephen Gundle translated *culturame* as "manure culture"; Gundle, *Death and the Dolce Vita*, 181. The aforementioned *Avanti!* article, "Presentiamo il governo dell'anno santo," of January 28, 1950, portrayed Scelba as the plume on the Fascist helmet; and "everybody remembers '*culturame*.'"

230. "Morte ad Anastasia," *Avanti!*, February 25, 1956; Paolo Pavolini, "Democristiani 1956," *Il Mondo*, February 14, 1956. The review conceded that Scelba handled the Trieste issue well, securing its resentry into the Italian nation.

231. IS Dir. Naz. Sc. 7, f. 107, "Giunta esecutiva del 29 Aprile 1950"; Dir. Naz. Sc. 7, f.108, "Giunta esecutiva del 5 Maggio 1950"; Dir. Naz. Sc. 7, f.95, "Verbale della adunanza della direzione del 5 Ottobre 1950." See also "Centro attività culturali," *Bollettino della Direzione Centrale D.C.* 4, no. 1 (October 15, 1950).

serve the cultural "Third Page" in the face of skeptics. He complained of a DC directive demoting cultural reporting from its third-page prominence to a corner of page five. Piccioni asked that the "Third Page," or some other page, remain entirely devoted to culture for even one day per week.[232] Gonella helped to preserve the "Third Page" and pressed on elsewhere. At the end of 1951 he promoted a meeting of provincial cultural representatives in order to "confront in an organic and radical way the delicate and too-long ignored problem of *cultural activity* [emphasis in original]. Let's immediately rid ourselves of the notion that cultural activity is marginal. . . . Christian Democracy has its cultural heritage and we cannot fail to address it. A simple glance around us tells us that we cannot do otherwise." Gonella wanted to revitalize the party's Office for Cultural Activities with three goals: to familiarize the public with DC "intellectual representatives," to coordinate disparate and isolated intellectual currents, showing that the party "appreciates their efforts and is happy to help them," and to study better ways to present the party's thoughts, through "publications, libraries, [and] institutes." It remained, however, a highbrow message. A typical report from May 1952 discussed a talk given by a professor from the Catholic University "to the intellectuals of Naples." But the desire to go to, or to connect *with*, the people became quite clear.[233] A month later a party conference recognized the necessity for immediate action on a number of fronts, including more provincial concerts, "radical revision[s]" for the Italian Olympic Committee (CONI), the workers' assistance agency (ENAL), changes in the government's approach toward cinema, and a reorganization of the SPES propaganda office.[234]

Elsewhere, by 1954 at the SPES, Mariano Rumor promoted the new emphasis before a meeting of provincial and regional secretaries. The party's strength, he argued, lay in its vision. As greater than the sum of its parts, ideology trumped specific programs. "The Party is always superior, through its ideological inspiration, to all of the programs on a concrete level that it proposes."[235] The "Heavy Party" would also show

232. IS Seg. Pol. Gonella Sc. 8, f. 4, Piccioni/Gonella, September 14, 1950.

233. IS Seg. Pol. Gonella, Sc. 10, f. 1 and 6. Gonella circular, December 26, 1951. In a September 28, 1951, circular, Gonella also discussed the Cultural Activities Office, particularly coordinating work with the "Artistic Activities Office" and in the creation of a speakers list for distribution in the provinces; IS Seg. Pol. Gonella, Sc. 10, f. 1. An article in *Il Mondo* described Gonella at the Ministry of Public Instruction as "intransigently Catholic" and a "ferocious clerical"; Paolo Pavolini, "Democristiani 1956," *Il Mondo*, February 14, 1956; Giuseppe Ermini, "Attività culturali," *Libertas*, May 8, 1952.

234. IS Direzione Nazionale Sc 12, f. 109, Verbali, June 5–6, 1952.

235. IS Sec. Pol. De Gasperi, Sc. 18, f. 11, Mariano Rumor (SPES) circular, June 18, 1954.

everybody that the DC and the church were back on the same page. Fanfani worked to improve relations with the Vatican, enjoying what the *Corriere della sera* described as a "very cordial" rapport with the pontiff. The new leader, however, did not enjoy positive relations with every cleric. He rarely saw eye to eye, for instance, with Archbishop Siri. On the other hand, Fanfani cultivated a particularly fruitful relationship with Angelo Dell'Acqua, who replaced Montini at the Secretariat of State when the latter left for his Milan exile.[236]

While the Office of Cultural Activities still aimed at sophisticated intellectuals and highbrows, during the Fanfani era it broadened and extended its scope. In a report, the Cultural Activities director from 1955 to 1957, the Umbrian Tommaso Bozza, emphasized the importance of establishing "a sympathetic current between the DC and intellectuals." On top of an art journal, *Taccuino delle arti*, founded in 1952, the office started to award its own prizes for young artists in 1957 and collaborated with other contests, such as the Viterbo and Milan's San Fedele awards. The *Taccuino* was joined in 1955 by a monthly cultural review from the Milanese Jesuits, *Leggere*; Bozza, however, hoped that the party directorate could create a journal "of even higher prestige."[237] The DC also opened its Cinque Lune publishing house in 1954.[238]

All this was too narrow for Fanfani, who in August of 1954 extended the party's influence further into Italian society by creating the Central Office of Popular Activities (*attività popolari*), an agency more relaxed than Cultural Activities. So that party members might better appreciate the broader culture, the party would deliver to "voters and Party sympathizers ... occasions of honest recreation" and promote provincial recreational initiatives. Four months later, in December, its head, the Apulian deputy Gabriele Semeraro, sketched the office's task to the first national congress of provincial delegates. This was not, he insisted, a propaganda office. Nevertheless, he seemed intent on "a program of propaganda and penetration intended to form a greater base for the formation of a democratic and Christian state."[239] Subsequent circulars

236. A. A., "I rapport fra Pio XII e il mondo politico italiano," *Corriere della sera*, October 10, 1958; Magister, *La politica vaticana e l'Italia*, 203–5.

237. IS Seg. Pol. Moro, Sc. 118, f. 9, "L'Ufficio delle attività culturali" report (by Tommaso Bozza), n.d. (probably early 1958). The Cultural Activities Office also established a Roman art gallery, the Alibert.

238. On Cinque Lune, see also "Attività culturali della CD," *Il Popolo*, October 29, 1955.

239. IS Seg. Pol. Fanfani Sc. 55, f. 11. Semeraro/Fanfani, December 16, 1955. Regarding Semeraro's aims, see also IS Seg. Pol. Fanfani Sc. 36, f. 11, Semeraro circular n.d. (late 1954). This document asks provincial DC leaders to nominate party members to serve in the local Popular Activities Offices. It

accorded Popular Activities a wide-ranging mission of (1) the development of a party social life, (2) tourism and folklore activity, (3) theater, (4) cinema, (5) "*arte varia*," by which it meant, in the mid-1950s, choral and orchestral work, endeavors apparently dear to Semeraro's heart, (6) radio and television, and (7) traditional, regional, and local festivals (*feste e radune*). Activity might also include a trip to World War I battlefields or a chess match.

Events like the DC Registration Days (*Giornate di tesseramento*) and Member's Festivals (*Feste del socio*) focused on the party faithful; but other activities extended well beyond, to the community at large. Touring Sicily in March and April 1955, for instance, *arte varia* troupes reached fully 80 percent of the island's small towns and, one memo noted, contributed to the happy outcome of local elections there.[240] The Member's Festivals, starting in January 1955, were marked by rallies and speeches across the nation. An article from *Il Popolo* on that first Member's Festival proclaimed that the dark clouds after the 1953 electoral debacle dissipated before the new leaders and a fresh spirit. It applauded Fanfani's ambitions to reach all corners of the nation and insisted that, as his reform of the party offices strengthened the union between leadership and the rank and file, a stronger bond would then form between art and nation. For the *Feste del socio* Fanfani led the way with visits to four local party offices and a discourse in Rome calling upon DC militants to brace themselves for a year of heightened action.[241] In its second annual meeting in March 1957, the Popular Activities office trumpeted a self-congratulatory tone. There, Semeraro recounted the expanding numbers of musical and folklore bands and comedy troupes and vowed to direct more energy toward film and television. To the delegates assembled in Rome, party secretary Fanfani hailed its work and noted the appreciation for it exhibited by party members and sympathizers alike. The work of

also asks to be informed of each provincial tourist official (EPT and ENAL) and their party affiliations.

240. IS Seg. Pol. Fanfani, Sc. 40, f. 28. L'Ufficio delle attività popolari, "Compiti, Organizzazione, Settori di Lavoro delle Attività Popolari," n.d. (probably December 1955). See also IS Seg. Pol. Fanfani, Sc. 57, f. 29; "L'Ufficio delle attività popolari dalla sua costituzione sino ad oggi," n.d., apparently 1956. The report listed that the office had at its disposal three "*Libertas*" lyric-symphony orchestras, three light music ensembles, a folklore band (left over from the Fascist Dopolavoro organization), and the services of the "Trinca" show circuit and its three musical comedy troupes. On the issue of propaganda and the Cultural Affairs Office, see the Faldella circular, which described a plan to spread the party's message among the public via the DC and sympathetic media; IS Seg. Pol. Fanfani, Sc. 40, f. 24, Minaj Faldella circular, August 25, 1955.

241. "Fanfani impegna la DC al Rinnovamento," *Il Popolo*, January 3, 1955; "Vasta ripurcussione del discorso di Fanfani e del rafforzamento organizzativo della D.C.," *Il Popolo*, January 4, 1955.

Popular Activities, he claimed, reached eight times the number of party voters.[242]

These internal party efforts, however, could yield mixed results, and reports revealed snags. In March 1954, for example, the vice director of the more highbrow Cultural Activities Office complained of a lack of resolve, particularly among the crucial provincial chairs, many of whom displayed little attention to their work and "in fact more often than not" were downright "inefficient" or even "absent."[243] Another report, in 1956, noted that the new Popular Activities Office work had still not reached much outside of Rome, although at the end of 1955, sixty provincial representatives came to the capital for two days of discussions and planned on another in the coming months. The office recognized, however, that it had "not always register[ed] a cordial collaboration" with incapable and irresponsible provincial delegates.[244] The Catholic media also could dampen the mood, as when, at the end of 1955, a *Discussione* piece by Giuseppe Rossini praised the endeavor up to a point. "To whoever looks at politics over these last few years," he wrote, "it will appear evident that a solution to the problem of rapport between cultural life and political life has been a long time coming." The party had been chained too much in short-sightedness and had neglected the serious thought that culture required. The results of a DC poll of 350 local Cultural Activities offices, he continued, were hardly exciting. The party, concluded Rossini, must fill the void and bring Catholicism's rich and ancient heritage to the table.[245] *Il Popolo* also expressed concern, noting that the old axiom against mixing politics and religion was still quite strong among a lot of people. But with firm direction, hoped the paper, the new office might contribute a valuable service to Christian Democracy, locating "sympathetic roads between the Party and the Italian cultural world."[246] As the aforementioned 1956 report emphasized, the Popular Activities Office work should extend well beyond elections, and "not to take advantage of this modern method of penetration would be a grave mistake."

242. "Fanfani apre il convegno per le Attività culturali della d.c.," *Il Popolo*, March 10, 1957.

243. IS Seg. Pol. De Gasperi, Sc. 18, f. 2, Minaj Faldella/Giuseppe Spataro, March 6, 1954.

244. IS Seg. Pol. Fanfani, Sc 57, f. 29, "L'Ufficio delle attività popolari dalla sua costituzione sino ad oggi." The "Ordine del Giorno" of the December 1955 meeting can be found in IS Seg. Pol. Fanfani Sc 55, f. 11, Semeraro/Fanfani, December 16, 1955.

245. Giuseppe Rossini, "Un'iniziativa culturale in ogni Sezione della DC," *Discussione*, December 4, 1955.

246. "N.R."; "Attività culturali della D.C.," *Il Popolo*, October 29, 1955.

Fanfani's new activism may have brought more focus to culture, yet it was usually just more a matter of degree than real change. The party's somewhat modest internal measures may not have lived up to expectations, but they enhanced the DC's commitment to joining the church and Catholic Action in the cultural battles. They also enabled the party to begin to catch up to its two partners, which had already been traveling that road for a long time. Catholic Action indicated that it welcomed the new direction and signaled its readiness to cooperate. Already in 1953, to a conference of the AC's elite *laureati*, Monsignor Adriano Bernareggi delivered the keynote discourse on "Italian Culture Today and Christian Thought." Sharing the stage with Gedda and Fanfani, he announced that Catholics now stood "reinvigorated in philosophy, narrative literature, theater, cinema and art." Engagement with fellow intellectuals was proper and inevitable; but now the *laureati* had to go beyond the intelligentsia and reach out to the people (*massa popolare*), a difficult task but a realistic one with God's help.[247] The DC, AC, and the church seemed to agree that they should devote much of their greatest effort to cultural questions, starting with the media and family matters.

247. "I lavori del congresso dei Laureati Cattolici," *OR*, January 5–6, 1953; "Cultura italiana e pensiero cristiano nella relazione di Mons. Bernareggi," *OR*, January 7–8, 1953.

Chapter 2

Media and Censorship

After he briefly succeeded Alcide De Gasperi as prime minister, Giuseppe Pella received a letter from a Milanese father alarmed that Christianity's foes were on the march. He urged more government action, not against the Muscovite threat but against "the greatest enemies of morality . . . [found in] movies and newsstands." Similar missives urging action regularly reached DC officials as well as Catholic Action leaders. For example, don Mario Gatti, a priest near Verona who had gained notoriety and some legal trouble for ripping offensive movie posters off walls, complained to the government that "every cinema and every newsstand are becoming schools of crime and corruption."[1]

Catholics agreed that something needed to be done regarding the media and the arts. The common answer, censorship, attracted many political factions. Even before De Gasperi's first ministry, in August of 1945 the Parri government set a post-Fascist precedent by ordering editors to present copies of all their publications to the local public defender's office for vetting before they reached kiosks. Most Italians agreed that pornography, at least, needed restrictions, and much of the law here derived not from the DC, but from the so-called Togliatti Decree of May 31, 1946, named for the then Communist minister of justice. At times, moreover, other non-Catholic groups pressured to censor or ban something, often beyond pornography. One such case from 1952 concerned veterans' groups who protested the Italian release of the American film *The Desert Fox*, a glamorized account of the German general Irwin Rommel and the Afrika Korps. In Rome, a protest by veterans against the

1. Maurizio Cesari, *La censura in Italia oggi (1944–1980)* (Naples: Liguori editore, 1982), 101–2.

motion picture confronted Interior Minister Mario Scelba's *celere* police squads, whom the Socialist *Avanti!* condemned as typical of Scelba'a ham-fisted style. However, the government also condemned the movie and announced that if it had been made in Italy it would have never received state assistance; and Catholics in general joined the veterans, urging that *The Desert Fox* not be shown.[2]

Few, however, considered censorship as a good unto itself or a universal panacea; in fact, the critic Giacomo Gambetti wrote, nobody ever really wanted it.[3] Catholics could reasonably fear that in the wrong hands censorship might restrain them along with everyone else. "Censorship has never enjoyed sympathy from anyone," wrote one Christian Democrat. "The censor's job," he continued, "is dark, cold, and obnoxious [*oscuro, arido ed odioso*]."[4] With Fascism very much a living memory, an era of real suppression remained vivid. Italy's new republican state could not simply or flippantly impound any publication or halt any film that offended it; and in any case, everyone accepted the Constitution's Article 21, which guaranteed artistic freedom. When they secured power in the 1920s, Fascists, not to mention Nazis and Communists, sequestered anything they wanted—ugly examples not to be repeated—and consequently the *Popolo* announced that Christian Democrats had no intention of such abuses. Those fears, it insisted, were "unfair, narrow-minded ... excessive and out of place."[5] Catholic Italy would refrain from book burnings.[6]

On the other hand, the Constitution's Article 7 obligations shielded the faith, the church, and the family and at some level pushed Catholics around to some acceptance of the necessity for censorship. Their dismay

2. "Sdegno in tutto Roma contro il film su Rommel," *Avanti!*, February 29, 1952; "Perchè non è stato proibito il film biografico su Rommel?," *Il Popolo*, March 1, 1952.

3. Giacomo Gambetti, *Cinema e censura in Italia* (Rome: Edizioni di bianco e nero, 1972), 19.

4. Renzo Helfer, "Liceità e necessità di una censura," *Rivista del cinematografo*, December 1960.

5. "La Legge sulla stampa," *Il Popolo*, July 2, 1952. In the same issue, Leone Piccioni wrote "Libertà d'espressione," which clearly linked Lay and Marxist trepidations to the recent placement on the Index of Alberto Moravia's works. Piccioni distinguished between government limits regarding censorship and the church's valid decision to warn "unwitting" Catholics of questionable literature. Furthermore, he continued, the Index was not a reflection on Moravia's estimable talent, just as it had not reflected poorly on the works of André Gide. On July 3 *Il Popolo* (in "Ancora sulla stampa") repeated and elaborated its argument on press censorship, noting that the editor of *Avanti!* also supported the revisions.

6. In his examination of book burnings in the early modern era, Christopher Black encountered an earlier streak of doubt among Italians. In contrast to the impressive amount of between ten and twenty thousand volumes that the Romans torched in March 1559, Florence's Duke Cosimo de'Medici decided that "in deference to scholars and 'poor booksellers,' [his] should be a 'fire for show ... more demonstration than effect'"; Christopher F. Black, *The Italian Inquisition* (New Haven, Conn.: Yale University Press, 2009), 169.

over Italy's relentless secular drive led to measures and actions that political foes interpreted as evidence of a clerical dictatorship. At the Vatican, Pius XI's 1936 encyclical *Vigilanti cura* recognized cinema's dangers and encouraged Catholic critics to take them seriously. The document applauded the work of the American Catholic Legion of Decency that, through pressure and persuasion, played a key role in informal film censorship. It was no coincidence that, to a conference of film critics and journalists that year, the pontiff said censorship "must be just, but justly severe."[7] Like the pope, Albino Galletto, one of the church's leading arts authorities, applauded America's self-censorship (*autocensura*) but worried in May 1951 that Italy's postwar measures, modeled on those principles, were failing and that "up until today the Italian code has not been applied." Why not?, he asked, and threw down the gauntlet. "We will be happy if the men of the cinema: producers, directors, scriptwriters and artists, would like to tell us in this regard." Although one American observer blamed the Communists, Galletto did not feel this to be the case. "If it were so, we would have to conclude that the moral convictions of filmmakers were superficial and their courage somewhat weak."[8]

Catholic Action had fewer reservations over censorship and hoped to influence government action through its Ente dello spettacolo. Created in 1944, the agency oversaw three organizations: Luigi Gedda's CCC, Centro cattolico cinematografico, founded in 1935 for film with its respected review, the *Rivista del cinematografo*, and digests *Segnalazioni* and *Disco rosso*; the CCR, Centro cattolico radiofonico, founded in 1940 for radio; and the CCT, Centro cattolico teatrale, established in 1943 for the stage.[9] The Ente dello spettacolo needed time to get its footing after the war, a frustrating delay for some of the more ambitious militants. Its "ecclesiastical assistant," Monsignor Ferdinando Prosperini (before he joined Gino Gavuzzo at the Morality Office), complained in April 1945

7. William Troy McCraw, "Political Sponsorship of the Arts: Subsidization and Censorship of Motion Pictures and the Performing Arts by the Italian National Government, 1943–1962," (Ph.D. diss., Stanford University, 1966), 185–86. See also Raffaele De Berti, "Dalla *Vigilanti cura* al film ideale," in *Attraverso lo schermo: Cinema e cultura cattolica in Italia*, vol. 2, *Dagli anni Trenta agli anni Sessanta*, ed. Ruggero Eugeni and Dario Viganò (Rome: Ente dello spettacolo, 2006), 79–88.

8. Albino Galletto, "Responsabilità morali della produzione," *Rivista del cinematografo*, May 1951. A rather lukewarm response from the producers came in "Rispondono gli industriali," *Rivista del cinematografo*, November 1951.

9. Centro Cattolico cinematografico, *Guida Cinematografica*, 1934–1962 (Rome: CCC, 1962), xxx–xxxiii. Pius XII ordered the creation of a television center (Centro cattolico televisivo) in January 1954; see also Stefano Pivato, *Clericalismo e laicismo nella cultura popolare italiana* (Milan: Franco Angeli, 1990), 175.

that, of the three, the film bench provided the only accomplishments, all thanks to Gedda's dynamism. But, continued the priest, Gedda was overextended, while the other two agencies, for radio and theater, languished. In the five months since Prosperini took the position, he submitted, the radio group had met only twice and the theater group never. The secretary of the theater branch, he wrote, should be fired and replaced with somebody competent.[10] Two years later little had improved. The Ente's new chief, Ugo Sciascia, reported in July 1947 that the theater office needed to start over, while the radio office possessed only one functionary who had secured a commitment from state broadcasting, the RAI, to transmit a fifteen-minute Sunday show, "News of the Catholic World," and an occasional special event. Even at the CCC, Gedda, Prosperini, and Sciascia sometimes squabbled over personnel. To manage the film office, for example, Gedda had just appointed Ildo Avetta. Primarily an architect, he won important Catholic Action commissions for retreats and study centers at Paestum and at Casale Corte Cerro near Lago Maggiore. Sciascia had nothing against that appointment, he wrote, "except for [Avetta's] complete lack of any aptitude on film." That only meant, he continued, the necessity of quality picks at the lower level, advocating two others "with or without Dr. Avetta," one of whom had a morning job that would limit his service to the afternoons. The architect, however, was a man to watch and took over the Ente dello spettacolo in 1952.[11]

Along with that panoply, the AC launched, on May 18, 1949, the Catholic Association of Film Exhibitors (Associazione cattolica esercenti cinema, or ACEC) as a lobby for the parish cinemas, those that the church owned outright.[12] On March 9, 1950, influential Catholics gathered in Rome to christen yet another organization, the UCIC (Ufficio Cinematografica Internazionale tra Cattolici), which was Italy's branch of the Office Catholique Internationale du Cinema (OCIC; the Italian branch was UCIC), under Igino Giordani. Giordani emphasized the gravity of the film problem, charging that the time was ripe "for effective

10. IPVI, Pg XV, b. 8, Prosperini report, April 10, 1945.

11. IPVI, Pg XV, b. 8, Sciascia report, July 22, 1947. On Avetta, see also Andrea Longhi, "Le architetture di Luigi Gedda: Committenza e cantieri (1949–1959)," in *Luigi Gedda nella storia della Chiesa e del Paese*, ed. Ernesto Preziosi (Rome: AVE, 2013), 277–302. Shortly after Sciascia's report, Turi Vasile took control of the theater office and Daniele Fabbri became head of the radio office.

12. IPVI, Pg XV, b. 8, Ente dello spettacolo circular, April 26, 1949, containing "Statuto dell'Associazione Cattolica Esercenti Cinema." See also De Berti, "Dalla *Vigilanti cura* al film ideale," in Eugeni and Viganò, *Attraverso lo schermo*, 2:88–89. Giuseppe Dalla Torre was among the directors of Universalia.

action by Catholics in this field."[13] ANICA (the Associazione nazionale industrie cinematografiche e affini) was another important association of film producers and distributors that, although not strictly a Catholic vehicle, enjoyed the confidence of DC governments. Founded in 1944, it linked itself to the big industry association Confindustria, while its leadership also sided with the Catholics. ANICA's first president, Alfredo Proja, was elected as a Christian Democrat to the Constituent Assembly and then to the Parliament. His successor in 1949 was Eitel Monaco, who began his career with important industry positions under the Fascists; but in 1943, rejecting their entreaties to come north and serve the RSI, he hid out in Rome until the liberation.[14]

The government's most prominent office for cultural affairs was the Undersecretariat of State for Press, Entertainment, and Tourism (Stampa, spettacolo e turismo), tucked in a nest of agencies within the prime minister's office. During the 1950s, however, the Undersecretariat morphed into many forms, a succession of alterations that reveal some Christian Democrat doubts over cultural policy's proper place; and the indecision must have acted as a brake on it. The Undersecretariat almost became a full-fledged ministry when Mario Scelba, who became the prime minister in 1954, tried to assemble something under a minister without portfolio. A press bureau and one for sports, furthermore, made on-again, off-again appearances in this scheme. To head the project, he designated Giovanni Ponti, the mayor of Venice and head of the city's *Biennale* art festival. That arrangement ended along with the Scelba government in July of 1955.

From 1946, Christian Democrats headed the Undersecretariat, starting with Paolo Cappa, then Giulio Andreotti, who really put his stamp on it. Teodoro Bubbio, Giuseppe Ermini, Oscar Scalfaro, Giuseppe Brusasca, Raffaele Resta, and Egidio Ariosto followed Andreotti, but none enjoyed his influence, which would extend past film and reach all corners of the art world. Another key office within the Undersecretariat was the General Directorate of Entertainment (Direzione generale dello spettacolo), which oversaw a number of cultural offices for film, theater, opera, and so on, and administered censorship. The Interior and to some ex-

13. IS Seg. Politica Gonella, Sc 13, f. 1, Igino Giordani/Giorgio Tupini, March 11, 1950, with "Relazione" of the first meeting on March 9. The ecclesiastical liaison for the new UCIC was Fr. Diego Dedel.

14. For a brief biography, see the entry "Monaco, Eitel," in http://www.treccani.it/enciclopedia/eitel-monaco_(Dizionario_Biografico)/ (accessed November 13, 2019).

tent the Postal and Telecommunications Ministries also had some say, particularly in their composition of censorship panels and, in the case of the Interior Ministry, enforcement of morality laws. In 1959 Umberto Tupini became the minister without a portfolio for Sport and Tourism and, finally, became Italy's first minister of Tourism and the Spettacolo in March 1960.[15]

Printed Matter

Cultural battles were frequently fought over the print media—newspapers, reviews, and other literary venues. Particularly vexing was Italy's vibrant "*cronaca nera*" press that emerged after the war and reveled in scandal and lurid accounts of the worst of the human condition. Calls for action predictably came from the church and Catholic Action and usually started with specific attacks on the *cronaca nera*. Monsignor Prosperini of the Morality Office declared this "dishonest press" as "danger number one" and urged a rigorous and scrupulous boycott. Never acquire it, never accept it from a friend, and never permit it into one's home. Furthermore, he concluded, regarding the bad press, the *stampa galeotta*, one must "resort to legal options to repress it."[16] The Vatican knew what needed to be done—simply more censorship, starting with those "poisonous" rags. In 1957, for instance, the *Osservatore* devoted a front-page article to what it felt was too broad a latitude given to shameful periodicals like *Confidential*. While respecting the right of political journals to promote any ideology, *Confidential* and similar magazines peddled a special "narcotic" that crossed into moral issues. The *Osservatore* urged that publishing needed a good cleaning.[17] Gedda's *Iniziativa* also advocated more press morality, claiming that the scandal sheets degraded the reader's conscience; that those who read them began to think like them. The Catholic press, such as *L'Avvenire d'Italia*, led the way by refusing to publish news of suicides. But prospects were bleak, considering that publishing was a business, was fixed on the bottom line, and was not too concerned with the moral health of its customers. "Business and morality in the field of journalism," stated *Iniziativa*, "are not the best of

15. Lorenzo Quaglietti, *Storia economico-politica del cinema italiano 1945–1980* (Rome: Riuniti 1980), 52–94.

16. Ferdinando Prosperini, "Per la difesa del costume," *Iniziativa*, April 1950.

17. "Mercato di stupefacenti," *OR*, October 23, 1957. The article prompted an exchange with *Il Tempo*. See "Nessuna confusione," *OR*, October 25, 1957.

friends."[18] As undersecretary for *spettacolo*, in 1956 Giuseppe Brusasca emphasized the importance of controls. Fearful that the DC's lay partners might undermine censorship, he urged that party chief Amintore Fanfani and the entire DC stick to their guns. "The argument is very important," he wrote to Fanfani, "the Church anxiously follows it and we must show that our energies are committed ... to the defense of spiritual, moral and social principles that inspire our actions."[19] He was preaching to the choir. Fanfani's father had in fact served as a military censor during the First World War.[20]

The Interior Ministry led the government action against the print media. Its police merely enforced the existing provisions found in the Constitution's Article 7, for example, or in the penal code. The ministry relied to some extent on Catholic Action's Morality Office, which kept track of objectionable literature via circulars to diocesan offices and alerts to the police. A revealing 1947 report claimed that Gavuzzo's operation identified seventy-two of "about" 150 periodicals subject to revisions and that, of those, twenty-three had suspended publication or had folded altogether.[21] In May of 1950, Gavuzzo reported fines against two mainstream newspapers, *Il Messaggero* and *Il Tempo*, along with the Communist *L'Unità*, for publishing grisly photos from a murder-suicide scene. Also that month, Nicola Archideacono of *Il Tempo* received a penalty of eight thousand lire and three months in prison for printing the "shocking and horrifying details" (*particolari impressionanti e raccapriccianti*) in the case of an old man who molested his mentally disabled daughter. Such details were such that they could "disturb the common sentiment," and their publication landed Archideacono in jail.

Along with Gavuzzo's work, in a 1951 report to De Gasperi, Carlo Costantini discussed the activity of his *Buon costume* association to survey censorship.[22] Upon monitoring 2,700 newspapers, 1,420 magazines (*riviste illustrate, periodici settimanali, quindicinali e mensili*), and 350 theater, cinema, and variety shows, it delivered 841 "alerts" (*segnalazioni*) to authorities as well as to private concerns, for which the courts issued

18. Fausto Vallainc, "Per la moralità della stampa," *Iniziativa*, June 1953.

19. AS Casale Monferrato Fondo Brusasca M 97, f. 302, Brusasca/Fanfani, November 9, 1956. The letter is also found in IS Seg. Pol. Fanfani Sc 79, f.6.

20. Vincenzo La Russa, *Amintore Fanfani* (Soveria Mannelli: Rubbettino, 2006), 7.

21. IPVI, Sg VI, b. 1, f. 3, "Relazione sulla attività degli uffici, segretariati ed enti della presidenza generale dell'ACI Novembre 1946–Ottobre 1947."

22. IPVI, Pg XII, b. 32, Associazione nazionale per il buon costume—Relazione all'assemblea dei soci sull'attività svolta dall'associazione nel quinquennio 1946–1950, January 7, 1951.

"about" 200 condemnations. The association, however, extended culpability far beyond conventional "pornographic" images of carnal lust. Besides such predictable titles as *Seduzione*, *Venus*, and *Scandalo in paradiso*, Costantini's list included main-line but left-wing publications—in particular *L'Unità* and *Paese Sera*. Finally, he predicted long and difficult fights against clever and resilient hedonists, citing the example of one smutty review, *Sette*, that had been sequestered only to resurface a week later as *Otto*.[23]

At the end of 1952, Gavuzzo announced in *Iniziativa* that the Catholic Action morality campaign had made significant progress regarding the print media. Through "repressive activity" (*attività repressiva*), certain obscene and indecent magazines had been forced to change their content or shut down altogether. But the struggle had not ended, and he urged continued vigilance, perfecting the laws, public education, and a judiciary that would "orient itself more rigorously in the interpretation of the laws on the books." Theater and cinema, furthermore, needed greater attention; and the movie poster issue that had brought trouble to don Gatti near Verona was being dealt with in Parliament. Guidelines for *Questura* offices to deal with them were forthcoming, while, unfortunately for Gavuzzo, questions of "coming attractions" would plague moralists into the 1960s. Nonetheless, he took pride that his work had "exquisitely positive consequences": the safeguarding of souls and the fight against the deterioration of public civility.[24]

By the mid-1950s, it appeared that more and more Catholics were rallying around tougher regulations. At the start of the decade the National Press Congress had passed a weak resolution that accepted some measure of self-censorship but rejected government controls. It failed to receive the endorsement of a key Catholic activist, Raimondo Manzini. The editor of *L'Avvenire d'Italia* almost since its founding in 1927, Manzini was a Paulist priest who left the order in 1947 to marry. He sat as a DC deputy from 1948 to 1963, and Pope John would appoint him editor of the *Osservatore Romano*. He enjoyed widespread confidence across the whole Catholic spectrum and had, in fact, already been at work on a censorship proposal with some DC colleagues in Parliament.[25] By the

23. IPVI, Pg XII, b. 32, Associazione nazionale per il buon costume. Along with the Costantino report on *Sette* and *Otto*, see "Il dopoguerra è finito ci dicono le riviste-sensazione," *Il Popolo*, February 4, 1950.

24. "L'Attività dei segretariati centrali," *Iniziativa*, December 1952.

25. Libertà di stampa e censura preventiva, *Il Quotidiano*, January 7, 1950. On Manzini, see Natal Mario Lugaro, *Raimondo Manzini: Giornalista cattolico* (Milan: NED, 1988).

middle of the decade, the DC's *Discussione* urged a "free but responsive press," and Manzini spoke of the limits to its freedom and its role in the "protection of public morality."[26] Little of this sat well with the Socialists at *Avanti!*, who answered in November 1954 that Catholic authoritarian tendencies toward the press had been apparent for some time and had begun to resemble Mussolini's moves in the mid-1920s toward muzzling it.[27]

Catholic censorship presented a dilemma to the lay and Marxist camps. Did opposition to it make them appear too enthusiastic in defending those who insulted the religion or, perhaps even worse, gave the impression that they were hedonists or pornographers? Communists, in particular, exerted special effort to prove their upright, almost puritan, sensibility.[28] Indeed, on occasion the Communists collaborated with the Christian Democrats to forge censorship as they did with some press legislation of 1946.[29] But the PCI and the rest of the Marxists and lay factions also criticized censorship by lamenting its sloppiness and imprecision. In the staid *Nuova antologia*, for instance, Renato Lefevre pitied "the poor magistrate" forced to deal with such familiar but nonetheless imprecise terms as "common sentiment" and "offends decency." From the Milan Tribunal, he quoted a May 1949 sentence, "That which offended decency in other times cannot offend such sentiments in our times."[30] At a conference in February of 1958, the Friends of *Il Mondo* issued a manifesto, "*La Stampa in allarme*," which denounced recent Catholic attempts to infringe on press freedoms and a "preventative censorship" of children's and youth literature through the creation of a special commission. It also expressed alarm over the "growing number of criminal proceedings against journalists, particularly regarding crimes of pornography, contempt, and defamation."[31]

26. "L'Opinione pubblica esige una stampa libera ma cosciente," *Discussione*, December 5, 1954; "L'autodisciplina della stampa in una conferenza di Raimondo Manzini," *OR*, February 4, 1955; "Ferme dichiarazioni di Manzini sulla tutela della pubblica moralità," *OR*, February 27, 1955. Manzini saw that the ancient democracies such as the United States and Britain also faced problems of public morality, that it had become universal; Manzini, "L'Autodisciplina della stampa," *Tabor*, December 1955.

27. Ferdinando Schiavetti, "Le minacce alla stampa," *Avanti!*, November 16, 1954.

28. Stephen Gundle, *Between Hollywood and Moscow: The Italian Communists and the Challenge of Mass Culture, 1943–1991* (Durham, N.C.: Duke University Press, 2000); and Sandro Bellassai, *La morale comunista: Pubblico e privato nella rappresentazione del PCI (1947–1956)* (Rome: Carocci editore, 2000).

29. Marco Barbanti, "Cultura cattolica, lotta anticomunista a moralità pubblica (1948–60)," *Rivista di storia contemporanea* 1 (1992): 150.

30. Renato Lefevre, "Stampa licenziosa, cronaca nera e stampa per ragazzi," *Nuova antologia* (April 1950): 385–94.

31. Adolfo Battaglia, "Una Stampa Libera," *Il Mondo*, March 4, 1958. Alongside Battaglia's piece, *Il Mondo* printed the February 23 manifesto "La Stampa in Allarme."

Children's Literature

Through one route or another, most arguments for greater media regulation began with concern for the moral health of children and adolescents. Comics (*fumetti*) consequently assumed a prominent place in censorship discussions. Not all comics were bad. In the nineteenth century, some writers, such as Carlo Collodi, who created Pinocchio, contributed to the *fumetti* genre; and in 1937, none other than Luigi Gedda launched a comic of his own, *Vittorioso*. However, comics were frequently identified with the United States, particularly with the prewar appearance of Topolino (Mickey Mouse); and Italians understood that American comics were a force with which to be reckoned. One sign of their strength, argued Luciano Tavazza, had been a printers' strike in New York that forced Mayor Fiorello La Guardia to read the funnies over the radio to chuckle-starved children. After the war, furthermore, "very powerful" comics syndicates combined with U.S. occupation troops to push *fumetti* onto the Italian market as never before, leading to a more repugnant product "dominated by gangsters, *femmes fatales*, by detectives, by the ugly power of the sadist, or by the evil craftiness of the blackmailer." Especially obnoxious was their "abnormal" treatment of women as either "viragos" or "baby dolls." The situation worsened in 1950 when the Communists got into the act and introduced *Pioniere*, a form of left-wing "political comics" that served as the organ for the Pioneer youth organization. Its circulation could not compare to that of *Vittorioso*, 65,000 to 300,000 in the mid-1950s, despite input from such luminaries as Carlo Levi and Pier Paolo Pasolini.[32]

Catholic horror stories also charged that *fumetti* endangered not only the souls of children, but even their bodies. In November 1949, a six-year-old Bolognese boy was murdered by a fifteen-year-old who, according to a Catholic Action report, had been worked into a frenzy by "dark" *fumetti* and a "certain disturbing and immoral cinema." Consequently, Catholics of Bologna organized a Save the Children Committee to honor "the little martyr."[33] Another case concerned one unfortunate Turin boy who had

32. Luciano Tavazza, "Il fumetto ieri ed oggi," in Azione cattolica italiana, *Stampa, cinema, radio per Ragazzi* (Rome: Ufficio centrale aspirante, 1952), 11–32; Silvia Franchini, *Diventare grandi con il "Pioniere" (1950–1962) Política: Progetti di vita e identità di genere nella piccola posta di un giornalino di sinistra* (Florence: Firenze University Press, 2006), 1 and 273, regarding Levi and Pasolini, and 23–24, regarding circulation figures.

33. IPVI, Pg VI, b. 2, f. 3, Carlo Salizzoni (President of the Executive "Save the Children" Committee)/Vittorino Veronese, December 11, 1949; Communiqué announcing the creation of the "Save the

been enchanted by tales of the Wild West. His fixation led to experimentation with Indian knots and nooses until one day in 1957 his brother discovered his dead body with a rope around his neck. The AC children's magazine *In Alto* printed the tragic story and lamented that the boy's "poor mamma vainly wanted to burn the stack of comics [that were] responsible for the death." But most parents, continued the article, shrug their shoulders. "'What's wrong with [such literature],' they ask, 'it's kids' stuff?'" To prevent such tragedies *In Alto* concluded emphatically with capital letters, "GIVE KIDS READING MATERIAL THAT IS HEALTHY AND SAFE FROM EVERY VANTAGE POINT."[34]

That comic books could kill meant that children needed special protection from the modern media culture. After the Bologna incident, Andreotti argued that a reexamination might be necessary, and at the Montecitorio, the DC deputy, Maria Federici, introduced a bill to control children's literature. As in other cases, however, many argued that the laws were on the books and needed only either minor modification or only proper enforcement. One even-handed observer in the prestigious *Nuova Antologia*, for example, referred to a 1906 Liberal press law that condemned "obscenity crimes and offenses against *buon costume*." The Penal Code's Article 528, he continued, rooted out such indecent publications. But the 1949 Bologna shock, he wrote, alarmed everybody. "Let's apply . . . the possibility that the Constitution offers us against the scandalous press [*cronaca nera*] and above all against the media that targets children [*ragazzi ed ai bambini*]. Let's apply it against the fumetti, against the comic books that any youngster can buy at the newsstands for a few pennies."[35] Catholic Action addressed the issue in myriad ways, speaking directly to youth via its many children's magazines and to parents through public meetings or publications. The need for vigilance was the message of *The Press, Cinema and Radio for Kids* (*Stampa, cinema, radio per ragazzi*), the proceedings of an April 1952 Catholic Action conference held to "create a public opinion line." In his preface to the conference proceedings, the tireless don Galletto noted that mother and father could not accompany their offspring every moment of the day and night. The little ones needed help in those unguarded occasions of sin

Children" Committee with the blessing of Bologna's Cardinal Archbishoop Giovanni Battista Nasalli Rocca, December 8, 1949; Veronese/Salizzoni, December 16, 1949.

34. "Un'altra vittima dei fumetti," *In Alto*, January 1957.

35. Renato Lefevre, "Stampa licenziosa, cronaca nera e stampa per ragazzi," *Nuova Antologia*, April 1950.

when he or she encountered "that magazine passed under the counter, those immoral advertisements, the radio in the house, [and] 'strong' movie scenes."[36]

A daunting task, but Catholics like Tavazza and others engaged the fight with confidence. In the *Osservatore Romano* Carlo Cappello urged the faithful to take heart and not "cry so much" over children's media because their own press led the way in the struggle. Fourteen healthy Catholic reviews, including the *Giornalino*, *Voci d'Oltremare*, *Vera vita*, *Il Corrierino*, and, for the smallest Catholic girls, *La Vispa Teresa*, with a combined circulation of over one million meant that they had nothing to be ashamed of.[37] The Catholic fortress was formidable, but the secular lure remained, producing a mix of confidence and urgency. In another talk from the April 1952 conference, Domenico Volpi concluded that "kids are in danger. We have good weapons for this battle: let's go fight it!"[38]

Literature

The left-leaning bastion of highbrow literature was another matter—a distinctly Communist, Socialist, and lay turf. Serious adult books, therefore, avoided the kind of scrutiny that film and the theater received.[39] The government targeted outright pornographers but left alone most mainline writers and publishers. Not very common was the case of the publisher Leopoldo Longanesi and Sebastiano Pavanello, who authored the book *Una donna al giorno* (One Woman a Day). In 1950, the Milan Tribunal absolved the two, but in 1955 Catholic Action reported that, after a "diligent examination" of the text, the Appeals Court reversed the earlier sentence and condemned them to four months in prison with a 10,000 lire fine, a decision then confirmed by the Supreme Cassation Court.[40]

Catholics, moreover, were not entirely hopeless here and used their leverage when they saw the opportunity. Catholic Action could exert subtle but effective influence, as it did in 1955 when Gavuzzo success-

36. Azione cattolica italiana, *Stampa, cinema, radio per Ragazzi*, 5–7. The title was included in a series entitled *Quaderni di ragazzi*. Catholic concern regarding comics reflected, in some measure, Pope Paul IV's (Caraffa) order in the 1550s that the Index would include not only Erasmus, but fables as well; Black, *Italian Inquisition*, 160.

37. "La buona stampa per la gioventù," *OR*, May 21, 1953.

38. Domenico Volpi, "La nostra azione," in Azione cattolica italiana, *Stampa, cinema, radio per ragazzi*, 60.

39. Mino Argentieri, *La censura nel cinema italiano* (Rome: Editori Riuniti, 1974), 81.

40. IPVI, Pg XII, b. 34, Servizio informazione bulletin, February 2, 1955.

fully pressured the Mondadori publishing house to alter a promotional campaign. A December 2 Morality Office circular noted that prospective subscribers to Mondadori's women's magazine, *Grazia*, were invited to choose from a list of free books, including Gustave Flaubert's *Madame Bovary* and Alexandre Dumas's *The Lady of the Camellias*, two items that the Holy See had placed on the Index. Within two weeks, Gavuzzo happily reported that the publisher replaced the offensive titles with Dante's *Divine Comedy* and a collection of Shakespeare's plays.[41] On another occasion, *Il Popolo* went to the Morality Office to clear a toothpaste ad. Presented as a list of "psychological" questions, the last one asked the husband, "Would you give up your faithful Durban's toothpaste if your wife gave you any other brand?" Gavuzzo had no objectons.[42]

For the most part, however, the Marxist and lay literary establishment confidently operated with the knowledge that Catholic threats wouldn't amount to much. Marxists and former *azionisti*—for example, Leone Ginzburg, Massimo Mila, Carlo Antonicelli, Augusto Monti, and Franco Venturi—ran Turin's Einaudi publishers, arguably Italy's premier house.[43] Consequently, the Catholic press hardly bothered to discuss Italy's most distinguished book prizes, the Strega, the Bagutta, and the Viareggio, dismissed as not worth the effort. In 1957, a *Discussione* article charged that the Strega Prize was rigged "for better or worse." Sometimes these competitions recognized real quality work, such as Corrado Alvaro's *Quasi una vita* in 1951; but sometimes not, such as in the case of Mario Soldati's 1954 Strega winner, *Le lettere da Capri*.[44] After the crisis that ran through the Communist world triggered by the 1956 Hungarian revolution, *Discussione*'s Enzo Maizza detected an improvement of sorts at the Viareggio Prize; that the all-powerful PCI's grip had apparently slipped. But now the prize was dominated by the smothering regime of the big lay publishers—Einaudi, Garzanti, and Mondadori. The "pusillanimity" and "indolence" of the prize judges, furthermore, and their "collective lack of character," had degraded the literary competition into a mere "beauty contest" wherein the big houses gobbled up for themselves the bulk of the awards.[45]

41. IPVI, Pg XII, b. 2, Gavuzzo circulars, no. 136 of December 2, 1955, and no. 138 of December 15, 1955.

42. IPVI, Pg XII, b. 33, Antonio Loi (of *Il Popolo*)/Gavuzzo, May 17, 1954; Gavuzzo/Loi, May 18, 1954.

43. Massimo Teodori, *Storia dei laici nell'Italia clericale e comunista* (Venice: Marsilio, 2008), 44–45.

44. Angelo Paoluzzi, "Bene e male sul premio Strega," *Discussione*, July 14, 1957.

45. Enzo Maizza, "La Torta di Viareggio in dodici fette," *Discussione*, September 8, 1957.

Still, the faithful had options. On occasion, they just shrugged their shoulders and tried to downplay the ideological problems; indeed, as often as not, Catholic critics applauded the work of lay and Marxist writers. It helped, of course, when the writer broke with the party, as in the case of Italo Calvino, whose defection from the Communists earned him high marks from Leone Piccioni, who in *Il Popolo* noted that the "newly won autonomy" would serve him well.[46] Making the best of it, however, only went so far. In the fall of 1948, from Gavuzzo's Morality Office, Ferdinando Prosperini took a "no prisoners" view in an exchange of letters with Federico Alessandrini, the editor of Catholic Action's *Il Quotidiano*. The priest objected to the paper's tepid discussion of Alberto Moravia, one of Italy's most important writers and an ardent Communist. Prosperini emphatically protested to Alessandrini when the *Quotidiano* condemned Moravia's work on an aesthetic basis rather than a moral one. "No! dear Director!," he wailed, "We, I want to say we Catholics, in a Catholic Action organ can *never* avoid moral judgment. If we don't do it, who will?" Alessandrini tried to placate Prosperini in a light-hearted reply, hinting that the cleric perhaps had overreacted. Nonetheless, he argued that Moravia's work needed to be discussed and that the article *did* explicitly condemn it as pornographic. He affirmed complete agreement with the Holy Office and implied that *his* position was closer than Prosperini's to church authority. This failed to amuse the priest, and Alessandrini, sensing this ("I see that you took my joke seriously"), pledged his continued devotion to the Morality Office. In May 1952 the Holy Office settled the question by placing all of Moravia's works on the Index.[47] Shortly afterward the writer won the Strega Prize for his *I Racconti*. In *Il Popolo* Leone Piccioni chastised Moravia's acceptance speech, which declared the award as a nod to the freedom of expression. This veiled attack, he wrote, was misplaced in that the Index was only a Catholic guide for the faithful and that Moravia was no victim. His book was published, after all; and it won a prestigious award. Moravia was, rather, pandering to "anticlerical attitudes [which] reach from the communist camp to the most sectarian and utopian liberals."[48]

Perhaps no author earned as much Catholic opprobrium as did the

46. Leone Piccioni, "Ritratto di Calvino," *Il Popolo*, September 1, 1957.

47. IPVI, Pg XII, b. 31, Prosperini/Alessandrini, October 29, 1948; Alessandrini/Prosperini, November 1, 1948; Prosperini/Alessandrini, November 4, 1948; Alessandrini/Prosperini, November 9, 1948. At one point Prosperini made it clear that Gavuzzo shared his opinions.

48. Leone Piccioni, "Libertà d'espressione," *Il Popolo*, July 2, 1952.

French Roger Peyrefitte. While no Moravia, he was *sui generis*, a writer who peppered his aim to embarrass the church with a very open homosexuality and hedonism. The times determined that the Catholic disdain for homosexual activity enjoyed widespread consent. In the 1950s, no political party supported gay rights as such, although the church confronted some individuals who championed the cause—namely, Peyrefitte, the self-styled "Pope of the Homosexuals." A minor diplomat during the 1930s who served in France's embassy at Athens, Peyrefitte also exhibited an inclination to pederasty that prompted his expulsion, although his adventures continued. Later, in the mid-1960s, he met the "great love of his life" and business partner, a twelve-year-old boy. During the war, the Vichy Foreign Ministry put Peyrefitte back to work before he turned entirely to a literary vocation. His 1955 novel *The Keys of Saint Peter*, a sly critique of the workings of the Roman Church, was immediately banned under the terms of Article 7, although it apparently stayed in press and some bookshops still distributed it, occasionally suffering state retaliation. In February 1956, for instance, the head of Rome's Communist Rinascita bookshop was charged with a violation of the Civil Code's Article 352 on the sale of sequestered books. On February 22, 1958, the anticlerical *Paese Sera* pushed the envelope by publishing an inflammatory article by Peyrefitte. The piece, "Rome of the Popes," was a lewd historical treatment of the papal city with depictions of figures such as Pius IX's secretary of state, Cardinal Giacomo Antonelli, who "flitted" around Roman salons, brushing against the shoulders of the lovely ladies and burying his eyes in their cleavage. The cardinal, Peyrefitte continued, even fathered an illegitimate daughter. The article outraged the Holy See and triggered an extraordinarily blunt page-one essay in the *Osservatore* declaring that the Frenchman ventured "beyond all bounds" and demanding his prosecution. To that effect, on February 24 the Nuncio formally protested to Italy's Foreign Ministry in a *note verbale* and urged that Peyrefitte be brought up on charges for his violation of the Lateran Pacts. The next day, from his rented villa at Taormina, the "libellant" dismissed all accusations as "absurd and fantastic" and snapped that he was Italy's guest, not the Vatican's. *Paese sera* kept up the attack, claiming that Peyrefitte was a "disciplined believer" who appreciated Italian culture and, in fact, revered the great Liberal Benedetto Croce. They capped the piece with a photo of the Frenchman kissing the ring of New York's Archbishop Francis Spellman. Pressed by the

Holy See, on March 1 the DC government complied and filed *vilipendio* charges against Peyrefitte and the *Paese sera*'s assistant director, who had to answer for his superior, Mario Melloni, a parliamentarian who enjoyed immunity.[49] On March 3, the Milan police again began to sequester copies of *The Keys of Saint Peter*. The book's typographer finally agreed to cease printing, while the publisher, Longanesi, contacted bookstores, urging them not to comply and to sell as many copies as soon as possible.[50]

Peyrefitte presented difficulties for the lay press, which was reluctant to appear too supportive of such an outrageous hedonist but sympathetic to his struggle to freely publish. To *La Tribuna*, the Liberal Giovanni Malagodi wondered whether it made sense to herald the Frenchman as a new Voltaire, while the *Voce repubblicana* insisted that the sodomite did a disservice to the lay cause, deriding the *Paese Sera* for printing such "political filth" (*sozzura politica*). Nonetheless, the Republicans reluctantly admitted that the case was one of freedom of conscience, leaving them the distasteful but necessary job of defending Peyrefitte.[51]

49. Robert Aldrich, *The Seduction of the Mediterranean: Writing, Art and Homosexual Fantasy* (London: Routledge, 1993), 187–88. A biographical sketch of Peyrefitte can be found online in the entry, "Peyrefitte, Roger (1907–2000)," by Michael D. Sibalis, in *GLBTQ: An Encyclopedia of Gay, Lesbian, Bisexual, Transgender and Queer Culture*, at http://www.glbtqarchive.com/literature/peyrefitte_r_L.pdf (accessed November 13, 2019). See also Roger Peyrefitte, *The Keys to Saint Peter: A Novel* (New York: Criterion, 1957); Peyrefitte as "R.P," "La Roma dei papi," *Paese Sera*, February 22, 1958; "Oltre ogni limite," *OR*, February 24–25, 1958; "Nota di protesta del Vaticano per un articolo di Peyrefitte," *Avanti!*, February 25, 1958; "Per vilipendio al Papa, procedimento penale contro Peyrefitte e '*Paese será*,'" *Il Popolo*, February 25, 1958; "Peyrefitte: Sono l'ospite dell'Italia e non del Vaticano," *Paese sera*, February 25–26, 1958; Silvio Negro, "Nota del Vaticano a Palazzo Chigi per uno scritto ingiurioso di Peyrefitte," *Corriere della sera*, February 25, 1958, and "Nuovo vivacissimo attacco dell' 'Osservatore' a Peyrefitte," *Corriere della sera*, February 27, 1958; "Sarà la magistratura pontificia a giudicare la quarela di Peyrefitte," *Corriere della sera*, February 28, 1958; "A Colloquio con Peyrefitte nel 'ritiro' di Taormina," *Paese Sera*, February 28–March 1, 1958. The *Quotidiano* echoed the *Osservatore*'s judgment by branding "La Roma dei papi" "a collection of lies and nonsense" from the "new Voltaire"; "Un calunniatore," *Il Quotidiano*, February 23, 1958. At about the same time, *Paese sera* launched an incendiary series of articles on leading clerics. The first concerned Florence's Cardinal Elia Dalla Costa, whom the paper accused of Nazi sympathies. *Il Popolo* dismissed the reports as anticlerical lies and garbage while noting a similar "coattail" inquest in *Avanti!*; "Fuochi fatui anticlericali," *Il Popolo*, February 19, 1958; "Presentate le querele di Peyrefitte contro i giornali del Vaticano e dell' AC," *Avanti!*, March 19, 1958; "Peyrefitte denunciato d'ufficio per offese al Sommo Pontefice," *Il Quotidiano*, February 25, 1958; and "Trasmessa da Palazzo Chigi la protesta della Santa Sede," *Il Quotidiano*, February 26, 1958. On the 1956 *Rinascita* case, see IPVI, Pg XII, b. 18, Gavuzzo circular, February 29, 1956.

50. "Sequestrato a Milano un libello di Peyrefitte," *Il Quotidiano*, March 5, 1958.

51. "I soldali di Peyrefitte," *Voce repubblicana*, February 26, 1958. Two days later the paper expressed frustration in the Vatican tactic of lumping the lay and Marxist presses together as one, although it insisted again that Peyrefitte must be defended in principle; A. A., "Governo e DC si sforzano di fugare le apprensioni," *Corriere della sera*, March 4, 1958; "Laicismo strumentale," *Voce repubblicana*, February 28, 1958. That the lay forces did not march lockstep with the Communists was emphasized on March 2 by the head of the Republican Party, Ugo La Malfa, in his essay "Stato e chiesa," *Voce repubblicana*, March 2, 1958.

Oddly, Peyrefitte found one fan within the cabinet of Prime Minister Adone Zoli. Even in a case as black and white as this, the *Corriere della sera* embarrassed the DC government by identifying none other than the minister of foreign commerce, Guido Carli, who sent a laudatory note to the ribald author. Despite Carli's explanation that his was only a cordial message between friends, a red-faced government decided not to comment on the issue until it blew over. Gedda, however, circulated a criticism within the AC complaining, in a veiled reference to Carli, that the pontiff suffered slurs even from the Eternal City. Somewhat flummoxed, the *Quotidiano* disavowed Carli as one of the occasional technocrats brought into the government; that he was neither a "political" appointee nor a member of the Christian Democracy. However, continued the AC journal, for a sitting minister to send such a message was in the current circumstance "rather incredible."[52] Vatican Radio, moreover, used the Peyrefitte affair to scold the DC and call for stiffer resolve. "There are times," stated the announcer, "that require firm positions and decisive closings of ranks [*schieramenti decisi*], without the possibility of taking refuge in regrettable ambiguity."[53]

Against the criticisms reserved for writers like Moravia or Peyrefitte, praise for Catholics could be difficult, since few of the nation's literary "greats" identified themselves as particularly devout. Perhaps the most prestigious of that small number was Giovanni Papini, who had been thought of as an atheist and nationalist before the First World War, then collaborated with Fascism and embraced Catholicism by the 1920s. He subsequently became a third-order Franciscan and was lauded by *Il Popolo* and other journals upon his death in 1956.[54] By far, however, Italy's most popular Catholic writer was Giovannino Guareschi, the creator of the "don Camillo" series of novels, many of which were adapted to film. He enjoyed a huge audience, and his books outsold those of every contemporary. He was no highbrow; lay critics typically dismissed his work as lacking authentic political or ideological content, a judgment

52. "Il Processo a Peyrefitte sarà celebrato in Aprile," *Il Quotidiano*, March 2, 1958. *L'Unità* reported ("Peyrefitte è stato rinviato a giudizio," of March 2, 1958) that Zoli met with Carli, who insisted that the telegram only reflected a personal friendship between the two men; A. A., "Ne' dimissioni ne' crisi di governo per il telegramma di Carli a Peyrefitte," *Corriere della sera*, March 2, 1958; "Un telegramma a Peyrefitte rinfacciato al ministro Carli," *Avanti!*, March 2, 1958. For his part, Carli not only remained a member of the Zoli cabinet; in 1960, he became the governor of the Bank of Italy, a position he held until 1975.

53. "Sequestrato a Milano un libello di Peyrefitte," *Il Quotidiano*, March 5, 1958.

54. "È morto Papini," and Francesco Casnati, "Giovanni Papini, Cercatore della verità," both in *Il Popolo*, July 9, 1956; and Carlo Betocchi, "Il grande Papini," *Il Popolo*, July 10, 1956.

that begs reconsideration.[55] With "a wonderful gift for illustrating the spiritual dimension of everyday life," Guareschi became postwar "Italy's preeminent Catholic storyteller." Set in a Po valley town, the series depicted the White-Red contest between the parish priest, don Camillo, and the oafish Communist mayor, Peppone. In search of guidance, the plucky priest turned, literally, to discussions with Christ, an oracle much older and more venerable than Marx. Don Camillo chose not to cage his arguments with the mayor behind those bars of "political economy" and "dialectical materialism" demanded by Communists and materialist thinkers. Rather, his first impulse was to knock Peppone over the head and then apologize to il *Signore*. The burlesque notwithstanding, the dialogue between priest and Savior was always endearing, and the contest was real enough. Simply put and peppered with slapstick, it expressed itself in a language foreign to the deadly serious and dry forms of "modern," mid-twentieth-century political discourse. From the left, Moravia considered the film versions of don Camillo "reductivist," but positively so, and judged their impact more effective than "so many other anti-communist movies."[56]

Don Camillo offered a welcome face for the Catholic cause, although Guareschi himself proved an embarrassment to the Christian Democrats. Despite his sincere faith and the Catholic feel of his writings, he was a political maverick and identified not with the DC but with the Monarchists and some sectors of the far right. He found himself on Christian Democracy's bad side when he charged that, during the war, De Gasperi urged the Allies to bomb an aqueduct on the periphery of Rome in order to demoralize the Fascists. Guareschi based his case on two probably fraudulent letters that he published in his satirical review, *Candido*, and that the Communists reproduced in *L'Unità*. He chastised De Gasperi as "cold, ruthless, lacking any scruples and savage," the most dangerous man in Italy and a figure that even Christ could not pardon. Such "infamous attacks," announced the *Osservatore Romano*, on "a noble brother in the faith and a generous fighter on the political

55. Paolo Bertetto, "La costruzione del cinema di regime," in *Il cinema italiano degli anni '50*, ed. Giorgio Tinazzi (Venice: Marsilio, 1979), 138–39. Bertetto wrote that "in the don Camillo cycle concrete political or ideological debates are totally ignored." See also Daniela Treveri Gennari, *Post-War Italian Cinema: American Intervention, Vatican Interests* (New York: Routledge, 2010), 140–45.

56. Alan R. Perry, *The don Camillo Stories of Giovannino Guareschi: A Humorist Portrays the Sacred* (Toronto: University of Toronto Press, 2007), 25 and 184. Perry sketches the basic outline of Guareschi's life on 6–24. See also Alberto Moravia, "Il Secondo match tra Fernandel e Cervi," *Europeo*, October 4, 1953, 37. Moravia felt that the stories exhibited a humanity in the jousting between "an endearing and turbulent priest and the no-less-endearing and goodhearted revolutionary."

field," produced "misery not only on those who dared to make them and those who supported them, but also on the nation's *buon costume*." A court battle ensued, and Guareschi was found guilty of defamation, with a sentence of a year in prison and a 100,000 lire fine.[57] That blemish did not decrease don Camillo's popularity—later, Pope John even invited the writer to contribute to the project of a new catechism—and the don Camillo series continued even after Guareschi's premature death in 1968.[58]

The Stage

On the stage, Catholics took a bolder approach. With Catholic Action's Centro Cattolico Teatrale in the Ente dello spettacolo and the government's theater office, part of the Spettacolo Undersecretariat's General Directorate of Entertainment, Catholics were better prepared here than with the print media; and they felt a more urgent need to do something. Starting with variety shows, they took aim at a host of raunchy comedians and dancing girls in skimpy, provocative garb. Naples witnessed a flap in early 1956 over a Folies Bergère show that had already secured government permission and had previously run in Milan. It premiered to sold-out houses at the stylish Mercadante Theater with upper-crust audiences that included Naples' Catholic Action head, who claimed later that he and his entourage went merely to understand the reason for all the hubbub. The Folies Bergère show could, indeed, have befuddled him because it was loaded with contradictions. The local Morality Office felt that a tasteful "stained glass window" number with plenty of clothes and the strains of Charles Gounod's *Ave Maria* might not earn the censors' pass for the show in that it had been sandwiched between two "quasi" nude skits. The prefect of Naples could not report any public discontent over the Folies, although some grumbling surfaced when the director pulled the "Ave Maria" number. Oriana Fallaci in *L'Europeo*, however, wrote that Neapolitan high society came apart over the issue.

57. In 1950, Guareschi had already received an eight-month sentence for libel against President Luigi Einaudi. *Europeo* claimed in its May 15, 1955, edition that Guareschi was finishing his third "don Camillo" while serving his sentence. That sentence was then merged into the De Gasperi judgment. See also "Guareschi condannato a un anno di reclusione" and "La parola di giusztizia," both in *Il Popolo*, April 16, 1954; "Che le lettere siano state falsificate è immerse dalle prove oltre ogni dubbio," *Il Popolo*, April 15, 1954; and "Immondezza di candido," *Discussione*, January 31, 1955. The *Osservatore romano* quote was cited in "Guareschi condannato a un'anno di reclusione," *Il Quotidiano*, April 16, 1954.

58. Perry, *Don Camillo Stories of Giovannino Guareschi*, 184. The sixty-year-old Guareschi died of a heart attack.

Il Mattino labeled the show "family fare" and wondered how the Folies could cause a scandal when the Holy See had recently hosted Sophia Loren. Even the *Osservatore* in Rome felt obliged to comment in an article titled "Attenzione!," which the Foreign Ministry interpreted as a warning. The Lateran Pacts prohibited such vulgarity from coming to Rome, where the local Catholic Action head dutifully reminded the government against any such "indecorous" exhibitions.[59] Another issue that concerned the Morality Office was the level of homosexuality in the performances. Catholic Action therefore agreed to cooperate with the police in the "total elimination of the most deplorable and frequent references to homosexual vice" in variety shows and reviews. While this would not result in ripping pages from existing scripts, it would, Gavuzzo wrote, require vigilance for the future, particularly with the lower-class houses that employed little-known entertainers.[60]

Dealing with the legitimate theater could be trickier than the variety stage, where obscenity charges flew more freely. Theatrical censorship per force began before film; and, after some groundwork in 1864, the modern Italian state set the practice in legislation in 1888 and 1889.[61] After the Second World War, the case of Vincenzo Di Crescenzo's 1949 *Il Pellegrino di Piedigrotta* serves as an early example of the arrangement between the producers and the government Undersecretariat. Playing off the 1950 Holy Year, the play concerned some Neapolitans who preyed upon unsuspecting pilgrims. The doubts it cast on the integrity of the Holy Year concerned censors such that they gutted the work's religious angle, substituting references to the pilgrim (*pellegrino*) with tourist (*turista*) or foreigner (*forestiero*), and consequently insisting on a new title, *Il Forestiero di Piedigrotta*.[62]

A significant number of the playwrights targeted by censors were foreigners. The East German Berthold Brecht's play about the Thirty Years War, *Mother Courage and Her Children*, was banned, and the Ministry

59. IPVI, Pg XII, b. 37, Morality Office, "Appunto per s.e. Mons. Castellano," January 28, 1956; ACS, PCM 1959–61, 1-6-4 97605 s. 2, Prefect Naples report, February 11, 1956; Brusasca memorandum, February 1, 1956; Catholic Action Rome protest, February 3, 1956; and Ministry of Foreign Affairs/Brusasca, January 27, 1956. See also Oriana Fallaci, "Brutte ma nude," *L'Europeo*, February 5, 1956.

60. IPVI, Sg. XII, b. 5, Morality Office circular, April 9, 1953. The document cited Gavuzzo's *Guida* for guidance on dealing with stage shows.

61. Alessandro Clericuzio, *Tennessee Williams in Italy: A Transcultural Perspective* (Switzerland: Palgrave Macmillan, 2016), 74; Federica Festa, *Teatro proibito: In scena i tabù di una nazione* (Spoleto: Editoria and Spettacolo, 2011), 18–29; and *Censura teatrale e fascismo (1931–1944): La storia, l'archivio, l'inventario*, ed. Patrizia Ferrara (Rome: Ministero per i beni e le attività culturali, Direzione generale per gli archivi, 2004), 1:13–19.

62. Festa, *Teatro proibito*, 45–48.

of Foreign Affairs refused him and his troupe entry into Italy in 1951.[63] Even such a classic as Machiavelli's *La Mandragola* was not allowed, while Shakespeare's *Henry IV* and *Falstaff* both saw the sacred word "Madonna" cut from the scripts.[64] The most notable example of theatrical censure during the 1950s concerned Vitaliano Brancati's *La Governante*, which Andreotti rejected in 1951 owing to, among other things, a major character's lesbian inclination and a suicide. He told the author that the play was simply "indigestible." At *Il Popolo* Leone Piccioni believed that while he succeeded in publishing his play as a book, Brancati still relished his role as victim and martyr, "traveling through Italy, revealing his scars that the (clerical) tyranny inflicted on him." Brancati's relationship with tyranny, however, was complicated. He had, in fact, carved a comfortable career for himself in the 1930s as a protégé of fellow Sicilian Telesio Interlandi, editor of the anti-Semitic *Tevere*. But his second novel, *Singolare avventura di viaggio*, revealed an interest in awkward sexual attitudes, incest in this case, and gave the regime cause for concern. His wings clipped, he moved back to Sicily while keeping his Fascist ties. Mussolini even personally awarded him a grant for a book of essays on the poet Giacomo Leopardi. Brancati died in 1954, but his widow, the actress Anna Proclemer, soon petitioned that her own troupe might stage *La Governante*. When, at the Undersecretariat, Giuseppe Brusasca received letters from the Republican foreign minister Gaetano Martino and the Social Democrat vice chair of the Council of Ministers Giuseppe Saragat, he concluded that general agreement on the play had been reached—release it "with numerous cuts."[65]

Government censors felt more comfortable with plays based on Catholic themes. Giulio Cesare Viola's story of rich, thrill-seeking American youth, *Poveri davanti a Dio*, for example, was one of the era's first hits. A Liberal, Viola joined other writers like Bruno Cicognani, whose 1947 "neoguelph" drama depicted Spain's King Phillip II as *Yo el rey*; Carlo

63. Argentieri, *La censura nel cinema italiano*, 80–81; see also Clericuzio, *Tennesee Williams in Italy*, passim.

64. Cesari, *La censura in Italia oggi*, 75–79; Carlo di Stefano, *La Censura teatrale in Italia (1600–1962)* (Rocca San Casciano: Cappelli, 1964), 133. See also Giovanni Ozzo, "Sulla censura teatrale," *Il Ponte* 12 (August–September 1957). Ozzo saw as particularly troublesome the wide berth given to the prefects, causing *La Mandragola*'s censorship in Prato and not in Rome.

65. IS Seg. Pol., Fanfani Sc 79, f. 6, Brusasca/Fanfani, November 9, 1956, which includes attachments to the Prefecture of Milan and the letters from Martino and Saragat. Also found in AS Casale Monferrato Fondo Brusasca M 97, f. 302; Leone Piccioni, "Libertà d'espressione," *Il Popolo*, July 2, 1952. Brancati's earlier play, *Raffaele*, had been held up for six months in the *censura*. Guido Bonsaver discussed Brancati and the Fascists in his *Censorship and Literature in Fascist Italy* (Toronto: University of Toronto Press, 2007), 83–87. On the *Governante*, see also Festa, *Teatro proibito*, 55–57, 112–15.

Trabucco and Silvio Giovaninetti, who both wrote for *Il Popolo*; Valentino Bompiani, who founded a publishing house that bore his name; Turi Vasile and Diego Fabbri, both AC militants; and Ugo Betti, who, according to one observer, composed the day's "most profoundly religious works."[66] Yet even Betti was almost obliged to change the title of his play, *Corruption at the Courthouse* (*Corruzione al palazzo di giustizia*), during the Montesi scandal when the DC chafed at anything that hinted of mistrust of the government.[67] To emphasize the party's interest in theater, in the spring of 1955 Fanfani ordered the DC Office of Cultural Activities to work with Catholic Action in the creation of the Popular Little Theater (Piccolo teatro popolare). Its first production that June was *A Cathedral for the Island* (*Una cattedrale per l'isola*) by the Franco-Jewish playwright Jean-Jacques Bernard. The party office also promoted a "National Drama Festival."[68]

Diego Fabbri, too, enjoyed a status among the era's Catholic "prestige" playwrights. He maintained close ties with Gedda and collaborated with him on the film *Pastor Angelicus*, the paean to the pontiff on the twenty-fifth anniversary of his episcopal ordination. Gedda also trusted Fabbri with the direction of the Catholic AVE publishing house. The DC press, moreover, often lavished attention on the playwright. *Discussione*, for example, interviewed Fabbri after the Parisian success of his play *Processo di famiglia*. Although "one of the most representative figures of our culture," stated the article, "our theater and all the intellectual and cultural scenes," he remained unaffected by the haughtiness of *divismo*, remaining "a simple man without any pretentiousness," a polymath who spoke knowingly but with ease on subjects from Chekov to psychology, from religion to sports. While a review of the play in *Il Popolo* questioned some of the philosophizing at the end, it also stressed a reception of sincere, spontaneous, and popular applause, one not "sophisticated or forced," which revealed the bond that Fabbri enjoyed with regular folk. Theater, claimed the artist, must be a "testimony and echo of our social attitudes, the vision of our way of thinking and our everyday actions."[69]

66. Carlo Falconi, *La Chiesa e le organizzazioni cattoliche in Italia*, especially chapter 9, "Il teatro religioso," 212–60. For a DC estimate of Betti, see "Speranza tragica di Ugo Betti," *Il Popolo*, May 18, 1955.

67. Argentieri, *La censura nel cinema italiano*, 120.

68. IS Sez. Pol. Fanfani, Sc 57, f. 29, "L'Ufficio delle attività popolari dalla sua costituzione ad oggi," n.d., apparently 1956. Bernard's work was telecast and then released as a film in 1960.

69. Carlo Trabucco, "Al Teatro Eliseo: Processo di Famiglia," *Il Popolo*, February 9, 1954; Giuseppe Tedeschi, "Diego Fabbri reduce dal 'Processo,'" *Discussione*, October 30, 1955. On the following January 24, *Il Mondo* lauded Fabbri's "Processo a Gesù." The reviewer, however, needed to mention that some of Fabbri's theme corresponded to the work of the heretic Ernesto Buonaiuti; Nicola Chiaromonti,

Cinema

Of the various media, the battle over film was the most intense and dramatic. A struggle over huge cultural stakes to the extent that, as Gian Piero Brunetta wrote, through the difficult 1940s, film had become nothing less than a focal point of Italy's national identity.[70] One *Osservatore Romano* article stressed the "overwhelming" impact of film on culture and society, to the point that it had become a necessity of life for some people, particularly the young.[71] One who addressed this issue in 1950 was Albino Galletto. In 1948 he succeeded Ferdinando Prosperini as the ecclesiastical assistant with Catholic Action's Ente dello spettacolo and claimed that "film lacks a Christian face [and] why are the Catholics absent?"[72] As with serious literature, Catholics could not claim the screen entirely for themselves. One historian even wrote that "the Catholic press often demonstrated a pathological phobia of the cinema."[73] Recent scholarship has tempered some of this judgment. Regarding the motion picture community's suspicion of religion, one observer, Tim Cawkwell, discerned an "ambivalence toward the Catholic Church [that] has a habit of turning up in postwar Italian cinema and, when compared to other national cinemas, appears peculiar to it." Yet it was, as Cawkwell states, ambivalence but not disparagement. While some leading directors such as Luchino Visconti had little or nothing to do with the religion, a remarkable group did.[74]

During the immediate postwar years, the battle centered on neorealism, with its gritty "realist" look that portrayed the poor and working class and its rejection of conventional filmmaking techniques, most notably the use of professional actors or at least "movie stars." In that the war and often the Resistance experience informed nearly every early neorealist film and that they all condemned Nazism and Fascism, the

---

"Processo in parocchia," *Il Mondo*, January 24, 1956. In 1950 *Il Popolo* also found merit in Fabbri's *Inquisizione*: "Ha avuto successo 'Inquisizione,'" *Il Popolo*, February 15, 1950.

70. Gian Piero Brunetta, *The History of Italian Cinema: A Guide to Italian Film from Its Origins to the Twenty-first Century*, trans. Jeremy Parzen (Princeton, N.J.: Princeton University Press, 2003), 111.

71. Raffaello Lavagna, "Necessita 'dello spettacolo?" *OR*, October 4, 1953.

72. Albino Galletto, "I giudizi morali sui film," *Rivista del cinematografo*, February 1950.

73. Pierre Sorlin, *Italian National Cinema 1896–1996* (London: Routledge, 1996), 87. Sorlin cautioned, however, that "this may sound exaggerated."

74. Tim Cawkwell, "The Catholic Church in *Il bidone*: Salvation or Swindle?," in *Italy on Screen: National Identity and Italian Imaginary*, ed. Lucy Bolton and Christina Siggers Manson (Oxford: Peter Lang, 2010), 70–71. Daniela Treveri Gennari and Marco Vanelli convincingly emphasize the extent of Catholic-leftist collaboration in their "Did Neorealism Start in a Church? Catholicism, Cinema and the Case of Mario Soldati's *Chi è Dio?*," *New Review of Film and Television Studies* 8, no. 2 (June 2010).

left laid a claim on them. The movement's first rustlings came, paradoxically, during the Fascist era, particularly with Visconti's *Ossessione*. It blossomed, however, after the Liberation with Roberto Rossellini's powerful *Roma, città aperta* and *Paisà*, Visconti's *Terra trema*, and Vittorio De Sica's *Sciuscià* and *Ladri di biciclette*, works that brought a global prestige to Italian cinema.[75]

By far most Catholics initially wanted nothing to do with neorealism, although some may have chafed at the idea that the genre excluded them or relegated them to second-class artistic status. As usual, they blamed the Communists even beyond the end of neorealism's heyday in the early 1950s. "The PCI's policy toward film," wrote the *Popolo* in 1957, "has until now been imbued by a very narrow and closed dogmatism, a dogmatism, naturally, *ad personam*." It was a world in which the artist's beliefs classified him or her "in one of two camps, as a friend or an enemy."[76] Marcello Vazio probably expressed the majority Catholic view in the *Rivista del cinematografo*. There, with some political reservations, he advocated a film industry purge, urging suspect directors, critics, and actors to resettle in the Balkans.[77] The DC cultural activist Gabriele Semeraro, on another occasion, found fault with *Ladri di biciclette* when he asked on the chamber floor why a man would consider theft as the only remedy for poverty.[78] Perhaps the most famous example of political suspicions concerned Vittorio De Sica's *Umberto D*, which Andreotti famously criticized in the DC review *Libertas*. He appreciated the director's refusal of PCI membership and applauded his rejection of the USSR's Stalin Prize for his work. However, in the film's depiction of a retired, impoverished, and desperate government clerk, *Umberto D* not only raised the suicide taboo but performed a "disservice to [the] fatherland" in that it was so depressing and lacked "any principle, of either religious, or even human solidarity." It failed, furthermore, to recognize the "progressive social legislation" that Italy had accomplished. That De Sica was such an internationally acclaimed man of the arts, in fact, made things worse—people everywhere would want to see the movie

75. An enormous literature exists on neorealism. An excellent introduction in English, focusing on "Rome Open City," "Paisà," and "Bicycle Thieves," is Christopher Wagstaff, *Italian Neorealist Cinema: An Aesthetic Approach* (Toronto, Buffalo, and London: University of Toronto Press, 2007).

76. Tomaso Subini, *La Doppia vita di 'Francesco Giullare di Dio," Giulio Andreotti, Felix Morlion e Roberto Rossellini* (Milan: Lampi di stampa, 2011), 38; P. V., "Crisi della critica marxista," *Il Popolo*, February 28, 1957.

77. Subini, *La Doppia vita*, 40–41.

78. McCraw, "Political Sponsorship of the Arts," 203–4.

and its sad portrayal of Italy—and its acclaim in foreign festivals must have irked the DC.[79]

Yet some Catholics applauded neorealism, its honest portrayals of real people, for instance, something that the Belgian Dominican and critic Felix Morlion insisted was crucial in making a "Catholic film."[80] In 1948, he even claimed that Catholics coined the term "neorealist school." One of the principal Catholic figures in Italy's film world, Morlion possessed an intriguing past. After founding a Catholic version of the Anti-Comintern in Lisbon, during the war he developed a close relationship with don Sturzo and worked with William Donovan and the American Secret Service. After arriving in Italy in 1944 and aided by Andreotti, who apparently had a brief run as the Dominican's secretary, Morlion achieved a "celebrity" status as the founder in 1947 of Rome's International University of the Social Sciences "*Pro Deo*," which housed a cinema institute, and later as U.S. Ambassador Clare Boothe Luce's confessor.[81] He landed as a juror for the 1948 Venice *Biennale*, but the pontiff had a hand in removing him for 1949 after a photo surfaced that showed the Dominican enjoying, maybe a bit too much, a glance at Anna Magnani's low-cut gown.[82] Another Catholic intellectual, Angelo Solmi, was a critic and writer who hailed neorealism from its early "Rossellinian" visions in *Roma, città aperta* to De Sica's work and cited *La Terra trema* as a neorealist masterpiece.[83] Although more cautious, and despite his criticism of *Umberto D*, Andreotti might also be counted in this camp, announcing in the film review of *Bianco e nero* that while some

79. Giulio Andreotti, "Piaghe sociali e necessità di redenzione," *Libertas*, no.7, February 28, 1952, reprinted in Alfredo Baldi, *Lo sguardo punito: Film censurati 1947–1962* (Rome: Bulzoni, 1994), 147–50; with De Sica's tongue-in-cheek reply (150–51). In 1948 Giovanni Battista Montini also complained to Andreotti of film's portrayal of priests as "lazy or greedy or grotesque or idiotic"; Subini, *La Doppia vita*, 46–47.

80. Felix Morlion, "Esiste un film cattolico?," *Squilli fuori classe*, November 19, 1950.

81. Tag Gallagher, *The Adventures of Roberto Rossellini* (New York: Da Capo, 1998), 268. The claim was made in the June 1948 issue of *Bianco e nero*. The article has been reprinted and translated into English in *Springtime in Italy: A Reader on Neo-Realism*, ed., trans. David Overbey (Hamden, Conn.: Archon, 1978), 115–24. On Morlion, see Subini, *La Doppia vita*, 23–25; and David Alvarez, *Spies in the Vatican: Espionage and Intrigue from Napoleon to the Holocaust* (Lawrence: University Press of Kansas, 2002), 253–57.

82. Subini, *La Doppia vita*, 168–75. For 1950, Andreotti unsuccessfully tried to slip Morlion's name in his list of jury nominees. Morlion continued to attend "incognito."

83. Angelo Solmi, *Cinema, Specchio del tempo: Una storia del cinema in rapporto al costume* (Brescia: La Scuola, 1963), 167–69. More praise for neorealism can be found in the *Quotidiano*, where one article on the dignity of women ("Alcune risposte all'Inchiesta svolta dalla Gioventù femminile" of February 11, 1950) noted that, as "filthy" as it was, Giuseppe De Santis's 1949 film *Riso amaro* might be recommended as a serious and honest examination of the mistreatment of female workers in the rice fields. See also "Prof. A. Morlion," "Filosofia del neorealismo," *Squilli Fuori Classe*, March 18, 1951, and Pierantonio Bertè's "La Critica e il neorealismo," *Il Quotidiano*, February 24, 1950.

of the "neoveristic cinematographic school" might alienate Catholics, they had to reckon with it.[84]

Some Catholics, moreover, were determined to carve for themselves a stake in neorealist filmmaking. One option led to the creation of two production companies, Orbis and Universalia. The success of *Pastor Angelicus* inspired Gedda and Fabbri to develop Orbis during the Nazi occupation of Rome. After the liberation, in December 1944, Orbis SpA incorporated and in 1945 produced De Sica's *La porta del cielo* and a short by Mario Soldati and Fabbri, *Chi è Dio?* Ambition led to overextension, however, and the quick demise of Orbis. The two entrepreneurs immediately joined with the art director Salvo D'Angelo and the editor of *Osservatore Romano*, Giuseppe Dalla Torre, to replace it with a second company, Universalia, in the spring of 1946. Sometimes referred to as Orbis-Universalia, this business proved more successful and produced until 1950. It formally went out of business in 1958. It scored a huge early hit with *Fabiola*, about the early Christian saint, and produced *Daniele Cortis*, based on Antonio Fogazzaro's novel of a Catholic politician, that starred Winston Churchill's daughter, Sarah. Universalia's real coup, however, came with its production of Visconti's *La Terra trema*, which won the International prize at the 1948 Venice Film Festival, part of the *Biennale*. The tale of a poor family's struggle in the then humble Sicilian fishing village of Aci Trezza, it had been intended by Visconti as the first part of a PCI propaganda trilogy.[85] Carlo Trabucco in *Il Popolo*, however, argued that the film's exposition of Italian poverty was, indeed, "a noble aim" with which no one could find fault, and he compared it to Robert Flaherty's great Irish documentary *The Man of Aran*. Communist critics, he proposed, had only twisted the film's message and forced it to conform to their agenda.[86]

84. Elena Dagrada, "A Triple Alliance for a Catholic Neorealism: Roberto Rossellini according to Felix Morlion, Giulio Andreotti, and Gian Luigi Rondi," in *Moralizing Cinema: Film, Catholicism and Power*, ed. Daniela Treveri Gennari and Daniel Biltereyst, 117–18; Subini, *La Doppia vita*, 43–44.

85. Emilio Lonero and Aldo Anziano, *La Storia della Orbis-Universalia: Cattolici e neorealismo* (Turin: Effatà, 2004), particularly 121–23 regarding "La terra trema." See also Dario Edoardo Viganò, "The Roman Catholic Church, Cinema and the 'Culture of Dialogue': Italian Catholics and the Movies after the Second World War," in Treveri Gennari and Biltereyst, *Moralizing Cinema*, 39–40. On "*Chi è Dio?*," see Treveri Gennari and Vanelli, "Did Neorealism Start in a Church? Catholicism, Cinema and the Case of Mario Soldati's *Chi è Dio?*" Another important Universalia film was Alessandro Blasetti's 1950 *Prima comunione*, for which Cesare Zavattini worked on the script; Daniela Treveri Gennari, "Catholicism and Neorealism: Zavattini's Contribution to Universalia-Produced *Prima Comunione* (Blasetti, 1950)," in *Beyond Catholicism: Heresy, Mysticism, and Apocalypse in Italian Culture*, ed. Fabrizio De Donno and Simon Gilson (New York: Palgrave, 2014).

86. Carlo Trabucco, "La terra trema," *Il Popolo*, June 11, 1950. See also Falconi, *La Chiesa e le organizzazioni cattoliche in Italia 1945–55*, Chapter 10, "Il cinema religioso," 261–95.

Some, like Andreotti and Morlion, considered another option and felt that Catholics might better secure their place in neorealist film if they could identify and maybe collaborate with a well-known director. Together with the critic Gian Luigi Rondi, they formed what the film scholar Elena Dagrada called a "Triple Alliance for Catholic Neorealism" in a search for the Catholic artist.[87] Despite *La Terra trema*, the trio would not find it in Visconti, an anticlerical and pronounced Communist, someone whom Andreotti contemptuously dismissed as the "little snob."[88] Rather, they discovered Roberto Rossellini, whose film *Roma, città aperta* contained a memorable figure in Aldo Fabrizi's portrayal of Don Pietro Pellegrini, a self-sacrificing hero who died before a Fascist firing squad at the end of the film. The director, in fact, could not allow the "good" Italian troops to shoot the beloved priest, so, when given the order, they aimed wild or shot into the ground, forcing the "bad" Nazi to commit the vile deed himself. Rossellini followed *Open City* with *Paisà*, another work containing positive Catholic elements. Out of the studio, he even identified himself as a Christian Democrat, claiming to be a party member and even attending some meetings. Andreotti believed him.[89] Prospects were bright until complications emerged when Rossellini started work on his next film, *Stromboli*, starring the international diva Ingrid Bergman, who abandoned Hollywood to work in the neorealist hothouse. Morlion came aboard to touch up the script's second draft and make it more Catholic, so much so that the Italian title was altered to *Stromboli, Terra di Dio* (*Stromboli, God's Earth*). But behind the movie camera Rossellini launched an adulterous love affair with Bergman, sending him to Austria for a divorce from his long-jilted wife while Bergman divorced by proxy in Mexico. Word got around, and a fuming Cardinal Ruffini wrote to De Gasperi that if, indeed, the director had joined the DC, "he should have been expelled from the Party." The scandal not only gained the lovers worldwide press attention, mostly scorn, but also a son. Rondi learned of the child during the casting for Rossellini's next film. "Maybe it would be good that we talked," the director confessed to the critic. *Stromboli's* release and future work, he said, proceeded nicely, but, "after a long pause, and in a voice more and more embarrassed," Rossellini admitted that "for a few months Ingrid has been expecting a

87. Dagrada, "A Triple Alliance for a Catholic Neorealism," and Subini, "The Failed Project of a Catholic Neorealism," 114–34 and 173–85; see also Subini, *La Doppia vita*, 28–31.

88. Clericuzio, *Tennesee Williams in Italy*, 87.

89. Subini, *La Doppia vita*, 27–28.

baby . . . and I don't know if we'll be able to marry before it's born."[90] The union took place in May of 1950; Robertino was delivered in February.

Plagued by the Bergman controversy and countless rewrites, *Stromboli* fared poorly at the box office. Undaunted, the Catholics and Rossellini pressed on with another film, *Francesco, Giullare di Dio* (*Francis, God's Jester*, sometimes titled *The Flowers of Saint Francis*), which was shot between January and June of 1950. With more input from Morlion and another Dominican, Antonio Lisandrini, the film had the gritty neorealist look, with Francis and his followers sloshing around a rainy and muddy Umbria. These were simple, some would say ridiculous, medieval brothers, totally enthralled with and wonderfully elevated by God's love. The film was released in September of the Holy Year and, along with *Stromboli, Terra di Dio*, entered at the Venice Film Festival. Neither won, although Andreotti helped the cause by placing Rondi on the prize committee. *Francesco, Giullare di Dio* also triggered a huge debate and, in the words of one writer, "never has a film with such lousy grosses—less than $13,000 in Italy—spawned such controversy." One film historian called it "one of the biggest disasters of the postwar era." Some disagreed with Rossellini's vision of Francis as a "fool for Christ" and charged that he had turned the saint into an idiot. In Paris even the Nuncio Angelo Roncalli "put his hand on Roberto's arm and said, '*Poverino, poverino*, you don't know what you've done.'" On the other hand, critics, including many Catholics, adored the film and agreed with Aldo Palazzeschi in *Epoca*, who wrote that, exiting the theater, "you realize that you have walked along the mysterious cutting edge of poetry as along a razor."[91] Over ten years later, at the Second Vatican Council, the Holy See exhibited the film to eight hundred prelates and church officials, who greeted it with warm applause.[92]

In 1950, the *Osservatore*'s Pietro Regnoli regretted that commercial interests and the movie industry's desire to appeal to the broadest markets had edged out *Francesco, Giullare di Dio* at the Venice Festival. Nevertheless, he concluded that, along with Alessandro Blasetti's *Prima Co-*

90. Subini, *La Doppia vita*, 57–58 and 151–54 on the name change. On Bergman's pregnancy, Subini quoted a later piece by Rondi: "Rossellini e Bergman," *Nuova antologia* 138, no. 2226 (April–June, 2003). On Bergman in Italy, see William Bruce Johnson, *Miracles and Sacrilege: Roberto Rossellini, the Church and Film Censorship in Hollywood* (Toronto: University of Toronto Press, 2008), 264–69; Gallagher, *Adventures of Roberto Rossellini*, 353–58.

91. Dagrada, "Triple Alliance for a Catholic Neorealism," 114–34, and Subini, "Failed Project of a Catholic Neorealism," 173–85; Subini, *La Doppia vita*, 43–49; Brunetta, *History of Italian Cinema*, 134.

92. Viganò, "Roman Catholic Church, Cinema and the 'Culture of Dialogue,'" 36.

munione and Leonide Moguy's *Domani è troppo tardi*, which won the prize for best Italian film, *Francesco, Giullare di Dio* assured everyone that on moral balance the nation could hold its head high. Such praise came only a few months after the Rossellini divorce flap at the Turin Appellate Court, and Catholic publications struggled to separate the scandal from the film. Along with the aforementioned *Osservatore* piece, the *Quotidiano* hailed Rossellini's opus as "enchanted and touching" and recalled the critical success of *Stromboli*, praising Ingrid Bergman with no mention of scandal.[93] Morlion and Andreotti defended the director, both in print and on the floor of Parliament, where Andreotti argued that an artist's work must be considered apart from his personal life. That Bergman and Rossellini chose not to abort Robertino certainly also registered with Catholics as a good sign, one in which at least the prospect of new life might carry the couple closer to God. Morlion, no less, in a letter to Joseph Breen, head of the U.S. Legion of Decency, applauded Bergman's "courage in accepting the responsibility of motherhood."[94]

One historian concluded, however, that the courtship dance with Rossellini was the "failed project of Catholic neorealism," and it failed because many Catholics simply could not stomach him and his flouting of their morality. His accomplishments of *Roma, città aperta*, and *Paisà*, and his cooperation with *Stromboli, Terra di Dio* and *Francesco, Giullare di Dio*, could not erase the stain of Ingrid Bergman. The director did not help his cause when he made a two-episode film called *L'Amore* that contained the blasphemous "The Miracle," written by Rossellini and Federico Fellini, who also played a tramp who convinces a simple peasant (Anna Magnani) that he is St. Joseph. He seduces her; she discovers soon that she is with child, and to the derision of the townsfolk, believes it to be the Messiah.[95] Such a toxic plot left little doubt over the CCC's condemnation, although Gavuzzo revealed some difficulty in coming up with one. The producer in this case had refrained from the normal procedure of inviting a priest-reviewer to a private screening, no doubt, Gavuzzo surmised, from fear of certain censure. Instead, if he wished to assess the film, the cleric needed to view it in a public theater, something that

93. Mario Natale, "'*Francesco giullare di Dio*': Un omaggio al Santo degli umili," *Il Quotidiano*, August 27, 1950. The *Osservatore Romano* also noted that Bergman's performance in *Stromboli* was better than the film itself; OR, "Al XI Festival cinematografico," August 30, 1950.

94. Subini, *La Doppia vita*, 57, f. 82.

95. On "*L'Amore*," see Johnson, *Miracles and Sacrilege*, passim; Subini, *La Doppia vita*, 135–48 and 161–63, and Alessandro Carrera, *Fellini's Eternal Rome: Paganism and Christianity in the Films of Federico Fellini* (London and New York: Bloomsbury Academic, 2019), 27–34.

the Rome vicariate forbade. Entered at the 1948 Venice Festival, not even Morlion could vote for *L'Amore*. *Il Popolo*'s Trabucco defended the film, on the other hand, with praise for its "rare beauty," revealing some distance between the hardnosed Catholic Action and the DC's more political outlook. In 1950, furthermore, Rossellini won the *Premio Roma* from the party's Cultural Affairs office with Rondi's help. But the DC had its limits, and De Gasperi arranged that, out of embarrassment, the director not appear at the ceremony. Instead, Andreotti accepted the award. Later, in 1962, the critic Nazareno Fabbretti cleared the air and admitted in the Catholic review *Humanitas* what many others would not, that Rossellini had been a "director for hire" and, quite simply, a nonbeliever. In a 1974 interview, Rossellini finally confirmed Fabbretti's charge. Asked if he believed in God, the director answered simply, "No." To the query, did he believe back in 1950, he repeated, "No." In any God, in any type of mysticism, pressed the interlocutor, to which Rossellini retorted, "No, not at all."[96]

One more try at a Rossellini-Catholic rapprochement yielded *Europa '51*, but neorealism was by then running out of steam. The failed flirt, however, did not stop cineastes from debating film's Catholic element. In 1953, at a conference in Parma, Rondi declared that neorealism depended on a realist perspective that could only be informed by Christianity. Giancarlo Vigorelli agreed and felt that the Parma meeting probably ended "the Communist monopoly on neorealism." As late as 1955 the *Rivista del cinematografo* raised the question of the possibility of a Christian neorealism, although by then it had lost its place in the culture wars, and the Italian cinema transformed into what Lino Micciché described in a political sense as a "cinema of centrism."[97] If films had drifted over toward DC "centrist" views, Catholics generally welcomed the shift. In *Discussione*, for instance, Gian Luigi Rondi cited a 1953 DOXA poll that said that the public clamored for more "dramatic-sentimental" movies, followed "at some distance" by adventure films and comedies.

96. Subini, "Failed Project of a Catholic Neorealism," 179; and Dagrada, "Triple Alliance for a Catholic Neorealism," 120. On the trouble over a CCC review, see IPVI, Pg XII, b. 31, Gavuzzo's "Appunto per l'avv. Veronese," November 10, 1948. On the *Premio Roma* and the Fabbretti article, see Subini, *La Doppia vita*, 55–58, 161–63, and, regarding the 1974 interview, 80. See also Rondi, "Rossellini e Bergman," *Nuova antologia*, 322–23.

97. Emilio Lonero, "Note sul Convegno di Parma"; Giancarlo Vigorelli, "Fine di un Monopolio?," and Gian Luigi Rondi, "Neorealismo, arte cristiana," all in *Rivista del cinematografo*, January 1954; Antonio Covi, "È possibile un neorealismo cristiano?," *Rivista del cinematografo*, April 1955 (Covi was a Jesuit); Lino Micciché, "Dal neorealismo al cinema del centrismo," in Tinazzi, *Il cinema italiano degli anni '50*, 21–32.

But he felt that producers and directors still failed to appreciate this and were determined to force-feed highbrow productions to a public that did not want them. This frustrated filmmakers and caused them to lament condescendingly "that the public doesn't understand what we're giving them."[98]

The Ideal Film

The question remained, what kind of film could be called a *Catholic* work? While he searched for a neo-realist director, Father Morlion wondered whether a "Catholic film" could really exist, and he concluded that if, indeed, it could, it must display not only a moral but also a living, human dialectic.[99] To further such explorations, the Dominican established a "*cineforum*" film discussion group in 1947, the first in Italy, and one that inspired the creation of many more. Perhaps the most important one was attached to the Jesuits' San Fedele cultural center in Milan. A national *cineforum* association, Federazione Italiana dei Cineforum, was founded with its headquarters at Morlion's "Pro Deo" University in Rome. In these *cinefora*, or *Cineclubs*, the censor's heavy hand yielded to a spirit of education with clergy-led discussions, representing the church's positive approach to film as a vehicle for understanding.[100] The church itself strove to provide guidance on the proper approach to cinema, and Pius followed other high-level clerics along that line. Paris's Archbishop Maurice Feltin, for instance, delivered two talks on film morality in 1952; and in March 1953, Florence's Cardinal Elia Dalla Costa wrote on film and family values for the *Osservatore Romano*, arguing against movies that ridiculed Catholic principles like those on married life. "Good people remain bitter or deceived," he wrote, by pictures depicting marriage as something "funny" and harming the moral development of youngsters. A society that prohibits war toys, he wrote, should also keep children from such "irreverence."[101]

98. Gian Luigi Rondi, "I produttori non sanno quali film vuole il pubblico," *Discussione*, February 12, 1956.

99. Felix Morlion, "Esiste un film cattolico?," *Squilli fuori clase*, November 19, 1950. See also Zacheo, "Una lettera socchiusa a Padre Morlion," *Avanti!*, February 7, 1950.

100. Falconi, *La Chiesa e le organizzazioni cattoliche in Italia*, 92. See also De Berti, "Dalla *Vigilanti cura* al film ideale," Eugeni and Viganò, *Attraverso lo schermo*, 92–95; Treveri Gennari, *Post-War Italian Cinema*, 82–84; and Viganò, *Un Cinema ogni campanile: Chiesa e cinema nella diocesi di Milano* (Milan: Editrice Il Castoro, 1997), 102–3.

101. Elia Dalla Costa, "Problemi moderni dell'educazione," *OR*, March 6, 1953; "Anche i vescovi si interessano del cinema," *Noi uomini*, April 30, 1952; Mélisande Leventopoulos, "An Alternative Way

Pius continued on this line with his two lessons on cinema, delivered to filmmakers and distributors in talks on June 21 and October 29, 1955, remembered together as the discourses on "the ideal film." Later, his 1957 encyclical *Miranda prorsus* served as his principal document on the subject. *Il Popolo* considered Pius's first talk as a plea for self-censorship, delivered in St. Peter's Basilica to an estimated ten thousand Italian and foreign cinema representatives, including Giovanni Ponti, Oscar Scalfaro, and Luigi Gedda. The pontiff acknowledged film as "a vehicle so quick to yield good but also to spread evil," a medium of great power, particularly over the poor— for whom it was one of the few available forms of entertainment—and the young—for whom it provided "a quick and attractive means of quenching the natural thirst for knowledge and experience which the age promise[d] them." But film's ability to penetrate and influence the psyche's deep corners, for better or worse, via an actor's simple shrug or glance gave the medium a frightening power that validated state intervention to protect "the civic and moral heritage of peoples and families." In a more positive sense, Pius urged filmmakers to consider three questions regarding the "ideal film"—its impact on spectators, its treatment of the subject, and its effect on the whole community. Leaving the last two points for another talk, the pope charged film to respect the "dignity and nobility" of the spectator and appreciate his or her special place in God's order. This required the delivery of a good artistic product, one that satisfied the audience's legitimate wishes and dreams. At this point Pius added parenthetically that "the unjust and the amoral do not come into the question here," and later, that lapses "into vulgarity or unseemly sensationalism" were to be avoided. Censorship, he continued, was a reasonable option to defend a people's civil and moral heritage, although the industry should have a say in its application.[102]

---

of Moralizing Cinema: Father Flipo's Remedy for the Catholic Church's Propaganda Failure in France (1945–1962)," in Treveri Gennari and Biltereyst, *Moralizing Cinema*, 106–7.

102. On the *film ideale*, see Treveri Gennari, *Post-War Italian Cinema*, 23–27. She writes that the two speeches were "sophisticated" and "compelling"; "Il Papa indica agli uomini del cinema l'importanza e le responsabilità del loro compito," *Il Popolo*, June 22, 1955; "Provvide indicazioni e norme del Sommo Pontefice a quanti partecipano al 'mondo cinematográfico," *OR*, June 22, 1955. See also Mariagrazia Fanchi, "The 'Ideal Film,' On the Transformation of the Italian Catholic Film and Media Policy in the 1950s and 1960s," in Treveri Gennari and Biltereyst, *Moralizing Cinema*, 221–36. Also in the audience for the first talk were the directors, Alessandro Blasetti and Luigi Comencini, and the actors Paolo Stoppa, Alberto Sordi, and Dawn Addams. *Avanti!*'s piece on this first talk was respectful and noted that the actresses dressed in "simple [and] modest outfits"; "Pio XII esorta i cineasti a moralizzare la produzione," *Avanti!*, June 22, 1955. See also Pierre d'André, "Il Senso del peccato," *Rivista del Cinematografo*, March 1958, 78–80. On *Miranda prorsus*, see note 102.

In October, Pius resumed with his second discourse on the ideal film before an eclectic gathering that spilled in from two international conferences and included Gedda, the DC cultural activist Gabriele Semeraro, Sophia Loren, and De Sica, whom *Il Popolo* happily captured on page one rendering homage to the Holy Father.[103] The pontiff urged that cinema not ignore religion, which might be easily worked into scripts, particularly in treatments of evil, "of pride, excessive ambition, lust for power, greed, infidelity, injustice, [and] debauchery." Returning to his three issues, along with the spectator, the ideal film next considered the product, itself, its "specific goodness, its proper worth." Starting with "instructional films," Pius noted that the science documentary, in its revelation of "the infinite superabundance of the perfection and beauty of nature's Creator," could reach the "ideal" status. More of a problem, however, the "action" or "plot-film" ran the moral gamut. It could be a religious work that, handled properly, might illustrate Divine presence in mortal lives; and since most believed in him, "nothing, then, is more natural and more suitable than for due account to be taken of this in films." A good plot-film need not be some overt hagiography or life of Christ, then, but rather a simple and honest acknowledgment of the holy, "a word on God, a thought directed towards Him, a sigh of confidence in Him, an appeal for divine help." The ideal film, furthermore, did not deny the role of evil and the bad choices that people make, since, after all, one could locate similar tales throughout the Bible. Apologies for sin, nonetheless, or its glorification, were obviously out of the question. Finally, the pontiff's third aspect of the "ideal film" concerned its relationship to the community, beginning with the family. Many works unfortunately belittled the "vast treasury of good that the family can dispense." The ideal film depicted the proper family, starting with the father, "a man, endowed with a strong character, who does his duty, who dares and struggles, who knows also how to endure and wait, how to act manfully and firmly, and at the same time maintain and prove an unshakeable fidelity, sincere conjugal love and the constant solicitude of a father; again, of a woman, in the worthiest and noblest sense of the word, wife and mother of stainless conduct, open-minded, capable within and without the family, and at the same time devoted to home and its intimacy, because she knows how to find there all her happiness;

103. "Il Papa indica nel 'film ideale' un efficace strumento di elevazione," *Il Popolo*, October 29, 1955.

and again, of children, respectful to their parents, earnest in their ideals, serious in searching for the better things, always lively and jovial, but at the same time obliging, generous, intrepid." Pius concluded with brief discussions on the state, which like the family was a natural institution, and on the church, which rested "on the positive foundation of the Redeemer." As such, while one should approach the state with respect, the church transcended "the very possibilities of human instruments of expression." If mentioned in a film, it should receive absolute reverence.[104]

Two years after his "ideal film" teachings, on September 8, 1957, Pius issued his encyclical on the "communications field," *Miranda prorsus*. The document paid homage to Pius XI's 1936 *Vigilanti cura* on motion pictures but expanded it to consider radio and television. The technological advances made over the past twenty-one years inspired, with great opportunities to educate and spread the word of God, while at the same time it threatened to "disfigure [men's minds] with dark shadows, disgrace them with perversity, and expose them to unrestrained passions." That danger started with innocent children who needed the protection of clergy, Catholic Action, and Christian educators. The media needed restraint in "the sweet yoke of the law of Christ," and Pius entrusted the public authorities "bound, beyond all doubt, to oversee carefully these new means of communication." Both the 1936 and the 1957 encyclicals expressed an admiration for the American Catholic Legion of Decency as a model for film censorship, and in 1948 Pius established a Pontifical Commission for the Study and Ecclesiastical Evaluation of Films on Religious or Moral Subjects. He placed it under Bishop Martin John O'Connor, a native of Scranton, Pennsylvania, and rector of the North American College. The bishop remained at the helm when, in January 1952, it became the Pontifical Commission for Cinema, and he stayed there until his retirement in 1971.[105]

104. The two discourses can be found at www.vatican.va/holy_father/pius_xii/apost_exhortations/documents/hf_p-xii_exh_25101955_ideal-film_en.html (accessed November 13, 2019), and Viganò, *Cinema e Chiesa: I documenti del magistero* (Turin: Effatà Editrice, 2002), 74–104; De Berti, "Dalla *Vigilanti cura* al film ideale" and Viganò, "Il cinema di Pio XII," both in Eugeni and Viganò, *Attraverso lo schermo*.

105. *Miranda Prorsus*, in Claudia Carlen, IHM, *The Papal Encyclicals* (Wilmington, N.C.: McGrath, 1981), 347–64. It can also be seen through "Papal Encyclicals Online," at https://www.papalencyclicals.net/pius12/p12miran.htm and through the Vatican website at http://w2.vatican.va/content/pius-xii/en/encyclicals/documents/hf_p-xii_enc_08091957_miranda-prorsus.html (both accessed November 13, 2019). See also Giovanni Paolucci, "Gli Atti del symposium per lo studio della 'Miranda Prorsus,'" *Rivista del Cinematografo*, August 1959, 258–59. On the Legion of Decency, see Frank Walsh, *Sin and Censorship: The Catholic Church and the Motion Picture Industry* (New Haven, Conn.: Yale University Press,

The Hollywood Factor

Coming from the world leader, American films in particular posed many challenges, and Italian Catholic responses to them revealed much about the type of movies that they preferred or disdained. One can, moreover, read an impulse by Catholics to control their own films, to filter what the faithful should see for their own spiritual health. This aim was both negative and positive in the sense that film was a brave new tool for evangelization. Like Hollywood and Washington, Rome also exported culture and ideas. If America's cinema industry sent forth missionaries of the American way of life, it was pitted against a very seasoned and knowledgeable contender in Rome. Catholics had little positive to say about Hollywood, the capital of narcissism and vice, where so many young actresses met their downfall in search of the "Buick Eldorado" and where the stars confessed not to priests but to psychiatrists. One critic wrote that an American's "daily bread consists of statistics, psychoanalysis and spam." The *Rivista del cinematografo* discussed the American movie industry's obsession with "Freud's condemned theories" and its export in the art of Eugene O'Neill, Tennessee Williams, William Faulkner, and Ernest Hemingway.[106] U.S. productions often presented a vapid fascination with sex, with narcissistically irresponsible attitudes on marriage and the family. They were too quick to promote war and violence; they wallowed in the star system and the cult of *divismo*; and they often expressed ambivalent, unorthodox, or strange visions of Christianity.[107]

1996); Gregory Black, *The Catholic Crusade against the Movies, 1940–1975* (New York: Cambridge University Press, 1997); and Una M. Cadegan, "Guardians of Democracy or Cultural Storm Troopers? American Catholics and the Control of Popular Media, 1934–1966," *Catholic Historical Review* 87, no. 2 (April 2001): 252–82. Commentary on *Miranda Prorsus* from the Catholic press includes Salvatore Canals, "L'Enciclica 'Miranda Prorsus,'" *Rivista del cinematografo*, December 1957, 335–37; Antonio Petrucci, "Il Symposium per lo studio della 'Miranda Prorsus,'" *Rivista del cinematografo*, May 1958; and "Cinema, radio e TV in una Lettera Enciclica del Sommo Pontefice" and "Le moderne techniche audiovisive al servizio della verità e del bene," both in *Il Popolo*, September 12, 1957. For a brief historical sketch of the Pontifical Commission, see http://www.vatican.va/roman_curia/pontifical_councils/pccs/documents/rc_pc_pccs_pro_14101999_en.html (accessed November 13, 2019). It is today known as the Pontifical Council for Social Communications.

106. "Commenti d'arte" columns, *OR*, February 15, 1950, and May 6, 1951; A. L. M., "Hollywood in pericolo," *Rivista del Cinematografo*, May 1950; Francesco Dorigo, "Psicanalisi e complessi nel cinema," *Rivista del Cinematografo*, July–August 1957; Bruno P. F. Vanrooij, "Italy: Sexuality, Morality and Public Authority," in *Sexual Cultures in Europe: National Histories*, ed. Franz X. Eder, Leslie A. Hall, and Gert Hekma (Manchester: Manchester University Press, 1999), 130. On the Hollywood challenge more generally, see David W. Ellwood, *Hollywood in Europa: Industria, politica, pubblico del cinema 1945–1960* (Firenze: La Casa Usher, 1991).

107. Regarding DC reservations on *divismo*, see "I guai del divismo," *Il Popolo*, January 5, 1957; "La crisi del nostro cinema," *Il Popolo*, January 9, 1957; and Ferrucci Visconti, "La Fabbrica dei sogni," *Rivista del Cinematografo*, April 1959.

For many, the to and fro of movie stars, artists, and socialites from the United States, with occasional well-publicized marriages, revealed the cutting edge of Americanization. "The patricians, unfortunately," wrote the neo-Fascist journalist Mario Tedeschi, "like the plebeians, concerned themselves with ever-closer relations with the foreign victors," and throughout the era Rome witnessed a string of nuptials between Italian and American celebrities. Henry Fonda and Gary Cooper, for instance, both married well-connected Italian women in the 1950s. One of the more scandalous unions took place in April 1947 between the twice-divorced Admiral Ellery Stone and the aristocratic but much younger Renata Arborio Mella di Sant'Elia. As Allied commissioner in Italy at the war's end, Stone found that his military prestige and his peacetime status as a leading figure in the electronics industry helped him to secure church permission to marry again. His first wife, a Catholic, had died *after* their divorce, and his second wife, despite their split, was a Protestant. The bride's uncle, a *monsignore*, lamented, "An Arborio Mella who marries a divorced man . . . how did we get to this point?"[108]

The movie prince Tyrone Power helped to atone for the gaffe in 1949 when he and Linda Christian staged the wedding of the year at the Church of Santa Francesca Romana in the Imperial Forum, a bizarre mix of Hollywood kitsch and Italian Catholicism. The crowd of fans and onlookers required extra police on horseback and motorcycles and, according to Christian, caused the closure of neighborhood schools. "Tyrone's arrival at the church created a near-hysteria," she wrote, "and as my car arrived I heard the incessant roar of: 'Ty-ro-ne—*Magnifico!*' Even the motorcycle-police escort made no impression on the wall of humanity . . . 'Linda, Linda!' the crowds were screaming as they threw themselves in a solid block against the phalanx of policemen struggling to lead us to the steps of Santa Francesca Romana. People seemed to be everywhere, even hanging from the walls outside." Power's divorce, however, from the French actress Annabella only became effective that day (fortunately the two had only been joined in a civil ceremony), while the church was rearranged with "effect" in mind by such events as the replacement of the modest organ with a more majestic one. After the Nuptial Mass, the couple drove to St. Peter's for an audience with Pope Pius, "frail and ethereal," as Christian remembered him. "I am happy that you have chosen my country for your wedding," he told the newlyweds, "the people

108. Mario Tedeschi, *Roma democristiana* (Milan: Longanesi, 1956), 30.

love you here." The discussion turned to business, and the pontiff told Power, "Your industry can do a lot of good in the world, but it can also give bad examples. You must show everyone the meaning of a Catholic marriage."[109] Linda and Tyrone brought two daughters into the world before they divorced in 1956.

Eight years later, *Miranda prorsus* admonished actors to remember their special status and to serve as "an example of virtue in . . . private life." Hollywood seemed to reject that message, and the Catholic press disdainfully looked there for tales of wrecked marriages and adulterous affairs. The *Rivista del Clero* cited case after case of frivolous American movies stars' divorces, those of Ava Gardner and Frank Sinatra, for example, or Lana Turner and Lex Barker.[110] In a Catholic Action women's review, Sergio De Marchis contrasted socially conscious Italian neorealism with U.S. films mired in greed and divorce. "If a large part of American society," he wrote, "firmly believes in divorce as an ideal solution for family troubles, it is because Hollywood is not stingy in supplying kilometers and kilometers of film based on this subject . . . films that present . . . the moral validity of divorce . . . [whereas] in Italy the best neorealist films present a common message for the audience; [that] our people thirsts for . . . social justice." The films elevated Italian consciousness, whereas the materialist and hedonist American cinema contributed to the destruction of the family.[111] In the *Rivista del cinematografo*, Andreotti also raised the "moral danger" of American films that reduced divorce into some blasé occurrence among the smart set . . . "an insult [*vilipendio*] of sugar-coating divorced couples who retained their flair and remained 'good friends' with no consideration for the fate of the children." Impressionable Italians might watch these films and confuse their devil-may-care messages, he concluded with the almost obligatory Cold War paean to the greatness of the United States.[112] One U.S. film

109. Linda Christian, *Linda: My Own Story* (New York: Crown, 1962), 115–17. That busy day also included a meeting with Prime Minister De Gasperi. Stephen Gundle discussed the wedding in his essay "Memory and Identity: Popular Culture in Post-War Italy," in *Italy since 1945*, ed. Patrick McCarthy (Oxford: Oxford University Press, 2000), 190–92; his "Hollywood Glamour and Mass Consumption in Postwar Italy," *Journal of Cold War Studies* 4, no. 3 (2002): 101; and his *Death and the Dolce Vita: The Dark Side of Rome in the 1950s* (Edinburgh: Canongate, 2011), 64–67.

110. Francesco Olgiati, "Turlupinature divorziste," *Rivista del clero italiano*, September 1957.

111. Sergio De Marchis, "Capire il film," *Squilli fuori classe*," March 15, 1953.

112. Giulio Andreotti, "Censura e censure," *Rivista del cinematografico*, December 1952. He also criticized U.S. productions that sentimentalized gangsters—another frequent Catholic theme. The *Rivista del Clero* also cited case after case of frivolous divorces among star couples like Ava Gardner and Frank Sinatra, Lana Turner and Lex Barker, and others; Olgiati, "Turlupinature divorziste," *Rivista del clero italiano*, September 1957.

that suffered a Catholic scolding was William Dieterle's *September Affair*, wherein Joseph Cotten, intoxicated by Italy's charms, abandons his family in America to join his new love, an artist played by Joan Fontaine. The *Osservatore Romano*'s correspondent Piero Regnoli took offense precisely in that "Italy" had become an embarrassing character in the drama, the very cause of Fontaine's and Cotten's illicit love affair.[113]

Catholics also expressed clear distaste for American war movies, partly because distribution agreements determined that, having been banned by the Fascists, they now appeared on Italian screens and continued to do so well into the 1950s. "Enough with the war!" wrote Regnoli in 1950. Propaganda against the Japanese enemy particularly got on the Vatican's nerves. Another article from 1950 declared, "Enough with Japan!," lamenting the evil depiction of a nation of so many "heroic spirits," both pagan and Catholic. But the "anachronistic propaganda" continued, and the *Osservatore* unleashed another volley with "Again the Japanese" in 1951.[114] Condescending portrayals of Italians in movies such as 1947's *Story of G.I. Joe*, which contrasted savvy U.S. soldiers to ignorant Campanian peasants who could not understand the purpose for a phonograph record, also irked Catholics.[115] Regnoli's snub of *A Bell for Adano* was particularly scathing. "It would be easy just to let out a belch," he wrote in the *Osservatore Romano*, "but let's be more analytical." John Hersey's original story, he admitted, was "really very sweet, but Henry King has ruined its transfer to film."[116] In 1957 the *Osservatore* called for an end to war movies and suggested a "peace movie" genre.[117]

Catholics loathed one particularly American cocktail that blended movie stars with a cold, modern, and phony culture. The *Rivista del cinematografo*, for instance, sneered at Christmas layouts in Hollywood fan magazines, well-orchestrated by public relations managers but obviously fake with their gigantic Christmas trees "surrounded by . . . the most celebrated actors and their photogenic children." Their silly texts placed verses of Holy Scripture next to Dorothy Lamour's holiday recipes, while "wishes for peace and goodwill [sat] alongside descriptions of Ann Blythe's furniture." In the hope that it not appear petty, the *Rivista* reminded readers that "even in America there are simply normal people." A rare

113. "Al XI Festival cinematografico di Venezia," *OR*, August 28–29, 1950.
114. "Commenti d'arte" columns, *OR*, October 27 and November 1, 1950, and January 15–16, 1951.
115. "Commenti d'arte," *OR*, April 27 and 29, 1951.
116. Piero Regnoli, "Una Campana per Adano," *OR*, May 26, 1950.
117. "Il cinema e la pace," *OR*, August 23, 1957.

laudatory article concerned Gary Cooper's Catholic funeral in 1961, at which the outpouring of affection for the star contrasted with Hollywood's normal "squalid" funeral and revealed a spiritual "thirst" in that cultural desert.[118]

Catholics also attacked Hollywood for wrong-headed depictions of Christianity. The *Rivista del cinematografo*, for instance, hated one of the most iconic religious pictures of the era, 1959's *Ben-Hur*, which as a "commercial" and "industrial" work should never have won the Academy Award.[119] Earlier, in a series of articles dealing with Catholic film, Father Morlion condemned C. B. De Mille's *The Sign of the Cross* as a monstrosity and a fraud. At first glance, it looked like a Catholic film of heroic early Christians, but that just provided a cover. The real story concerned the "handsome and sporty" Marco, a "refashioned cowboy," who tried to seduce the "diaphanous" Marcia, who was in reality "a New England bigot." When Marco realized the futility of the seduction, he let the lions kill him in the arena in order to reunite with her in heaven, a ridiculous conversion story. Giorgio Nardoni in *Noi uomini* agreed and condemned *The Sign of the Cross* as "tremendously pagan and obscene."[120] On occasion Italian Catholic critics might split over a "religious" film, as in the case of Henry Koster's 1949 *Come to the Stable*, with Loretta Young and Celeste Holm as two young get-up-and-go nuns. The *Osservatore Romano* and the *Rivista del cinematografo* both liked it, but a Catholic Action girls' review had some reservations. Two "ultramodern sisters," it stated, racing around in a jeep, riding bicycles down dusty roads, and playing tennis was all right up to a point; but the whole idea seemed "subtly dangerous."[121]

Suspicion toward certain Hollywood productions, of course, did not match treatment of Soviet work, most of which Catholics ignored or that obtained minimal distribution in Italy. Hollywood, furthermore, occasionally made a movie that all Catholics could enjoy. Family pictures generally received good press. Ugo Sciascia liked *It's a Wonderful Life*,

118. "Panoramica," *Rivista del cinematografo*, January 1953; on the American style of Christmas, see "Gli Americani schiavi delle feste di natale," *Discussione*, December 25, 1960; on the Cooper funeral, see Eliseo Sgarbossa, "Una pausa nei cantieri della celluloide," *Orizzonti*, May 28, 1961.

119. Sergio Orlandi, "Ben Hur, Strage di Oscar," *Rivista del Cinematografo*, April 1960.

120. Felix Morlion, "Esiste un film cattolico?," *Squilli fuori classe*, November 19, 1950; Giorgio Nardoni, "Quattro passi," *Noi uomini*, June 15, 1950.

121. "Commenti d'arte," *OR*, March 3, 1950; "Un grande film di Henry Koster," *Rivista del cinematografo*, March 1950; "Vocazioni sullo schermo," *A Colloquio con le giovani*, April 9, 1950. Clare Booth Luce wrote the screenplay for *Come to the Stable*, much before she became the U.S. ambassador to Italy. Loretta Young also added weight to the film as one of Hollywood's leading Catholics.

Mrs. Minniver, and *Mrs. Parkington* because of their exaltation of the family. But he soured on 1944's *The Fighting Sullivans*, the true story of five Iowa brothers who died in the Pacific War when a Japanese submarine sank their ship. Although the Sullivans were Catholics, and the Vatican even expressed condolences to the family, Sciascia dismissed the picture because it exploited the horrible loss for the purpose of war propaganda.[122] More agreeable was the output from Walt Disney, whom *Noi uomini* hailed as "the only director who has always interested himself in childrens' cinema" and whom the Ente dello spettacolo feted on a visit.[123] His 1937 *Snow White* and 1950's *Cinderella* received praise, but some expressed reservations over 1951's *Alice in Wonderland*. It "doesn't entirely convince us," stated the *Osservatore Romano*, in that Disney might have become too much the technical perfectionist, leaving behind the humor and "delicate poetry" of *Snow White*. The Vatican paper followed up on this in a 1959 article that, while still positive, felt his productions had become more industrial and business-like.[124] The favorite American production may have been Delbert Mann's and Paddy Chayefsky's *Marty* of 1955 and released in Italy as *Marty, vita di un timido* (*Marty, Life of a Shy Guy*). The tale of an Italo-American butcher's search for a girlfriend and his long-suffering *mamma*, the film received effusive praise from Rondi in the *Rivista del cinematografo*, who wrote that its strength was precisely because it did not gleam with slick Hollywood brilliance. Rather, Ernest Borgnine's portrayal and those of the other actors "showed the faces of real people and how they live, feel and enjoy each other in a climate that . . . profoundly permeates Christian values." Although *Marty* was not entered at Venice, it took four Academy Awards for Best Picture, Best Director, Best Actor, and Best Screenplay; and at Cannes it won not only the Best Picture and the *Palme d'or*, but the Catholic OCIC prize.[125]

Despite resevations over U.S. films, however, as Italy moved away from neo-realism, a less gritty and more "American" look took over its productions, and the 1950s became known as the era of *commedia all'ita-*

122. Ugo Sciascia, "La Famiglia nel film," *Squilli Fuori classe*, February 24, 1952.

123. Giovanni Lucciolli, "Una favola a venezia, *Noi uomini*, August 31, 1950. An early aborted attempt at collaboration between the CCC and the Disney studio is discussed in Treveri Gennari and Vanelli, "Did Neorealism Start in a church? Catholicism, Cinema and the Case of Mario Soldati's *Chi è Dio?*," 202.

124. "Commenti d'arte," *OR*, December 23, 1950; "Disney e le favole," in "Commenti d'arte," *OR*, April 20, 1951; "Omaggio a Disney," in "Commenti d'arte," *OR*, August 3, 1951; "Disney soppesato a Venezia," *OR*, August 23, 1951; "Hollywood e i festivals," in "Commenti d'arte, *OR*, September 14, 1951; "Il Ciclo di Walt Disney," *OR*, March 11, 1959.

125. Gian Luigi Rondi, "L'Ottavo Festival," *Rivista del cinematografo*, June 1955.

liana. A more relaxed and playful style took hold identified with many younger entertainers such as Sophia Loren, Gina Lollobrigida, and Alberto Sordi.[126] Italian cinema's own greatest box office success of the 1950s was a comedy, the film version of Guareschi's *The Little World of don Camillo*. Released in 1952, it enjoyed high praise from the Catholic press. The prime mover in getting the novel to the screen, Felix Morlion ran into some snags in his search for a director. Many shied away from getting involved in its Cold War issues and in possibly upsetting the PCI. De Sica, for example, rejected the offer and announced, "I have been accused several times of being a communist. To prove that I am not a communist, I do not need to do an evidently anti-communist film." Morlion eventually found his director in France with Julien Duvivier, who, ironically, preferred his own colleagues and kept the Dominican from working on the script.[127]

Options

Beyond the Rossellini experiment and ambivalence over the American model, Catholics considered other ways to address and tame cinema. Venues for action included discussions of a Latin film alliance, the Venice Festival, control of parish cinemas, and censorship. Many found attractive the idea of Latin or Catholic cooperation. Catholics are inclined to extend their hands across frontiers. The church, of course, thinks globally. Catholic Action situates itself in a worldwide family of sister organizations. Christian Democracy, moreover, found some of its first footing not in Italy but at an 1867 meeting at Malines, Belgium. In 1956, Christian Democratic Parties held a conference in Paris to form their own organization, a Christian Democratic International.[128] Italians interested in promoting Catholic culture, therefore, looked abroad in search of friends and allies, explorations that focused on Latin Catho-

126. Peter Bondanella, *A History of Italian Cinema* (New York: Continuum, 2009), chapter 7. Quoting a number of filmmakers, Bondanella notes, however, that, besides the lightness, a "current of social malaise" distinguished much of the *commedia all'italiana*, "quite courageously and more successfully than overtly ideological films"; Rondi, "L'Ottavo Festival," 181.

127. Subini, "The Failed Project of a Catholic Neorealism," 179; see also Subini, *La Doppia vita*, 50–52.

128. Roberto Papini, *L'Internazionale DC: La cooperazione tra I partiti democratici cristiani dal 1925 al 1985* (Milan: Franco Angeli 1986), 280–83. Peter Kent discussed the idea of a Latin Bloc from France's perspective in his *The Lonely Cold War of Pope Pius XII: The Roman Catholic Church and the Division of Europe, 1943–1950* (Montreal and Kingston: McGill-Queens University Press, 2002), 166. David W. Ellwood also wrote about the concept of a Latin alliance during the reign of Leo XIII; Ellwood, *The Shock of America: Europe and the Challenge of the Century* (New York: Oxford University Press, 2012), 28–29.

lic countries. Based in Belgium, OCIC advocated these searches, as did the DC government. Indeed, for the *Rivista del cinematografo*, the Interior Ministry's Oscar Scalfaro emphasized the need for international coordination, starting with France, Germany, and Spain.[129]

The *Osservatore*'s Piero Regnoli in April 1951 advanced the idea of a "Latin" film bloc to counter those of the "extreme west" and "extreme east." Under Stalin's thumb, the East produced more heavy-handed political fare designed "for a mind [*psicologia*] less complex than ours." The American-dominated West, however, used subtler methods, particularly the star system (*divismo*), to promote democratic ideals. Regnoli claimed that the Italians, French, Spanish, and, oddly, Austrians were less susceptible than others to such propaganda.[130] Perhaps Italy could meet the challenge through some kind of film alliance with other Catholic nations. In spring 1952, the *Rivista del cinematografo* showed that the Italians were not alone in considering this, reprinting a French piece that urged Catholics to strike while the iron was hot. Italy's successful film industry, moreover, destined it to lead Europe, creating a marvelous opportunity for the Latin nations (Italy, France, and Spain). "We predict," stated the article, "a real Latin alliance . . . as solid and as important as the Anglo-Saxon one."[131] Creation of the Common Market, of six predominantly Catholic nations added to many hopes for a new bloc. After the 1957 Treaty of Rome gave life to the community, European film concerns met in Munich and Milan to discuss their next step and the problem of myriad film laws. They took a timid step forward in early 1958, but, as one disappointed observer wrote in the *Rivista del cinematografo*, a lasting arrangement was a long way off. "While one can say that a real common market for film is near, there are still many problems to solve, first among them is the moral one, otherwise the cinema will lose a great opportunity."[132]

An unsigned *Osservatore* article from July 1951 threw Latin America into the mix. The continent was "particularly interesting" because of a growing international significance of Argentina and Brazil and the continent's "Latin and Catholic traditions." In union with European Catho-

129. Oscar Scalfaro, "Problemi e aspetti della cinematografia per ragazzi," *Rivista del Cinematografo*, March 1955.

130. Piero Regnoli, "Commenti d'arte," *OR*, April 6, 1951.

131. "Per una cinematografia latina," *Rivista del cinematografo*, March 1952.

132. Eitel Monaco, "Cinema Europeo," *Rivista del cinematografo*, May 1957; Vittorio Bruno, "Lento a partire il MCC," *Rivista del cinematografo*, April 1958; Antonio Petrucci, "In Attesa della legge," *Rivista del cinematografo*, December 1958.

lics, Latin Americans would add to a resurgent "anti-materialist" force and present an alternative to the Washington or Moscow paths.[133] Such an event would also, according to another article, solve problems of different national traditions like Sweden's or Japan's.[134] Consequently, the Catholic press devoted much effort to covering and applauding the Punta del Este film festival in Uruguay and Spain's very Catholic one in Valladolid.[135] President Giovanni Gronchi emphasized the possibilities in much-publicized trips to Brazil in 1958 and to Uruguay, Argentina, and Peru in 1961.

Promoting Latin partnerships, however, offered some risk. While Italy and France developed a lively business of co-productions, creating 250 between 1950 and 1958, France also famously exported more cinematic filth than any other nation. And while the CCC judged 38 percent of Italian films either "inadvisable" or "excluded" in 1953, the corresponding French figure was 59 percent.[136] One Catholic optimist, however, found something positive in Paris' crackdown on *Tarzan* comics. Even French censors, he wrote, "maybe can teach us something."[137] In hopes for a Latin alliance, Iberia's dictatorships presented other issues. As in the debacle of Operation Sturzo, images of Antonio Salazar and, especially, Francisco Franco continued to float around somewhere in Catholic minds. In the case of film, however, the press devoted much favorable mention to the two regimes. While Italy banned children under sixteen from certain films, *Noi uomini* applauded a Portuguese measure that prohibited entrance to cinemas for all children between six and thirteen except for special screenings. "Apparently," wrote the review, "in Portugal the financial interests of the producers, distributors and theater owners do not win over the child's sacrosanct right to grow up free from evil."[138] Franco's Spain churned out reels and reels of religious movies and gave Italian Catholics one of their favorites, *Marcelino, pan y vino*, released in Italy as *Marcellino, pane e vino*. Gian Luigi Rondi's afore-

133. "Verso il tramonto dell'era materialista?," *OR*, July 28, 1951.

134. Andre Ruszkowski, "Il II Festival di Cinema di Punta del Este," *Rivista del cinematografo*, March 1952.

135. See also "Cronache minori del Festival del Punta del Este," *Rivista del cinematografo*, March 1952; "Il I Festival si concluse felicemente con il trionfo dei prodotti italiani," *OR*, February 17, 1952; "Nuove speranze per un cinema migliore," *Rivista del cinematografo*, July 1959.

136. "Crisi morale del cinema," *Rivista del cinematografo*, January 1954. The *Rivista* later reported that the French Catholic hierarchy lamented the disgrace of their nation's film industry, something "ben noto in Italia"; Antonio Petrucci, "I furbi tacciono," *Rivista del cinematografo*, April 1960.

137. "Cinema e morale," *Noi uomini*, February 15, 1954; Luciano Tavazza, "Il fumetto ieri ed oggi," in Azione cattolica italiana, *Stampa, cinema, radio per ragazzi*, 32.

138. "Film Buoni per i nostri ragazzi," *Noi uomini*, January 15, 1952.

mentioned discussion of the 1953 DOXA poll and what Italians wanted in film criticized the survey in that it did not consider those "rare" spiritual pleasures such as this Spanish import, one of the hits of the 1955 season and winner of a "special" OCIC prize at Cannes, alongside its award for *Marty*. The disarming story of a waif who holds conversations with his Lord in a Spanish monastery, redolent of Guareschi's don Camillo, this beloved tale required only a small cast of a boy and twelve monks—eliminating any need of Hollywood-style star power, according to Rondi.[139]

Along with dreams of a Latin film alliance, Catholics saw another opportunity in the Venice *Biennale*. One of the most prestigious art shows in the world, it presented postwar Italy a marvelous chance to recapture a lofty cultural presence, and the DC was determined to control it. Andreotti in particular worked toward this from the start. Party influence was facilitated in the figure of Giovanni Ponti, a Christian Democrat who had been active in the Resistance, served as Venice's first postwar mayor, and was a prime mover in the festival's resurrection. As mayor, Ponti assumed the chair of the *Biennale*'s governing Ente and prepared for the 1948 exhibition. He met a bump in the road in March 1946 when a Communist, Giovanni Battista (Giobatta) Gianquinto, replaced him as mayor, and should have replaced him at the Ente as well, but Rome opted to maintain Ponti with the title Extraordinary Commissioner (*commissiario straordinario*). Ponti thus ran the *Biennale* through 1954 (he was reelected mayor in 1951 but resigned for health reasons) and then again in what has been described as a coup, from 1957 until 1960, a year before his death in 1961.[140]

Much of the *Biennale* was devoted to the international cinema festival, an annual event that began its postwar life in 1946, ahead of the rest of the show. The film festival was a plum of cultural politics and

139. Gian Luigi Rondi, "I produttori non sanno quali film vuole il pubblico," *Discussione*, February 12, 1956. In 1958 Totò issued his own spin on the Spanish film *Totò e Marcellino*, which received a favorable judgment from the CCC; "*Totò e Marcellino*," *Segnalazioni* 43, no. 20 (1958).

140. Nancy Jachec, *Politics and Painting at the Venice Biennale, 1948–1964: Italy and the Idea of Europe* (Manchester: Manchester University Press, 2007), 5–7, 36–63; Jahec, "Anti-Communism at Home, Europeanism Abroad: Italian Cultural Policy at the Venice Biennale," *Contemporary European History* 14, no. 2 (May 2005): 201–2. Subini records Andreotti's interest in controlling the *Biennale* in *La Doppia vita*, 128–29. Fanfani called Ponti back to head the *Biennale* in 1957 after the failed tenure of the Liberal Massimo Alesi. A DC pro-memoria described the choice of Alesi as "a mistake" and "a misfortune." His tenure corresponded to the first Segni coalition cabinet, which was in coalition with the Liberals. On Alesi, see Vincenzo Gagliardi/Fanfani (with pro-memoria), August 9, 1957, in IS Sec. Pol. Fanfani, Sc. 79, f. 18.

invariably provoked discussion, envy, and dissent. What lessons might be drawn, for instance, from the entries that had no connections to the Catholic world? Should there be a Catholic presence in the film festival, and, if so, what form should it take? Catholic activists never doubted the answer, and the Cold War's secularist or anticlerical struggles often targeted the contest.[141] The *Biennale* nonetheless flowered under Ponti and his director of the film festival, Andreotti's man—Antonio Petrucci, who, upon the end of his tenure, penned an open letter to his boss. Five years before, he wrote, he had arrived at an operation in shambles, without an organization, archives, or even a projector. But thanks in great measure to "cordial and intelligent support" from Andreotti and his assistant at the General Directorate of Entertainment, Nicola De Pirro, Ponti revived the gala "to the glory of Italy and Venice." Petrucci's last festival was 1953. Ottavio Croze, who ran it under the Fascists, replaced him briefly until the job went to Luigi Floris Ammannati in 1956.[142] Despite Catholics at the top, however, they rarely engaged in ham-fisted control. Venice was just too big and too international to risk embarrassments, or as one scholar wrote, "a safe haven for artists and critics, light years away from the general public and from censorship."[143]

The church itself possessed one potent weapon in the war for good films: its network of parish cinemas that it owned and operated, the *sale parrocchiali*. By 1951, Italy had 3,500 of them out of a total of 8,138 cinemas. At the end of the decade, Parliament determined that the respective numbers had risen to 4,500 out of 12,366. Limited to showing only films included in the first two categories—"for everyone" and "for everyone with reservations"—they provided young people with a wholesome alternative to the works found in many private movie houses. Thus, about one-third of Italy's movie theaters were automatically censored to the church's liking. A student of the Italian cinema cautioned, however, that parish cinemas tended to be concentrated in the smaller towns; they hosted smaller audiences than did the private halls, and

141. See, for example, Tommaso Riccardi, "In crisi a Venezia il cinema marxista," *Discussione*, September 19, 1954.

142. "Cinque anni di vita operosa della vita della Mostra di Venezia," *Il Popolo*, January 1, 1954. In a 1960 article, *Avanti!* insisted that Petrucci had almost ruined the festival. Cannes had surpassed it, and the hoteliers on the Lido were calling for help; "Il direttore della Mostra del cinema di Venezia non piaceva più ai monsignori," *Avanti!*, February 28, 1960. On Andreotti and De Pirro, see Subini, *La Doppia vita*, 34.

143. Clericuzio, *Tennesee Williams in Italy*, 87.

since they provided movies only four nights of the week, they probably failed to live up to their potential, especially in the more competitive large cities. Since the church considered them as vehicles for evangelism and not profit, tickets at parish cinemas cost less, often much less, than those at first-run movie houses. Their box-office profits, therefore, constituted only 5 percent of the national total. As early as 1956, however, Catholics saw that despite a general expansion in numbers, something was happening. Television was hurting the precarious situation of many little parish cinemas.[144]

Interested in the health of the *sale parrocchiali*, in the spring of 1957 the Spettacolo undersecretary Brusasca polled the priests in Piedmont who operated them. Regulations, taxes, and the cost of renting the films constituted a universal plague; but above all the encroaching box, TV, had become, as one respondent stated, "the tomb of the parish cinema." Attendance had already plummeted; most fall-offs stood at around 30 or 35 percent, but some declines reached 75 percent. One priest from Asti put it another way—that he counted 4,650 spectators in 1955 and 2,563 in 1956. With television's challenge barely a few years old, some theaters had already closed. Regarding TV audience preferences, Mike Bongiorno's hugely popular game show *Lascia o raddoppia* consistently topped the list, followed often by another, *Telematch*. One highbrow cleric from Mondovì followed it with "the occasional opera." "The laborer," he wrote, "loves above all to relax from his day's work with calming and happy shows." To Brusasca's question on films with best customer responses, most answered generically—Westerns, historical dramas, detective and adventure stories, and musicals. As for suggestions, some wanted to restrict television, limiting broadcast times, for example, particularly on Sundays; or as one cleric wrote, regulate it like the state railways. Most called for more religious and wholesome works such as, specifically in at least one case, *Marcellino, pane e vino*. Another, from Tortona, preferred "beautiful films" like the neorealist *Roma, città aperta*, or *The Count of Montecristo*, although, he added, "cut the kisses and the overly prominent bust lines."[145] Lorenzo Quaglietti's study of parish cinemas

144. McCraw, "Political Sponsorship of the Arts," 192–95. See also Viganò, "Roman Catholic Church, Cinema and the 'Culture of Dialogue,'" 38–40; Mariagrazia Fanchi, "Non censurare, ma educare! L'esercizio cinematografico cattolico e il suo progetto cultural e sociale," in Eugeni and Viganò, *Attraverso lo schermo*, 103–13; Treveri Gennari, *Post-War Italian Cinema*, 68–71; and Wagstaff, *Italian Neorealist Cinema*, 419. Also on the parish cinemas, see the contributions in Gianfranco Gori and Stefano Pivato, eds., *Bianco e nero: Gli anni del cinema di parrocchia* (Rimini: Maggioli Editore, 1981).

145. The responses to Brusasca's poll are found in AS Casale Monferrato, Fondo Brusasca, M90 f. 174.

shows that some of the priests' gripes and fears might have been overblown in that a generous tax arrangement had already been settled with them in 1946. To nip in the bud the problem of declining attendance, moreover, in 1957 the government reached an agreement wherein one of every three new movie theaters would be a parish cinema. But the issue remained of filling the seats.[146]

Film censorship was another tool at the government's disposal. An ancient weapon, the church wielded it in the *Index Librorum Prohibitorum*, which it unveiled as a Tridentine reform in the sixteenth century. In modern times, the liberal state applied censorship, as did its successor, the Fascist regime. Italy's first serious stab at film censorship came well before the Lateran Pacts, when the so-called Facta (or Giolitti) Law of May 1, 1913 (number 785) gave the Interior Ministry veto power, withholding the *nulla osta* over anything shown onscreen. To receive the *nulla osta* meant that the movie had passed muster and could be exhibited in theaters. Denial meant that the work had, according to Article 1, caused offenses "to morality, to *buon costume*, public decency and private citizens; national decorum and public order; and to the prestige of institutions and public authorities." Also subject to censorship were "grim, repugnant or cruel scenes, including those harmful to animals; frightful crimes or suicides; and in general perverse actions which might teach criminal acts, rouse spirits [*turbare gli animi*] or incite evil."[147] The Fascists incorporated the liberal guidelines in their own censorship decree of September 24, 1923 (number 3287), adding only a prohibition on works inciting class division. Emboldened later by the example of National Socialist control of the German arts, Mussolini in 1935 took a more activist road and created the Ministry of Popular Culture. With his son-in-law Galeazzo Ciano at the helm, the government pledged intervention "to the fullest with precise aims in the cinema field." The regime, however, continued to rely on the old rubrics, broadening them with only a few new Fascist ideas such as purging regional dialects and banning Jews from the industry.[148]

146. Lorenzo Quaglietti, "Quell'anche fu la questione dei 'parrocchiali,'" in Gori and Pivato, *Bianco e nero*, 45.

147. Ernesto G. Laura, ed., *La censura cinematografica: Idee, esperienze, documenti* (Rome: Edizioni Bianco e Nero, 1961), 6–7; Baldi, *Lo sguardo punito: Film censurati 1947–1962*, 13. Laura incorrectly listed the Facta law as 1914. See also McCraw, "Political Sponsorship of the Arts," 164–70. McCraw refers to the measure as the "Giolitti Law," since Giovanni Giolitti was prime minister when it was enacted. McCraw also states that the guidelines came with a decree of May 31, 1914, no. 532, issued by the then Minister of the Interior Antonio Salandra.

148. McCraw, "Political Sponsorship of the Arts," 175–76; RDL 3287 of September 24, 1925, and RDL 2125 of November 30, 1939; Quaglietti, *Storia economico-politica*, 13–33.

A good portion of Fascist measures was nationalist and meant to stem the flood of U.S. films into the Italian market, an arrangement ended by defeat in 1943 and Anglo-American military occupation. After Allied troops entered Rome in June 1944, a temporary Commission for Cinema worked out of the American embassy. Along with embassy personnel, it included figures from the U.S. Psychological Warfare Branch (PWB), Francesco Libonati, the undersecretary of state for Press, Entertainment (*spettacolo*), and Tourism, and representatives from industry and labor. Its task, to craft a new film law, resulted in DLL, October 5, 1945 (number 678), a measure that complied with Allied wishes and lifted all restrictions on the import of U.S. films except for those blocked by the military censor. The floodgates thus opened, and Italy was inundated with American productions, prompting the historian Lorenzo Quaglietti to conclude that the law unleashed an era of unbridled capitalism and scandal. By 1951, of 524 films shown on the Italian circuit, 328 were American.[149]

After the war and the Anglo-American departure, for cinema matters De Gasperi and his successors relied on the Undersecretariat for spettacolo, which, as stated previously, existed in many forms within the prime minister's office. The Genoese Christian Democrat Paolo Cappa served as undersecretary from July of 1946 until May 31, 1947, when De Gasperi formed his third government. During his tenure the Constituent Assembly approved the so-called Cappa Law on May 16, 1947 (number 379), which resurrected Mussolini's 1923 censorship framework. Although it had been enacted in the Fascist era, one scholar concluded that the 1923 measure did not give too much pause after the war. Mussolini's coalition cabinet had not even been a year old, and the dictatorship was a while off. The 1923 measure, furthermore, drew most of its provisions from the earlier 1913 liberal one; and its first line, that "the production of films is free," must have worked a consoling effect on many. Neither De Gasperi nor the "leaders of the Italian left as well as of the center and right accepted without protest this retention of censorship powers." In Constituent debates, furthermore, Aldo Moro, who managed the draft of the charter's freedom of expression clause, Article 21, tried to allay fears over the continuation of censorship by emphasizing its focus on

149. Quaglietti, *Storia economico-politica*, 40, 43–44, 48–51. An example of Allied censorship in practice can be found in Victoria Belco, *War, Massacre and Recovery in Central Italy, 1943–1948* (Toronto: University of Toronto Press, 2010,) 112–13.

buon costume and not on politics.[150] Some of Moro's guarantees rang hollow, however, in that this was largely an old-fashioned "cut" and "ban" censorship. Timing also played a role when, in the two weeks between the measure of May 16 and his departure on May 31, Cappa took the controversial opportunity to select as head of the General Directorate of Entertainment Nicola De Pirro, who had been the *Duce*'s Director General for the Theater. Upon his arrival, De Pirro raised eyebrows by promptly staffing the new agency with many Fascist-era colleagues.[151] The heat intensified when De Gasperi named as Cappa's successor Giulio Andreotti, who would hold the office until August 1953. Devoted to Pius XII and a social traditionalist much to the liking of Catholic Action, Andreotti was another FUCI alumnus who fought in the front ranks against immorality. He subsequently occupied other government chairs, including that of prime minister seven times; but for decades to come Andreotti would serve as a lightning rod in Italian cultural politics and an *eminence grise* in Italy's film world.[152]

The DC followed the Cappa Law with a coupling of the "little law" (*leggina*) of July 1949 and the so-called Andreotti Law of December 29, 1949 (number 958) that again affirmed the framework from the 1923 measure and established an incentive system of state subsidies to producers based on ticket sales that fostered the production of broadly popular films instead of highbrow ones. The Cappa and Andreotti acts created a two-tiered system of financial bonuses for filmmakers, funding for which came from a "dubbing tax" on imports. Those Italian motion pictures cleared with the *nulla osta* received another 10 percent of their box-office profits, while those judged by the government to be of special "artistic and cultural value" took an additional 8 percent. An ANICA survey revealed much about how the whole thing worked. It found that in 1951–52, 5 percent of mainstream films failed to get the *nulla osta*; 15 percent received just the 10 percent award, while 80 percent took the full 18. As Daniela Treveri Gennari concluded, this system trumped the Constitution's Article 21. But it also had an Achille's heel. The censor-

150. McCraw, "Political Sponsorship of the Arts," 177–82, 196–200.

151. Argentieri, *La censura nel cinema italiano*, 67–69; on De Pirro's Fascist past, see also Bonsaver, *Censorship and Literature in Fascist Italy*, and Rhiannon Evangelista, "The Particular Kindness of Friends: Ex-Fascists, Clientelage and the Transition to Democracy in Italy, 1945–1960," *Modern Italy* 20, no. 4 (2015): 411–12.

152. In 1957 the Communist *Vie Nuove* reported that, four years after he left the undersecretariat, Andreotti remained an "object of deference, mixed with fear, in many corners of the cineaste world"; "Cosa vuole sua eccellenza?," *Vie nuove*, May 11, 1957. This article can been found at IS Archivio Andreotti Cinema, b. 1073, f. 6.1.

ship panels, or commissions, that processed the films were subject to personal whims and a lack of hard-and-fast guidelines. Therefore, one panel might interpret things very differently from another. Some minor modifications waited down the road, but the Cappa and Andreotti Laws, combining prevention and incentive, set the agenda for the state's dealings with film at least until 1962.[153]

From the Palazzo Balestra in the via Veneto, the Central Film Office (Ufficio centrale per la cinematografia) within the Undersecretariat's general directorate vetted the films. Here was where one found the real work of the censorship and its weaknesses: as Gavuzzo told Andreotti in a 1949 report, the process was too bureaucratic.[154] The Ufficio centrale strongly urged that production companies submit screenplays to it ahead of time before proceeding with the project, a sensible step where a preliminary judgment could save a lot of trouble later on. Visconti and Suso Cecchi D'Amico, for example, apparently chose to make *Senso* in 1954 after such a warning aborted their plan to adapt Erich von Stroheim's silent classic *The Wedding March*.[155] After the opening cautionary steps, the First Level Censor Commission (Commissione di censura di primo grado) undertook the task of the initial, and hopefully final, formal review of the film. This panel awarded the *nulla osta* or withheld it, stipulating cuts to be made before the movie could be released. An appeals panel, Commissione di secondo grado, heard challenges in case of a contested decision. The Cappa Law directed that a representative of the Ufficio centrale chair the First Level Censor Commission, joined

153. Daniela Treveri Gennari, *Post-War Italian Cinema*, 39–55. Her point on Article 21 is found on page 52; McCraw, "Political Sponsorship of the Arts," 33–37. Like the "Cappa Law," the "Andreotti Law" had a forerunner in the Fascist "Alfieri Law" of 1938, named for Dino Alfieri, Mussolini's minister of popular culture. Andreotti's defense of the industry in the face of American encroachment has earned him a certain, perhaps grudging, respect from earlier detractors. An April 1951 agreement between ANICA and the American Motion Picture Export Association, for instance, reflected his thinking and launched a string of measures limiting the amount of U.S. films that could be shown on Italian screens. Another cinema law in 1956 further reduced U.S. influence by expanding to one hundred hours per quarter the time in which Italian films should be shown on Italian screens. See Treveri Gennari, *Post-War Italian Cinema*, 9; see also Brunetta, *History of Italian Cinema*, 113–15. Employment of a certain number of Italian workers for Italian productions was also mandated, while the Andreotti Law specified jobs for graduates of the government's Experimental Film Center (Centro sperimentale). "This memory of Andreotti, the ogre who sought to destroy neorealism, has endured," wrote Brunetta (*History of Italian Cinema*, 114), "while few remember him as a benevolent figure who made a significant contribution to the protection and renewal of Italian film production."

154. IS Archivio Andreotti, b. 1072, f. 2.3, Gavuzzo/Andreotti, December 19, 1949.

155. Henry Bacon, *Visconti: Visions of Beauty and Decay* (Cambridge: Cambridge University Press, 1998), 60. Bacon notes that the production company, Lux, was reluctant to involve itself in the divorce debate and shied away from the project. Visconti and Cecchi D'Amico then turned to Camillo Boito's story, *Senso*, which they successfully completed as a film. Camillo was the brother of the acclaimed librettist and composer Arrigo Boito.

by a judge and someone from the Interior Ministry. The undersecretary or his proxy chaired the appeals panel and was joined, again, by a judge and an Interior Ministry figure. This arrangement seems to have been malleable in that sometimes a priest or, as the Fascists had stipulated, a father or mother "*di famiglia*" might appear in the mix. The proper composition was endlessly debated and probably improvised on occasion, as in 1959, when the *Rivista del cinematografo* stated that not three but five members comprised each panel. Although final decisions might reveal the nuts and bolts of the deliberations, much happened behind the scenes, with frustrated filmmakers confronting officials at the Palazzo Balestra in tones anywhere from angry to flattering. Some government minister, moreover, an ecclesiastical official, or Gavuzzo's Morality Office might try persuasion, often resulting in confused, uneven, and unfair application of norms that nobody completely understood.[156]

Debates over censorship and the new measures enlivened the press. In a sign of things to come, six months after Andreotti took office, *L'Unità* attacked him in an open letter from many of Italy's leading film directors. Their manifesto expressed an anxiety over "a tendency [that revealed] a return to the Fascist practice of controlling film production." The directors denied that this was an issue of *buon costume*, but "rather of a true and genuine *censura* of an ideological and political nature."[157] Many of the more ardent Catholic culture warriors argued on the other hand that the Andreotti Law did not go far enough and that the government presented a rather milquetoast image. Their opinions surfaced

156. Alberto Anile, *Totò proibito: Storia puntigliosa e grottesca dei rapporti tra il principe De Curtis e la censura* (Turin: Lindau, 2005), 13–16. See also Antonio Petrucci, "Diritti e doveri della libertà," *Rivista del cinematografo*, January 1959. Petrucci lists the constitution of the first level commission as: 1. a "functionary" from the Direzione dello spettacolo; 2. an ordinary judge; 3. a representative from the Interior Ministry; 4. a representative from the Ministry of Public Instruction; and 5. a film critic nominated by the prime minister's office (most likely the undersecretary), from a list submitted by the National Press Federation (Federazione nazionale della stampa). The Appeal Commission consisted of: 1. the undersecretary of the spettacolo; 2. a judge from the Cassation Court; 3. a functionary of the Interior Ministry; 4. a representative from the Ministry of Public Instruction; and 5. a film critic (probably like the other one in the first commission). The Fascist panels as directed by the law of June 24, 1929, number 1103, had nine members, including someone from the Colonial Ministry. On this, see Giovanni Battista Guzzetti, "Il clero e la nuova legge censura," *Rivista del clero italiano*, July 1962. Regarding Gavuzzo, he alerted Andreotti about a film, *Il Cantante sconosciuto*, in 1949. Apparently, the censor had missed a scene where a naked woman steps from a bathtub. Andreotti agreed and reported that the movie received the proper cuts; IPVI, Pg XII, b. 31, "Appunto per s.e. L'Onorevole Andreotti," July 3, 1948; and Andreotti/Gavuzzo, August 2, 1948.

157. McCraw, "Political Sponsorship of the Arts," 201–2; Cesari, *La censura in Italia oggi*, 83–85. Among others, the letter bore the signatures of Michelangelo Antonioni, Alessandro Blasetti, Giuseppe De Santis, Vittorio De Sica, Federico Fellini, Pietro Germi, Alberto Lattuada, Roberto Rossellini, Luchino Visconti, and Luigi Zampa. The Italian text (from *L'Unità* of December 10, 1947) was printed in Domenico Tarantini, *Processo allo spettacolo* (Milan: Edizioni di comunità, 1961), 197–98.

in parliamentary debates from October 1950 over the Interior Ministry budget, wherein some Christian Democrats deplored the lack of controls in defense of morality and *buon costume*. A DC deputy from Verona, Fiorenzo Cimenti, promoted tighter surveillance of film, reminding the assembly that while the Constitution's Article 21 guaranteed freedom of expression, it also prohibited "the publication, performances [*spettacoli*] and all other manifestations contrary to *buon costume*" and that "the law provides adequate measures to prevent and punish [*a prevenire e a reprimere*] transgressions." Cimenti delivered a backhanded compliment in applauding his and Mario Scelba's Christian Democracy for its "defense of the family and healthy education for youth," but, "as a father and as a representative of hundreds of thousands of fathers," he admitted to a certain "bitterness" over society's tendency to "demolish the moral principles assiduously inculcated in the family, and . . . an executive power [that] does not always intervene with timeliness and necessary firmness." He then turned his fire on the lay deputies who labored to remove Christianity from state schools but gave their own children Jesuit educations. When Cimenti cornered one such legislator, he received the advice, "Dear colleague, politics is one thing, fatherhood is another."[158]

In December 1952, Andreotti lamented in an open letter to don Galletto that the censor was stuck between a rock and a hard place. From one side, he argued, criticism came from both Communists and "self-styled *benpensanti*," with their lay vision of an ultimate secular good devoid of "any solid rule of morality or conduct." They condemned censors as "maniacal distributor[s] of fig leafs" or "sadistic" philistines engaged in a war on art. The other side derided censors as "tepid or lax," and Andreotti cited a recent Catholic publication from Varese, dismissing them as "either crooks or idiots." Censorship, moreover, was not simply about low necklines and naked legs; and Andreotti re-posed the question of what needed to be done: "Has the State done enough to assure the moral improvement of cinema?" He praised a recent proposal by two DC deputies, Pia Colini Lombardi and Maria Pia Dal Canton, to facilitate funding for children's films, and finished with a call for a measure to reinforce censorship commissions with "more medical and psychological experts."[159]

158. "L'Ordine morale e l'ordine pubblico nella discussione del Bilancio degli Interni," *OR*, October 21, 1950; *Atti parlamentari*, Legislatura I, Camera dei Deputati, Discussioni—seduta del Ottobre 19, 1950, 22,932–36.

159. Giulio Andreotti, "Censura e censure," *Rivista del cinematografico*, December 1952; regarding

More and more Catholic calls for tougher measures followed the 1953 elections and the fall of De Gasperi. To a Catholic Action crowd in 1953, Gedda insisted that cinema promote God's message and counter Communism's anti-Christian campaign. Representing the administration, Andreotti's successor as undersecretary of the Spettacolo Teodoro Bubbio agreed and offered his full collaboration.[160] Matters came to a head in 1954, when the 1949 Andreotti Law was scheduled to expire and Catholics considered their next move, although the government ended up proroguing the measure. At the DC, in *Discussione*, Arnaldo Forlani announced that the new situation required that the party display its many cultural and social faces and interests, paying particular attention to film.[161] Alongside Fanfani's adoption of the activist "heavy party," moreover, the Marian year intensified focus on film, reflected in a January *Osservatore* assertion that the industry shirked its moral duty and aggravated social ills.[162] The same month, *Iniziativa* announced that, in keeping with Catholic Action's dedication of the year to Christian comportment, 1954 would be devoted "toward a moral entertainment which required more of commitment on the parish and diocesan levels."[163] Toward that end, seminars for teachers of religion would examine questions of "art, entertainment [theater, film, and television], sport and tourism," coming from the premise based on God's plan, that good conduct always beats ignorance.[164] Catholic Action continued to press the DC for more censorship. Gedda's call for as much at a March 1955 conference, for example, was presented as a final motion and endorsed by the vicar general of Rome, Cardinal Clemente Micara. At a Florentine film meeting the following year, don Galletto also advocated for tighter film controls, with similar calls at congresses in Bologna and Genoa at the end of 1956.[165]

Italy's cinematic success, the revenues it provided, and, above all, the eight-hundred million paying customers (probably one billion if one

---

the Andreotti letter, see also "Voci nel deserto," *Rivista del cinematografo*, March 1953, and "Paternalismo e censura," *Cinema nuovo*, February 4, 1953.

160. G. G., "Cinema e television," *Noi uomini*, November 30, 1953.

161. Arnaldo Forlani, "La Propaganda democratica Cristiana," *Discussione*, October 16, 1955.

162. "Sullo schermo e dietro lo schermo," *OR*, January 19, 1954, cited in V. S. "Il passivo morale del cinema costituisce un grave problema sociale," *Il Popolo*, January 20, 1954.

163. "Per un costume cristiano dello spettacolo," *Iniziativa*, January 1954.

164. Luigi Cardini, "Insegnanti di religion a convegno," *OR*, August 19, 1953.

165. "Cronaca di Roma," *OR*, March 21–22, 1955; "Un Congresso di studi sulla cinematografia," *OR*, November 19–20, 1956; "Necessita 'di maggior controllo sulla cinematografia per la gioventù," *OR*, November 22, 1956; "Il convegno sul cinema per la gioventu,'" *OR*, November 24, 1956; and "I requisiti essenziali del film per ragazzi illustrate al Convegno di studi sulla cinematografia," *OR*, December 4, 1956.

counted those who somehow entered the theater without payment) demanded Parliament's attention. The Andreotti legislation still needed to be revised or extended, and, thankfully, the new Spettacolo undersecretary Giuseppe Brusasca announced that the government would introduce a new law soon.[166] Brusasca was wrong: new legislation would be slow in coming. Patchwork measures gave Parliament more time on a new censorship, and a special commission was formed to work it out, but arguments dragged on and on when, in May 1956, Giuseppe Sala, the DC head of the Centro sperimentale film school, blamed the delay on Communist "blackmail"—something made worse by the rising costs of doing business and by the new challenge of television.[167] *Il Popolo* also blamed the Communists in Parliament for blocking progress, citing accusations from Mario Alicata, a member of the special commission, that the PCI's role only became apparent when it was needed for something. Consequently, they linked their opposition with a deal that included easier distribution in Italy for Soviet films.[168] The frustrations of 1956 dragged on into 1957 and through December 1958, when Rondi wondered in *Concretezza* if the new law would ever come. The latest delay ran until the end of the year, he wrote, and then Italy would have no censorship law.[169] More delays came, however, pushing the day of reckoning into the next decade.

Cutting and Banning

L'Unità declared 1954 one of the most difficult years for cinema and censorship.[170] Upon taking office in February, Prime Minister Scelba took a tough approach that reflected Fanfani's desire for a more activist DC. For film, Scelba relied not only on Giovanni Ponti, his minister without portfolio, but also on his undersecretary, Giuseppe Ermini, and on his protégé in the Interior Ministry, Oscar Scalfaro, a rising darling of the culture militants who later took Ermini's position. Ermini came to the office in Fanfani's first cabinet of January–February 1954 and continued under Scelba until September 19, 1955, when he became minister

166. Gian Luigi Rondi, "Cinema e società," *Discussione*, October 30, 1955.

167. "Il comune per lo sviluppo dell'industria cinematografica," *Il Popolo*, May 17, 1956.

168. "Il problema morale sullo schermo," *OR*, January 15, 1956; "Dipende dalle sinistre l'approvazione della legge sulla cinematografia," *Il Popolo*, February 15, 1956.

169. Gian Luigi Rondi, "La legge di censura," *Concretezza*, December 1, 1958.

170. Franco Giraldi, "Personaggi femminili di un anno di cinema," *Unità*, January 6, 1955.

of public instruction. Originally from Frosinone, he was a "fish out of water," it was said, who rarely even went to the movies. As Scelba's assistant before he replaced Ermini, Scalfaro had already been involved in censorship. He came from Novara in Piedmont with a background in Catholic Action, read law at the Catholic University, and became a FUCI activist. He lost his twenty-year-old wife in 1944 during the birth of their daughter. After the war, Scalfaro became a prosecuting attorney until, representing Turin, voters sent him to the *Costituente*. There he launched a political career that culminated with his election to the presidency of the republic in 1994.

In July of 1950, Scalfaro earned a special notoriety and some legendary credentials in the culture wars. During that particularly hot summer month, he and one or two other DC deputies lunched at Chiarina's, a restaurant on the fashionable Via delle vite. At a nearby table sat Edith Mingoni Toussan, a young woman who at one point during the meal took off her *bolerino*, a Spanish-style shawl, exposing her shoulders. The Christian Democrats, offended by the sight, approached the woman, and Scalfaro "ordered" her to cover herself. Toussan told them more than once to mind their own business, and the confrontation escalated into a tumult where, it was said, Scalfaro slapped her in the face. Somebody called the police, and the skirmish ended in front of "a very embarrassed functionary" at the local Trevi police station. Toussan's father and her husband, both military men, challenged Scalfaro to duels, to which he replied that, as a Christian, he did not engage in such things.[171]

Under Scelba, Ermini, and Scalfaro, noted one observer, the government "authorized the banning or ordered the revision of a greater number of films that year than had Andreotti in any of his tenure, and the censorship activity of the *Direzione Generale* reached its height."[172] Government representatives discussed these issues with a group from Parliament led by Gabriele Semeraro, the head of the DC's cultural activities office who complained of spotty and uneven government regulations that led to anxiety among filmmakers and decreased production.[173] By October 1955 the film critic Rondi discussed this sterner government attitude toward film. Back in 1949 he had written, "Cinema was not a se-

171. On the Chiarina restaurant incident, see Anile, *Totò proibito*, 79–81, and "Le spalle della bella signora non avevano l'imprimatur," *Avanti!*, July 22, 1950. As with urban legends like this, some details remain disputed. Anile says that one deputy accompanied Scalfaro, the Socialist paper says two, including Vittoria Titomanlio. Anile believes that the slap was later invented. *Avanti!* did not mention a slap.

172. McCraw, "Political Sponsorship of the Arts," 208; Argentieri, *La censura nel cinema italiano*, 105.

173. R. C., "Il Gruppo parlamentare dello spettacolo," *Rivista del cinematografo*, March 1955.

rious problem"—a thing of "Charlie Chaplin's sadness, some actresses in search of a fortune, of some financier in search of easy money"; and consequently Giulio Andreotti proved to be a man ahead of his time, almost single-handedly pushing his film law through the chamber. Now, however, Rondi concluded that the old laxness was dead.[174]

If censorship panels had problems with a movie, they could either refuse it the *nulla osta* or they could order the producers and directors to make cuts. This second option became much more common, although everyone seemed to have opinions on where to make the cuts. The prefect of Reggio Emilia, for instance, requested a cut in Alberto Lattuada's *La Spiaggia* for a scene in which a traveler offers the Communist *L'Unità* to a priest who indignantly refuses it.[175] Another concerned the 1954 *Adventures of Casanova*, directed by Stefano Vanzina, known as Steno. The film had already passed the censors, but Scalfaro interjected and ruled it "offensive to decency, morality and *buon costume*," mysteriously revoking the *nulla osta*, perhaps, it was said, because of clerical pressure. In the end, Steno accepted certain cuts and modified the title from *The Adventures and Loves of Casanova* to *The Adventures of Casanova*. Scelba stepped in, agreed to the revisions, and overrode Scalfaro.[176] And what could be wrong with Mario Camerini's 1957 *Suor Letizia* starring Anna Magnani as a Neapolitan nun who runs an orphanage, a role for which she won an award at the Venice Film Festival? The censor, however, cut two scenes, one of which concerned a child playing in the sand with the sister. Magnani loses her coif (*cuffia*), revealing her hair and prompting the astonished child to respond, "Hey, you really are a woman!" (*Allora, tu sei proprio una donna!*). Such circumstances revealed the bonds that permeated the Catholic movement. When some Franciscan sisters registered their complaint over the controversial scenes, they went straight to Andreotti, who, despite his new position as finance minister, still maintained a certain gravitas at the film office and assured them of the cuts, particularly concerning the little boy, which he considered "unintentionally vulgar." He expressed regret over the affair but was happy to deal with the concerns of "the good Franciscan sisters."[177]

174. Gian Luigi Rondi, "Cinema e società," *Discussione*, October 30, 1955.

175. Mino Argentieri and Ivano Cipriani, "Censura e autocensura," *Il Ponte* 13, August–September 1957, 1353.

176. ACS, PCM 1955–58, 3-2-12, f. 5999, b. 216, Salvatore Corapi (the lawyer for firms that produced *Casanova*)/Scelba, March 11, 1955.

177. Argentieri and Cipriani, "Censura e autocensura," *Il Ponte* 13, August–September 1957, 1344–45; IS Archivio Andreotti Cinema b. 1072, f. 2.3, Andreotti/"Reverenda Madre," August 4, 1956.

The decade's most celebrated censorship case was arguably that over *Totò e Carolina*. The government's handling of it illustrates a complicated crusade against vice accompanied by doses of personality and politics. Produced by Carlo Ponti and Dino De Laurentis for Lux Pictures, directed by Mario Monicelli, and written by Ennio Flaiano, it starred Antonio De Curtis, universally known as Totò, Italy's greatest comic actor, who portrayed a widowed police officer from the *Buon costume* squad. In the film, a police sweep of prostitutes at the Villa Borghese yields Carolina, a good girl who had been dealt a bad hand in life and contemplates suicide. But the kind-hearted Totò saves and shelters her with fatherly concern. In September 1953 the movie in preparation was denied the *nulla osta* from the commission headed by Annibale Scicluna Sorge, one of De Pirro's ex-Fascists who had come from Malta before the war to serve Mussolini. But Scicluna's ruling did not stop the actors and crew, who proceeded anyway and finished their work in early 1954. On February 17, aware that they were now in trouble, the producers conceded that revisions would be necessary; but on February 22 the Undersecretariat ruled against *Totò e Carolina* and prohibited its circulation as an "offense to morality, to *buon costume* [and] public decency, as well as to the decorum and prestige of functionaries and agents of public security." In short, *Totò e Carolina* floundered in a murky moral and political swamp. In its condemnation, forwarded to and signed by Ermini, the commission referred to the 1923 censorship measure.[178] A back and forth ensued that ultimately resulted in eighty-two cuts to the film, many of which appear absurd. The name was even changed from *Addio Carolina*; Totò's character was also changed, from Callarone to Caccavallo. The censors objected when a band of flag-waving workers in the picture sang the Communist anthem, *Bandiera Rossa* (*Red Banner*), and so it first became the innocuous "Workers' Hymn" ("Inno dei lavoratori") before ending up as the partisan song "Di qua e di là dal Piave" ("Along the Piave"). In another scene a policeman delving for evidence of illicit sex at the Villa Borghese opens and shuts the door of a parked car, muttering an embarrassed "excuse me your Excellency," implying a government minister inside. The line ended up as the more mundane "excuse me sir" (*scusa commendatore*).

178. Cited in Vittorio Boarini, "L'avventura censoria," in *Totò e Carolina*, ed. Tatti Sanguinetti (Ancona: Transeuropa, 1999), 144–46. Ermini reviewed the decision and confirmed it. This was not Totò's first encounter with the censor. His 1951 *Totò e i re di Roma*, for instance, was held up for about a year; Alberto Anile, *I film di Totò (1946–1967): La maschera tradita* (Genoa: Le Manni, 1998), 124–28, 140–45; Anile, "Gli altri Totò tagliati," in *Totò e* Sanguinetti, *Carolina*, 199–201.

Ultimately, the cuts did the trick. *Totò e Carolina* received the *nulla osta* on December 8, 1954, and, while cineastes had already held a few clandestine screenings, the film opened legally on March 8, 1955. In a letter to Scelba, Morlion was glad to see it released, which also nipped in the bud any chances for Communist maneuvering. He reassured the prime minister that the film offended neither the *celere* police nor the church, while the portrayal of a "ridiculous" parish priest caused no problems. Furthermore, he reported, a number of DC leaders, from Fanfani to Scalfaro and Andreotti, had no objections.[179] In November, moreover, the government awarded *Totò e Carolina* the full 18 percent bonus. The last step came in 1958, when Rome allowed its distribution abroad, although by then Lux was in receivership. In his study of the film, Alberto Anile attributes some of the delay to the fact that two more of Ponti's productions, *La romana* and *Mambo*, faced censorship problems at the time. Scelba's excessive concern over the reputation of *his* police might have also held things up. During this long drama, attention bestowed on *Totò e Carolina* certainly fanned the public's interest, and it was marketed accordingly. "After a year of trepidation," ran the text on the movie poster, "the most talked-about film in its original version [*sic*] hits all screens.... After Marilyn Monroe, Jane Russell and Sophia Loren, now Totò has his 'prohibited film.'" Ten years later, and proud of its "eighty-two cuts," the comic declared that *Totò e Carolina* was his best work. In *L'Unità* Ugo Casiraghi mockingly charged that, in mutilating the work the censors surely convinced themselves that they had defused a revolution.[180]

Frustration with confused and erratic Catholic censorship methods frequently surfaced in the opposition press. In February 1956 *Avanti!* polled important artists and intellectuals for their judgments on censorship. Antonio Banfi, a respected Communist philosopher, claimed that one set of government controls operated alongside another vague one operated by the church. The result was an irrational and incoherent mishmash of prizes and subsidies that crippled Italian cinema production from one "once so young, vigorous and audacious—now numb, paralyzed by respectability or by a childish fascination with stars' breasts or clownish snickers." Former Prime Minister Ferruccio Parri added that

179. ACS, PCM 1955–58, 3-2-12, b. 216, f. 193, Morlion/Scelba, December 27, 1954.

180. Alberto Anile, "Due Totò per un celerino," in Sanguinetti, *Totò e Carolina*, 27. The movie poster can be seen on the book's frontispiece. See also Anile, *Totò proibito*, particularly chapter 4; and Ugo Casiraghi, "Totò e Carolina mutilati e invalidi," *Unità*, March 7, 1955. A September 9, 1953, judgment on the film, the Casiraghi article, and other reviews can be found in ACS, MTS (Fondo Ministero del Turismo e dello spettacolo), CF (Lungometraggi) 1798.

the state had "sterilize[d] art" and that "censorship and the police never halted any process of decay, but rather aggravated it and sped it up." Other figures who lent their voices to *Avanti!*'s series included Carlo Levi, Riccardo Bauer, and Guido Calogero, who declared "no censorship of any kind, not religious, not philosophical, not ideological, not political, not photographic, not for shows, not for conduct, in no case, for no reason, not even for emergencies."[181]

Government censorship also continued to confuse and disappoint Catholics. In 1957, Brusasca complained that one review panel, headed by Scicluna, somehow passed a Brigitte Bardot film, *La sposa troppo bella* (released in the United States as *Her Bridal Night*). Bardot's "ample displays of legs and breasts [along with her] marked displays of sensuality" shocked Brusasca, who wondered how the committee did not just ban the movie to children under sixteen. That the same panel then repeated the blunder by approving Dino Risi's *Poveri ma belli* triggered angry letters to Brusasca and to the prime minister, prompting the immediate suspension of Scicluna's committee.[182] Brusasca's action, moreover, may also have been a Catholic slight against De Pirro and his group of ex-Fascist underlings.[183]

Movie Posters

More straightforward was the issue of movie advertisements. The Catholic press targeted offensive advertising, either in racy "coming attractions" that slipped in between otherwise decent films or in posters found around towns and cities. Catholic Action's *Noi uomini* lashed out at the coming attractions in a 1951 piece, while the *Rivista del Clero Italiano* in 1953, citing the Italian Penal Code's Article 528, advocated action against ads that "offend the common sentiment." The faithful, continued the *Rivista* piece, must not simply lament (*mugulare*) and grumble (*borbottare*), but, rather, do something. Indeed, they should emulate Milan, where some had collectively complained and achieved real results, "precise interventions [of] small, documented actions conducted with good human and Christian sense."[184] The *Osservatore Romano* joined in when it

181. "La Censura in Italia," *Avanti!*, February 15, 21, 23, and 25, 1956.

182. AS Casale Monferrato Fondo Brusasca M89, f. 149, Brusasca/De Pirro, March 15, 1957.

183. Argentieri, *La censura nel cinema italiano*, 112–13.

184. "Secondo Noi," *Noi uomini*, February 15, 1951; Carlo Demetrio Faroldi, "Concretezza di metodi nella buona battaglia contro l'immoralità," *Rivista del Clero*, January 1953, 17–18.

announced in 1954 that unlimited press freedoms could unleash a "hellish storm" in the battle for comportment. Real freedom, rather, freed citizens from the pernicious influence of the press (and cinema ads).[185]

Some frustrated militants, anxious that their government was not doing enough, took matters into their own hands. Near Verona, the aforementioned don Mario Gatti lost a November 1950 judgment for ripping down what he saw as obscene movie posters. Upon witnessing parish children ogling the dirty images and hearing their vulgar talk, the priest petitioned the Carabinieri to remove the posters. When he realized that the police would be of no help, don Gatti acted on his own, a bit of boldness that Gavuzzo cited and lionized in his *Guida* and that inspired Giulio Andreotti to compose a sympathetic letter to the priest. Later, in 1954, don Gatti protested yet again to the government, this time to Andreotti, regarding the poster for Alessandro Blassetti's *Too Bad She's Bad* (*Peccato che sia una canaglia*), which was based on an Alberto Moravia story and starred Sophia Loren. His letter illustrated the sentiment that the DC was not doing enough in the battle for morality. "Why," wrote the priest, "aren't the real criminals in the cinema and the press put under arrest? Why doesn't the government do something, or why does it do so little to hold back the nefariousness of modern life?" In Rome no less a figure than Cardinal Alfredo Ottaviani of the Holy Office complained to Gavuzzo, notably rather than to the government's Undersecretariat or the Ministry of the Interior, about the film's lavish attention to Loren's body, urging that something be done "effectively to end these scandals." Others agreed. From the Ente dello spettacolo, don Galletto called for tougher censorship in 1951 and protested in 1957 to Eitel Monaco at ANICA about movie ads in newspapers, urging greater vigilance and obliging him to remind producers and distributors of their responsibilities. Aware of the charge, Undersecretary Brusasca professed full agreement with Galletto but pinned the blame on the judiciary.[186]

To the dismay of Gatti and Galletto, the DC government seemed incapable of regulating movie posters. Things came to a head in 1957 when two particularly repugnant images reached the streets of the Eter-

185. "Voci ed echi," *OR*, August 4, 1954.

186. Gavuzzo, *Guida*, 225, f. 1. The 1954 Gatti protest to Andreotti can be found in David Forgacs and Stephen Gundle, *Mass Culture and Italian Society: From Fascism to the Cold War* (Bloomington: Indiana University Press, 2007), 231; AS Casale Monferrato Fondo Brusasca M89 f.149; Galletto/Monaco (copied to Brusasca), May 13, 1957; and Brusasca/Galletto May 15, 1957. The Ottaviani protest can be found in IPVI, Pg XII, b. 34; Ottaviani/Gavuzzo, March5, 1955 and Gavuzzo/Ottaviani, March 10, 1955; Cesari, *La censura in Italia oggi*, 101.

nal City: advertisements for the Bridget Bardot film *Miss Spogliarello* (or *Miss Striptease*, first released in France as *En effeuillant la marguerite* and in the United States as *Plucking the Daisy*), and Anita Ekberg's *Zarak Khan*. It was said that the pontiff had spotted the offensive art while being driven through the city. Then, in a Lenten message, Pius criticized the government for allowing such filth to pollute Roman streets and pointed to the Lateran Pact obligations to maintain the city's sacred character and to "impede . . . everything that could be in contrast with that character." To the question of whether the government fulfilled that commitment, he concluded, "We are sorry to have to respond no" because of those two "pornographic" movie posters, seven meters wide and three high, that shocked and imperiled the morality of every good Catholic, local or pilgrim.[187] *Il Popolo* applauded the pope's message and regretted the "very sad phenomenon" born in America that now "propagated like a plague," and the paper urged Undersecretary Brusasca to focus more attention on the issue. Nor could the journal resist a rather nasty swipe at Bardot, whose "scrawny" body and "squashed" nose, "Pekinese" style, hardly warranted celebrity status except for the fact that each successive film revealed her in less and less clothes.[188] A lay and left backlash promptly formed. *L'Unità* complained that Rome's legal sacred status had turned it into a "ghetto" that resisted the laws of the Italian Republic. The inaugural ruling of Italy's new Constitutional Court in 1956, moreover, seemed to deny the government's authority over displaying posters, although the long reach of the Lateran Pacts in the Constitution's Article 7 might contradict that, especially in Rome. The *Voce repubblicana* also resented the church's "ham-fisted" (*goffaggine*) response to the posters. To their charge that the pope really wished for a return to the old Fascist laws, a page-one editorial in the *Osservatore* emphasized that Pius's was not a voice in the wilderness. In the preceding November, for instance, the local tourist board had already called for preemptive measures against dirty advertisements after a Socialist senator also urged tighter controls.[189] Consequently, one disgusted state worker took Catholic Ac-

187. "Fervide sollecitudini ed esortazioni del Sommo Pontefice Pio XII nell'incontro con i Parroci e i Predicatori Quaresimalisti di Rome," *OR*, March 6, 1957. The transcript of Pius's speech fills most of that issue's first page.

188. P. T., "Film e manifesti," *Il Popolo*, March 7, 1957. Brusasca was not mentioned by name. The paper referred to his title only—the undersecretary of the Spettacolo. See also IPVI, Pg XII, b. 18, Gavuzzo circular, March 15, 1957.

189. N. A., "Precisazioni," *OR*, March 9, 1957. See also (all in *OR*) "Commenti in margine," of March 10, 1957; "Obbiettivi rilievi," of March 15, 1957, regarding more criticism in *La Tribuna*; and "Volgari ironie," of March 16, 1957, regarding a piece in *Il Mondo*. On the Constitutional Court, see chapter 4.

tion's prompting seriously and filed his own complaint over the posters that had "disturbed and damaged" his four children. In June 1958, the case went to Tribunal, where fines were placed on three distribution company employees who marketed the Bardot and the Ekberg films.[190] Two years later, on December 12, 1960, the Migliori Law on movie posters (no. 1391) mollified Catholics. The Morality Office was optimistic and asked the AC leadership to consider that, instead of the usual position against tougher laws and only for better prosecution, for years, in fact, "we wished for a *tougher* law than that which existed." The Migliori Law "finally offers" that.[191]

Discussions on the propriety of movie posters, particularly those for *Miss Spogliarello*, begged the question, "Why was the film released at all?" —a query not lost on many Catholics. Brusasca assured the Catholic Action Morality Office of Bolzano, for instance, that the government had already remedied the film with many cuts and banned it from children. Gino Gavuzzo also wrote to Brusasca, acknowledging the "patient, assiduous and difficult action" that the job required. But when faced with the outrage over *Miss Spogliarello*, he wondered to what extent financial interests influenced such decisions. The undersecretary assured him that lucre was not a factor, but only "our spiritual, moral and social responsibilities to the spectators." That said, he summoned the three members of the censorship panel, all respectable fathers with young children, to remind them "of the seriousness of their decision."[192]

Miss Spogliarello revealed again that confusion ran through the censorship project. The church, various Catholic Action agencies, the DC, and, after 1953, its partners in government all wanted input on what got censored or banned. One observer might see nothing wrong with a film or a play, while another wanted action taken against it. A general attitude might reign among the Catholics that could evaporate when they got down to specific cases. In the spring of 1957, trouble over Brusasca illu-

190. "In Cassazione la vertenza per i manifesti di Bridgette Bardot e di Anita Ekberg," *Corriere della sera*, September 3, 1958.

191. IPVI, Pg XII, b. 3, Morality circular, March 25, 1961; Rodolfo Venditti, *La Tutela penale del pudore e della pubblica decenza* (Milan: Giuffrè, 1963), 51–61; and an interesting website on censured films, "Le Mutande della censura," at http://www.fotogrammidicarta.it/album_censura/censura_paginaoo.htm (accessed October 3, 2019).

192. AS Casale Monferrato, Fondo Brusasca, M93, f. 227, Verona Morality Office/Brusasca, March 20, 1957; Bolzano Morality Office, March 22, 1957, Brusasca/Bolzano, March 27, 1957; Brusasca/Francesco Penotti (Columbia Pictures), March 12, 1957; Gavuzzo/Brusasca, March 4, 1957; Brusasca/Gavuzzo, March 7, 1957; AS Casale Monferrato, Fondo Brusasca, M89, f. 149, Gavuzzo/Brusasca, March 15, 1957; Brusasca/Gavuzzo, March 27, 1957. Gavuzzo had also pressured to cut at least one scene from *Miss Spogliarello*; IPVI, Pg XII, b. 2, Gavuzzo circulars of March 6 and 12, 1957.

strated this. On March 20, *Avanti!* spotted discord in DC ranks, identifying a plot hatched by Andreotti and the undersecretary's two predecessors, Scalfaro and Ermini, to label Brusasca too soft on bad films. The Socialist paper, like the Communist *Vie nuove*, felt that Brusasca had, in fact, brought a much-needed civility to the censor's office, a gentility not much appreciated by his colleagues. Then, after reading pieces in *Concretezza* and one by Rondi in *Discussione* insinuating lethargy or softness, an incensed Brusasca complained to Party Secretary Fanfani. He also fumed in an eight-page letter to Andreotti, citing case after case where Catholics disagreed among themselves, including on issues between him and his predecessor. He cited, for instance, the imbroglio over Jules Dassin's crime story, *Rififi*, which had been banned and then released a year later. To Andreotti, Brusasca conceded what he would not admit to Gavuzzo, that indeed business played a role. The film had been banned while the LUX organization handled it; but the second time around Italo Gemini of CEI INCOM successfully pressured a skeptical Brusasca to release it. Gemini brought in none other than Albino Galletto, who "confidentially" told the undersecretary that, with a few cuts and prohibiting it only to those under seventeen, *Rififi* could be released. As a crime picture, then, a still-skeptical Brusasca checked with the head of the police, who opposed it until some interventions from Prime Minister Antonio Segni's secretary secured his assent; the censorship panel then awarded its *nulla osta*, and *Rififi* reached screens across Italy. Brusasca pointed to other examples, including *Miss Spogliarello*, with which, despite Andreotti's own condemnation and outside of the title and the notorious poster, he personally found little to offend. Other examples included the 1956 American *The Bad Seed*, released in Italy as *Il Giglio nero*, concerning a murderous little girl, a work that the CCC condemned but *Il Popolo* lauded, and the Italian *Poveri ma belli*, chastised by the Vatican despite a favorable review from *Il Quotidiano*. Brusasca could go on, he told Andreotti, but finished with "the most singular case" of Federico Fellini's *Le Notti di Cabiria*, a work unanimously acclaimed by the selection committee for the Cannes festival and by Genoa's very conservative Archbishop Giuseppe Siri, who secretly viewed it in a private screening arranged by Fellini's friend, the Jesuit Angelo Arpa. But somehow the Interior Ministry's representative to the censorship panel condemned it.[193]

193. IS Sez. Pol. Fanfani, Sc 79, f. 18, Brusasca/Fanfani, March 29, 1957, with attachments: Brusasca/Andreotti, c. March 15, 1957, and Brusasca/De Pirro, March 15, 1957; AS Casale Monferrato, Fondo Brusasca, M89, f. 148, Brusasca/Andreotti, March, 22, 1957; "Vestire i titoli ignudi," *Avanti!*, March 20,

Broadcasting

At least as much as their rivals, Catholics appreciated the power of the broadcast media and pounced to control it at the end of World War II. As early as the "45 Days" after Mussolini's downfall in 1943, Gedda offered a deal to Prime Minister Pietro Badoglio in which Catholic Action would collaborate in nominating figures to administer many of the old Fascist agencies, including the state radio, EIAR.[194] Gedda's arguments, however, were moot in that the system was in shambles. Through sabotage, dismantling, and forced transfer to the north, Italy's radio network had practically vanished. In August 1944, however, and with heavy Allied guidance, the government resurrected the EIAR and in October renamed it the Radio Audizioni Italia (RAI). This ended up as a quasi-government entity with controlling interest in the hands of a Piedmontese electric company, the SIP, and the RAI administration soon fell under Catholic control. By August of 1946, shortly after the referendum and elections to the *Costituente*, the DC's Giuseppe Spataro replaced the non-DC Catholic intellectual Arturo Carlo Jemolo as president. He was followed in 1951 by Cristiano Ridomi, who had been Mussolini's press attaché at the Berlin embassy and, later, De Gasperi's spokesman. Thanks to a twenty-year agreement signed in January 1952, the giant state holding company, the IRI, took control of RAI, creating what, on the floor of the chamber, the Communist Pietro Ingrao derided as neither a state nor a government monopoly, "but more precisely a party monopoly, even [exercised] by the dominant current within the Christian Democracy." All of this was too much for the opposition; and by 1958 a Communist deputy, Aldo Natoli, bemoaned "radio's shameful subjugation to the aims of government and clerical propaganda."[195]

1957, and "Cosa vuole sua eccellenza?," *Vie nuove*, May 11, 1957. These articles can been found in IS Archivio Andreotti Cinema, respectively, b. 1072, f. 2.3 and b. 1073, f. 6.1; on Arpa and Siri's secret screening, see also Carrera, *Fellini's Eternal Rome*, 53. Fellini felt that Siri must have slept through most of the movie.

194. Giovanni Miccoli, "Chiesa, partito cattolico e società civile," in Valerio Castronovo, *L'Italia contemporanea* (Turin: Einaudi, 1976), 195–96; Teodoro Sala, "Un'offerta di collaborazione dell'Azione Cattolica Italiana al governo Badoglio (Agosto 1943)," *Rivista di storia contemporanea* 4 (1972); Luigi Gedda, *18 aprile 1948: Memorie inedited dell'artefice della sconfitta del Fronte Populare* (Milan: Mondadori, 1998), 85–86; and Mario Casella, *L'Azione cattolica alla caduta del fascismo: Attività e progetti per il dopoguerra (1942–'45)* (Rome: Studium, 1984), 51–59. Casella concluded that Gedda did not presume any succession after Fascism but rather a maintenance of Catholic spirit in Italian society.

195. Franco Monteleone, *Storia della Radio e della televisione in Italia* (Venice: Marsilio, 1992), 160, 196–97, 231–42; Monteleone, *Storia della RAI dagli Alleati alla DC (1944–1954)* (Rome and Bari: Laterza, 1980), 63–64. The 1952 agreement was reprinted in "Centro Studi Economico Sociali," *La Radiotelevisione in Italia: Legislazione, Documenti Parlamentari dal 1958 al 1963* (Milan: Studium, 1963), 41–61. Regarding

At first, before television, radio alone drew Catholic concern in its ability to invade the home. Radio enabled, at any moment, unwanted sounds, feelings, and ideas to cross that last and most sacred of thresholds. The *Osservatore Romano*'s media critic, Guido Guarda, labeled the radio program an "involuntary show." But while it "penetrat[ed] the community of the family," it could not monopolize the listener's attention.[196] Despite Christian Democracy's domination of the RAI, Italians could access other systems. Vatican Radio always existed alongside Italian state broadcasting, although Catholics found nothing to complain about there. From beyond the Alps, however, foreign waves penetrated the nation's airspace. Above all, Italian-language broadcasts from Radio Prague provided a Communist voice, while Yugoslavia produced Radio Capodistria from 1949, and, as of 1966, Radio Montecarlo transmitted more mainstream programming.[197] Still, the DC's heavy hand manipulated the RAI to serve its ends. Certain words, such as Christ, Jesus, and bed, were banned. The news program *Giornale Radio*, in fact, became little more than an extension of the party. Opposition voices were simply refused airtime. Sometimes little tricks served to do the job; for instance, early on, in December 1948, the Socialist response to a De Gasperi speech was cut due to technical difficulties. In November 1947 *L'Unità* argued that radio had returned to the days of Fascist propaganda, and, two years later, a group of eleven Communists, ten Socialists of varying stripes, two independents, and two Liberals presented a motion in the chamber protesting *Giornale Radio*'s partiality. Such efforts proved futile, however, and by the time of RAI's 1952 absorption into the IRI, DC domination was complete.[198]

The issue of newsreels in movie theaters added to concern over control of news outlets. Mussolini's video propaganda came from LUCE, which did not effectively recover from the war until the 1960s. Italy's chief postwar news footage company, therefore, was Settimana Incom. A private concern, its day-to-day administrator was Sandro Pallavicini, who began his career under the Fascists and had married a distant cousin of Franklin Roosevelt in a Protestant ceremony, later divorcing

---

Ingrao, *Atti parlamentari*, Legislatura II, Camera dei Deputati, Discussioni—Seduta del 13 Marzo 1958, 40,935–44.

196. Guido Guarda, "Responsabilità della radio," *OR*, June 2, 1950, and his "Responsabilità della televisione," *OR*, September 1, 1950.

197. Brief sketches of Radio Capodistria and Radio Montecarlo can be found, respectively, at http://www.rtvslo.si/radiocapodistria/chi_siamo and at http://www.radiomontecarlo.net/ (both accessed October 3, 2019).

198. Monteleone, *Storia della Radio e della televisione in Italia*, 231–39; Cesari, *La censura in Italia oggi*, 68–74.

her. While Pallavicini was not known as a Catholic, Settimana Incom's vision owed much to the fact that the DC senator Teresio Guglielmone acquired controlling interest in the company in 1948 and launched a legacy of government support.[199]

As elsewhere, however, the party's control of the medium sometimes failed to please Catholic Action militants. In April 1953 Daniele Fabbri of the Centro cattolico radiofonico reviewed the RAI and detected "a certain indifference regarding religious and moral content, a certain spirit of laicism ... [and] an evident tendency to hide ... [religious] values." Fabbri claimed that 95 percent of radio programming was "the product of an intransigent lay worldview." He had no problem with children's shows but felt that variety programs displayed an "excessive irreverence (or indifference) toward the family." Songs were often "erotic," and comedies were "basically flawed," which might be all right for the stage but must not be broadcast into homes. Two "external" controls vetted programming, one from the Undersecretariat, which "never intervenes," and the other, a "Central Committee for Radio Vigilance," nominated by the Ministry of Posts and Telecommunications, approved everything "after endless discussions." Fabbri concluded by calling for Catholic inclusion, particularly to give a voice to the radio listeners. He also urged a "penetration of national programming" with Vatican Radio, one that would not compromise "its spiritual function."[200]

On January 3, 1954, at 11:00 A.M., the Rome studios joined those in Turin and Milan to launch the national television network—RAI's channel

199. Luciano Cheles and Lucio Sponza, eds., *The Art of Persuasion: Political Communication in Italy from 1945 to the 1990s* (Manchester: Manchester University Press, 2001), 50–52; Luigi Fossati, "Cercansi notizie dell'Istituto Luce," *Avanti!*, October 24, 1953; *La Settimana Incom: Cinegiornali e informazione negli anni '50*, ed. Augusto Sainati (Turin: Lindau, 2001), particularly Sainati's introduction and the essays from Pierre Sorlin and Piero Craveri. See also "Pallavicini, Sandro," in the *Treccani Encyclopedia*, http://www.treccani.it/enciclopedia/sandro-pallavicini_%28Dizionario-Biografico%29/ (accessed November 13, 2019).

200. IPVI, Pg XV, b. 6, Fabbri/Bastoncini (C.C.R. report), April 20, 1953. For an ACI women's paper, Fabbri urged radio audiences, particularly the young, to be more active listeners. "Radio 1952," *Squilli Fuori Classe*, January 27, 1952. Control of radio extended beyond waves to the print media when in April 1950, the Catholic Action leader Vittorino Veronese complained to Giuseppe Spataro about some questionable material found in a recent issue of the guide *Radio-Correre*. In a note that reflects the close relationship between Catholic Action and Christian Democracy, Veronese began with an introductory endearment, "Peppino," then made sure that Spataro still headed the organization. Veronese reasoned that since the magazine reached "homes everywhere and into the hands of the even the very youngest," could "Peppino" guarantee that "similar embarrassments [*inconvenienti*]" do not occur in the future?; IPVI, Pg VI, b. 4, Veronese/Spataro, April 13, 1950. Veronese also attached a memorandum on risqué lyrics heard on the "Briscola" radio program. A nostalgic song about a house of prostitution was bad enough; but the show extended the theme to a comedy sketch of a Holy Year pilgrim who lamented the closing of an old haunt.

one. At the Monte Mario broadcasting center, RAI's President Ridomi, Mayor Rebecchini, and Giuseppe Spataro joined Cardinal Micara, who blessed the equipment and made a short speech, invoking the hope that TV remember its educational, moral, and spiritual responsibilities. The mayor added the wish that the antennae send and receive messages of faith and love.[201]

Television thus joined radio at RAI, and, while the acronym remained the same, the Radio Audizioni Italia became the Radiotelevisione italiana. Before its formal debut, TV was an infant project that, beyond a few experiments in Turin and Milan and limited French-assisted Vatican transmissions during the Holy Year, had yet to make its mark. The church expressed early interest in it, and in 1949, when the first trial cameras arrived at Genoa from America, a cardinal was on hand to bless them.[202] Starting with Pius, Catholics nevertheless recorded mixed feelings. On January 1, 1954, the pope issued an "Exhortation" on the new medium. He had just expanded Bishop O'Connor's Pontifical Commission for Cinema into the Pontifical Commission for Cinema, Radio and Television to promote shows that "conform to the Christian spirit," to "protect the faithful from morally negative [productions]," to keep track of those media, and to coordinate with other agencies, specifically the Catholic cinema, radio, and television centers, OCIC and UNDA, the worldwide Catholic agency for radio and television. Along with the announcement, Pius lauded TV's potential to spread the gospel, protect children, and promote healthy family life.[203] A patron saint would also help the cause. In the summer of 1952, therefore, during construction of the main transmitter on Monte Penice in the Ligurian Apennines, Pius dedicated television to the archangel Gabriel, confirming this in *Miranda prorsus*, and putting his statue next to the structure. In 1958, however, the pontiff decided that St. Clare was better suited for the task. The thirteenth-century holy woman, it was said, lay dying in bed while her

201. "Da ieri la televisione italiana ha iniziato i suoi programmi regolari," *Il Popolo*, January 4, 1954.

202. Arturo Gismondi, "Inchiesta sulla Radio-Televisione," *Il Ponte* 13, August–September 1957, 1419–20, 1431. Regarding the cardinal's blessing in Genoa, see Arturo Gismondi, *La Radiotelevisione in Italia* (Rome: Editori Riuniti, 1958), 75. Gismondi did not identify the cardinal, and although Giuseppe Siri had been the archbishop of Genoa since 1946, he was not made a cardinal until 1953.

203. "I vantaggi e pericoli della TV," *Il Quotidiano*, January 3, 1954; "Le responsabilità della televisione," *Il Quotidiano*, January 17, 1954; Albino Galletto, "La Pontificia Commissione," *OR*, February 27, 1955. The text of the pontiff's December 16, 1954, announcement can be found at: http://www.vatican.va/roman_curia/pontifical_councils/pccs/temp/hf_p-xii_lett_16121954_statute-cinema-radio-tv_it.html (accessed October 3, 2019). See also "Esortazione all'Episcopato per la trasmissione della televisione," *Il Popolo*, January 3, 1954. UNDA (the Latin word for "wave") merged with OCIC in 1998 to form "Signis," the world Catholic association for communication.

companions left her for a Christmas Eve Mass. When Clare sighed to her Lord that now only the two remained together, a miraculous image appeared on her wall—that of the Mass taking place in the room below—and perhaps heralding the television to come.[204]

Still, concern persisted over an unwelcomed invasion of programming into the family sanctuary, something aggravated by the invention's accessibility at the hands of children. "Everyone knows well," Pius wrote in *Miranda prorsus*, "that, very often, children can avoid the transient attack of a disease outside their own home, but cannot escape it when it lurks within the home itself. It is wrong to introduce risk in any form into the sanctity of home surroundings."[205] The Catholic press echoed papal concern with television. In May 1953, with national broadcasting just around the corner, Guido Guarda in the *Osservatore Romano* wrote of the "marvelous but disturbing" invention, in this case, regarding children's programming. This "new toy" was "something more dangerous than the atomic bomb, if left in the hands of those who have no idea how to use it." Already, Guarda warned, the "unscrupulous and libertine" nature of America's television experience gave Italy something to ponder.[206] In the January 1956 issue of *Famiglia Cristiana*, one mother complained that while she had no problem with televised puppet shows, programs later in the evening brought images of theft and violence into her home. She couldn't control everything that her children saw and expressed alarm that they had even begun to act out the offensive scenes. "Have we become so uncivilized," she asked, "as to simply take whatever is given to us? What sort of education is this?"[207] *Discussione* also raised the "Ameri-

204. "Il Breve Pontificio che proclama S. Chiara Patrona della Televisione," *OR*, August 11–12, 1958; and "Santa Chiara di Assisi Patrona della Televisione," *OR*, August 10, 1961. It is interesting to see that in 2015 on their website, Franciscan broadcasters of "AirMaria" relay their disappointment in the medium: "Unfortunately, in regard to content, Modern TV is the total opposite of what Clare saw in her vision from afar. Instead of Holy Sacrifice for the removal of sin, TV wholly promotes sin and self-indulgence through indecent content"; http://airmaria.com/st-clare-patron-of-tv/ (accessed November 13, 2019). Regarding the archangel Gabriel, see Gismondi, *La Radiotelevisione in Italia*, 76.

205. Pius XII, *Miranda Prorsus*, http://w2.vatican.va/content/pius-xii/en/encyclicals/documents/hf_p-xii_enc_08091957_miranda-prorsus.html (accessed October 3, 2019).

206. "Televisione per ragazzi," *OR*, May 4–5, 1953. Less than one week later, Raffaello Lavagna wrote in the same journal that America might also provide some useful models in that U.S. Catholics, particularly Bishop Fulton Sheen, had gone onto the attack and had begun to tame the savage box; Lavagna, "Responsabilità della televisione," *OR*, May 10–11, 1953. Three years later the *Osservatore* noted that a "rebellion" against the TV had begun in America, where surveys revealed that, glued to the screen, children were starting to sacrifice the benefits of team sports. It also feared the "dumbing down" (*intontimento*) of a TV generation; "Ribellione contro la TV negli Stati Uniti," *OR*, April 9–10, 1956. On the "unscrupulous and libertine" nature of American TV, see Stefano Pivato and Anna Tonelli, *Italia vagabonda: Il tempo libero degli italiani dal melodramma alla pay-tv* (Rome: Carocci, 2001), 129.

207. Damiano Garofalo, *Political Audiences: A Reception History of Early Italian Television*, trans. Michael Sarnoff-Wood (Milan: Mimesis International, 2016), 73–74.

ca" question when it examined television. Was it a "valid and useful" device that brought "truth to the people" or a mere publicity mechanism, particularly in political campaigns? The article urged Italians to look at the United States where the medium had already taken the form of "an invisible but omnipresent web."[208] The *Rivista del clero italiano* cautioned of TV waves invading the home and urged that only parents control access to the box. Children, servants, and guests should not be allowed to touch it. At school, moreover, its educational value made it a "necessity." Still, of course, as a luxury, as a seduction, and as a time-waster, the TV should not enter a priest's dwelling. Doing so would only diminish his standing among the faithful.[209] Cardinal Siri, in fact, wanted to prohibit televisions in all Catholic places. However, that the state, meaning Christian Democracy, controlled these matters led Guarda to conclude in the *Osservatore* that the problem would be "serenely confronted." For Catholic Action, accommodation was possible, and less than three months after TV's inauguration it organized "Radio-Television Weeks" of study at parishes across the nation, asking militants to compile subscriber lists for those who could then receive helpful brochures on the new device. It also called for the establishment of "Radio-Tele Clubs" along the lines of Morlion's successful *Cineclubs*. The DC's Office of Cultural Activities aimed to channel interest into *Teleclubs* that would organize "TV evenings" for discussions and conferences. Unwilling to shake the old "enlightenment" notions, Semeraro insisted that TV was not merely "simple entertainment" (*svago*) but had the ability to elevate cultural awareness.[210]

Despite the occasional ambiguity among Catholics, they had at least started to develop an approach to television well ahead of their rivals. On the left, occasional Communist grumbling over DC control did not hide a sense of resignation. In some ways redolent of the clergy, the PCI maintained an aloofness toward "vulgar" television, "where superficiality and cultural approximations are represented in their most slovenly and grotesque forms." The party maintained this attitude, banning sets

208. Renato Venturini, "Agenti di pubblicità per gli uomini politici," *Discussione*, October 24, 1954.

209. N.A., "Attività in programma per le giunte parrocchiali," *Iniziativa* supplement, January–February 1954; Luigi Oldani, "Appunti morali sulla televisione," *Rivista del clero*, December 1956.

210. IS Sez. Pol. Fanfani, Sc 57, f. 29, "L'Ufficio delle attività popolari dalla sua costituzione ad oggi," n.d., apparently 1956; IS Sez. Pol. Fanfani, Sc 49, f. 64, Semeraro/Fanfani, n.d. (1957). On Siri and television, see Andrea Riccardi, "Chiesa di Pio XII e chiese italiane," in *Le Chiese di Pio XII*, ed. Andrea Riccardi (Rome and Bari: Editori Laterza, 1986), 35–36. Regarding television's pedagogical promise, see also "Televisione educativa," OR, June 24, 1955, and "Radio Televisione e Cultura," OR, July 10, 1955.

from its offices and the Case del popolo centers at least through the end of the 1950s, although, as one scholar noted, "nobody listened," and many places acquired them anyway. Some clever official in the Tuscan Christian Democracy proved something in 1954 by awarding a television set to "a worker family," which obediently installed it in the local PCI offices, causing a rift among the Communists. "The Stalinists immediately denounced the new device as 'priest stuff,'" recalled a Catholic worker, "while the other, more moderate half gathered every evening at the Party seat to watch the television programs."[211]

Now securely in charge of the RAI and in the bloom of Fanfani activism, the DC looked at the management of nascent television as "an essential moment in the Catholic re-foundation" and named a director with impeccable credentials. This meant that Ridomi and his chief assistant, Salvino Sernesi, would soon get the axe; and it fell after angry calls flooded the Turin RAI switchboards over lavish exposure of dancers' legs during some early broadcasts. Mario Scelba, who assumed the prime minister's chair in February 1954, also found objectionable some rose-colored passages in a broadcast on Soviet architecture. Consequently, as the old Radio Audizioni Italia was jettisoned, so was the hapless Ridomi. Fanfani and Scelba demoted the RAI presidency beneath the office of administrative delegate (*Amministratore delegato*, which might be translated as chief executive officer). There they placed the stalwart Filiberto Guala.[212] A FUCI militant in his youth, the devout Guala was a Piedmontese Catholic Action leader with close ties to Giuseppe Dossetti and Giorgio La Pira, an early patron, to Montini, Carlo Carretto, Franco Costa, and the charismatic Don Luigi Orione, a figure of special importance in his development. Guala also enjoyed a reputation as an able technocrat, first at the Turin water authority and later as Fanfani's right hand at the public housing project, Ina-Casa. Prime Minister Scelba personally urged him to take the RAI appointment, saying, "There is no one else among the Catholics that we can place [in the position]." Guala accepted but soon faced internal opposition from the so-called "mandarins," the entrenched "anticlerical" bureaucracy, rooted in Fascism, those who either associated with business-oriented factions or,

211. Garofalo, *Political Audiences*, 54–56; Massimo Scaglioni, "Cavalcare la tigre: TV italiana e culture storiche," in *Storia e culture della televisione italiana*, ed. Aldo Grasso (Milan: Mondadori, 2013), 32–34.

212. The new RAI president would be the physicist Antonio Carrelli. The DC knew that Sernesi had been one of the key Fascists in the RAI and said as much in an unsigned party circular; IS Pol. Sec. Moro Sc. 118, f. 8.

like Ridomi, first owed their positions to Mussolini. Ettore Bernabei, who would assume the RAI helm in 1961, identified the clique's *eminence grise* as the Torinese lawyer Marcello Bernardi, the "vice-director general," an indestructible bureaucrat who reigned "as the real boss" without interruption from the mid-1920s into the 1960s. His cadre called the venerable Turin Whist Club home. One DC report, in fact, acknowledged that these Fascist belligerents linked to the old EIAR were out for Guala's head. The new executive immediately added to the storm when he brought in his own cadre of young Catholic militants, among them Umberto Eco, who would later find fame as an academic semiotician, popular essayist, and novelist, all members of a vanguard that complemented Fanfani's aims and one that, noted an observer, called for closer ties with the church, "isolation of the Marxist left, antipathy for lay culture, and moral rigor." *L'Unità* countered that the choice of Guala served Catholic Action's agenda and that he led "a group of Fanfani fanatics and incompetents who help[ed] themselves to public funds and push[ed] their own propaganda." The new boss's Catholic fervor, described by some as "volcanic," certainly startled RAI personnel, as it must have at an early meeting at the Turin office, where he reportedly announced, "I'm here to chase out the pederasts and Communists."[213]

Guala's motivation can be discerned in his use of a "Code [*norme*] of self-discipline" that he circulated secretly (*segretissima*) through the RAI. The code stated that television should devote itself to "healthy family recreation [and] to the education and the moral and cultural elevation of citizens." The broadcaster, therefore, needed to question whether a

213. Monteleone, *Storia della radio e della televisione in Italia*, 288–90; on Guala, see *Filiberto Guala: L'imprenditore di Dio*, ed. Monastery of San Biagio (Casale Monferrato: Edizioni Piemme, 2001); on Scelba's plea, see 16. See also Pivato and Tonelli, *Italia vagabonda*, 126–31; Francesco Malgeri, *La Stagione del centrismo: Politica e società nell'Italia del secondo dopoguerra* (Soveria Mannelli: Rubbettino, 2002), 310–11; Monteleone, *Storia della RAI dagli Alleati alla DC (1944–1954)*, 170–72; Scaglioni, "Cavalcare la tigre," and Marco Damilano, "I partiti all'assalto di Viale Mazzini," both in Grasso, *Storia e culture della televisione italiana*; Menico Caroli, *Proibitissimo! Censori e censurati della radiotelevisione italiana* (Milan: Garzanti, 2003), 30–31, 42; Franco Chiarenza, *Il Cavallo morente: Trent'anni di Radiotelevisone italiana* (Milan: Bompiani, 1978), 66–80; Umberto Eco, *Il costume di casa: Evidenze e misteri dell'ideologia italiana* (Milan: Bompiani, 1973); "Il Signor Guala e il controfagotto," *L'Unità*, December 22, 1955; "La RAI consegna all'Azione Cattolica?," *L'Unità*, June 2, 1954; Pietro Ingrao, "E la RAI?," *L'Unità*, May 16, 1954. The "pederasts and communists" quote came from the PCI critic Giovanni Cesareo. It has been cited in a number of places, including Giulia Guazzaloca, *Una e divisibile: La RAI e i partiti negli anni del monopolio pubblico (1954–1975)* (Florence: Le Monnier, 2011), 14–19, 24–25, and 58n28. She writes, "That [Guala] was a difficult personality can be understood through myriad anecdotes, found somewhere between reality and legend, that have been attributed to him." On Fascists and the old EIAR spirit in the RAI, see IS Sez. Pol. Moro, Sc. 118, f. 9, unsigned report on RAI, n.d. (c. 1960); Ettore Bernabei and Giorgio Dell'Arti, *L'Uomo di fiducia: I retroscena del potere raccontati da un testimone rimasto dietro le quinte per cinquant'anni* (Milan: Mondadori, 1999), 91–97.

show depicted "dishonesty, vice, and crime" in such a way as to produce imitation. Did it discredit the institutions of the family, the law, or the nation? Did it cause shame or offend *buon costume* or public decency? Did it exalt "deplorable sentiments such as hate, violence, vendetta, or brutality, including against animals"? The code went on to address more specific issues of civil and religious order. Murder, slaughter, kidnapping, dueling, and euthanasia were all subject to censure, as was suicide, "which must never appear as a solution to life's difficulties." "Sacrilege, profanation, blasphemy . . . [and] gestures that offend God" were prohibited, while church dogmas and commandments were to be treated "with absolute reverence." "The health of matrimonial ties and respect for the institution" occupied a central place, with a list of taboos including adultery, illegitimacy, rebellion against parents, and, of course, divorce. Not part of the code itself, RAI also circulated a list of banned words. "Armpit" (*ascella*) was unacceptable, as were "sweat" (*sudore*), "bedroom" (*alcova*), and "bridal chamber" (*talamo*). "Thighs" (*cosce*) could be applied only to chickens. "Lover" (*amante*) was out of bounds, even for "lover of beauty," "lover of freedom," and "lover of fine wine." Such semantic measures led the RAI to change the name of one telecast from *The Bandit's Girlfriend* to *The Bandit's Wife*. In his study of TV censorship, Menico Caroli related how, on another occasion, the writer Curzio Malaparte caused a flap by stating on a live interview show that Italy unfortunately still had no legal divorce. A "red-faced" director of programming, Bernardi's man Sergio Pugliese, stormed into the studio from the control room and cut Malaparte's microphone, and the writer never again received an invitation to appear on the program.[214]

Of singular importance was the RAI's vision and promotion of a feminine ideal that it captured in a group of announcers who became known as the "*signorine buonasera*." Starting at the very birth of TV broadcasting and continuing until 2016, they announced each evening's programming and became household names unto themselves. RAI made sure that, as one observer wrote, "They must be very beautiful but reserved, neither aggressive nor sexy. Very elegant, no make-up, a discrete smile:

214. Caroli, *Proibitissimo! Censori e censurati della radiotelevisione italiana*, 30–41. The *norme di autodisciplina* can be found in Gismondi, *La Radiotelevisione in Italia*, 157–77. On the code, see also Enrico Menduni, "La Nascita della tevevisione in Italia," in *Il Miracolo economico italiano (1958–1963)*, ed. Antonio Cardini (Bologna: Il Mulino, 2006), 126–29. Pugliese was another old EIAR hand with ties to Nicola De Pirro, as well as to Bernardi. One author identified Pugliese as the chief thinker regarding the form RAI television would take, a man whose vision directly contradicted Guala's more culturally based aims; Scaglioni, "Cavalcare la tigre," 36–38.

she is the image of the woman on TV, who must not rouse the Italians, who must suggest the idea of the wife and not that of a lover."[215] The *signorina buonasera* was in a class by herself, often becoming a celebrity in her own right. But as the public faces of the RAI, they were joined by other women who raised different problems. Writers and directors brought their own stars and showgirls to the screen, with the result that controversies surfaced over dancers' legs and issues of décolleté. The most celebrated case concerned the bandleader Xavier Cugat and his American wife, Abbe Lane, who costarred in one of Italian television's first hits, Sunday night's *Casa Cugat*, which premiered on December 4, 1954. Although the pair had respectfully attended the pontiff's second talk on the "ideal film," the voluptuous Lane, who, one enthusiastic fan raved, made Jayne Mansfield look like a boy, displayed provocative dance numbers and pushed the envelope more than Catholics liked. Following a lusty first episode, for Lane's second show the hapless director placed a large rose in her cleavage and urged her to "wiggle less." The performance still outraged the censors, so much so that Guala ordered her removal from the air. A few weeks later, however, and no doubt after some discussion, she reemerged on the screen more modestly draped and with less suggestive moves. By then, however, *Casa Cugat*'s days were numbered, and the show ended its controversial run for good the subsequent March.[216]

The overwhelming majority of RAI programming, however, did not showcase programs like *Casa Cugat*. Sports, particularly soccer, occupied large swaths of weekly schedules, as did musical shows and games like *Lascia o raddoppia*, with Mike Buongiorno. The RAI also gave generous attention to religious programs such as the televised Mass and the very popular Padre Mariano's various shows, starting with *Padre Mariano's Mail*

215. Monteleone, *Storia della radio e della televisione in Italia*, 303; Gundle, "Signorina Buonasera: Images of Women in Early Italian Television," in *Women in Italy, 1945–1960: An Interdisciplinary Study*, ed. Penelope Morris (New York: Palgrave, 2006). The last broadcast for the signorine *buonasera* came on May 28, 2016, according to "'Le signorine buonasera' vanno in pensione: Oggi è l'ultimo giorno," Sì24.it, May 27, 2016 (accessed September 28, 2017).

216. Michele Galeani, "Suggeriamo qualche ritocco a 'Lascia o radoppia,'" *L'Europeo*, January 8, 1956. See also Monteleone, *Storia della radio e della televisione in Italia*, 347; Caroli, *Proibitissimo! Censori e censurati della radiotelevisione italiana*, 40–41. Born a Brooklyn Jew, Lane's work and marriage with Cugat launched her successful and controversial nightclub career. The American columnist Frank Thistle described Lane in an article, "The Swingingest Sexpot In Show Business," *Adam* 7, no. 4 (1963), found at http://javasbachelorpad.com/abbeadam.html (accessed October 3, 2019). See also Renato Tomasino, *Abbe Lane, Mirella Freni, Valeria Moriconi, Amy Whitehouse: Quattro sirene* (Alessandria: Edizioni Falsopiano, 2014), 24–27, and "1955: Abbe Lane è troppo sexy," *Il Giornale.it*, August 1, 2006, accessed through: http://www.ilgiornale.it/news/1955-abbe-lane-troppo-sexy.html (accessed October 3, 2019).

(*La posta di padre Mariano*) in 1955. The Capuchin's comforting and engaging manner at times attracted the greatest RAI audiences.[217] The struggle against what little smut existed on the tube nonetheless continued, and Guala's "clear the decks" gusto collided not only with wishes for more programs like *Casa Cugat*, but also with the old EIAR group and lay and Marxist political factions. Guala, however, still could count on Fanfani, who, at a February 1956 meeting of the DC leadership, the Consiglio Nazionale, expressed frustration over a state television that was out of control. No DC agency, he stated, "should be a vehicle ushering into the home something that the Church condemns." "Radical measures" had become necessary because "what [was] happening with television [was] an intolerable scandal."[218]

Finally came the confrontation. What *L'Unità* described as a "defenestration" started with Aldo Passante, a Mason and member of the old guard whom Guala had demoted. Passante, it was said, "inspired" a nasty polemic by Alfredo Panicucci in the pages of *Epoca*, on the heels of which Guala offered his resignation on June 27, 1956. While developments at RAI were not his purview at the Spettacolo Undersecretariat, Brusasca composed a letter of solidarity. "Your virtue and strengths, and the Christian example of your life," he wrote, have left their mark and will become more apparent with time. "The Lord, for whom you work at the RAI," concluded Brusasca, will reward you. Even the Communists expressed some, perhaps grudging, sympathy for a man who had suffered "defenestration" at the hands of big money—in this case, they felt, certain state-run power companies with interest in the RAI.[219]

A new, more sedate team led by the Neapolitan aristocrat Marcello Rodinò as *Amministratore delegato*, assisted by the DC journalist Rodolfo Arata (as director general), replaced Guala and his cohort. Under them, and although as loyal as ever to Fanfani, the RAI took a more lay-friendly turn and launched what one historian characterized as its "greatest

217. Monteleone, *Storia della Radio e della televisione in Italia*, 304. See also the somewhat hagiographic Rinaldo Cordovani, *Padre Mariano: Il parroco di tutti gli italiani* (Padua: Edizioni Messagero Padova, 2011), 145–52.

218. IS Consiglio Nazionale Sc 23, Minutes from meetings of February 26–27, 1956.

219. AS Casale Monferrato, Fondo Brusasca, M100, Brusasca/Guala, June 29, 1956; "Guala defenestrato dalla RAI e sostituito da un uomo dei monopoli," *L'Unità*, June 28, 1956. Sympathy might also have come from the fact that two of Guala's close circle at RAI, Mario Motta and Pieremilio Gennarini, had significant links to the Communists; Ada Ferrari, *Milano e La RAI un Incontro Mancato? Luci e ombre di una capitale di transizione (1945–1977)* (Milan: FrancoAngeli, 2002), 150. See also Chiarenza, *Il Cavallo morente*, 72–73. Bernabei had a different story: that Guala had been set up by Bernardi and Pugliese and that Prime Minister Segni, a critic of the Fanfani faction, did nothing to defend him; Bernabei and Dell'Arti, *L'Uomo di fiducia*, 98–99.

season," one of technical and professional polish.[220] In a May 1959 interview with *Discussione*, Rodinò dismissed questions of controls in that the RAI censored itself as would any theatrical or film impresario.[221] Two breakthroughs in 1957 were RAI's first real on-screen kiss and its first commercials, famously well-made and bundled together in the hugely successful and long-running show *Carosello*. Catholic struggles to keep the screen clean nevertheless continued, as did the controversies; and state censorship still provided nightmares for the artists. One actor known for "histrionics," Vittorio Gassman, landed in trouble, for example, over his show *Mattatore*, which premiered in 1959. An anthology of skits, often satirical, the program enjoyed popular acclaim but pushed the censors too far, and *Mattatore* lasted barely two months. One early test for Rodinò concerned Maria Luisa Garoppo, a "tobacco girl" who, shortly after Guala's resignation but still in the summer of 1956, appeared as a contestant on *Lascia o raddoppia*. Her form-fitting dress accentuated an ample bosom and created a presence that was, as *Avanti!* cheerfully observed, "hard to ignore." *Il Popolo* denounced the disgrace, while the Socialist paper claimed that the flap over *signorina* Garoppo's chest reached into the RAI boardroom. The scandal worked itself out, however, and on her next appearance she appeared in more modest attire that "could not offend the harshest critic or the most dour and diffident Trappist."[222]

This Socialist criticism proved prophetic, because four years after his RAI debacle Guala joined the Trappists, with whom he happily spent the rest of what turned out to be a long life. *L'Europeo*'s Achille Campanile predicted in an "open letter" that someday St. Filiberto Guala, the "video Trappist," would join Saint Clare as copatrons of the medium. "In the meantime," he wrote, "reverend father, pray for TV, which has so much need of prayer; and help and enlighten those who run TV, they who have so much need of help and enlightenment."[223]

220. Monteleone, *Storia della radio e della televisione in Italia*, 298–99; Caroli, *Proibitissimo! Censori e censurati della radiotelevisione italiana*, 50.

221. "Non esiste una 'censura televisiva,'" *Discussione*, May 10, 1959.

222. On *Mattatore*, see Caroli, *Proibitissimo!*, 56–58; see also "Il diavolo sui teleschermi," *Avanti!*, August 19, 1956, and "La Garoppo sui teleschermi in abito 'permesso a tutti,'" *Avanti!*, August 21, 1956. *L'Unità* ("Neppure le trovate dei censori della TV frenano le esuberanze della Garoppo," on August 31, 1956) reported that she had received thirty-six marriage proposals, only one of which had been taken back. Three years later, *L'Europeo* reported that Garoppo opted for a brief fling on the striptease stage; Achille Campanile, "Finti o veri la censura non li accetta," *L'Europeo*, August 2, 1959.

223. Achille Campanile, "Lettera aperta al Trappista del video," *L'Europeo*, December 11, 1960.

Chapter 3

Family Matters

Catholic arguments of *costume* and culture sooner or later turned to the family, which the church always acknowledged to be something of unquestionable importance.[1] In his aforementioned talks on the "ideal film," Pope Pius XII assured everyone that the family was "the source and channel of the human race and of mankind. Masterpiece of the Creator's supreme wisdom and goodness, from Him has it received the laws, the prerogatives, the duties which open for it the road towards the fulfillment of its own high destiny. Based on love and for love, the family can and should exist for its members: spouses, parents, children, their own small world, refuge, oasis, earthly paradise in the fullest measure attainable here below. Thus it will be in reality, if it is allowed to be what the Creator willed, what the Savior confirmed and sanctified."[2] The *Osservatore Romano* echoed the pontiff and confirmed in 1957 that "the Church, forever faithful to its teaching continues to struggle . . . against all currents adverse to the stability of the matrimonial bond."[3]

The commitment reached far beyond the Vatican hill. The *Settimane sociali* were conferences that the church organized on a different topic each year. The 1954 "social week" focused on women and society, which, as usual at such conferences, meant marriage and motherhood. The 1954 meeting was true to form, and the audience gathered in Pisa heard

1. One observer wrote that, historically, "the most important institution governing the family was without any doubt the Catholic Church"; Bruno P. F. Wanrooij, "Italy: Sexuality, Morality and Public Authority," in *Sexual Cultures in Europe: National Histories*, ed. Franz X. Eder, Leslie A. Hall, and Gert Hekma (Manchester: Manchester University Press, 1999), 115.

2. From Pius XII's exhortations on the "ideal film" of October 28, 1955; http://www.vatican.va/holy_father/pius_xii/apost_exhortations/documents/hf_p-xii_exh_25101955_ideal-film_en.html (accessed October 17, 2019).

3. V. F., "A tutela del matrimonio," *OR*, March 11–12, 1957.

Genoa's Archbishop Giuseppe Siri emphasize the sacramental power of matrimony that surpassed all human strengths. Only the priesthood and the family, he continued, "of all human institutions with social scope, possess sacramental grace [*decoro*]." The meeting—on women and society—in fact, issued a final document emphasizing the church's regard for the family as "a total and organic vision," whose "moral health is the indispensable foundation for the well-being of society." It reminded Catholics that the family was as "the safeguard of Christian comportment."[4]

The ideal setting for the healthy Catholic family was rural Italy, the last redoubt, reasonably free of modern vices and ills, and something to protect. The Piedmontese Christian Democrat Giuseppe Brusasca provided a personal testament to this when he commissioned the sculptor Giannino Castiglioni to create a bas relief monument to the "Peasant Defender of Liberty" in his native village of Gabiano.[5] While the simple faith of the *contadini* and their world of the village parish remained a comforting Catholic dream, economic development presented challenges, chief among which was that the rural world was shrinking. Industrialization, the expanding tertiary sector, and urban prosperity pushed more and more peasants off the land, leaving the small village poorer and more untenable and creating a crisis for Catholics. Agricultural Molise and Basilicata lost 10 percent of their populations in the 1950s, while the figure for Italian cities with over 100,000 inhabitants rose between 1950 and 1970, from twenty-six to forty-five, predominantly in the center and north of the country, while the number of people who lived in those cities grew from nine million to sixteen million. Many migrants ended up in massive suburban slums, the *borgate*, that ringed the great cities; and those who went north faced a great deal of prejudice. Poverty, alienation, moral confusion, fears, and bitterness, moreover, affected those who left as well as those who stayed behind.[6] As the party of prosperity, the DC did little to alter this pattern.

4. Siri's speech was transcribed as "Tendenze sociali e valori permanenti della famiglia cristiana." It and the concluding resolution of the 1954 *Settimana sociale* are included in "Le conclusioni della Settimana di Pisa," both in OR, September 29, 1954.

5. Information and an image of the monument can be seen at http://www.cantinadelrubino.it/territorio.htm (accessed October 17, 2019).

6. Guido Crainz, *Storia del miracolo italiano: Cultura, identità, trasformazioni fra anni cinquanta e sessanta* (Rome: Donzelli Editore, 1998), 103–12. The journalist Giorgio Bocca, for example, discussed the strain on families caused by the migrations. One of the most vexing problems was the detachment of young couples from their relatives. He described the situation as an issue of "he and she, alone amid sparkling appliances"; Giorgio Bocca, *La scoperta dell'Italia* (Bari: Laterza, 1963), 36.

The pontiff, however, issued a call to protect rural life in a letter to the 1947 *Settimana sociale*. To the conferees assembled that year in Naples, Pius wrote that the pure, clean air of the countryside contributed to the nation's moral health. "Neopagan morality," however, threatened to pollute the air, creating "the greatest danger of our times." In 1953, at the first meeting of the newly formed Italian Episcopal Conference (Conferenza episcopale italiana, or CEI), Padua's Archbishop Girolamo Bortignon discussed modernization's assault on rural Catholicism. Focusing on the rural north, he identified three types of country parish. The first, found mostly in the Veneto, Piedmont, and some parts of the *Mezzogiorno*, remained untouched by the modern world and lived "in full Christianity," observing the sacraments, where children studied their catechism and "a fervid spirit" prevailed. The second was infected with the lay mentality, where "wise guys" (*furbi*) commit adultery and the "pure" becomes "stupid." At the other end, the third type of parish was dead. Barely Christian communities, "the church and the priest remain[ed]" but only women and children attended Mass. The men were gone. The worst areas were Emilia-Romagna, Tuscany, and certain corners of Piedmont. Better, Bortignon concluded, to ring the alarm today than suffer tomorrow.[7]

Catholic Action joined the church to address the moral issues of the great migration. The first "Congress of Rural Youth," for instance, in October 1950 lamented that so many had pulled up stakes to settle in cities, where they "burned out" and fell prey to hedonist culture. Not all was bucolic nostalgia, and one speaker queried if staying in a miserable rural homestead was preferable to an alienated urban existence: "We must ask—is the house habitable?"[8] One found such treatments across the spectrum of Catholic publications. In a series of articles in late 1953 and early 1954, the Catholic Action women's review, *A Colloquio con le dirigenti diocesane*, blamed the effects of the World War, the rise in salaries, and technological progress. Rural culture, wrote one author, was a human culture, "integral and Christian"; but it was challenged by proletarian and bourgeois ones, born of the Enlightenment and tinged with materialism and atheism. Italy, concluded the review, needed to repair the damage and restore dignity to rural life.[9] Elsewhere, worries emerged

7. Francesco Sportelli, *La Conferenza episcopale italiana (1952–1972)* (Galatina: Congedo Editore, 1994), 45–47.

8. A. Maria Lelli, "Migliore comunità rurale," *Squilli per militanti rurali*, October 22, 1950.

9. N. A., "Il problema di una cultura rurale," *A Colloquio con le dirigenti diocesane*, June 7, 1953. The

in advice columns. One 1954 note from a *contadina* to an AC magazine for young rural women, *Squilli casa e campi*, identified the problem. Many of the girls she knew were unhappy and expressed the wish to leave the villages for urban jobs—departures, however, that would be "washed in tears." A year later a seventeen-year-old Sardinian girl confessed to the same column that her hard life on the land made the city, "where one works less," a real attraction. But, she conceded, moving there would also bring shame. What would her *paesani* think if she "abandoned" her brothers, sisters, her dad and mom, even "Catholic Action and the *Casa e campi* journal that I love so much?" The review responded with a warning of the dangers of urban life and that many relocate with insufficient preparation, while, on the other hand, back home she still enjoyed the warmth of her loved ones.[10]

Catholics especially pointed to the woman as the vital vessel of hope for the fragile *mezzogiorno*, holding families together in an area that was losing its young men to northern or even foreign industrial employment. Emblematic of their concern was a 1956 Centro italiano femminile (CIF) conference on the southern woman held in Naples, where Archbishop Marcello Mimmi welcomed 400 attendees and the CIF president, Contessa Amalia di Valmarana. The DC minister of agriculture Emilio Colombo delivered the keynote address on the realities of the postwar south, promising agrarian reform. Colombo also insisted that the southern woman held an integral place in this coming "motor of growth and expansion" through an "exaltation" of cultural and educational values, women's work, and, above all, by bringing a "Christian approach" to the problems of the *Mezzogiorno*.[11]

If modernity endangered rural life, it also brought transformational opportunities for all women, something with which Catholics seemed fairly comfortable, up to a point. Numbers helped to bring the issue into focus. Monsignor Prosperini reported in the April 1950 *Iniziativa* that virtually all AC men were fathers and that 86 percent of its women were

review's series on "Problemi rurali," by Emma Schwarz, appeared in the November 8, 1953, December 6, 1953, January 24, 1954, and February 7, 1954 issues.

10. From the "Microfono è vostro" column of *Squilli casa e campi*, from January 24, 1954, and January 30, 1955.

11. "Il Card. Mimmi e il Ministro Colombo al convegno sui compiti della donna nel Mezzogiorno," *OR*, March 5–6, 1956. Women's roles served as the subject of another conference, a "Social Week" in L'Aquila, which recognized that in the modern democratic order, "the woman can and must make her precious contribution in all sectors which do not contrast her dignity and feminine delicacy [*delicatezza*], for the good of the family, the fatherland and the Church"; "Una Settimana Femminile a L'Aquila sulla 'Dignità e Missione Sociale della Donna,'" *OR*, November 11, 1956.

mothers "and the others mostly teachers."[12] The DC also understood these issues in part because women constituted 35 percent of its membership and probably the majority of its votes, compared to 25 percent at the Communist Party.[13] In an *Osservatore Romano* piece on "education of children in the Christian family," the archbishop and jurist Giuseppe D'Avack urged mothers to stay home and educate their offspring; but he carefully admitted that such counsel might be impractical. "I don't mean," he wrote, "to speak of those parents and above all of those mothers who for real and profound necessity are obliged to work outside the house." Rather, D'Avack concerned himself with pampered middle- and upper-class mothers who neglected their children for "'social proprieties,' visits, functions [and] bridge."[14]

In an elocution of October 21, 1945, the pontiff urged support for women's engagement and a "reawakening" of their activity. Women and their "continual worry of obtaining daily bread" demanded them a place in the public workforce. "It is therefore in vain," said Pius, "that one preaches for her return to the hearth as long as the common conditions persist that constrain her to stay away."[15] The many Catholic Action reviews dedicated to women, naturally contained the greatest praise for women's work outside the home, frequently lauding and promoting it, if with occasional condescension. In that, the more Protestant and north European "cult of domesticity" never found much traction among Italians whose Catholic culture, particularly informed by Christian notions of the nobility of labor as well as a strong peasant tradition, affirmed work as central to a woman's identity. For another AC women's review, furthermore, Claudio Pettinato very matter-of-factly posed no objections to women entering the university.[16] On June 8, 1954, *Il Popolo* got in on the act, inaugurating its "women's page" with an article, by a man, comparing Geneviève De Galard, the French "angel of Dien Bien Phu" in Vietnam, to Marilyn Monroe and concluding that men were, indeed, the weaker sex.[17]

12. Ferdinando Prosperini, "Per la difesa del costume," *Iniziativa*, April 1950.

13. Molly Tambor, *The Lost Wave: Women and Democracy in Postwar Italy* (Oxford: Oxford University Press, 2014), 47–48.

14. Giuseppe D'Avack, "L'educazione dei figli nella famiglia Cristiana," *OR*, July 8, 1950.

15. Cecelia Dau Novelli, *De Gasperi nell'età del centrismo*, ed, G. Rossini (Rome: Cinque Lune, 1984), 295; Wendy Pojmann, *Italian Women and International Cold War Politics, 1944–1968* (New York: Fordham University Press, 2013), 59.

16. Claudio Pettinato, "Donne all'Università?" *Squilli fuori classe*, May 20, 1951.

17. Giorgio Ceccherini, "Le rivendicazioni femminili alla luce dei valori morali," and "Grazia" "La moda questa tirannia," both in *Il Popolo*, June 8, 1954. The Catholic Action militant Elsa Conci

The aforementioned *Settimana sociale* in Pisa also lauded "woman's presence in social and political life." Similar issues had been raised at the 1910 Naples gathering and one in 1927 at Florence. For the 1954 meeting Pisa welcomed, among others, Amintore Fanfani, Archbishop Siri, and Professor Innocenzo Gasperini from the University of Sassari, who spoke on "family balance." One paper by the DC Parliamentary deputy, Maria Federici, took a swipe at nascent feminism that, "despite its promises," failed to "identify components of equilibrium" between old values and new ones. Nello Palmieri of the Forensic Medicine Institute (Istituto di medicina legale) at the University of Naples spoke on marriage choices and family preparation. Spousal preference depended too much, he stated, on "erroneous, ephemeral and one-sided criteria" as well as on the gamble of sexual attraction that, over time, often yields disappointment.[18]

The tenth anniversary of women's suffrage in 1956 prompted more discussion on public activism. The January *Rivista del clero italiano* published a collection of talks from one such conference on "The Hour of Catholic Women." Its introductory essay admitted the skepticism still held by some priests toward a woman's "vital importance" for the country, an obstacle that she would ultimately vanquish. One monsignor added that a whole new world was opening to women, one that called for a new mental attitude redolent of the pontiff's call, "Your time has come, Catholic women and girls, public life needs you." The review drew from a speech by Carmela Rossi, the president of the Unione donne, on women's postwar "sacrifice to raise the family, to put it back together, and to reintegrate into normal life the men who returned tired, sick, deluded, or burdened with hate. The woman: humble housewife, heroic in the difficult task of rebuilding her destroyed nest, of squaring the budget, looking for work, caring for the sick and the psychologically hurt. How much the nation owes to these women." All of the authors, priests, and women were Catholic Action activists, and all joined in the call to mobilize and meet the challenge of dynamic modern life.[19] Catholic Action hosted another conference, in April 1957 at Potenza, on the social role of women that emphasized their duty to participate in "institutions

introduced the page with a short piece, "La nostra iniziativa." Next to it the editor placed an essay on "the tyranny of fashion."

18. "La presenza della donna nella vita sociale e politica," OR, September 23, 1954; "La scelta matrimoniale e la preparazione alla famiglia," OR, September 24, 1954.

19. AAVV, "L'Ora delle donne cattoliche," *Rivista del clero italiano*, January 1956.

of secure Christian inspiration" that could guarantee respect for their "dignity and womanhood." Luigi Gedda concluded that meeting with a lecture on citizenship.[20]

Sports

Catholics also became more open to women's participation in sports, something about which the Holy See had long expressed doubts. In the 1920s, while prominent clerics like Agostino Gemelli applauded a form of feminine "Catholic gymnastics," Pius XI condemned them as modern paganism, in part from Fascism's use of sport and as an expression of "Catholic prudery." Clothing also entered the picture, and Gino Gavuzzo's Catholic Action *Guida* made specific mention of women's sporting attire, urging that militants remain on the alert regarding its "correctness."[21] For traditionalists, the historian Victoria De Grazia wrote, "childbirth was the best exercise, of course, and all physical culture was to facilitate that purpose."[22] Work, sports and all other emancipations, must concede priority to motherhood, the noblest vocation for any lay woman. *Mamma* still reigned supreme at cradle and hearth. A 1950 CIF poll could not have surprised many in that ninety percent of women respondents, predominantly primary-school educated, felt very comfortable and "in command" in the home, on their turf.[23] The Catholic press endlessly lauded the sacrifice, sobriety, humility and generosity of the Christian woman, devoted to her husband and offspring. In March 1952, one comment in the *Osservatore Romano* contrasted the pagan view of a woman, as a "trinket" (*gingillo*), with her Christian status as equal to

20. "La presenza della donna nella società alla 'settimana sociale femminile' di Potenza," *OR*, April 10, 1957. Catholics held periodic "women's social weeks" across Italy. Florence hosted one in 1955, dedicated to the 'woman's mission in social life." Mayor La Pira thanked the participants for the "wealth of grace and Christian poetry" that they brought to the city; "La Settimana sociale femminile chiusa dal Card. Dalla Costa a Firenze," *OR*, April 28, 1955. In September of 1957 the more broadly aimed thirtieth *Settimana sociale*, chaired by Cardinal Siri, highlighted the problem of agricultural women as part of rural transformation. Among the final resolutions was a measure expressing concern for the continued presence of the Mass in that population; "La conclusion della XXX Settimana Sociale," *OR*, September 30–October 1, 1957.

21. Gino Gavuzzo, *Guida per la difesa della moralità: Indicazioni, legislazione, giurisprudenza*. (Rome: Segretariato centrale per la moralità, 1952), 57. Gavuzzo cited (59n1) a November 1946 Ministry of Public Instruction directive that secondary schoolgirls in gym class should dress themselves in knee-length shorts.

22. Victoria De Grazia, *How Fascism Ruled Women, Italy, 1922–1945* (Berkeley: University of California Press, 1992), 218–19.

23. Clelia d'Inzillo, "Le donne prefiriscono 'comandare' a casa," *Il Popolo*, January 19, 1950. Of the respondents, 60 percent were housewives, 30 percent were listed as "peasant and worker [*elemento contadino e operaio*]," and 10 percent were engaged in white collar work.

man. Nonetheless, the article placed her in her essential and "sovereign" role within the family, as wife and mother, "her first and most important mission."[24] About a year later, the same paper printed the tragic story of the supreme sacrifice made by a thirty-year-old, Angela Zanetta, who suffered complications in childbirth and learned that she or her baby had to die so that the other might live. She implored the doctor to save her child, then "clearly and serenely faced death." In the end, however, both mother and child succumbed. The journal honored Zanetta as a woman, a mother and a Christian. Nonetheless, the *Osservatore Romano* sensed that the mainstream lay press would sneer, "So who was she? She wasn't a screen or stage actress; she led no adventurous life of sad loves, or divorces; with careless disregard toward children, tragedies, and bad manners [*malcostume*]." Her legacy, rather, served to remind the faithful of sublime Christian duty, "teaching everyone that there exist obligations that demand the price of life."[25]

Despite such misgivings, Catholic attitudes toward women in sports modified. After all, according to the CSI's review *Stadium*, physical activity was a "biological necessity for every human being."[26] DC leaders, furthermore, eagerly enrolled young women into their Libertas sport ranks. By the end of 1951 Libertas's Angelo Priore reported that programs for women were being organized, with basketball leading the way. Libertas would work closely with the DC Women's Movement, the Movimento femminile (MF), to the extent that the director of women's activities for each Polisportiva Libertas would also be a member of the MF.[27]

"Sports, exercise, culture, new professions, fashion, entertainment, various associations, activities, new attitudes, tastes, events in private and public life," wrote one author, "have all taken women and sent them along completely new roads." The vice president of the AC's Women's Union in Milan reminded the readers of unfinished work, including moral education for the media and shelters for unwed mothers, "fallen women" and released convicts. Catholic Action women's reviews struck the same optimistic note in two articles from the summer of 1956, surveying young women from a Ligurian parish and one in Sicily, findings

24. Pio Giardina, "La donna e i femminismi," *OR*, March 20–21, 1952.

25. "Voci ed echi," *OR*, April 16, 1953. Mario Marazziti noted that the Zanetta case had become a *cause célèbre* among Catholics in 1953; Mario Marazziti, "Cultura di Massa e valori cattolici: La Famiglia Cristiana," in *De Gasperi nell'età del centrismo*, ed G. Rossini (Rome: Cinque Lune, 1984), 321.

26. Stefano Pivato, *Clericalismo e laicismo nella cultura popolare italiana* (Milan: Franco Angeli, 1990), 215.

27. IS Seg. Pol. Gonella, Sc. 11, f .8, Angelo Priore, Centro nazionale sportive Libertas Circular no. 17, December 10, 1951.

that indicated that woman's lot was improving and on the right path.[28]

The establishment of Catholic Action's Federazione Associazioni Sportive Cattoliche Italiane (FARI) at the War's end also sent a clear signal for those who doubted. Given the opening, the young women of FARI could be seen chafing at the bit for more acceptability from above. Its clerical liaison, Francesco Delpini, sympathized, advocating more exercise for women to balance their often monotonous, "painful and debilitating" jobs that demanded little physical activity. In particular, he suggested gymnastics and track events. Among more traditionally manly sports, moreover, Father Delpini favored soccer as neither immoral nor dangerous while the brutality of boxing and wrestling put them beyond discussion.[29]

The Summer 1960 Olympic games in Rome, however, showed how Catholic doubts over women and sports persisted, approaching the event with a mixture of pride and embarrassment. The DC was proud of the planning and construction that went into the games and expressed hope for their success.[30] Emphasizing that the capital of Catholicism welcomed the athletes, the *Quotidiano* denounced "a certain campaign conducted by the left-wing press" to downplay any religious angle to the games. The paper estimated that 2,500 of the athletes were Catholics and to serve them, Rome's vicar general, Cardinal Clemente Micara designated the basilica of Santa Croce in via Flaminio near the Olympic park, and staffed it with extra multilingual priests.[31] The notorious American anti-Catholic Paul Blanshard, however, claimed that the Catholic Church prohibited its seminarians from viewing swimming and female diving competitions as well as boxing and wrestling contests.[32] At the same time, as Nadia Zonis has written, the event defied some notions of *buon costume*. Contestants, particularly women she noted, came to Rome not just for the thrill of competition, but also for a dose

28. "Bello e brutto il mondo di oggi," July 29, 1956; "Andiamo verso un'epoca migliore?," August 26, 1956; both in *Squilli effettive e giovane*. The *Squilli* articles were often printed in more than one location.

29. Francesco Delpini, "Morale e sport," *A Colloquio con le dirigenti diocesane* June 3, 1951. Some information on the FARI can be found at https://www.isacem.it/it/fondi-archivistici/federazione-attivita-ricreative-italiane-1949–1972-fari (accessed December 20, 2019).

30. See, for example, "Roma ha dimostrato con le Olimpiadi di essere ben incamminata sulla via del progresso," *Il Popolo*, November 4, 1960, or Giulio Andreotti, "Olimpiadi," *Concretezza*, August 16, 1960, and Andreotti, "Pensieri Olimpici," *Concretezza*, September 1, 1960.

31. "Fervore di assistenza religiosa agli atleti del Villaggio Olimpico," *Il Quotidiano*, August 27, 1960.

32. R. J. B. Bosworth, *Whispering City: Rome and Its Histories* (New Haven, Conn.: Yale University Press, 2011), 242.

of the "3 S's"—sun, spaghetti and sex. Coverage of the events, moreover, had consequences for the Catholic morality campaign. RAI broadcasted for the first time myriad and no doubt shocking images of naked legs, particularly those of swimmers and track and field participants. Reacting to some of this, the *Osservatore Romano*'s Sunday edition, the *Osservatore della Domenica* published a "stunningly belligerent editorial," "Le galline" ("The Hens"), on foreign women and their conduct. The Rome Olympics, concluded Zonis, "dealt a significant blow to the old assumptions about what behaviors were appropriate, and possible, for Italian women."[33]

But for women and athletics the bottom line remained motherhood. In 1953 one women's review made this very plain when, discussing sports, it said that the body has certain limits and the duty of the female athlete was to know when arduous activity endangered "a possible maternal future."[34] At the Montecitorio, Catholic legislation and governance regarding women aimed less at their independence and emphasized family assistance, to make their lives easier as mothers and wives. Maintenance of the ONMI support mechanism for young mothers, for example, aided them, as did "the most progressive maternity law of the time," number 860 of August 26, 1950, a happy cooperative result from the PCI's Teresa Noce and the DC's Maria Federici. Elsewhere, the historian Molly Tambor cited Federici's work in the chamber toward "loans and insurance to protect marriage and for family salaries [and] equal access to the workplace and marketplace, and [women's] right to protection from exploitation of their work and their property."[35]

Sexual Relations

Women's questions turned delicate when the embarrassing but unavoidable issue of sexual relations entered the conversation. In the aforementioned 1950 *Iniziativa* article, Monsignor Prosperini wrote that Catholics must fight "the most widespread, the deepest, the most inveterate, the

33. Nadia Zonis, "City of Women: Sex and Sports at the 1960 Rome Olympic Games," in *Women in Italy, 1945–1960: An Interdisciplinary Study*, ed. Penelope Morris (New York: Palgrave, 2006), 80 and 88–89. Damiano Garofalo also recounted one woman's 1965 letter to *Famiglia Cristiana*, complaining about the short skirts worn in ice skating competitions. "I can't watch," she wrote, "not even alone the ice skating programs on TV without feeling ashamed"; Damiano Garofalo, *Political Audiences: A Reception History of Early Italian Television*, trans. Michael Sarnoff-Wood (Milan: Mimesis International, 2016), 122.

34. "Possiamo divertirci?," *Squilli lavoratrici*; December 20, 1953.

35. Tambor, *The Lost Wave*, 103–4 (regarding the law on maternity leave) and 64–65, 71 (on Federici's measures).

most powerfully organized and industrialized of disorders: lust."[36] Marco Barbanti recognized this determination when he wrote, "The morality campaign tended to gravitate ... toward the dimension of sexuality." It was concerned with portrayals of sex in the media, "through beachwear ... dancing, beauty pageants [or] tourism" and, above all, "adultery, divorce, abortion, birth control, homosexuality, prostitution, artificial fertilization, and illegitimate births."[37] As seen elsewhere, on sexual matters the Italian police cooperated with the Catholics, particularly with Gavuzzo's office; many of their tasks resembled the activity of vice squads in other nations during the 1950s. In April 1954, alarmed by news reports that sensationalized the city's "world of the pleasure-loving, the idle, vagabonds, misfits, prostitutes, homosexuals, perverts, drug addicts, ... pimps, drug traffickers, gamblers [*biscazzieri*], card sharks and other disgusting parasites," Rome's *Questore* Arturo Musco, who replaced the Montesi-tainted Saverio Polito, issued a report on police vigilance toward the maintenance of "public morality and *buon costume*." To fight miscreants required "organic, constant and energetic" police work, "astutely conducted" without a "pietism" that might attract unwanted publicity and "compromise the good name of the Capital or adversely affect tourism." Musco urged action against prostitution that endangered girls and boys, and he targeted homosexuals at their gathering spots—scenes of "repugnant obscenity, absolutely intolerable," adding that a tendency toward "frightening blood crimes" made them especially perilous. Beyond the reprobates, those who profited from these crimes or who "favor[ed] corruption,"—pimps, for example, or barkeeps who turned the blind eye—required more vigilance.[38] Such campaigns received not only Catholic support but that of others, particularly the Communist Party, which, in *L'Unità*, applauded the crackdown on "repugnant vice that unites men with men in unnatural relations."[39]

While Catholics were not alone here, sometimes they needed to tread lightly or invite ridicule as prudes. In the early 1960s the DC bastion of Catania in Sicily might have crossed the line in an experiment that separated the sexes on the number 27 bus line. For a few days, the transport officials reserved one bus for women and the next for men,

36. Ferdinando Prosperini, "Per la difesa del costume," *Iniziativa*, April 1950.

37. Marco Barbanti, "Cultura cattolica: Lotta anticomunista a moralità pubblica (1948–60)," *Rivista di storia contemporanea* 1 (1992): 144.

38. IPVI, Pg XII, b. 33, Questura Report, April 26, 1954. A copy of this fell into the hands of Giovanni Battista Montini in the Vatican, who forwarded it to Gino Gavuzzo.

39. Barbanti, "Cultura cattolica," 151.

the so-called "moustache bus," until they abandoned the whole thing as a total failure, prompting the journalist Giorgio Bocca to scoff that Catania had come to resemble a puritanical Muslim town.[40] The flame of sin, however, burned in other spaces that needed to be watched. One observer for *L'Europeo*, for instance, discussed a "particularly energetic" church warning (*monitum*) on sin, concluding that some clergy identified the two chief dangers as "kissing and dancing."[41] Kissing emerged as an issue, oddly, in Turin, where the *Questura* launched in 1955 a campaign against excessive necking in movie theaters. An earlier Cassation ruling permitted public kissing as "simple manifestations of affection," although it couldn't elaborate on where the manifestations turned into something else. One newspaper doubted that the Turin police understood that line. Based on the Penal Code's Articles 527 and 726 concerning public obscenity and offensiveness, the city's police dispatched "anti-kissing squads" (*squadre antibacio*) to enforce *buon costume*. Transgressors risked one month in jail and fines of up to sixteen thousand lire. A Morality Office report from Monsignor Prosperini felt that the trouble of erotic scofflaws extended far past Turin; but the issue failed to achieve the notoriety it deserved because of well-meaning people who opted to turn away. *Noi uomini* also complained that the Turin situation went "past all grades of toleration" and applauded the police who enforced laws based on "profound and patient educative intentions according to Christian principles." Questions remained through the decade and into the next. In 1960 *L'Europeo* submitted a tongue-in-cheek article on the still-unresolved kissing issue, addressing the new minister of Tourism and the Spettacolo, the DC's Umberto Tupini, who took a stab at a rubric. First, to be offensive, reported the *Europeo*, the minister stressed that the kiss needed to take place in a public area—that is, where people would be able to bear witness. Then it had to meet two criteria. The kiss could neither be excessively long nor "exaggerated."[42]

Other suspicion came from "Lidia," who wrote advice columns in some of the AC's women's reviews. Many Catholics, particularly the clergy, shared her reservations about dance. Attendance at too many dances, for instance, might damage reputations and end hopes of be-

40. Bocca, *La scoperta dell'Italia*, 205.

41. Renzo Trionfera, "Il diavolo a passo di cha cha cha," *L'Europeo*, August 13, 1961.

42. "Signorine, non baciate i ministri," *L'Europeo*, June 5, 1960; R. M., "Educazione e vigilanza," *Noi uomini*, January 31, 1955.

coming a godparent.[43] Italy's greatest mass-circulation magazine, *Famiglia Cristiana*, urged those wanting "to maintain Christian serenity within the family" to turn off the television when dancers appeared on the screen.[44] The aforementioned *L'Europeo* article quoted a Dominican's alarm over "extended contact" dances like the tango, the "slow" fox trot, the one-step, and the Boston. The appearance of the Twist caused much anguish. A column in *Orrizonti* answered the question of "why can't we dance the Twist?" with the argument that civilized nations needed to do everything possible to protect themselves from such "stupidities."[45]

Modernity seduced fathers, mothers, and children, making them forget their responsibilities, accept "stupidities," and rebel against the faith of their ancestors. Many of the faithful considered juvenile delinquency, birth control, prostitution, and fashion, particularly women's fashions, as battlefields in the contest against moral decay, and discussions about them tell us a great deal about *costume* and the Catholic family vision. By the mid-1950s, their considerations of juvenile delinquency and its impact on the family took cues from foreign images and icons, such as James Dean, and terms, as in Britain's "Teddy Boys."[46] From Milan in 1955, Archbishop Montini identified this malaise among the young as one of "skepticism, doubt, irreverence [and] inertia."[47] The phenomenon emerged as a particular problem in many national cinemas, beginning with such U.S. films as *Rebel without a Cause* and *Blackboard Jungle*, both released in 1955. The Franco-Italian coproduction of Marcel Carné's *Les Tricheurs* (*The Cheats*), released in 1959 in Italy as *Peccatori in Bluejeans* (*Sinners in Bluejeans*), triggered a debate and produced a flurry of Catholic commentary. In the Milanese Jesuit review *Letture*, Enrico Baragli lambasted Carné's "burned youth" as self-absorbed phonies who "don't study, don't work, dance to the latest [Gerry] Mulligan beats, snog and steal . . . they drink, they swear . . . then they talk about suicide." But because "Carné is Carné," continued Baragli, censorship would encounter difficulties from those who flaunted immorality behind the shield of "art."[48]

43. David Forgacs and Stephen Gundle, *Mass Culture and Italian Society: From Fascism to the Cold War* (Bloomington, Ind.: Indiana University Press, 2007), 257.

44. Garofalo, *Political Audiences*, 110–11.

45. Renzo Trionfera, "Il diavolo a passo di cha cha cha," *L'Europeo*, August 13, 1961; "Si/No" column, *Orizzonti*, January 25, 1962.

46. Stefano Pivato and Anna Tonelli, *Italia vagabonda: Il tempo libero degli italiani dal melodramma alla pay-tv* (Rome: Carocci, 2001), 135–36.

47. Giorgio Vecchio, "Il conflitto tra cattolici e comunisti: caratteri ed effetti (1945–1958)," in AAVV, *Chiesa e progetto educativo nell'Italia del second dopoguerra (1945–1958)* (Brescia: Editrice La Scuola, 1988), 468.

48. Enrico Baragli, "La morale dei 'Tricheurs,'" *Lettura*, February 1959.

Concern with juvenile delinquency, however, came during a time when, paradoxically, the problem seemed to be on a statistical decline. Although *Il Popolo* claimed that Italy had one of the lowest rates in Europe, the Chamber of Deputies discussed the issue on January 21, 1960. Much of the talk was anecdotal; that Roman gangs had appeared on the Aventine and Oppian Hills, or regarding a recent incident at Lake Bracciano. Justice Minister Guido Gonella confirmed that from 1896 to 1950 youth offender condemnations had fallen by over half, from forty-one thousand to twenty thousand, and that the decline continued through the early 1950s. Yet, he continued, the trend might have undulated since 1954.[49] Gonella and other officials regularly received letters from Catholic constituents, worried over this and linking it to the Spettacolo. The AC's Morality Office in Bergamo, for instance, asked Gonella in 1960 when the state would get serious about the application of laws that regulated cinema, theater, and the press and that protected public morality.[50] Apparently government revocation the year before of all licenses for pinball machines, known in Italy as "flippers," failed to impress them.[51]

Prostitution exerted another moral pall. As elsewhere, the "oldest profession" functioned in Italy for millennia. Terms for bordellos, itself an Italian word, include "houses of tolerance" (*case di tolleranza*) and "closed houses" (*case chiuse*), recalling an ancient law in the Papal States that required such places to keep their window shutters closed. The historian David I. Kertzer noted a historical unevenness before the fall of the Papal States, and concluded that "although the popes had periodically allowed prostitution in the past, by the early decades of the nineteenth century they again banned it as sinful and criminal."[52] After the conquest of Rome in 1870, Pius IX asked King Victor Emmanuel II to close the city's bordellos, but the request went unanswered. After the *Risorgimento* a long debate on prostitution began, with Catholics relegated to the sidelines. As Sandro Bellassai noted in his study of "the law of

49. *Atti parlamentari: Camera dei Deputati.* III legislature, *discussioni*, January 21 1960, 12,593–609; "Il ministro Gonella annuncia una legge sulla delinquenza minorile," *Il Popolo*, January 22, 1960; Gavuzzo cited the *Popolo* claims in his June 15, 1960, circular (IPVI, Pg XII, b. 18); see also Uberto Radaelli, "Andamento e tendenze della delinquenza minorile," *Concretezza*, April 16, 1961. Radaelli's moderate tone echoed Gonella's, that a problem existed, although it was probably not as bad as some made it out to be. Such a response might have been self-serving for the Christian Democrats.

50. ACS, PCM 1959–61, b. 102, 1.6.4, f. 97605, s. 0, ACI Morality Office (Gianfranco Goisis)/ Gonella, January 30, 1960.

51. "Da ieri aboliti i 'flippers' in tutta Italia," *Unità*, July 2, 1959.

52. David Kertzer, *Sacrificed for Honor: Italian Infant Abandonment and the Politics of Reproductive Control* (Boston: Beacon, 1993), 57. See also Mary Gibson's *Prostitution and the State in Italy, 1860–1915* (Columbus: Ohio State University Press, 1999); particularly, for our concerns, her conclusion, 207–16.

desire," since Count Cavour undertook the first steps toward regulation measures in 1860, the debate over abolition had been confined largely to the secular world.[53] By 1950, however, legal prostitution had ended in many nations, such as France, which abolished it in 1946. Catholic input accelerated. In January 1949, in fact, the DC unsuccessfully sponsored a bill to close the *Case chiuse*. The Sicilian deputy Giuseppe Caronia introduced the measure and shared sponsorship with a Liberal, a Monarchist, and a thirteen-member DC group that included four women, Maria Jervolino, Pia Colini Lombardi, Angela Maria Guidi Cingolani, and Maria Federici. When criminalization of prostitution finally did come, in February 1958, most Italians must have found it ironic that a Socialist deputy, Lina Merlin, guided the measure. Catholics, however tried to hijack the law for themselves. The DC deputy Antonio Boggiano Pico worked on it with Merlin but then took credit for it as a victory of the "morality campaign."[54] However, closures never enjoyed widespread support. A 1949 poll showed that over 80 percent of respondents believed that ending the *case chiuse* only removed prostitution from state-regulated houses and put it on the streets. Most felt that the state provided positive regulatory and health guidance in a necessary and inevitable evil, reasoning that criminalization would force prostitution into the shadows to no one's benefit. A 1951 Gallup poll conducted in Varese revealed that almost 59 percent opposed outlawing prostitution, while 28 percent remained undecided on the subject. Among women, only 9 percent advocated closing the houses.[55] On the other hand, many Catholic leaders supported the Merlin Law. *Concretezza* greeted the end of the double standard that let the man off the hook. Discussing its significance on Il *Popolo*'s new women's page (page 4), furthermore, the DC deputy Ida D'Este hailed the end of government regulation, born of "male egoism and sensuality" and a system of "guilt- and remorse-free vice." The Merlin Law was a step forward in the "struggle against vice, exploitation, pimping [*lenocinio*], and prostitution."[56]

53. Sandro Bellassai, *La legge del Desiderio: Il progetto Merlin e L'Italia degli anni Cinquanta* (Rome: Carocci editore, 2006), 17–18.

54. The chamber approved the so-called Merlin Law on January 29, 1958, by a vote of 385 to 115. It was issued as the law of February 20, 1958, number 75. Merlin was also responsible for a law (January 9, 1963, no. 7) that ended the practice of firing female employees when they married. See also Tambor, *The Lost Wave*, particularly chapter 8, 108–40.

55. Tambor, *The Lost Wave*, 124–25; Carlo Falconi, "La Crisi della parrocchia in Italia," *Nuovi argomenti*, July–August 1953.

56. Luigi Scremin, "Case chiuse e 'doppia morale,'" *Concretezza*, January 15, 1957; Ida D'Este, "Significato di una legge," *Il Popolo*, February 10, 1958. A protégé of Giovanni Ponti, D'Este worked in the

The law, as feared, did not end prostitution but pushed it onto the streets, creating greater dangers for the prostitutes. *Time* magazine noted that, in fact, a surge in the trade followed criminalization, and state-registered syphilis cases doubled between 1957 and 1960, an increase, the review implied, that may have partly resulted from the Merlin Law restrictions.[57] Such questions prompted concern from the DC deputy Maria Pia Dal Canton, who understood that the legislation permitted police intervention only to stop "scandalous" or violent circumstances as they happened. Citing the notorious murder of Rosemarie Nitribitt, a high-class German call girl in October 1957, Dal Canton felt the need for something more to "protect and aid" prostitutes as well as other women and children in dangerous situations. As president of the Italian Committee for the Moral and Social Defense of Women (Comitato Italiano di Difesa morale e sociale della Donna, or CIDD), another DC deputy, Pia Colini Lombardi (Merlin was the vice president), linked Catholic Action Citizens Groups and the CIDD to work closely with the Interior Ministry in aiding ex–*case chiuse* personnel. On the diocesan level, church offers to help to ex-prostitutes sometimes proved disappointing. In Albegna, for example, the bishop opened an office and made provisions to place the women and any children in a Genoese refuge. Only four women showed up at the office: two elderly, one forty-year-old with her daughter, and one thirty-year-old with her three children. None was interested in the refuge. The DC understood the need to protect these newly jobless people, and with that in mind, on June 13, 1958, Dal Canton proposed a bill in the chamber for women police units. Ten colleagues endorsed it, of which six were DC women. Dal Canton had been calling for some time for a special force to deal with "women's social activity," and the Merlin Law paved the way for her. "It's time to launch the act on women police," announced *Discussione* in April 1959, and eight months later, on December 7, the proposal became law number 1083. The police (*pubblica sicurezza*) established a training regimen, and the first class of seventy-three graduated in August 1961. Only one of the students was married, a woman who had been allowed to join in recognition of her experience with the postwar Allied occupation of Trieste. The Catholic press all expressed support for the new "vice inspectors," assigned to morals cases or those involving women and children,

Venetian Resistance during the war. She was captured and tortured by the neo-Fascists; http://www.anpi.it/donne-e-uomini/ida-deste/.

57. "Italy: The Klaxon Girls," *Time*, October 10, 1960.

who would be given duties in the main cities across the peninsula, "The smile is replacing handcuffs," hailed *Orizzonti*. One of the few cautious articles came from the girls' review *In Alto*, where Olga Barbieri stressed the "hard and tough" road ahead and, without wanting to interfere, hoped that all Catholics might in some way help.[58]

Dress

Fashion, particularly women's fashion, often linked to brazen American or French consumer cultures, also had the power to seduce and endanger the family. Fashion provoked, and sex followed. One historian has written that the new styles provided "some of the most obvious and visible ways in which the new Italy of the miracle was manifesting itself... the long-standing battle on morality was waged as much over clothes as it was over relationships."[59] Catholic interest in comportment extended to Italian *moda*, an industry and a culture that blossomed after the war and began to make great strides against its competitors in France. The Powers-Christian nuptials of 1949, for instance, provided wonderful press for the shop of the Fontana sisters who made the bride's dress.[60]

As seen elsewhere, the faithful might fear going too far and appear as unbending blue noses—in this case over modern fashion. But here they could happily point to the church's rather liberal stand on certain aspects of style. In the 1940s don Michele Peyron, the brother of Turin's mayor, established his own Catholic-inspired house of Alta Moda, the Turris Eburnea. An attempt to reach young women through "the language of *moda* and elegance," it rendered friendly advice on the latest fashions, choosing the right wedding dress and so forth.[61] Later, in

58. F. Dalmazzo, "In tema di 'polizia' femminile," *OR*, November 15, 1955; "È ora di varare la legge sulla polizia femminile," *Discussione*, April 26, 1959; "Che cosa fanno le donne della polizia italiana?," *Orizzonti*, April 30, 1961; "Il sorriso sostituisce le manette," *Orizzonti*, September 3, 1961; Olga Barbieri, "Polizia femminile," *In alto*, January 1962; Perry Willson, *Women in Twentieth Century Italy* (New York: Palgrave Macmillan, 2010), 147. On the CIDD, see IPVI, Pg XII, b. 2, Archbishop Mario Castellano/Episcopal Commission for the Direction of Italian Catholic Action, June 23, 1958, with "Segnalazione urgente del segretariato centrale per la moralità." In the same folder: Gavuzzo circulars, April 21 and May 22, 1958. The chamber discussed Pia Dal Canton's bill on June 24 and July 15, 1959. On the Albegna case, see IPVI, Pg XII, b. 90, Albegna Segretariato per la moralità, "Relazione attività anno sociale 1957 = 1958."

59. Niamh Cullen, "Morals, Modern Identities and the Catholic Woman: Fashion in Famiglia Cristiana, 1954–1968," *Journal of Modern Italian Studies* 18, no. 1 (2013): 40.

60. Stephen Gundle, "Hollywood Glamour and Mass Consumption in Postwar Italy," *Journal of Cold War Studies* 4, no. 3 (2002): 109.

61. "Sì e No" column, *Orizzonti*, December 3, 1961. There is very little information on the Turris Eburnea, which, as of 2017, was still in operation, with representation around the world. It has no archives but maintains a website: http://www.turriseburnea.it/ (accessed April 20, 2021).

1955, *Famiglia Cristiana* launched a fashion advice column with a more open attitude toward current attire.[62] Pope Pius's treatment of the Fontana sisters, perhaps Rome's most famous designers of the 1950s, also revealed some openness. They raised some eyebrows with a tight-fitting dress for Ava Gardner, called the *pretino*, part of the *cardinale* line, and obviously inspired by clerical garb. Nevertheless, in July 1957 this did not stop the pontiff from welcoming the sisters and their staffs to the Vatican and complimenting them on their achievements. He even joked that, since black was the preferred Fontana hue, the Holy See must have been responsible for a lot of their business.[63] Some months later, in September, Pius delivered another notably conciliatory address to industry representatives on "the moral problem of fashion." Style often focused on the exterior, he said, rather than the interior, and, badly directed, it could be a place where "provocation and seduction, worship of things and luxury, or simply silliness dwell." The chief problems stemmed from immodesty and luxury. However, the pontiff shied away from blaming or condemning fashion as long as it maintained its proper role in "the decoration and ornamentation of the body." "Monotony" and "severity," he insisted, were unnecessary.[64] A year later, in a young women's Catholic Action review, "Rita" announced that "fashion is blessed." The church does not condemn fashion, she stated, but respects it for the admirable goal of "harmonizing the beauty of the human body" to make it attractive to the opposite sex with the intention of creating a family. It simply was not true, she continued, that the Gioventù femminile (Catholic Action's young women's organization) "wanted everybody to walk around dressed in black with violet veils over their heads, sleeves down to the wrists in the summer heat and thick socks." Not wishing to be seen as too negative and in an effort to placate well-meaning if not-quite-so-militant Catholics, even Gavuzzo issued a list of respectable but chic beach outfits, their prices, and distributors' addresses. He went so far as to recommend a special issue of *Gioia* magazine "dedicated to the summer 1948 season."[65]

A less generous attitude existed elsewhere in Catholic Action's Mo-

62. Cullen, "Morals, Modern Identities and the Catholic Woman," 38.

63. Shawn Levy, *Dolce Vita Confidential: Fellini, Loren, Pucci, Paparazzi, and the Swinging High Life of 1950s Rome* (NY: W. W. Norton, 2016), 169–70.

64. "Il discorso del Pontefice sul problema morale della moda," *Il Popolo*, September 11, 1957.

65. "Rita," "La moda è benedetta da Dio," *Squilli effettissime e giovanissime*, April 6, 1958. See also an article in the AC review for working women, *Squilli lavoratrici*, "La moda, che passione!," of May 19, 1957. For the Gavuzzo concession to fashion, see IPVI, Sg. XII, b. 1, Gavuzzo circular, June 10, 1948.

rality Office, where Monsignor Prosperini wrote in 1954 that *moda* and *morale* belonged closer together, prompting readers to remember that clothing protected people from three things: cold, heat, and, especially, the "fire of passion." In all of this, he continued, the faithful seemed to have forgotten the importance of clothing. To correct this, they should understand the deeper issues of shame and decency inherent in dress; and they should look to the Bible, a guide for everything from the simple robes of Jesus and Mary to the repulsive "sensuality" of Herod's or Salomè's attire. Fashion, concluded Prosperini, formed the ring of petals that surrounds the "wonder of life."[66] Two years later, the *Osservatore Romano* questioned the wisdom of the industry in that what had formerly passed as fashion, based on aristocratic whims, had now "democratized" into a world determined by movie stars, sports, travel, department stores, and the leading houses (the *grandi sarti*). This collage of influences produced parallel systems, one inhabited by those "great tailors" who created "works of art" for refined tastes and the other characterized by a silliness leading to "mature men who dress like little boys."[67]

In keeping with the convergence of *moda* and *morale*, everyone, but particularly women, needed to adopt simple and modest dress. Catholic reviews saw conservative clothing as an expression of *buon costume*. One easy way to distinguish between the two sides of Italy's culture wars was the presence of "page six," or cheesecake photos, that regularly appeared in the lay or left press, where shots of Italian and foreign "sex pots" in various states of undress were de rigueur. Such images did not exist in Catholic publications, which regularly depicted women in modest dress, business suits, peasant garb, or clerical habits. At *Famiglia Cristiana*, Father Atanasio's "unbending" advice column to women frowned on summer impulses to dress with less and even to bare one's arms. The Madonna certainly dressed appropriately, he wrote in one column, so Italian women must also make the sacrifice.[68] In 1954, the *Osservatore Romano* complained about the rising numbers of women in pants, a "shameful exhibition and an insult to the beauty of women," and something that demanded more surveillance at the entries to the great basilicas.[69] Foreign tourists nonetheless pushed the envelope. Responding to the Vatican paper's discussions during the summer of 1957 and to

66. Ferdinando Prosperini "La moda e la morale," *Iniziativa*, March 1954.
67. "E," "Considerazioni sulla moda," *OR*, June 4–5, 1956.
68. Cullen, "Morals, Modern Identities and the Catholic Woman," 45–46.
69. Lorenzo Bracaloni, "Le vere donne," *OR*, August 14, 1954.

circulars from Rome's *Questore* cracking down on indecent attire, the lay *L'Europeo* published "The Crisis Is Arriving in Short Pants," noting that, while sacristans had been "tacitly authorized" to turn a blind eye to blue jeans in churches, shorts could never be tolerated. But what of "places of respect," such as museums, mischievously continued the piece, where so many naked statues might trigger some smirks over a ban on shorts? Large sections of the beach at Nettuno, furthermore, might have to be closed to bathers, since they sit within eyeshot of Saint Maria Goretti's tomb.[70] Sometimes push came to shove, as in the 1956 case of a young woman fined one thousand lire for sporting shorts in Monterosso near La Spezia. She had been stopped on a street that led to the beach. On appeal, however, one month later the court waved the fine.[71]

Vacations

Particularly vexing was the never-ending issue of vacations and holiday resorts, the *villeggiatura*. In these moral-free danger zones, many, especially foreigners, lost their inhibitions, made fools out of themselves, and imperiled innocent women. In 1963, even the lay journalist Giorgio Bocca warned of a new vacation culture where "everything is available, promiscuous and approachable." Acknowledging the implicit moral challenges, he especially alerted his readers to a homosexual subculture, created mainly to serve foreigners, a sophisticated demimonde with prices to match. Venice charged the most.[72] Mountain zones caused concern, but with so many vacationers tanning in their bikinis, beaches raised the most alarm.[73] Greater and greater numbers of transient merrymakers, intoxicated with the salt air or stronger stuff and cavorting far from the gaze of the parish priest, aroused Catholic Action anxiety from the top down. Among the most extreme solutions might have been found in a 1955 letter from a parish priest to congratulate the local DC

70. Vittorio Zincone, "La crisi sia arrivando in calzoncini," *L'Europeo*, September 1, 1957. See also "Il turismo in calzoncini," in the "Voci ed echi" column, OR, August 14, 1957; and the "Voci ed ehi" column of August 29, 1957. Zincone also recorded some frustration on the part of Roman restauranteurs over tourist problems with fettucine and other *primi* in a diet-conscious time.

71. IPVI, Sg. XII, b. 12, Gavuzzo *Relazione*, December 1, 1960.

72. Bocca, *La scosperta dell'Italia*, 190, 221.

73. On clerical concern for mountain vacations, see don Marino Grassi, "I problem montani della villeggiatura," *Rivista del clero italiano*, June 1954. On the inspiration from the *Base Missionaria*, see Bruno Paparella, "Parliamo bene della villeggiatura," *Iniziativa*, May 1953. The author noted that the movement had taught militants to mingle among their neighbors and coworkers. Then came the next step—to expand their missions to the summer resorts and vacation centers.

government for allocating separate men's and women's zones on Calabrian beaches.[74] Elsewhere, few Catholics went as far as the prefect of Brescia who, in 1948, urged that bathing zones be "imbued with seriousness and severity." But just how much fun would the Catholic regime allow? In an advice column to female Catholic workers, "Lidia" asked, "Can we enjoy ourselves?" After hedging on most subjects and specifically condemning some divertissements like modern dance, she concluded with a barely more encouraging, "Enjoy yourself, yes! Sin, No!"[75]

The AC's "Campaign for a Christian Comportment" of the 1954 Marian Year directed a sharp light on *costume* and launched a special "sub-campaign for the moralization of *villeggiatura*," although its aim was largely of degree rather than change. It placed more emphasis, for instance, on AC presence in tourist zones, focusing on religious activities for the young, organizing exhibits, circulating Mass schedules, and so on. One booklet for women made particular mention of young hotel workers who might be wooed by guests or colleagues or exposed to racy literature left by departing patrons. Or perhaps worst of all, they might fall victim to the traps of envy and jealousy. To fight these dangers she should pray, take frequent communion, and keep sight of Catholic Action, whether in reading its reviews or, more abstractly, maintaining "faith in [her] commitment" to the organization.[76]

For *Iniziativa*, one author, probably Gavuzzo, expressed the problems of the *centri balneari* from the seashore resorts to lakeside and pool decks. He suggested that churches in the tourist zones, along with the faithful (particularly those in Catholic Action) who lived there year-round donate their services for the spiritual assistance of vacationers, many of whom, he advised, came from foreign "latitudes" where behavior was "less correct" (*men castigato*) and religious sensitivity was less developed than that found in Italy.[77] Catholics understood differences between foreign and Italian cultural sensibilities and sometimes portrayed them in human form. In his "states of spirit" column for the *Osservatore Romano*, for example, Lorenzo Bracaloni chastised the foreign female tourist

74. PCM 1959–61, 1-6-4, 97605, s.1, don Michele Tarzia/Antonio Segni, August 7, 1955.

75. "Lidia," "Possiamo divertirci?," *Squilli lavoratrici*, December 20, 1953, 2–4. The Brescia statement is found in an AC Morality report (no. 85) of June 30, 1948; IPVI, Pg XII, b. 16.

76. Azione Cattolica (Giunte Diocesane), *Campagna "Per un costume cristiano," 3rd period, Summer Assistance* n.p., n.d. (probably 1954). See also Olga Barbieri (Unione donne)/Luigi Gedda, February 24, 1954, both in IPVI, Pg VII, b. 20.

77. N. A., "Vita religiosa e costume cristiano in villeggiatura," and G. G., "Iniziative pratiche: Quello che si può fare per la pubblica moralità," both in *Iniziativa*, June 1, 1957.

for her improper dress, particularly when she visited Italy's artistic and religious treasures. She presented a "ridiculous" figure in "tight and rolled up pants," an insult to the beauty of "real women." Fortunately, at the doors of Italy's great churches, attentive guards barred entry to this "worldly woman," who, concluded Bracaloni, took the wheel of the car and even competed with men in motorcycle races.[78]

Concern with the seashore and vacations persisted. In July 1955, an alarmed member of the Milan AC's Morality Office contributed an article for the *Rivista del clero italiano* on "the grave problems of religious and moral order" at the beach, issues of "dress and comportment [that] cause frequent scandal and serious damage to individuals and families." To confront the threat, the author urged that Catholic book fairs or other such events take place in resort areas; but, more important, he urged that the law be respected and applied.[79] Frequent memoranda from Gavuzzo's desk referred to the state's enforcement role and the need to work closely with the authorities to root out violations of dress, conduct, and "obscene acts." Circulate leaflets among the vacationers, he wrote in 1954, in both Italian and in foreign languages to acquaint them with the law and customs.[80] Along with enforcing morality laws and bringing a Christian sensibility to resorts, Catholic Action's *Noi uomini* added in 1956 the simple suggestion that the best vacations were those undertaken together by the whole family. Not only could parents and their offspring enjoy fun and relaxation, but they could also devote some of their holiday to searching out local sanctuaries and participating in Confession and Holy Communion.[81]

Beachwear proved to be among the hottest items in the battle for *buon costume*, and discussion focused overwhelmingly on women. In Milan, Archbishop Montini lashed out at its "perfidious esthetic"—fla-

78. Lorenzo Bracaloni, "Le vere donne," OR, August 14, 1954. On the subject of host reception to tourists, see Jeremy Boissevain, ed., *Coping With Tourists: European Reactions to Mass Tourism* (Providence, R.I.: Berghahn, 1996). In his introduction (p. 6), Boissevain noted that in the Mediterranean (specifically Malta), "remarkably little friction" marred relations between hosts and tourists. "This is because both are celebrating their leisure." His conclusion would certainly have been truer for Italy in 1996 than for Italy in 1956.

79. Giovanni Bellaviti, "Il problema della moralità e le spiagge," *Rivista del clero italiano*, July 1955. This article cited the Scelba circular as issued in 1948.

80. IPVI, PgVII, b. 20, Gavuzzo circular, March 26, 1954. *Noi uomini* printed one of the Catholic Action fliers. Written in Italian, French, English, German, and Spanish, it said (in the English translation), "Other countries, other customs. We beg you not to offend the modesty of our people: your manner of dressing is contrary to the Christian customs in our land. From your behavior will be judged the education and civilization of your country"; P. Erbe, "La Morale non va in vacanza," *Noi uomini*, May 26, 1957.

81. Carlo Carbone, "Turismo e vita familiare," *Noi uomini*, June 30, 1956.

grant disregard for proper comportment—bred in summer as "corporal exhibitionism."[82] Gavuzzo never relented on bathing suits, and his *Guida* specifically referred to them, lamenting that no particular laws dealt with them, leaving only the option of Article 527 regarding obscene acts. Nevertheless, a clutch of Interior Ministry circulars showed that the DC and AC saw eye to eye on bathing suits and acted in concert in a war without truce that continued for almost two decades. The *Guide* reprinted many of these directives, beginning with one from July of 1947 alerting authorities to the "prohibition against undressing on the open beach, leaving proper swimming areas in bathing suits or excessively skimpy apparel [*abiti eccessivamente succinti*], and attending dances in bathing suits or robes."[83] This circular was revived by the ministry and praised by Gavuzzo every year throughout the 1950s, reflecting persistent alarms of debauchery on the hot sands.[84] Much of the fury concerned women's two-piece bathing suits, although men were targeted, too, in their use of so-called *slips* (the term for immodest bathing suits). Every year, wrote Scelba, "certain bathers and tourists disparage shame [*pudore*] and decency, creating grave scandal, especially for children." To control this, the state would employ the Penal Code, starting with Article 726 regarding acts offensive to public decency. The AC Morality Office closely followed events. In 1957 it applauded, for instance, militants in the Savona area who, for documentary evidence, photographed those whose beachwear demonstrated a "complete lack of respect" for decency. Albegna, on the Riviera, however, described the campaign for Christian comportment as moribund with "scarce" results, specifically the distribution of a questionnaire in the schools. Its Morality Office, however, had participated in some magazine sequestrations and had "intervened with scholastic authorities" over the length of girls' gym shorts. The Albegna report concluded glumly that "a broad sense of mistrust snakes through our ranks" and that Catholic Action initiatives met with "little enthusiasm and without conviction. The work of the diocesan leaders seem[ed] sterile in vain attempts of persuasion." Gavuzzo took note, furthermore, that already in 1951 and 1953, judges in Pavia and Milan threw wrenches in the works when they declared that "slips" broke no laws.[85] Nonetheless, the struggle continued throughout the

82. "A Venezia come a Rimini," in the "Voci ed echi" column, *OR*, August 14, 1957.

83. Gavuzzo, *Guida*, 62–68.

84. See, for example, Rome *Questura*, circular of July 6, 1951, in IPVI, Pg XII, b. 32.

85. IPVI, Pg VI, b. 15, f. 7; IPVI, Pg XII, b. 16, Gavuzzo circular, January 15, 1953; and IPVI, Sg. XII,

decade. From banning bathing suits in areas off the beach to prohibiting two-piece ensembles at beauty contests and pressing the issue on tourist violations, the government expressed its commitment to keep the seaside clean.[86] And not only on the sand. In 1959, *Iniziativa* lamented the "deplorable habit" of wearing scandalous bathing suits into bars and restaurants (*pubblici locali*) and "even into dance halls and theaters."[87]

In 1953, a Catholic Action activist from the Veneto, don Adeodato Padovan, complained to Gavuzzo of a situation in Jesolo where, without any changing stations on the beach and most seafront property taken up by hotels, scantily clad bathers had to wander along the boulevards and into the town. The cleric added, perhaps with some chagrin, that the mayor was a Christian Democrat and head of the local Catholic Action.[88] Elsewhere, clashes between beachgoers and Catholic militants marred the 1957 season at Rimini when some holidaymakers in bathing suits or shorts spilled out of the surf and into a bar on the busy Corso Augusto (although the corso sits significantly inland), causing a heated confrontation with local Catholics. The *Osservatore Romano* defended the militants and insisted that articles on the skirmishes, from *L'Unità* and some mainstream dailies, formed part of a "seaside anti-clericalism."[89]

Franco's Spain provided some beach guidance. The bishop of Majorca in the Balearic Islands, for instance, enlightened Florence's Cardinal Dalla Costa, who related as much to the *Osservatore Romano*. On Majorca, wrote the cardinal, hotelkeepers advised tourists who were garbed in the more casual northern look not to go outside lest they be subject to the governor's sanctions. Italy could learn from such measures, and foreign slaves to fashion should remember "that our home [*dimora*] is profaned by people who are immodestly dressed." Parents, furthermore, should remember the Gospel of Luke when their own children approach the altar for Communion in that Christ was wrapped in simple and humble clothes; or Saint Paul, who in his Letter to the Romans (12:1) portrayed the body as a temple, "dedicated and acceptable to God."[90]

---

b. 5, Gavuzzo circular, April 8, 1953. Regarding the Savona case, see IPVI, Pg XII, b. 90, Giuliano Marconcini (Morality Secretary for Savona)/Gavuzzo, October 17, 1957; and Gavuzzo/Marconcini, October 22, 1957. The Albegna reports can be found in IPVI, Pg XII, b. 104.

86. Marco Barbanti, "La classe dirigente cattolica e la 'battaglia per la moralità,' 1948–1960: Appunti sul 'regime clericale,'" *Italia contemporanea*, no. 189, December 1992, 614.

87. *Iniziativa*, May 15, 1959.

88. IPVI, Pg XII, b. 86, Padovan/Gavuzzo, September 2, 1953.

89. "Anticlericalismo balneare," *OR*, August 5–6, 1957; "Voci ed echi," *OR*, August 10, 1957; and "L'Argomento di stagione," *OR*, August19–20, 1957.

90. Cardinal Elia Dalla Costa, "Problemi moderni dell'educazione," *OR*, March 6, 1953.

For Catholics, particularly irksome was the union of provocative beachwear and the beauty contest. In 1939, Italy held its first real tournament, crowning "*Miss Sorriso*" (Miss Smile) at a resort in Stresa. After a wartime suspension, competitions revived in 1946 as "*Miss Italia*." The 1950 event was the first one transmitted across Italy via radio, and soon the Catholic world could not afford to ignore the spectacles that it abhorred and condemned.[91] Catholic Action's *Squilli effettive e giovanissime* for young girls took a lead in lamenting the "invasion" of such competitions, known colloquially as *le Miss*, with their images of wholesome young women degraded on the judging platform for "an hour of fame." One article reminded the contestants, "poor creatures," that when the inevitable age lines appear and time eats into their youth, then God will still be there to provide them with the only true happiness.[92] Not surprisingly, two months later the *Rivista del clero italiano* joined the *Squilli* in passionate denunciations of *le Miss*. What could possibly motivate contestants to parade around dressed in next to nothing?, the Franciscan Grey Friar Serafino Guarise asked rhetorically. He answered his own question by pointing a finger at the "growing sexual promiscuity" that everywhere manifested itself "from work to sport to culture" and twisted a young lady's "innate wish to present herself pleasingly on all occasions [*in ogni evenienza*]." But other, greedy factors were at work, too, like the desire to make money or manipulate the contests to find a potential husband. Guarise, furthermore, stressed the contests' foreignness, emphasizing the influence of the British and Americans with their "failed marriage statistics." Men must also do their part and, with good hearts, join the battle against *le Miss*. Remember the warning of Matthew's Gospel, he continued, that "he who looks at a woman with impure desire commits adultery in his heart." Money and greed again took much of the blame, and the Franciscan again referred to the apostle, who asked, "What, then, will anyone gain by winning the whole world and forfeiting his soul? Or what can a man give in exchange for his soul?" Guarise fin-

91. Stephen Gundle, *Bellissima: Feminine Beauty and the Idea of Italy* (New Haven, Conn.: Yale University Press, 2007), 116–21. In his study *Death and the Dolce Vita: The Dark Side of Rome in the 1950s* (Edinburgh: Canongate, 2011), Gundle notes (p. 225) that one of the chief suspects in the Montesi affair, Ugo Montagna, had served as a judge at beauty contests. On another occasion, in 1911, for the fiftieth-anniversary celebrations of the foundation of the Kingdom of Italy, a "poor girl from Trastevere" was crowned as the queen of the festival. The Catholic and the Liberal press both denounced the event; R. J. B. Bosworth, *Whispering City: Rome and Its Histories* (New Haven, Conn.: Yale University Press, 2011), 149.

92. Lidia Macor, "Voglio anch'io essere una 'Miss'!," *Squilli effetttive e giovanissime*, April 4, 1954. See also "Voci ed echi," *OR*, September 13, 1953.

ished by calling on militants and other responsible citizens to raise their voices for more "energetic intervention" from the public authorities to save "our still-healthy Italy."[93] Those public authorities included Mario Scelba at the Interior Ministry, who in May 1953 argued for closer inspection of what he called those "indecency fairs." That underaged girls might slip in as contestants triggered frequent alarms, not an unreasonable fear, since, three years earlier a fifteen-year-old Sophia Loren (under an earlier name) competed unsuccessfully for *Miss Italia*. On February 2, 1954, an Interior Ministry report alerted every prefect in the country to the danger of girls under eighteen participating in beauty pageants. This directive took the opportunity to remind colleagues of Scelba's 1953 circular, which banned two-piece bathing suits from these events. Furthermore, "the clothing and, often, the behavior of tourists and vacationers" at such venues, Scelba insisted, justified extra vigilance.[94]

Class, too, surfaced as a factor in Catholic judgments. In 1950 the *Osservatore Romano* saw little difference between leftist assaults on the traditional family and the "Miss Europe" pageant that had been recently staged in Salsomaggiore. The "depravations of the bourgeoisie, bad manners of the rich, scandals at the beach and at the 'high class clubs,'" it noted, were real and required just as much disapproval as did the sins of the working class.[95] Don Padovan's letters from Venice also raised the class issue. In one he wrote that "the people are tired and indignant ... particularly the women" and cited a petition of fifty thousand signatures to that effect. "I know the spirit of the People," he continued, "because I am a son of the People. I am a chaplain for workers and I well know the spirit of the worker because before I was a priest I was a worker. Even if they hold silly ideas, they're good people and we need to care for their morals so that they can become better and more faithful."[96]

The church did not limit its response to denunciations, but also undercut the *Miss* competitions by advocating an alternative Catholic femininity. During the Marian year it promoted a counter-competition for

93. Serafino M. Guarise, "Il fenomeno delle 'Miss,'" *Rivista del clero italiano*, June 1954. See also Don Umberto Cicogna, "Le elezioni delle 'Miss,'" *Rivista del clero italiano*, April 1957; FVC Fondo Gedda, b. 240, Rome File, Interior Ministry circular, February 2, 1954. See also IPVI, Sg. XII, b. 5, Gavuzzo Circular, July 13, 1953. Regarding Guarise's quotes, the Jerusalem Bible inserts "life" for "soul."

94. N. A., "In vacanza anche la morale nel period estivo?," *Iniziativa*, March 1954; "Principiis obsta," *OR*, February 16, 1955; IPVI, Sg. XII, b. 5, Gavuzzo circular of June 23, 1953, which reprinted the Interior Ministry circular of May 25, 1953. The February 2, 1954, Interior Ministry circular can be found in FVC Fondo Gedda, b. 240, Rome.

95. Onorio Cairoli, "Fine stagione," *OR*, September 30, 1950.

96. IPVI, Pg XII, b. 32, Padovan/Gavuzzo, June 26, 1951.

the "Ideal Woman." In 1954 representatives from Italy's regions as well as from expatriate communities in Switzerland, San Marino, and Egypt met at Acqui Terme as part of the challenge. There, the women demonstrated "domestic capacities" as well as proficiency at sports. Folkloric costumes assumed a special place in the competition, and, in fact, wrote one observer, the only bathing suits in evidence were seen at the swimming event.[97] A year later, *Osservatore Romano* readers learned of a similar competition in L'Aquila for the "most beautiful and good [*bella e buona*] Abruzzese maiden." "No strip-tease," continued the article, "no runway, no judgments from severe artists, cinematographers and journalists . . . [but rather] the proper and honest woman, the type that Dante loved, that all men marry." In place of lurid body measurements, she knew how to "render a gracious household, [and] an inviting table" and served as "an eloquent and noble example" for all.[98] The Catholic woman, of course, stood in sharp contrast to her Marxist sister. The *Rivista del clero*'s editor, Francesco Olgiati, for example, claimed that Communist women comported themselves even more scandalously than did the men. He decried their "anti-clerical rage, anti-religious furor, blasphemous and implacable hate, [their] passion that translates into the most vulgar impudence, the most ferocious invective [and] in the basest immorality." What kinds of children, he asked, are reared by such mothers?[99]

Children, Malthus, and the Pioneers

The church taught that children completed the union of husband and wife. Children were to be cherished, taught well, and protected. The Gospel of Mark related when Christ admonished the apostles for not paying enough attention to them. "People were bringing little children to Him, for Him to touch them. The disciples scolded them, but when Jesus saw this He was indignant and said to them, 'Let the little children come to me; do not stop them; for it is to such as these that the kingdom of God belongs.'" Mark says elsewhere, "Taking a child He placed it in their midst, and putting his arms around it He said to them, 'Whoever receives one child such as this in my name, receives me; and whoever

97. "Voci ed echi," OR, September 15, 1954.
98. "Voci ed echi," OR, September 28, 1955.
99. Francesco Olgiati, "Pessimismo ed apostolato nell'ora presente," *Rivista del clero italiano*, February 1957, 61–72.

receives me, receives not me but the One who sent me.'"[100] The fight against birth control, or "Malthusianism," therefore, was necessarily—and perhaps literally—vital to Catholic family politics. Pius XI condemned the practice in his 1930 encyclical *Casti connubii*, and the Fascist "Rocco" penal code's Article 553 banned the dissemination of birth control "propaganda." Postwar Catholics saw no reason to modify this. In an article from a series on *costume cristiano* prompted by the Marian Year, Carlo Carbone identified "egotistical calculations" among those with no wish to marry or among self-centered spouses as an important factor that kept down family size. Government had a responsibility to encourage child-bearing and provide hard and substantial material support for those who took seriously the duty of parenthood.[101] At the AC Morality Office, Gino Gavuzzo took note of one case against a Hungarian-born author, Sandro Lenard, brought to trial for his book on birth control. While the court did not consider his work "Malthusian" propaganda and absolved him, his publisher still received a sixteen thousand lire fine for its dissemination.[102] In case there were doubts, the pontiff twice emphasized the church's stand—on October 29, 1951, to a meeting of midwives and obstetricians, and before members of the Family Front and others on the following November 27. For the *Rivista del clero* Angelo Civera condemned the modern attitude of "Enjoy but don't generate children; use methods to evade them." Birth control, according to Civera, was a hubris that led to "vice, perversion, clandestine prostitution, adultery, voluntary abortion [and the view] of offspring as a weight and an economic worry." In the practical understanding that certain options might be occasionally called for, however, he recommended continence or the "Ogino-Kraus theory," also known as the rhythm method.[103]

Marxist and lay Malthusians mounted a formal attack on November 30, 1953, in a parliamentary proposal from the Social Democrat Luigi Preti to abrogate Article 553 and lift the punishment of three years in confinement for those who "publicly promote" birth control. Preti en-

100. Mark 9:36–37, 10:13–14.

101. Carlo Carbone, "Benemerenze e diritti delle famiglie numerose," *Noi uomini*, May 15, 1955.

102. IPVI, Sg. XII, b. 5–15, Morality Office circular, July 29, 1950.

103. Apparently not considering Ogino-Krauss, the *Osservatore Romano* also proclaimed, "Catholic morality never admits the use of any method [of birth control]"; "Voci ed echi," *OR*, January 4, 1953; Angelo Civera, "Il controllo di nascite, *Rivista del clero italiano*, January 1951. Pius's October 1951 discourse can be found at https://www.papalencyclicals.net/pius12/p12midwives.htm (accessed October 11, 2019); and for his November one, see https://w2.vatican.va/content/pius-xii/it/speeches/1951/documents/hf_p-xii_spe_19511127_associazioni-famiglie.html (accessed October 11, 2019).

joyed support from the entire "lay front"—from Communists and Socialists through Republicans and Liberals. The *Osservatore Romano*, however, condemned his "initiatives that [had] nothing in common with Christian morality."[104] The DC saw to it that Preti's idea went nowhere in the chamber, but the fight had just begun. Shortly after the bill's defeat Roman members of the Italian Association for Demographic Education (Associazione italiana per l'educazione demografica, or AIED) pressed on and, to promote its agenda, organized a celebrity committee that included a Socialist, a Social Democrat, a Liberal, a Republican (notably, Ugo La Malfa), and the author, Alba DeCespedes. That this committee included no Communists may indicate that the PCI was less enthusiastic than its lay allies on birth control.[105]

Beyond Malthusianism, Catholics kept a sharp eye on rival political activity that might lure children from their camp. They showed special concern over the Pioneers Association of Italy (Associazione pionieri d'Italia, or API), which the Communists founded in 1949 for boys and girls from the ages of seven to fourteen. Distinct from the PCI's Youth Front (FGCI), the API focused partly on sports and recreation and partly on education and indoctrination in an attempt, as the *Rivista del clero* charged, "to ape" Catholic Action "and the scouting model of the Catholic Explorers."[106] The Pioneers' founder and director, Carlo Pagliarini, in fact brazenly aspired to "tear thousands of boys and girls from the ideological and organizational influence of the clergy and the AC." API children supported strikes in Milan, declared solidarity with African Americans in the U.S. civil rights struggle, and sided with Julius and Ethel Rosenberg in the celebrated espionage case. In his study of Communist morality, however, Sandro Bellassai wrote that, for the overwhelming

104. "Sarà permessa la propaganda antiprocreativa?," *L'Europeo*, December 1953; "Una proposta di legge," *OR*, December 17, 1953; and "Il matrimonio cristiano," *OR*, December 20, 1953, both written by Federico Alessandrini. See also "Voci ed echi," *OR*, September 22, 1954, which retaliated against an article in the popular *Oggi* magazine about a Jesuit who advocated birth control for overpopulation. "We need," retorted the *Osservatore Romano*, "to control the stories in their overpopulation of fantasies." See also Arturo Carlo Jemolo, *Church and State in Italy, 1850–1950*, trans. David Moore (Philadelphia: Dufour, 1961), 310.

105. IPVI, Pg XII, b. 33. Regarding the AIED press release, see Gavuzzo/Antonio Colini (president of the *Fronte della Famiglia*), March 3, 1954.

106. Tommaso Toschi, *Le Maschera e il volto: Verità su l'opera antireligiosa del P.C.I.* (Bologna: Editrice A.B.E.S., 1952), 33–45. See also Toschi, "L'Opera nefasta delle API alla luce di nuove documentazioni," *Rivista del clero italiano*, April 1952. Two months later, Toschi wrote a more general piece on Communist anticlerical plans for youth. The pernicious goal, he wrote was to "form youth to a materialist conception of life, hardening them to the spirit of struggle and take them to militant atheism"; Toschi, "L'Opera antireligiosa del P.C.I. fra la gioventù," *Rivista del clero italiano*, June 1952. See also Francesco Olgiati, "Per un'Italia cristiana," *Rivista del clero italiano*, May 1953.

majority of clergy and Catholic activists, "the simple existence" of such organizations created "a scandalous situation . . . a satanic growth to be immediately destroyed." The API was never a great success; it was based mostly in Emilia and Tuscany and some northern cities until Palmiro Togliatti disbanded it in 1962.[107] It nonetheless provided Catholics with plenty of outrage, such as in 1950 when it participated in a Communist youth festival at Piacenza where, during "four days of fun," a phony "Marriage and Divorce Office" united couples in unholy wedlock. The *Quotidiano* did not find this funny and grieved over the "disgraceful" festival aimed at the "spiritual ruin of children" and the derision of the institution of marriage.[108] Papal actions fortified Catholic reaction. Pius's encyclical *Summi maeroris* of July 10, 1950, ostensibly directed against the Soviet Bloc, could easily apply to Italian Communists on at least one point. "Through errors, calumnies and every kind of indecency," he wrote, "they draw the people, especially the tender youth, away from integrity of morals, from virtue and innocence, to the allure of vice and corruption."[109] Two weeks after *Summi maeroris*, on July 28, a Holy Office *monitum* specifically extended the 1949 excommunication of Communists to the API and the families that belonged to it.[110] From Milan, Cardinal Schuster denounced Communist "schools of corruption where children are systematically initiated into vice," and at Catholic Action Monsignor Urbani called for "the moral defense of children, besieged by a vile contempt never dared before . . . especially from the associations of the API." The Romagnole priest Lorenzo Bedeschi authored an exposé of the Pioneers as part of a Soviet toehold in Italy and servitude to Moscow. The Pioneers, he wrote, were taught to spy and inform on everyone—"an acquaintance, a friend and even relatives" and reportedly took their loyalty oaths before a representative of the USSR's youth organization, the Komsomol.[111]

Tensions mounted between Communist youth on one side and Cath-

107. Sandro Bellassai referred to the API as the most "hard pressed" (*stentata*) of the Communist organizations; Bellassai, *La morale comunista: Pubblico e privato nella rappresentazione del PCI (1947–1956)* (Rome: Carocci editore, 2000), 321–28.

Carlo Pagliarini, born in 1926, maintains a website with useful information about the API experience: http://www.carlopagliarini.it/database/archiviopagliarini/archiviopagliarini.nsf/Pagine/B8EA0A2DB88A3833C1256FE9004B76C9?OpenDocument (accessed October 11, 2019). The website states that the organization disbanded in 1960.

108. "Giorni di matrimonio simbolico" and "Difesa urgente," in *Il Quotidiano*, July 26, 1950.

109. The Vatican website, www.vatican.va, contains the text of *Summi maeroris*.

110. "Il Monitum del S. Officio," *Rivista del clero italiano*, October 1950. Alessandro Naccarato, *Angeli o demoni i nostri bimbi? Storia di una montatura anticomunista; Il processo ai pionieri di Pozzonovo* (Verona: Cierre edizioni, 2011), 26–27.

111. Lorenzo Bedeschi, *Dissacrano l'infanzia! I Pionieri d'Italia* (Bologna: Editrice A.B.E.S., 1950), 20.

olics and the state on the other. After the bishop of Reggio nell'Emilia received a disturbing report of obnoxious API children swearing, spitting on the Madonna's image, and interrupting the rosary with cackles and whistles, prosecutions ensued. Another case in Tuscany involved two children who attempted to shoot their parish priest. After the DC deputy from Verona Fiorenzo Cimenti made a spirited parliamentary denunciation of the API in October 1950, the government shut twenty-seven of its youth camps. Seven more closed the following year. Near Siena, the prefect took over an API site and proposed to transfer the children to a nearby Catholic camp.[112]

The case against the API took a more scandalous turn during the Pozzonovo affair.[113] In the small agricultural community of Pozzonovo, situated in the DC stronghold of Padua province, Catholics believed that they uncovered hard evidence of vile API acts. There, in early July 1953, Sister Battistina Gurian grew suspicious of some shocking language that came from the mouths of the little sons and daughters of certain Communist families. She listened in horror while a three-and-a-half-year-old girl sang an obscene song littered with Pioneer references. The sister presently discovered a group of Pioneer counselors who had turned their makeshift day camp (*asilo*), located in the town's PCI headquarters, into a "school of corruption" and a locus of "satanic orgies," where thirty to forty youngsters learned that the Vatican would soon be theirs and that the pope would burn at the stake. The Communists turned innocents into delinquents who blasphemed and insulted God, the Madonna, the pontiff, and the church. Sexual depravity pervaded the indoctrination where, in the dark, the leaders undressed the older children and subjected them to filth and ugliness.

News of Sister Gurian's investigation reached the office of Padua's Bishop Bortignon, who, on October 2, examined the "ghastly evidence" and denounced the API for pushing the young "toward materialism,

112. Bellassai, *La morale comunista*, 328. In 1952, furthermore, Rome contracted with the Vatican agency, the Pontificia opera di assistenza (POA) to administer for five years property inherited from the former Fascist youth organization the Gioventù italiana del littorio. On Cimenti's denunciation, see Chamber of Deputies, *Atti parlamentari*, Legislatura I, Discussioni—seduta del Ottobre 19, 1950, 22,935.

113. For discussions of the affair, see Giorgio Tosi, "Pozzonovo," in *La Bilancia e il labarinto: Istruttorie e processi esemplari*, ed. Giorgio Tosi (Padua: Il Poligrafo, 2000), 31–46; Bellassai, *La morale comunista*, 328–32; Andrea Colasio, "Forme del conflitto politico nel Veneto degli anni '50; Il processo ai 'Pionieri di Pozzonovo,'" *Venetica* (2) 1984: 40–62; Dolores Negrello, *A pugno chiuso: Il Partito comunista padovano dal biennio rosso alla stagione dei movimenti* (Milan: Franco Angeli, 2000), 99–105; Barbanti, "La classe dirigente cattolica e la 'battaglia per la moralità' 1948–1960," 617–18; Barbanti, "Cultura cattolica," 157–71; and Naccarato, *Angeli o demoni i nostri bimbi?*, passim.

atheism, sacrilege, cursing, immorality, [and] hate." The organization stood guilty of the "violation of childhood's sacred essence." On the seventh, he issued a diocesan letter to parents, instructing them never to trust "lay outsiders" in their children's education but rather to leave that task for the clergy.[114] The Pioneers and the Communists responded in denials and counteraccusations. On October 7, the Paduan Communist weekly, *Il Lavoratore*, dismissed the bishop's indictment as a pack of "ridiculous lies." At the national meeting of API leaders in June 1954, Pagliarini identified a "religious terrorism" against his organization, in which the church used the rites of First Communion and Confirmation as weapons.[115] The issue had already come to the attention of the authorities, and on September 8, 1953, the state prosecutor requested an inquiry. On the following October 29, the inquest began in nearby Padua, where the seven camp counselors were charged with eight crimes, including showing pornographic films, corruption of minors, and rape (*violenza carnale continuata*). On December 29, 1954, the case went to tribunal. Already, however, even before the inquest began, some of the children began to retract their stories, admitting that they had lied to Sister Gurian and to the parish priest who had acted as the chief inquisitor. The tribunal considered the church's evidence, therefore, as fundamentally flawed and, on January 28, 1955, absolved the API counselors, a verdict upheld by a Venetian appeals court the following November. A week after the tribunal decision, the DC-controlled Padua city council, in a vindictive mood that *L'Unità* labeled "clerical fanaticism," banned the Communist Party from the use of the city's major meeting venues.[116] In a speech to about 1,200 clerics in Padua's *duomo*, Bishop Bortignon expressed his bitterness "as a priest, a teacher, judge of good and evil [and] defender of his flock against rapacious wolves." But the problem, he announced, was not the judgment. One later account, in fact, concluded that the church never even wanted to risk a trial but only to embarrass the API and the Communists. The real issue now, continued Bortignon, had to confront the anticlerical chorus "over an empty victory." Keeping in mind Communism's goals to crush religion in the hearts of all children and to gain absolute power "to do whatever they want to

114. Naccarato, *Angeli o demoni i nostri bimbi?*, 37–42.

115. Naccarato, *Angeli o demoni i nostri bimbi?*, 29–30, 42.

116. "I clericali isolati impongono a Padova un illegale provvedimento anticomunista," *L'Unità*, February 9, 1955. The ban was more bluster than anything else and was never applied; Naccarato, *Angeli o demoni i nostri bimbi?*, 97. One of the defendants died in a car crash before the trial began.

do," the bishop urged all priests to maintain their "zeal and courage" in the church's defense.[117] Responding to statements from the Communist Concetto Marchesi, who had testified for the defense as an "expert in morality and sexual prudence," that the trial reminded everyone of the age-old religious obsession with sex, the *Osservatore Romano* simply hoped that the Padua decision not "provide anybody the right to dishonor religious morals."[118] In February 1955 the Paduan DC launched a collection to purchase the scene of the alleged crime—the cursed *asilo*. Upon the resolution, a first installment of fifteen thousand *lire* was raised by the party members who, noted the *Popolo*, stood in line behind a woman, clearly of modest means, who donated 500.[119]

Divorce

The Gospel of Mark records Christ's response to the Pharisees' questions on marriage wherein man and woman, he said, no longer are two, but become one flesh. Their union is God's will, and no one may separate them. Anyone who divorces his or her spouse commits adultery. Along with divine teachings, Catholics instinctually viewed divorce as a particular menace to the family. On November 29, 1949, to a group of Catholic jurists, Pius counseled that secular judges not require people to commit "intrinsically immoral" acts due to state measures contrary to "the laws of God and of the Church."[120] Such acts included divorce, which in 1949 was still legally out of the question. Consequently, Italians stuck in unhappy marriages could either simply leave their spouses or approach the church for an annulment, or they could go abroad and get a divorce. In a 1955 series of articles on "Christian comportment in the family" for *Noi uomini*, Carlo Carbone outlined Catholic Action's position. Marriage, he wrote, based itself on three characteristics: first, that it was a sacred thing, not just among Christians but for the faithful of all religions, for every epoch, for every place and every civilization. Second, marriage was a monogamous union between a man and a woman. And

117. Naccarato, *Angeli o demoni i nostri bimbi?*, 75–80.

118. "Sciocchezza e iniquità 'osculatae sunt,'" *OR*, February 3, 1955. See also Agostino Maltarello, "Difendiamo i nostri fighi," *Noi uomini*, February 15, 1955. In his study of Pozzonovo, Andrea Colasio notes that, on this occasion, the Catholics received support from the *Corriere della sera*, which considered the defendants guilty; Colasio, "Forme del conflitto politico nel Veneto degli anni '50," 58.

119. "La sezione D.C. di Padova per l'asilo di Pozzonovo." *Il Popolo*, February 22, 1955.

120. Mark 10:2–12; Alceste Santini, *Stato e chiesa nel processo contro il Vescovo di Prato* (Rome: Giovanni Semerano, 1958), 50–51.

third, marriage was indissoluble, otherwise, Carbone reasoned, people would enter the union too lightly, always with the nagging suspicion that it might not last. The horrid result of divorce was to reduce marriage to "an enjoyment, a caprice, a passion," the woman to an object of pleasure, and the children to victims.[121] Such arguments, however, were almost moot because, first, the Catholic stance was so well known and, second, divorce was not an option in Italy. As the ruling party, the DC stood against the legalization of divorce; but so did most of the political spectrum and society. Between 1947 and 1970 the DOXA polling organization ran eleven surveys, each of which showed that a constant majority of Italians opposed it. One poll from 1952 revealed that 62.5 percent of the population objected to it, with an even higher tally among women.[122] Many Marxists, furthermore, concurred. Togliatti often spoke against divorce, and the Socialist leader Lelio Basso recalled that even though, as a delegate at the Constituent Assembly, he voted to drop the "indissoluble" modifier to marriage, he would never have endorsed divorce because of "the moral and social level of Italian life."[123] Only among lay political factions did one encounter noteworthy sympathy for divorce; and a few courts served their agenda in recognizing it or annulment decrees issued abroad in such places as Austria, Mexico, and the Communist Bloc. Romanian judges posed particular problems that stemmed from an 1880 convention with Italy. In keeping with "the new [postwar] political climate," however, a pliant Liberal, Giuseppe Grassi, who succeeded Togliatti as attorney general, advised prosecutors and magistrates at the end of 1947 that foreign, particularly Romanian, annulments needed to be vetted by Italian courts.[124]

Catholics everywhere identified the Turin Appeals court under Judge

121. C. C., "Il matrimonio," *Noi uomini*, March 15, 1955.

122. Giorgio Vecchio, "Il conflitto tra cattolici e comunista," 460; Douglas Wertman, "The Catholic Church and Italian Politics: The Impact of Secularization," in *Religion in West European Politics*, ed. Suzanne Berger (London and Totowa, N.J.: Frank Cass, 1982).

123. Martin Clark, David Hine, and R. E. M. Irving, "Divorce—Italian Style," *Parliamentary Affairs* 27 (1974): 336–37. On Togliatti, see Fiamma Lussana, *L'Italia del divorzio: La battaglia fra Stato, Chiesa e gente comune, Con lettere dei "fuorilegge del matrimonio"* (Rome: Carocci, 2014), 20–21. Togliatti's wife, Rita Montagnana, a delegate to the *Costituente*, contributed a polemic of her own, *La famiglia, il divorzio, l'amore*, to the case against divorce. Her husband left her in 1948 to live openly with Nilde Iotti; Lussana, *L'Italia del divorzio*, 24–25; and the entry "Montagnana, Rita," in the Treccani Dizionario Biografico degli Italiani, vol. 75 (2011), at http://www.treccani.it/enciclopedia/rita-montagnana_(Dizionario-Biografico)/ (accessed October 10, 2017).

124. Guido Neppi Modona, "La magistratura dalla Liberazione agli anni cinquanta: Il difficile cammino verso l'indipendenza," in *Storia dell'Italia repubblicana*, vol. 3, ed. Francesco Barbagallo et. al., part 2, "L'Italia nella crisi mondiale: L'Ultimo ventennio" (Turin: Einaudi, 1997), 107–10; Lussana, *L'Italia del divorzio*, 77; Alessandro Coletti, *Il divorzio in Italia: Storia di una battaglia civile e democratica* (Rome: Giulio Savelli editore, 1974), 124.

Domenico Peretti-Griva as the main culprit in the campaign against God's marriage contract. Also known as an accomplished photographer, Peretti-Griva was a nephew of the former prime minister Ivanoe Bonomi. He joined the bench in 1910 and remained there through the Fascist era, although he never joined the party and even once ruled against three Blackshirts who were defended by Roberto Farinacci.[125] By the 1950 Holy Year, Peretti-Griva had established a reputation based on rejection of the Grassi advice regarding validation of foreign divorces and annulments. The *Osservatore Romano* reckoned that the judge had ruled on 1,800 separation cases since 1945. In a speech to launch the new year in the courts, the state prosecutor, Gaetano Miraulo, singled out Turin as a real problem. Within weeks of Miraulo's complaint, Peretti-Griva reaped more wrath by ratifying a Vienna tribunal's divorce grant for the renowned film director Roberto Rossellini, paving the way for his marriage to the diva Ingrid Bergman.[126] The Rossellini-Bergman affair ignited on the set of *Stromboli, terra di Dio* and provided tabloids from Rome to Hollywood with a hurricane of ink. To make matters worse, the director already had a wife (his second), and, worse still, he had been dating the star Anna Magnani, whom he callously dropped in order to clear the deck for his new *inamorata*. The tabloids accordingly bestowed martyr status on Magnani. In the meantime, with a proxy Mexican divorce, Bergman left her Swedish husband, Petter Lindström, and rendered defunct a marriage that had already produced a daughter, Pia. Ingrid's union with Rossellini yielded a son, Robertino, in February; and the two wed in a civil ceremony the following May. Already, on January 17, 1950, the outraged *Quotidiano* charged that, since the director's first marriage had been Catholic, Peretti-Griva violated the Concordat's Article 34, which placed church weddings on an equal footing with civil ones and left ending marriages to church tribunals. The Lateran Pacts, in fact, placed annulment jurisdiction in the hands of eighteen diocesan boards with ultimate and appellate authority in the Roman *Rota* and, theoretically, the Supreme Tribunal of the Apostolic *Signatura*. Twelve days later, the *Quotidiano* denounced the Turin court's argument as based on a "fraud ... a sham ... an invention ... [and] lies."[127] On January 19,

125. Peretti-Griva's biography can be seen in the online Treccani, http://www.treccani.it/enciclopedia/peretti-griva-domenico-riccardo_%28Dizionario-Biografico%29/ (accessed October 17, 2019).

126. Achille Battaglia, *I Giudici e la politica* (Bari: Laterza, 1962), 155–56. The decision was also noted in a Morality Office *relazione* of January 15, 1950; IPVI Sg. XII, b.16.

127. "La Corte dei divorzi," *Il Quotidiano*, January 17, 1950; G. B. Migliori, "Questa volta è Rossellini," *Il Quotidiano*, January 29, 1950. The *Quotidiano* also claimed that the Turin Appeals Court had

the Vatican paper, on page 1, condemned Peretti-Griva's decision to accept the Austrian decision of "mental infirmity" in the Rossellini case, one that ran "contrary not only to the thinking of the top jurists, but also to decisions of the Cassation Courts."[128] The Catholic press, moreover, tended to assail Peretti-Griva much more than it did Rossellini, who, as we saw regarding the cinema, was cultivating something of a Catholic identity.

Six months later, the Vatican paper criticized the Turin Appellate Court after it learned of yet fifty more annulments. One case concerned a professor who abandoned his wife of sixteen years (she had been his student) and obtained a decree, later ratified in Turin, from a particularly notorious Romanian Judge Ilfov. Peretti-Griva again clearly rejected Grassi's advice. Ilfov agreed that the husband had suffered a "serious mental illness" on his wedding day and "that (after the birth of two children) . . . " he insisted "he had not lived with his wife for even one day." He had since moved to the United States, married another of his students, and fathered two more children. "*Et ab uno disce omnes*," concluded the *Osservatore Romano*—the one case illustrated the larger issue—that the sanctity of the family had been sacrificed to the secular state (*il laicismo dello stato*).[129]

Parliament finally retaliated with an act of July 30, 1950, number

declared its "open rebellion" against the Italian legal system; "Diminuita la criminalità," *Il Popolo*, January 6, 1950. In fact, Rossellini had two earlier marriages. The first, to the Italo-Russian actress Assia Noris, ended in annulment. Then, in 1936 he married Marcella De Marchis. That union was clearly in trouble by 1944 when Rossellini courted the actress Anna Magnani on the set of his *Rome, Open City*. On reaction to the Rossellini-Bergman story in the United States, see William Bruce Johnson, *Miracles and Sacrilege: Roberto Rossellini, the Church and Film Censorship in Hollywood* (Toronto: University of Toronto Press, 2008), 265–69. The Concordat's Article 34 can be found on the Vatican website: http://www.vatican.va/roman_curia/secretariat_state/archivio/documents/rc_seg-st_19290211_patti-lateranensi_it.html#CONCORDATO_FRA_LA_SANTA_SEDE_E_LITALIA (accessed October 17, 2019). Regarding the Roman Rota, see Mauro Mellini, *Così annulla la sacra rota: Divorzio di classe nell'Italia clericale* (Rome: Edizioni Samonà e Savelli, 1969), 72–77; see also Lussana, *L'Italia del divorzio*, 46.

128. "A proposito di una sentenza," *OR*, January 19, 1950. The 1,800 figure came from an article written by the editor, Federico Alessandrini, "In difesa del matrimonio," *OR*, July 20, 1950. On September 26, 1936, Rossellini had married Marcella De Marchis in a Civitavecchia church, although he argued to the Austrians that he did so under the influence of drugs. The *Osservatore Romano* article and Rossellini's divorce were also discussed in Father Saturnino Manzoni, "La Magistratura italiana ed il divorzio," *Rivista del clero italiano*, June 1950. This article mentions that Rossellini's divorce was granted in Eisenstadt, Austria, south of Vienna and situated at that time in the Soviet occupation zone. The verdict had also caused a sensation in Vienna, where the minister of justice sequestered the court proceedings, and one newspaper wondered if Austria had become "a second divorce haven, after Reno." The Rossellini-Bergman union, however, was doomed, and the two split when the scandal-plagued director met a new paramour, Sonali Gupta, on his 1957 trip to India, an outrage so shocking on the subcontinent that government support for his film project there dried up, and Prime Minister Nehru personally helped the disgraced woman to leave the country. Gupta soon became Rossellini's final wife; Tag Gallagher, *The Adventures of Roberto Rossellini* (New York: Da Capo, 1998), 342, 465–96.

129. "Sic et simpliciter," *OR*, June 23, 1950.

534, dubbed the "law against Peretti-Griva" wherein, by votes of 133 to 83 in the Senate and 254 to 112 in the chamber, Article 72 of the Code of Civil Procedure was altered to strengthen the public prosecutor's power against the appellate court by giving him more ability to question its decisions. The Catholic press emphasized that this was no mere correction of the judicial system, but rather a victory in the protection of marriage. The *Popolo* regarded the battle as the "defense of the family against matrimonial deception [*frodi matrimoniali*]." Another article declared that the modifications would protect mothers and employed women. Federico Alessandrini praised the vote in the *Osservatore Romano*, noting that opposition was led by the "anticlerical" Social Democratic jurist Piero Calamandrei, with some Communist and Socialist support. However, Alessandrini continued, the secret ballot allowed a few "lay deputies" to vote their consciences, and the measure won the day. Writing in the *Quotidiano*, he criticized the lay parties, which generally sided with the Marxists in the debate over Article 72. These factions were untrustworthy, occasionally allied with the DC but only for opportunistic reasons, and committed to, in an odd choice of words, "universal" values—not Catholic ones. *Avanti!* condemned Article 72 as a government blow against an independent judiciary.[130]

Catholics mostly considered such open battles as options of last resort. Beyond a few militants like Guido Gonella, many DC leaders preferred to leave well enough alone and keep divorce from turning into a cause celèbre. And by mid-decade, it seemed that restraint was paying off. Fights over divorce were unnecessary because, by crediting the "vast Catholic Action campaign for Christian comportment in the family," *Il Popolo* tracked fewer failed marriages, from 10,697 separation requests in 1947 to 7,875 in 1953.[131] Calls to arms, however, still emerged from the clergy and Catholic Action. Ready or not, they seemed to say, divorce was coming to the agenda. In the *Rivista del clero* Luigi Mengoni detected

130. "Difesa della familia contro le 'frodi matrimoniali,'" *Il Popolo*, May 11, 1950; Federico Alessandrini, "In difesa del matrimonio," *OR*, July 20, 1950. The bill focused on the wording of the Code of Civil Procedure's Article 72. See also the following *Quotidiano* articles: "Il Voto del Senato sansisce la necessaria tutela del matrimonio," May 12, 1950; "Art. 72," May 13, 1950 (of Alessandrini); "Confermato alla camera l'art 72 del Codice di P.C.," July 15, 1950; and "Contrabando dei divorzi," July 19, 1950; see also "Il clericalismo ottiene una vittoria di stretta misura," *Avanti!*, October 11, 1950; and Coletti, *Il divorzio in Italia*, 125. Although Calamandrei opposed Article 72, he also argued against including women's rights in the Constitution. See also Tambor, *The Lost Wave*, 70–71; Mellini, *Così annulla la sacra rota*, 25; Lussana, *L'Italia del divorzio*, 77.

131. "In costante diminuzione le separazioni matrimoniali," *Il Popolo*, February 22, 1955. The 1947 number was probably higher in part because the end of the war led to more divorces and separations in many countries.

more and more divorce talk in the air, thanks, he felt, to the "inauspicious" 1953 election.[132] Whether as new proposals in the legislature, or Italian courts validating foreign decrees, or stories of Hollywood movie stars "with their habits and inclinations to divorce," the *Osservatore Romano* confirmed one year later that the divorce camp was preparing new attacks.[133] Their suspicions proved correct because, in October 1954, the Neapolitan Socialist Renato Sansone proposed in the chamber what became known as the Little Divorce, which allowed the termination of marriage after one spouse tried to murder the other, or had been institutionalized for mental illness for at least five years, or had received a prison sentence of fifteen years. Such modest provisions prompted the historian Mark Seymour to note that Sansone's plan "was so extraordinarily conservative that it was barely a divorce at all." Sansone often denied that his was an attack on marriage itself, but rather an attempt to resolve the problem of illegal separations. In 1954 *La Stampa* reported, for example, that each year something like sixty-seven thousand couples simply broke up on their own and moved on to other arrangements. Milan alone, it was said, contained eighty thousand people in this limbo. The press dubbed this growing mass "the marriage outlaws" (*fuorilegge del matrimonio*).[134]

For Catholics, however, there was much at stake, and the AC Morality Office said as much in a July 1954 circular. It was not a question, it stated, of a modest proposal that would permit very few divorces. The numbers didn't matter, but rather "a matter of principle," continued the analysis, "which cannot be nullified without the collapse of the family, itself."[135] The *Quotidiano*, moreover, described the Little Divorce as just a sneaky attempt to wedge a secular foot in the door. Why did the proposal's text,

132. Luigi Mengoni, "Considerazioni sul divorzio," *Rivista del clero italiano*, February 1955. Among other statistics, he noted that divorced people had the highest rate of French suicides.

133. "Voci ed echi," OR, September 22, 1954.

134. Mark Seymour, *Debating Divorce in Italy: Marriage and the Making of Modern Italians, 1860–1974* (New York: Palgrave, 2006), 169. See also Diana De Vigili, *La battaglia sul divorzio: Dalla Costituente al Referendum* (Milan: Franco Angeli, 2000), 35–38; and Coletti, *Il divorzio in Italia*, 127–29. In 1956 *Il Mondo* reported Sansone's estimate that four million Italians lived in an "extralegal" limbo, the result of marriages only on paper; Anna Garofalo, "Il Sonno del Piccolo Divorzio," *Il Mondo*, September 11, 1956. Sansone had also supported Luigi Preti's birth control measure in 1953. In a "Voci ed echi" column of July 23, 1954, the *Osservatore Romano* reported somewhat different, but stiffer, requirements for a divorce, apparently from an earlier draft of Sansone's plan. It specified issues such as the existence of a twenty-year prison sentence for murder or some other horrible crime (*delitto infamante*); abandonment of fifteen years; incurable mental illness for the past ten years in a psychiatric hospital; and attempted murder (*tentato o mancato omicidio in danno dell'altro coniuge*). The paper took note that Domenico Peretti-Griva applauded the Little Divorce in the pages of *La Stampa*; "Voci ed echi," OR, August 1, 1954.

135. IPVI, Pg XII, b. 17. Morality circular, no. 231, July 31, 1954.

it asked, use the word "termination" (*scioglimento*) instead of "divorce"? Sansone "and his comrades," continued the piece, knew perfectly well that "'little divorce' was really a 'big divorce'" of the Italian people from their traditions. Look at the particulars. With her husband in prison, the wife might remarry and then find out that he was innocent, after all. Attempted murder? The idea of divorce might provoke him even more. And using the incurable mental illness excuse sounded too much like racial selection.[136] Anyone who doubted this, wrote Silvio Chini in the *Rivista del clero*, need only look to the United States for proof of the damage that divorce exerted on society. Americans entered lightly into marriages and just as flippantly dissolved them, thus creating a social "plague of vast proportions."[137] Elsewhere, the *Rivista*'s editor, Francesco Olgiati, viewed the Sansone plan as one more stick of dynamite in the campaign to blow up the Christian *domus* and linked it to the notorious Peretti-Griva court, where "wealthy big shots [*ricchi signori*] . . . tired of the marriage bond" no longer bothered to go abroad for divorces; but rather found a 'free haven' [in Turin]." Fortunately, wrote Olgiati, "our DC" was prepared to challenge Sansone and the Socialists.[138] Needless to say, the party came to the rescue, and, thanks in part also to a lack of Communist enthusiasm, the "*piccolo divorzio*" crashed twice. Sansone's 1954 proposal never came to the floor in debate. In June 1958 he tried again, this time cosponsoring it with Giuliana Nenni, the daughter of the Socialist leader. Like the first attempt, however, it died before it could be argued.[139]

Love and the Bishop of Prato

Throughout the decade no challenge to traditional marriage stirred as much controversy as did the case of Pietro Fiordelli, the bishop of Prato—an issue that laid bare church-state arguments and became, in the words of the Socialist leader Lelio Basso, "the central fact of Italian public life."[140] On Sunday, August 12, 1956, thirty-three-year-old

136. "La ipocritica e sovvertitrice proposta per il 'piccolo divorzio' in Italia," *Il Quotidiano*, November 14, 1954.

137. Silvio Chini, "A Proposta della campagna divorzista III," *Rivista del clero italiano*, May 1957.

138. Francesco Olgiati, "Gli assalti attuali contro la famiglia Cristiana," *Rivista del clero italiano*, January 1955. Gedda's paper echoed this when it criticized the wealthy divorce hunters as "devoid of any moral scruples"; "Troppi compiacenti divorzi sono stati omologati in Italia," *Quotidiano*, May 11, 1950.

139. Seymour, *Debating Divorce in Italy*, 170.

140. Lelio Basso, "Respingere la provocazione," *Avanti!*, March 4, 1958. On Prato, see Vittorio De Marco, *Le Barricate invisibili: La Chiesa in Italia tra politica e società (1945–1978)* (Lecce: Congedo, 1994), 135–56. See also Crainz, *Storia del miracolo italiano*, 56–59.

Mauro Bellandi joined twenty-five-year-old Loriana Nunziati in a civil marriage at the City Hall of Prato, a small industrial city near Florence. Though both had been baptized in the faith, they chose not to confirm their bond with a Catholic wedding, and, consequently, that same day, during Mass, Bishop Fiordelli singled them out as "public concubines," a charge that subjected them to an array of ecclesiastical penalties. The newlyweds sued their bishop and their parish priest for defamation of character and launched a scandal in which Fiordelli became the first Italian bishop tried by the state since Mussolini and Cardinal Gasparri signed the Lateran Pacts.

Tuscany, where the bishop of Prato lived, with its sister regions of Umbria, Marche, and Emilia Romagna, formed Italy's Marxist "Red Belt." Some DC pockets existed here and there, like "white" Lucca, and Tuscany's capital, Florence, which was governed by Giorgio La Pira from 1951 until 1957 and again from 1961 until 1965. Prato, however, was more typically Tuscan. As in the Renaissance, its twentieth-century success rested on textiles; but by the 1950s modern industrial workers had replaced fifteenth-century artisans. In the 1953 elections for the Chamber of Deputies, Prato's Communist-Socialist alliance earned 26,400 votes over the Christian Democrats' 19,746, and the 1956 administrative vote yielded 39.6 percent for the Communists alone.[141]

Along with possible challenges from the working-class left, the diocese of Prato was just getting back on its feet. The city had had no residential bishop since the 1650s when Pope Innocent X joined it to Pistoia. Pius XII resurrected the diocese only in 1954, firing some ancient and fierce civic pride, a dose of joyous revenge against Pistoia. The new bishop, Fiordelli, arrived in October and was "triumphantly welcomed." Born in Città di Castello, where he was ordained in 1939 and served as ecclesiastical assistant to the local Catholic Action before moving to Prato. At thirty-eight, he was Italy's youngest bishop and enjoyed a reputation as a smart and progressive up-and-comer, announcing, "I will be the bishop of all the *Pratesi*." "Even revolutionaries and the most radical lay people," he felt, must understand this as a statement of reconciliation, a "promise of a truce [and] the good-natured cynicism of the Italians [that] is always open to friendly reconciliation of opponents." Fiordelli nevertheless considered Prato "an atheist city and dominated

141. P. Vincent Bucci, *Chiesa e Stato: Church-State Relations in Italy within the Contemporary Constitutional Framework* (The Hague: Martinus Nijhoff, 1969), 109.

by nonreligious parties [*partiti areligiosi*]." To confront this, he aimed to detach (*strappare*) the working class from the Communists, pull the DC together, mobilize Catholic Action, and penetrate the city's social and economic life.[142]

The bishop's test came on that Sunday when Bellandi joined Nunziati in marriage. The bride, her parents, and the groom's family were observant and worshipped in the parish of Santa Maria del Soccorso, but the dutiful Nunziati submitted to her *fidanzato*'s demand that the local government and not the church join the couple. With a strong anticlerical streak, Bellandi had been a member of the PCI, fought the Fascists in the armed resistance, and spent time in Buchenwald concentration camp. The couple's ceremony, therefore, transpired at City Hall with Prato's Communist mayor Roberto Giovannini. Bishop Fiordelli had long been determined to stem civil matrimonies done without church blessings; his first pastoral letter affirmed that only a marriage celebrated "before God and the Church" validated the constitution of the family, and he used the Bellandi-Nunziati marriage as his line in the sand.[143] Earlier, and aware of the impending event, he summoned Loriana to the chancery, where she responded and professed her Catholic faith to the bishop. There had not been much doubt on that account. Only a few months before, in March of 1956, her parents had, in fact, accompanied Fiordelli on a pilgrimage to Pompei. Nonetheless, at the chancery she confirmed her decision to submit to her future husband's wishes and forgo a church wedding. In response, the bishop warned her and, on a separate occasion, her parents, that this course of action would warrant episcopal condemnation.[144] In the first days of August, then, Fiordelli notified don Danilo Aiazzi, the pastor at Santa Maria del Soccorso, that, starting with the 6:00 A.M. Mass on August 12, four hours before the scandalous act would occur at City Hall, he and every other priest celebrating Mass in the diocese would read to the parishioners a letter from their bishop concerning the Bellandi wedding. Despite the church's efforts to "prevent the very grave sin," stated Fiordelli's declaration, Bellandi and Nunziati, baptized parishioners, refused a religious marriage and offended the clergy and the faithful. "This open gesture,

142. Pietro Farinelli, *Il Vescovo di Prato alla sbarra del Tribunale penale, ossia il suo "famoso caso" alla luce dei fatti e del diritto* (Pistoia: Tipogafia Pistoiese, 1958), 2.

143. Farinelli, *Il Vescovo di Prato*, 8.

144. Luigi Rosa, "Il Caso di Prato," *Aggiornamenti social*, April 1958. The author of this article had access to a number of church and Catholic Action documents, particularly a *pro-memoria* of Bishop Fiordelli.

a contemptuous repudiation of religion has prompted great distress for the clergy and the faithful. Therefore, you, by the light of Christian morality and the laws of the Church, will label the two as public concubines and, according to the norms . . . of canon law, will consider Mr. Mauro Bellandi a public sinner and Miss [*signorina*] Loriana Nunziati a public sinner" who would henceforth be denied the Holy Sacraments. Their home would not enjoy a church blessing, they could not stand as godparents, and they would be refused Catholic funerals. Their parents, furthermore, would be denied the blessing of Holy Water at Easter. Mauro Bellandi later claimed that the announcement did not reach him and his wife right away in that they left immediately after the ceremony for their honeymoon at Cortina in the Alps. The bishop's supporters, however, disputed this assertion, noting that after the ceremony the couple enjoyed a "sumptuous feast" at a restaurant adjacent to the cathedral and then formed a receiving and photo line in front of the church as the faithful exited after midday Mass. In any case, when the newlyweds returned to Prato about two weeks later, a young girl came to their door and then ran away after she had thrust into Bellandi's hand an envelope containing the parish bulletin, *Richiami*, in which don Aiazzi published the terrible news.[145]

On September 6, the Bellandis sued Bishop Fiordelli and Aiazzi for defamation, an offense covered in the Italian penal code. Loriana's father and Mauro's mother followed with separate accusations on the ninth. The bishop had not only brought a cloud over Mauro and Loriana's new lives together, but his denunciation separated them from old friends and led to a decline in the family grocery business. The Italian judicial system, based on the Napoleonic Code, placed the inquest (*istruttoria*) in the hands of the Florence procurator general, Giuseppe Ognibene. On May 11, 1957, Ognibene rejected the Bellandis's charges, ruling that the bishop merely exercised his religious duty, something that did not constitute a crime (*il fatto non costituisce reato*). Padua's Bishop Bortignon argued along similar lines after the Pozzonovo trial in 1955.[146] Fiordelli and Aiazzi operated in a religious sphere, Ognibene concluded, not a civil one, sanctioned in the Lateran Pacts and in the Constitution's Article 7. The plaintiffs' reputation, the judge continued, had "not been

145. Bocca, "Sposarsi in municipio è motivo di scandalo?," *L'Europeo*, November 10, 1957. The bishop's letter was published in the parish bulletin on August 31, 1956. On the wedding feast, see Farinelli, *Il Vescovo di Prato*, 9.

146. Naccarato, *Angeli o demoni i nostri bimbi?*, 74–80.

injured because it is extraneous to the religious reputation they enjoy as Catholics." No law, therefore, had been broken. But the clerics could not relax for long, because the Bellandis appealed, and a second inquest convened in October under Aldo Sica. To the surprise of many, Sica's second judgment reversed Ognibene's, rejecting the notion of separate civil and the religious spheres and ordering the case to trial.[147] *Discussione* saw immediately the Communist hand and that of *Il Mondo*, home of "the most acidic Italian laicism."[148] A week later, the DC review wrote, perhaps too optimistically, that "for over ten years, Italy has enjoyed a substantial, freely sought, religious peace." But now the lay/Marxist alliance was ready to launch an anticlerical attack; "the sickness," stated the front page editorial, "has become an epidemic."[149] At this point, the "case of the Bishop of Prato" became a national, even international, scandal.

Early indications of this were Fiordelli's calls for help in mid-November to Catholic Action, to DC members of Parliament, and to his episcopal brothers across Italy.[150] On November 24, the *Osservatore Romano* first discussed the controversy in a front-page article, "A Legal Case." "If two Catholics, refusing Catholic matrimony, unite with only a civil ceremony," it stated, "the Church has the right and the duty to condemn them." To hamper the bishop in the exercise of his spiritual duty was to trample on church rights and violate the terms of the Lateran Pacts.[151] Whatever their perspectives, the press reminded readers of the greater context, that of the struggle between the church and secularist forces. The Prato controversy addressed growing anxiety over what Catholics referred to as "the Christian family," and it would foster discussions of

147. Bucci, *Chiesa e Stato*, 38–42. See also Giuseppe M. Fazzari, *L'esercizio della giurisdizione ecclesiastica in Italia: Riflessioni sulla motivazione della sentenza contro il Vescovo di Prato* (Naples: M. D'Auria Editore Pontificio, 1958), 22. In a page 1 *Osservatore Romano* editorial, the Vatican insisted that, contrary to claims found in such anticlerical publications as *L'Unità*, the Lateran Pacts, indeed, protected the bishops and their exercise of authority; "Gregge costituzionale," *OR*, December 2–3, 1957.

148. Mario Malvesto, "Laicisti e sinistre contro il codice e contro la logica," *Discussione*, November 17, 1957.

149. r.l.v., "A chi giova?," *Discussione*, November 24, 1957. In a discussion of the divorce proceedings between Ingrid Bergman and Roberto Rossellini, the Vatican paper lamented that, because of their celebrity, the issue had become an item entertained in the press "which pretends to be educator, moral guide, and mind of the people"; "Voci ed echi," *OR*, December 6, 1957. On November 11 *Il Popolo* claimed (in "La morale corrente") that writers for *L'Unità* and *Avanti!* had simply lost their minds.

150. "Anche il vescovo di Prato ha ascritto un memoriale," *Avanti!*, November 17, 1957.

151. "Un caso giuridico," *OR*, November 24, 1957. One report noted that language became an issue at a few points in the two pretrial hearings in that canon law did not use terms like "public sinners" and "concubines." In reply, one advocate remarked that Italy's penal code described a "thief" but did not use the word; Mario Cervi, "Perchè il P. G. chiese l'assoluzione e la sezione istruttoria rinviò a giudizio," *Corriere della selá*, February 23, 1958.

family issues, particularly those of divorce. To *Il Popolo*, Giorgio La Pira defended the bishop. As one who had been instrumental in the incorporation of the Lateran treaties into the Constitution, the mayor emphasized that the sacraments formed "the substance of the Church." How could Fiordelli *not* defend them? Failure to do so, said La Pira, would be a sign of "indifference and laziness."[152] The left and the lay press, in turn, intensified their attacks on the bishop and clerical power, denouncing the Lateran Pacts as Fascist relics that demanded reconsideration.[153] During the trial, Piergiovanni Permoli, in the *Voce repubblicana*, reached the "clear fact [that] we now face dangerous and grave threats of clerical intrusion and enormous ecclesiastical authority [*strapotere ecclesiastico*]," although he was not as pessimistic as the Communist Giuseppe Chiarante, who argued in *Nuovi Argomenti* that the bourgeoisie had surrendered to that power.[154] In December, Bellandi's supporters pointed to a case in Bologna as another example of clerical intolerance. There, an "atheist" tramworker had "blasphemed" at work and was arrested on the charge of "contempt for the state religion" (*vilipendio della religion dello Stato*).[155]

Under President Antonio Paganelli, the Florence Tribunal heard the Fiordelli case from February 24 until March 1, 1958. Well-known attorneys represented both sides. The Bellandi family's legal team was led by Achille Battaglia and Leopoldo Piccardi, two of Italy's most activist and committed *laicista* lawyers and central figures in the Friends of *Il Mondo* organization. The clerics were represented by a three-man team of Ugo Fortini, Giacomo Delitala, and the respected professor of canon law Pietro Agostino D'Avack, a cousin of Archbishop Giuseppe D'Avack.[156] About fifty or sixty journalists attended the proceedings in the narrow and overflowing courtroom, contesting for space with spectators from off the street. Joking that impartiality might be a problem in a building

152. "Il parere di un costituente," *Il Popolo*, November 6, 1957.

153. *Avanti!* responded to "Un caso giuridico" (see note 151) primarily in Lelio Basso's "Sudditi pontifici?" of November 26, 1957. The *Osservatore Romano* discussed this and other left retorts in "Latrati contro le leggi" ("Barks against the laws"), a part of its "Voci ed echi" column on November 25–26, and in a separate article, "Trilogia critica," of November 28, 1957. It reiterated that since Nunziati was a "clearly observant Catholic," the church had every right to discipline her and call into doubt the validity of the marriage.

154. Piergiovanni Permoli, "Intemperenza confessionale," *Voce repubblicana*, March 2, 1958.

155. "Voci ed echi" columns, in *OR*, December 9–10, December 21, and December 27–28, 1957.

156. Battaglia had also been on the defense team in the appeal case for the Bardot and Ekberg movie posters. D'Avack published an influential study on homosexuality and canon law: Pietro Agostino d'Avack, "L'omosessualità nel Diritto Canonico," *Ulisse* 3, no. 18 (1953): 680–97. During the 1960s he would serve as the rector of the University of Rome.

that had once been a convent and now sat in a piazza named for a saint (San Firenze), with a courtroom that had once been a chapel, one Socialist reporter's jest illustrated the complicated issue of Italy's Catholic heritage and sense of self.[157]

Large partisan crowds, furthermore, spilled out of the grandiose baroque tribunal and into the piazza San Firenze. Already a week before the trial, a Civic Committee activist noted that the Communists, *laicisti*, and the "so-called 'rationalists for divorce'" had commandeered the piazza's choice shaded areas, and he urged that the bishop's support get there at least a few days before the start of the proceedings.[158] *L'Unità* found a greater Catholic presence inside the courtroom, with "priests and activists [who tended to] express themselves in a revolting manner."[159] From Rome, shortly before the trial's start, Judge Vincenzo Renis raised some eyebrows when he was promoted to head the Florence Appellate Court, the work of Guido Gonella, who had become Italy's justice minister in May of 1957. The left and lay press challenged Gonella's move, in that Renis had publicly expressed confidence in Fiordelli and should the bishop fare badly in the tribunal, he could count on a friendly face on appeal.[160] Parliament also followed the trial and debated it on February 27 during discussions over a bill submitted by the Communist Fausto Gullo that would further check the church's involvement in politics.[161]

Two figures who did not appear at the trial were don Aiazzi and the bishop himself, who wrote to Paganelli that his attendance might automatically confirm state dominion over the church. He pleaded that the "sons of darkness" in their "hatred of the religion" labored against *his* mission "to defend the dignity of the Sacrament, the sanctity of the family hearth, persuaded as they are that in the Christian health and integrity of the family rest[ed] the fundamental and real well-being of the

157. "Il vescovo di Prato si rifiuta comparire davanti un tribunale che deve giudicarlo," *Avanti!*, February 25, 1958.

158. Vittorio Bellucci, letter to Padre Lucio Migliaccio (Civic Committee Headquarters), February 17, 1958; FVC Fondo Archivi Personali Gedda, Faldone 53, "Emilia-Romagna, Toscana." Another unsigned report (Faldone 20) noted that discussions often overheated and required police intervention. It made particular mention of the Masonic element in enemy ranks.

159. "Secondo I defensori le leggi dello stato non valgono per giudicare il vescovo," *L'Unità*, February 28, 1958.

160. "Il trasferimento di alcuni magistrati rinfocola la polemica sul caso di Prato," *Corriere della sera*, January 10, 1958. Gonella also transferred Francesco Rotella to Trent. Rotella had been involved in the first stages of the case and was known to have advocated charges against Fiordelli. See also Giorgio Sgherri, "Fissato al 24 febbraio il processo al vescovo di Prato," *L'Unità*, January 5, 1958.

161. "Il dibattito alla camera sull'invadenza clericale," *Voce repubblicana*, February 27, 1958. Gullo's comrade, Mario Alicata, asserted that a movement was afoot in Italy to surrender proper state functions over to the Catholic Church.

Church and the nation." Finally and predictably, Fiordelli requested that the state honor its commitment in Article 7 of the Constitution and leave him to the "spiritual governance of the faithful."[162] In court, Piccardi vehemently denounced the bishop's letter. "Rarely," he announced, "have I seen such an insolent document . . . [it] is an act of war, a clear act of war."[163] Judge Paganelli nonetheless agreed with Fiordelli and excused the prelate.

Like Fiordelli and Aiazzi, Mauro Bellandi did not attend the hearing, but for reasons of health rather than principle. Bellandi had succumbed to what at the time was considered a cerebral hemorrhage, although a final diagnosis never seems to have emerged. His illness, however, contributed to the lore of the trial. Some Catholics felt that Mauro suffered some kind of fit upon hearing that Loriana, in the hospital maternity ward, had permitted baptism for their newborn son (which was true). Others simply interpreted Mauro's condition as "the finger of God" at work: punishment for his effrontery. The Socialist *Avanti!* retaliated against the "superstitious [and] the bigoted" (*superstiziosi, bigotti, beghini*) who would come up with such rubbish, proof that "even great nations and modern cities like Prato are still home to barbarity and the dust of the Middle Ages."[164]

Despite Mauro's condition and her own, Loriana *did* attend the trial and was often photographed with her celebrated attorneys. The *Quotidiano* described her as a "shapely" woman who frequently looked around

162. Mario Cervi, "Assenti il vescovo e il parroco al processo per gli 'sposi di Prato,'" *Corriere della sera*, February 25, 1958; Vittorio Citterich, "L'Inizio del processo al Firenze del Vescovo di Prato," *Il Popolo*, February 25, 1958. In an editorial on the next day, Panfilo Gentile rejected the bishop's argument. If the tribunal accommodated Fiordelli, he wrote, what would prevent all clergy from becoming a privileged class?; Panfilo Gentile, "Il processo di Firenze," *Corriere della sera*, February 26, 1958.

163. Mario Cervi, "Illegittima second la parte civile la forma seguita dal Vescovo per la censura," *Corriere della sera*, February 26, 1958.

164. "Atmosfera di caccia alle streghe," *Avanti!*, November 20, 1957. See also Giovanni Pieraccini's editorial, "Ritorni medievali" in the same edition. The baptism was also discussed during the second day of the trial when the priest involved, don Stefanacci, recounted that after the bedside ceremony Loriana asked to be "brought back among the holy" (*rientrare in santo*), upon which the cleric blessed her. Don Stefanacci then countered Loriana's pleas not to tell her husband with the counsel that he should also know of the baptism, although timing may be a factor in that confession. The mother then denied the priest's testimony, claiming that she had not been present during the baptism, although later consented when don Stefanacci asked her if she wanted to *rientrare in santo*; "La presa di posizione del Vescovo," *Voce repubblicana*, February 26, 1958. *Il Popolo* wrote that the baptism was a "dirty little secret" that no one on the left wanted to discuss; t.a., "La paura," *Il Popolo*, November 21, 1957; Philip S. Land, "A 'So-Called' Marriage," *America*, December 21, 1957. On Mauro Bellandi's health, see also "Chi tocca al vescovo," *Avanti!*, November 18, 1957; and Cervi, "Lunedì il processo per diffamazione contro il vescovo di Prato e un suo parroco," *Corriere della sera*, February 22, 1958. Cervi, who handled most of the reports for the Milanese daily, wrote that despite Bellandi's "gigantic stature," his right arm had become completely paralyzed and that he could barely move his right leg.

at the courtroom throng. *L'Unità* reported that a chorus of Catholic jeers accompanied her entrance into the hall. One Civic Committee priest confronted her with the question, "Why don't you stay home? You're only here to be photographed." A "burly" Carabinieri officer separated the two before she could slap the cleric while insisting on her right to be present.[165]

In court, the Catholic lawyers D'Avack and Fortini argued that the bishop and don Aiazzi had acted within their religious purview, *as clerics*, as guaranteed by the Constitution and the Lateran Pacts; that the affair was a religious matter between clergy and parishioners. The church, indeed, recognized the fact of civil marriages, which had been legal in Italy for about one hundred years. But Italian Catholic culture still frowned on civil marriages without the church's blessing. Even the anticlerical hero Giuseppe Garibaldi agreed to a church wedding at least once. Since the war's end, moreover, nuptials among celebrities had made Italians accustomed to stories of simple, church-free civil marriage. In 1956, the same year as the Bellandi wedding, the Swedish bombshell Anita Ekberg married the British heartthrob Anthony Steel in the Florence City Hall. The Peretti-Griva court and notoriously volatile movie star marriages, moreover, helped bring the issue to the public's attention. As cited earlier, Ingrid Bergman and Roberto Rossellini pledged their love without the church in a civil ceremony after the birth of their son. Hoping to court him, however, Catholics directed their glare elsewhere. They showed less generosity with the young and glamorous film siren Sophia Loren, who earned opprobrium for her scandalous civil marriage in 1957 to the divorced and significantly older movie producer Carlo Ponti. *Noi uomini* chastised them in an article, "The Diva and the Divorced Man" ("La diva e il divorziato"), which, without naming the principals—their fame made that unnecessary—charged that they had committed two sins. First, the producer, "the old divorced man," had rid himself of his first wife by taking advantage of Mexico's "convenient" laws for a quick divorce. Second, he and his new bride resorted to a civil ceremony, "which before God, Church and conscience, has no value." To rub salt in the wounds, the Catholic Action review lamented that Loren had been "stupidly" proclaimed the "ambassadress of Italianness [*Italianità*] in America." The *Osservatore Romano* echoed *Noi uomini* in 1959 when it dismissed

165. "La Prima udienza del processo di Firenze," *Il Quotidiano*, February 25, 1958; "Secondo I defensori le leggi dello stato non valgono per giudicare il vescovo," *L'Unità*, February 28, 1958.

her as the "international diva" who made her reputation by taking off her clothes and marrying a divorced man.[166] But those were all secular hedonists, while traditional Catholics married with a different set of rules. If Fiordelli had "trampled the flowers in the Boboli Gardens," wrote the Jesuit Giuseppe Fazzari in his study of the trial, the state would have every right to prosecute him. But the Bellandis were not tulips. They were baptized Catholics and subject to the bishop's spiritual authority.[167]

Bellandi's lawyers argued against that spiritual authority and that Fiordelli's decision to brand the couple's marriage a "scandalous concubinage" carried a very cruel message that warranted censure. "Here we are in Italy," declared Piccardi, "and in Italy the expression 'scandalous concubinage' [*scandaloso concubinato*] has a very precise meaning. It is not easy to define legitimately married spouses as concubines."[168] References to intolerance or medieval ignorance and fanaticism also became daily fare for the Bellandi lawyers and their sympathetic press.[169] On February 23, the day before the trial began, to a meeting of the Friends of *Il Mondo* in Rome, Battaglia railed against Catholic "illiberal prejudices" and, in a "tirade" on the church's past intolerance, cited the persecuted heretics Giordano Bruno and Tommaso Campanella and the sixteenth-century artist Daniele Da Volterra, dubbed il *Braghettone* for painting drapery over Michelangelo's naked figures in the Sistine Chapel.[170]

As the trial drew to a close, Fiordelli appeared to have already won. Representing the state, Manlio Mazzanti urged the court to absolve the bishop who, despite some excess in his choice of words, had only done his duty.[171] At 9:30 on the evening of March 1, however, after over five hours of deliberation, the Florence Tribunal reached a verdict against the bishop, imposing a minimal fine of forty thousand lire and court costs. Catholic Action immediately offered to cover the fine, although

166. "La diva e il divorziato," *Noi uomini*, October 6, 1957; "Voci ed echi," *OR*, September 7–8, 1959. For the Mexico nuptials, Loren was represented by a proxy. On Loren, Gina Lollobrigida, and other Italian divas, see Gundle, *Bellissima*, 2007, and Daniela Treveri Gennari, "Forbidden Pleasures: Voyeurism, Showgirls and Catholicism in Postwar Italy," in *Italy on Screen: National Identity and Italian Imaginary*, ed. Lucy Bolton and Christina Siggers Manson (Oxford: Peter Lang, 2010), 101–14.

167. Fazzari, *L'esercizio*, 42.

168. Cervi, "Illegittima secondo la parte civile la forma seguita dal Vescovo per la censura," *Corriere della sera*, February 26, 1958. On February 26 *Il Quotidiano* answered Piccardi's point on concubinage (in "Gli errori di Piccardi"), stating that canon law declared a civil marriage to be an "inexistent" one, thus permitting the "concubine" label.

169. On medieval references, see for example, Giovanni Pieraccini, "Ritorni medioevali," *Avanti!*, November 20, 1957.

170. p.p., "Pregiudizi illiberali per una stampa libera," *Il Popolo*, February 24, 1958.

171. Cervi, "L'Assoluzione del Vescovo e del parroco chiesta dal P.M. al Tribunale di Firenze," *Corriere della sera*, February 27, 1958.

the bishop was given five years to pay it. The verdict absolved don Aiazzi of all guilt. Paganelli and his fellow judges agreed with the earlier Sica ruling that the Catholic Church indeed operated under Italian law and the norms of the penal code on defamation. D'Avack turned to Fortini and remarked, "It couldn't have gone any worse." The victors exited the courtroom and were met outside by a crowd of well-wishers, while in Prato between 150 and 200 gathered at the diocesan offices to express their solidarity with the church. The bishop stayed secluded in prayer until Fortini phoned with news of the verdict, whereupon the crowd urged him to emerge from the chancery chapel and speak. "Pray and forgive," he responded, "for our diocese, for the church . . . I am content. Whatever happens on Earth occurs because God has willed it and His designs are infinite." The bishop of Prato then returned to the chapel.[172]

According to *Il Popolo*, the verdict stunned Prato's faithful, "those who know their archbishop personally and who deeply love him." With tears and choked words, on March 2 Fiordelli celebrated Mass before an overflow throng at the cathedral, where he spoke of forgiveness, humility, and love. But then, "in a stronger voice," he announced that the verdict would not muzzle him. "If," he continued, "someone thinks that, after these sad events, your bishop will become silent, that person is seriously mistaken." Fiordelli went on to chastise "atheist and inhuman Marxism . . . rampant immorality [and] wretched laicism, the ruin of our Italy. I will defend the right of little ones," he continued. "to become children of God through baptism; I will defend the right of the sick and dying to have a priest next to them; and with all my strength I will defend the Christian family which I honor and love."[173]

On the evening of March 4, the same day that Fortini filed for the *pro forma* appeal, Oscar Scalfaro and Italy's ambassador to the Holy See called on the Vatican. Both sides, however, emphasized that the visits were routine and had nothing to do with the verdict.[174] Italy's Marxist and lay cultures claimed victory, a fact recognized in the Jesuit *Civiltà Cat-*

172. Cervi, "Condannato il Vescovo di Prato per diffamazione a 40 mila lire di multa," *Corriere della sera*, March 2, 1958; "Pregate e perdonate," *Il Quotidiano*, March 2, 1958. To Fortini's news of the verdict, Fiordelli responded, "It is the Lord's will."

173. "Il vescovo invita al perdono e riafferma i diritti della Chiesa," *Il Popolo*, March 3, 1958.

174. Cervi, "Verrà riesaminata in appello la causa per gli 'sposi di Prato,'" and U. I., "L'ambasciatore Migone e l'on: Scalfaro in Vaticano mentre si escludono conseguenze diplomatiche," both in *Corriere della sera*, March 5, 1958. The Italian government at first denied the Scalfaro visit but later admitted it. Ambassador Migone made another visit the following day to the editor of the *Osservatore Romano*, again insisting that the meeting had no connection to the Prato case; U. I., "'L'Osservatore Romano' invita a 'ricondurre le cose all'equilibrio,'" *Corriere della sera*, March 6, 1958.

tolica, where Salvatore Lener lamented that the March verdict provoked "jubilation" among "the church's enemies [who] have intensified their heavy [*massicci*] attacks on it." The *Quotidiano* expressed comparable sentiments. "The mask has dropped," it insisted, revealing the true colors of the Marxist-lay alliance. But euphoria would only last, continued the journal, until the enemies of the church realized that theirs was only a pyrrhic victory.[175]

The Marxist and lay press had, indeed, staked much on the trial. *L'Unità* pointed to the verdict as a triumph for modern Italy, something echoed in *Avanti!*, which hailed it as the confirmation of the rule of law. Lelio Basso dismissed Fiordelli's cause as "a wave of clerical *sanfedismo*" and "a crusade against the independent and sovereign state," which tested the Christian Democracy and found it wanting. The *Voce repubblicana* identified the trial as an examination of "exceptionally grave questions . . . regarding the authority and sovereignty of the Italian state before the church," of whether or not the clergy could form "a state within a state."[176] For the more temperate Republicans, the case served as a "warning" to all for moderation, but particularly to the church, which needed to reconsider its political activity and to Christian Democracy, which "must serve the democratic state without compromises."[177] Lay and Marxist factions, however, could not assume that the Catholics had no tricks left up their sleeves. The left expressed alarm that, on the day after the verdict, at 2:30 in the afternoon the RAI substituted radio shows on its second channel with programs piped directly from Vatican Radio that condemned the Florence verdict, something *Avanti!* labeled an act of "airwaves theft."[178]

175. Salvatore Lener, "La condanna del vescovo di Prato," *Civiltà Cattolica* I, q. 2586, March 8, 1958, 641; "La maschera è caduta," *Il Quotidiano*, March 5, 1958.

176. "Davanti ai giudici il vescovo di Prato," *Voce republicana*, February 25, 1958; "Significativa vittoria dell'Italia moderna," *L'Unità*, March 2, 1958; Lelio Basso, "Respingere la provocazione," *Avanti!*, March 4, 1958.

177. "Un ammonimento," *Voce repubblicana*, March 4, 1958. After the verdict, the Republican paper conducted an exclusive interview with its "friend" Battaglia, who recalled how "the civilization of Florence, of the Florentines" struck him. The daily sight of crowds waiting at the courtroom doors, citizens of all classes, hoping to be admitted; their tolerance and fair-mindedness caused him to recall the liberal Catholic sentiments of Baron Ricasoli in the nineteenth century; "Intervista con Achille Battaglia," *Voce Repubblicana*, March 4, 1958. On Republican and Liberal moderation over the verdict, see also A. A., "Le polemiche fra i partiti per la sentenza di Firenze," *Corriere della sera*, March 3–4, 1958. The cautious tone of the more centrist lay parties might also be read in a page 1 editorial of the March 5, 1958, *Corriere della sera*, "Moderation," by Panfilo Gentile.

178. See, for example, "Su ladri di onde," *Avanti!*, March 4, 1958; "La RAI sospende le trasmissioni per rendere possibile l'ascolto di violenti attachi dalla Radio vaticana alla Magistratura," *L'Unità*, March 3, 1958; "La RAI ha ceduto i microfoni alla Radio Vaticana," *L'Unità*, March 3, 1958; and "Un uomo e un giorno," *Paese Sera*, March 3–4, 1958.

Beyond Italy, much of the world's mainstream press expressed satisfaction with the verdict. Britain's *Economist* applauded the judges in discharging "an invidious task with credit and discretion." While the modest penalty "soothed" church anxieties, the verdict "upheld the state's duty to safeguard the freedom of conscience of all its citizens whether they do, or do not, believe in God."[179] From Washington, Glenn Archer of Protestants and Other Americans for Separation of Church and State, hailed the conviction as "one of the most significant victories of religious tolerance in our times." The foreign Catholic press, of course, saw things differently. The Jesuit *America* and the British Catholic *Tablet* both condemned the verdict, while France's *La Croix* feared that the trial had created a lay and Marxist union against the church in preparation for the coming national elections.[180]

An accident of history aggravated the passions surrounding the Bishop of Prato in that the controversy around the French writer Roger Peyrefitte occurred at the same time. Journals and reviews across the spectrum, therefore, discussed Fiordelli's trial and the "French libeler" literally on the same pages and sometimes in the same article. The Bellandi lawyers, Battaglia and Piccardi, even served on Peyrefitte's defense team. Just as Prato fueled arguments, noted the *Corriere della sera* on February 28, "now it [was] the turn of the Peyrefitte case."[181] *Avanti!* charged that Prato prepared the way for the new issue by exposing as phony the church's cries of foul, which still enjoyed protection from the Lateran Pacts and the Constitution's Article 7. Instead, claimed the Socialists, it was clergy like Fiordelli, "with the tacit and at times expressed consent of the Christian Democratic Government," who truly endangered the charter, a situation aggravated by the fact that a foreign country, the Vatican City State, had prompted the case against Peyrefitte. The real scandal, noted another article, came from the fact that an alien power twice insisted on "prompt punishment" in an Italian legal matter and that Italian authorities showed such a "quick obedience."[182]

Catholics closed ranks around the pontiff, who had, according to the *Osservatore Romano*, in "conditions of bitterness, of sadness and of outrage," suspended celebrations for the nineteenth anniversary of his

179. "The Bishop Loses," *Economist*, March 8, 1958, 839.

180. *New York Times*, March 3, 1958.

181. "Sarà la magistratura pontificia a giudicare la quarela di Peyrefitte," *Corriere della sera*, February 28, 1958.

182. "Nota di protesta del Vaticano per un'articolo di Peyrefitte," *Avanti!*, February 25, 1958; "Proseguono le polemiche sullo scandalo Peyrefitte," *Avanti!*, February 26, 1958.

coronation. Pius then addressed thousands of well-wishers at a Mass in St. Peter's, thanking them for their "unshaken loyalty and devotion to this Apostolic See."[183] The dean of the Sacred College, Eugene Cardinal Tisserant, assured Pius that he and his colleagues shared the "grave bitterness" caused by Prato and by Peyrefitte; the Cathedral of St. John Lateran, the pope's church, led other parishes across the peninsula in penitential services.[184] In a letter to the clergy of Genoa, Cardinal Siri wrote that the Fiordelli verdict attacked the church and its defense of the family through the sanctity of matrimony.[185] The Holy See announced an ipso facto excommunication *latae sententiae* of all concerned, starting with Bellandi and Nunziati and extending to the lawyers, judges, and even the hapless public prosecutor, based on canon measure 2334, which was directed against anyone who "either directly or indirectly impedes the exercise of ecclesiastical jurisdiction." Both *Il Quotidiano* and Vatican Radio argued that the Paganelli court not only violated the Lateran Pacts, but placed the bishop in the same boat with persecuted clerics in the Soviet Union and Communist China, a sensitive point for *L'Unità*, which criticized such a "disproportionate and counterproductive reaction." Bologna's Cardinal Giacomo Lercaro assumed the mantle of the member of the hierarchy most critical of the verdict. He had already manifested his commitment to marriage during the Marian Year by inaugurating a "village for young married couples," an ambitious housing complex that would provide them with almost four hundred units. After the Prato verdict, Lercaro personally sent to Fiordelli a statement of solidarity and announced that the Church of Bologna would observe a week of mourning, with doorways draped in black and the sound of bells for five minutes each evening at six.[186] The Lombard bishops joined the

183. *New York Times*, March 10, 1958; "Il genetliaco del Papa solennemente celebrato," *Corriere d'informazione*, March 3–4, 1958. This was the afternoon edition of the *Corriere della sera*. See also Gentile, "La condanna," "Il Papa sospende la festa dell'Incoronazione: Scomunicati coloro che trassero in giudizio il Vescovo," and "Fervidi attestazioni a mons: Fiordelli della solidarietà del mondo cattolico," all in *Corriere della sera*, March 4, 1958. The DC paper discussed the "Church's bitterness over the anticlerical rush" in "Amarezza della Chiesa per l'ondata anticlericale," *Il Popolo*, March 4, 1958.

184. *New York Times*, March 8, 1958.

185. U. I., "Si esclude ogni conseguenza nei rapporti fra Chiesa e Stato," *Corriere della sera*, March 7, 1958.

186. "Il Cardinale Lercaro pone la prima pietra del Villaggio per giovani sposi," *OR*, December 14–15, 1953. The article noted that the "happy ceremony" was well attended by "all the civil and military authorities," but no officials attended from the Bologna administration, "the center of atheist Italian Communism." By December 1954 the first nineteen dwellings were ready, and residents were being chosen by lottery; "Il Cardinale Lercaro inaugura a Bologna il 'Villaggio dei giovani sposi,'" *OR*, December 9–10, 1954; "La Chiesa di Bologna prende il lutto," *Il Quotidiano*, March 1, 1958. On the excommunication, see "La scomunica per i protagonisti del processo," *Il Quotidiano*, March 4, 1958; "L'Osservatore romano annuncia la scomunica dei giudici di Firenze," *Avanti!*, March 4, 1958.

chorus on March 4 with a letter that denounced a "conspiracy . . . among various sectors of Italian public life against the Church . . . the bishops . . . the Pontiff . . . and our religion."[187] Fiordelli also received international support. The Foreign Ministry reported that the Argentine and Brazilian churches expressed solidarity.[188]

More response came from Francesco Olgiati, who defended the right of the "Church in mourning" to defend itself. "As priests," he wrote, "we do not want to insert ourselves in the political field [and] confuse religion and politics . . . but [citing Communist, socialist, and lay attacks] . . . no one can make us forget our right and our duty to be concerned over faith and Christian morals, to defend and react against those who would tear them from the heart of our people."[189] Some sympathy might be discerned, moreover, in an article by the president of Catholic Action's Young Women organization, Alda Miceli, who deplored the politicization of a simple religious matter in which the bishop was just fulfilling his duties. As someone who worked with young women, however, Miceli expressed particular grief in Nunziati's choice, made by a young Catholic woman like herself, of a sinful life over fidelity to divine law.[190]

The faithful protested in rallies across Italy. At Catholic Action Gedda dismissed the verdict, since "men cannot condemn the will of God." On the bright side, he continued, the verdict exposed as frauds those who, despite pronouncements of loyalty to the church, turned out to share "the worst anti-religious *laicismo* of our foes."[191] Gavuzzo's Morality Office received over two hundred telegrams from diocesan chapters, either to lodge formal protests against the "defamation" and the "violent anti-Catholic campaign" or to plan public demonstrations.[192] A Catholic Action press release termed the verdict "a bitter chalice." In an open letter, Gedda assured Pius that all Catholics stood with him at a difficult time made worse by "a vast campaign of calumny and defama-

187. "L'aggressiva campagna anticlericale denunciata dall'Episcopato lombardo," *Il Quotidiano*, March 5, 1958. On March 9, observing the nineteenth anniversary of Pius' coronation, Archbishop Montini also lamented the "facts harmful not only to the honor and right (*diritto*) of the Pope and the Church, but also to the honor, prestige and concord of our civil life." The letter was printed in the unsigned article "Solidarietà e carità," *Aggiornamenti sociali*, April 1958.

188. IS Fondo Gonella, Serie 3.2.4, b. 57, f. 9, Foreign Ministry/Gonella, March 17 and March 26, 1958.

189. Francesco Olgiati, "La chiesa in lutto," *Rivista del clero italiano* 39, April 1958. On other reactions within the church, see "Cronaca contemporanea, Santa Sede," *Civiltà Cattolica* I, q. 2586, March 8, 1958, 645–48.

190. Alda Miceli, "Un vescovo in tribunale," *Squilli effettive e giovanissime*, December 1, 1957.

191. "Speculazioni sulla condanna del vescovo," *Avanti!*, March 5, 1958.

192. IPVI, Pg VIII, b. 6, f. 6.11, f. 6.12. See also IPVI, Pg XII, b. 18, *moralità relazione*, no. 316–17, February 15 and 28, 1958.

tion against the bishops and the clergy [marked by] a more antireligious and partisan spirit," concluding with a prayer for the conversion of the church's tormentors. Among the Christian Democrats, Scelba characterized the judgment as "very grave," and, to a crowd in Trent, Fanfani lamented that it "grieves us."[193] The verdict came under a *monocolore* cabinet, under Adone Zoli, which contained only DC (or technocrat) ministers. Zoli, who was in Florence, sent his son to the bishop to extend his best wishes; the day after the announcement, the prime minister agreed to an interview with the editor of the *Giornale del Mattino*. Asked for his reaction, Zoli's face registered an expression "different from the serene one that everybody knows." Agitated, he rose without saying a word, escorted the editor to the door, and shook his hand, but in a gesture "different from a normal 'how do you do.'"[194]

With technically no domestic political allies in the *monocolore* cabinet, then, the Christian Democracy and the Catholics received a full barrage from across the political spectrum. The *Voce repubblicana* charged on March 6 that Prato placed "the democratic state in dire straits and pushed the lay parties up against a wall." The paper felt that Pius's and Lercaro's actions had only exacerbated the situation "in an atmosphere of Holy War." The Republicans and the Socialists also sensed dissonance within Catholic ranks. Although Fanfani sent a letter of support to the pontiff, who in turn thanked him and the DC for its "clear affirmation of Christian principles," the Republicans detected a DC response more subdued than those from the church and Catholic Action. On the other hand, as the government party, despite Adone's *monocolore* cabinet, the DC always had to tread more carefully. *Il Popolo* answered the charges by rejecting the verdict, but, it continued, to compare Prato to Beijing, as Catholic Action and Vatican Radio had done, was a bit of a stretch.[195] The Vatican, too, quickly modified its approach, placing it more in line with the DC's. On March 6 the *Osservatore Romano* devoted a front-page editorial, *Comprensione*, to the qualities of "'proportion,' of 'non-exaggeration,' of

193. Crainz, *Storia del miracolo italiano*, 56–59. For the Gedda letter, see "L'Azione Cattolics italiana si stringe attorno a Pio XII," *Il Quotidiano*, March 1, 1958; A. A., "Le polemiche fra i partiti per la sentenza di Firenze," *Corriere della sera*, March 3–4, 1958. Fanfani had also sent the pope his best wishes on the anniversary of his coronation, a message cited in gratitude by Florence's auxiliary bishop Angelo Dell'Aqua. The *Osservatore Romano* welcomed this exchange as a positive sign of Catholic unity; U. I., "L'ambasciatore Migone e l'on: Scalfaro in Vaticano mentre si escludono conseguenze diplomatiche," *Corriere della sera*, March 5, 1958.

194. A. A., "Governo e D.C. si sforzano di fugare le apprensioni," *Corriere della sera*, March 4, 1958.

195. "La DC oppone l'appoggio vaticano," *Voce repubblicana*, March 6 1958; "Speculazioni sulla condanna del vescovo," *Avanti!*, March 5, 1958.

serene objectivity . . . the straight [*non smentito*] good sense of the Italian people."[196]

Six months later, it looked like Catholic fortunes might have turned for the better. In October, upon appeal, Bishop Fiordelli was absolved. The Bellandis were ordered to pay court costs, although this time the prestigious lay journal, *Il Ponte*, offered to cover them. Other news might have heartened the faithful. Many engaged couples, perhaps intimidated by the trouble that haunted the Bellandis, opted less for civil weddings alone, which, in Milan, dropped 25 percent. Rome's figure, moreover, was 28 percent, with 45 percent in Modena, 48 percent in Venice, and 57 percent at Reggio Calabria. More good news came when the *Quotidiano* announced a decision by two Communists to marry in church. The couple had been joined six years earlier in a "Lenin Hall" ceremony but now chose to wed in a House of God, Rome's San Francesco a Ripa, after which the two planned to honeymoon in Prato for a show of unity with the bishop. But the damage had been done. The church had been hauled into court, and, even in filing an appeal, the bishop implicitly recognized state authority, something that the press recognized immediately.[197]

The spring of 1958 began in the wake of Bishop Fiordelli's trial and the nuisance of the Peyrefitte scandal. Troubled Catholics then had to consider national elections scheduled for May 23. In Parliament, DC insistence on a political voice for the church prompted heated debate on March 6, again launched by Fausto Gullo's aforementioned motion to restrict clerical interference in politics—a proposal doomed this time by a show of hands, although not before a fistfight erupted among twenty members on the chamber floor.[198] The newly formed Italian Episcopal

196. "Comprensione," *OR*, March 6, 1958. See also "Il Vaticano invita alla moderazione," *Voce repubblicana*, March 7, 1958. The Republicans, moreover, surmised that the Vatican would make the best out of the lost cause of Fiordelli and extend an olive branch to the judiciary in anticipation of a case against Peyrefitte.

197. Cervi, "Il vostro Vescovo non tacerà dopo questo doloroso avvenimento," *Corriere della sera*, March 3–4, 1958. The paper reasoned that in filing for the appeal Bishop Fiordelli repudiated his argument for not attending the trial; U. I., "L'ambasciatore Migone e l'on: Scalfaro in Vaticano mentre si escludono conseguenze diplomatiche," *Corriere della sera*, March 5, 1958. On the decline in civil marriages, see Aldo A. Mola, "Il Caso del vescovo di Prato," in AAVV, *Il Parlamento Italiano, 1861–1988* (Milan: Nuova CEI, 1988), 17:29. On the Communist couple, see "Due ex comunisti sposano col rito religioso," *Il Quotidiano*, March 5, 1958.

198. *New York Times*, March 7, 1958; Gentile, "Due autorità," *Corriere della sera*, March 8, 1958. Gentile reported that Gullo's measure was rejected in great part because of its obvious partisan grandstanding in view of the upcoming elections.

Conference, anxious to avoid a repeat of 1953's electoral sting, urged or, according to the *Quotidiano*, "warned" the faithful to unite in defense of religious freedom and Christian values. In the meantime, the lay and left press again accused the bishops of violating the Lateran Pacts by directing parish clergy to break the law and pressure Catholics to vote for the Christian Democracy. The *Quotidiano* agreed with the Episcopal Conference on the need to defend the Catholic vision. It reprinted a piece from the Family Front's review, *La Famiglia italiana*, which identified Sansone's Little Divorce and the bishop of Prato's trial as the two main attacks on the marriage bond and the sanctity of the family since 1953, assaults that came from the lay parties and their allies at the Italian Divorce Movement and the Italian Association for Demographic Education, which advocated Malthusianism. The DC, it continued, clearly and forcefully supported "the protection of children and the family against any actions that menace their health and integrity" and for "the defense of public morality, respect for civil institutions, and the political and religious convictions of citizens."[199]

The May 1958 elections yielded back some of the ground that the Christian Democracy lost in 1953, going from 40.1 percent of the vote to 42.3, which provided ten more seats in the chamber, from 263 to 273 out of a total of 596. In the lay and Marxist camps, the Socialists won the most, adding 9 seats (to 84) while the Communists, despite a slight gain in the popular tally, lost three (to 140). The Social Democrats gained four (to twenty-three), while the Republicans and Liberals each added one (to six and fourteen, respectively). The big losers were on the far right, where nineteen seats were lost. Many of those voters clearly rallied to the DC as they had done in 1948.

Bad news from the Vatican, however, sobered Catholic optimism. The holy father's health had been deteriorating for a few years. The year 1954 had been particularly bad for him, producing scares in all those around him; on one occasion he even received the last rites, prompting the composition of an obituary. Pius never completely recovered from those maladies, and a faulty "capacity for lucid judgment and effective governance" darkened the last years of his life.[200] His aloofness and self-inflicted lone-

199. "La profonda risonanza del monito dei vescovi," May 4, 1958; "Il monito dei Vescovi italiani al centro dei commenti politici," May 5, 1958; and "Votare per la famiglia," May 22, 1958, all in *Il Quotidiano*.

200. Robert Ventresca, *Soldier of Christ: The Life of Pope Pius XII* (Cambridge, Mass.: Harvard University Press, 2013), 288–89, 292; Crainz, *Storia del miracolo*, 59–61.

liness made the situation worse.[201] Then, on October 6, 1958, at Castel Gandolfo, the pontiff's final agonies began when he suffered a stroke. He languished for a few days and expired early in the morning on Sunday, October 9. Eugenio Pacelli, Pope Pius XII, the Vicar of Christ, was dead.[202] Palmiro Togliatti announced that his passing brought the long age of Constantine to an end.[203] The historian John Pollard wrote that Pius's death ended the faith's last "best chance to re-establish its absolute hegemony in Italian society, to carry to completion [his] great project of a 'Christian restoration of Italian society.'" That hope was expiring before the "resilience of lay, anti-clerical forces," the Marxist parties and, most importantly, "the massive social and cultural changes generated by both the economic 'miracle' and Anglo-Saxon influences."[204] At first glance it might appear that the biographer of Federico Fellini, Tullio Kezich, appreciated the transition differently, although perhaps his analysis was not too far removed from Pollard's point. Kezich claimed that as long as Pio was pope, Rome lacked a significant nightclub scene. That, too, would soon change, with real impact on the sacred image of the Eternal City.[205]

201. Ventresca, *Soldier of Christ*, 235–37.

202. Ventresca, *Soldier of Christ*, 294–98; John Pollard, *The Papacy in the Age of Totalitarianism, 1914–1958* (Oxford: Oxford University Press, 2014), 442–45.

203. Daniela Saresella, *Cattolici a sinistra: Dal modernismo ai giorni nostri* (Rome and Bari: Laterza, 2011), 115–17; Peter Nichols, *The Politics of the Vatican* (New York: Praeger, 1968), 2.

204. Pollard, *Catholicism in Modern Italy: Religion, Society and Politics since 1861* (New York: Routledge, 2008), 129.

205. Tullio Kezich, *Federico Fellini: His Life and Work* (New York: Faber and Faber, 2006), 195.

Chapter 4

The *Dolce Vita*

About a month after Pope Pius died, one of the most emblematic events of postwar Italian culture occurred over the Janiculum Hill from the Vatican, at Rugantino's nightspot in Trastevere. There, in early November, members of Rome's smart set gathered at a birthday party for one of their own, the aristocrat Olghina di Robilant. The countess was a bit down on her luck, and so the American millionaire Peter Howard Vanderbilt bankrolled the evening. The swanky guests included the Swedish actress and "sexpot" Anita Ekberg; Linda Christian, freshly divorced from Tyrone Power; the local police chief, who probably felt a bit out of his element; and Sergio Pastore, a rising figure in the film world. Pastore came with a date, Aiché Nanà, a Turkish dancer who ended up hanging around the bar alone when a suspicious di Robilant approached her. Nanà got nervous and ran to the dance floor, where, frenzied by tunes from the "New Orleans Jazz Band" and later claiming to have been drugged, she launched into a striptease, a *spogliarello*. Seeing the room crowded with celebrity photographers, the police chief intervened and confiscated the rolls of film. But he missed one. The resourceful Tazio Secchiaroli, a legend in the paparazzi world, managed to hold on to his; and those revealing pictures of Nanà appeared in *L'Espresso* and other mainstream publications, igniting a national scandal over high-class debauchery. Rugantino's eventually closed, and today the building houses a bank. But a plaque outside, at number 40 Piazza Sonnino, commemorates that evening's revelries: "In this place, once Rugantino's restaurant, on the night of 5 November 1958, the *Dolce vita* began."[1]

1. "Morte a 78 anni Aiché Nanà: Addio alla ballerina della Dolce vita," *Corriere della sera* (Rome),

The historian Silvio Lanaro recognized this era, the end of the 1950s and start of the 1960s, as an "acceleration" of an economy that had been growing with gusto for about a decade and creating the *dolce vita*. Notwithstanding a brief recession in 1963 and 1964, he continued, the good times persisted until 1970.[2] This impressive postwar expansion, with its corresponding social and cultural developments, what Guido Crainz called the "great transformation," seemed to be felt most intensely and discussed most passionately from about 1958 until 1963, a time and a phenomenon famously described three ways. With *il boom* (the boom) Italians borrowed an English word that invites measuring their nation to the American standard. *Il miracolo* (the miracle) is a term taken from religion and reminds us that, as in the case of the German *Wirtschaftswunder*, the stratospheric economic figures were not only miraculous; they somehow complemented the rule of a religious party, the Christian Democracy. A newspaper, the *Corriere dell'informazione*, coined the third term, but it became most associated with the cinema world. *La dolce vita* (the sweet life) presents a vision still linked to the director Federico Fellini and his iconic film of the same name about the fast, immoral, and amoral world of movie stars, paparazzi, and nightlife on the via Veneto.[3]

In observing this era, the historian Ernesto Galli della Loggia wrote that "old habits and modes, sometimes very old, dissolved; fashions, things, consumer goods, new mentalities triumphed . . . a whole cultural tradition exhausted itself and died."[4] Statistics and anecdotes illuminate the nature of the change. In 1957, Italy's first supermarket opened in Milan. At the 1958 San Remo music festival, Domenico Modugno popularized what came to be considered the anthem of *dolce vita* Italy—*Il*

January 30, 2014, found at http://roma.corriere.it/roma/notizie/cronaca/14_gennaio_30/morta-78-anni-aiche-nana-addio-ballerina-dolce-vita-f5723520–8988–11e3-be5b-d457abaa7165.shtml (accessed December 20, 2019). On the party, see also "The Roman 'Orgy' That Kicked Off La Dolce Vita," *Independent*, October, 23, 2011—an interview with di Robilant, http://www.independent.co.uk/news/world/europe/the-roman-orgy-that-kicked-off-la-dolce-vita-1031222.html (accessed December 20, 2019). For his part, the paparazzo Secchiaroli professed repugnance and described the party as "the most sinful, transgressive thing that I had ever photographed"; Shawn Levy, *Dolce Vita Confidential: Fellini, Loren, Pucci, Paparazzi, and the Swinging High Life of 1950s Rome* (New York: W. W. Norton, 2016), 251. The police sequestered the edition of *L'Espresso*.

2. Silvio Lanaro, *Storia dell'Italia repubblicana: L'economia, la politica, la cultura, la società, dal dopoguerra agli anni '90* (Venice: Marsilio, 1992), 223; Guido Crainz, *Storia del miracolo italiano: Culture identità, trasformazioni fra anni cinquanta e sessanta* (Rome: Donzelli, 1998), 83. See also Vittorio Zincone, "L'Italia dipinto di blu," *L'Espresso*, February 1, 1959.

3. Stephen Gundle provides an excellent depiction of "Hollywood on the Tiber" in chapter 5 of his *Death and the Dolce Vita: The Dark Side of Rome in the 1950s* (Edinburgh: Canongate, 2011). He identifies the origin of the term *dolce vita* on page 272.

4. Galli della Loggia, quoted in Yannis Voulgaris, *L'Italia del centro-sinistra, 1960–1968* (Rome: Carocci editore, 1998), 84.

blu dipinto di blu, more popularly known as *Volare*. From 1955 until 1960, the number of motor scooters in circulation increased from one million to four million. Italy's automobile production rose from 148,000 in 1959 to 760,000 in 1963, figures that reflected the increased number of cars on the road—from one million in 1956 to five and a half million in 1965. Arrivals at Italian airports rose from 485,574 in 1955 to 2,374,664 in 1962 and 3,664,134 two years later. But such glittering figures reflected mainly the better-off part of the population. Purchases of nonessential or luxury items reveal that, of the 1,500,000 record players in Italy in 1959, one-half of the nation's students owned one, while only 8 percent of manual workers and 2 percent of peasants did.[5]

In a February 1960 *Iniziativa* article, Giuseppe Orlandi presented a metaphor for Italy in Feronia, a village of 3,000 souls and 120 TV sets, and a place where shepherds and sharecroppers came into town to catch the latest installment of *Canzonissima*. The rural village ways, he wrote, were yielding to those of "a new town," and he tolled the bell for "the old *osteria*," which was evolving into a "neon-lit bar." Orlandi took particular note of Feronia's young women, who presented a bad omen for the future. No longer did they work with their mothers in the fields. Now they squandered their time in self-indulgence and envy (*sartine*).[6] The following year, *Discussione* wrote critically about the "attack" on Italian markets from the big department stores and mentioned a DC proposal in the chamber to restrict their opening hours.[7] Nor was the priesthood spared from change. In discussing the clergy, the historian Maurilio Guasco used the term "climate change," noting how an issue of the *Rivista dei seminaristi* from 1958 included an insert on something previously considered taboo in such journals—namely, the seminarians' biological families.[8]

All of this, of course, was a celebration of materialism, and many Catholics took note. "Despite the anti-communist crusade of the Cold War years," wrote one scholar, "it was the explosion of prosperity and consumerism in the late 1950s, and the ever-growing presence of Amer-

5. Crainz, *Storia del miracolo italiano*, 83–85; Antonio Cardini, ed., *Il Miracolo economico italiano (1958–1963)* (Bologna: Il Mulino, 2006).

6. Giuseppe Orlandi, "La vecchia osteria diventa un bar col neon," *Iniziativa*, February 15, 1960. Orlandi was vague about Feronia's exact location, although one town by that name sits in Lazio a bit north of Rome.

7. "I Grandi magazzini all'assalto del mercato italiano," *Discussione*, July 9, 1961.

8. Maurilio Guasco, "Il modello del prete fra tradizone e innovazione," in *Le Chiese di Pio XII*, ed. Andrea Riccardi (Rome and Bari: Laterza, 1986), 98–99.

ican and American-style mass culture that was to offer a more insidious threat to the Vatican's place in Italian society in the long run."[9] Indeed, despite the usual Catholic suspicions, Marxist atheism did not figure as a prominent factor here; rather, the new robust business climate and its corresponding to notions of acquisition, gain, and modernity were primary factors. Catholic interpretations could even sound a bit rooted in class terms—that Italy's hot economy, which favored corporate moguls and the managerial class, also harmed the spirituality of the workers. Referring to the film industry and moral degradation, for example, Catholic Action's *Noi uomini* blamed "producers of boundless greed [who] offend the sense of justice and menace the institutions of the state." The DC's *Discussione* took a nuanced approach to the problem. It examined one poll of five thousand Catholic laborers that revealed the difficulties in keeping Sundays holy and saw business coercion as an answer. Forty-eight percent of workers responded that they could not take off on the Lord's day, forcing the analyst to admit that even Protestant Britain complied better on Sunday closings and did a superior job of maintaining its Christian status.[10] Sometimes overworked employees were simply too exhausted to go to church. In his advice column for *Famiglia Cristiana*, Father Atanasio ran across one such case, "a Piedmontese girl" who, tired at the end of the week, preferred to skip Sunday Mass and pray the Rosary instead. The *padre* found this unacceptable and dismissed her as lazy.[11] Should he have blamed her, since a whole new society seemed bent on more materialism with its corollaries of hedonistic fun and self-absorption? At least she prayed the Rosary. Somewhat paradoxically, the challenges of modernity also included the problem of free time, something that triggered anxiety among Catholics. The clerical liaison with Catholic youth tourism, don Giuseppe Rovea, commented on it in 1962. He took seriously a number of predictions of a world, forty years hence, where 90 percent would work in the tertiary sector, where robot labor would allow humans to enjoy 344 vacation days a year, and where

9. Niamh Cullen, "Morals, Modern Identities and the Catholic Woman: Fashion in *Famiglia Cristiana*, 1954–1968," *Journal of Modern Italian Studies* 18, no. 1 (2013): 37.

10. "La ormai famosa lettera del Ministro Tupini," *Noi uomini*, July 24, 1960; Roberto Bencivenga Jr., "Di Domenica gli Italiani non riposano," *Discussione*, March 24, 1957. See also "Inosservato in Italia il terzo Comandamento," *Il Quotidiano*, September 14, 1960. Here was another case where the Catholics relied on a Fascist law; RDL, no. 370, February 22, 1934. One more odd occasion of Italian Catholic envy of Protestant Britain concerned the canceled presentation there of a don Camillo film because London censors would not allow God's voice on the soundtrack; Leone Piccioni, "Libertà d'espressione," *Il Popolo*, July 2, 1952.

11. Cullen, "Morals, Modern Identities and the Catholic Woman," 46.

one would only need employment from about age twenty-five to about forty-five. These may have been dubious prophesies, but to don Rovea the warning was clear—"immense problems of culture . . . of education of the spirit" were just around the corner. Would the new opportunities lead to the "recuperation of genuinely human and spiritual values," or would they be wasted? Law number 326 on vacation homes (*case per ferie*) settled don Rovea's nerves. He applauded the legislation in its aim of keeping families together on vacation. The choice of the word "*casa*" pleased him because it spoke "of stability, of permanence. "*Casa*," he continued "says family."[12] Don Rovea's qualms resonated in a broader context for an *Iniziativa* article. There, Bruno Maioli "diagnosed" the era's ills as "instability, disorder, uncertainty and fear," which stemmed from an abandonment of God in the Enlightenment and in nineteenth-century Romanticism. Far from God, he wrote, the people "search in vain for certainty, peace, light, [and] freedom."[13]

In addition to being affected by economic and social developments, Catholic militants lost key leaders, starting with Pope Pius in 1958, who, shortly before his demise, said that "Rome has a long way to go before it lives up to what God wants."[14] Mario Missiroli, therefore, had reason to wonder in the *Corriere della sera* whether the church would stay on Pius's road now that he was gone.[15] He had his answer when, on October 28, 1958, after three days of deliberation and eleven ballots, the Conclave elected his successor, the seventy-six-year-old Angelo Roncalli, patriarch of Venice, who took the name John XXIII.[16]

John would, indeed, change course, and signs of a new direction appeared right away. The day after his first Christmas as pontiff, he stunned everybody with a call on Rome's Regina Coeli Prison.[17] A crush of "authorities, photographers, prisoners, warders" swamped him, he recalled, "but the Lord was close." On April 11, 1961, during a state visit from Prime Minister Fanfani, John pulled another surprise by accepting Italy's

12. Giuseppe Rovea, "Il problema della villeggiatura," *Rivisto del clero italiano*, June 1962.

13. Bruno Maioli, "Diagnosi del nostro tempo: instabilità, disordine, incertezza, paura," *Iniziativa*, November 30, 1960.

14. Ermanno Graziani, *Il Carattere sacro di Roma: Contributo all'interpretazione dell'Art.1, CPV., Conc.* (Milan: Dott. A. Giuffré editore, 1961), 8.

15. Mario Missiroli, "Le vie dell'avvenire," *Corriere della sera*, October 10, 1958. See also Indro Montanelli, "Un'Apparizione," in the same issue.

16. Peter Hebblethwaite, *Pope John XXIII: Shepherd of the Modern World* (New York: Doubleday, 1985), 270–84.

17. Hebblethwaite, *Pope John XXIII*, 303.

1870 annexation of Rome as part of God's plan and calling for a "wider Tiber"—that is, greater separation between the Holy See and the Italian government. At the same time, he urged the Italian Episcopal Conference to refrain from interference in electoral affairs.[18] John's ascent to St. Peter's throne, furthermore, triggered personnel developments with consequences for the lay Catholic world. The new pope accepted Giuseppe Dalla Torre's retirement from the *Osservatore Romano* and replaced him with Raimondo Manzini, who went to the Vatican and found it "absorbing [and] the occasion august . . . I am at the feet of John XIII, alone." John asked him, "Do you want to recite the *Angelus* with me?" Such was, he thought, the pope's "humble and holy goodness." Manzini piloted the *Osservatore* until 1978 and employed the pope's spirit of *aggiornamento*, bringing the church up to date with the rapidly changing society, by making the newspaper "livelier, more open to cultural affairs and social issues."[19]

Beyond Italy, as the head of a global religion, Pope John promoted his notion of *aggiornamento* above all by calling the Second Vatican Council, which met in Rome from October 1962 until December 1965; it outlasted John, who died in June 1963 and left his successor, Giovanni Battista Montini, Pope Paul VI, to finish it. The Vatican Council would alienate figures associated with Pius XII's triumphalist style. The isolated Father Lombardi sensed friction with his Jesuit colleagues, and he wondered whether he might no longer be considered a Soldier of Christ. That the Holy See in January 1962 condemned his book *Concilio: Per una riforma della carità* made his sense of ostracism all the more complete.[20] About this time, Lombardi began to turn more seriously to interests in Latin America, where he would spend many of his remaining years.[21] At the Holy Office, Cardinal Ottaviani grew concerned over progressive sounds coming from the Council. He corralled a group of conservatives—including archbishops Giuseppe Siri of Genoa, Ernesto Ruffini of Palermo, Piero Parente, also of the Holy Office, Pericle Felici from the Curia, with experience in the Roman *Rota*, and Bishop Luigi Carli of

18. Maria Elisabetta de Franciscus, *Italy and the Vatican: The 1984 Concordat between Church and State* (New York: Peter Lang, 1989), 70–71; Hebblethwaite, *Pope John XXIII*, 360–61.

19. Natal Mario Lugaro, *Raimondo Manzini: Giornalista cattolico* (Milan: NED, 1988), 46–49.

20. Arnaldo Chierici, *Una Speranza per la Chiesa: Padre Lombardi ed il Movimento Mondo Migliore* (Rome: Editrice Rogate, 1984), 36–37; Giancarlo Zizola, *Il Microfono di dio: Pio XII, Padre Lombardi e i cattolici italiani* (Milan: Mondadori, 1990), 448–71.

21. Chierici, *Una Speranza per la Chiesa*, 174. In 1968, Lombardi would attend the Latin American episcopal "CELAM" conference at Medellín, Colombia, a meeting which is often understood as the birth of Liberation Theology—at least from the Vatican's perspective.

Segni—a faction that John labeled "the prophets of doom." And John was right. The writing on the wall became apparent during Ottaviani's speech of October 30, when he bluntly inquired, "Are the Fathers planning a Revolution?" After going some minutes past his time allotment, someone pulled the plug on the cardinal's microphone and cut him off. Some in the assembly applauded this measure, and Ottaviani, angry and humiliated, boycotted the procedures for two weeks.[22]

More change was underway at Catholic Action. Three days after his coronation, John met with Cardinal Siri to discuss Luigi Gedda and in 1959 replaced him at the top with Agostino Maltarello. At the start of 1960, moreover, the stalwart Ildo Avetta succeeded Gedda at the helm of the *Rivista del cinematografo*.[23] To rub salt in the wounds, Montini arranged for Father Agostino Gemelli to blackball Gedda's efforts for admission in the Pontifical Academy of Sciences. "He's not a nice man," Montini said to Pope John. But Gedda did not bend under the degradations and turned to other pursuits, including marriage at sixty to Teolinda Romano in December 1962. The sympathetic Siri, moreover, helped him to revitalize the Civic Committees in the summer of 1959 at an organization meeting in Paestum with provincial delegates and Piedmontese industrialists eager to provide support.[24]

Albino Galletto was another victim of the purge, ousted in September of 1959 from the Ente dello spettacolo, its CC-Television, and from the CCC, where he had been the ecclesiastic assistant since 1948. According to the left-wing *Paese*, Galletto had served in Catholic Action's "holy war against Brigitte Bardot's legs, and never missed an occasion to exalt state censorship, the necessity of its intervention. But monsignor Galletto did not recognize the changing times." He had no diplomatic skill, claimed the paper, and so got the axe.[25] Like Gedda, however, Gal-

22. Xavier Rynne, *Vatican Council II* (New York: Farrar, Straus and Giroux, 1968), 68–69; John W. O'Malley, *What Happened at Vatican II?* (Cambridge, Mass.: Harvard University Press, 2008), 137–38. In his study of the Council, O'Malley discussed (110–12) the broader faction of conservatives that labeled itself the "International Group of Fathers." This included the archbishop of Dakar Marcel Lefebvre, who later suffered excommunication. Giuseppe Alberigo edited the most extensive history of the Second Vatican Council, the five-volume *History of Vatican II*, English version edited by Joseph A. Komonchak (Leuven: Peeters, and Maryknoll, N.Y.: Orbis, 1995).

23. Marco Muscolino, "La 'Rivista del Cinematografo' dalla nascita al 1968," in *Attraverso lo schermo: Cinema e cultura cattolica in Italia*, vol. 2, *Dagli anni Trenta agli anni Sessanta*, ed. Ruggero Eugeni and Dario Viganò (Rome: Ente dello spettacolo, 2006), 193.

24. Benny Lai, *Il Papa non eletto: Giuseppe Siri cardinale di Santa Romana Chiesa* (Rome and Bari: Laterza, 1993), 146 and 146n5; Nicla Buonasorte, *Siri, Tradizione e novecento* (Bologna: Il Mulino, 2006), 210–11.

25. "Galletto verrà estromesso," *Il Paese*, September 20, 1959; "Dimissioni (e no) del Senatore Ponti," March 16–17, 1960, and "La Biennale alla deriva," March 19–20, 1960, both in *Voce repubblicana*.

letto persisted, and his voice would still be heard in such venues as the *Rivista del cinematografo* and at the Venice *Biennale*. At the Morality Office, Gino Gavuzzo avoided the block.

Along with John's revolution and new faces at Catholic Action, the DC witnessed a changing of the guard in late January 1959, when Fanfani lost his party secretary position to Aldo Moro, stepping down as prime minister a few weeks later. Like Galletto and Gedda, however, Fanfani was not finished. He would return as prime minister for the first time in the summer of 1960 and then again as DC boss in 1973–74.[26] Moro, the head of the party's volatile *dorotei* faction, has been described as "a politician's politician." Fanfani's bitter enemy (although the two would soon cooperate in arranging an alliance with the Socialists), the man from Apulia, had, it was said, an "oriental patience" and was "legendary for the obscurity of his ideas."[27] It has been said that the party program most concerned Fanfani, while Moro's turf was the more purely political world of alliances and deals. But the contrasts extended to personalities. Contrary to his feisty predecessor, Moro seemed less militant, almost lethargic, a trait that hid a certain cunning. Signs of a new tone appeared at an October 1959 conference to commemorate the death of don Luigi Sturzo, where even Mario Scelba, who had supported Moro's bid, denied that Christian Democrats were zealots and fanatics. "Our program," he declared, "is a temperate one and not an extreme one; we're democrats but we deny the exaggerations of demagogues; we call for freedom but we don't surrender to the temptations of libertinism [*la licenza*] . . . the DC is, in its constitutional essence, a centrist party."[28]

Not everyone was happy. Some militants soldiered on while facing what seemed to be inevitable—a more secular Italy. The historian Andrea Riccardi observed that, during the late 1950s, Catholic ranks developed a defensive "traditionalism" associated with Genoa's Archbishop Siri, "truly a bishop at the heart of Pius XII."[29] At the Holy Office, Cardinal Alfredo Ottaviani had become known as one of the most

26. Francesco Malgeri, "Gli anni di transizione: Da Fanfani a Moro (1954–1962)," in *Storia della democrazia cristiana*, ed. Francesco Malgeri (Rome: Cinque Lune, 1988), 3:187–98.

27. Agostino Giovagnoli, *Il Partito italiano: La Democrazia cristiana dal 1942 al 1994* (Rome and Bari: Laterza, 1996), 114; Frederic Spotts and Theodor Wieser, *Italy: A Difficult Democracy* (New York: Cambridge University Press, 1986), 29.

28. Giovagnoli, *Chiesa e democrazia: La lezione di Pietro Scoppola* (Bologna: Il Mulino, 2011), 34. Scelba is quoted in Giuseppe Carlo Marino, *La Repubblica della forza: Mario Scelba e le passioni del suo tempo* (Milan: Francoangeli, 1995), 33.

29. Andrea Riccardi, *Il Potere del papa da Pio XII a Paolo VI* (Rome and Bari: Laterza, 1988), 73–77; Buonasorte, *Siri, Tradizione e novecento*, 154–71.

vocal traditionalists. In January 1958, the combative Ottaviani used the columns of the *Quotidiano* to vent his anger in a barely veiled attack on the DC. His page 1 article, "To Serve the Church and Not to Serve Her" (*Servire la Chiesa e non servirsene*), illustrated how deep ran his resentment by lamenting that in such dangerous times, some in power, "even Catholics," adopt policies harmful to the church, and by blasting "certain" party leaders as "undisciplined" and potential "traitors" to the Catholic cause. The cardinal held that the church's enemies were winning and that their strength was "the fault of our weakness and evil." The immediate object of his outburst was the DC's Rinaldo (Dino) Del Bo, who had been promoting closer relations with the Soviet Union and who had, in fact, arranged for President Giovanni Gronchi's visit to Moscow. Del Bo was merely one irritant, however, and Ottaviani's anger spread farther afield—certainly prompted by Bishop Fiordelli's trial in Prato. "The Bride of Christ," he wrote, "must be defended not only from those who persecute her, but also from those who would sully her and compromise her." The cardinal vilified those "Catholics in positions of political authority who dare to assume the roles of those who not only offend but butcher [*massacra*] the Church," attributing the strength of its enemies to "our weakness and cowardice." Even the *Osservatore Romano* considered Ottaviani's piece too incendiary and issued an explanation that the cardinal was only speaking for himself. In the next issue of the *Quotidiano*, however, Igino Giordani echoed Ottaviani's call with the "Pathology of Laicism," urging the faithful to stand up and confront those who would "get rid of the Church—[under] the pretext of laicism and materialism" and transfer its powers, rights, and conscience to the state.[30] From the other side, Il *Mondo* could not resist comment and followed on February 4 with "The Trumpets of the Holy Office" (*Le trombe del Sant'Uffizio*), sarcastically bestowing an almost mythic status on Ottaviani's letter and assuring its readers that his caustic words "would not be undervalued or forgotten." The cardinal had exposed for all to see the church's attack on the state's autonomy, although, admitted il *Mondo*, some lay parties were also guilty of collaborating with the DC and failing to confront the

30. Alfredo Ottaviani, "Servire la Chiesa e non servirsene," *Il Quotidiano*, January 21, 1958; Igino Giordani, "Patologia della laicità," *Il Quotidiano*, January 22, 1958. On the controversy surrounding the Ottaviani piece, see "Il Papa era d'accordo," *L'Europeo*, February 2, 1958; Ottaviani, "Precisazioni del Vaticano sull'intervento del card," *Corriere della sera*, January 23 and 26, 1958; and "Cronaca contemporanea, Santa Sede," *Civiltà Cattolica*, q. 2584, February 8, 1958, 425. "Servire la Chiesa e non servirsene" was reprinted in Alfredo Ottaviani, *Il Baluardo* (Rome: Edizioni Ares, 1961), 67–73. See also Sandro Magister, *La politica vaticana e l'Italia 1943–1978* (Rome: Editori Riuniti, 1979), 221–23.

"process of clericalization."[31] In February, Ottaviani's angry message reached the chamber floor, where Ambrogio Donini, the PCI's chief Vatican analyst, charged the cleric with meddling in Italian politics and violating the Constitution's "independence of church and state" clause. In a heated debate, Prime Minister Adone Zoli refuted accusations of clerical control and charged that no one in his cabinet could ever be forced to act against his conscience. "However," he continued, "I want to declare, as a citizen and as a Catholic, I cannot ignore the teachings issued from a lofty throne," a response that brought applause from the center and right of the hall.[32]

The DC, nevertheless, soldiered on. Just before the cardinal's *cri de coeur*, and from the party's conservative wing, Giulio Andreotti put an optimistic spin on things in November of 1957. Before a crowd in Como, he proclaimed that the DC had arrived as a permanent force in Italian civic life; that it had become the essential collaborator in the solution of all the nation's political problems.[33] That same month *Il Popolo* delivered a darker reading. The bishop of Prato case, it proffered, presented an opportunity to seriously discuss Italy's moral decline and the assault on marriage, issues lost on the left in its self-made hysterical smoke. Reporters dropped the ball and missed cataclysmic developments, especially among the young, toward a pathological culture where Prato's "concubines" might transform into "champions of a 'new,' more 'progressive' and 'modern' type." Down that road, one encountered "models" of modernity such as the American hotel queen Barbara Hutton, newly detached from her sixth husband, or the movie star Rita Hayworth, who waded through five of them. Still, while Italy's moral health left it better off than what many supposed, Italians were still subject to new temptations and corruptions and needed the "strong roots" that only the church provided.[34]

Another signal of shifting times came in the long-delayed inauguration of the Constitutional Court. The 1948 Constitution had called for it, but the enabling legislation waited until 1953. Then, in 1956, the court

31. Adolfo Battaglia, "Le trombe del Sant'Uffizio," *Il Mondo*, February 4, 1958.

32. "Zoli nega che la Chiesa abbia tentato di menomare l'indipendenza dello Stato," *Corriere della sera*, February 13, 1958.

33. "Andreotti: La D.C. è forza permanente della vita italiana," *Il Popolo*, November 11, 1957.

34. r.l.v., "La morale corrente," *Il Popolo*, November 20, 1957.

began to hear cases and soon created headaches for Catholics. Its first decision that June struck down a Fascist law of June 18, 1931, no. 773, that, among other things, required police permission to distribute fliers on the street and prohibited public gatherings contrary to morality and *buon costume.*[35] This held immediate consequences for the activity of Protestant missionaries, who would no longer suffer legal harassment at the hands of the police. Four years later, the L'Aquila Appeals Court underscored the decision by ruling for a Baptist pastor who had been condemned to two weeks' confinement for circulating flyers insulting to the Catholic Church. "The L'Aquila ruling," noted the *Voce repubblicana*, "affirms in substance that the Catholic religion does not constitutionally enjoy any legal privilege with respect to other ... confessions." Hence, reported *Time* magazine, "Protestants face nothing worse than occasional bureaucratic delays in getting permission to build churches, and the expectable problems of being a minority." One Baptist missionary told the magazine of the conversion of an entire family except for "one daughter, who feared that nobody in the village would marry her if she left the Catholic Church."[36] The Constitutional Court's second ruling in 1956, that "morality" could not reach such a level of importance to limit freedoms, must also have given pause to many.[37]

A new secularist political faction also emerged to try Catholic patience. The militantly lay Radical Party formed in 1956, mostly from disaffected progressive Liberals and its leadership included names familiar to readers of Mario Pannunzio's *Il Mondo*, the new *L'Espresso*, and other similar publications—Leopoldo Piccardi, Ernesto Rossi, Leo Valiani, Eugenio Scalfari, and Marco Pannella. With their goal to become "a democratic and reformist alternative to the Communist Party," they sometimes gathered as the Friends of *Il Mondo*. Among their first aims

35. On the Constitutional Court, see Norman Kogan, *A Political History of Italy: The Postwar Years* (New York: Praeger, 1983), 105–9; and the court's website, http://www.cortecostituzionale.it/documenti/download/pdf/Cc_Checosa_2012.pdf (accessed November 5, 2019). The 1956 ruling can be found at http://www.cortecostituzionale.it/actionSchedaPronuncia.do?anno=1956&numero=1 (accessed November 5, 2019); the wording of the law of June 18, 1931, no. 773, can be found in Rodolfo Venditti, *La Tutela penale del pudore e della pubblica decenza* (Milan: Giuffrè, 1963), 238. Mussolini amplified the 1931 law, along with the 1923 censorship measure, in the law of May 6, 1940, no. 635; Paolo Barile, "I censori fra la costituzione e i giudici," *Il Ponte* 17, no. 11 (1961): 1481. At about the same time as the creation of the Constitutional Court, a Superior Council of the Judiciary emerged in 1958 that fostered greater Independence among the judges.

36. "Importante sentenza sulla libertà religiosa," *Voce repubblicana*, March 9, 1960; "Protestants: Getting Ahead in Italy," *Time*, June 4, 1960.

37. Barile introduction in Camera dei deputati, Segretariato Generale, *Orientamenti Giurisprudenziali in tema di buon costume* (Rome: Servizio studi legislazione e inchieste parlamentari, 1972), 6.

was to delete Article 7 and the Lateran Pacts from the Constitution.[38] Although their numbers were small, with their impressive intellectual credentials the Radicals consequently provoked the ire of both Palmiro Togliatti's Communists and the Christian Democrats.

Of greater immediate political impact was the DC's 1963 "opening to the left" (*apertura alla sinistra*), which accepted the Socialists as ruling, but junior, government partners.[39] Many Catholics saw this as either a mistake or a defeat and dug in their heels. Hardliners came from the Italian Bishops Conference, which had already discussed an *apertura* at its 1956 meeting. There, Archbishop Enrico Nicodemo of Bari promptly denounced it. "Any possibility of an opening to the left," he argued, "constitutes today an extremely grave danger not just to religion, but for democracy itself and free institutions in Italy."[40] In April 1959, the *Osservatore Romano* reemphasized the church's condemnation of those who voted for Marxist parties, and, the following January, the feisty Ottaviani took his turn to denounce "those men who hold responsible positions in the West ... and who call themselves Christians but shake the hand that slapped Christ." From Milan, in May 1960, Archbishop Montini also condemned any "opening."[41] Catholic Action and the Civic Committees received bundles of letters from disgruntled priests, including one from Pisa branding Fanfani as worthless and the PSI as really only an arm of the PCI. "If you're on your way to destruction," the cleric continued, "here's the road."[42]

To better gauge the church's feelings on the *apertura*, between May and October of 1962, Moro dispatched party and government figures to probe the Curia and the episcopate, and the answers were probably better than he expected. Bypassing some like cardinals Siri and Urbani, who had already taken strong positions against the deal, Moro's interviewers and questionnaires reached 254 churchmen, and the answers encouraged him. Of the 138 clerics interviewed, 60 percent accepted the

38. Massimo Teodori, *Pannunzio, Dal "Mondo" al Partito radicale: Vita di un intellettuale del Novecento* (Milan: Mondadori, 2010), 181.

39. In chapter 11 of his essential *Political History of Italy*, Norman Kogan provided a useful discussion of the politics of the *apertura*. The presidential election in 1955 of the left-wing Christian Democrat Giovanni Gronchi served as a sign that they were more open to an arrangement with the Socialists; Kogan, *Political History of Italy*, 84–85.

40. Francesco Sportelli, *La Conferenza Episcopale Italiana (1952–1972)* (Galatina: Congedo editore, 1994), 94–99.

41. Voulgaris, *L'Italia del centro-sinistra*, 87, 91–92. Eliana Versace also recounted a particular flap in Milan between the archbishop and Fanfani, who had been attacked in a Lombard Catholic weekly, *Il Cittadino*; Versace, *Montini e l'apertura a sinistra: Il falso mito del "vescovo progressista"* (Milan: Guerini, 2007), 224–25.

42. FVC, Faldone 20, "Atti politici, Pisa," Don Giulio Corallini/Lucio Magliaccio, October 2, 1962. Magliaccio was one of Gedda's chieftans in the Civic Committees.

government plan and 40 opposed it, a ratio that closely mirrored the written submissions. Some, like Prato's Bishop Fiordelli, emphasized the need for unity among Catholics, perhaps burying their own reservations about the *apertura*. Pistoia's Mario Longo Dorni urged for efforts to calm fears, "especially among women."[43]

Beyond Moro's poll, however, others in the church feared that the "opening" signaled an opportunity for the PCI and that, at best, the Socialists were only dupes. "We are certain," wrote Francesco Olgiati in the *Rivista del clero italiano*, "that COMMUNISM IS SILENTLY ADVANCING.... The barbarians are advancing. And they dream of the day when their mechanical and materialist civilization will replace Christian civilization, our historic glory and salvation of our fatherland, the world and our souls."[44] On another occasion, during the 1960 administrative elections in Cosenza province, one angry Civic Committee activist was disturbed to see the hammer and sickle on Socialist propaganda. Suspicious of a "diabolical pact" between the Socialists and a "dangerous" DC faction that was less interested in principles than in doling out jobs, he wrote, "Whoever abandons the fight is a coward; whoever betrays the cause is a traitor; and which label shall we place on the worthy leaders of the local DC?" Perhaps, he added, Catholics might look elsewhere and dump the Christian Democrats altogether.[45] Along with such dissent, Moro discovered how many doubts existed even within his own ranks. At a March 1959 meeting of the DC's National Council, Raimondo Manzini asked if the party had lost its course, forgetting some of its mandate to build "a humanistic state, a Christian state whose values are eternal [and] not those of class."[46] In Parliament, a DC opposition formed around Mario Scelba and Guido Gonella. Thirty-eight deputies and eighteen senators, including Maria Pia Dal Canton, Oscar Scalfaro, and Giuseppe Ermini, joined this faction of contrarians.[47]

Lay figures, on the other hand, provided some support for at least the spirit of an *apertura*. Arturo Carlo Jemolo, among the most respected, wrote early on in *La Stampa* that secularists might now explore their own tolerance and reach an "opening to the Catholics." In *Il Ponte* Tristano

43. Augusto D'Angelo, *Moro: I vescovi e l'apertura a sinistra* (Rome: Edizioni Studium, 2005), 39–41; Guido Bisori/Moro, April 10 and 17, 1962, in IS Sez. Pol. Moro, Sc. 92, f. 22.

44. Francesco Olgiati, "I barbari avanzano," *Rivista del clero italiano*, January 1961. Capital letters in the original.

45. FVC, Fondo Gedda, B. 65, Cosenza report by Elio Gliosci (Civic Committee activist) to DC and CC headquarters, November 19, 1960.

46. IS Consiglio nazionale, sc. 30, March 14, 1959.

47. D'Angelo, *Moro: I vescovi e l'apertura a sinistra*, 90.

Codignola dismissed Jemolo's argument as moot because history sided with *laicismo*. Most baptized Catholics, he wrote, were in fact already free thinkers, not a "clericalized minority" trapped in the DC's clutches. Extending a hand to the hierarchy, therefore, was a waste of time, since clerical parties were inherently doomed and the DC's day would come, as was happening in France with the Mouvement Républicain Populaire.[48]

Heartened by Pope John's "benevolent neutrality," John Kennedy's victory in the American elections, and by his reading of the bishops, Moro reckoned that partnership was in the cards.[49] For its part, the left had turned a corner in 1956 with the Hungarian uprising and Nikita Khrushchev's "secret speech" in the Soviet Union that denounced Josef Stalin. In Italy, these events facilitated PSI efforts to distance itself from the PCI, leading Socialist chief Pietro Nenni to recall "his own statements from the 1920s and 1930s about the historic differences between the socialist and communist traditions" and break from what many considered his embarrassing policy of slavish subservience to the PCI.[50] Socialists had taken part in every struggle for liberty and democracy for seventy years, wrote Nenni in 1962, often at the front of the line, "paying a heavy toll, even in human lives, for every advance of political democracy." But, he stated, "the PSI is not, and never was, a copy of the Communist Party." He initiated talks with the Social Democrat Saragat for a reorientation of a reunited Socialist party toward the political center—that is, toward the Catholics.[51]

The Socialists, at their Milan congress in March 1961, and the DCs, in Naples the following January, cleared much of the way. In March 1962, Fanfani formed a preparatory center-left government with Social Democrats and Republicans, and finally, in December 1963, Moro assembled his first cabinet with Socialist participation—the *apertura* was now a fact. Nenni announced that "from now on everyone is freer," and on April 12, 1965, Pope Paul VI thanked him personally for his work.[52]

48. Tristano Codignola, "Una scelta per i cattolici," *Il Ponte*, December 1957.

49. Paul Ginsborg, *A History of Contemporary Italy: Society and Politics 1943–1988* (New York: Palgrave Macmillan, 2003), 258–61; Giovagnoli, *Chiesa e democrazia*, 69.

50. Alexander De Grand, *The Italian Left in the 20th Century* (Bloomington: Indiana University Press, 1989), 124. At the PSI's 1955 Turin congress, Nenni declared himself ready for a compromise with the DC; Kogan, *Political History of Italy*, 84.

51. Pietro Nenni, "Where the Italian Socialists Stand," *Foreign Affairs*, January 1962.

52. Giovagnoli, *Il Partito italiano*, 117. Crainz, *Il Paese mancato: Dal miracolo economico agli anni ottanta* (Rome: Donzelli editore, 2005), 82; Ginsborg, *History of Contemporary Italy*, 267–75; De Grand, *The Italian Left*, 126–27.

Beneath all of these developments lurked deeper problems for which Catholics braced themselves. From Milan, for instance, Montini discussed the state of the faith in 1958 and found it wanting. Italy was a Catholic nation, he said, and "*per fortuna*," the great majority of Italians were baptized. But "we must recognize that the greatest part of our faithful are unfaithful; that the number of those far away [from the Church] is greater than those near."[53] Some of the other bleak judgments came from the church, like Monsignor Olgiati's alarmist article "Return to Paganism" at the end of 1959. In an era obsessed with sensual pleasure, he wrote, "In every nation, in every city, in every village morality is becoming more and more an insignificant and faded memory." He found signs of degeneration everywhere, from the notorious party at Rugantino's to "delinquents in blue jeans" to Brigitte Bardot, the "striptease expert," although Olgiati gladly noted that even "BB" had declared "enough with *spogliarelli!*"[54] Also disturbing for the clergy must have been the decline in adult weekly church attendance, falling from 69 percent of the population in 1956 to 53 percent in 1961 and 48 percent by 1968.[55] The DOXA Institute, Italy's premier polling organization, investigated religion and published its findings in September 1958. While two-thirds of respondents felt that the clergy had the right to speak their minds, it also depended on the subject: 56 percent answered that priests could publicly discuss marriage matters, and 58 percent acknowledged their right and duty to "intervene in the private lives of citizens." About two-thirds agreed that they should be able to speak on media and school questions, but a majority doubted that they should opine on labor and political issues.[56]

In November 1958, Gavuzzo added to the discussion, speaking on "The State of Public Morality" to a convention of diocesan leaders. His targets ranged from printed material to the Spettacolo to women's fashion. He judged as "very bad" conditions in almost all sectors. Printed matter of all kinds was in a disastrous state, and only regarding periodicals sold in kiosks did Gavuzzo see circumstances not entirely hopeless, chastising his audience, furthermore, for not speaking out enough

53. Andrea Riccardi, *Vescovi d'Italia: Storia e profili del Novecento* (Milan: Edizioni San Paolo, 2000), 9. Eliana Versace has illustrated something of a panic in Milan over the sad moral state found there during the Montini years; Versace, *Montini e l'apertura a sinistra*, 74–79.

54. Olgiati, "Il ritorno al paganesimo," *Rivista del clero italiano*, December 1959.

55. Martin Clark, *Modern Italy: 1871 to the Present* (Harlow, Essex: Pearson Longman, 2008), 444–46.

56. G. B. Penco, "L'opinione pubblica italiana e I problemi religiosi," *Rivista del clero italiano*, March 1959.

on this dismal problem. Moving on, Gavuzzo had nothing good to say about the Spettacolo, where things had gotten so abysmal that comics employed sexual humor, even jokes about homosexuality, to arouse titters from teenagers and children. On women's fashion, the morality secretary could only see "big worries to come." He finished with a grouse over the penetration everywhere of obscene graffiti and questionable advertisements "in public, judicial and administrative offices, railroad stations, stores, staircases of apartment buildings, and even in Church."[57] In the spring of 1959, the situation had not improved for Gavuzzo, who embarked on a tour of the striptease scene out of which he composed two reports for Undersecretary Oscar Scalfaro at the Interior Ministry. The morality secretary attended a number of shows in Rome, Bologna, Genoa, Turin, and Milan, sometimes observing the same performers in different locales. He wrote, for example, of how he saw "Miss Tamara" at two places in the capital. Gavuzzo made particular mention of one of these, a spot in the via Nazionale where the proprietor brazenly posted a photo of her bare breasts at the entrance. A piece of tissue paper intended to cover the offending flesh had slipped down, exposing Miss Tamara's chest to passers-by. Gavuzzo also reported with some frustration that the "very grave filth" he witnessed was only the tip of the iceberg; and even more galling, from an employee at a Bologna strip joint he learned that the *Questura* "tolerated" the shows. He believed that the state had dropped the ball, and his disappointment even reached all the way to office of the heretofore-trusted Scalfaro, whose lack of enthusiasm left Gavuzzo "confused, distressed, and very worried." Shortly afterward, in a separate report, he wondered why the state had not banned these "satanic" shows and exhibited no indication that it would anytime soon.[58]

By the end of 1959, in a letter to diocesan lay and clerical leaders, Gavuzzo "tearfully" lamented that many Italians simply turned a blind eye to such goings-on. Anxious to escape life's ugly side, they had lost their "sense of sin."[59] Shortly thereafter, in February 1960, a dismayed

57. IPVI, Pg XII, b. 18, Gavuzzo Circular, November 15, 1958; A memorandum to Gavuzzo repeated and emphasized much of his circular; IPVI, Pg XII, b. 36, "Appunto per il segretario generale," April 3, 1959.

58. IPVI, Pg XII, b. 25, Gavuzzo/Scalfaro, April 30, May 21, and June 10, 1959; and Scalfaro's response to Gavuzzo, June 6, 1959. See also Gavuzzo's 1960 report: IPVI, Pg XII, b. 38, Gavuzzo "Risposta al questionario 20 gennaio 1960: Moralità pubblica in Italia," February 2, 1960.

59. IPVI, Pg XII, b. 3, Gavuzzo letter to Ecclesiastical Consultants and (AC) Secretariats, November 3, 1959.

Gavuzzo expanded on this in another gloomy report, a twenty-six-page account of "public morality."[60] "The 'sense of sin,'" he wrote, even in healthy areas, "appear[ed] profoundly weakened." Expressions like "the occasion of sin" had fallen into disuse. A lowered moral level in theaters, public conduct between couples, a notable spread of vulgar language, diminished outrage over men who "parade their homosexual vice," all served as illustrations and causes of "grave moral decay." Regarding the last point, Gavuzzo noted that the state had scored only one victory in a Treviso case against a pornographic review. Beyond that, a fickle public barely reacted to "moral disorders," only to deplore them and then blame the government for failing to stop them. Only Catholic Action militants provided any real public indignation, although even then, few possessed the stomach for "public and personal engagement." And for their trouble, fighting for better public conduct and locating scandal, Gavuzzo noted sadly (*doloroso*), they labored in a secular arena of public ridicule. He also found "highly unsatisfying" the quality of the AC morality offices at the diocesan level, most of which, if they operated at all, were grossly inefficient or operated on a shoestring budget. Of the satellite organizations, the National *Buon Costume* Association under the "incomparable" Carlo Costantini and then his successor was a one-man show that had seen better days, although recent activity indicated some sign of life. The Family Front was still active, but the states' attorneys' offices and magistrates, particularly Turin's, but also Milan's and Bologna's, showed "scant sensibility." Only Rome's prosecutors seemed capable of addressing the morality issue. In the government, Gavuzzo complimented the work of Oscar Scalfaro and Guido Bisori at the Interior Ministry and of the local police, which often developed close relationships with AC's Morality Offices.

Beyond hopes for a more effective cinema law, Gavuzzo proposed nothing new, just more of what existed. He urged more police crackdowns on illegal but persistent prostitution and on lewd public comportment by couples, specifically citing parked cars as the locus for this. He called for "greater rigor" on film and theater censorship commissions and "an active police presence" at variety reviews. Of course, the state must "rigorously prohibit everywhere" strip shows. *Questuras* needed more vigilance in vetting publications, especially foreign printed ma-

60. IPVI, Pg XII, b. 38, Gavuzzo "Risposta al questionario 20 gennaio 1960: Moralità pubblica in Italia," February 2, 1960.

terial that circulated in Italy. Gavuzzo also pointed to television, calling for "diligent and rigorous investigations" of all complaints, clearly on the assumption that most grievances came from Catholic Action militants or kindred spirits. RAI management should warn offenders that, if their outrages continued, they would be sacked.[61]

Such arguments were not lost on the faithful in their protests over Italy's moral degradation. Alarmed that their approach to film was failing, Catholics sounded the bells. In 1958, Albino Galletto wrote that with each year more and more films fell into the CCC's "excluded" category.[62] Two years later, he turned up the heat, announcing that despite a movie's commercial success, CCC ratings could paint a different and darker picture. Whereas in 1957 13 percent of productions received the most positive score, "for everybody," he wrote, in 1959 that number sank to about 7.5 percent. For the same period, works rated either "S" (unadvisable) and "E" (excluded) rose from 19 to 31 percent. Galletto concluded that the "honest public" had reached its limit and must rally to end the "gall" (*spudoratezza*), this attempt "to unhinge and corrupt every moral value."[63]

Still, discontent among the militants was widespread. In February of 1961, Verona witnessed fifty thousand march with the mayor and other dignitaries and behind Archbishop Giuseppe Carraro to protest the decline of *costume*. Before the Duomo, Carraro urged his flock not to lose the sense of sin, the sense of moral evil, and the sense of goodness and justice. The media offended such sentiments, he said, through their "truly pathological *divismo*" or their vulgar exhibitionism displayed without any pretense to art. Christians must unite, concluded the archbishop, to help the "innocent and the weak," those first victims of people who would "desecrate love, dissolve the family, deride religion, [and] shake the foundations of social order."[64] A month later, the Italian Episcopal Conference joined the battle with a letter condemning the "growing [pattern of] immorality on the nation's screens." Of particu-

61. IPVI, Pg XII, b. 38, Gavuzzo "Risposta al questionario 20 gennaio 1960."

62. Albino Galletto, "Arte e morale in vacanza," *Il Quotidiano*, February 27, 1958.

63. The 1960 figure for the "S" and "E" categories rose again to 33 percent; William Troy McCraw, "Political Sponsorship of the Arts: Subsidization and Censorship of Motion Pictures and the Performing Arts by the Italian National Government, 1943–1962" (Ph.D. diss., Stanford University, 1966), 190; Albino Galletto, "Bilancio morale in passivo nel cinema italiano del '59," *Il Quotidiano*, January 31, 1960; this was also printed in *Il Popolo* and the *Rivista del cinematografo*. See also "Bilancio negativo del cinema nel 1961," *Noi uomini*, January 28, 1962.

64. "Manifestazione penitenziale a Verona contro le degenerazioni del pubblico costume," *OR*, February 27–28, 1961. On the same page was a shorter discussion of a similar protest in Genoa, "Un comitato a Genova contro l'immoralità degli spettacoli."

lar concern was the cinema's cavalier handling of family values, of love, and of its insulting treatment of women, "usually seen as instruments of fun and pleasure." These films, continued the letter, disparaged authority, mocked sacrifice, and exalted "money, luxury and easy success." Mothers and fathers especially must guide their children, using tools like the CCC film suggestions, rejecting immoral offerings and selecting for them motion pictures that "present authentic contributions to mankind's intellectual and moral growth."[65] Applauding that effort, however, Monsignor Prosperini at the Morality Office lamented that Catholics lacked discipline; that "everybody—or almost everybody—on one pretext or another, goes to see everything."[66] In the April 2, 1961, issue of *Orizzonti*, Eliseo Sgarbossa noted that the situation had become worse in that the share of Italian products in the *sconsigliabili* and *esclusi* categories had reached over 60 percent, significantly higher than the foreign portion of approximately 35 percent.[67]

An Entertainment Ministry

For almost ten years after end of the war, the Christian Democrats scattered the leisure-oriented fields of *spettacolo*, sports, and tourism among various offices, mostly in the Council of Ministers with a vague idea that one day they might be reconstituted in one place. Prime Minister Mario Scelba, in February 1954, took a decisive step toward that end when he gave all three to the head of the Venice *Biennale*, Giovanni Ponti, as minister without portfolio. In January 1955, Ponti appeared before the Senate to present the government's case for a full-fledged "Ministry of Tourism, Spettacolo, and Sport." He argued that it made sense to coordinate myriad organizations, including the Italian Olympic Committee, under one roof. Growth in these fields led to a popular demand for such a move, he said, and the new ministry would fill the need while "acting as a suitable instrument for the moral, spiritual and physical elevation of the Italians."[68] Catholics were still uncertain about the duties and the

65. The letter was reprinted in many places, including, "Un messaggio dei Vescovi sul cinema," *A Colloquio FARI*, April 1961. See also "La Conferenza episcopale italiana per la moralità degli spettacoli," *Noi uomini*, April 2, 1961. Cardinal Siri provided an interpretation of the letter to Catholic Action that was reprinted in *Bianco e Nero*, April–May 1961, 137–44.

66. IPVI, Pg XII, b. 3, Prosperini circular, July 14, 1962.

67. Eliseo Sgarbossa, "Il cinema nella tomba," *Orizzonti*, April 2, 1961.

68. Atti parlamentari, Senato della Repubblica no. 899, Disegno di legge, January 19, 1955; found in AS Casale Monferrato Fondo Brusasca, M 88, f. 68.

reach of the new agency. To a reporter from the *Quotidiano*, Ponti emphasized that it was still a work in progress and a "possibility." The Commissariat for Tourism, for example, in the prime minister's office, would still function.[69] The momentum for a real ministry subsided, however, when Scelba left office in July 1955. During the next government, under Antonio Segni, the old arrangement resumed with another undersecretary, Giuseppe Brusasca, and with the reappointment of Pietro Romani as high commissioner for Tourism. Fanfani briefly raised the possibility of incorporating the Undersecretariat into the Education Ministry, a "grave error," in the opinion of the *Rivista del cinematografo*. Segni's second ministry (February 1959–March 1960), then, finally saw the birth of a real Ministry of Tourism and the Spettacolo, created by Law number 617 of July 31, 1959. Some of the difficult knots of tourist boards and hotel associations still had to be dealt with, and a last-minute agreement dropped "sport" from the title, but the Senate approved Aldo Moro's final draft, and the ministry was cleared for launch. Umberto Tupini, whom Segni had already appointed as minister without portfolio, became the first minister of Tourism and the Spettacolo. Before that, Tupini had served in two CLN governments as justice minister and followed Salvatore Rebecchini as Rome's mayor from 1956 until 1958. He would stay on as the Spettacolo minister through the Segni cabinet and that of his successor, Fernando Tambroni. When he returned as prime minister in July of 1960, Fanfani replaced Tupini with Alberto Folchi, who remained at the ministry until December 1963.[70] From a venerable Roman noble family, Folchi stood among the DC's old guard. A PPI activist, he emerged with De Gasperi's followers after World War II. Shortly before he moved to the new ministry, Folchi outlined what he saw as many of Italy's cultural challenges in a letter to Cardinal Siri. Noting the "negative influence" of cinema and movie posters, he found particularly infuriating the circulation of movies without the censors' cuts and coming attractions that slipped through without proper vigilance. New legislation and coordination among the ministries, he felt, might help.[71]

Although the *Rivista del cinematografo* hailed the ministry as a positive step that would clear the air, it might also be said that the act pinned

69. "Le funzioni del nuovo dicastero per lo Spettacolo, Sport e Turismo," *Il Quotidiano*, February 25, 1954.

70. "Varato a Palazzo Madama il nuovo Ministero per il turismo e lo spettacolo," *Voce repubblicana*, May 23, 1959.

71. ACS, PCM, 1959–61, 1-6-4, f. 97605, s.3, Folchi/Siri, June 16, 1960.

the DC regime between a rock and a hard place.[72] Previously, the undersecretary could hide, buried in the prime minister's office. But now he stood out in the open and subject to attacks on all fronts and from all sides. In January of 1960, Tupini expressed some of his anxieties in a letter sent to a "cinema and culture" conference in Milan. He had no fear of a *censura* (or its revision) but admitted that he walked a thin line between those in the opposition who cried that "censorship is a noose that strangles freedom and artistic inspiration" and those who blamed the government for allowing the circulation of films that poison the "spirit of the audience, and particular youth." By this "opposition of a different tendency" Tupini clearly meant Catholic Action militants, some of whom published an open letter in the *Rivista del cinematografo* to remind him that he was one of them and as such must use the same "clarity and firmness" with which, they said, Andreotti had distinguished his tenure. Above all, that meant an effective application of real censorship. Action, Tupini felt, must protect art but also carry the obligation to defend culture and families, two impulses that could be reconciled. He therefore could proclaim that "art is like the [rays of the] Sun: it can touch mud without getting dirty. True art is never dangerous."[73] Still, Tupini needed to feed the rank and file with hard-nosed declarations. In February 1960, he announced in the chamber a tougher policy toward racy floor shows that accompanied films, particularly at the big urban theaters.[74] The following June, in an open letter to Eitel Monaco, the president of the producers' association ANICA, Tupini promised that "from this moment on I will be very severe in censorship matters," and after the recent laxness found in the censorship program, he would refuse, "as is my right, [to issue] permits for films in public, even if the censorship commissions passed them."[75] When Folchi replaced Tupini as minister in July 1960, the bold embrace of censorship continued. In December his undersecretary, Renzo Helfer, called it "lawful and necessary." No one wanted "gratuitous persecution," he wrote in the *Rivista del cinematografo*, but neither could one cure a thief by foregoing prison and

72. Emilio Lonero, "Motivi di un'anno," *Rivista del cinematografo*, November–December 1959.

73. Umberto Tupini, "Censura e libertà," *Rivista del cinematografo*, February 1960; "Lettera aperta al Ministro Tupini," *Rivista del Cinematografo*, August 1959. The Catholic Action film review claimed full credit for the creation of the new ministry.

74. "Saranno disciplinati per legge gli spettacoli di 'arte varia,'" *Il Quotidiano*, February 20, 1960.

75. Gavuzzo quoted extensively Tupini's letter in his circular; IPVI, Pg XII, b. 18, Gavuzzo circular, June 15, 1960. Shortly afterward Tupini backtracked, denying any intent to restrict artistic freedom; "Tupini precisa sulla censura," *Il Quotidiano*, July 7, 1960.

allowing him to steal again.[76] Such pronouncements from the government would contribute to controversies over films like *La dolce vita* and *Rocco e i suoi fratelli* and, along with the appointment of Emilio Lonero to head the Venice Film Festival, prompted some to see 1960 as the year "of the reawakened dinosaur."[77] The old monster seemed to have returned.

DC actions, however, once again called into question its firmness and commitment. One of the *apertura's* first casualties in 1963 was the Ministry of Tourism and the Spettacolo, which Folchi handed over to Achille Corona, a Socialist who gained some experience as the head of Pesaro's tourist office. The result was not, however, a complete handover. Behind Corona, the ministry's second rank continued to be staffed by DC stalwarts. Corona remained at the top until June 1968, when a Christian Democrat, Domenico Magrí, once again became the minister in Giovanni Leone's second cabinet.

La dolce vita

Gian Piero Brunetta claimed that in 1960 "the Italian cinema had reached the peak of its success." Italy still led the world with cinema attendance, and receipts reflected this.[78] The greatest motion picture controversies in Italian history, however, also came in 1960 with Fellini's *La dolce vita*, followed by Luchino Visconti's *Rocco e i suoi Fratelli*, and soon joined by other works, like Michelangelo Antonioni's *L'Avventura*. These controversies exposed deep and potentially dangerous arguments that ran through Catholic sentiment toward *buon costume*. At the turn of the new decade, Catholic determination to bowdlerize artistic production found a second wind. With renewed gusto, the faithful took aim at a number of works, some of which achieved iconic status in Italian cultural history. Fellini's masterpiece *La dolce vita* occupies a special place here. Upon its debut at Rome's *Cinema Fiamma* on February 3, 1960, it lent its title to an era. Fellini cast Marcello Mastroianni as the anti-hero, Marcello, the "*giornalista alla moda*," who leads the audience on a tour of profligate café society or, as Director of the Spettacolo Nicola De Pirro's evaluation of the script put it, "all the Rugantinos." The journey began in

76. Renzo Helfer, "Liceità e necessità di una censura," *Rivista del cinematografo*, December 1960.

77. Aldo Bernardini, "Cattolici e cinema italiano: Spunti per un bilancio," in *Bianco e Nero: Gli anni del cinema di parrocchia*, ed. Gianfranco Gori and Stefano Pivato (Rimini: Maggioli Editore, 1981), 76; Mino Argentieri, *La censura nel cinema italiano* (Rome: Editori Riuniti, 1974), chapter 8, 147–69; "Il risveglio del dinosauro," *Paese sera*, November 20, 1960.

78. Gian Piero Brunetta, *The History of Italian Cinema: A Guide to Italian Film from Its Origins to the Twenty-first Century*, trans. Jeremy Parzen (Princeton, N.J.: Princeton University Press, 2003), 167.

the skies over Rome with a helicopter suspending a statue of Christ. The film continued from a nonstop party around an over-the-top voluptuous Hollywood glamor queen played by Anita Ekberg, to the decision of a cerebral but troubled father to kill himself and his two children, and to the final scene where guests spill out onto a beach after a debauched bacchanal and *spogliarello*.[79] The striptease clearly referred to the Rugantino episode, and Fellini then linked his picture to another national shame, the aforementioned Montesi scandal. He filmed the conclusion on the beach chillingly close to where Wilma Montesi spent her last evening, perhaps at much like the all-night party that Fellini depicted. "There can be little doubt," wrote one student of the affair, that the wretched "sea monster" dragged up from the surf by the fisherman at the film's end represented the ghastly reality of Montesi's corpse.[80]

The DC censorship process turned out to be the least of Fellini's worries, and De Pirro's committee's initial read-through of the script raised no significant issues. The film received the *nulla osta* in February 1960, and the financial bonus came the following winter.[81] Rather, the director encountered problems elsewhere, starting on day one of shooting—the first scene to be filmed was a playful treatment of Ekberg's climb to the top of St. Peter's dome, recreated in Cinecittà's Studio Sixteen. Fellini adorned the Swedish "bombshell" in a dress that resembled a clerical cassock and recalled the scandalously tight-fitting frock that Rome's Fontana sisters made earlier for Ava Gardner. In the hubbub, some called for Ekberg's arrest for imitating a priest.[82]

In release, Fellini's work struck many nerves. The well-heeled crowd at the Rome premiere met it with icy silence, and, after the performance, one audience member threatened the director to a duel. In Milan, another spat in his face. Fellini professed not to understand the harsh reaction to his film, which he felt had been informed by a powerful Christian sensibility, a work that treated life in modern decadent Rome with sym-

79. ACS, MTS, CF2990, "Dolce vita," Divisione generale spettacolo, "Revisione cinematografica preventiva," February 19, 1959. Gian Piero Brunetta reminds us that Alessandro Blasetti's 1959 film *Europa di notte* also included a *spogliarello*; Brunetta, *History of Italian Cinema*, 211.

80. Karen Pinkus, *The Montesi Scandal: The Death of Wilma Montesi and the Birth of the Paparazzi in Fellini's Rome* (Chicago: University of Chicago Press, 2003), 17–20.

81. ACS, MTS, CF2990, "Dolce Vita," *Nulla osta*, February 9, 1960, and Folchi/Riama Film, Sp.A., January 23, 1961.

82. Gundle, *Death and the Dolce Vita*, 281. On the making of the film, see Tulio Kezich, *Federico Fellini: His Life and Work* (New York: Faber and Faber, 2006), particularly chapter 23, "The Summer of Via Veneto." On the dress, see Nicola White, *Reconstructing Italian Fashion: America and the Development of the Italian Fashion Industry* (New York: Berg, 2000), 140–42. White notes that, with such controversy swirling around the "cassock dress," the Fontana line was "assured commercial success."

pathy, perhaps empathy, and sadness. He had no interest in polemics, he told the prestigious film review *Bianco e Nero*; his film was a "fable played as a ballet." Indeed, the director had worked with Roberto Rossellini, albeit in the embarrassing *L'Amore* but also in such masterpieces as *Roma, città aperta* and *Francesco, Giullare di Dio*. He acknowledged his own faith; and many such as Pier Paolo Pasolini defended Fellini's "broadly Catholic ideology, his loving and sympathetic optimism."[83] The picture became the talk of Italy. Arturo Chiodi in the DC's *Discussione* reported that "what do you think about *La dolce vita*?" had become the question of the day, an unceasing chatter reflected in the packed theaters. Everyone agreed. The PCI felt that arguments went beyond cinematic criticism and triggered a political row not seen for a long time, pitting democrats against "blind conservatives and reactionaries."[84] In the Communist *Rinascita* Rino Del Sasso lauded the film's demolition of the upper class "code of silence and hypocrisy," revealing its "true nature." Fellini, he wrote, exposed the "parasites who use religion as an instrument of their power, who live in tiresome antics and black masses, sucking the blood of others and avoiding taxes."[85]

As one scholar later put it, in an Italy perched "on the ridge between modernity and tradition," the film ignited "a real ideological *casus belli*."[86] It received reproach from many quarters, not just Catholic. Noble and heraldic societies, for instance, protested the film's treatment of the aristocracy, while some industrialists resented its portrayal of the

83. The British *Guardian* claimed that a man spat on Fellini, although Father Arpa recorded that it was a "noblewoman"; https://www.theguardian.com/theguardian/2012/feb/25/archive-1960-la-dolce-vita; Angelo Arpa, *La Dolce vita: Cronaca di una Passione* (Naples: Parresía, 1996), 23; Enrico Baragli, "Dopo 'La Dolce Vita 1,'" *Civiltà cattolica*, q. 2646, September 17, 1960; and Baragli, "Dopo 'La Dolce Vita 2,'" *Civiltà cattolica*, q. 2648, October 15, 1960. Pasolini's judgment was recorded for *Filmcritica* 6 (February 1960), which was translated as "The Catholic Irrationalism of Fellini," by Frank and Pina Demers, in *Film Criticism* 9, no.1 (Fall 1984). On Fellini's Catholic sensibility, see Tim Cawkwell, "The Catholic Church in *Il bidone*: Salvation or Swindle?," in *Italy on Screen: National Identity and Italian Imaginary*, ed. Lucy Bolton and Christina Siggers Manson (Oxford: Peter Lang, 2010); and Angelo Solmi, *Storia di Federico Fellini* (Milan: Rizzoli, 1962). Solmi recounts (47) how, when asked which historical figures he would like to meet, Fellini answered St. Francis and the eighteenth-century scoundrel Cagliostro. In a 1976 interview, the director exuded his esteem for Pope John: "He was a poet. What a beautiful man!" Fellini also said that, although he was not too rigorously Catholic, he was a believer. "My Christianity is rough and ready," he continued, "I don't go to the sacraments, but I think prayer can be thought of as an exercise to bring us closer and closer to the supernatural"; Federico Fellini, *Fellini on Fellini*, trans. Isabel Quigley (New York: Delacorte Press and Seymour Lawrence, 1976), 56–57, 64–66.

84. Arturo Chiodi, "Nessuno si salva?," *Discussione*, February 14, 1960; Rino Del Sasso, "La dolce vita," *Rinascita*, February 1960.

85. Rino Del Sasso, "La dolce vita," *Rinascita*, February 1960.

86. Tomaso Subini, "La lagrimetta negata nel finale de 'La dolce vita,'" in *Federico Fellini: Analisi di film; Possibili letture* (Milan: McGraw-Hill, 2006), 58, accessed in users.unimi.it/cinema/Tomaso_Subini_-_Pubblicazioni_files/Subini_Dolce vita.pdf (accessed February 8, 2013).

bourgeoisie.[87] Among Catholics, *La dolce vita* and the complexity of Fellini's message proved to be a source of rancor. Their reaction was not monolithic, and arguments revealed fissures and dissent in the ranks. While some scenes certainly offended many, in its own way *La dolce vita* critiqued hedonism and narcissism as well as any priest could on a Sunday morning. Some initial reviews were positive. Mario Verdone, in *Il Quotidiano*, for instance, and *Il Popolo*'s Paolo Valmarana gave it favorable appraisals. A difficult and challenging film that needs to be seen, wrote the latter, a motion picture that blessed Fellini with "preeminence among contemporary directors."[88] *Discussione* saw a complicated work of art—one that rejected simple judgments of "beautiful or ugly, positive or negative, sublime or shameful." Marcello's *dolce vita* was a world "without faith, without spiritual light, without joy" represented by the grotesque sea beast dragged from the surf in the last scene and contrasted to Paola the servant girl (Valeria Ciangottini), the "symbol of purity and innocence" that had become sadly "hopelessly lost."[89]

On the other hand, the *Osservatore Romano* was quite clear in its denunciation. In two unsigned inflammatory pieces (but generally attributed to Oscar Scalfaro), "Basta" (Enough) and "La sconcia vita" (The Filthy Life), the Vatican paper expressed "overwhelming disgust" with a film hypocritically masquerading as art. It was time, stated the paper, for the spectators to shout "enough!" From *Il Quotidiano* an angry head of the Rome AC charged that *La dolce vita* offended Catholicism and the family and that new laws would not help. "We don't want to invoke the Inquisition or the pyre for Italy's cinema," he wrote, "we only want the current laws to be applied." Many similarly blamed the government. One small-town mayor who secured promises from the local exhibitors not to show the film earned praise from the *Osservatore Romano* for accomplishing something that Rome "still hasn't done." Agostino Greggi, a young Christian Democrat cultural firebrand who served with the state's case over the *Miss Spogliarello* posters and in 1963 would win a seat in the chamber, asked at a public rally, "What would Cavour and Mazzini have said if they saw *La dolce vita*?"[90] Angry letters filled government mailboxes. To Prime Minister Segni and Tupini, the women's organiza-

87. Enrico Baragli, "Dopo 'La Dolce Vita 1,'" *Civiltà cattolica*, q. 2646, September 17, 1960.

88. Mario Verdone, "Prime del cinema—La dolce vita," *Il Quotidiano*, February 6, 1960; Paolo Valmarana, "Fellini preso nella dolce vita," *Il Popolo*, February 5, 1960.

89. Chiodi, "Nessuna si salva?," *Discussione*, February 14, 1960.

90. Claudio Cutolo, "L'A.C. romana insoddisfatta della risposta alla Camera per il film, 'La dolce vita,'" *Il Quotidiano*, February 23, 1960; Argentieri, *La censura nel cinema italiano*, 154–55. On Greggi, see

tion, the CIF, sent a formal protest that deplored the film's treatment of religion.[91] The Palermo AC expressed outrage over the laxness of the censorship commissions that passed *La dolce vita* and other films like it. It feared the developing situation where youth "went down a road believing that everything was easy, that a moral code did not exist . . . [heralding] the slow, continuous pernicious collapse of moral values."[92]

A real catastrophe occurred in Milan at the Jesuit San Fedele Center, which had already established a reputation as a progressive and independently minded organization through its programs and events and in its reviews, *Aggiornamenti sociali* and *Letture*.[93] In 1958 the Jesuits had raised eyebrows at the beleaguered Venice festival with their praise for Eduard Hofman's *The Creation of the World*, an animated Franco-Czech entry. In the *Letture* Father Nazareno Taddei, who had founded the Spettacolo center at San Fedele, considered it acceptable for mature audiences and rather a good film.[94] This judgment, however, contrasted with harsh Catholic condemnation elsewhere, particularly from the *Osservatore Romano*. From the Ente dello spettacolo and as a representative of the international Catholic film organization OCIC, an infuriated Albino Galletto complained about the Milan Jesuits to Archbishop Montini. Galletto pronounced the 1958 festival a failure, and the OCIC withheld its prize due to a lack of worthy entries. The flattering *Letture* article by Taddei was the last straw. "This review's attitudes, particularly toward the cinema," Galletto huffed, "stand in net contrast to the directives of the ecclesiastical authorities, to judgments from the national office and all the other offices under OCIC. This situation causes grave confusion among Catholics."[95] Gino Gavuzzo added his voice in support of Gal-

---

also "Una nuova crociata contro Brigitte Bardot," *L'Unità*, January 4, 1958; and "Zoo di vetro: Agostino Greggi," *L'Unità*, May 3, 1958.

91. "La protesta del CIF per il film di Fellini," *Il Quotidiano*, February 20, 1960.

92. ACS, MTS, CF2990, "Dolce Vita." This file contains ACI Palermo/Segni, February 23, 1960, and a number of other Catholic Action and diocesan protests to the prime minister's office and the new ministry.

93. A collection of organizations such as the Centro di Studi Sociali and the Centro culturale San Fedele, it was (and still is) commonly and simply known as the Centro San Fedele because of its location in Milan's Piazza San Fedele close to the Duomo.

94. Nazareno Taddei, "Mostra del documentario e cortometraggio," *Letture*, November 1958. On *Letture*, see Gianfranco Bettetini, "Chiesa cattolica e cinema: Dal sessantotto a oggi," in Eugeni and Viganò, *Attraverso lo schermo*, 3:82–83. Bettetini claims that Taddei originated the televised Mass.

95. "Premiata una parodia blasfema," *OR*, August 2, 1958; "Voci ed echi," *OR*, August 8, 1958; ASDM, Fondo Montini, B. 116, f. 364, Tardini/Montini, December 2, 1958, with Galletto attachment; Tardini/Montini, February 24, 1959, with Galletto attachment. Alberto Bassan, the Jesuit superior of the San Fedele Center in Milan, which published *Letture*, answered Galletto's objections in a letter to Montini dated January 13, 1959 (also found in f. 364). In defense of the Center, Bassan explained the goal of keeping open a dialogue on film.

letto in a February 3, 1959, memorandum. The Morality Secretariat, he wrote, stood in solidarity with the Ente dello spettacolo, although their cause suffered when "moral and *religious*" (emphasis in original) evaluations of artistic works were "not shared by all Catholics," specifically blaming the *Letture* group for "the very difficult situation."[96]

Despite the earlier flap, the San Fedele Center proved well disposed to *La dolce vita*, and Fellini's friend, the Jesuit Angelo Arpa, arranged for a January 31 preview at its Milan auditorium. The evening ended in a lively debate. None of this sat well with one who would never see the film and who already had strained relations with the center: Archbishop Montini.[97] For some time, the Milan archdiocese had been experiencing a moral backlash toward cinema. In January 1959, the Lombard Episcopal Conference came down hard on films in the "adult" and "excluded" categories, obligating priests to alert their flocks to their showings even in public theaters, and the following March the AC men's organization there protested the "'resurgence of immorality' that must not pass in silence."[98] A glowing appraisal of Fellini's film from *Letture*'s Father Taddei did not ameliorate things. He used the review's pages to applaud *La dolce vita* as a well-told tale of how the via Veneto's fast life dulled Marcello's "noble aspirations," which lingered from his roots in provincial Cesena. Fellini, he wrote, lovingly portrayed authentic characters of his film, an accomplishment that, despite some reservations, was "substantially Christian" and "positive," and laudably pushed film in new directions.[99]

Taddei's review sharply contrasted with the CCC's judgment that *La dolce vita* was simply another serving of smut that deserved the *escluso* rating. In an attempt to get Fellini a fair hearing, Father Arpa revisited his successful strategy for *Notti di Cabiria* and arranged for another private screening for Cardinal Siri, this time in Milan. While the Genoese archbishop did not find *La dolce vita* wholly negative, he was perhaps sensitive about offending his colleague Montini and reluctant to go out on a limb on this film as he had on the earlier occasion. Consequently, when the Holy Office condemned Fellini's film, the cardinal agreed, calling it

96. IPVI, Pg XII, b. 36, Gavuzzo "Segnalazione," February 3, 1959.

97. Montini had a falling-out with the San Fedele group over his suspicions of left-leaning Christian Democrats Luigi Granelli and Dino Del Bo; Versace, *Montini e l'apertura a sinistra*, 165–77, 204, particularly note 20.

98. "L'Episcopato Lombardo sui problem dello spettacolo," *Rivista del cinematografo*, February 1959; Giambattista Migliori, "Immoralità e sentiment commune," *Iniziativa*, April 25, 1959.

99. Nazzareno Taddei, "La Dolce vita," *Letture*, March 1960. Taddei also noted that the structure of the film, with stories swirling around Marcello, made *La dolce vita* a work of art akin to Raphael's painting of *The School of Athens*. He also noted Ekberg's "violent beauty."

"particularly dangerous" and admonishing Arpa.[100] Four months and four issues after its initial review, a chastened *Letture* issued an unsigned "clarification," regretting the "inopportune occasion of scandal" and emphasizing that the review staff had not "intended to distance ourselves from, much less to correct, the normative judgment of the CCC." Perhaps they had insufficiently stressed the movie's negative moral element, and the "clarification" wished to "underline and in part develop" its reservations such as those concerning the "images' violence and dangers." *La dolce vita* blurred the line between good and evil and therefore "the moral edict must be all the more severe."[101] Soon after, Montini ordered Taddei to cease publishing reviews and exiled the head of Centro San Fedele, Alberto Bassan, to Padua.[102] Aware of the mess in Milan, the shaken Fellini attempted without success to meet with the archbishop. "I was wrong after all," the artist told Taddei; "My movie causes 'evil'—and I thought I'd made a Catholic movie." To his friend Father Arpa, the director instructed, "If you ever meet Cardinal Montini, you can tell him that his refusal to see me hurt a lot."[103]

In the *Civiltà cattolica*, the Jesuit critic Enrico Baragli delivered the final ambiguous judgment on *La dolce vita*. Some of the greatest rubbish (*madornali sciocchezze*) had come from the Catholics, he wrote, but while Fellini was no Marxist and may or may not have been a believing Catholic, Baragli apparently took him at his word that the film was just a fable. Yet although *La dolce vita* approached vice with a sense of frustration and disgust, "in no instance" did it "open to Christian values." Nonetheless, as a film, it was "*naturaliter cristiano*"; its values were "not outside of the Christian message."[104]

To outsiders, arguments in the DC and in the Catholic world appeared fratricidal. *L'Unità* happily noted the internecine fights brought on by Fellini's "slice of the Italian cadaver [*Italia cadaverica*]."[105] At a February 1960 meeting of Catholic Action's "Central Junta," Monsignor Ismaele Castellano, who replaced Urbani in 1955 as the church's

100. Kezich, *Federico Fellini: His Life and Work*, 209–10; Buonasorte, *Siri: Tradizione e novecento*, 136. Almost at the same time Montini quarreled with the San Fedele over its treatment of Vittorio DeSica's film adaptation of Alberto Moravia's novel *Two Women*.

101. "Chiarificazione," *Letture*, July 1960.

102. ASDM, Fondo Montini, B. 113, f. 321, Bassan/Montini, February 23, 1961, and Montini/Bassan, February 26, 1961.

103. Kezich, *Federico Fellini: His Life and Work*, 210–11.

104. Solmi, *Storia di Federico Fellini*, 213–15; Enrico Baragli, "Dopo 'La Dolce Vita 1,'" *Civiltà cattolica*, q. 2646, September 17, 1960.

105. "I cattolici nettamente divisi nella polemica sulla 'Dolce vita,'" *L'Unità*, February 11, 1960.

chief liaison, recognized the difficulties presented by the government's clumsy handling of the film and urged that the matter not further divide Catholics. "No matter how much certain DC attitudes and shortcomings grieve us," he wrote, "we must maintain the Catholic unity as desired by our superiors." He proposed some kind of document, grouping all Catholic organizations in a common front. To the gathered AC leaders, he pleaded that this also meant not playing favorites and avoiding "the impression that the AC support[ed] one or another [DC] faction [*corrente*]."[106]

In the chamber, neo-Fascist and rightist criticism erupted, and the party witnessed something of a rebellion in the ranks when three DC deputies demanded an account from Tupini's Ministry of Tourism and the Spettacolo. Did the government, they asked, not recognize the public's wrath toward the film that insulted the "people of Rome and the dignity of Italy's and Catholicism's capital?" On February 17, the undersecretary Domenico Magrí went to the Montecitorio to defend the state's reluctance to act. On the floor, he acknowledged that while the film's scenes of "squalid degradation" were "unworthy of Rome and of our civilization," it did not celebrate decadence but only offered a frank portrayal of it. Furthermore, he continued, the government was working on a new and better censorship process. Magrí was followed by one of the three DC petitioners, Renato Quintieri, who accepted the government's explanation but lamented that it had yet to produce solid legislation for the moral health of the nation. Worse, he added, was the problem of the censorship panels. "We are not satisfied with the conduct of these commissions."[107]

Rocco e i suoi fratelli

Arguments over *La dolce vita*, however, seem almost courtly next to those that erupted over Luchino Visconti's *Rocco e i suoi fratelli* from the moment in September when it premiered at the 1960 Venice *Biennale*. It is the story of a southern family, a widow, Rosaria Parondi, and four of her five children, who move north in search of work, joining a fifth son, Vincenzo, who had already settled in Milan. Trouble immediately starts, however, with bad blood between the Parondis and the family of Vincenzo's fiancé. Two other brothers, Rocco and Simone, take different paths,

106. IPVI, Pg VIII, b. 24, Minutes of AC giunta centrale, February 13–14, 1960.

107. *Atti parlamentari: Camera dei Deputati*, III legislature, *Discussioni*, February 17, 1960, 13,222–13,227; "I criteri adottati per il *nulla osta* alla 'Dolce vita,'" *Il Popolo*, February 18, 1960.

although both end up as boxers and as rivals for the heart of Nadia, a prostitute. The film spirals through a sordid and violent demimonde on the fringe of the sprawling and cold northern metropolis, ending tragically with Nadia's murder at Simone's hands. *Rocco e i suoi fratelli* brought to the screen ugly issues of north-south bigotry, alienation, illicit sex, and crime, particularly among youth, uncomfortable subjects for many Italians, particularly devout Catholics.[108]

Anxious over a Catholic backlash against their film, Visconti and *Rocco*'s writers, including Suso Cecchi D'Amico and Vasco Pratolini, appealed to the *Voce repubblicana*, which responded in November 1960 that Italy was in their debt for challenging the absurdity and "breaking the circle of conformism."[109] The Republican paper's arguments brought a direct rebuttal from *Il Popolo*: an editorial that echoed Tupini's proxy address to the earlier conference on cinema and culture. Both the minister and the party organ expressed the DC's growing frustration with the whole system. *Il Popolo* found the "polemical brutality" a bit too much and led to a clarification that the DC had always opposed "all political censorship" and "political limits on freedom of expression." It had no wish to "impose conformity" on the nation and had nothing against stories about "southern immigrants in Milan or the bitter *dolce vita* of Rome's privileged classes." Still, continued the editorial, some movies "lull the conscience" in carnal excitement, stories that "depict women of our nation as prostitutes, all men as crazed maniacs and families as nests of vipers."[110]

The Communist arts review *Il Contemporaneo* reported that before a rally at the close of the November 1960 administrative elections campaign, Andreotti branded Italian intellectuals as a "legion of opportunists" who, "from their gilded trenches of the via Veneto struggle in the service of Togliatti against the DC." In this, Andreotti raised the issue of Visconti's film. "We prefer," he said, "the Olympic youth over those so dear to the Communists, those of *Rocco e i suoi fratelli*."[111] Among the most outraged Catholics was the critic Fabrizio Schneider, who wrote "Defenestrate the Cinema" for *Discussione*. A *grido di dolore* against "the wave of immorality that invests the country and now bears fruit,"

108. A useful treatment and bibliography of *Rocco e i suoi fratelli* can be found at www.filmreference.com/Films-Ra-Ro (accessed November 5, 2019).

109. "Cinema e teatro: Procura e censura," *Voce repubblicana*, November 14–15, 1960.

110. r.l.v., "Censura e libertà," *Il Popolo*, November 19, 1960.

111. Domenico Tarantini, *Processo allo spettacolo* (Milan: Edizioni di comunità, 1961), 222–23; also cited in McCraw, "Political Sponsorship of the Arts," 213–14.

Schneider charged that audiences carried some of the guilt in their indifference and resignation; and he pointed to the movie crowd that defended filmmakers who continue "educating the public on the latest rape techniques." But the guiltiest, he insisted, were the Communists and their allies, "perfectly happy in their pigsty," launching missiles against the "clerics and the priestly regime that governs Italy." Schneider concluded that "we are fed up and we have the right to be." At the ministry, Alberto Folchi joined the chorus against the "flood" of immoral cinema and theater offerings. The overwhelming majority of Italians, he announced to an audience at Rome's Teatro Appio, was "tired" of the trash. New and improved censorship measures could not come too soon.[112]

In production, *Rocco* had already experienced difficulties during the previous spring, not from Rome but from the Milan prefecture and the DC-led provincial council (*giunta*), which abruptly refused Visconti permission to shoot the last outdoor location scenes at the city's seaplane airport. With the schedule tightening, on April 9, 1960, the production company Titanus petitioned the new Ministry of Tourism and Spettacolo for help; and on the fourteenth a group of critics urged Tupini to allow the shooting to finish. Even the hardnosed De Pirro dispatched a sympathetic note to his boss, citing the financial difficulties that would arise if production were cut.[113] Visconti was able to complete his film; but he then encountered opposition from the Milan Tribunal's public prosecutor (*procuratore*), Pietro Trombi, and Carmelo Spagnuolo, the Appeals Court prosecutor. Claiming that the film led to "the progressive lowering of moral barriers—sentiment of decency, family order, and understanding of social relations—that constitute the sole and irreplaceable safeguard of every civil society," Trombi threatened to ban it. The day after its October 14 advance showing at Milan's Capitol Theater and despite the *nulla osta* from the ministry in Rome, Spagnuolo pulled *Rocco e i suoi fratelli* and then ordered the deletion of some scenes. After negotiations with the Appeals Court, the producer Goffredo Lombardo agreed to make four cuts that totaled about fifteen minutes of screen time. He did so, however, without consulting Visconti, who promptly retaliated

112. Fabrizio Schneider, "Defenestrare il cinema," *Discussione*, November 13, 1960; "Allarme per il dilagare della corruzione nei film," *Il Quotidiano*, October 21, 1960; and "Il pubblico è stanco del cinema immorale," *Il Quotidiano*, November 2, 1960.

113. ACS Ministry of Tourism and the Spettacolo (henceforth MTS), CF 3282, *Nulla osta*, November 12, 1960; Titanus/MTS, April 9, 1960; Milan critics/MTS, April 14, 1960; De Nicola/Tupini, April 9, 1960.

by taking legal action. He also announced that he would not direct Gaetano Donizetti's *Poliuto* at La Scala and would refuse new engagements in Italy. The *Voce repubblicana* expressed solidarity with Visconti against this "authentic Fascist menace" to freedom, civilization, and the future. Milan's application of what became known as the *supercensura* established its court as the harshest of censors, rendering somewhat as a "joke" the Ministry of the Spettacolo in Rome. Four days later, the Republicans wondered how foreigners might view the Milan events, and how Italians of the *Mezzogiorno* might do so. The *Procuratore* and his allies, continued the Republicans, were evidently uninterested in the plight of those southerners who migrated to the northern cities.[114]

In *Rocco*'s case, however, Catholics could not be entirely blamed for heavy-handed censorship. Despite charges such as the *Voce repubblicana*'s that this was a "clerical attack" on freedom, the prosecutors were not known as Catholic militants, and, at one point, Trombi emphasized to the press that "we judges are the agents of no one."[115] Neither the *Osservatore Romano* nor the DC's *Concretezza*, moreover, had much to say about the two men and did not place the controversy in any specifically Catholic context. Trombi and Spagnuolo, nevertheless, clearly enjoyed support from many of the faithful. The Catholic newspaper *Italia* applauded their measures, which addressed the shouts of "enough" from a people tired of immorality and obscenity on the screen. In the AC men's review *Noi uomini*, Rosario Mazzone felt "unconditionally pleased" in the magistrates' actions, which affirmed the rights of families. After all, he wrote, the censorship panels at the ministry can make mistakes.[116] Public meetings across Italy brought up the familiar discussions of clerical domination versus a nation on the path to damnation. One priest in

114. Gianni Rondolino, *Luchino Visconti* (Turin: UTET Libreria, 2006), 390–416; "Rocco dietro le velline," *Voce repubblicana*, October 28–29, 1960. On the consequences for southerners, see "Miracolo e supercensura," *Voce repubblicana*, November 1–2, 1960; McCraw, "Political Sponsorship of the Arts," 219–22; and Mino Monicelli, "La Settimana dell'effetto notte," *L'Europeo*, November 6, 1960. See also Henry Bacon, *Visconti: Visions of Beauty and Decay* (Cambridge: Cambridge University Press, 1998), 102–4. Regarding Visconti's refusal to work at La Scala, see "La Procura di Milano sequestra 'La giornata balorda,'" *Voce repubblicana*, November 17–18, 1960. In a 1965 speech to inaugurate the new judicial year in Milan, Trombi again denounced the "decline in *costume*"; "Il procuratore generale Trombi denuncia il declino del costume," *Corriere della sera*, January 12, 1965.

115. e.b., "Cultura e censura," *Voce repubblicana*, November 18–19, 1960; Trombi was quoted in McCraw, "Political Sponsorship of the Arts," 221.

116. r.m. (Raimondo Manzini?), "Polemica forzata," OR, January 13, 1961; M. Valdoreto, "Censori e giudici," *Concretezza*, November 16, 1960; "Basta agli spettacoli corruttori della società," *Italia*, November 16, 1960, found in ACS, MTS, Divisione teatro, f. 19353; Rosario Mazzone, "Giudici e censura," *Noi uomini*, January 8, 1961. Spagnuolo, in fact, later turned up on the list of members in the notorious P-2 Masonic Lodge scandal of the 1980s.

Sardinia, however, tried a different tactic and, in the square behind the parish church, burned five hundred copies of the town paper that carried lurid ads for a minor film, *Un mandarino per Teo*.[117]

The aforementioned promises from Tupini and Folchi for tougher application, moreover, might have inspired the magistrates to take matters into their own hands or fostered an atmosphere that permitted that. Trombi and Spagnuolo's actions, however, were irregular. Censorship decisions previously came from the Undersecretariat, the Interior Ministry, and now the Ministry of Tourism and the Spettacolo, not maverick prosecutors; and, indeed, their move apparently took the ministry by surprise. Undersecretary Renzo Helfer insisted that no communications between Milan and Rome preceded the action. The 1923 censorship law, however, had allowed the "minister . . . on his own initiative," to "recall the film," although it had already received the *nulla osta*. Helfer urged caution and confessed that he told as much to the Titanus producers.[118] A few weeks later, the December 1960 *Rivista del cinematografo* drew no links between the magistrates and the Catholic movement. While its tone was sympathetic, the article hinted at some reservations toward the magistrates' actions. "Censorship, therefore, is necessary," it stated, "but only if it's regulated wisely."[119] Looking for the root of the trouble, *L'Europeo* interviewed the tough-looking Trombi and found him a man of "uncommon intellectual and moral rigor" whose chief aim, as he put it, was "defending and protecting" defenseless youth. The magazine found Spagnuolo less "puritanical" and blessed with a sense of humor. Catholic Action's *Orizzonti* could only claim that his thoughtful considerations revealed "a profound internal discourse, meditated as in prayer."[120]

In a speech in Rome Folchi blamed the Communists, troublesome hypocrites who relied on friendly magistrates against "fascist" censorship then turned around to attack them when they issued inconvenient

117. ACS, Interno gabinetto, 1961–63, B. 324, f. 17083, s.1., Cagliari prefecture report, February 17, 1961. This folder contains a number of prefectural reports on the public gatherings.

118. ACS, PCM, 1959–61, 1-6-4, B. 102, f. 97605, s. 3, MTS report by Renzo Helfer, October 21, 1960, with cover letter Folchi/Fanfani, October 22, 1960. On November 25, the Milan chapter of the National Magistrates Association voted to disavow Trombi's and Spagnuolo's actions; "La Procura di Milano non rappresenta la Magistratura," November 26–27, 1960; "La censura ministeriale contro il film 'La francese e l'amore,'" November 29–30, 1960, both in *Voce repubblicana*.

119. Lugaro, "Censura, male inevitabile," *Rivista del cinematografo*, December 1960.

120. Giovanni Bonetto, "Il nemico dell'Arialda," *Orizzonti*, March 12, 1961. There may have been some rivalry between the two men. Trombi had only recently arrived in the city, and Spagnuolo, a Milanese since 1935, bragged that he had long been taking a tough stance; Mino Monicelli, "Cala la tela," *L'Europeo*, March 5, 1961.

verdicts. Catholic Action, on the other hand, applauded the sequestrations of works even though they had received the government's *nulla osta*: more reason for a tougher censorship. A divergence, however, might be discerned between the moderate Christian Democracy and the more militant Catholic Action. To Monsignor Castellano a worried Gavuzzo revealed that the sequestration implicitly led to AC support for the two magistrates and criticism of the DC government, something that, although "entirely justified," was best kept from the public. That the Morality Office kept mum, moreover, did not stop it from receiving letters of endorsement for the two judges from dioceses across Italy.[121]

The controversies continued, and the two magistrates even broadened their attacks to other films. In October 1960, they went after Alberto Lattuada's *I Dolci inganni* (released in English as *Sweet Deceptions*) and Michelangelo Antonioni's *L'Avventura*, the big Italian offering at the Cannes Film Festival, which the audience there booed. In November, using the Criminal Code's Article 528, they sequestered two more works, Mauro Bolognini's *La Giornata Balorda* (released in English as *From a Roman Balcony*, based on one of Alberto Moravia's Roman tales) and even André Cayatte's *Crossing the Rhine*, which won the Golden Lion at Venice. This attitude spread to other cities such as Foggia and Pavia, where prosecutorial enthusiasm led to more film seizures.[122] It also reached abroad. In November, the censor's range extended to Britain, where the cast of Tennessee Williams's *The Roman Spring of Mrs. Stone* received word that they would not be permitted to enter Italy and begin production. The bewildered producer, Louis de Rochemont, stated that he had not received any reason for Rome's action. The bulk of the film was consequently shot in London. This was a national disgrace, something "absolutely illegal and absolutely intolerable," cried the *Voce repubblicana*. Italy lived in a surreal existence, they wryly stated, a land "absolutely clean, chaste, and comfortable" of "virtuous women and Olympic victors."[123] Critics knew that they stood on firm legal ground. In *Cinema nuovo*, a

121. "Discorso del ministro Folchi sui problemi dello spettacolo," *Il Popolo*, November 2, 1960; IPVI, Pg XII, b. 38, Gavuzzo/Castellano, November 29, 1960.

122. Bolognini's *La Giornata Balorda* encountered trouble for a scene in which a thief snatches a ring off a corpse's finger. For Cayatte's *Il Passaggio del Reno*, it came in a scene where an escaped prisoner strips a woman to keep her from betraying him to the authorities; "Sequestrato il film *La Giornata Balorda*," *Il Popolo*, November 17, 1960.

123. Alessandro Clericuzio, *Tennesee Williams in Italy: A Transcultural Perspective* (Switzerland: Palgrave Macmillan, 2016), 129–36; "Cinema e teatro: procura e censura," *Voce repubblicana*, November 14–15, 1960; "Lo sconfinamento di potere della procura di Milano alla CS della Magistratura," *Voce repubblicana*, November 3–4, 1960.

University of Pavia law professor Pietro Nuvolone argued that prosecutors had no authority to apply their own censorships.[124]

The question was taking its toll among Catholics, and, a year later, in November 1961, another crisis over the film *Non uccidere* aired more embarrassing arguments in public and illustrated still more fissures in the DC position. Directed by France's Claude Autant-Lara and with a mostly Yugoslav cast, it told the story of two conscientious objectors after the Second World War. The film triggered diverse reactions. Some approached the motion picture as a tale of honest feelings, while others saw disrespect and delinquency. France delayed the film's release there until 1963, and it failed to receive the *nulla osta* in Italy. The Jesuits in *Letture*, moreover, pronounced it "morally ambiguous and confused"; but in Florence, Giorgio La Pira admired the idea behind the work. Having returned to the mayor's office after a four-year hiatus, he hadn't seen it yet, but he took matters into his own hands, ignored Folchi's ban, and showed the film to an audience of journalists and intellectuals. Criticisms of the DC leader soon surfaced in the Catholic press. In the *Osservatore Romano*, Raimondo Manzini quoted La Pira's introduction to the guests at the screening, admitting that the last film he had seen was *Snow White and the Seven Dwarfs* and implying that his spotty knowledge of film disqualified him from any real judgment. Otherwise, Manzini asked, how could such a Catholic see any worth in such an obviously anti-Catholic film? An angry Andreotti attacked La Pira in an open letter, charging that he had placed himself above the law and above morality.[125] The mayor responded to criticisms in an open letter to Manzini, asking which Catholic groups had condemned the motion picture and likening the response to the Soviet Union's persecution of the writer Boris Pasternak. In turn, the editor gave La Pira a list of Catholic organizations that condemned *Non uccidere*, starting with OCIC, and reminded him that Italy was a democratic country that only censored for the "common good" and not a totalitarian nation that hounded writers like Pasternak.[126]

124. Pietro Nuvolone, "La Supercensura del signor Procuratore," *Cinema Nuovo*, December 1960, 486–89.

125. "I gesuiti contro 'Non uccidere,'" *L'Unità*, November 18, 1961; Raimondo Manzini (r.m.), "Ribalta dei fatti," *OR*, November 20–21, 1961; "Sì e No," *Orizzonti*, December 3, 1961.

126. "Ribalta dei fatti," *OR*, November 23, 1961. The Soviet government persecuted Pasternak after the publication of his *Doctor Zhivago*. He died in 1960. See also ACS, Interno Gabinetto, 1961–63, f. 17083, s. 16, b. 324; and PCM 1959–61, 1-6-4, f. 97605, s. 3; ACS Interno Gabinetto 1961–63, f. 17083, s. 16, b. 324; and "Obiezione di coscienza tutto cominciò con un film," *La Stampa*, October 21, 2011, http://www.lastampa.it/2011/10/21/cultura/obiezione-di-coscienzatutto-comincio-con-un-film-Bi96KGbnyvOEBdPynDHWFP/pagina.html (accessed February 17, 2017).

Lay figures of all political stripes protested what was coming to be seen as the censorship debacle. The Friends of *Il Mondo* organized a conference on clerical control of the media and published the proceedings. At a crowded meeting at Rome's Corso cinema, the National Union of Cinema Journalists called for a strike in November 1960.[127] In its April–May 1961 issue dedicated to censorship, *Bianco e Nero* sampled the views of states attorneys across Italy, most of whom supported their Milanese colleagues, maintaining that the government had an obligation to protect youth from the "violence, horror, and sadism" found in film.[128] *Il Ponte* also published a special issue on the subject in November of 1961, combining short opinion pieces from all sectors with longer articles from the lay perspective. At the Morality Office Gavuzzo dismissed *Il Ponte*'s censorhip issue as a collection of "the usual phrases about 'Fascist measures,' of the 'holy furor from the moral hypocrite,' and about 'ethics free from the prejudices of sects,' *et cetera*."[129]

Catholic cineastes, however, also soured. In *Discussione* Renato Filizzola confessed that things were getting out of hand; and when the judges took aim at *I Dolci inganni*, he could only moan "another week, another sequestration." He agreed with Spagnuolo, who insisted that he only applied the law. But the censorship question had become more bewildering than ever: "confusion and incoherence" reigned, and Filizzola argued that one must get to the root of all evil: the "Fascist" legislation of 1923. The Italy of 1960, he concluded, was not the Italy of 1923, and it demanded new rules.[130] Battle fatigue affected other Catholic critics at about the same time. In *Il Popolo* Paolo Valmarana expressed doubts over the state's wisdom, and Nazareno Fabbretti criticized the simplistic thought in some parish cinemas that a film's morality depended on a snip of kissing or crime footage.[131] Qualms extended even to the top of the censorship bureaucracy. Alberto Folchi confessed to Aldo Moro in February of 1961, "I have always thought that the 'moral' issue of cinema

127. "In sciopero il mondo del cinema," *Paese sera*, November 2, 1960.

128. "La censura cinematografica: Idee, esperienze documenti," special issue of *Bianco e Nero* 22, no. 4–5 (April–May 1961). The quote about protecting youth came from the state's attorney of the Naples Appeals Court, 82.

129. Paolo Barile, "I censori fra la costituzione e i giudici," *Il Ponte* 17, no. 11 (1961): 1,484–85, 1,496–97. See also F. Di Giammatteo and G. Moscon, "Al limite," 469–71, in the same issue; IPVI, Pg XII, b. 19, Gavuzzo Circular, January 31, 1962.

130. Renato Filizzola, "Gli inganni dell'avventura balorda che si chiama 'guerra alla censura,'" *Discussione*, December 4, 1960.

131. Paolo Valmarana, "Molte proteste per nulla," November 2, 1960, and Nazareno Fabbretti, "Oltre le etichette," November 6, 1960, both in *Il Popolo*.

could not just be resolved with the application of censorship." The industry, he said, needed redirection. Better days, he continued, were on their way thanks to a steady hand and "some intelligence."[132]

L'Arialda

As controversy swirled around his *Rocco e i suoi fratelli* and the other films, in the fall of 1960 Luchino Visconti found himself in a different scandal over his staging of Giovanni Testori's play *L'Arialda*. Unlike the *Rocco* case, where Trombi and Spagnuolo muddied the waters, this was more clearly one of organized Catholic censorship. Born in 1923, the illustrator and writer Testori could easily be classified as a Catholic artist. After the war, he attended classes at the Catholic University, where he befriended the respected intellectual Father David Maria Turoldo and produced quite a few works on religious themes, including the well-received *Caterina di Dio*. His work *Il Ponte della Ghisolfa*, in fact, provided some inspiration for Visconti's *Rocco*. Testori's *L'Arialda*, however, soon ran afoul of the authorities. After a first read, the new ministry reported back on October 26, 1960, that the story centered on the love-starved Arialda and her "pederast" brother, Eros. The play stood on shaky ground from the start, but, from the script's page 135 until the final curtain, Testori seemed to have abandoned all caution. The report noted that the text became "ever more repugnant" until it evolved into "an open apologia for homosexual passion." The theater censorship committee met on the twenty-eighth. One member, Carlo Brancoli from the Labor Ministry, started the discussion by denouncing *L'Arialda*, which "justifies and stimulates ... homosexual vice [and] damages the moral personality of the spectator." A general agreement with Brancoli's accusation followed, although De Pirro, who also served on the committee, argued that the end of the play offered a "glimmer of redemption" and urged that the company might alter the script. Nevertheless, based on a unanimous decision, the ministry alerted the Rome Questura to halt any production of *L'Arialda*, a work of "clear offense to the foundation principles of the family."[133] The Communists interpreted this as "clerical obscurantism," and the Republicans scorned the "wave of phony moralism that ... bat-

132. IS Sez. Pol., Sc. 148, f. 39, Folchi/Moro, February 11, 1961.

133. Ministry of Tourism and the Spettacolo, "Relazione on L'Arialda," October 26, 1960; the ministry's Commissione consultiva per la censura teatrale, minutes of its October 28, 1960, meeting; and Renzo Helfer, undersecretary in the Ministry of Tourism and the Spettacolo/Rome Prefecture, October 30, 1960. All can be located in ACS, MTS, Divisione Teatro, f. 19353, L'Arialda.

tered Italy's show business."[134] Consequently, at Rome's Eliseo Theater, Visconti, Testori, and the show's producers, Paolo Stoppa and Rina Morelli, arranged for a reading of the script before an audience of the city's principal critics. One Communist, in fact, designated this improvised production as the high point of the theatrical season. Debates within the ministry continued. The ex-Fascist De Pirro would again, perhaps ironically, rise to Testori's support, claiming that, with the exception of Eros and his lover, Oreste, all the characters possessed at least *some* redemptive qualities. The DC undersecretary Helfer would not back down and charged that the play and its characters were entirely devoid of any morality. On November 14, however, De Pirro's position, to cut rather than ban, won the day.[135] Testori obliged with cuts on forty pages, almost a third of the script, and rewrote the dialogue between Eros and Oreste. Finally, on the twenty-first, the censorship committee met and approved the release of *L'Arialda*, which opened at the Eliseo on December 22.[136] *Il Popolo* predictably found the play offensive and "the dialogue and characters . . . simply repugnant." *Avanti!* saw little to like in a play about "homosexuals, pimps, trollops and blackmailers."[137]

Visconti and Testori, however, encountered more opposition in February 1961 when their show reached Milan, where Spagnuolo condemned it for its "turpitude and triviality" and closed it after one performance. The Communists gave *L'Arialda* a more sympathetic hearing when the "unchained" Trombi and Spagnuolo shut down the production and sequestered copies of the text from bookstores. *L'Unità* felt that the two treated Testori's work the same way as they would deal with pornographic films or obscene publications. In *L'Europeo* Indro Montanelli (writing as

134. "La Censura contro l'Arialda," *Voce repubblicana*, November 9–10, 1960. A week later the Republican paper feared that, taken with the film cases, including the trouble over "The Roman Spring of Mrs. Stone," the censors had run riot and that the intolerance and hypocrisy had reached cretinous levels; "'L'Arialda' vietata: La censura assume pieni poteri," *Voce repubblicana*, November 15–16, 1960. On *Il Ponte della Ghisolfa*, see Maria Vittoria Sala, "I giovani del *Ponte della Ghisolfa* di Giovanni Testori e *Rocco e i suoi fratelli* di Luchino Visconti: Un confronto," found on Griseldaonline, http://www.griseldaonline.it/didattica/i-giovani-del-ponte-della-ghisolfa-sala.html (accessed November 5, 2019). See also Bruno Schacherl, *Il critico errante: Anni Sessanta e dintorni a teatro in cerca di Storia* (Florence: Le Lettere, 2005), 124–26. The Marxist critic Schacherl believed that the whole affair was part of a clerical vendetta against Visconti.

135. ACS, MTS, Divisione Teatro, f. 19353, L'Arialda, minutes of the November 14, 1960, meeting of the Commissione consultiva per la censura teatrale.

136. ACS, MTS, Divisione Teatro, f. 19431, Testori/Ministry of Tourism and the Spettacolo, November 21, 1960; Giovanni Raboni, introduction, xxiv–xxv, in Giovanni Testori, *Opere 1943–1961*, ed. Fulvio Panzeri (Milan: Bompiani, 1996); see also Federica Festa, *Teatro proibito: In scena i tabù di una nazione* (Spoleto: Editoria and Spettacolo, 2011), 115–18.

137. "Precisioni sul divieto alla commedia l'Arialda," *Il Popolo*, November 20, 1960; Chigo De Chiara, "Movimentata 'prima' dell'Arialda all'Eliseo," *Avanti!*, December 23, 1960.

"Marmidone") expressed a "here we go again" frustration. Even without the police order, he wrote, the Milan premiere was a disaster in which the critics panned it and the great majority of the audience registered their disgust by whistling as the curtain fell. A long run was out of the question, so, he asked, why "in the name of God, would the judges want to insert themselves in this?" The good name of Milan, he maintained, had become synonymous with "intolerance and oafishness."[138] Three years later, the case against Testori and Gian Giacomo Feltrinelli, who published *L'Arialda* in book form, finally went to court. On the defense team, one of Italy's most prestigious legal scholars, Giuliano Vassalli, argued that the two defendants committed no crimes. The court agreed and absolved them on April 23, 1964.[139]

Emilio Lonero and the Venice *Biennale*

As part of his more aggressive tactics in the spring of 1960, Tupini attempted to strengthen the Catholic presence at the Venice film festival by replacing Luigi Floris Ammannati with a new director. Catholic Action had initially promoted Ammannati's nomination in 1956, but he since acquired a rather relaxed reputation. The new director would be the more militant Emilio Lonero, also from Catholic Action. The new man had been building a career for himself in the Catholic film world. Part of the old Orbis crew, he moved on to head the CCC and direct the *Rivista del cinematografo*, where many of his articles dealt with the *Biennale*. But his nomination stirred a great deal of controversy. In *L'Europeo*, Renzo Trionfera contended that Lonero came to the *Biennale* after an aborted takeover of the Experimental Film Center, where the faculty resented him and the director, also a Catholic, appealed to Tupini. Lonero then undertook a new campaign for the Venice post and approached his "protectors," Galletto and Gedda, who marshaled on his behalf influential clerics like cardinals Mimmi, Micara, and Lercaro. After a breakfast meeting between Tupini and Gedda, a "reluctant" Giovanni Ponti, head of the *Biennale*, agreed to accept Lonero for the Film Festival.[140] *Avanti!*

138. "L'Arialda sequestrate nelle librerie," *L'Unità*, March 2, 1961; "Marmidone," "La denuncia milanese e la battaglia per *l'Arialda*," and "Ancora l'Arialda: I critici, il pubblico, il tribunal," *L'Europeo* (respectively), March 12 and April 9, 1961.

139. "Non è oscena: assolta 'L'Arialda,'" *Corriere della sera*, April 24, 1964; "Assolta 'L'Arialda' con formula piena," *Avanti!*, April 24, 1964.

140. Renzo Trionfera, "Il censore in gondola," *L'Europeo*, March 13, 1960. This article was summarized in the *Voce repubblicana* as "L'Attacco clericale al cinema," March 10–11, 1960. See also "La 'longa

dismissed the "foolishness" and predicted more trouble—"a clerical offensive against our cinema."[141] Lonero at the helm, insisted the Socialists, would ruin Venice's international status, "something that even the Fascists were unable to do."[142]

For his part, Ponti denied in *Il Popolo* any religious maneuver to take over the *Biennale*.[143] Lonero did not help his cause, however, when he announced his intention to steer the festival on a more "spiritual" course, or his statement upon taking office, on March 7, 1960, that cinema's mission was to "culturally and ethically elevate" the public. Lonero's appointment outraged the film festival's selection jury so much that they collectively resigned, including, significantly, the Catholic critic Gian Luigi Rondi. This act was followed by resignations from other members of the *Biennale*. One jurist, the journalist Gino Visentini, stated that the choice had jeopardized the "long tradition of liberality" to which Ammannati had adhered, and the *Voce repubblicana* predicted that the attempt to place the festival "in the hands of clericals [*clericali*] seem[ed] destined to fail."[144]

Along with Rondi's resignation, problems with Lonero's appointment emerged elsewhere in Catholic quarters. In Liguria, a DC paper lamented that the loss of Ammannati was "not good news for those who love without reservations cinematic art." He cut a "courteous and competent" figure marked by "taste and gentility," known across the Italian Riviera for his work at a comedy film festival in Bordighiera, which the paper hoped would continue.[145] *L'Unità* detected more Catholic dissent when it chronicled Ponti's frustrated attempts to assemble a new jury. Important Catholics, it noted, such as the *Quotidiano*'s film critic, Mario Verdone, flatly rejected participation.[146] On March 10 the paper reported that Lonero and Ponti had been hard-pressed to replace the members, although some names circulated, particularly Giovanni Gigliozzi, a Catholic convert from Marxism and, despite his denial, Verdone, both

manus' di monsignore Galetto [*sic*]," *Avanti!*, March 2, 1960. Lonero's articles on the *Biennale* include "Venezia 1956," *Rivista del cinematografo*, September/October 1956, which stated that the 1956 event restored faith in the festival and augured well its role as "a real fact of culture and art."

141. "Il direttore della Mostra del cinema di Venezia non piaceva più ai monsignori," *Avanti!*, February 28, 1960.

142. F. m., "La lunga notte del censore," *Avanti!*, March 10, 1960.

143. "Dichiarazione di Ponti sulla Biennale veneziana," *Il Popolo*, April 10, 1960.

144. "La Commissione di Venezia si dimette al completo," *Voce repubblicana*, March 2, 1960; "Insediato a Venezia il direttore della Mostra Cinematografica," *Il Quotidiano*, March 8, 1960.

145. "Una nomina che ci addolora," *Popolo Ligure*, March 4, 1960. This article can be found in FVC, Fondo Gedda, B. 392, f. 911.

146. "I Cattolici divisi anche sul caso Lonero," *L'Unità*, March 6, 1960.

of whom the Republicans dismissed as "names of no consequence in the cultural field."[147] Ponti enticed the wayward committee members to return through guarantees of Lonero's liberality and the offer to draft a new charter for the group. Some returned, but more did not, and *Il Popolo* dismissed their stand as an overwhelmingly radical one that had created an "unbridgeable divide." On March 16, the Milanese *Il Giorno* revealed that Senator Ponti's own resignation as head of the *Biennale* had been sitting on Tupini's desk for fifteen days.[148]

The tempers and confusion exacted a toll on the event. The lay *Belfagor* called the 1960 Venice Festival "scandalous" and "the worst and the dullest" ever. On September 7, to a chorus of "loud whistles, catcalls and jeers of disapproval," the reconstituted jury of eleven, headed by the French screenwriter Marcel Achard, awarded the Golden Lion to André Cayatte's *Crossing of the Rhine*. Sentiment among the outraged fairgoers was that the *Biennale* had snubbed Visconti's *Rocco e i suoi fratelli*. A Russian member of the committee, in fact, accused Achard of rigging the process to favor his fellow Frenchman and deny the prize to Italy's "authentic work of art." Upon word that Visconti's film would instead receive a "special" prize, the angry producer cabled Lonero that he would refuse it.[149] Catholics scrambled for a response. One critic defended the festival but saw the problem in the state of film art where productions came from either the far left or "unscrupulous merchants." Another, in the *Rivista del cinematografo*, chastised the *Biennale* for "wrongly" presenting the Golden Lion to *Crossing of the Rhine* but felt that the "special" award for Visconti's film was sufficient.[150]

Lonero waited until after the awards to answer his critics, and consequently, on September 8 he denounced "the sabotage of certain film professionals." Catholic Action's *Quotidiano* took up the cudgels for Lonero and charged that vengeful "lay speculation" regarding him had gone "beyond belief." Not only had the attack been aimed at Lonero and the festival, it was also an assault on Catholic Action. For the *Quotidiano* the challenge was quite clear: lay factions "don't want him because he's

147. "Nuove proteste per Lonero," *Voce repubblicana*, March 9, 1960. See also "Il caso Lonero," March 6, 1960. On March 8 the paper reported that the respected Catholic critic Renato May declined to participate on the reformed committee; "Lonero in difficoltà," March 8, 1960.

148. "Dimissioni (e no) del Senatore Ponti," *Voce repubblicana*, March 16–17, 1960; "Troppi statuti per Venezia," *Il Popolo*, May 24, 1960.

149. Giorgio Moscon, "L'Ultimo festival di Venezia," *Belfagor*, September 30, 1960; "French Film Gets Top Venice Prize," *New York Times*, September 8, 1960.

150. N. a., "Venezia, Tiro a segno," and Leandro Castellani, "Un Ripertorio non eccezionale ma superiore a quello dello scorso anno," both in *Rivista del cinematografo*, September–October, 1960.

Catholic," and the paper urged the government not to succumb to the loudest clatter. On behalf of the government, Gabriele Semeraro issued the obligatory declaration that the twenty-first film festival was a success, thanks to the heads of the *Biennale* as well as the selection committee.[151] Lonero, nonetheless, suffered the fallout from the disastrous twenty-first festival and lost his position to Domenico Meccoli. A critic and screenwriter, the replacement had served on the Cannes committee and had composed the script for a notable "Catholic" film under the Fascists, 1939's *Abuna Messias*. Meccoli also dabbled in acting, costarring with Marcello Mastroianni and Pedro Armendariz in 1955's *Tam Tam Mayumbe*. It may not have been a coincidence, moreover, that on October 1, just after the festival, Monsignor Galletto left his liaison position with the Ente dello spettacolo to focus on his work with the Pontifical Commission for Film, Radio, and Television. Giovanni Ponti also completed his tasks when he died in December 1961.[152]

Revising Censorship

From the end of the war until 1962, Italy's legislature entertained at least sixteen unsuccessful proposals to replace or seriously modify the old 1923 censorship framework. The most important of these was the 1949 Andreotti measure, which expired in 1955, but the government could not supplant it with anything new. The Constitutional Court did not act on it, either, because, as a code (*regolamento*) and not a law, the 1923 ordinance stood outside its jurisdiction.[153] A cinema law of July 31, 1956, no. 897, therefore, simply extended Andreotti's system and, as one scholar remarked, "continued the life of the 1923 code." After 1956, the provisions were then merely annually renewed through 1961. The DC Senator Mario Zotta tried without success to pilot on-again off-again ventures with the intention of cobbling together a new law. In October 1961 he raised eyebrows on the left by implying on the Senate floor that a real censorship might also extend to the press. Arguments went back and forth on the composition of the review committees: judges, for example, or law professors, professors of pedagogy, psychologists, and

151. "Il direttore della Mostra di Venezia reagisce alle critiche 'non obiettive,'" *Il Quotidiano*, September 9, 1960; "Speculazioni laiciste," *Il Quotidiano*, September 18, 1960.

152. "Monsignor Galletto lascia l'Ente dello spettacolo," *Rivista del cinematografo*, September–October 1960.

153. McCraw, "Political Sponsorship of the Arts," 222–23.

representatives of directors, of the motion picture industry, and of cinema journalists. Controversy triggered by *La dolce vita* and then by Trombi's and Spagnuolo's actions forced more examinations of the creaking censorship process.[154]

The DC and their new allies on the left finally crafted a censorship act of April 21, 1962, no. 161. Seen as part of the *apertura*, however, the Socialists and Social Democrats pressured to forge the 1962 law in that spirit. This meant breaking the DC's grip and placing the first read of scripts in the hands of seven-member commissions, picked by the minister of Tourism and the Spettacolo, no longer the Interior. A magistrate chosen by the judicial establishment would chair each panel, which was to include a psychologist, a teacher, an author, a cinema journalist, and an industry representative.[155] In his study of politics and the arts, William Troy McCraw added that the 1962 law partly resulted from Common Market developments. Article 2 of the Treaty of Rome aimed to curb protectionist practices such as government subsidies and bonuses that had been in practice since the law of May 16, 1947 and revised in the law of July 31, 1956.[156]

In any case, the new measure shook the Catholics, who feared any relaxation of censorship or even that this was the beginning of its end. Claims from lay and left factions no doubt fed such worries. Citing an *Avanti!* article by the deputy Luciano Paolicchi, the *Voce republicana* credited the new law as "a step in the secular march toward the liberalization of thought."[157] The *Rivista del cinematografo*'s March 1962 edition covered a conference on "Marxism and *laicismo* in the Italian Cinema," where one speaker, the Jesuit Enrico Baragli, claimed that the Andreotti Law's expiration in 1955 gave the lay-Marxist alliance the opportunity to slowly gnaw away at censorship, with its "total abolition" now in sight.[158] Such fears troubled the Milanese theologian Giovanni Battista Guzzetti, who saw nothing of value in the new censorship law. The old hope, that it should contribute to a more Christian Italy and extend to the common good, seemed on the wane. Still, Catholics, he argued, should not settle for less. "We have the impression," Guzzetti continued, "that not enough is demanded of producers, operators of cinemas, spectators

154. McCraw, "Political Sponsorship of the Arts," 34, 180–81.
155. McCraw, "Political Sponsorship of the Arts," 222–43.
156. McCraw, "Political Sponsorship of the Arts," 219–43.
157. "Il censore travestito," *Voce repubblicana*, March 10–11, 1964.
158. Filippo Russo, "Marxismo e laicismo nel cinema italiano," *Rivista del cinematografo*, March 1962.

and parents." He also condemned state subsidies of films "that harmed the public good." Lawmakers might expand the definition of *buon costume* or change the Constitution, but, Guzzetti confessed, neither seemed likely.[159] In January 1963 the Interior Ministry, led by the DC's Paolo Emilio Taviani, expressed concerns, too, particularly over a relaxed *Nulla osta* process and minors gaining access to questionable films. To combat this the ministry would rely on the new women's police units for vigilant observance and frequent visits to theaters. The doomsday mentality pervaded Catholic thinking, and *Orizzonti* bluntly asked whether or not the new law was, indeed, just a surrender.[160] Six months later Antonio Petrucci echoed this resignation in the *Rivista del cinematografo* and blamed the DC for most of it. Petrucci lauded Andreotti's earlier measures, but he fought the good fight by himself, abandoned by the party elite. Such figures humbly deferred to the left and, particularly "lay and secularist" (*laica e laicista*) mainstream journals while maintaining both a "well-intentioned suspicion and secret admiration for entertainment" (*spettacolo*).[161]

Ettore Bernabei at RAI

As late as 1962 the church still agonized over television's effects and devoted its thirty-fifth "social week" to the question. Chaired by Cardinal Siri, the clerics and scholars met in Siena to deliberate the box's educational value and its moral dangers to youth.[162] Two years later, in *Concretezza*, Evelina Tarroni also questioned TV's worth, but from the woman's angle. Advertising made it essential, she wrote, that television enter the private home—but respectfully. Citing Vance Packard's 1957 sensation, *The Hidden Persuaders*, Tarroni felt that advertisers took advantage of women, who were "more emotive [and] given to emotions and impulses." Consequently, she feared that TV had spawned not an evolution but something of a "messy revolution."[163]

159. Giovanni Battista Guzzetti, "Il clero e la nuova legge censura," *Rivista del clero italiano*, July 1962.

160. Mario Guidotti, "La censura s`è arresa?," *Orizzonti*, April 5, 1962. Gavuzzo circulated the Interior Ministry analysis of January 16, 1963. See IPV, Sg. XII, b. 3, Gavuzzo circular "Compiti del Corpo di polizia femminile," September 28, 1963. See also "Questa censura," *Noi uomini*, April 22, 1962; and Enrico Baragli, "Una battaglia da non perdere," *Rivista del cinematografo*, February 1962.

161. A. P. (probably Antonio Petrucci), "Si raccolgono i frutti d'una politica culturale," *Rivista del cinematografo*, June 1963.

162. Antonio Ferrace, "Le incidenze sociali dei mezzi audiovisivi," *Concretezze*, October 16, 1962.

163. Evelina Tarroni, "Chiediamo una evoluzione non una rivoluzione," *Concretezza*, February 16, 1964.

The RAI, however, remained a DC monopoly, a situation persistently criticized by the Communists. Pietro Ingrao, for example, wrote that "the RAI is a closed institution dedicated exclusively to clerical propaganda." After the somewhat freer 1948 electoral campaign, the DC used the RAI to clamp down for the 1953 vote and those of 1958 when *L'Unità* reported a parliamentary exchange over Catholic control between Prime Minister Adone Zoli, the Republican Ugo La Malfa, and the Liberal Bruno Villabruna. The DC, concluded the Marxists, had isolated itself.[164] Ernesto Rossi and the *Mondo* group followed with more attacks through a gathering of lay dissidents, the proceedings of which he published in 1959 as *Verso il regime (Toward the Regime)*. Their approach, which considered Italian democracy and DC control of the RAI as mutually exclusive, yielded a Communist measure in 1959 that Ingrao and some lay colleagues proposed in Parliament but failed to reach a vote. Why should the Communists get airplay, queried Zoli, when they already enjoyed the Italian language transmissions of Radio Prague?[165]

A July 1960 ruling from the Constitutional Court, however, aided the revolt and decided that the Catholic grip on news could not continue. It voided a 1936 measure on which the DC based its control, and the following October, Fanfani announced to Parliament that all political factions would be allowed a number of aired "press conferences" before the upcoming administrative elections. Soon opposition leaders appeared on *Tribuna elettorale*, a new show of political speeches and discussion that became *Tribuna politica* the following year. "For the first time in Italy," stated the Turin daily *La Stampa*, "electioneering will appear on television."[166]

On January 4, 1961, Ettore Bernabei took the director general's chair at RAI. The office had been elevated over that of the *Amministratore delega-*

164. "La DC isolata sul problema della RAI," *L'Unità*, April 17, 1958. See also Menico Caroli, *Proibitissimo! Censori e censurati della radiotelevisione italiana* (Milan: Garzanti, 2003), 65–66.

165. Giulia Guazzaloca, "The 'Revolution That Never Was': Rai-TV and the Launch of *Tribuna politica*," *Modern Italy* 14, no. 3 (2009): 277–80. Guazzaloca also deals with this issue in *Una e divisibile: La RAI e i partiti negli anni del monopolio pubblico (1954–1975)* (Florence: Le Monnier, 2011), 87–95. On the Zoli statement, see Crainz, *Storia del miracolo*, 8. On the PCI's judgment, see Damiano Garofalo, *Political Audiences: A Reception History of Early Italian Television*, trans. Michael Sarnoff-Wood (Milan: Mimesis International, 2016), 57.

166. The Constitutional Court sentence was number 59 of July 13, 1960, http://www.giurcost.org/decisioni/1960/0059s-60.html (accessed November 7, 2019). See also "La costituzionalità dell'esercizio statale per i servizi di T.V.," *Il Popolo*, July 14, 1960; Edoardo Novelli, *Dalla TV di partito al partito della TV: Televisione e Politica in Italia* (Florence: La Nuova Italia, 1995), 4–13; Crainz, *Storia del miracolo italiano*, 204–6; On *Tribuna politica*, see also Antonio Catolfi, *Televisione e politica negli anni Sessanta* (Urbino: QuattroVenti, 2006), particularly chapter 2, "Nasce la politica in televisione."

to, in which Marcello Rodinò remained in a reduced role. Although the Moro faction had replaced Fanfani's and Bernabei was close to Fanfani, they registered no objections to his appointment.[167] He came as a newspaperman, with stints first at Florence's *Giornale del Mattino* and then *Il Popolo*. Like Filiberto Guala, Bernabei also identified with the DC's progressive La Pira faction. According to one observer, his lengthy tenure at the helm, serving until 1974, ensured "that the RAI remained for a long time firmly in the Fanfani camp."[168] And as was so often the case in the DC, the ties were personal. Fanfani's son, Giorgio, was not only La Pira's godson, he married Bernabei's daughter.[169] Also like Guala, Bernabei was known as a hothead and admitted as much. "Yes, unfortunately," he confessed, "when I get angry I turn all red, even blue in the face [*paonazzo*], and I shout and, God forgive me, use bad words." He was quick to point out that he did not blaspheme.[170]

Bernabei, however, did not share Guala's star-crossed fate. When asked if anyone surpassed him as Italian TV's "supercensor," he answered with a blunt "no" and continued, "I did it and I'd do it again."[171] Bernabei, nonetheless, possessed a political astuteness that came in handy as he piloted the RAI through the "opening to the left" while maintaining the DC's guiding presence. He could bend when necessary.[172] Under Bernabei, the rigid Code of Self Discipline and list of banned words appear to have been much relaxed, if indeed they were even seriously applied. Female legs provide another illustration. Among the RAI's big finds of the era were the Kessler twins, two German blondes from a Berlin nightclub who, quite famous for their legs, received lavish attention from the RAI. This earned the familiar negative reactions from Catholics. One angry viewer announced that "these women who dance on TV have lost all sense of shame and modesty . . . making a show of their nudity without reserve." Later asked why he would tolerate such extravagant play on Italian screens and court such responses, Bernabei insisted that despite his "harsh point of view," the Kesslers were "elegant and full of style, never vulgar." "When a woman's

167. Ettore Bernabei with Giorgio Dell'Arti, *L'Uomo di fiducia: I retroscena del potere raccontati da un testimone rimasto dietro le quinte per cinquant'anni* (Milan: Mondadori, 1999), 101–2, 109.

168. Guazzaloca, *Una e divisibile*, 32–33; Franco Chiarenza, *Il cavallo morente: Trent'anni di Radiotelevisione italiana* (Milan: Bompiani, 1978), 131–55.

169. Vincenzo La Russa, *Amintore Fanfani* (Soveria Mannelli: Rubbettino, 2006), 54 and 277.

170. Bernabei with Dell'Arti, *L'Uomo di fiducia*, 17.

171. Caroli, *Proibitissimo!*, 68.

172. Chiarenza, *Il cavallo morente*, 109.

legs are so lovely, it's no sin to show them in tights [*calzamaglia*]." Asked if the Catholics understood this, he replied, "It was a tough argument, on the razor's edge."[173]

Bernabei even went so far as to endorse, and later regret, the involvement of the controversial husband-and-wife team Dario Fo and Franca Rame for the 1962 season of the very popular *Canzonissima*, a variety show wrapped around a song contest. The two made their careers out of satirical, critical, and often radical attacks on the political establishment. But, recalled Bernabei, whose pragmatism may have rivaled his devotion, "one in four Italians was communist . . . and a greater percentage was anti-Christian democrat. We were DC but we knew our public." Thinking that Fo and Rame might succeed without offending, he concluded that "it was like the Kesslers' legs." The two, however, probably went too far too quickly, and neither Bernabei nor Italian TV was prepared for what one observer called their "grotesque humor satirizing capitalist exploitation." After a number of run-ins and censorial touches to their sketches, Bernabei fired the couple at the end of the season. The RAI sued Fo and Rame, destroyed all of their *Canzonissima* recordings, and effectively banished them from television screens for fourteen years. "Yes, I censured Dario Fo," Bernabei concluded, "I didn't want to have him use TV as a wedge between classes."[174]

Bernabei started work at RAI with a number of key personnel changes to indicate that the agency would not be considered a DC bailiwick. He came in with a new president, for example, the Liberal aristocrat and intellectual Novello Papafava, who served until June 1964. Of the old EIAR cohort that had given Guala so much trouble, the unsinkable Marcello Bernardi remained untouched at his post. Only death would end his tenure in 1969. Another of the ex-Fascists, Sergio Pugliese, had died four years earlier, in 1965. Early on, moreover, Bernabei replaced another member of the old clique, Antonio Piccone Stella, who had led the postwar RAI journalism office for radio and then for radio and television. On the other hand, when Bernabei promoted Guala's protégé Luigi Beretta Anguissola, apprehensive lay observers caused such an uproar that some of the governing board resigned, including the noted writer Giorgio Bassani. In the rubble of the news divisions, Bernabei tapped

173. Bernabei with Dell'Arti, *L'Uomo di fiducia*, 122–23; Garofalo, *Political Audiences*, 121–22.

174. Tony Mitchell, *Dario Fo: People's Court Jester* (London: Methuen, 1999), 72–75; Joseph Farrell, *Dario Fo and Franca Rame: Harlequins of the Revolution* (London: Methuen, 2001), 59–64; Bernabei with Dell'Arti, *L'Uomo di fiducia*, 125–26.

Enzo Biagi to direct the primary news broadcast, *Telegiornale*. No Christian Democrat, Biagi had fought in the Resistance with the anti-Fascist Justice and Liberty faction before he joined the Action Party. In charge, he promptly terminated one of the DC's key propaganda practices, that of broadcasting ceremonies such as inaugurations and ribbon-cuttings, gratuitous events that highlighted party leaders and invariably included Catholic prayers and blessings.[175] In November 1961, RAI branched out with an alternative channel, RAI 2, which would be administered by Angelo Romanò, a former radio stalwart hand-picked by Bernabei because "he was a good man and believed in God." Bernabei conceded here that Christian Democrats had no monopoly on faith and that it could tap decent people from outside of the party. Romanò, in fact, later stood in elections as a Communist and with RAI 2, the left now had its foot in the door. Bernabei deftly controlled things through the decade, prompting the PCI to believe that television was still a propaganda tool of their "Christian Democratic enemy." But the monopoly was slipping. Never thrilled by the medium, Guido Gonella grumbled and, significantly, conflated its political fallout with the moral issue. "The worst thing that TV did," he announced, "was to have brought Togliatti and the Kessler Twins into the heart of Italian families."[176]

The Artist Retaliates

The prim "blue nose" and the moralist hypocrite like Nathaniel Hawthorne's Arthur Dimmesdale have been comic foils, tragic or detestable figures in much of modern Euro-American fiction.[177] One scholar wrote that Italians tend to see the "moralist" as a fraud, as one "who gratuitously blathers about virtue, not one who pierces [the bubble of] the blatherer."[178] Here and there, a film surfaced that teased or criticized the censors and the campaign for *buon costume*. An early example, 1952's *Art. 519 Codice penale*, hinted that state meddling might actually cause marital problems. The story concerned Renato, who seduces the object

175. Bernabei with Dell'Arti, *L'Uomo di fiducia*, 140–41; Chiarenza, *Il cavallo morente*, 110–11; 136, regarding Berretta and Bassani; and 163–64, regarding Bernardi.

176. On Romanò, see Bernabei with Dell'Arti, *L'Uomo di fiducia*, 148. In 1979 RAI added a third channel, which the Communists administered. On the Second Channel, RAI due, see Videografo, "È arrivato il secondo canale," *Concretezza*, November 16, 1961.

177. On British depictions, see Faramerz Dabhoiwala, *The Origins of Sex: A History of the First Sexual Revolution* (Oxford: Oxford University Press, 2012), 69.

178. Saverio Vertone, ed., *La Cultura degli italiani* (Bologna: Il Mulino, 1994), 14–15.

of his intentions, the under-age Clara. A scandal ensues and gets him condemned to two years in prison. Article 519, however, provided that marriage between the two would cancel the sentence, and so they tie the knot, only to discover that they hate each other and opt to separate. The newlyweds get back together in a happy ending, perhaps softening any attacks from the CCC that, indeed, felt that although *Art. 519* portrayed a "thorny" subject, it was not without value. The CCC awarded the film an "Ar" rating, for "fully mature adults."[179]

At the end of the decade, another work took aim at moralists and turned the censors themselves into objects of ridicule. 1959's *Il moralista* poked fun at the fictional "OIMP," an international morality association that, much like Catholic Action, pressured for government standards. Vittorio De Sica played its jaded president, who seemed to derive some pleasure by perusing indicators of moral decline, while Alberto Sordi was his assistant who actually ran the organization based on his own insufferably holier-than-thou standards. Both men succumb to temptation, however, and the film ends as the police take Sordi away in handcuffs. The *Rivista del cinematografo* delivered a blistering review, denouncing its "ingredients" of "sex, easy and vulgar laughs, technical weakness and mediocrity [*banalità del gusto*]." It would not merit any comment at all except that, unfortunately, it was so typical of Italy's pathetic film production. The CCC began its *Segnalazioni* judgment of *Il moralista* more moderately, as a "satire of certain self-described moralists although their own moral guilt is greater than that of everyone else," thereby quashing any suspicions that the work was a veiled criticism of Catholic morality organizations. The film, in fact, carefully distanced De Sica's and Sordi's characters from any hint of Catholicism. Nonetheless, its depiction of "night clubs, some dances, racy clothing, *spogliarello*, etc.," made the target clear enough and earned it the harshest rating, *escluso*—that is, no one should view it. As had clearly become the case, however, an *escluso* had little to do with the government's *nulla osta*, which *Il moralista* received on August 7, 1959.[180]

After *La dolce vita*, Fellini waited until 1962 to get some revenge. That year RAI television gave him further reason to resent the censor when it presented his 1953 film *I vitelloni* but with significant cuts. Fellini pro-

179. "Art. 519 Codice penale," in *Segnalazioni cinematografiche* 32, no. 24 (1952): 190.

180. "Il moralista," *Rivista del cinematografo*, November–December, 1959; "Il moralista," *Segnalazioni cinematografiche* 46, no. 14 (1959); ACS, MTS, CF 3086, *nulla osta*, August 7, 1959. Before the producers decided on "*Il moralista*" as a title, they considered "*L'Arriviste*" and "*Hula Hoop*."

tested in *Il Ponte* that the snips had destroyed "the film's value" and only served to "defraud the public."[181] He got his last laugh, though, in a Franco-Italian coproduction, *Boccaccio 70*, an episode work with three other directors. Its title was a hint that it would push the envelope. Fellini's story, "The Temptations of Doctor Antonio," had a personal axe to grind, starting with a reenactment or mockery of the famous incident at a Rome restaurant when Oscar Scalfaro allegedly slapped a woman for her bare shoulders. Peppino De Filippo portrayed the Scalfaro figure, Doctor Antonio, a militant who contributes to Catholic publications. *L'Europeo* described the character as "a fanatical bigot and moralist." Antonio's rigid life of dogmatic certainty crumbles when a billboard promoting the public to "drink more milk" appears within eyeshot of his bathroom window. The vehicle for this message comes in the form of a gigantic reclining Anita Ekberg, who quickly becomes the object of Antonio's obsession. The voluptuous colossus descends one night from the billboard and playfully torments him. He calls her "Sodom and Gomorrah" but ends up the next morning, clad only in underwear, deranged and straddling the top of the billboard. As an ambulance transports him away, he can only mutter "Anita!" while a giggling little Eros rides on top. The CCC gave *Boccaccio 70* its *escluso* rating, and the *Rivista del cinematografo* clearly recognized Fellini's determination to parody the "hypocritical moralists" who had made life miserable for him with *La dolce vita*. "The Temptations of Doctor Antonio," continued the review, began in satire but descended into farce of doubtful taste.[182]

Among other critical motion pictures, 1961's *Divorce Italian Style* (*Divorzio all'italiana*) had the greatest impact. Based on Giovanni Arpino's novel *A Crime of Honor* (*Un delitto d'onore*) Pietro Germi directed the film, which took direct aim at what it saw as Italy's antiquated marriage laws. Set in Sicily, the movie depicted an impoverished noble played by Marcello Mastroianni. Dissatisfied with his drab wife, he discovers the greater pleasures of his much younger cousin played by Stefania Sandrelli and is delighted to discover her interest in him. Since divorce is illegal, the baron decides to murder his wife "*all'italiana*" in an absurd but legal crime of honor. Fiasco ensues, but eventually Mastroianni ends

181. Maurizio Cesari, *La censura in Italia oggi (1944–1980)* (Naples: Liguori editore, 1982), 186.

182. Giuseppe Marotta, "L'Impossibile coabitazione di quattro superbi galli in un pollaio," *L'Europeo*, March 11, 1962; "Boccaccio 70," *Segnalazioni cinematografiche* 51, no. 16 (1962); "Boccaccio 70," *Rivista del cinematografo*, April–May 1962; Gian Luigi Rondi, "Da 'La Strada' al 'Deserto Rosso,'" *Concretezza*, January 1, 1965.

up with Sandrelli, who promptly begins searching for an improvement on him. Although the CCC's *Segnalazioni cinematografiche* acknowledged *Divorzio all'italiana*'s entertainment value, it still gave the film the *escluso* rating because its authentic "brio" could not justify the reality of what actually appeared on the screen. The *Rivista del cinematografo* had little good to say for Germi's work and considered it a "grotesque vulgarization" of a serious subject. Both reviews, however, downplayed the film's divorce element and emphasized instead the crime of honor, identified in the *Rivista*'s piece as Article 587 of the Penal Code.[183] The Communist *Noi donne*, on the other hand, in a long review praised not only the film, but Germi's "courage" in dealing with the subject. In his study of divorce, Mark Seymour wrote that "in Italy, perhaps more than anywhere else in Western Europe," this immensely popular film represented the "high point" in the clash between the nation's "extraordinary and sudden economic advancement" and its old customs and traditions.[184]

At the Holy See, few Italians saw in Paul's new pontificate much of the confidence of Pius XII's years or the pure goodness of John's. After the Vatican Council, Montini confused observers with bold measures like his encyclical *Populorum progressio* of 1967 or *Humanae vitae*, one year later.[185] The remaining ten years of Paul's reign (he died in 1978), consequently, proceeded from one crisis to another, as he piloted St. Peter's barque and its Italian passengers through dangerous currents and the great secular storm.

183. "Divorzio all'italiana," *Segnalazioni cinematografiche* 51, no. 15 (1962): 160; "Divorzio all'italiana," *Rivista del cinematografo*, February 1962; see also Pietro Germi and Giorgio Moscon, *Divorzio all'italiana* (Rome: Edizioni FM, 1961).

184. Mark Seymour, *Debating Divorce in Italy: Marriage and the Making of Modern Italians, 1860–1974* (New York: Palgrave, 2006), 174–77.

185. Hebblethwaite, *Paul VI: The First Modern Pope* (New York and Mahwah, N.J.: Paulist Press, 1993), 480, 519.

Chapter 5

"Because This World as We Know It Is Passing Away"

In his consideration of the developed West, the church historian Hugh McLeod found the 1960s "religiously explosive not because of one key ingredient, but because so many currents of change, initially separate, interacted with one another." Chief among these was "the impact of affluence," which he placed ahead of feminism, theological radicalization, and sexual revolution.[1] Ahead of all political developments, affluence holds center place in the emerging Italy, where a perfect secular storm gathered that would destroy serious Catholic attempts to tame media and the arts and deliver a devastating blow to the church's vision of the family—the legalization of divorce between 1970 and 1974.

Affluence worked with its secularizing siblings such as modernity, urban growth, and consumerism, all pushing Italy from its sense of traditional self. And the indicators accelerated and multiplied. By the 1960s, Italy's urban population skyrocketed and revealed a corresponding rural crisis. The number of cities with populations over 100,000 increased from twenty-six in 1951 to forty-five in 1971. Where in 1951 nine million Italians lived in those cities, twenty years later sixteen million

The chapter title is a quote from Paul, 1 Corinthians 7:31.

1. Hugh McLeod, "The 1960s," in *Religion and the Political Imagination*, ed. Ira Katznelson and Gareth Stedman Jones (Cambridge: Cambridge University Press, 2010), 255. He included radicalism from opposition to the Vietnam War as another factor. Elsewhere, McLeod cited Rene Remond's point that "after religion it is morality that ceases to be a matter for society," wherein "individual conscience" replaces morality; McLeod, *The Religious Crisis of the 1960s* (Oxford: Oxford University Press, 2007), 238. In his broader study of cultural revolution, Arthur Marwick understood the volatile sixties as "c. 1958–c. 1974"; see Marwick, *The Sixties: Cultural Revolution in Britain, France, Italy, and the United States, c. 1958–c. 1974* (Oxford: Oxford University Press, 1999).

did. From 1951 to 1961, on the other hand, 70 percent of communes, almost entirely the smaller ones, declined in size.[2] From 1954 to 1964, the agricultural slice of the job force shrank from 40 percent to 25 percent; the industrial sector rose from 32 to 40 percent, and the tertiary went from 28 to 35 percent. Factories churned out 370,000 refrigerators in 1959 and 1,500,000 in 1963, and it took just seven years, from 1958 to 1965, for the number of households that owned one to shoot from 13 percent to over 50 percent. Ten years later, the figure reached 94 percent. In 1960, 20 percent of homes owned a television; that figure rose to 99 percent in 1975.[3]

Such phenomena nurtured the growing sense of alarm among the faithful, like Pietro Scoppola, who wrote that, coming as fast as it did, this was not an evolution but a break (*rottura*) that led to "a jump into an ethical void."[4] In April 1963 Catholic Action's *Noi uomini* charged that Italy had lost its "moral sense." The angry author pointed to the effects of rapid economic and social transformation, all chipping away at the Catholic cultural presence. "Things are tolerated today which a few years ago couldn't have existed." He deplored "a certain moderate elasticity" of comportment and a new "freedom of expression" that everywhere spawned "vulgar and unnatural" scenes. Now came the time to say "enough" and rally everyone to "halt this ruinous descent."[5] Catholics were losing on the cultural front to materialist, lay, and hedonist barbarians who had entered the gates, provoking the faithful to wonder if, indeed, their handle on the arts and society was any better than that of the secularists. In this gloomy vein, the *Rivista del cinematografo* in 1963 approvingly cited an article by Brunello Vandano from the mass circulation magazine *Epoca*, claiming that the faithful lost the culture war because their leadership never understood the propaganda value of art, a variant of the old argument that the Catholics had no art. Vandano argued that only Andreotti appreciated culture, but his efforts at the end of the 1940s were stillborn. *Epoca*'s analysis, the *rivista* argued, "was spot on." In fact, the Catholic elite, "inevitably composed by the middle class," deferred to the lay press and expressed a certain cavalier

2. Guido Crainz, *Storia del miracolo italiano: Cultura, identità, trasformazioni fra anni cinquanta e sessanta* (Rome: Donzelli editore, 1998), 83.

3. Crainz, *Il Paese mancato: Dal miracolo economico agli anni ottanta* (Rome: Donzelli editore, 2005), 13–18.

4. Pietro Scoppola, *La Nuova cristianità perduta* (Rome: Edizioni studium, 1986), 141–47.

5. Domingo Rapallo, "Spettacoli, censura, senso morale," *Noi uomini*, April 21, 1963.

or aloof attitude toward *spettacolo*, even perhaps "a secret admiration" for it.[6] The Italian Episcopal Conference (CEI) also understood the secular challenge and expressed it at its June 1966 assembly at the Domus Mariae outside Rome. There, Cardinal Giovanni Urbani, who had recently succeeded Giuseppe Siri as president, declared that the roots of the crisis were not spiritual but rather came from the "impact of material comforts. There's no time for God." Another conference in 1968 called for a "new evangelization." To the Secretariat of Nonbelievers in 1971, Pope Paul VI, too, recognized "secularization" as "a danger to avoid," although his 1975 encyclical, *Evangelii nuntiandi*, modified this to distinguish between neutral secularization and the edgier secularism with its assault on the church.[7]

The Christian Democrats had long existed in a bind over secularization in that the nation's prosperity, for which they claimed credit, had created a great deal of the problem. But the DC was not alone here. The Catholic Church itself also played an unwitting hand in the secularization process that diminished its own role in society and culture. Repercussions from the Second Vatican Council (or Vatican II) and the new face it gave to the church contributed to a change in thinking. The historian Tony Judt wrote that Vatican II achieved or at least facilitated and authorized "the final divorce between politics and religion in continental Europe."[8] His judgment may have been premature in the Italian case, although he had a point in that some Council documents undercut the premise that Catholic politics were the only way. In October 1965, for example, *Nostra aetate*, on non-Christians, and December's *Dignitatis humanae*, on religious freedom, presented what some considered a new relativism and rendered moot Catholic claims on the inferiority of other cults, while advising that the state, like Italy's, should not disadvantage or persecute them. On December 7, 1965, the Council's final day, the *Pastoral Constitution on the Church in Today's World*, known as *Gaudium et spes*, modified the church's traditional suspicion of democracy and allowed for competing political visions. "Christians should recognize," it an-

6. A. P., "Si raccolgono i frutti d'una politica," *Rivista del cinematografo*, June 1963.

7. Francesco Sportelli, *La Conferenza episcopale italiana* (1952–1972) (Galatina: Congedo Editore, 1994), 234–35, 262; Danielle Menozzi, *La Chiesa cattolica e la secolarizzazione* (Turin: Einaudi, 1993), 4. On Siri, see Xavier Rynne, *Vatican Council II* (New York: Farrar, Straus and Giroux, 1968), 208; and Benny Lai, *Il papa non eletto: Giuseppe Siri, cardinal di Santa Romana Chiesa* (Rome: Laterza, 1993), which states on p. 223 that Siri received the official announcement that Paul accepted his resignation as CEI chief, although he had never submitted it. Urbani became a cardinal in 1958.

8. Tony Judt, *Postwar: A History of Europe since 1945* (New York: Penguin, 1945), 375.

nounced, "that various legitimate though conflicting views can be held regarding the regulation of temporal affairs." The church was "bound to no particular form of human culture nor to any political economic or social system." In March 1967, Paul followed up with his encyclical, *Populorum progressio*, which implied an international redistribution of wealth and appeared to many as dangerously leftist. The pontiff's biographer, Peter Hebblethwaite, claimed that the document enabled him to "look the Latin Americans and the Africans in the eye, and think of going there [and that he] was on their side." The *Wall Street Journal* dismissed it as "warmed-over Marxism." Four years later, the pope declared in his 1971 encyclical *Octogesima adveniens* that "the same Christian faith can lead to different commitments."[9] In his new "design," it appeared that Montini even retreated from his premise, and that the Italian core was no longer Catholic. The CEI followed in 1973–75 with a plan to spread the gospel in Italy. "It does not seem excessive to say that Italy is mission territory [*un paese da evangelizzare*]."[10]

In December of 1965, Paul issued a *moto proprio* that reached the heart of Catholic traditionalism when he turned the Supreme Congregation of the Holy Office into the Congregation for the Doctrine of the Faith, a blow to its head, the arch-conservative Alfredo Ottaviani. The old cardinal stayed on for a while, even conceding that the old Holy Office possessed a "dictatorial" nature and announcing that the Index of Prohibited Books would be left to die. Defeated and dismayed, however, Ottaviani's heart was not in the new order, and on January 8, 1968, he resigned just short of the fifteenth anniversary of his appointment by Pius XII. The Yugoslav cardinal Franjo Seper replaced him.[11] More shake-up came with Paul's Apostolic Constitution *Regimini ecclesiae universae* of August 17, 1967,

9. *Populorum progressio* can be located on the Vatican website: http://w2.vatican.va/content/paul-vi/en/encyclicals/documents/hf_p-vi_enc_26031967_populorum.html (accessed December 31, 2019). See also Peter Hebblethwaite, *Paul VI: The First Modern Pope* (New York and Mahwah, N.J.: Paulist Press, 1993), 480–81; and Mari Rapela Heidt, "Development, Nations, and 'The Signs of the Times': The Historical Context of *Populorum Progressio*," *Journal of Moral Theology* 6, no. 1 (2017): 1–20. *Octogesima Adveniens* can be found at http://w2.vatican.va/content/paul-vi/en/apost_letters/documents/hf_p-vi_apl_19710514_octogesima-adveniens.html (accessed December 31, 2019). See also Francis X. Murphy, "Vatican Politics: Structure and Function," *World Politics* 26, no. 4 (July 1974): 549; Paul Furlong, "The Italian Christian Democrats: From Catholic Movement to Conservative Party," Hull Papers in Politics no. 25 (Hull: University of Hull, February 1982), 12–13.

10. Guido Formigoni, *Alla prova della democrazia: Chiesa, cattolici e modernità nell'Italia del '900* (Trent: Il Margine, 2008), 34; Vittorio De Marco, *Le Barricate invisibili: La Chiesa in Italia tra politica e società (1945–1978)* (Lecce: Congedo, 1994), 289–310.

11. John W. O'Malley, *What Happened at Vatican II?* (Cambridge, Mass.: Harvard University Press, 2008), 285–89; "Cardinal Concedes Holy Office Acted Dictatorially," *New York Times*, April 17, 1966; Maurizio Cesari, *La censura in Italia oggi (1944–1980)* (Naples: Liguori editore, 1982), 168.

and the *Regolamento generale della curia romana* of the following October 22, which launched a top-to-bottom reorganization of the Vatican's bureaucracy, abolishing the papal aristocracy and limiting officeholders in the household to five-year terms.[12]

Beyond the church, the optimism of the Second Vatican Council stood in strange contrast to a realization that the Catholic experiment was drawing to an unsatisfying close. The DC was not immune to this malaise. Agostino Giovagnoli noted that by 1964 and 1965, talk of defeat could be heard in the party's inner circles.[13] Already, the period of two of Aldo Moro's governments in the mid-1960s prompted the Catholic historian Pietro Scoppola to bemoan a certain deterioration or "emptiness" of ideas.[14] Elsewhere, Giovagnoli concluded that the DC, itself, had become less of a Christian party.[15] To address the sense of "detachment and isolation" and the continual dearth of the faithful in culture, in April 1967 Mariano Rumor, who succeeded Aldo Moro as DC party secretary, hosted a conference at Lucca on "Catholic Italians during Christianity's new era," an expression of post–Vatican II soul-searching. For three days in the old walled Tuscan city, he mixed Catholic intellectuals and party leaders looking for an identity. In his keynote address, Gabriele De Rosa set the tone by blaming some of Italy's "despiritualization" on its economic success. Moro urged that the party should conduct a self-examination, one that, while crediting the DC for success in economic development and political freedom, would surely reveal that it came up short in other areas. But the congress took place under a cloud. Many of the leading Catholic journals boycotted it, and Scoppola wondered whether it was an "oasis" or only a "mirage," exerting no effect on the DC. In any case, the party, he claimed, failed to take seriously any lessons from Lucca, and the meeting represented a key break between it and Catholic intellectuals.[16]

12. Murphy, "Vatican Politics: Structure and Function," 544–46.

13. Agostino Giovagnoli, *Chiesa e democrazia: La lezione di Pietro Scoppola* (Bologna: Il Mulino, 2011), 69.

14. Scoppola, *La repubblica dei partiti* (Bologna: Il Mulino, 1991), 352, cited in Crainz, *Il Paese mancato*, 65.

15. Giovagnoli, "La Stagione democristiana," in *La Nazione cattolica: Chiesa e società in Italia, 1958-oggi*, ed. Marco Impagliazzo (Milan: Guerini, 2004), 53 and 66.

16. *I Cattolici italiani nei tempi nuovi della Cristianità: Atti del convegno di studio della democrazia cristiana, Lucca 28–30 Aprile 1967*, ed. Giuseppe Rossini (Rome: Cinque lune, 1967); Mario Cuminetti, *Il dissenso cattolico in Italia (1965–1980)* (Milan: Biblioteca Universale Rizzoli, 1983), 130; Scoppola, *La Nuova cristianità perduta*, 131; Damiano Garofalo, *Political Audiences: A Reception History of Early Italian Television*, trans. Michael Sarnoff-Wood (Milan: Mimesis International, 2016), 37–38; Giovagnoli, *Il Partito Italiano: La Democrazia cristiana dal 1942 al 1994* (Rome and Bari: Laterza, 1996), 124–27; Giovagnoli, *Chiesa e democrazia*,

Vatican II also shook Catholic Action, which began to crack. Gedda's successor, Agostino Maltarello, certainly encountered despair among the rank and file in a survey he commissioned in early 1964. Responses from militants across Italy were almost uniformly pessimistic. One reply from Volterra described the AC's presence in the community as "poor and hardly effective." A representative from Città di Castello in Umbria claimed, "We are isolated in the diocese, we have no voice." In Reggio Calabria, the morality program was "spotty [*episodico*] and sometimes not even expressed in a suitable and timely manner."[17] Many offered suggestions on how to reactivate the organization. From the Pescara area came a call to empower the Ente dello spettacolo and Gino Gavuzzo's Morality Office. Amid all the chaos, furthermore, it cannot have been entirely inconsequential that in Vatican II's wake, Catholic Action numbers collapsed along with much of the spirit behind the battle for *buon costume*. From over 3,500,000 members in 1962, its roster shrank to 1,600,000 in 1970. It would continue to slip and eventually stabilized at around 300,000. Along with the AC, other Catholic organizations transformed themselves at this time: for instance, the Catholic labor union, the CISL, ceased political activity, and the Christian Associations of Italian Workers (ACLI) left the fold altogether, seeking alliances or even affiliation with Marxists.[18]

Pope Paul delivered another shock to Catholic politics on January 30. 1965, when he addressed Luigi Gedda and fourteen hundred Civic Committee leaders, the first such meeting since one hosted by Pius in 1957. Searching to redefine the CC, Paul referred to it as "an intermediary" with the task of educating and guiding. Certainly recalling his Operation Sturzo experience twelve years before, he insisted that it and, by implication Catholic Action, must never aspire to active participation in politics, much less evolve into a political party.[19] In 1964, moreover, Paul substituted Maltarello with Moro's friend Vittorio Bachelet to head the AC. Two individuals more in keeping with the Vatican II spirit, Bachelet

---

96–97. Rumor's memoirs are quoted in Andrea Riccardi, "Il Cattolicesimo della repubblica," in *Storia d'Italia*, vol. 6, *L'Italia contemporanea*, ed. G. Sabbatucci and V. Vidotto (Rome and Bari: Laterza, 1999), 267.

17. The responses to Maltarello's circular can be found in IPVI, Pg VIII, b. 5.

18. Crainz, *Il Paese mancato*, 176; Massimo Faggioli, "The New Elites of Italian Catholicism: 1968 and the New Catholic Movements," *Catholic Historical Review* 98, no. 1 (Winter 2012): 25–26; Daniela Saresella, "Ecclesial Dissent in Italy in the Sixties," *Catholic Historical Review* 102, no. 1 (Winter 2016): 50–54; Cuminetti, *Il dissenso cattolico in Italia*, 173–78. On the ACLI, see Domenico Rosati, *L'Incudine e la croce: Mezzo secolo di AC* (Turin: Edizioni Sonda, 1994), 202–15; Sportelli, *La Conferenza episcopale italiana*, 271–76 and 282–85.

19. F. D. S., "Delimitati dal papa i compiti dei comitati civici," *Corriere della sera*, January 31, 1965.

and Catholic Action's ecclesiastic assistant Franco Costa, worked to "curb support for the DC and end any form of interference in Italian political life."[20]

Inspired by the Council, Bachelet and Costa proclaimed a new evangelical road, a "religious choice" (*scelta religiosa*), better geared toward an "intimate" spirituality and dedicated to good works and charity. Bachelet later described the move as a "cultural shift" leading to a "centrality in the liturgy, in prayer, in culture the seed to change the world. . . . This is the *scelta religiosa*." This was not only a radical shift for Catholic Action. The historian Sandro Magister called it a refoundation, and, as Danilo Veneruso put it, the *scelta religiosa* was "antithetical" to Christian Democracy.[21] After he succeeded Bachelet in 1973, Mario Agnes continued his reforms and spirit.[22]

Such changes did not always sit well, and many militants grew worried. To calm them, in his January 1965 address the pontiff urged AC members not to let the Council's breathtaking developments shake them into despair. "We understand you," he told them, noting in particular the need to hold onto "certain and indisputable" truths. Bachelet and Costa also detected worry in the ranks. To the *Corriere della sera*, Bachelet, in fact, confessed some second thoughts. The December 12, 1964, meeting of AC's Central Junta discussed "a society violently shaken by a current and rapid transformation," and it wondered how to maneuver. A bleak agenda written to prompt the conversation raised the issue of militants who now dealt with a "new democratic reality" of atheist and lay ideologies that viewed man in terms "naturalist or hedonist, classical or capitalist but always economic." This modern attitude stood in contrast to the Christian life. Proper comportment, accordingly, came under attack, "sometimes clandestinely, sometimes with arrogance" in the "novels, movies and television" of modern urban living, a

20. Mario Casella, *L'Azione cattolica nell'Italia contemporanea (1919–1969)* (Rome: AVE, 1992), 555–56.

21. Antonio Acerbi, "La Chiesa italiana dalla conclusione del Concilio alla fine della Democrazia Cristiana," in *La Chiesa e l'Italia: Per una storia dei loro rapporti negli ultimi due secoli*, ed. Antonio Acerbi (Milan: Vita e Pensiero, 2003), 449–520, in particular, 456–67; see also Giorgio Vecchio, ed., *L'Azione cattolica del Vaticano II: Laicità e scelta religiosa nell'Italia negli anni sessanta e settanta* (Rome: AVE, 2014); Casella, *L'Azione cattolica nell'Italia contemporanea*, 555–87 (Bachelet's statement can be found on 559); De Marco, *Storia dell'Azione Cattolica negli anni settanta* (Rome: Città Nuova, 2007), 15–39; Danilo Veneruso, "L'Azione Cattolica," in Impagliazzo, *La Nazione cattolica*, 237–49; and Sandro Magister, "Catholic Action and Internal Conflicts in the Catholic Church," in *Italian Politics: A Review*, ed. Raffaella Nanetti, Piergiorgio Corbetta, and Robert Leonardi (London: Pinter, 1987), 2:25–40.

22. Vecchio, "L'ACI nella nuova stagione del laicato: Indicazione per una storia del ventennio 1965–1985," in *La Generazione del Concilio: Tra cronaca e storia*, ed. Rosy Bindi and Agostino Moscatelli (Rome: AVE, 1986), 79–115; see also Saresella, "Ecclesial Dissent in Italy in the Sixties."

culture of "lucre and pleasure." This dialectic, furthermore, developed in a church where "religious practice had already been reduced to a mechanical and exterior devotion (particularly among peasants)" and Catholic ceremonies had turned into mere social gatherings for white collar and bourgeois edification. Added to the mix was the evolution of the family "from a patriarchal structure to one more simply conjugal." The report took heart that in this age of transition, wherein some new developments might be misunderstood, positive signs still included a developing liturgical movement and the fact that Catholicism had made a healthy turn to ideas of justice and charity.[23]

Catholic Action's next step was to rewrite its statutes. After three years of raucous debate, its new "magna charta" went into effect on November 1, 1969. Rejecting the tone of the earlier 1946 statutes, the new measure shied away from attributing any sense of leadership or exclusivity to the AC, replacing terms like "dependence" on the hierarchy with "collaboration."[24] The Morality Office fell victim to the reorganization. As a kind of farewell to the troops, probably written in 1969, Gavuzzo confessed that large strata of Italy's population simply no longer possessed "the sense of sin, of evil, or moral well-being." "Today's grave evil," he wrote, was not so much immorality as it was amorality. An emptiness was taking over wherein the person did not fight a battle against norms and laws but simply lived without them. "The palate," Gavuzzo continued, "doesn't taste flavor."[25] Paul's reaction, however, was at best oddly lukewarm. Indeed, as the theologian Massimo Faggioli wrote, the organization's attempts at reform "were not rewarded by the Holy See," which instead sought ties to the new laity "that were more reliable than the 'old guard.'" The new statutes also ended the distinctions between men's and women's movements, something that proved especially devastating for the latter. Cecilia Dau Novelli has shown how merging the two ended the separate and vital world of the women's branches. "A history," she wrote, "concluded."[26] The militant vanguard of Catholic politics, the Civic Committees, too, lived in perpetual crisis

23. IPVI, Pg IX, b. 1, "Considerazioni circa i "punti nodali" della società in trasformazione," December 12, 1964; F. D. S., "Paolo VI esorta a non cedere allo scetticismo," *Corriere della sera*, January 4, 1965.

24. Casella, *L'Azione cattolica nell'Italia contemporanea*, 584–87; Giacomo Martina, *La Chiesa in Italia negli ultimi trent'anni* (Rome: Studium, 1977), 149–51.

25. IPVI, Pg XII, b. 22, "Segretariato per la Moralità," n.d., c. 1969.

26. Cecilia Dau Novelli, "Azione Cattolica e questione femminile," in *Storia dell'Azione Cattolica: La presenza nella Chiesa e nella società italiana*, ed. Ernesto Preziosi (Soveria Mannelli: Rubbettino, 2008), 286–88.

since Pope John's shake-up brought Luigi Gedda's demotion. In 1968, one disgruntled priest from Pisa complained to the CC's ecclesiastical liaison that the organization had become moribund. He blamed the tight reins with which the Holy See and the CEI held the bishops—reins that muzzled the movement and ended the wild days of "noisy propaganda." But so much remained to be done—tasks, wrote the priest, that the Catholics were "too stupid or blind" to grasp. "We see that not even [the issue of] divorce sparks a crusade; so [alluding to the old parallel between the 1948 elections and the battle of Lepanto] the Turks won't come but divorce will." His pessimism found an echo three years later from Grosseto, where another cleric charged that the Civic Committees languished with only "the usual elements" in each parish who did all the work. He called for new recruits, new training, new leaders, and a new call to arms.[27]

Censorship and the Arts

The arts remained a cultural battlefield. *Buon costume* still mattered, but embarrassments continued to surface, leading many of the faithful to dismiss the April 1962 censorship measure as toothless, wrong-headed, or misdirected. Some pointed to Giovanni "Tinto" Brass's first film, *In capo al mondo* (*On Top of the World*), which premiered at the 1963 Venice festival to positive reviews, although the censorship panel had refused it the *nulla osta* for Italian distribution. Then, after the appeals panel upheld the suspension, according to *Il Ponte*, Brass simply changed the title to *Chi lavora è perduto* (*He Who Works Is Lost*), resubmitted it to the ministry, and received the *nulla osta*.[28] For militants who lost hope in the censorship process, the courts theoretically still provided some option in prosecuting offensive and obscene entertainment. Yet here, too, Catholics might think again before relying on judges like the one in Venice who, in 1962, saw nothing wrong in Pier Paolo Pasolini's use of vulgarities like "*fiore di merda*" and "*pisciata*" in his film *Mamma Roma*.[29]

27. FVC, b. 20, "atti politici," "Pisa," Don Guido Corallini/Migliaccio, April 25, 1968. In a May 23 follow-up letter in the same folder, Corallini lamented that Catholic Action had lost the old "Gedda rhythm"; FVC, b. 20, "atti politici," "Grosseto," Don Giorgio Gaggioli/Migliaccio, November 11, 1971.

28. Cesari, *La censura in Italia oggi*, 199; "Giova ripettere," *Rivista del cinematografo*, November 1963.

29. Rodolfo Venditti, *La Tutela penale del pudore e della pubblica decenza* (Milan: Dott. A. Giuffrè Editore, 1963), 111, f. 103. Catholic Action found at least one bright spot—applauding the actress Virna Lisi for refusing a part in a Roger Vadim film that would have required her to remove her clothes; "Punte Secche," *Noi uomini*, July 2, 1963.

In July of 1961, the Socialists detected DC duplicity when, alarmed by the rising number of racy films in Italy, *Avanti!* charged that after Andreotti killed off the noble neo-realist experiment, his party had, indeed, fostered dirty filmmaking. In contrast to Umberto Tupini's fraudulent aspirations to be the "savior of 'morality' and the 'fatherland,'" the Socialist paper claimed that, tired of neo-realist portrayals of the poor, Andreotti called for "less rags and more legs" (*meno stracci, più gambe*), a phrase also carried in a paper from the Veneto, the *Gazzettino*. After Gavuzzo at the Morality Office urged him to "set the record straight," Andreotti responded to both papers. His note to the *Gazzettino* was the more explicit of the two and adamantly denied any responsibility for the line. Both letters emphasized, moreover, his respect for and, indeed, admiration of neo-realism.[30]

Marxist and lay critics, however, were not alone. Wondering how such cynical duplicity could exist in a Catholic nation, many of the faithful blamed their Christian Democratic leaders. In 1963, the AC's Morality Office in Vicenza issued a typical complaint about two-faced government "interpreters and defenders of Christian values" whose apparent sympathy for "advocates of a misplaced freedom" triumphed over "legitimate and grave worries of parents and teachers." The note expressed an ever-increasing annoyance among militants who called for Christian Democrats to work harder for the Catholic commonweal—a goal that seemed to be slipping away.[31] For the November 1963 edition of the *Rivista del cinematografo*, Antonio Petrucci announced the failure of government censorship. Incoherent and probably on the way out, it had become a ridiculous political football, and the whole program was falling to pieces.[32] Even *Discussione* contributed a February 1963 piece, admitting that censors looked like "deaf and bigoted henchmen for an antiquated law."[33] Two years later, citing one DC deputy who challenged the government for "protecting immoral films," the respected Catholic *Eco* of Bergamo showed more generosity. Obviously, it argued, neither Prime Minister Aldo Moro nor Interior Minister Paolo Emilio Taviani could be blamed, not even the Socialists—namely, Pietro Nenni or the Socialist

30. IS Archivio Andreotti Cinema, Serie 2, b. 1077, s. 1, Gavuzzo/Andreotti, July 11, 1960; Andreotti/Giuseppe Longo (*Il Gazzettino*), July 15, 1960; Andreotti/Giovanni Pieraccini (*Avanti!*), July 15, 1960. This file also contains a copy of the *Avanti!* article "Le Menzogne di Tupini" of July 6, 1960.

31. IS Sec. pol. Moro, Sc. 156, f. 30, Report from Secretary Pio Rumor of Vicenza Morality Office, April 5, 1963 (cosigned by the ecclesiastic consultant Giovanni Sartori).

32. Antonio Petrucci, "Giova ripetere?" *Rivista del cinematografo*, November 1963.

33. "Arte e censura nello spettacolo," *Discussione*, February 1963.

Minister of Tourism and the Spettacolo Achille Corona, who took the reins in December 1963, thanks to the *apertura*. Rather, continued the *Eco*, the problem of immoral films derived from simple sloth, an inertia that reaped depravity. "Evil always benefits from the good walking in its sleep," it concluded, and the government goes for months and even years "without lifting a finger."[34] For *Discussione*, Fabrizio Schneider had already expressed his frustration in January of 1964 regarding the film *Ieri, oggi, domani*, which starred Mastroianni and Loren. Not only did the state permit eighteen-year-olds to enter, he complained, it even admitted fourteen-year-olds. And, he continued, it was not even an "art film." "It is absolutely inadmissible," he concluded, "that we make laws and then allow them to be trampled on as if they didn't exist." In February 1965, the same month as the *Eco* article, Schneider recalled this sentiment for *Discussione*, branding the new censorship machinery a "national shame." The state's eight panels, chaired by magistrates, reneged on their task of "protecting *buon costume*" and proved useless against "the wave of eroticism, vulgarity and obscenity that [had] invaded the Italian market." Particular humiliation must have come from the Communist review *Noi donne*, which admitted that it could not blame the Catholics' operation for "excessive moralism."[35] One month later, the *Rivista del cinematografo* ran "The Useless Censor," a poignant and posthumous testament of personal exasperation. The piece extracted parts of a diary kept by the motion picture director Giovanni Paolucci, whom Minister Folchi appointed to the censorship commission at the end of May 1962. Paolucci did not last long and soon resigned. He died in March 1964. His journal entries expressed a bitterness over vetting endless newsreels and banal discussions where colleagues quit over films under consideration, specifically pointing to a fight over Luis Buñuel's *Viridiana*. Paolucci believed that the censorship experiment had reached its end and now accomplished nothing. Replace it, he concluded, with a simple "adults only" rubric that would keep the children out. "Thus ends," he concluded, "my time as a useless censor."[36]

In the Chamber of Deputies, more and more ire erupted among DC deputies, furious that the government did not merit their trust and that the party leadership had surrendered on the Catholic cultural mission.

34. "Il Governo protegge il cinema immorale?," *Eco di Bergamo*, February 14, 1965; found in ACS, PCM 1962–64, b. 108, f. 7880.1, 1.1.14; Giulia Guazzaloca, *Una e divisibile: La RAI e i partiti negli anni del monopolio pubblico* (1954–1975) (Florence: Le Monnier, 2011), 35.

35. Fabrizio Schneider, "Vergognosa abdicazione," *Discussione*, January 19, 1964; and Schneider, "Una vergogna nazionale," *Discussione*, February 21, 1965.

36. Giovanni Paolucci, "Il censore inutile," *Rivista del cinematografo*, March 1965.

How else, they reasoned, could censors commit such blunders? In October 1963, for instance, Tommaso Sorgi asked his fellow deputies how censorship commissions could pass seventy-six unquestionably dirty films, virtually all of which were Italian. Even worse, he continued, the censorship panels failed to see that words in the titles like "sexy," "nude," and "prohibited" should have been immediate tip-offs.[37] Such feelings found an echo the following March, when Catholic Action's *Noi uomini* claimed that two of the censorship panels allowed the circulation of over one hundred "sexy" films.[38] Indeed, the historian Gian Piero Brunetta later described "an explosion of films with titles that included the word 'sexy.'" Along with works like *Sexy ad alta tensione*, he wrote, production in the early to mid-1960s included "fake documentaries that explored the female body as if it were the landscape of an undiscovered continent."[39] The head of Florentine Catholic Action submitted a scathing complaint to Maltarello's aformentioned 1964 survey. "Find me," he wrote, "a Catholic minister or deputy who dares to effectively protest [state] financing of 'putrid' films.... We no longer tolerate their hypocritical presence among us, as our representatives, and we want that they comport themselves as Christians."[40]

The rebellious DC deputies formed what became known as the "53," which included Sorgi and such disparate figures as Flaminio Piccoli, who became party secretary in 1969, and Agostino Greggi, who left the Christian Democrats in the 1970s to join the neo-Fascist MSI.[41] They pointed to films like Vittorio DeSica's *Yesterday, Today, and Tomorrow* (*Ieri, oggi, domani*) of 1963 to illustrate the fiasco of government (and DC) measures. When it received the *nulla osta* without even an "adults only" rating, despite some *spogliarello* by Sofia Loren, the "53" charged in a March 1964 letter to the DC's president of the chamber, Brunetto Bucciarelli Ducci, that Italy was now in the business of exporting sin. In Parliament, to Sorgi's question of how this could have happened, the minister, Corona, shirked and passed the blame onto the censorship panel.[42]

37. "Sexy nudo proibito," *L'Europeo*, October 27, 1963.

38. "Cinema e censura," *Noi uomini*, March 10, 1964.

39. Gian Piero Brunetta, *The History of Italian Cinema: A Guide to Italian Film from Its Origins to the Twenty-First Century*, trans. Jeremy Parzen (Princeton, N.J.: Princeton University Press, 2003), 211.

40. IPVI, Pg VIII, b. 5, President of Catholic Action for the Diocese of Florence/Maltarello, April 21, 1964.

41. IPVI, Pg XII, b. 19, Gino Gavuzzo, "Relazione Morale 461, April 30, 1964. On Greggi, see Andrea Mammone, "The Transnational Reaction to 1968: Neo-Fascist Fronts and Political Cultures in France and Italy," *Contemporary European History* 17, no. 2(May 2008): 223.

42. "Cinema italiano peccato sociale," *Noi uomini*, April 7, 1964; and "I Cattolici si muovono in

Beyond the "53," outrage over the flawed program spread to many outside the government. By September 325,000 protest letters had crossed Bucciarelli Ducci's desk, and the number climbed to 450,000 a month later.[43] Some were "fill-in" petitions torn from presumably Catholic Action publications, like one from a Capuchin community in the Marche. It not only denounced "immoral cinema," but charged that the DC, "elected by Catholics," must accept its duty and defend "*buon costume* and Christian morality." Bucciarelli Ducci was not the only recipient of these letters. Party secretary Rumor received a long missive from Greggi, complaining that the "over-the-top vulgarity" in film made him "ashamed to be Italian." If Christian Democrats ran on the promise to clean up motion pictures, he continued, they should live up to those promises and not betray theit electoral base. Moro also received letters, including one from the prior of the Certosa San Bruno in Calabria, lamenting that only fifty-three Christian Democrats closed ranks on the issue. Where were the rest?—the other DC "lost sheep"—asked the cleric, who finished his letter with the war cry "Christians unite!"[44]

The government made one last stab at effective film control in the law of November 4, 1965, number 1213, dubbed the "Corona Law" after the Socialist minister.[45] It changed little, and Catholic malaise reflected this, as in a December 1966 *Rivista del cinematografo* stock-taking article, "The Cinema Law One Year Later." Everything, it stated, floundered in chaos. The law established a committee of experts that changed every year, but, in violation of the act, the one for 1966 had yet to convene. The Prize Committee for full-length films had also failed to meet, not even for 1965, nor had a panel dealing with credit for filmmakers, "and no one knows why." A panel on youth films had only completed its work up through the summer of 1964.[46]

difesa della moralità," *Noi uomini*, August 11, 1964; *Atti Parlamentari*, Camera dei Deputati, IV Legislatura, *Discussioni*, March 10, 1964, 1,468–69.

43. "325,000 Proteste contro il cinema immorale," *Noi uomini*, September 15, 1964; "La battaglia per il cinema continua," *Noi uomini*, October 27, 1964. The aforementioned August 1964 article, "I Cattolici muovono in difesa della moralità," stated that Bucciarelli Ducci had received 20,000 letters and telegrams.

44. Greggi/Rumor, November 16, 1964. The immediate object of Greggi's complaint was a four-episode film, 1964's *L'idea fissa* (released in the United States as *Love and Marriage*). Greggi claimed that the movie offended him so much that he had to walk out after the second chapter. Both letters and many more can be found in ACS, PCM 1962–64, b. 108, f. 7880, s. 1.3, 1.1.14.

45. The legislation can be read at http://www.adquattrone.org/CINEMA/LEGGE%204%20NOVEMBRE%201965.htm (accessed December 31, 2019).

46. Antonio De Gregorio, "La Legge sul cinema un anno dopo," *Rivista del cinematografo*, December 1966.

Pasolini

Beyond censorship and sequestration, many Catholics still hoped that their church could play a more positive role in the arts. At the start of 1964 the *Rivista del cinematografo* still asked for the best strategy to make cinema into "an instrument of Christianization, a vehicle of authentic religiosity."[47] The Vatican Council helped by reemphasizing the apostolate of cinema "and other means of communication" in *Inter mirifica*, its decree of December 4, 1963. " Pope Paul's 1964 Apostolic Letter *In fructibus multis*, furthermore, breathed new life into Pius XII's Council for Social Communication and led to the 1971 encyclical *Communio et progressio*, which Dario Edoardo Viganò characterized as "the 'Magna Charta' of the Church in the field of communication."[48] Father Giovanni Rossi's Pro Civitate Christiana organization in Assisi seemed to be at the right place at the right time and maintained a high profile. Despite the depressing news on censorship and the appearance of more and more vulgarity and immorality on screen, he nonetheless launched a new quest for a "Catholic" film director.[49]

By the early 1960s the Roberto Rossellini debacle had receded into memory, and now Rossi was willing to relaunch a search with new enthusiasm. This time he targeted Pier Paolo Pasolini. Even more than Rossellini, however, Pasolini and the Catholics developed an awkward and difficult relationship. The artist often found himself in trouble with the police, sometimes for violent crimes, and he never hid his atheism. At least Rossellini pretended to be one of the faithful and courted the Catholics at least as much as they courted him. Pasolini even refused to do that. Trouble, it seems, plagued his life. After the end of World War II, he had joined the Communists as a young teacher in Italy's northeast Friuli region, but in 1949 a homosexual scandal linked him to some of his students and cost him his job and his party membership. *L'Unità* condemned Pasolini in an editorial that compared him to Andre Gide, Jean-

47. Francesco Alberoni, "Per una politica culurale dei cattolici," *Rivista del cinematografo*, January 1964.

48. Luigi Storace, "L'Episcopato italiano destina un premio al cinema," *Noi uomini*, March 30, 1965. On *Inter Mirifica*, see Sinaldo Sinaldi, "Cinema e dialogo ad Assisi," *Noi uomini*, October 25, 1966; and "Uno Spirito nuovo," *Rivista del cinematografo*, March 1966; Dario Edoardo Viganò, "The Roman Catholic Church, Cinema and the 'Culture of Dialogue': Italian Catholics and the Movies after the Second World War," in *Moralizing Cinema: Film Catholicism and Power*, ed. Daniela Treveri Gennari and Daniel Biltereyst (New York: Routledge, 2014), 38.

49. Giancarlo Zizola, *Don Giovanni Rossi: L'Utopia cristiana nell'Italia del '900* (Assisi: Citadella Editrice, 1997), 352–403.

Paul Sartre, "and other poets and decadent men of letters who, in reality, represent the very worst aspects of bourgeois degeneration."[50]

Meanwhile Pasolini underwent a crisis of faith that accompanied his wartime partisan experience and continued after 1945.[51] He expressed his complicated feelings in a collection of poems, *The Nightingale of the Catholic Church* (*L'Usignolo della Chiesa Cattolica*), written between 1943 and 1949 but published only in 1958. The work was in part a collection of meditations on the Passion of Christ, Pasolini's "serene poet, wounded brother."[52] The artist relocated to Rome, where he turned his attention to the cinema and collaborated on a number of films, including doing some scriptwriting for Fellini's *Notti di Cabiria*. He acknowledged Rossellini's work and praised *Francesco, Giullare di Dio* as "among the most beautiful in Italian cinema." Pasolini released his own first film, *Accattone*, in November 1961, shortly before his arrest for armed robbery.

Pius XII's triumphalist Rome haunted the troubled Pasolini, who admitted his sins but refused to accept the church's forgiveness. Such prejudices continued after the pontiff's death because, as the film scholar Tomaso Subini noted, Pasolini at first failed to appreciate the new world of John. But now, as he became a better-known writer and filmmaker, Pasolini grew closer to the church and would even cooperate with it. He did so thanks in large measure to the efforts of don Rossi at Pro Civitate Christiana in Assisi. Rossi's focus on film led to his inauguration in the summer of 1959 of a series of "Cineaste encounters," the first of which attracted the attendance of Umberto Tupini and Nicola De Pirro. In 1965, the CEI began to use the occasion of the assemblies to award Assisi prizes intended "to encourage the production of films that present Christian values in everyday language."[53]

In 1961, Rossi decided to court Pasolini when he asked a friend to name the film director who stood "the farthest from Christian faith and morals." His immediate response, "Pasolini," prompted Rossi to

50. Sam Rohdie, *The Passion of Pier Paolo Pasolini* (London: British Film Institute; Bloomington: Indiana University Press, 1995), 26–29. Rohdie acknowledged that Pasolini's dismissal from the party resulted from the scandal, although he believed that the writer's support of dialect literature drew more ideological fire from his erstwhile comrades.

51. Tomaso Subini, "Il dialogo tra Pier Paolo Pasolini e la Pro Civitate Christiana sulla sceneggiatura de 'Il Vangelo secondo Matteo,'" in Eugeni and Viganò, *Attraverso lo schermo*, 3:223–37. See Pasolini's comment on Rossellini in Tag Gallagher, *The Adventures of Roberto Rossellini* (New York: Da Capo, 1998), 355.

52. Pier Paolo Pasolini, *L'Usignolo della Chiesa Cattolica* (Turin: Einaudi, 1976), 8. Longanesi first published it in 1958.

53. "Nuove speranze per un cinema migliore," *Rivista del Cinematografo*, July 1959; "L'episcopato italiana destina un premio al cinema," *Noi uomini*, March 30, 1965.

dispatch his associate to Rome to make contact. The meeting did not go well, and the envoy later reported that Pasolini "look[ed] at me as though I were stupid." By October of the following year, nonetheless, the director agreed to attend a film conference in Assisi. When given the best guestroom in the house and told that Pope John had slept there, Pasolini asked that it be exorcised. But the visit to the city of St. Francis left a real impression on him, and rumors flew that don Rossi had even converted the artist. Perhaps still burned by his experience with Rossellini, a suspicious Gian Luigi Rondi telephoned the priest and warned him to "cut all business with this monster."[54]

Pasolini did not convert, but he *did* soften toward the church and the late Pope John, and in 1964 he expressed a fondness for a man who had, he wrote, brought "something new in the Church, humor, irony.... Pope John laughed at himself as pope."[55] Pasolini never hid the fact that he was not a believer, but he could sound like one; and he shared with the Catholics at least one of their cherished visions, that of the holiness of peasant life, something that never sat well with colleagues in the avant-garde art world. In her study of the artist and the sacred, Stefania Benini states that, for Pasolini, "the new industrial order represented first and foremost the worst enemy of the sacred: the commodification of objects and relationships that had replaced the sacredness of life."[56] In 1961, this awareness led to a trip to India with Elsa Morante and Alberto Moravia, who maintained that Pasolini found and celebrated there a world that was quickly passing.[57]

Two years later, in 1963, Pasolini contributed one episode, *La ricotta*, to a four-part collaborative film, *RoGoPaG*.[58] *La ricotta* tells the story of making a movie, directed by Orson Welles, about Christ's death on the cross. The central figure, however, is "Stracci," who plays one of the two crucified thieves on Golgotha and who, between takes, gorges himself on food while the cast and crew egg him on. Time for the big scene, but Stracci suffers a gastric attack and dies, literally on the cross. While

54. Zizola, *Don Giovanni Rossi*, 320–34.

55. Stefania Benini, *Pasolini: The Sacred Flesh* (Toronto: University of Toronto Press, 2015), 46–47.

56. Benini, *Pasolini: The Sacred Flesh*, 11. Benini writes on page 42 that "Pasolini clearly sees the binary dynamism between the Church and the peasant world, both of which present themselves as repositories of the sacred."

57. Rohdie, *Passion of Pier Paolo Pasolini*, 37. Pasolini wrote a book on his voyage, *L'Odore dell'India*, and produced a 1968 film, *Appunti per un film sull'India*, on the subject. Rohdie records (57–58) Pasolini's comparisons of Mumbai and Calcutta with Naples and other locales, such as Friuli and Matera.

58. The film title represents the names of the four directors: Rossellini, Godard, Pasolini, and Gregoretti.

Pasolini intended this as a Marxist and Christian critique of capitalist excess, he was right when he predicted in the film's foreword that the subject matter would bring trouble. And so, while it received the *nulla osta* and enjoyed some clerical support, such as that from faculty members of the Gregorian University, on March 1, less than two weeks after the film's premiere, a Roman judge, Giovanni Di Gennaro, sequestered it and charged Pasolini with *vilipendio*. In his study of *La ricotta*, Subini advanced the idea that the real problem stemmed from a personal insult; that Pedoti, the movie's nastiest character, was inspired by Pasquale Pedote, a judge who had condemned a friend of Pasolini. Judge Di Gennaro, furthermore, considered himself a cineaste. To examine evidence in the trial, he personally ran a moviola machine, a first in Italian juridical history, and he used the proceedings as a platform to protect Catholics from the "superman of eccentric tastes and feelings ... the Trojan Horse of Pasolini." For his part, the artist later dismissed the judge's histrionics as an example of the "Grand Guignol and the ridiculous ... the oral masterpiece of the clerico-Fascism of the fifties." Pasolini lost his court case, but appealed his four-month jail sentence, which was eventually cancelled.[59]

Against all odds, for Catholics, Pier Paolo Pasolini remained the most intriguing prospect. Rossi and others, like Giorgio La Pira and don Francesco Angelicchio at the CCC, continued to hope that collaboration between the artist and the church might yield fruit. While he was in Assisi, however, Pasolini recalled that he stayed in his room and read St. Matthew's Gospel, a "hard yet tender text, so Jewish and hot-tempered." Yet "there, that day, in those hours," he decided to put the story on celluloid.[60] Those thoughts led to his 1964 film *Il Vangelo secondo matteo* (released in Britain as *The Gospel according to Matthew* and in the United States as *The Gospel according to St. Matthew*). Pasolini always remained adamant that, as he told the Pro Civitate Christiana people, he wanted to make a poetic film, "not a religious work in the current sense of the term, nor a work in some way ideological. To put it simply and frankly,

59. Erminia Passananti, "Pasolini's Deconstruction and Reformulation of Italian Catholic Identity in *La ricotta*," in *Italy on Screen: National Identity and Italian Imaginary*, ed. Lucy Bolton and Christina Siggers Manson (Oxford: Peter Lang, 2010), 77–99. On Pedote, see Tomaso Subini, *Pier Paolo Pasolini: La ricotta* (Turin: Lindau, 2009), 44–45. See also Benini, *Pasolini: The Sacred Flesh*, 52–62; and Barth David Schwartz, *Pasolini Requiem* (New York: Pantheon, 1992), 415–20. Schwartz recounts (391–92) an earlier problem for Pasolini that resembled the Pedote issue. In 1962, a DC ex-deputy, Salvatore Pagliuca, sued the director for defamation regarding *Accattone*. An evil figure in the film was named Pagliuca. The charges were dismissed.

60. Benini, *Pasolini: The Sacred Flesh*, 62; Zizola, *Don Giovanni Rossi*, 320–22.

I don't believe that Christ is the son of God."[61] Disagreements inevitably arose on the set between the director and Pro Civitate Christiana, questions about whether or not to depict Mary breastfeeding Christ or how far ancient Holy Land peasants should resemble modern industrial proletarians.[62]

As before, Gian Luigi Rondi was one Catholic who refused to join the hosannas for Pasolini. In *Concretezza*, he dismissed *Il Vangelo secondo Matteo* and the other entries at the 1964 *Biennale* as mediocrities. One month later, Rondi specifically addressed the film, according it some credit for innovation, although he found it confused. In contrast to the convert Giovanni Papini's inspired biography of Christ, he continued, Pasolini applied an atheist interpretation that portrayed miracles and angels as myths. Rondi didn't even like the film's music by J. S. Bach. Perhaps, he suggested, audiences might better appreciate Pasolini "in the library" rather than on the screen.[63]

With the government's *nulla osta*, *Il Vangelo secondo Matteo* premiered at the 1964 *Biennale*, where youths from the radical right pelted Pasolini with tomatoes and eggs. Police had to quell the disturbances and protect the filmgoers as they entered the theater. Despite the tumult, OCIC bestowed its prize on Pasolini's film, probably bringing director and church closer together than they ever would be again. For his part, Pasolini expressed a change of heart when he dedicated his completed work to Pope John's "dear, happy, familiar memory," while the *Osservatore Romano* praised the picture and Pope Paul held a private screening.[64] On October 5, 1964, furthermore, OCIC arranged with the secretariat in charge of the Vatican Council to show it to 800 of the "conciliar fathers." The ever-skeptical Pasolini regarded this screening as something of a *frondiste* affront, a sure signal to anyone who still harbored Catholic hopes for the artist.[65] Pasolini's 1968 *Teorema* marked the end of his "di-

61. Millicent Marcus, *Filmmaking by the Book: Italian Cinema and Literary Adaption* (Baltimore and London: Johns Hopkins University Press, 1993), 111–12.

62. Subini, "Il dialogo," 231–33. Some questioned whether Pasolini made Herod look like the Egyptian dictator Gamel Nasser. See also Schwartz, *Pasolini Requiem*, chapter 18.

63. Gian Luigi Rondi, "Alla Mostra di Venezia tutto da rifare," *Concretezza*, September 16, 1964. Another film in the running was Jean Delannoy's production of Roger Peyrefitte's *Les amitiés particulières*, "a devious defense of homosexuality and a polemic against the Catholic school in France"; Rondi, "Pasolini e Padellaro," *Concretezza*, October 16, 1964.

64. Subini, "Il dialogo," 227; Schwartz, *Pasolini Requiem*, 451–57; Laura Betti, ed., *Pasolini: Cronaca giudiziaria, persecuzione, morte* (Milan: Garzanti, 1977), 149–53.

65. Dario Edoardo Viganò, "Il cinema: Ricezione, riflessione, rifiuto," in *Cristiani d'Italia*, ed. Alberto Melloni (Rome: Istituto della Encyclopedia Treccani, 2011), n.p. The Fondazione dello spettacolo kindly made Dr. Viganò's study available to me.

alogue" with the church. The film examined an upper-class Milanese family and their maid, all of whom succumb to the erotic temptations of a Christ-like "Visitor." Astonishingly, considering the blasphemous content, OCIC still awarded *Teorema* its prize at the 1968 *Biennale*, something inconceivable only a few years before. Pope Paul, however, responded with an attack on "inadmissible films," and the OCIC board capitulated, expressing regret that it had ever lauded Pasolini's film. The director then fired back that "the International Catholic Office for Cinema [could] keep their award, and take back the one they gave me for *Il Vangelo secondo Matteo*."[66]

Il Vangelo secondo Matteo's bumpy ride at the Venice *biennale*, moreover, had an impact not only for Pasolini, but for what remained of any cultural project among the Catholics who no longer deemed control of the Festival feasible or even desirable. In 1961, Emilio Lonero's exit and Giovanni Ponti's death delivered serious blows to Catholic hopes in Venice. Only one year later, by the time of the 1962 festival, Nazareno Fabbretti wondered in *Orizzonti* what had become of the Catholics. Beyond the "external" OCIC presence, they had vanished.[67] By 1964, *Noi uomini* blasted the *Biennale*'s "so-called art" in an article titled, "The Museum of Horrors."[68] In January of that year, an exchange between Giulio Andreotti and the president of the festival, Mario Marcazzan, confirmed the divorce. Speaking specifically about painting, Andreotti could have been discussing any field, insisting that the state had no artistic policy. To "shut the doors," moreover, on rebellious artists or for the state to ridicule or curb any artist's production was un-Italian and more typical of Khrushchev's Soviet Union. The next day, Marcazzan declared that the *Biennale*'s choices and decisions were entirely independent of

66. Benini, *Pasolini: The Sacred Flesh*, 49; 111–46. In the waning days of the Pasolini flirtation, some Catholics expressed a brief interest in the young director Liliana Cavani, who in 1966 released her first major picture, the promising *Francesco di Assisi*. An RAI production, it was broadcast in two parts and naturally invited comparisons with Rossellini's and Pasolini's works. It received positive reviews except from the neo-Fascists, who didn't like it. According to her biographer, Cavani's film "was acclaimed as the most controversial and successful program of the year." The Catholic *Orizzonti* invited her, Pasolini, and others to discuss *Francesco di Assisi*. Pasolini considered the Protestant "beatnik" Lou Castel's portrayal of Francis too bourgeois for his tastes. The fling was brief, however, because Cavani went off in other directions, with films like the celebrated *The Night Porter* in 1974. She nonetheless returned to the saint in 1989 with *Francesco*, starring Mickey Rourke as Francis and Helena Bonham Carter as Clare; Gaetana Marrone, *The Gaze and the Labyrinth: The Cinema of Liliana Cavani* (Princeton, N.J.: Princeton University Press, 2000), 17–33; Bianca Sermonti, "Liliana Cavani," part of a series, "Quando il regista è donna," *Rivista del cinematografo*, April–May 1967, 259–62.

67. Nazareno Fabbretti, "Assenti i cattolici alla mostra di Venezia?," *Orizzonti*, September 20, 1962.

68. Lorenzo Martiena, "Il Museo degli orrori," *Noi uomini*, July 21, 1964.

the state.[69] A couple of years later, the AC men's review condemned the festival as a mere stunt, a "regurgitation of the smart set" on behalf of the local tourist industry.[70] The *Biennale*'s film festival, furthermore, was entering its own era of doubt. It suspended prizes in 1969 and undertook a complete reorganization in 1973. The drought of awards would last until 1980. A critic for the *New York Times*, John Canaday, wrote at the end of 1969 that the *Biennale*'s demise might rather be the healthiest development on the world's art scene.[71]

Abandoning Pasolini and Venice, by the 1970s Catholics might have taken heart that some of their tools still worked. In December 1970, the Constitutional Court affirmed the validity of the Penal Code's articles 527, 528, and 529 on morality; the following year a number of films still managed to encounter trouble from the censors. The government briefly delayed the releases of Ken Russell's *The Devils* and Ingmar Bergman's *The Touch*, while authorities in Bari sequestered Pasolini's *Decameron* for a time. Through 1971, the minister of Tourism and the Spettacolo, the Social Democrat Gianmatteo Matteotti, engaged in yet another give-and-take over a new censorship measure.[72] The old debates resurfaced in 1973, when the public defender in Benevento sequestered Pasolini's *Canterbury Tales* after the court had cleared it for showing, and in Bologna, where the Appeals Court ordered the same for Bernardo Bertolucci's *Last Tango in Paris*. In a verdict that *Avanti!* considered "absurd," the judge also ordered jail time for the director and thirty-thousand lire fines all around, including for the stars, Marlon Brando and Maria Schneider.[73] But these arguments seemed more and more concerned with vogue, celebrities, or the scandal *du jour* and illustrated that the government's erratic activity meant a lack of coherent policy. The old Catholic concerns resurfaced with the 1980 seizure of the entertainer Renzo Arbore's film *Il Pap'occhio* (*In the Pope's Eye*) for which the state leveled the reliable *vilipendio* charge of insulting the pontiff. Less obviously religious motives

69. "Una dichiarazione del Ministro Andreotti," *Il Popolo*, January 22, 1964; "Dichiarazione del presidente della Biennale," *Il Popolo*, January 23, 1964; see also "Dichiarazioni di Andreotti sulla Biennale di Venezia," *Corriere della sera*, January 22, 1964.

70. "Venezia: Cinema senza morale," *Noi uomini*, October 11, 1966.

71. John Canaday, "A Few Worsts, Bests, and Mosts," *New York Times*, December 28, 1969.

72. Giacomo Gambetti, *Cinema e censura in Italia* (Rome: Edizioni di bianco e nero, 1972), 7–18. Gianmatteo Matteotti was a son of Giacomo Matteotti, whose murder in 1924 triggered the great crisis of the early Fascist regime.

73. "Un film può essere bloccato anche se un giudice lo assolve," *Il Messagero*, April 3, 1973; also located in IS Archivio Andreotti Cinema, b. 1072, f. 2.3; and "Assurda sentenza di condanna per il film di Bernardo Bertolucci," *Avanti!*, June 6, 1973.

prompted the government's ban on 1981's *Lion of the Desert* by the Syrian director Moustapha Akkad. A critique of Italy's colonial administration in Libya, the film centered on an indigenous revolt against Mussolini's troops. The Republican Giovanni Spadolini, Italy's first non-DC prime minister since 1945, considered it insulting to the army and denied its release in theaters. Although it was shown around the world, in Italy the film languished until 2009, when it finally appeared there on television's Sky Cinema.[74]

After the Pasolini debacle, however, more distress lurked around the corner. Already in a 1965 piece for *Epoca*, Grazia Livi claimed that Italy was generally sliding into a pornographic culture, something that began with Fellini's *La dolce vita*. The public had grown numb to it, even acting as "sheepish" accomplices in the decay. Each year since 1960, she continued, along with new films, more obscene words entered circulation—along with new off-color expressions or more ribald (*boccaccesca*) situations. One screenwriter confessed to Livi that "every season . . . represent[ed] one more stop on the road to [that] vulgarity."[75]

Livi had a point. By April 1969, the flood of pornographic movies along with the futility of the vetting process led to the resignations of five frustrated judges from their posts as chairs on censorship commissions. A representative for the group charged that the 1962 measure remained seriously flawed and stifled their ability to do their job. Another interjected that the law "only protected producers [rather than], as it should, work for *buon costume*." *La Stampa* reported that since only three of the eight commissions really functioned at all, and since most authors and cinema journalists had been boycotting the commissions from the start, the resignations would cause serious delays for the whole system. By the mid-1970s, almost half of Italy's film production could be considered "erotic."[76]

As one historian put it, "Toward the end of the 1970s full-fledged pornographic theaters began to appear in Italy, initially just a handful, then tens and hundreds of them. Unfortunately, for every one of these red-light theaters that opened, at least ten, or even twenty, second-

74. Guido Bonsaver, "Censorship from the Fascist Period to the Present," in *The Italian Cinema Book*, ed. Peter Bondanella (London: Palgrave Macmillan, 2014), 71–72. See also "Musical stravagante per niente blasfemo," *La Repubblica*, October 19, 1998, posted on the newspaper's website: http://www.repubblica.it/online/cinema/papocchio/papocchio/papocchio.html (accessed December 31, 2019).

75. Grazia Livi, "Italia pornografica," *Epoca* (754), March 7, 1965.

76. "Cinque magistrati si ritirano dalle commissioni di censura," *La Stampa*, April 23, 1969; also located in IS Archivio Andreotti Cinema, b. 1072, ff. 2.3.

or third-run theaters in small towns and the outskirts of big cities closed."[77] Add to the mix the collapse of all ticket sales by 75 percent between 1977 and 1989. The obvious casualties here were the legitimate theaters, which declined by 50 percent in those years, and the parish movie house. As late as 1967, Catholics still depended on the roughly six thousand parish halls that constituted about half of Italy's movie theaters. There, patrons might not have been treated to much first-run fare, but they could enjoy acceptable family films. Like other religious organizations in the 1960s, however, erosion was setting in, and thirty years later the one-in-two ratio of movie theaters that were housed in parish halls sank to just one in ten.[78]

Television

At RAI Ettore Bernabei successfully maintained his balancing act, accomodating the "opening to the left" while keeping TV in the DC camp. His only real problem, in fact, came from inside the party when, in April of 1965, Moro planted a factotum, Gianni Granzotto, in the organization to keep an eye on Bernabei, who was always considered Amintore Fanfani's man. Granzotto lost that battle, however, and was soon out.[79] But television as such continued to worry Catholics. In 1969, *Famiglia Cristiana* conducted a survey that asked viewers if and how the box changed them and their families. Results showed that Catholics believed that television alienated people and weakened family life. One viewer complained of its effect on daughters who took their cues from the questionable conduct of actresses, while others lamented the rampant consumerism in shows, particularly *Carosello*.[80] Television under Bernabei, however, still offered some hope for Catholics. Indeed, already at the end of 1963, wrote Antonio Petrucci in the *Rivista del cinematografo*, the talk on the Montecitorio was that the DC had abandoned film in order to devote all its energies to television, which may have been true, considering reaction to the 1962 and 1965 censorship measures.[81] Nonethe-

77. Brunetta, *History of Italian Cinema*, 212; Edward Bowen, "'Take Notice of the Red Light!' A History of Adult Cinemas in Rome," *Journal of Italian Cinema and Media Studies* 4, no. 1 (2017): 3–21.

78. Gianfranco Bettetini, "Chiesa cattolica e cinema: Dal sessantotto a oggi," in *Attraverso lo schermo: Cinema e cultura cattolica in Italia*, vol. 3, *Dagli anni settanta ai nostri giorni*, ed. Ruggero Eugeni and Dario E. Viganò (Rome: Ente dello spettacolo, 2006), 3:80.

79. Franco Monteleone, *Storia della Radio e della televisione in Italia* (Venice: Marsilio, 1992), 368–70. Granzotto replaced Marcello Rodinò. Regarding Moro's opinion of Rodinò, see Franco Chiarenza, *Il cavallo morente: Trent'anni di Radiotelevisione italiana* (Milan: Bompiani, 1978), 130.

80. Garofalo, *Political Audiences*, 132–33.

81. Antonio Petrucci, "Giova ripetere?," *Rivista del cinematografo*, November 1963.

less, in the mid-1960s one viewer asked *Famiglia Cristiana* why, with the DC monopoly on RAI, the schedule did not consist entirely of Catholic programming, and in 1964 the *Rivista del cinematografo* admitted that despite Catholic control, TV's "Christianizing role was not very elevated."[82] Some outside the DC, of course, disagreed and felt that TV was entirely too Catholic. Easy targets were the RAI's various Padre Mariano programs, *Eyes on the World* (*Sguardi sul mondo*) and, later, *Padre Mariano's Mailbag* (*La posta di Padre Mariano*). In 1967, rumors circulated that the popular Capuchin's show would be yanked, prompting *Famiglia Cristiana* to respond with an article intended to calm the fears: "Padre Mariano Will Remain on TV." The review blamed the DC's Socialist junior partners at RAI for mischievously stirring the pot.[83]

Bernabei remained at the helm through the 1960s and into the next decade until two decisions by the Constitutional Court, numbers 225 and 226 of July 1974, acted as a "cold shower" and broke decisively the DC's monopoly over television broadcasting. He left the RAI that September, the same month that Silvio Berlusconi changed the face of Italian television by unveiling his cable station, *Telemilano*.[84] Soon even housewives, who a decade or two before would never have considered such a shameful thing, performed the *spogliarello* on TV to win domestic appliances; and in a few years contestants stripped on an immensely successful show, *Colpo Grosso*, produced from 1987 until 1992 by Berlusconi's Fininvest corporation for the Italia 7 channel.[85] Censorship activity clearly declined, although some significant cases emerged here and there, and Catholic influence at the RAI informally continued. *Paese sera*, in fact, reported in 1974 that although Bernabei seemed to be on the way out, he ensured that key staff members would remain, including Emilio Rossi, "the black soul at the center of RAI TV," and Vincenzo Incisa, who kept tabs on scripts and programming.[86] In the 1980s, one functionary confessed to Jeff Pratt, a British scholar, that television provided the pope with extensive coverage and still respected the church as "untouchable." "This kind of censorship, which applies to other key

82. Garofalo, *Political Audiences*, 125; Francesco Alberoni, "Per una politica culurale dei cattolici," *Rivista del cinematografo*, January 1964.

83. Garofalo, *Political Audiences*, 127–28.

84. Franco Chiarenza, *Il cavallo morente*, 215; Monteleone, *Storia della Radio e della televisione in Italia*, 387–88.

85. John Ellis, *Seeing Things: Television in the Age of Uncertainty* (London: I. B. Tauris, 2000), 49.

86. Ivano Cipriani, "La RAI-TV davanti al referendum per il divorzio," *Paese sera*, March 7, 1974, also located in IS Fondo Gonella Series 3, B. 55, f. 30.

areas of national life," wrote Pratt, "is so total as to pass virtually unnoticed."[87] Another study took note of the "capricious" persistence of the old *vilipendio* laws wherein a grapefruit advertisement had to be pulled because it featured a questionable image of the Last Supper.[88]

The *Deputy* Controversy

Along with its treatment of film, the April 1962 reform ended theatrical censorship, although the government still possessed some resources to protect the church from what it saw as anticlerical assaults on the stage. The most notorious case concerned Rolf Hochhuth's *Der Stellvertreter*, an indictment of Pope Pius's wartime conduct regarding the Holocaust. The play premiered in West Berlin in February 1963, in London in September as *The Representative*, and in New York in early 1964 as *The Deputy*. Britain's chief censor, the Lord Chamberlain, blocked the release of Hochhuth's play until a compromise allowed the Catholic Church to insert an "answer" in the theatergoers' programs.[89] In Bonn, the papal nuncio looked for guidance on whether the state could prosecute Hochhuth for defamation. The government replied that the prelate should not pursue the matter, since "in the current climate critics of the church had to be allowed a certain leeway."[90] In Italy, it appeared that critics of the church's conduct during the Holocaust had already taken a turn toward the personal by naming names. In 1958, for instance, soon after Bishop Fiordelli's first verdict, *Paese sera* charged that Florence's Cardinal Archbishop Elio Dalla Costa had collaborated with the Nazis. *Il Popolo* dismissed the calumny as a petty and ridiculous bit of fiction and *cronaca nera*.[91]

The Deputy, however, aimed for the top. Its portrayal of a cold-hearted and cowardly Pius, insensitive to Nazi savagery, was the last straw. Catholic outrage came immediately, most famously in a letter from Archbishop

87. Jeff C. Pratt, *The Walled City: A Study of Social Change and Conservative Ideologies in Tuscany* (Aachen: Rader Verlag, 1986), 255n1.

88. Frederic Spotts and Theodor Wieser, *Italy: A Difficult Democracy* (New York: Cambridge University Press, 1986), 164.

89. Peter G. Richards, *Parliament and Conscience* (London: George Allen and Unwin, 1970), 120–21. Another of Hochhuth's plays, *Soldiers*, briefly encountered censorship trouble in Britain.

90. Jacques Kornberg, *The Pope's Dilemma: Pius XII Faces Atrocities and Genocide in the Second World War* (Toronto: University of Toronto Press, 2015), 17.

91. "Fuochi fatui anticlericali," *Il Popolo*, February 19, 1958. *Paese sera* leveled the same charge at Giorgio LaPira. In 2012, Dalla Costa (who died in 1961) posthumously received the honor of "Righteous among the Nations" from Yad Vashem.

Montini to the British Catholic paper the *Tablet*. In their preface to the letter, printed on June 29, 1963, the editors stated that they received the missive one hour after Montini's election to the papal throne.[92] Based on his "close contact" with Pius and intimate knowledge of the wartime Holy See, the new pope challenged Hochhuth's misrepresentation as an "artificial manipulation of facts" and "pseudo-reality." The slander denied the truth—Pius's actions had been, in fact, "vigilant, persistent, disinterested and courageous." "What is the gain to art and culture," Montini concluded, "when the theatre lends itself to injustice of this sort?"

Der Stellvertreter reached Italy as *Il Vicario* (*The Vicar*). It came to Rome in 1965, although clearly in violation of *vilipendio* measures. Directed by Carlo Cecchi and with Gian Maria Volontè, fresh from work on Sergio Leone's *A Fistful of Dollars*, the play was privately staged in the cellar (*scantinato*) of a deconsecrated church. The government got wind of it, and on February 13 about fifty police and Carabinieri arrived at the scene. They blocked the little via Belsiana, just off the via del Corso, provoking scuffles, and nightstick-wielding police arrested two showgoers. Other showgoers suffered injuries. The Socialists first insisted that the police shut down the performance on the "ridiculous excuse" that the locale did not meet safety standards. On February 15, however, the prefect of Rome revealed the state's intentions, citing the Lateran Pacts, the offense of *vilipendio* toward the sacred essence of the city and the pope, therefore banning the production anywhere in the province. In the Senate on February 17, Mario Scelba's successor as interior minister, Paolo Emilio Taviani, reiterated the government's ban and its commitment to Rome's holy status. None of this intimidated the troupe, which, on the same day as the prefect's declaration, performed *Il Vicario* to a select group, after hours and in the back room of the Feltrinelli bookshop in the via del Babuino, not far from the first site. The Milan-based Feltrinelli had published Hochhuth's play in book form and had just opened its Rome store, which quickly became one of the city's literary nerve centers. The audience included members of Parliament, the writers Alberto Moravia, Carlo Emilio Gadda, Pasolini, Carlo Levi, and Natalia Ginzburg, and the American activist and writer Mary McCarthy. No police action disturbed the gathering.[93]

92. "Pius XII and the Jews," letter written by Giovanni Battista Montini to *The Tablet*, June 29, 1963. The letter can be accessed at the *Tablet* archive site: https://reader.exacteditions.com/issues/71550/page/18?term=Montini+%22pius+XII+and+the+Jews%22 (unfortunately now a pay site).

93. Emiliano Perra, "Il Dibattito pubblico italiano sul comportamento del Vaticano durante la

The via Belsiana incident prompted more arguments between those who charged anticlericalism and those who claimed that Lateran Pact protections had gone too far. The *Osservatore Romano* moaned that Hochhuth's insults hit a city that, not too long before, had hailed Pius as *Defensor Civitatis*. Giulio Andreotti located Hochhuth's support among Communists and "priest eaters" who had always loathed Pope Pius, but also among Germans wanting to spread the guilt of their Nazi past. The government had to take action, he wrote, although now that theatrical censorship had ended, Rome's prefect still had every right to seek the protection offered by the Constitution and its Article 7.[94]

On the left, the DC's Socialist partners were prudent, and *Avanti!* took a restrained tone, deploring a rather mediocre play that did not merit much artistic praise. At the same time, the Socialist paper was disturbed by offended Catholics who sought isolation in a comfortable bubble, a sorry lot compared to the "vitality" of Pope John's Church and the Vatican Council.[95] In the chamber, on February 18, 1965, a group of deputies proposed a discussion of the *Vicario* controversy with government representatives. One of the most prominent of the "53," for example, Agostino Greggi, wanted an explanation for the "incredible and absurd attempt to present [in Rome] a work that everyone judged devoid of historic value and without any artistic merit like *Il Vicario*."[96] The debate came on April 2, when the chamber treated a motion from the Communist literary figure Mario Alicata to lift the prefect's ban. The Venetian deputy Vincenzo Gagliardi led the Catholic response, joined by Oscar Scalfaro and others who repeatedly condemned the play as an insult and a jumble of lies. Greggi rose to point out that many behind Alicata's measure had voted for Article 7 at the Constituent Assembly. In his defense of the government, Minister Taviani emphasized that all argument stopped at Article 7—it could not be changed—something that a recent Cassation Court decision had affirmed. Caught in the middle,

---

Shoah: La Ricezione presso la stampa de Il Vicario, Rappresaglia e Amen," *Italianistica Ultraeictina* 3, 2008, accessed on December 31, 2019, at https://dspace.library.uu.nl/bitstream/handle/1874/33904/article.pdf?sequence=2&isAllowed=y. On the opening controversy: "La polizia impedisce la recita del "Vicario," February 14, 1965; "Niente Vicario a Roma in base al Concordato," February 16, 1965; and "La vicenda del 'Vicario': Un'esempio da non imitare," February 18, 1965, all in *Avanti!* See also "La risposta di Taviani," *Corriere della, sera*, February 18, 1965. On the Feltrinelli role, see "'Il Vicario' rappresentato privatamente in una libreria," *Corriere della sera*, February 16, 1965, and http://roma.corriere.it/roma/notizie/arte_e_cultura/13_luglio_26/chiude-libreria-feltrinelli-babuino-2222343733094.shtml?refresh_ce-cp (accessed December 31, 2019).

94. Giulio Andreotti, "Il Pro-Vicario," *Concretezza*, March 16, 1965.

95. Ugo D'Ascia, "Mobilitazione conformista contro 'Il Vicario,'" *Avanti!*, March 24, 1964.

96. Atti Parlamentari, Camera dei Deputati, IV Legislatura, *Discussioni*, February 18, 1965, 13,066.

twelve Socialists walked out of the hall when the voting began and Alicata's proposal failed.[97]

One historian wrote that, on the bottom line, *Il Vicario* was forever denied a (legal) showing in Rome. Indeed, the affair may have been the republic's most effective application ever of Lateran Pacts–based censorship. Yet this was not the case in other Italian cities—those not as strictly bound by the Lateran regulations as was the Eternal City. Within days of the via Belsiana incident, for instance, a student group staged the play in Florence, and by the spring even provincial cities like Savona were scheduling performances.[98]

While the *Vicario* controversy simmered, Catholics still hoped for a theater that reflected their vision and, despite the end of censorship, still scored an occasional victory. They found some solace in the director Orazio Costa, who directed Fabbri's *Processo a Gesù* and was broadly known for his devotion. In 1965, and with Pope Paul's blessing, he founded the Teatro Romeo to promote spiritual works on stage. The *Osservatore Romano* commented that now the public would be able to see productions that "too many impresarios and directors, deliberately or not, ignored or pretended to ignore." Costa's first offering at the Romeo was a production of Silvio D'Amico's *Mystery of the Nativity, Passion, and Resurrection of Our Lord* (*Mistero della Natività, Passione e Resurrezione di Nostro Signore*).[99]

Social Change and the Perfect Secular Storm

In February and March 1970, the *Osservatore Romano* ran a series of articles from one of Italy's chief Catholic thinkers, Augusto Del Noce. He condemned the triumph of "eroticism" in Western society and charged that moderns had grown numb to the lewdness all around them. Discussing Del Noce's claims in *Civiltà cattolica*, the Jesuit Salvatore Lener concurred. Looking back over recent times, he wrote, he realized that Italy and the developed world had suffered "an explosion of obscenity—in books, in

97. Atti Parlamentari, Camera dei Deputati, IV Legislatura, *Discussioni*, April 2, 1965, 14,151–220. The Cassation verdict was from October 23, 1964; *Foro Italiano* 87, no. 11 (1964): 2,084.

98. "Proteste a Savona per 'Il Vicario,'" *OR*, May 10–11, 1965; see also "Niente 'Vicario' a Roma in base al Concordato," *Avanti!*, February 16, 1965; and "La Vicenda del 'Vicario': Un esempio da non imitare," *Avanti!*, February 18, 1965.

99. "Le origini spirituali e religiose della creazione artistica riaffermate nel 'Teatro Romeo' di Orazio Costa," *OR*, April 5–6, 1965. On Costa see also http://www.cdrc.it/mmlOraz.html (accessed December 11, 2019).

the press, in *spettacoli*, in all methods of social communication." This did not just refer to "scurrilous language and exhibitions of nudity" but extended to "comportment and sexual degeneration," exaltations of prostitution, sexual exhibitionism, and homosexuality on a level never seen in "the history of modern civilization."[100]

Del Noce and Lener wrote when new attitudes toward sex and the family were surfacing, in an era also known for significant student and labor trouble linked to Italy's expanding economy and affluence. The literary world had already launched the revolution. Secularist journalists and intellectuals had been discussing new vistas in their essays and other works, considered to have been imported from abroad; and since the government refrained from challenging the *stampa* with the vigor that characterized their approach to the rest of the media, literature could promote social evolution with greater clarity and force. By 1960, therefore, *Iniziativa* recognized mainstream publishing as "the vice industry." An early shock came ten years before, in 1950, with Bompiani's Italian translation of Alfred Kinsey's *Sexual Behavior in the Human Male*. The publisher followed in 1955 with Kinsey's *Sexual Behavior in the Human Female*. The early sixties witnessed the publication, sometimes after long delays, of translations of a number of groundbreaking books, indicating that Italy's sexual revolution was on its way. In 1963, Feltrinelli issued Wilhelm Reich's 1936 *The Sexual Revolution*. Simone de Beauvoir's 1949 *The Second Sex* appeared in 1961, while Betty Friedan's 1963 *The Feminine Mystique* enjoyed a more timely Italian publication date of 1964. Also of note, in 1960 the German psychologist Fritz Kahn published his *Encyclopedia of Love* (*Enciclopedia dell'amore*) in Rome. This popular work, which claimed that "marriage is a form of biological life found in all classes of higher animals, insects, fish, birds and mammals," saw four editions through 1965.[101] Italian authors also began to write more openly of sex and sexual repression. Gabriella Parca's *Italian Women Confess* (*Le Italiane si confessano*), a collection of letters from women and girls to advice columns, appeared on many of 1959's must-read lists. Her book went through seven

100. S. Lener, "La difesa penale contro l'osceno," *Civiltà cattolica* 122, no. 2895, February 6, 1971. The Del Noce series "L'erotismo alla conquista della società" appeared in the February 26 and 28 and March 2–3, 5, and 12, 1970, issues of *Osservatore Romano*.

101. Crainz, *Il Paese mancato*, 10–11; Perry Willson, *Women in Twentieth-Century Italy* (New York: Palgrave Macmillan, 2010), 126–27; Carlo Barduzzi, "L'Industria del vizio," *Iniziativa*, May 15, 1960. On Kinsey, see Penelope Morris, "'Let's Not Talk about Italian Sex': The Reception of the Kinsey Reports in Italy," *Journal of Modern Italian Studies* 18, no. 1 (2013). On *The Encyclopedia of Love*, see Hervé A. Cavallera, *Storia dell'idea di famiglia in italia: Dall'avvento della Repubblica ai giorni nostri* (Brescia: Editrice La Scuola, 2006), 106–7, regarding Kahn and 109–11 regarding Reich.

printings by 1962 and came out again in 1964 with an introduction from Pasolini. The Lombard psychologist Luigi De Marchi trailblazed in this regard with his books *Sex and Civilization* (*Sesso e civiltà*) in 1959, *Sociology and Sex* (*Sociologia e sesso*) in 1963, and *Sexual Repression and Sexual Oppression* (*Repressione sessuale e oppression sessuale*) in 1965.[102] Many disgusted Catholics viewed such titles as mere pornography. When Alberto Moravia dedicated an issue of the *Nuova Antologia* to erotic literature, the DC's *Concretezza* could only condemn the esteemed review's slide into "immorality and libertinism ... corruption and perversion."[103]

The literary elite was one thing, but among the public, frank discussions of sex remained uncommon, at least before the mid-1960s. In 1963, for example, reviewing three new books on the subject, *Il Mondo* regretted that Italy might be the most backward European country regarding sex education. Schools "ignore it completely," claimed the author, and families weren't much better.[104] That same year, not long after the *vilipendio* trial over *La ricotta*, Pasolini's documentary film *Comizi d'amore* probed relations between the sexes, with interviews of everyone—from children in a schoolyard to men in a café, from the Bologna soccer team to writers Oriana Fallaci and Camilla Cederna on the Venetian Lido. Pasolini, a "gentle inquisitor," asked them questions like, "Where do babies come from?" and "Why do some men become homosexuals?" At one point, he stopped a pair of young ladies in a Milan ballroom to see if they had ever heard of "sadism" and "masochism." He added occasional commentary from "Italy's pop psychoanalyst Cesare Musatti and Moravia, the novelist of sex *par excellence*." In the end, as one observer put it, Pasolini painted a picture of "a hypocritical, boorish [*becera*], morbid, but real Italy." *Comizi d'amore* scored miserably at the box office, although this may have been the result of poor distribution. The filmmaker lamented that only "cinephiles and sociologists want to see it," and maybe the public saw itself reflected only too well in this production.[105]

More and more challenges to the traditional culture surfaced through the 1960s. Two female entertainers who pushed the envelope in the early

102. Cavallera, *Storia dell'idea di famiglia in italia*, 115–16. On De Marchi, see also his obituary in *La Repubblica* on July 25, 2010, found at http://www.repubblica.it/persone/2010/07/25/news/luigi_de_marchi-5825748/ (accessed January 28, 2015).

103. "Eroticismo," *Concretezza*, November 1, 1961; Amalia Signorelli, "Women in Italy in the 1970s," in *Speaking Out and Silencing: Culture, Society and Politics in Italy in the 1970s*, ed. Anna Cento Bull and Adalgisa Giorgio (London: Legenda, 2006), 42–68.

104. Vittoria Olivetti, "Il costume sessuale," *Il Mondo*, February 26, 1963.

105. Fiamma Lussana, *L'Italia del divorzio: La battaglia fra Stato, Chiesa e gente comune, Con lettere dei "fuorilegge del matrimonio"* (Rome: Carocci editore, 2014), 81; Schwartz, *Pasolini Requiem*, 437–43.

1960s were the actress Carla Gravina and the pop star Mina, who both had children out of wedlock. In 1961, Gravina and her lover, Gian Maria Volonté, who was wedded to another woman, produced a daughter. Mina carried on an affair with a married actor, Corrado Pani, who fathered her child in April 1963. The RAI banned the very popular Mina from the air, but public outcry brought her back by the start of 1964. Ironically, Olghina di Robilant, whose party at Rugantino's had caused a stir six years before and who, in 1959, had delivered her own child out of wedlock, published an ambivalent article on the Mina scandal that contrasted the star's "bad example" with her positive decision to deliver the child, recalling the earlier inconsistency toward Ingrid Bergman.[106]

Other women unintentionally prompted questions about sexual relations and marriage. The horrific case of Franca Viola served as another "strong signal of change." In December 1965 a young gangster, Filippo Melodia, helped by a dozen accomplices, kidnapped and raped Viola, a seventeen-year-old Sicilian. After eight days, he released his victim but, to avoid prosecution, proposed marriage to her, an act that would transform his brutality into a case of *fuitina*—a tradition of elopement between young lovers. Viola, however, surprisingly and boldly refused the gangster's offer, thus sending him to prison. Instead, she chose to marry her childhood sweetheart, which she did in 1968. *Fuitina* and other archaic traditions had little to do with Catholicism. Such customs, whether or not strictly Catholic, reinforced a woman's legal subservience to her husband, and many even remained on the books. A Milan Tribunal in 1958, for instance, affirmed that a man could prohibit his wife from leaving the house without him and that he might beat her for disobedience. In November of 1961, a Sardinian Tribunal ruled that husbands had the right to hit their wives "with the intent of correcting her [*a scopo di correzione*]."[107] As late as 1965, a Cassation Court ruled that husbands were within bounds when they prohibited wives from working outside the home. Even *Famiglia Cristiana*, in 1959, suggested that the husband might "moderately chastise his wife with words or even hit her" for serious enough reasons. By the 1960s, however, government and church tried to distance themselves from such attitudes. Shortly after the Viola

106. Natalia Aspesi, "Cronaca e costume," in *Le donne italiane: Le chi è del '900*, ed. Miriam Mafai (Milan: Rizzoli, 1993), 23–24; Rachel Haworth, "Scandal, Motherhood and Mina in 1960s Italy," *Modern Italy* 22, no. 3 (2017); on Gravina, see http://www.agoravox.it/Quando-nel-Transatlantico-c-era-la.html (accessed February 1, 2015).

107. Camera dei deputati, Segretariato Generale, *Orientamenti giurisprudenziali in tema di buon costume* (Rome: Servizio studi legislazione e inchieste parlamentari, 1972), 326.

affair, for example, the Constitutional Court threw out a Fascist measure that distinguished male from female adultery. The government, furthermore, modified the Penal Code's Article 587, which dealt with honor killings, something that factored in discussions of Pietro Germi's *Divorzio all'Italiana*. The church clearly condemned the acts of Viola's tormentors, and, in fact, Pope Paul received her and her husband at the Vatican.[108]

The historian Wendy Pojmann illustrated the quandary that the new feminism presented to Catholic women activists. "The older generation now had to confront an even larger range of issues," she wrote. "Was female chastity a virtue or part of an old bourgeois culture whose values no longer served a purpose? . . . Would feminism put an end to femininity?"[109] Those who advocated a greater female presence in the workplace found little resistance from Catholics, as long as it balanced with traditional obligations to family and children. In the 1940s and 1950s Catholic leaders, first Maria Badaloni and then Maria Cocco, pressed for women's access to the bench. Such efforts yielded a first step in the so-called Moro Law of December 27, 1956 (no. 1441), named for Aldo Moro, who was the DC minister of justice at the time and who advanced the bill. Then, in August 1960, Cocco introduced another proposal to open most government positions to women. Parliament tweaked it over the next two years with measures like an amendment from Fanfani to extend the employment of women to the diplomatic corps. Pope John also encouraged the idea in a speech to the CIF in 1960. Finally, February 9, 1963, saw the introduction of Cocco's law number 66. That year, furthermore, closed a legal loophole that had permitted the firing of female employees who married.[110]

Another significant controversy concerned homosexuality. Many, especially Catholics, found disturbing even its mention—a taboo that,

108. Crainz, *Il Paese mancato*, 186; Molly Tambor, *The Lost Wave: Women and Democracy in Postwar Italy* (Oxford: Oxford University Press, 2014), 179; Maria Pia Di Bella, "'Il caso di Franca Viola': La ragazza che disse di no," in her *Dire o tacere in Sicilia: Viaggio alle radici dell'omertà* (Rome: Armando editore, 2011), 167–86; "Sicilian Girl Who Refused to Wed Abductor Sees Pope," *New York Times*, December 19, 1968. On Article 587, see "Reale: A febbraio una legge per abolire il delitto 'd'onore,'" *Avanti!*, January 5, 1966. On the *Famiglia Cristiana* article, see Stefania Bernini, "Natural Mothers: Teaching Morals and Parent-Craft in Italy, 1945–1960," *Modern Italy* 9, no. 1 (May 2004). For this, Bernini quotes Mario Marazziti's chapter on *Famiglia Cristiana* in *Pio XII*, ed. Andrea Riccardi (Rome and Bari: Laterza, 1984), 24.

109. Wendy Pojmann, *Italian Women and International Cold War Politics, 1944–1968* (New York: Fordham University Press, 2013), 155.

110. Tambor, *Lost Wave*, 154–65, 179; see also Signorelli, "Women in Italy in the 1970s," in Bull and Giorgio, *Speaking Out and Silencing*, 52–53; and Lussana, *L'Italia del divorzio*, 61–62. The law that admitted women into public office and the professions was Legge 9 febbraio, 1963, no. 66; and the one to curtail firing of married women was Legge 9 gennaio, 1963, no. 7.

like suicide, they preferred to exclude from public discussions. Menico Caroli claimed that the RAI never even uttered the word "homosexual" until 1975, when it reported on the murder of Pasolini.[111] As a flamboyant gay man, Roger Peyrefitte in the 1950s served as a rare challenge to that rule, reinforcing for many the idea that sodomy was not an Italian vice as much as it was imported by foreigners, like the French novelist on the prowl for attractive Italian youths.[112] Reluctant to touch the issue, Italy had no explicitly anti-sodomy laws and traditionally entrusted the church to handle such questions before Mussolini's Rocco Code addressed "vices against nature."[113] Catholics referred to the Bible, starting with Old Testament proscriptions of Leviticus 18:22 and 20:13, that those who committed the "abominable" act should be put to death. Catholics, furthermore, were not alone on this. Disdain spread across the spectrum, from *L'Unità*'s aforementioned classification of sodomy as a "bourgeois degeneration" to the three attempts in the early 1960s to criminalize it: two by the neo-Fascists and a third from the Social Democrats. In an earlier case, in 1956, Parliament criminalized homosexual acts and punished them with a two-year prison sentence, but this required a change in the penal code, and the project fizzled.[114]

The case of Aldo Braibanti dragged the question into the volatile 1960s. Portrayed at varous times as a professor of philosophy, writer, poet, and Resistance fighter, Braibanti sequestered one, later two, of his students who reportedly lived with him, or spent a lot of time with him, in a Roman boardinghouse (*pensione*), where he pressed on them "strange ideas and habits." In 1964, the father of one of the young men brought the case to the attention of the state, which, with nothing better, charged Braibanti with violating Article 603 of the penal code, the crime of plagiarism (*plagio*). By dominating the young men, argued the state, the professor had robbed, or plagiarized, them of their identities, "choice, criticism and will." He had, it maintained, "enslaved" them. It was an odd but not unprecedented charge. In 1956, the state accused a

111. Menico Caroli, *Proibitissimo! Censori e censurati della radiotelevisione italiana* (Milan: Garzanti, 2003), 72.

112. Introduction, *Sexual Cultures in Europe: National Histories*, ed. Franz X. Eder, Leslie A. Hall, and Gert Hekma (Manchester: Manchester University Press, 1999), 7; on homosexuals as foreign predators, see Robert Aldrich, *The Seduction of the Mediterranean: Writing, Art and Homosexual Fantasy* (London: Routledge, 1993).

113. For a sketch of the era before the DC ascendancy, see Gianni Rossi Barilli, *Il Movimento gay in Italia* (Milan: Feltrinelli, 1999), 1–24. On the three proposals to criminalize homosexuality, see 37.

114. Giambattista Scirè, *Il divorzio in Italia: Partiti, chiesa, società civile dalle legge al referendum (1965–1974)* (Milan: Mondadori, 2007), 12.

man in the Abruzzo with *plagio* in that he beat and intimidated his wife while keeping her prisoner in a hovel. A priest brought the matter to light when he reported it to the Vatican, although in the hearing the wife defended her husband's actions, and the case fell apart.

Braibanti's *plagio* trial lasted almost four years, and he received aid from a number of intellectuals including Moravia, Morante, and Pasolini and the Radical Party leader Marco Pannella, as well as the journals *Il Mondo*, *Belfagor*, and *Astrolabio*, a review founded in 1963 by Ernesto Rossi and Feruccio Parri. Even the reserved *Il Ponte* defended Braibanti to the extent that, disturbingly, it praised the professor and dismissed any notion that he had abused the young men. The trial did not figure much in the Catholic press, although one nuanced response came from Gabrio Lombardi, a professor at Rome's Pontifical Lateran University. Before a meeting of Catholic jurists, Lombardi detected in the Braibanti case a "subtle echo between the lines of an existential remorse emerging from the depths of the *id*." Many Italians, he continued, had fallen into a "pseudo-culture" that only confronted moral issues with "alibis, uncertainties, specious pseudo-scientific reasoning and cowardice," a self-centeredness that threatened the idea of community. In December 1967, the court condemned Brabanti to nine years in prison, the first man in Italy ever to have been convicted of *plagio*. His sentence was immediately reduced by two years because of his wartime partisan experience; and two years later, in 1969, the appellate court ordered his release after the defense showed that one of the two victims had not lived in the boardinghouse during the ordeal but rather at home.[115] Like so many other developments in the 1960s, the Braibanti case helped to direct light onto sexual issues. Here, it preceded publications like *Diario di un*

115. The most complete work on the Braibanti case is Gabriele Ferluga, *Il processo Braibanti* (Turin: Silvio Zamorani editore, 2003). Oddly missing in his analysis, however, is the Catholic reaction. See also Rossi Barilli, *Il Movimento gay*, 43–45; "Italy Will Set Free a Professor Jailed for Brainwashing," *New York Times*, December 1, 1969. On *Il Ponte*, see Marco Ramat, "Contro il 'plagio,'" *Il Ponte* 24, no. 8 (August 31, 1968); Enzo Panareo, "Famiglia Sotto Processo," *Il Ponte* 25, no. 3 (March 31, 1969); and Enzo Enriques Agnoletti, "Braibanti," *Il Ponte* 25, no. 11 (November 30, 1969). On the Abruzzo *plagio* case, see "Teneva la moglie in stato di schiavitù," *Avanti!*, August 25, 1956. Ferluga also identified a few precedents for the Braibanti conviction—men who had abducted women—although these were not specifically for *plagio* but more in line with Article 605 of the penal code, for "sequestration"; Ferluga, *Il processo Braibanti*, 28–34. See also Gabrio Lombardi, "Diritto e moralità pubblica in Italia," in *Quaderni di "Iustitia,"* ed. Unione Giuristi Cattolici Italiani (Rome: Giuffrè and Iustitia, 1969), 3–36. Lombardi's talk took place in Naples on November 14–16, 1968. Aldo Braibanti died in 2014; see his obituary in *La Stampa*, "Aldo Braibanti, il suo plagio scandalizzò l'Italia del '68," April 9, 2014, http://www.lastampa.it/2014/04/09/cultura/aldo-braibanti-il-suo-plagio-scandalizz-litalia-del-pJjdqrVIvnVQPtsoZrnoyL/pagina.html (accessed September 20, 2019). Gabrio, Pia, and Riccardo Lombardi were siblings.

omosessuale (*Diary of a Homosexual*) by Giacomo Dacquino and published by Feltrinelli in 1970.[116] But an Italian gay movement emerged, very modestly, in the early 1970s. Later, in the spring of 1976, Roger Peyrefitte surfaced in the weekly *Tempo* to accuse Pope Paul of homosexual behavior and an affair with a minor actor, Paolo Carlini. The defamation first appeared in an interview that Peyrefitte granted to a French gay publication and was now translated into Italian. On April 4, the pontiff denounced the "horrible insinuations" and thanked Cardinal Vicar Urbani and the CEI for their support against Peyrefitte's calumny.[117]

Sexual controversies tended to compound another development discerned by the mid-1960s—Italy's birthrate crisis. Already in 1961, the bishop of Novara complained in the *Rivista del clero* about the strange but visible reluctance of many husbands and wives to procreate. The perpetual Catholic struggle against birth control, he wrote, must also not lose sight of "the horrible plague of onanism and abortion."[118] In 1965, the Constitutional Court made matters worse by accepting arguments from Renato Sansone, Paolo Barile, and Giorgio Moscon that invalidated the Criminal Code's article 553, thus ending the government's ban on disseminating birth-control information.[119] The state tried to modify the ruling's effect by filing charges against a pharmacist in Pisa who kept a prophylactic dispenser in her store. It accused her of breaking the Penal Code's Article 528 on obscenity. In February of 1967, the Pisa Superior Court (*Pretura*) dismissed the case as "not constituting a crime." "The trial did not go well," wrote the local morality secretary to Gavuzzo.[120] The pope then issued his encyclical on birth control, *Humanae vitae*, in July of 1968. One theologian wondered if the world could have welcomed anything from the church in that crisis-filled year; as it was, the avalanche of criticisms blindsided Paul. Arguing that the "consequences of methods and plans for artificial birth control . . . could open wide the way for marital infidelity and a general lowering of moral standards," Peter Hebblethwaite wrote that popular reaction to the encyclical unfairly skew-

116. Rossi Barilli, *Il Movimento gay*, 47–51. Bruno P. F. Vanrooij identified some activity by homosexual advocates in the early 1950s, particularly a short-lived magazine, *Sesso e Libertà*. See also Vanrooij, "Italy: Sexuality, Morality and Public Authority," in Eder, Hall, and Hekma, *Sexual Cultures in Europe*, 133.

117. "Pope Paul Denounces 'Horrible Insinuations,'" *New York Times*, April 5, 1976. See also Peyrefitte's interview, "Mea culpa? Ma fatemi il santo piacere," *Tempo*, April 4, 1976.

118. Gilla Vincenzo Gremigni, "Dove va la famiglia Cristiana?," *Rivista del clero italiano*, April 1961.

119. A copy of the decision can be found at http://www.giurcost.org/decisioni/1965/0009s-65.html (accessed May 23, 2018).

120. IPVI, Pg XII, b. 73, Pisa Morality Secretary/Gavuzzo, March 12, 1967.

ered him. Reaction to this teaching on birth control may have surprised him, and he pleaded that despite having been "submerged in a sea of documents," he could not "[give] in to contemporary opinion" on the issue. "Yet in his engaging simplicity," continued Hebblethwaite, "Paul did not realize how counterproductive his tone of pathos could sound. Those overwhelmed by the demands of bringing up children were not impressed by someone who was overwhelmed merely by paper." The encyclical clearly had no effect on Italy's declining birth rate.[121]

Concerns over the birthrate naturally directed focus on another element in the gathering storm—the youth question. The Italian youth revolution manifested itself in varied forms, sometimes hardly related to each other. Some acts were political, some cultural and sexual more atuned to lifestyle issues; but everywhere the rebels engaged in what the historian Guido Crainz called a "rapid and not very sad funeral mass for the old society."[122] The mass circulation *Famiglia Cristiana* illustrated some of the lifestyle changes in small ways. As miniskirts became more and more the rage, in 1964 the appearance on its pages of a naked knee certainly raised eyebrows. Father Atanasio's hard-bitten advice column for the magazine ended in 1966, replaced by quips from the softer don Giuseppe Zilli. The review ceased to condemn dancing as an absolute evil in its May issue, merely demoting it as a careless act that might lead to sin. A year later the magazine approved a young woman's choice of pants or culottes in the city while riding a Vespa.[123]

By 1964, the "topless" look reached Italian beaches, and trouble followed. *Il Ponte* noted one incident in Positano where two British tourists purchased the scandalous bathing suits from a local merchant. The Carabinieri tracked them down, brought them into the station, and persuaded them to forgo the beachwear.[124] A summer 1964 issue of *Concretezza* doubted that the new suits would go far. Simple feminine modesty would help draw the line, and the swimwear industry itself rejected the spread of the topless look, since one-piece suits necessarily yielded less profit—one must cost half of a bikini. Such nonsense stole

121. *Humanae vitae* is posted on the Vatican website: http://w2.vatican.va/content/paul-vi/en/encyclicals/documents/hf_p-vi_enc_25071968_humanae-vitae.html (accessed September 20, 2019); Hebblethwaite, *Paul VI: The First Modern Pope*, 516–20.

122. Crainz, *Il Paese mancato*, 19.

123. Niamh Cullen, "Morals, Modern Identities and the Catholic Woman: Fashion in *Famiglia Cristiana*, 1954–1968," *Journal of Modern Italian Studies* 18, no. 1 (2013): 47–48.

124. Cesari, *La censura in Italia oggi*, 166.

the focus from what some Catholics saw as a new problem at the shore, that of narcissistic young men who strutted up and down the beach with their chiseled physiques. Honed in gyms, the "new *licei*," claimed a 1964 *Concretezza* article, these peacocks stole the spotlight away from the poor beauty queens.[125]

Inspired by the Vatican Council and anxious that the faith not slide into irrelevance, some looked to music as one way to connect to youth culture. By the end of the 1960s, a few priests in working-class districts celebrated "beat" masses with guitars, an idea even adopted at the Pontifical Marianum College. In 1970, Rome's vicar general, Angelo Dell' Acqua, went unannounced to one such mass at the church of the Canadian Martyrs, where he watched from the back, "completely moved and . . . ecstatic to see the church full of young people singing, playing instruments and praying with such fervor and enthusiasm." Dell'Acqua could not resist giving the group a "lively and warm" word of encouragement. Soon after, Paul himself opened a mass at St. John Lateran with "la musica beat."[126]

In early 1966, the new times reached Milan's elite Liceo Parini, where three students—two boys and the daughter of the city's former *questore*—surveyed nine female students for the campus paper, the *Zanzara* (*Mosquito*). They printed their findings in an article, "What Today's Girls Are Thinking," which expressed concerns over parental relations, premarital sex, and religious guilt. Sex education based on medical texts served no one, said the respondents; rather, they called for a much broader vision which, one teenager insisted, required "sexual freedom and a complete reevaluation." Another argued that "when love exists, there cannot and must not be religious curbs." The *Zanzara* article triggered a backlash. The state launched an inquest and summoned the three authors, along with the head of the *liceo* and even the owner of the shop that printed the review. Based on an old Fascist mandate, furthermore, the youngsters had to submit to medical examinations for evidence of "defects" (*tare*). The two boys complied, but the questore's daughter refused. The *Zanzara* article had quickly become the *Zanzara* affair, and twenty thousand students took to the streets to protest the government's heavy hand. Despite the *apertura* coalition that still functioned under Prime Minis-

125. Mino Caudana, "Inchiostro simpatico," *Concretezza*, July 16, 1964.

126. Marco Impagliazzo, *La diocesi del Papa: La Chiesa di Roma e gli anni di Paolo VI (1963–1978)* (Milan: Guerini, 2006), 99–101.

ter Moro, Pietro Nenni came out in support of the students and wrote a public letter of support to the two boys' fathers, who turned out to be party comrades. In Rome, the Socialists organized a meeting at the Eliseo Theater, where those speaking for the students included Loris Fortuna, who had begun his work on divorce legislation. The Feltrinelli bookstore in the via Babuino enhanced its dissident reputation with an evening discussion devoted to the Zanzara affair. On the other side, the DC with neo-Fascist support sided with the Milan authorities. After five days, the inquest ended in acquittal for all except the printer, who received a fine for not submitting a copy of the offending edition with the courts. The Socialists declared it "a just sentence for modern Italy." The *Zanzara* affair quickly located itself in a rash of controversies over school politics and the press. Three other Milan *licei* had similar occurrences over articles on, for example, Vietnam or the Franco Regime in Spain. Turin also experienced some trouble, and in March 1966 Bologna's police sequestered another student paper, *Lo Spillo* from the Marconi Technical School.[127]

Licei, like the Parini, and universities took center stage in the youth revolt. Warning signs had already surfaced by the end of the 1950s, when almost half of Italian youngsters left school by age thirteen and only 20 percent completed their middle school education. The 1960s followed with an explosion in student numbers. A PCI reform bill in 1962 set the leaving age at fourteen for both sexes and helped to expand the number of secondary school students from 1.1 million in 1959 to 1.9 in 1969. At the same time, relaxation of university entrance requirements caused enrollments there to swell from 268,181 in 1960–61 to more than 450,000 in 1968, of which about one-third were women. The state tried to address the situation with a larger education budget, but everywhere students faced shortages, from textbooks to classroom space.[128] The "classic" revolts began as student protests against costs and overcrowding with an occupation of Milan's Catholic University in November of 1967. Trent followed in January with more occupations, demonstrations, and

127. Robert Lumley, *States of Emergency: Cultures of Revolt in Italy from 1968 to 1978* (London: Verso Press, 1990), 94–95; Crainz, *Il Paese mancato*, 205–8; Lussana, *L'Italia del divorzio*, 86–89; Cesari, *La censura in Italia oggi*, 167. On Milan protests and the events at the Eliseo and Feltrinelli's, see "Esempio di maturità e compostezza la marcia degli studenti," and "Manifestazione a Roma per i ragazzi del Parini," *Avanti!*, March 24 and March 25 (respectively), 1966. The Socialist paper published Nenni's letter to the father-comrades in the issue of March 25, 1966. On the verdict, see "Assolti," *Avanti!*, April 2, 1966. One of the defense lawyers was Giacomo Delitala, who had defended Bishop Fiordelli in his 1958 trial.

128. Lumley, *States of Emergency*, 51–56; Pojmann, *Italian Women and International Cold War Politics*, 171.

riots spreading across the peninsula and boiling through the year and into the next. That the trouble began at the Catholic University shocked many and stirred embarrassment and anger among others. The rector's first response was to expel one hundred and fifty students. Some Catholic rebels later landed in even more radical, revolutionary action, like Continuous Struggle (Lotta continua) and the Red Brigades (Brigate rosse).[129] In the CIF review *Cronache e opinion*, one observer huffed over these spoiled students, whose cheek grew from unrealistically self-absorbed ambitions.[130] The student revolts sometimes connected with growing labor unrest, which was aggravated by an economic slump at the end of the decade. Protests and strikes culminated in the "Hot Autumn" of 1969 and carried on into 1970.[131] Controversies over sex, youth culture, and revolt tossed Catholics into a chaos that led to what became their twin nightmares, legalization of divorce in 1970 and the referendum of 1974. Sandro Magister called this four- to five-year period "the Church in the storm," which ended with a "bitter awakening."[132]

Divorce

For the two or three decades after the war, in their determination to protect Catholic marriage and the family, Christian Democrats shied from mentioning divorce too much, hoping that the discussion would not spill out into open debate. On rare occasions when the Catholic reviews broached divorce, they often took aim at the United States and ridiculed Hollywood's hedonistic and vapid lifestyles, as Francesco Olgiati did for a 1957 issue of *Rivista del clero*.[133] The tactic of avoiding the subject seemed to work through the 1950s. One casualty of this was Renato Sansone's Little Divorce, which limped along—going nowhere—through the decade and into the early '60s. In 1961, Novara's archbishop thanked God in the *Rivista del clero* that Sansone's project enjoyed no traction and that Christian Democratic Italy would not share the fate of weaker governments that folded under what he saw as the international assault on marriage.[134] In 1960, however, a meeting of women jurists in Turin took

129. Richard Drake, "Catholics and the Italian Revolutionary Left of the 1960s," *Catholic Historical Review* 94, no. 3 (July 2008); Crainz, *Il Paese mancato*, 225–35; Lumley, *States of Emergency*, 77–86.

130. Pojmann, *Italian Women and International Cold War Politics*, 171–72.

131. Crainz, *Il Paese mancato*, 321–62.

132. Sandro Magister, *La politica vaticana e l'Italia 1943–1978* (Rome: Editori Riuniti, 1979), 391 and 447.

133. Francesco Olgiati, "Turlupinature divorziste," *Rivista del clero italiano*, September 1957.

134. Gremigni, "Dove va la famiglia Cristiana?" *Rivista del clero italiano*, April 1961.

up the larger subject of the indissolubility of marriage, and arguments pro and con became so fierce that the meeting threatened all semblance of collegiality and led to a decision to table all resolutions. Four years later, *Concretezza*'s article about another congress of women jurists, this time in Pesaro, sounded like a postmortem for the Little Divorce. Sansone spoke to the jurists while, outside, women of the Catholic CIF posted bills throughout the town proclaiming that "all women reject[ed] attempts to destroy the family." The drive to legalize divorce had been abandoned, insisted *Concretezza*, and now the women jurists could "return to occupy themselves with issues more serious, more pressing and more in keeping with the temperament and needs of Italian women."[135]

In October 1965, the Socialist Loris Fortuna took a turn at breaking the ice and introduced a new divorce bill, one regarding "cases of the breakdown of marriage" (*casi di scioglimento del matrimonio*). Less rigid than Sansone's earlier proposals, it permitted divorce for reasons of child abuse, five years of abandonment, mental infirmity, and recognition of foreign decrees. Fortuna's bid, however, seemed headed in the same direction as the earlier attempts. In her study, Diana De Vigili concluded that, by the end of the year, "divorce seemed destined to remain an academic question." Polls showed that, indeed, a large majority still opposed it. One such inquest from 1965 put the figures at 71 percent for men and 77 percent for women. Fortuna, in fact, found himself somewhat alone in his own PSI ranks and faced a skeptical party leader, Nenni. Some PCI factions, however, like the group associated with the review *Vie Nuove*, were open to the divorce option—supporting, for instance, Sansone's 1954 measure. And in 1956, a womens' group behind the review *Noi donne* had come around and urged some revisions on the party's position. But Togliatti's opposition to divorce dominated even after his death in 1964, and the PCI shied away from seriously addressing the issue until Pietro Ingrao raised it at a May 1969 meeting of the party Directorate, when it finally declared itself ready to fight.

The cause received another shot in the arm when in 1968 Fortuna encountered crucial backing in the lay camp, including a cosponsor in the Liberal Antonio Baslini, who brought the PLI's full support. To keep the issue on the right track, the editors at the pro-divorce magazine ABC arranged a meeting of the two sponsors with the Radical Marco Pannella,

135. Gigi Ghirotti, "Processo al matrimonio," *L'Europeo*, June 5, 1960; Clelia d'Inzillo, "Piccolo-divorzisti al convegno di Pesaro," *Concretezza*, October 1, 1964.

and the Fortuna-Baslini proposal took on steam. Polling, moreover, indicated shifting opinions. A DOXA survey taken in the summer of 1969 revealed that over 56 percent felt that divorce should be legal. Just under 30 percent still opposed it, and 14 percent remained undecided. But the numbers went back and forth. A year later, those opposed to divorce again outnumbered those who wanted it, 49 percent to 45.[136]

Divorce was emerging as a hotly debated topic, and charges flew on all sides. Between October 1965 and March 1966, *ABC* urged its readers to write in support of the Fortuna proposal, a push that resulted in thousands of letters and postcards delivered to his box at the Chamber of Deputies. Some of this, however, may have troubled the *divorzisti* camp, because, as the missives revealed, their supporters were overwhelmingly men, who wrote 22,774 notes—against 8,159 from women.[137] Along with already championing Braibanti, the Radical Party assumed an importance in this and other struggles for sexual liberation. A Radical Party–sponsored conference at the end of 1965 produced a League for the Institution of Divorce (Lega per l'istituzione del divorzio, or LID), which was formally launched in April 1966. Pannella led the organization with the assistance of Bruno Villabruna, an ex-Liberal who had served in the Scelba cabinet, but now stood among the founders of the Radical Party, and Judge Mario Berutti, who had just resigned the presidency of the National Magistrates Association over the Zanzara case. The LID maintained a newsletter with a circulation of 150,000 and enjoyed the support of a big mainstream magazine, *ABC*, which the state sometimes sequestered for its glossy photos of women in various stages of undress. In 1969, the Radical Party Congress gave birth to another organization, the Movement for the Liberation of the Woman (Movimento di liberazione della donna, or MLD), which joined the ranks with less mainstream but edgier feminist organizations, DEMAU and Rivolta femminile.[138]

On the other side, the Italian Episcopal Conference roundly denounced the divorce project, and, to the Catholic *Avvenire*, Cardinal Urbani expressed his concern on "the direct and immediate danger regard-

136. Scirè, *Il divorzio in Italia*, 26–27; Diana De Vigili, *La battaglia sul divorzio: Dalla Costituente al Referendum* (Milan: Franco Angeli, 2000), 41; Lussana, *L'Italia del divorzio*, 48–49, 52, 82–83, 100; Martin Clark, David Hine, and R. E. M. Irving, "Divorce—Italian Style," *Parliamentary Affairs* 27 (1974): 351.

137. Lussana, *L'Italia del divorzio*, 92–93. Fortuna claimed 36,000 letters; Alessandro Coletti, *Il divorzio in Italia: Storia di una battaglia civile e democratica* (Rome: Giulio Savelli editore, 1974), 134–35.

138. De Vigili, *La battaglia sul divorzio*, 44–47; Mark Seymour, *Debating Divorce in Italy: Marriage and the Making of Modern Italians, 1860–1974* (New York: Palgrave, 2006), 195; Coletti, *Il divorzio in Italia*, 132–37; Signorelli, "Women in Italy in the 1970s," in Bull and Giorgio, *Speaking Out and Silencing*, 53–55. On the Berutti resignation, see "Sempre più divisi i magistrati sul Parini," *Avanti!*, March 27, 1966.

ing the stability of the family."[139] In April 1966, the CEI called upon all of the faithful to defend the family against the challenges of "polygamy, the pain of divorce, so-called free love and other distortions [*deformazioni*]."[140] Pope Paul followed in 1967 with two discourses against divorce—at St. Peter's Square in his January 8 *Angelus* and shortly after to the Roman *Rota*, the church's top annulment tribunal.[141] Such pronouncements prompted the authors of one 1968 book to denounce the anti-divorce camp's "irrational fear fed by false and shoddy propaganda."[142]

The pro-divorce (*divorzisti*) camp always happily noticed when famous Catholics waffled or misstepped. Such an incident occurred toward the end of the Second Vatican Council when the Egyptian Melkite archbishop Elias Zoghby called for some accommodation to help wounded spouses in marital breakups. Although on the following day the Holy See roundly condemned that position, the damage was done, and papers announced that the church had modified its position on divorce.[143] Twice, to a meeting of the Italian League for Divorce and on the chamber floor, Loris Fortuna even claimed that Zoghby's speech persuaded him to present his proposal at the Montecitorio. He declared that what "could be peacefully discussed in the Vatican could also be peacefully discussed in the Parliament of the Italian Republic."[144]

The sixties had quietly been taking their toll, and suddenly the DC's tactic of evasion appeared to be failing. As a vote on the Fortuna Baslini bill approached, panic spread among the Catholics, and a glance at their media reveals a new resolve to engage the *divorzisti* head on. By 1966, *Noi uomini*, for example, presented argument after argument illustrating how the attack on indissolubility would destroy marriage, family, and even love.[145] In March 1967, at Catholic Action headquarters, Raimondo Manzini expressed anxiety over the sorry state of Catholic response in the face of firm and determined secularist adversaries, while Camillo Rossi declared the old reluctance to face the issue squarely now yielded only "bitter fruits."[146] Such accusations were aimed mostly at the DC and its

139. Sportelli, *La Conferenza episcopale italiana*, 274–75.

140. Lussana, *L'Italia del divorzio*, 94.

141. Seymour, *Debating Divorce in Italy*, 199–200; Lussana, *L'Italia del divorzio*, 102–3.

142. Piero Fortuna, Luciana Jorio, and Attilio Pandini, *Rapporto sul divorzio in Italia* (Milan: Longanesi, 1968), 5.

143. O'Malley, *What Happened at Vatican II?*, 260–61.

144. Fortuna, Jorio, and Pandini, *Rapporto sul divorzio in Italia*, 49–51; Lussana, *L'Italia del divorzio*, 80–81.

145. "Matrimonio in serie?," *Noi uomini*, August 2, 1966.

146. IPVI, Pg IX, b. 6, Minutes of *Giunta centrale* meeting, March 11–12, 1967.

policy of avoiding divorce discussion in Parliament. At a summer 1969 meeting of party leaders, however, Mariano Rumor, who became prime minister in December 1968, again pushed the avoidance ploy.[147] The Holy See resented this, and the scholar Agostino Giovagnoli wrote that divorce brought relations between the church and the state, the DC state, to their lowest ebb since Mussolini's anti-Semitic decrees in 1938.[148]

In October 1969, with a month to go before the chamber vote, the CEI approved the pastoral document "Marriage and Family Today in Italy." Italy had ceased, it said, to be a country where most families were large, lived in rural zones or "centers of production," and followed the wishes of husband and father. Now, continued the document, families lived in urban "centers of consumption" where husband and wife shared their authority more equally. Factors in the story included the demographic slide, industrialization, democracy, secularization, and the "intensified study of human sexuality," although the church reminded everybody that it "never taught that sex was bad." Rather, unguided youthful exuberance required better "education in chastity." New awareness of women's dignity, continued the document, warranted special attention. Drawing mostly from *Gaudium et spes* and *Humanae vitae*, the CEI emphasized that despite all modern developments, the twofold purpose of sexual relations remained—to unite husband and wife and to produce children. The pastoral document identified the indissolubility of marriage as essential to a family's stability and, therefore, it concluded with a "declaration on divorce." Although the bishops recognized that many problems in marriage needed to be addressed, indissolubility, they affirmed, guaranteed the dignity "of the person, the spouses, and the children."[149]

When the Fortuna-Baslini bill first came to a vote in the chamber on November 28, 1969, the DC found that, with only some embarrassing neo-Fascist support, it stood alone in its opposition to divorce.[150] Consequently, the bill passed by a count of 325 to 283 and moved on to the

147. Scirè, *Il divorzio in Italia*, 47–48. Already in May of 1968 Rumor privately confessed the ultimate impossibility of holding the line on divorce; Eliana Versace, "Giovanni Battista Montini—Paolo VI e la questione del divorzio," *Studium* 110, no. 3 (May–June 2014): 422.

148. Giovagnoli, *Il Partito Italiano*, 138–42.

149. CEI, *Matrimonio e famiglia oggi in Italia*, found at http://www.progettoculturale.it/cci_new/documenti_cei/2015-09/11-1047/Matrimonio_e_famiglia_oggi_in_Italia.pdf (accessed September 20, 2019). The text was published in the November 15, 1969, issue of *Notiziario della conferenza episcopale italiana*.

150. De Vigili, *La battaglia sul divorzio*, 39–41, 82; Scirè, *Il divorzio in Italia*, 36–37, 45; Maria Elisabetta de Franciscis, *Italy and the Vatican: The 1984 Concordat between Church and State* (New York: Peter Lang, 1989, 79; Seymour, *Debating Divorce in Italy*, 202–3.

Senate. In a Christmas letter to Andreotti, Paul bitterly confessed that he found no comfort in the "great wound inflicted . . . on the stability and sacredness of the family." On the following January 30, the Holy See lodged a formal protest with the Italian Embassy: that legalization of divorce violated the Concordat's Article 34 regarding matrimony.[151] Church irritation also surfaced in the diaries of Italy's ambassador to the Vatican, Gian Franco Pompei. In March of 1970, for example, an increasingly frustrated Pope Paul refused to meet with Rumor despite his firm declaration against divorce, although he had once counseled the prime minister on the need to take firm control of the party.[152] In a memorandum of June 15, Paul worried about the damage that divorce would inflict on the nation. "What misfortune would [it] bring on Italy," he wrote, "for its legal tradition, for the health of the social fabric [*compagine sociale*], for the teaching of *costume* and of the real concept of love, for the sense of duty, for so many children—orphans of parents with no sense of responsibility, for the split among souls and for the duty among the faithful and the Church to protest. It would be a very unfortunate 'political' act."[153] Ten days later, on June 25, Paul's deputy secretary of state, Archbishop Giovanni Benelli, bluntly warned Pompei that the movement toward divorce preoccupied the pontiff, who "as Primate of Italy and bishop of Rome" considered it "a profound offense to the basic moral norms of the Christian conception of life." After Aldo Moro confided to him that Paul's obstructionist stance endangered the Rumor government, the diplomat reported to a third party that Moro sympathized with "*povero* Pompei" who had to deal with "duplicitous" characters.[154] On August 6, a rattled Rumor resigned and was replaced as prime minister by his DC colleague Emilio Colombo. "Moro told me in great secrecy," recorded Pompei, "that the crisis was directly determined by the Vatican."[155]

Naturally, many DC leaders, like Giorgio La Pira, strongly identified with the anti-divorce camp. He appealed to the socialism of president

151. Sportelli, *La Conferenza episcopale italiana*, 276; Versace, "Giovanni Battista Montini—Paolo VI e la questione del divorzio," 424; Gian Franco Pompei, *Un ambasciatore in Vaticano: Diario 1967–1977* (Bologna: Il Mulino, 1994), 52–53 128–29n4.

152. Pompei, *Un ambasciatore in Vaticano*, 57; Riccardi, "Il Cattolicesimo della repubblica," in Sabbatucci and Vidotto, *Storia d'Italia*, 266.

153. Gian Maria Vian, "Montini e il divorzio trent'anni dopo," *Vita e pensiero*, no. 3 (2003): 103.

154. Pompei, *Un ambasciatore in Vaticano*, 85–91.

155. Pompei, *Un ambasciatore in Vaticano*, 100. See also Pompei's entry for July 30, 1970 (103–4), which rejected a charge from *Il Mondo* that Archbishop Casaroli had a hand in the Vatican's campaign against Prime Minister Rumor.

of the chamber Sandro Pertini and urged him to consider divorce as a decrepit remnant "of aged capitalist and bourgeois society."[156] He tried the same thing with the Communists twice, in November of 1969 and September of 1970, insisting to Ingrao and Nilde Iotti that opposition to divorce was a revolutionary and anti-bourgeois act. Not Togliatti, he claimed, nor Gramsci, nor Lenin would ever have voted for it.[157] If asked to identify the face of the anti-divorce sentiment in the late 1960s, however, one might have picked Guido Gonella, who campaigned tirelessly against it. A *divorzista* leaflet aimed at Gonella circulated in 1966 by the Italian Movement Favorable to Divorce (MIFAD), challenging his position point by point. It claimed that Gonella erred when he said that the gospels did not permit divorce. Archbishop Zoghby's infamous statement exposed that as false, as did the Greek Orthodox Church's accommodation of divorce. Gonella argued that support for dissolution came mostly from big guns and fat cats, "the corrupt and Voltairean bourgeoisie and cinema billionaires." He also maintained that, as a purely economic institution, the Common Market should have nothing to say on divorce. Its first impulse had been economic, but, noted the MIFAD circular, and as Gonella knew perfectly well, it planned to expand into politics and social issues. Besides, it continued, the famous American Catholic Senator Robert Kennedy had voted for divorce.[158] On April 17, 1970, a tired and dispirited Gonella signaled to Andreotti that he would only vote out of party loyalty. The DC had made some bad decisions in other fields, but first and second on his list were the pending breakup of the family and the coming challenge to religious peace through "violations of the Concordat."[159]

After the first chamber vote in November 1969, Fortuna-Baslini went to the Senate, where, after some modifications from the DC's Giovanni Leone, a revised version passed, 164 to 150, on October 9, 1970. It then returned to the chamber for a final vote. All eyes turned to the Montecitorio, and, in front of it, the Piazza di Monte Citorio became a theater of protests, placards, and histrionics. There, on November 10, Pannella and another Radical declared a hunger strike until the question's resolution. At the end of the month, Cardinal dell'Acqua urged the Roman

156. Scoppola, "Gonella e la crisi degli anni Settanta," in *Guido Gonella tra Governo: Parlamento e Partito*, ed. Giuseppe Bertagna, Alfredo Canavero, Augusto D'Angelo, and Andrea Simoncini (Rome and Soveria Mannelli: Istituto Luigi Sturzo—Rubbettino Editore, 2007), 1:290–91.

157. Scirè, *Il divorzio in Italia*, 54–55 and 78.

158. IS Fondo Gonella, Series 3, b. 51, f. 2, MIFAD circular, 1966.

159. IS Fondo Gonella, Series 3, b. 51, f. 3, Gonella/Andreotti, April 17, 1970.

faithful to pray for Italy's deliverance "from the pain of divorce." On November 29 parishes across the city instituted prayer vigils for the defeat of the bill, to which the LID retaliated with a "divorce vigil" in the piazza.[160] Inside, forty-two DC deputies led by Gonella, Scalfaro, and Greggi tried a last-ditch effort to derail the bill, but to no avail. Finally, at the end of a record-setting six-day session, and after some exhausted deputies had collapsed on the floor, at 5:40 in the morning of December 1, 1970, Pertini announced that by a tally of 319 to 286, the Chamber of Deputies approved the reconciled Fortuna-Baslini bill as law number 898. Divorce had come to Italy. LID offices quickly transformed themselves into clearinghouses for couples in search of information and help. The first to file were a man and woman from Modena, "the very opposite of the film stars whose marriage failures had previously grabbed the attention of the press," wrote one scholar. "They were ordinary people who just wanted to get on with their separate lives." The Jesuit review *Aggiornamenti sociali* pointed to this moment as one "destined to affect profoundly the social and political life of a nation." Approval of divorce, continued the analysis, ended the "juridical protection" of the family and put one spouse at the other's mercy.[161] Pope Paul heard the news while on his tour of East Asia and Australia. The Holy See released a statement to express his "deep grief" but also to remind the government that implementation of the measure would violate the Lateran Pacts. Back in Rome a week later, to about sixty thousand of the faithful in St. Peter's Square, Paul divulged his anguish that derived, as Ambassador Pompei reported, from the feeling that his beloved flock had let him down.[162] Similar laments rose from pulpits across the peninsula. The archbishop of Siena called on his "dearest children" to return to God. "Today," he wrote, "the family is in crisis." "Changed social conditions" had made "individual liberty . . . the supreme law, although it reveals itself in the social body as a law of fragmentation and death. The family is the mirror of God, and if the mirror is dirtied or broken, we will never understand the love of God."[163]

160. Coletti, *Il divorzio in Italia*, 145–50.

161. Seymour, *Debating Divorce in Italy*, 205–14; Coletti, *Il divorzio in Italia*, 155; Angelo Macchi, "Divorzio e referendum," *Aggiornamenti sociali*, January 1971.

162. "Grief Voiced by Pope on Divorce Law," *New York Times*, December 2, 1970; de Franciscis, *Italy and the Vatican*, 119–20.

163. Pratt, *Walled City*, 191–94; de Franciscis, *Italy and the Vatican*, 80.

The Referendum

DC deputies reacted at once to their parliamentary defeat. Within hours of the bill's approval, a group of twenty-five of them, including Sergio Cotta, La Pira, and Greggi, along with the renegade Socialist Lina Merlin, announced their goal to find the one-half million signatures needed to call a referendum on the divorce issue. Gabrio Lombardi and Merlin agreed to serve as president and vice president of a new National Committee for the Divorce Referendum (Comitato nazionale per il referendum sul divorzio, or CNRD). Their drive enjoyed overwhelming success, presenting the Cassation Court with 1,370,000 names, well ahead of schedule and with over 800,000 more signatures than needed.[164] Red tape and other snags, however, plagued the Catholics. Since the government had to determine a date for the vote, the quick signature drive proved moot—they weren't ready for it. The DC decided against holding the vote in 1972, since they feared that the public might confuse it with upcoming national elections. But this also turned out to be irrelevant, as the law did not permit staging such an election and a referendum in the same year. Delay, then, meant postponing the divorce vote until May of 1974 and losing it in a maelstrom of regulations that has been called "a marvel of Italian complexity."[165] Holding the referendum almost four years after the parliamentary vote could not yield any positive consequences for the DC.

In his study *Divorce in Italy*, Giambattista Scirè labeled the time between the legalization of divorce in December 1970 and the May 1974 referendum "without a doubt, one of [the Republic's] most important moments of caesura. [It] ... closed one historic phase and opened another."[166] British observers queried, "If it is true that there are only three things in life worth discussing—politics, religion and sex—then it is no wonder that the Italian Referendum on divorce of 12 May 1974 aroused so much interest. The debate was a fascinating one, involving serious discussions of Church-State relations, of clericalism and anti-clericalism, of women's place in society, of marriage and family, of civil liberties and the institution of the popular referendum."[167] The referendum also placed in

164. De Vigili, *La battaglia sul divorzio*, 79–80; Seymour, *Debating Divorce in Italy*, 214; on the referendum, see also Crainz, *Il Paese mancato*, 498–506.

165. Seymour, *Debating Divorce in Italy*, 214. Arthur Marwick's decision to identify 1974 as the end of the "Long 1960s" that began with 1958 holds particular relevance for Italy; Marwick, *Sixties*.

166. Scirè, *Il divorzio in Italia*, vii.

167. Clark, Hine, and Irving, "Divorce—Italian Style," 333.

a clear light the extent of Catholic Italy's "incomprehension of the secularization processes." Many considered it in the narrow contexts of one's own well-being or political battles; and it was said, probably unfairly, that Amintore Fanfani, who returned in 1973 as DC secretary, wished to use the vote only as a vehicle to rally the party.[168]

Regardless of Fanfani's motives, the church had more at stake with the referendum, and it scrambled to emphasize possible alternatives for couples in bad marriages. During the 1960s, it had been working to make annulment less costly and quicker, and numbers expanded from over three hundred granted in 1965 to more than eight hundred in 1970. In his *motu proprio* of March 28, 1971, *Causas matrimoniales*, Paul sped up the process even more and promised reforms in a revised Code of Canon Law. He followed this in October 1972 with another decree to reduce legal fees at the *Rota*.[169] But these appeared as half-measures, and the threat of clerical fracture on the issue certainly troubled the pontiff. Peter Hebblethwaite pointed to Pope Paul's considerable caution on the matter with which he and many of his brother bishops approached the referendum, while Massimo Faggioli also discerned Paul's significant moderation, especially by 1973. The pontiff informed the Episcopal Conference that he would abide with any decision they made, though he might personally disagree with it. At the CEI, Paul's chief representative was the secretary general and a friend, Archbishop Enrico Bartoletti, who displayed the same forbearance, although even he admitted to being perplexed by the pontiff's shifting. Paul's stance, however, hardened in 1974, making life more difficult for his factotum.[170]

The divorce crisis and the referendum energized much of the Catholic militant base. In 1968, Mario Missiroli in the *Messaggero* announced

168. Scoppola, "Tra Chiesa e società: il problema storico della Democrazia Cristiana," in Acerbi, *La Chiesa e l'Italia*, 388–89. Scoppola draws from Ambassador Pompei's memoirs, *Un ambasciatore in vaticano*. Pierluigi Castellani concluded that Fanfani was convinced of victory and that the vote would bring the Catholic Movement together; Pierluigi Castellani, "La Democrazia cristiana dal centro-sinistra al delitto Moro (1962–1978)," in *Storia della Democrazia Cristiana*, vol. 4, *Dal Centro Sinistra agli 'Anni di Piombo' (1962–1978)*, ed. Francesco Malgeri (Rome: Edizioni cinque lune, 1989), 73–74.

169. The English translation of *Causas matrimoniales* can be found at the Vatican website: https://w2.vatican.va/content/paul-vi/en/motu_proprio/documents/hf_p-vi_motu-proprio_19710328_causas-matrimoniales.html (accessed September 20, 2019). See also Mauro Mellini, *Così annulla la sacra rota: Divorzio di classe nell'Italia clericale* (Rome: Edizioni Samonà e Savelli, 1969), 113; Coletti, *Il divorzio in Italia*, 163–64; and Clark, Hine, and Irving, "Divorce—Italian Style," 341.

170. Mellini, *Così annulla la sacra rota*, 116–26. Figures sometime vary, often to include the dispensation of marriage vows because of one party's inability to consummate the marriage. As the CEI's number-two man, Secretary General Bartoletti served under Angelo Poma, president from 1969 until 1979; Massimo Faggioli, "Tra referendum sul divorzio e revisione del Concordato: Enrico Bartoletti segretario della CEI (1972–1976)," *Contemporanea* 4, no. 2 (April 2001): 263; Versace, "Giovanni Battista Montini—Paolo VI e la questione del divorzio," 430; Hebblethwaite, *Paul VI: The First Modern Pope*, 619–21.

"Gedda's return." Three years after Pope Paul's rebuke, he wrote, Gedda emerged with a speech in Milan and an appearance on Vatican Radio. Then, with national elections scheduled for May 1972, on March 19 Gedda issued the first edition of *Ripresa*, an "independent weekly" that identified with the Civic Committees. Gedda explained that the review's title came easily. "The delicate moment through which the nation passes," he wrote, "urgently demands a quick reawakening [*ripresa*] and a stong committment on the part of the Catholic world." For *Ripresa*'s first issue, Gedda rejected Paul's political moderation and boldly called for a "strong party of Catholics" similar to that which won the day in 1948. Asked about "some priests" who had been distancing themselves from politics, Gedda stated that such disengagement masked exhaustion and lack of courage. As unpleasant as it may have been for Gedda, he saw Italy's salvation hinged on a DC win; and since Catholic Action "isn't what it was twenty years ago," the Civic Committees must step up to assist the party. But the DC also had to stick to its guns and protect the nation from "an arrogant and malicious lay minority." Voting for Catholic members of opposition parties was useless because none of them ever lifted a finger against divorce when they had the chance. If Italy failed to go with the Christian Democrats, concluded Gedda, abortion was just around the corner, followed by "the end of Catholic schools and religious instruction, and who knows what else?"[171]

Anticipating the referendum, the DC's research office circulated a list of charges and rebuttals on divorce. To the accusation that divorce had become truly popular, for example, the Christian Democrat should answer that its acceptance remained anchored in the wealthy bourgeoisie. Party members should also consider the superficial nature of polling questions that evaded deep worries or dismissed them as simplistic: the fate of children and the wife, for example, or parents' fears that their children would grow up in a community without bearings. To the claim that divorce was just a private affair, the Catholic should insist that marriage was a bedrock social institution and that if the bonds between husband and wife unraveled, so too would those that held society together.[172]

The pope called the referendum "an audacious risk," and the Christian Democrats understood the perils, too. To bolster the DC's anti-

171. Mario Missiroli, "Il ritorno di Gedda," *Il Messaggero*, May 5, 1968; "Gedda: Necessario un forte partito di cattolici," *Ripresa*, March 19, 1972.

172. IS Fondo Gonella, Series 3, b. 51, f. 3, DC Sezione Inchiesta circular, April 3, 1974.

divorce camp with reliable troops, Gedda's Civic Committees had plenty of work to do. Despite the fight left in some sectors, however, Catholic Action's depressing membership collapse at the time must have dampened some of the enthusiasm. *Paese sera* pointed to a poll of CC members, citing one militant from Faenza who "bitterly admitted" that "Catholic Action, the ACLI, unions, parishes, priests and certain factions in the DC" had already abandoned the cause.[173] Along with the CCs, the DC also counted on the new Communion and Liberation organization, founded in Milan in 1954 and reformed in 1969. Yet it became clearer and clearer that the referendum was breaking Catholic unity; and indeed, as Scirè noted, almost every faction cracked on the divorce question. Some even declared themselves part of a Catholics for No movement with the aim of maintaining divorce's new legality. Members included Pietro Scoppola, Mario Gozzini, Ruggero Orfei, Pasquale Saraceno, the future prime minister Paolo Prodi, and Piero Pratesi, the editor of *Il Popolo*, who later switched his allegiance to the PCI. The ex-leader of Catholic Action youth (GIAC), Carlo Carretto, who suffered defeat at Gedda's hand in 1952, also joined the fray. Now a cleric, he declared himself on the "no" side despite a Vatican warning (*monito*). The FUCI, representing Catholic university students, declared in favor of divorce in 1971.[174] DC journals tended toward skepticism or even defeatism, and some predicted "electoral suicide," while the *Avvenire* and *Famiglia Cristiana* seemed surer of a positive outcome. In Parliament, except for the neo-Fascists and a tiny Monarchist faction, none of the DC's major allies stuck with it.[175] The historian Mark Seymour suggested, furthermore, that the party unwisely relied on many voters who backed it because it was the bulwark of anti-Communism rather than because it was a Catholic party. They might not fall in line for a narrowly sectarian idea like the battle against divorce. The "most obvious" fear, however, among Catholics "was the political undesirability of doing anything that might throw them into [the MSI's] arms ... which would tarnish their image and alienate the

173. Pope Paul's comment came in a memorandum he wrote in November 1971; Vian, "Montini e il divorzio trent'anni dopo," 104; Mario Lenzi, "L'esercito della salvezza," *Paese sera*, March 6, 1974, article also located in FVC Fondo Gedda, b. 347; Magister, *La politica vaticana e l'Italia*, 409. Despite Paul's caution, Eliana Versace pointed out that he had been thinking of a referendum on divorce as early as 1968; Versace, "Giovanni Battista Montini—Paolo VI e la questione del divorzio," 428.

174. De Vigili, *La battaglia sul divorzio*, 144; Lussana, *L'Italia del divorzio*, 160–61; Scirè, *Il divorzio in Italia*, ix; on the FUCI, see Sportelli, *La Conferenza episcopale italiana*, 270–71; Zizola, "I vescovi e il referendum," *Testimonianze*, April–May 1974, 299.

175. De Vigili, *La battaglia sul divorzio*, 96; Norman Kogan, *A Political History of Italy: The Postwar Years* (New York: Praeger, 1983), 283–84.

party's left wing." The *Voce repubblicana* offered another explanation for the lack of gusto. So many of the faithful, they argued, would simply never divorce anyway, so why charge into a fight to keep it illegal?[176]

The worries of Pope Paul and Luigi Gedda, moreover, might have been well founded in that the anti-divorce camp could not even count on full support from the clergy. Most clerics proved moderate on the issue, and many refrained from using the pulpit to discuss it. While it could fall into line with statements on the referendum that recalled the Tridentine era, the CEI also suffered internal acrimony. Archbishop Bartoletti floated a draft that, while recalling the "principles of Christian marriage," nevertheless urged Catholics to vote their consciences in the spirit of the Vatican Council. The CEI shot down the Bartoletti draft at its February 18, 1974, meeting.[177] One month later, Catholic Action, frustrated at being "set adrift" by the Episcopal Conference, adopted a progressive document that recalled the Bartoletti draft and cautioned against viewing the referendum as a crusade, as well as cautioning against those projects designed "to pollute" democratic actions and "erode the institutions of the nation."[178] Relations had grown so bad that the AC's President Agnes received instructions from the pontiff to "reestablish at least a formal common line between Catholic Action and the CEI."[179] Elsewhere, clergy raised their voices against what they considered the official stiff-necked stance. Jesuits at the Gregorian University, for instance, in the light of Vatican II, questioned the validity of "coercive" secular laws to enforce morality. Don Giulio Girardi, a young professor of philosophy at the Pontifical Salesian Athenaeum, known for promoting dialogue with Marxists, also invited controversy by promoting legal divorce.[180] Elsewhere, for second-guessing the *anti-divorzisti* camp, the Benedictines suspended from the order the abbot of Saint Paul outside the Walls, while the patriarch of Venice sent letters to twenty priests ordering them to avoid *divorzista* events. Just before the referendum, the archbishop of Ravenna condemned a Catholics for No manifesto signed by forty-

176. Seymour, *Debating Divorce in Italy*, 148; "Cattolici sempre più divisi," *Voce repubblicana*, May 4, 1974; Sandro Bonella, "Contro l'integralismo," *Voce repubblicana*, May 5, 1974.

177. Douglas Wertman, "The Catholic Church and Italian Politics: The Impact of Secularization," in *Religion in West European Politics*, ed. Suzanne Berger (London and Totowa, N.J.: Frank Cass, 1982); Faggioli, "Tra referendum sul divorzio e revisione del Concordato," 262–63; Zizola, "I vescovi e il referendum," 295.

178. De Marco, *Storia dell'Azione Cattolica negli anni settanta*, 130–31. The accusation of being "set adrift" as well as "political blackmail" can be found on 136.

179. Zizola, "I vescovi e il referendum," 299.

180. Scirè, *Il divorzio in Italia*, 57–58 and 73–74.

seven clergy. In another case near Viterbo, a priest speaking for moderation was heckled by a "Brother Giuseppe" who had come from the local monastery.[181]

With their backs more and more up against the wall, a siege mentality took grip among many Catholics. Perhaps bouncing off ABC's pronouncement that the war over divorce was a second *Risorgimento*, Ambassador Pompei compared the Italian kingdom's 1870 attack on papal Rome to what he labeled the "new Porta Pia." Gonella continued to stump tirelessly, often with Cardinal Ugo Poletti, but confessed in his review, *Società nuova*, that with the writing on the wall, Italian politics had come full circle—that the Communists were exacting their revenge for the 1948 election.[182] The *Corriere della sera* reported in April that, with a month to go before the referendum, Fanfani even warned husbands that divorce would allow "your wives to leave you and run off with a young girl." That same month, in Taranto, a desperate Fanfani assured wives that under the current laws their men may wander a bit, but most would return to the nest. "Tomorrow," he continued, "with divorce, who knows?"[183] Andreotti cynically added that *divorzista* victory would lead to abortion, "unnatural loves," legalization of drug use and dealing, and support for emerging radical terrorist organizations.[184] Moro, on the other hand, distanced himself from the campaign.[185] Only a few days before the vote, on May 8, the *Osservatore Romano* asked how a marriage could survive if, with divorce, it faced its demise at any moment. Day by day, the paper stated, spouses would come to ask themselves, "Do we continue or do we end it?"[186] The DC received one final blow before the big vote, a series of scandals that stretched from Christmas to Easter. Concerning Mideast oil, bribery, and phony stock quotes, as one report said, "the party emerged from the affair badly scathed." In her study of divorce in Italy, Fiamma Lussana concluded that "the Catholic world [was] in shambles."[187]

181. Clark, Hine, and Irving, "Divorce—Italian Style," 350–51; "Due preti, un frate e un insegnante di religione," *Voce repubblicana*, May 3, 1974; "Il Vescovo di Ravenna ai sacerdoti dissenzienti," *OR*, May 10, 1974.

182. Scoppola, "Gonella e la crisi degli anni Settanta," 290; "Il gregge abandonato," *Voce repubblicana*, May 7, 1974; Faggioli, "Tra referendum sul divorzio e revisione del Concordato," 264. On ABC, see De Vigili, *La battaglia sul divorzio*, 57–58.

183. Scirè, *Il divorzio in Italia*, 1; Seymour, *Debating Divorce in Italy*, 220.

184. Impagliazzo, *La diocesi del Papa*, 110–11. Andreotti used the term "Tupamaros" as a blanket term for the radicals on the left.

185. Clark, Hine, and Irving, "Divorce—Italian Style," 350.

186. Giovanni Sales, "Continuiamo o chiudiamo?," *OR*, May 8, 1974.

187. Clark, Hine, and Irving, "Divorce—Italian Style," 350; Lussana, *L'Italia del divorzio*, 165.

Italy voted on May 12. Accounting for between 2 and 3 percent blank or mutilated ballots, the "yes" (end divorce) tally was just under 13.2 million, or 40.9 percent, while the "no" (keep divorce) camp totaled just over 19 million, or 59.1 percent. "No" beat "yes" among both men and women. It beat "yes" in the north by 62.6 percent to 37.4; in the center by 65.2 to 34.8; and in the islands by 52.9 to 47.1. Only in the south did "no" surpass "yes": 52.1 to 47.9 percent.[188] The Communist leader Enrico Berlinguer declared it "the first mass lay victory in Italian history."[189] The *Corriere della sera* praised Italy's "civic maturity," while *La Stampa* declared, "Italy is a modern nation."[190] Three days later, to an audience of newlyweds, Pope Paul confessed his "shock and pain," particularly toward "not a few" clerics who refused to close ranks with the rest of the church. He told the new couples, however, not to lose heart because "God's law [hadn't] changed."[191] *Avvenire* attributed the loss to Italy's "profound transformation of *costume* and culture," while the *Osservatore Romano* saw the struggle as one between "cowardice and martyrdom." A bitter Gedda blamed the DC, sick with "autoagression," as the cause of its own downfall. Even worse, he wrote, were the parish priests, the religious, and religion teachers who flocked to the "no" camp and gave the PCI one-third of its new recruits.[192]

Headaches among the faithful did not end with the referendum, which had yanked the last optimism from them and put them on the perennial defense. Agostino Giovagnoli noted that "the Catholic question" erupted with the events of 1974—a rejection of "Italian Catholic backwardness [that was] incompatable . . . with a nation moving toward modernity." This resulted in "a broad-based attempt to isolate, culturally and politically, the DC, and separating it from the Catholic world."[193] Barely more than a year after the May vote, the DC faced another serious defeat when regional elections in June 1975 brought the Communist Party to within less than two points of it. The historian of the DC, Francesco Malgeri, believed that the referendum and the 1975 vote marked "the most difficult crisis in [the party's] long history."[194] As Pierluigi

188. "Il voto del 12 maggio," *Concretezza*, June 1, 1974.

189. Francesco Barbagallo, *Enrico Berlinguer* (Rome: Carocci editore, 2006), 201.

190. Diego Galli, *Pannella: La vita e l'eredità* (Rome: Castelvecchi, 2016), 44.

191. "Paolo VI agli sposi: 'La legge di Dio non è cambiata,'" *OR*, May 16, 1974.

192. Luigi Gedda, "Dove va l'Italia cattolica?," *Ripresa*, September 27–28, 1975.

193. Giovagnoli, *Chiesa e democrazia*, 115.

194. Francesco Malgeri, Introduction, in *Storia della Democrazia Cristiana*, vol. 4, *Dal Centro Sinistra agli 'Anni di Piombo' (1962–1978)*, ed. Francesco Malgeri (Rome: Edizioni cinque lune, 1989), p.vii; Cuminetti, *Il dissenso cattolico in Italia*, 244–45.

Castellani put it, "the end of . . . Christian Democratic hegemony" had arrived.[195] Sensing that the knives were drawn, Pope Paul employed his trusted Bartoletti to help save the battered Fanfani as DC secretary. With little faith in his task, Bartoletti wrote, "Fanfani doesn't understand the situation. He only thinks in tactical maneuvers, sincere, but unfit." In the end, rancor and, as Bartoletti put it, a "witch hunt" took over and led to Fanfani's replacement by Benigno Zaccagnini as party leader.[196] Twice more, nevertheless, Fanfani would serve as prime minister in the 1980s. Yet the stocky dynamo was always easily parodied, and he remained the butt of Marxist and lay derision. June 1975, for instance, saw the stage premier of *Fanfani Kidnapped* (*Fanfani rapito*), a brutal skewering from the renegade Dario Fo. In the play, the prime minister is abducted by what he believes are Red Brigade terrorists until he learns that Andreotti was the real culprit behind the deed, hoping to gain sympathy votes out of it. To save his own skin, the gutless prisoner immediately blames others, from De Gasperi to Scelba and Gonella, for the party's problems. The farce continues after Fanfani dies, when he pleads his case in heaven before the *Padreterno*, the Madonna, and Christ. Christ is boiling water when Fanfani meets him, prompting the question, "What are you going to have to eat?" "It's not for eating," answers the Savior, "It's for the trial . . . it's for you!" It is hard to think of Fo's play now without recalling the real kidnapping and murder of Aldo Moro less than three years later. During the days of theatrical censorship, the Christian Democrats probably could not have prevented the staging of *Fanfani rapito* based on its politics, although they might have had a better argument with its depiction of heaven.[197]

With his long ears and perpetual shrug, Andreotti also became the butt of jokes, often portrayed as a cartoonish bat or vampire. He sensed the defeat, and the referendum caused him to feel a sudden loneliness in the Catholic movement—one that, he feared, would lead to some "macabre trips."[198] Moro also lamented that Christian Democracy had transformed itself from the Catholic party to "the party of the state," an organization devoid of a spirit and only "condemned to govern."[199] The

195. Castellani, "La Democrazia cristiana," 73.

196. Faggioli, "Tra referendum sul divorzio e revisione del Concordato," 271–73.

197. Dario Fo, *Il Fanfani rapito* (Verona: Bertani editore, 1975); Joseph Farrell, *Dario Fo and Franca Rame: Harlequins of the Revolution* (London: Methuen, 2001), 152–55.

198. Andreotti, "Troppi autogoals," *Concretezza*, June 1, 1974.

199. John Pollard, *Catholicism in Modern Italy: Religion, Society and Politics since 1861* (New York: Routledge, 2008), 147–49.

future, he said after the catastrophic mid-1970s, "is no longer entirely in our hands."[200] Four years almost to the day after the referendum, on May 9, 1978, Moro fell victim to the terrorist Brigate Rosse, an act about which the embittered Cardinal Siri supposedly said, "He got what he deserved" (*Ha avuto quel che si meritava*).[201] Three months later, on August 6, Pope Paul died.

Pier Paolo Pasolini, in a strangely sympathetic voice, reflected some of the Catholic despair. In the days before the referendum, he contributed a number of articles to the *Corriere della sera*, mourning Italy's collapse into a land of hedonist motivation, shirking self-sacrifice and turning toward "parliamentary fascism." Observing a Good Friday procession at the Colosseum, he also pronounced dead the church's prestige and values, writing a few months later that it had betrayed the peasants who now embraced consumer culture. In January of 1975, not too long before his life ended brutally in November, Pasolini not only lamented Italy's slide into the disenchanted blandness of modernity, but also, in an article for the *Corriere della sera*, came out against abortion.[202]

Along with the regional elections in June, other jolts came, starting in 1975. In May, Parliament approved a new "Family Law" that challenged the traditional roles of husband and wife by introducing fundamental changes to the status of women, acknowledging the equality of spouses, thus making the mother equal to the father in parental authority and ending the husband's exclusive control of property.[203] That same year, Rome portioned land for the construction of a Muslim mosque that, designed by two Italians and an Iraqi, opened in 1995.[204] More shocks followed. In August 1976, the art historian Giulio Carlo Argan became Rome's first Communist mayor, ending the DC's unbroken line of rule that had begun with Salvatore Rebecchini in 1946.

Gedda's and Andreotti's predictions, furthermore, that abortion was the next step, soon proved correct. On January 15, 1975, Pannella declared in Rome's Piazza Navona that the battle had just begun. The

200. Giovagnoli, *Il Partito italiano*, 171. See also Moro's speech to the DC Congress in July 1974 in Martina, *La Chiesa in Italia negli ultimi trent'anni*, 180–81.

201. Saresella, *Cattolici a sinistra: Dal modernismo ai giorni nostri* (Rome and Bari: Editori Laterza, 2011), 156. Two years later the Red Brigades assassinated Vittorio Bachelet.

202. Pier Paolo Pasolini, *Scritti corsari* (Milan: Garzanti Editore, 1975), 38–41, 44–49, 100; Pasolini, "Sono contro l'aborto," *Corriere della sera*, January 19, 1975.

203. Thomas Glyn Watkin, *The Italian Legal Tradition* (Dartmouth: Ashgate, 1997), 164–65, 175, and 185; De Vigili, *La battaglia sul divorzio*, 29.

204. R. J. B. Bosworth, *Whispering City: Rome and Its Histories* (New Haven, Conn.: Yale University Press, 2011), 275–76.

cover of the progressive *L'Espresso*'s January 19 edition caused a scandal by depicting the crucifixion of a woman, naked and pregnant. Next to her ran the headline, "Abortion, an Italian tragedy." The state sequestered the offensive issues and charged *L'Espresso* with *vilipendio*.[205] But, like divorce, the Catholics would ultimately lose this battle, too. On June 6, 1978, ironically during Andreotti's fourth cabinet, abortion became the law of the land. Perhaps to clear the stain of the 1974 debacle, Catholics tried to reverse the abortion law with another referendum. Held in 1981, it too failed, prompting the historian John Pollard to conclude that for everyone "Italian society had become more secularized, thereby strengthening the hand of the reformers."[206]

The divorce referendum also accelerated the modification of the 1929 Concordat that had served the Catholic morality agenda. By the mid-1960s, inspired no doubt by *Gaudium et spes* and other Vatican Council documents, sentiment for revision already had begun to pick up momentum. Only the neo-Fascists insisted on maintaining things as they stood—after all, Mussolini had negotiated and signed the Lateran Pacts in 1929—while the only consistent call for abolition came from the Liberal Party. All others, including notably the Christian Democrats, carved out a middle ground, believing in the wisdom of at least some adjustments or, as Gonella called it, "cautious revisionism." Parliament first took up the discussion on March 11, 1965, when the moderate Socialist Mauro Ferri connected the issue to Hochhuth's *Il Vicario*. Angry that the state's treatment of the play derived from the obligation to maintain Rome's sacred character, Ferri urged his fellow deputies to step back and reexamine the Concordat itself. Only six days later, however, the Socialist Lelio Basso's formal proposal for reexamination fell flat.[207] Two years later, however, in 1967, Basso felt that a resubmission might now be in order. This time his scheme enjoyed a better reception, and, after two days of debate, on October 5, 1967, the chamber endorsed a bid from the DC's Zaccagnini, the Republican Ugo La Malfa, and Ferri to establish an investigative committee on Concordat revision. In 1969, Gonella took the chair and held it until he died thirteen years later.[208]

205. Impagliazzo, *La diocesi del Papa*, 19. In the preceding March the Communists also captured the Lazio region; "Pannella: Siamo all'inizio della battaglia sull'aborto," Corriere *della sera*, January 16, 1975; Galli, *Pannella*, 45–46.

206. Pollard, *Catholicism in Modern Italy*, 153–56.

207. Scirè, *Il divorzio in Italia*, 32; Lussana, *L'Italia del divorzio*, 109–11.

208. De Franciscis, *Italy and the Vatican*, 76–79; in 1980 Gonella lamented "the discouraging poverty" of cultural activity on the part of political parties. "And few recognize," he continued, "[that this is] one

Talks with the Holy See began but were suspended after the legalization of divorce. Pope Paul allowed them to start again after the referendum, and serious talks resumed in 1976. Significantly, some detected that by this time, the revision issue had begun to bore people; and until the last couple of years, when one could see that a new Concordat was in the offing, television and print coverage of the talks dwindled and in some cases even vanished.[209] Finally, on February 18, 1984, Bettino Craxi, Italy's first Socialist prime minister, and Cardinal Agostino Casaroli signed the new accords between Italy and the Holy See. Parliament ratified them on March 25, 1985. A far cry from the documents signed by Mussolini and Cardinal Gasparri fifty-six years earlier, the new Concordat ended Catholicism's status as the state religion and modified Rome's sacred image, declaring only that "the Italian Republic acknowledges the particular significance that Rome, the Episcopal See of the Supreme Pontiff, has to Catholicism."[210]

Epilogue

As cited earlier, the convulsions of the 1960s and 1970s affected much of the developed West. Italy was not alone, although it might have weathered the storm better than some other nations. According to the sociologist Callum Brown, for example, by 1963 most indices of British Christianity pointed to a free fall. This was not just the decline of Christianity, he continued, but "the death of a culture."[211] Indicators of this breakdown varied from country to country, and moral issues might strike chords in one nation while not in another. For obvious logistical reasons, Italians argued about bikinis more than the British did. On the other hand, more heat charged the British debate there over capital punishment, while it was hardly a concern in Italy, which had resolved the question

---

of the prime causes of weakness in the democratic system"; Gonella, introduction to Vittorio Cervone and Giacomo Cesaro, *La Formazione politica* (Naples: Società Editrice Napolitana, 1980), 7.

209. De Franciscis, *Italy and the Vatican*, 107.

210. Pompei, *Un ambasciatore in Vaticano*, 35. One can view the text of the agreement at http://home.lu.lv/~rbalodis/Baznicu%20tiesibas/Akti/Arvalstis_ligumi/Italijas&Sv.Kresla_konkordats.pdf (accessed September 20, 2019).

211. Callum G. Brown, *The Death of Christian Britain: Understanding Secularization 1800–2000* (New York: Routledge, 2009), 187–93. Canada also presents some striking parallels to Italy. Quebec experienced similar developments after Vatican II—what Kevin J. Christiano called a "crumbling of tradition"; see Christiano, "The Trajectory of Catholicism in Twentieth-Century Quebec," in *The Church Confronts Modernity: Catholicism since 1950 in the United States, Ireland and Quebec*, ed. Leslie Woodcock Tentler (Washington, D.C.: The Catholic University of America Press, 2007), 21–93. See also Mark Noll, "What Happened to Christian Canada?," *Church History* 75, no. 2 (June 2006).

at the end of the war.[212] Italy, moreover, experienced nothing like Britain's Wolfenden Report on homosexuality. Sir John Wolfenden chaired a parliamentary committee to investigate the controversy, and, in 1957, after three years, its findings urged the decriminalization of homosexual acts between consenting adults. The report's distinction between sin and crime prompted a skeptical Lord Devlin to advocate a state role in protecting moral values for society's good. But who decided which morals to uphold? Lord Devlin's response echoed Italian Catholic arguments on *comune sentimento*—"the reasonable man, the man on the Clapham omnibus or twelve of them seated together in the jury-room." Pressure groups formed to urge action on the report, prompting many to even question the morality of the subject. Parliament debated decriminalization for the last time in 1966 and 1967, when the measure was almost torpedoed, notably by a group of Labour MPs, mostly from working-class and Catholic Liverpool districts, in an attempt to protect the merchant marine. They failed, and, as of July 1967, the offensive acts no longer warranted prosecution.[213]

In 1964, the powerful British Board of Film Censors gave up the fight when its secretary, John Trevelyan, bluntly declared that his agency could "no longer assume responsibility for the guardianship of morality."[214] On British television, with new programs in 1965 that would have been inconceivable only a few years before, the BBC announced it could not even assume most of its audience as Christian.[215] Britain's stage censorship, based in the Lord Chamberlain's office, appeared more centralized and elitist than Italy's until the 1968 Theaters Bill ended it.[216] Up north, the 1970 report of the Moral Welfare Committee of the Church of Scotland welcomed Britain's decriminalization of homosexuality, legalization of abortion, and liberalization of divorce. But it could not ignore a gathering crisis rooted in the "'moral turn' in female sexuality"—that is, the "death of pious femininity [that] destroyed the entire house of cards." Brown wrote that "the committee grasped the central issue" in

212. Richards, *Parliament and Conscience*, chapter 3.

213. Lord Devlin's argument is summarized in Richards, *Parliament and Conscience*, 7–19. See also Richards, *Parliament and Conscience*, chapter 4, and Patrick Higgins, *Heterosexual Dictatorship: Male Homosexuality in Postwar Britain* (London: Fourth Estate, 1996), 15–148.

214. Richard Maltby, "'D' for Disgusting: American Culture and English Criticism," in *Hollywood and Europe: Economics, Culture, National Identity: 1945–1995*, ed. Geoffrey Nowell-Smith and Steven Ricci (London: British Film Institute, 1998), 109–10.

215. McLeod, *Religious Crisis of the 1960s*, 240–41. To the BBC's charge, the bishop of Leicester retorted, "The real reason is that the non-Christian element has become more militant."

216. Richards, *Parliament and Conscience*, chapter 6.

one sentence: "It is the promiscuous girl who is the real problem here." Italian Catholics would have understood this.[217]

~

As discussed throughout this book, from 1948 until 1974, Italy's Catholics tried to hold the line against the challenges of secularization and secularism to their vision of traditional Christian culture, one of modesty, of respect for family, and of obedience to the church. They pictured their enemies as a relentless tide that offered Italians fewer social and cultural rules and, arguably, more fun. A glance today at Italian beaches or comportment on the street might indicate that those militants correctly predicted the slide into a hedonist future, and, consequently, their efforts to stop the slide failed. The 1960s almost killed Catholic Action. The next few decades saw the total capitulation of the Christian Democracy. Nine months before his own murder in November 1975, Pasolini saw the end coming, sounding at turns nostalgic and bitter regarding the old "firefly" days. But by then those were only memories, he continued; the party had lost its peasant and Christian base and discovered crime as a way of life.[218] Finally, in 1994 the Democrazia cristiana closed shop at its suburban Palazzo Sturzo and at the old headquarters in the Piazza Gesù. As the DC collapsed in the early 1990s, the historian Mark Donovan concluded that it "may have won many battles, but the war to build a Christian Democracy in Italy [had] been lost."[219] The DC, however, shared the same fate as everything else on Italy's political spectrum. Not long after the new Concordat, at the end of the 1980s and the start of the '90s, Italy's entire political world crumbled, soon replaced by a new system that bore little resemblance in the twenty-first century to that created after World War II.[220] The PCI fell first. Shortly after the end of the Berlin Wall in 1989, the party chief Achille Occhetto announced radical reforms, a case of too little too late, and the Italian Communist Party ended its seventy-year existence in 1991. In 1994, the Socialists collapsed, then tried to reform in 2007 with no success.

As the parties went, so did their presses. *Il Popolo* limped along for a while after the DC's demise, ending operations in 2003. *L'Unità* died

217. Brown, *Death of Christian Britain*, 179–80.

218. The "firefly" essay was quoted in Giovagnoli, "La Stagione democristiana," 53.

219. Mark Donovan, "Democrazia Cristiana: Party of Government," in *Christian Democracy in Europe: A Comparative Perspective*, ed. David Hanley (London: Pinter, 1994), 84–85; see also Donovan, "Italy: A Dramatic Case of Secularization?," in *Religion and Mass Election Behavior in Europe*, ed. David Broughton and Hans-Marten ten Napel (London: Routledge, 2000).

220. Crainz, *Il paese reale: Dall'assassinio di Moro all'Italia di oggi* (Rome: Donzelli, 2012), 225–313.

in 2014, resurfaced briefly, then expired again in 2017, while *Avanti!* declared bankruptcy in 1994. Elsewhere, *L'Europeo* folded in 1995, revived in 2001, and closed for good in 2013. Rizzoli acquired *Il Mondo* in 1969 and turned it into a more neutral and mainstream newsmagazine until it, too, went under in 2014. *Noi uomini* and many of the other Catholic Action reviews ended publication when the new statutes came into force in 1969. One of the chief survivors among AC publications has been the *Rivista del cinematografo*, which continues today. The strictly church-operated publications like the *Osservatore Romano*, *Famiglia cristiana*, and *Civiltà cattolica* weathered the storms and emerged intact.

The state of Catholic culture, however, is one of broader and more complicated nuance. In 1982, Paul Furlong noted that "despite over thirty years of supposed Catholic-inspired government, Italian society [did] not appear any more Christian, and indeed legislation of a distinctly non-Catholic aspect now appears on the Statute book in the shape of divorce law and abortion law."[221] In the fall of 1983, the *Civiltà cattolica* announced that, although 97 percent of Italians still baptized their children, the country had become a land of "religious indifference." Seen through the lenses of Christian practice and comportment (*costume*), continued the article, "[Italy] is no longer 'Catholic.'"[222] Such post-mortems, however, may have been somewhat exaggerated. In 1985, 88 percent of Italians still identified themselves as Catholic, and, in 1987, just over 67 percent reported that they *believed* in God and in the Catholic Church.[223] Despite a dip in the 1990s, the 88 percent figure reappeared in a 2006 Eurispes poll. Almost 37 percent, moreover, practiced the religion with regularity, a figure that hadn't changed much for over forty years. Well over half of all Italians still attend Mass at least a few times every year.[224]

The sociologist Luca Diotallevi concluded in a 2002 study that secularization had not hit Italy as hard as it hit other countries. In the late 1990s, for example, Italy still ordained between 400 and 500 diocesan priests annually compared to between 100 and 150 in France. The stability of weekly Mass attendance, notably higher than many other European nations, led Diotallevi to attribute this vitality to myriad Catholic

221. Furlong, "Italian Christian Democrats," 23–24.

222. Scoppola, *La Nuova cristianità perduta*, 138.

223. Franco Garelli, *Religione e chiesa in Italia* (Bologna: Il Mulino, 1991), 42.

224. "Italia: Quasi l'88% si proclama cattolico," *Corriere della sera*, January 18, 2006, which one can consult at http://www.corriere.it/Primo_Piano/Cronache/2006/01_Gennaio/17/cattolici.shtml (accessed September 20, 2019).

options, or "firms," some of which had been founded earlier, like the Focolari and Opus dei, and others of later derivation like Communion and Liberation and the Saint Egidio Society. Some of these firms stood on the left and some on the right, but they all channeled many of the faithful who had drifted from the established church, Catholic Action, or the DC. Even Gedda founded his own Mario Fani clubs to retaliate against the AC's *scelta religiosa*. This "strategy," the sociologist wrote, "allowed Italian Catholicism to reverse, or at the very least to resist, the originally anticlerical nature of the modernization process, transforming it into 'protected' or 'defensive' modernization."[225]

In 2007, Enzo Pace also wrote that, whatever difficulties the Catholic Church experienced, there was "no decline of popular religion in Italy." Observance remained high, and local cults and adoration or saints remained "as vigorous as ever"—citing traditional ones like St. Anthony of Padua and newer ones devoted to Padre Pio or transformed ones like San Francesco de Paola, whom many motorcyclists have embraced as their patron.[226] Stefano Allievi felt Italian Catholicism to be in decent health compared to other nations in the Christian tradition in 2014. He found twenty-first-century Italian religion vibrant in its diverse manifestations, a "growing pluralization within the Catholic camp" and a "progressive increase in other religions or of other ways of being religious, as well as a variety of ways of not being religious."[227]

Catholicism and Catholic culture still maintain a presence in Italy's politics. In 1982, Pope John Paul II established a Pontifical Council for Culture, aimed in part to address the "galloping urbanization and cultural rootlessness" of modern life.[228] Prime Minister Silvio Berlus-

225. Luca Diotallevi, "Internal Competition in a National Religious Monopoly: The Catholic Effect and the Italian Case," *Sociology of Religion* 63, no. 2 (2002): 139–40. Diotallevi drew some of this reasoning from Renato Moro's "Il 'modernizzazione buono' e la 'modernizzazione' cattolica tra fascismo e postfascismo come problema storiografico," *Storia contemporanea* 19, no. 4 (1988); Saresella, "Ecclesial Dissent in Italy in the Sixties," 65–67; Cuminetti, *Il dissenso cattolico in Italia*, 130–46; see also Faggioli, "New Elites of Italian Catholicism." Faggioli identifies Catholic scouting as among the other beneficiaries of the Vatican II outlook.

226. Enzo Pace, "A Peculiar Pluralism," *Journal of Modern Italian Studies* 12, no. 1 (2007).

227. Stefano Allievi, "Silent Revolution in the Country of the Pope: From Catholicism as 'Religion of Italians to the Pluralistic 'Italy of the Religions,'" in *Beyond Catholicism: Heresy, Mysticism, and Apocalypse in Italian Culture*, ed. Fabrizio De Donno and Simon Gilson (New York: Palgrave, 2014), 286–313. More generally, see Grace Davie, *Religion in Modern Europe in the 21st Century: The Facters to Take into Account; A Memory Mutates* (New York: Oxford University Press, 2000); and her *Europe: The Exceptional Case; Parameters of Faith in the Modern World* (London: Darton, Longman and Todd, 2002).

228. Regarding the Pontifical Council for Culture, see http://www.cultura.va/content/cultura/en/organico/profilo.html (accessed September 20, 2019), and its 1999 document, "Toward a Pastoral Approach to Culture," http://www.vatican.va/roman_curia/pontifical_councils/cultr/documents/rc_pc_pc-cultr_doc_03061999_pastoral_en.html (accessed September 20, 2019).

coni described his Forza Italia in 2004 as "liberal, Catholic, social and popular."[229] But Catholic ideas reached beyond Berlusconi (who had first identified with the Socialists) and surfaced in figures across the political spectrum who started their careers in Catholic Action, other organizations like scouting, or the old DC. Many Italian notables started somewhere in the Catholic movement. These include those on the center-right—Rocco Buttiglione, for instance, Pier Ferdinando Casini, Angelino Alfano, and the family minister in Giuseppe Conte's first cabinet, Lorenzo Fontana—as well as those of the center-left, like Rosy Bindi, Romano Prodi, and Matteo Renzi. One scholar detected that, even in film, a kind of nostalgic memory of religion persists on Italian screens. Catholicism, purged of its imperfections, provides Italian cinema with a postsecular "shared and surprisingly monolithic identity."[230]

Initiatives like the Base missionaria may have withered, and, after the early victories of the late 1940s and early '50s, the faithful lost many of their battles at Pozzonovo, at Prato, over censorship, the fight for a Catholic cinema, and divorce. But their struggles left a significant legacy of social conservatism. Although the government in 1987 reduced the separation time before final divorce from five to three years, Italians still expressed less enthusiasm for it than did those in other countries. Chiara Saraceno reported that in 1998 only about 10 percent of Italian marriages ended in divorce, a small figure next to those in most West European and other developed countries. The United Nations confirmed that from 2002 until 2006, Italy and Ireland maintained Western Europe's lowest divorce rates, and Saraceno found in 2004 that "marital instability in Italy . . . [remained] still quite low." By 2018, however, Italy's divorce rate jumped to about 25 percent of marriages, a number still less than half of most of its neighbors. Across the continent, only countries with large Muslim populations—Bosnia, Montenegro, and Albania—boasted lower figures.[231] Despite legalization, abortion rates, too, remained low, at least on paper, since the nation's birthrate collapsed. By the mid-1970s, Italian fertility was ranked among the lowest in Europe and the world, a particular embarrassment for a Catholic country. By the

229. Paul Ginsborg, *Silvio Berlusconi: Television, Power and Patrimony* (London: Verso, 2004), 176.

230. Claodagh Brook, "Post-Secular Identity in Contemporary Italian Cinema: Catholic 'Cement,' the Suppression of History and the Lost Islamic Other," *Modern Italy* 22, no. 2 (2017).

231. Chiara Saraceno, "The Italian Family from the 1960s to the Present," *Modern Italy* 9, no. 1 (2004). For the U.N. numbers, see https://unstats.un.org/unsd/demographic/products/dyb/dyb2006/Table25.pdf (accessed September 20, 2019). The OECD published updated figures in 2018. See https://www.oecd.org/els/family/SF_3_1_Marriage_and_divorce_rates.pdf (accessed September 20, 2019).

mid-1990s, what might euphemistically be termed a "negative birthrate" hit bottom at 1.2 children per woman, rendering moot some of the old lay-Catholic arguments over the family.[232] Nevertheless, Franco Bolzonar reported that, after over thirty years of legal abortions, in 2012, 27 percent of Italian gynecologists still refused to engage in the practice, a figure that actually had grown over the preceding decade and reached 80 percent in some regions. Catholics, furthermore, scored a victory in the 2005 referendum on stem cell research. Anxious to defeat the measure, Pope Benedict XVI urged the faithful to boycott the vote to ensure that the 50 percent threshold for validation not be reached. And the majority complied, with only 26 percent casting their votes. Another indication of influence might be gay marriage. Identification with the traditional family, despite demographic collapse, remains strong. Thanks in no small measure to the Catholic Church, Italy has resisted efforts to recognize same-sex matrimony, something for which, in 2015, the European Court of Human Rights even censured it; as of 2021, the state still only allowed civil unions and restricted marriage to a man and a woman.[233] Militants may have suffered many defeats at the hands of the secular Devil, but Catholicism remains alive in Italian culture, politics, and society—albeit more subtly now than it did fifty, sixty, and seventy years ago.

232. On Italy's demographic crisis, see Marcantonio Caltabiano, Maria Castiglioni, and Alessandro Rosina, "Lowest-Low Fertility: Signs of a Recovery in Italy?," *Demographic Research* 21, no. 23 (November 6, 2009), found at https://www.demographic-research.org/volumes/vol21/23/21–23.pdf (accessed September 20, 2019); and S. Philip Morgan, "Is Low Fertility a Twenty-First-Century Demographic Crisis?," *Demography* 40, no. 4 (November 2003). For more of a historical perspective, see Massimo Livi-Bacci, *A History of Italian Fertility during the Last Two Centuries* (Princeton, N.J.: Princeton University Press, 1977).

233. Franco Bolzonar, "A Christian Democratization of Politics? The New Influence of Catholicism on Italian Politics since the Demise of the Democrazia Cristiana," *Journal of Modern Italian Studies* 21, no. 3 (2016): 447; "Vote on Fertility Law Fires Passions in Italy," *New York Times*, June 11, 2005.

Bibliography

AAVV. *XV Congresso eucaristico nazionale: L'eucaristia: "Sacramentum unitatis, vinculum caritatis."* Lecce, 1956.

———. *Legge penale e libertà del pensiero.* Padua: Cedam—Casa editrice dott. Antonio Milani, 1966.

———. *La riforma del diritto di famiglia: Atti del Convegno di Venezia svolto presso la Fondazione Giorgio Cini nei giorni 30 aprile—1 maggio 1967.* Padova: Cedam, 1967.

———. *Chiesa e progetto educativo nell'Italia del secondo dopoguerra (1948–1958).* Brescia: Editrice La Scuola, 1988.

———. *Il Parlamento Italiano, 1861–1988.* Milan: Nuova CEI, 1988.

———. *Il lungo decennio: L'italia prima del 68.* Edited by Carmelos Adagio, Rocco Cerrato, and Simona Urso. Verona: Cierre Edizioni, 1999.

———. *La storia dei giubilei.* Vol. 4, 1800–2000. N.P.: BNL Edizioni, 2000.

Aceti, Guido. *Monsignor Francesco Olgiati nel I centenario della nascita (1886–1986).* Milan: Vita e Pensiero, 1986.

Acerbi, Antonio. *Chiesa, Cultura, Società: Momenti e figure dal Vaticano I a Paolo VI.* Milan: Vita e Pensiero, 1988.

———, ed. *La Chiesa e l'Italia: Per una storia dei loro rapporti negli ultimi due secoli.* Milan: Vita e pensiero, 2003.

Acquaviva, Sabino. *The Decline of the Sacred in Industrial Society.* Translated by Patricia Lipscomb. New York: Harper and Row, 1979.

Adilardi, Guglielmo. *Chiesa cattolica e massoneria: Antiche lotte—Nuovi orizzonti.* Foggia: Bastogi, 2009.

Agnes, Mario, and Mario Casella, eds. *Vittorio Bachelet: Discorsi (1964–1973).* Rome: AVE, 1980.

Agosti, Aldo. *Palmiro Togliatti: A Biography.* London: I. B. Tauris, 2008.

Alberigo, Giuseppe, ed. *History of Vatican II.* 5 vols. English version edited by Joseph A. Komonchak. Leuven: Peeters; Maryknoll, N.Y.: Orbis, 1995.

Alberigo, Giuseppe, and Andrea Riccardi, eds. *Chiesa e papato nel mondo contemporaneo.* Rome and Bari: Laterza, 1990.

Aldrich, Robert. *The Seduction of the Mediterranean: Writing, Art and Homosexual Fantasy.* London: Routledge, 1993.

Alloway, Lawrence. *The Venice Bienniale 1895–1968: From Salon to Goldfish Bowl.* Greenwich: New York Graphic Society, 1968.

Allum, P. A. *Politics and Society in Post-War Naples.* Cambridge: Cambridge University Press, 1973.

Allum, Percy, and Ilvo Diamanti. '50/'80. *Vent'anni: Due generazioni di giovani a confronto*. Rome: Edizioni lavoro, 1986.

Almond, Gabriel A. "The Political Ideas of Christian Democracy." *Journal of Politics* 10 (1948).

Alvarez, David. *Spies in the Vatican: Espionage and Intrigue from Napoleon to the Holocaust*. Lawrence: University Press of Kansas, 2002.

Ambrosini, Giangiulio. *Referendum*. Turin: Bollati Boringhieri, 1993.

Amfitheatrof, Erik. *The Enchanted Ground: Americans in Italy, 1760–1980*. Boston: Little, Brown, 1980.

Andreatta, Beniamino. *Divorzio e referendum*. Bologna: Il Mulino, 1972.

Andreotti, Giulio. *Trento-Vienna-Roma: De Gasperi e il suo tempo*. Milan: Mondadori, 1956.

———. *De (prima) Re Publica: Ricordi*. Milan: Rizzoli, 1996.

Anile, Alberto. *I film di Totò (1946–1967): La maschera tradita*. Genoa: Le Manni, 1998.

———. *Totò proibito: Storia puntigliosa e grottesca dei rapporti tra il principe De Curtis e la censura*. Turin: Lindau, 2005.

Arata, Rodolfo. *Il futuro è in mezzo a noi*. Rome: Edizione Cinque Lune, 1970.

Argentieri, Mino. *La censura nel cinema italiano*. Rome: Editori Riuniti, 1974.

Arpa, P. Angelo. *La Dolce vita: Cronaca di una Passione*. Naples: Parresía, 1996.

Atkin, Nicholas, and Frank Tallett. *Priests, Prelates and People: A History of European Catholicism since 1750*. New York: Oxford University Press, 2003.

Atti del convegno di studio della Democrazia Cristiana. *I Cattolici Italiani nei tempi nuovi della Cristianità*. Edited by Giuseppe Rossini. Rome: Edizioni Cinque Lune, 1967.

Atti della tavola rotunda organizzata a Roma il 2 marzo 1967 dall'Ufficio Problemi del Tempo Libero della Democrazia Cristiana. *Il turismo sociale*. Rome: Edizioni Cinque Lune, 1968.

Augias, Armati. *Roma in Nera: I grandi delitti tra cronaca, storia, costume*. Rome: Palombi Editori, 2006.

Azara, Lilioza. *Lo stato Lenone: Il diabattito sulle case chiuse in Italia 1860–1958*. Melzo: Editrice CENS, 1997.

Azione cattolica italiana. *Stampa, cinema, radio per Ragazzi*. Rome: Ufficio centrale aspirante, 1952.

Baccetti, Carlo. *I Postdemocristiani*. Bologna: Il Mulino, 2007.

Bachelet, Vittorio. "L'Azione cattolica dopo il concilio vaticano II." *Humanitas* 1966.

———. *Il nuovo cammino dell'Azione Cattolica*. Rome: AVE, 1973.

Bacon, Henry. *Visconti: Visions of Beauty and Decay*. Cambridge: Cambridge University Press, 1998.

Baget-Bozzo, Gianni. *Il Partito Cristiano al Potere: La Dc di De Gasperi e di Dossetti 1945–1954*. Florence: Vallechi, 1974.

Baget-Bozzo, Gianni, and Giovanni Tassani. *Aldo Moro: Il politico nella crisi 1962–1973*. Firenze: Sansoni Editore Nuova, 1983.

Baldi, Alfredo. *Lo sguardo punito: Film censurati 1947–1962*. Rome: Bulzoni Editore, 1994.

———. *Schermi Proibiti: La censura in Italia 1947–1988*. Venice: Prima edizione, 2002.

Ballini, Pier Luigi, Alfredo Canavero, Maria Eleonora Guasconi, and Franco Boiardi. *Mario Scelba Contributi per una biografia*. Edited by Pier Luigi Ballini Rome: Soveria Mannelli: Rubbettino Editore, 2006.

Baragli, Enrico, SJ. *Cinema cattolico: Documenti dalla S. Sede sul cinema*. Rome: Città nuova editrice, 1965.

Barbagallo, Francesco. *Enrico Berlinguer*. Rome: Carocci editore, 2006.

Barbagallo, Francesco, et. al., eds. *Storia dell'Italia repubblicana* . Vol. 2, La trasformazione dell'Italia, sviluppo e squilibri. Part 2, "*Istituzioni, movimenti, culture*," edited by Francesco Barbagallo. Turin: Einaudi, 1995. Vol. 3, L'Italia nella crisi mondiale: L'ultimo ventennio. Part 2, "*Istituzioni, movimenti, culture*." Turin: Einaudi, 1997.

Barbanti, Marco. "La classe dirigente cattolica e la 'battaglia per la moralità,' 1948–1960: Appunti sul 'regime clericale.'" *Italia contemporanea*, no. 189 (December 1992).

———. "Cultura cattolica, lotta anticomunista a moralità pubblica (1948–60)." *Rivista di storia contemporanea* 1 (1992).

Barra, Giovanni. *Preti d'oggi*. Milan: Vita e Pensiero, 1953.

Bates, Anna. *Weeder in the Garden of the Lord: Anthony Comstock's Life and Career*. Lanham, Md.: University Press of America, 1995.

Battaglia, Achille. *I Giudici e la politica*. Bari: Laterza, 1962.

Battaglia, Adolfo. *Dibattito sulla scuola*. Bari: Laterza, 1956.

Baum, Gregory, and John Coleman, eds. *The Church and Christian Democracy*. Edinburgh: Concilium, 1987.

Beales, Derek, and Geoffrey Best. *History, Society and the Churches: Essays in Honor of Owen Chadwick*. New York: Cambridge University Press, 1985.

Bedani, Gino, and Bruce Haddock. *The Politics of Italian National Identity: A Multidisciplinary Perspective*. Cardiff: University of Wales Press, 2000.

Bedeschi, Lorenzo. *Dissacrano l'infanzia! I Pionieri d'Italia*. Bologna: Editrice A.B.E.S., 1950.

Belco, Victoria C. *War, Massacre and Recovery in Central Italy, 1943–1948*. Toronto: University of Toronto Press. 2010.

Bellassai, Sandro. *La morale comunista: Pubblico e privato nella rappresentazione del PCI (1947–1956)*. Rome: Carocci editore, 2000.

———. *La legge del desiderio: Il progetto Merlin L'Italia degli anni Cinquanta*. Rome: Carocci editore, 2006.

Benini, Stefania. *Pasolini: The Sacred Flesh*. Toronto: University of Toronto Press, 2015.

Berger, Suzanne, ed. *Religion in Western European Politics*. London and Totowa, N.J.: Frank Cass, 1982.

Berlin, Isaiah. *The Crooked Timber of Humanity: Chapters in the History of Ideas*. Edited by Henry Hardy. New York: Knopf, 1991.

Bernabei, Ettore, and Giorgio Dell'Arti. *L'Uomo di fiducia: I retroscena del potere raccontati da un testimone rimasto dietro le quinte per cinquant'anni*. Milan: Arnoldo Mondadori, 1999.

Bernini, Stefania. "Natural Mothers: Teaching Morals and Parent-Craft in Italy, 1945–1960." *Modern Italy* 9, no. 1 (May 2004).

———. *Family Life and Individual Welfare in Postwar Europe: Britain and Italy Compared*. New York: Palgrave, 2007.

Bertagna, Giuseppe, Alfredo Canavero, Augusto D'Angelo, and Andrea Simoncini, eds. *Guido Gonella tra Governo, Parlamento e Partito*. Vol. 1. Rome and Soveria Mannelli: Istituto Luigi Struzo/Rubbettino Editore, 2007.

Betti, Laura, ed. *Pasolini: Cronaca giudiziaria, persecuzione, morte*. Milan: Garzanti, 1977.

Biffi, Giacomo. *Risorgimento stato laico e identità nazionale*. Casale Monferrato: Piemme, 1999.

Biltereyst, Daniel, and Roel Vande Winkel, eds. *Silencing Cinema: Film Censorship around the World*. New York: Palgrave Macmillan, 2013.

Bindy, Rosa, and Agostino Moscatelli, eds. *La generazione del concilio: Tra cronaca e storia*. Rome: AVE, 1986.

Bireley, Robert. *The Refashioning of Catholicism, 1450–1700: A Reassessment of the Counter Reformation*. Washington, D.C.: The Catholic University of America Press, 1999.

Bisel, Jane Ferrel. "Advertising and the 'American Myth' in Italy: 1945–1955." Unpublished Master's Thesis. Montreal: McGill University, 1985.

Bisori, Guido. *Guido Bisori: Scritti e discorsi*. Prato: Edizioni del Palazzo, 1982.

Bizzarri, Libero, and Libero Solaroli. *L'industria cinematografica italiana*. Firenze: Parenti Editore, 1958.

Black, Christopher F. *Church, Religion and Society in Early Modern Italy*. New York: Palgrave, 2004.

———. *The Italian Inquisition*. New Haven, Conn.: Yale University Press, 2009.

Black, Gregory. *The Catholic Crusade against the Movies, 1940–1975*. New York: Cambridge University Press, 1997.

Bocca, Giorgio. *La scoperta dell'Italia*. Bari: Laterza, 1963.

Bocci, Maria, ed. *Non lamenta ma azione: I cattolici e lo sviluppo italiano nei 150 anni di storia unitaria*. Milan: Vita e pensiero, 2013.

Boissevain, Jeremy, ed. *Coping with Tourists: European Reactions to Mass Tourism*. Providence, R.I.: Berghahn, 1996.

Bolton, Lucy, and Christina Siggers Manson, eds. *Italy on Screen: National Identity and Italian Imaginary*. Oxford: Peter Lang, 2010.

Bolzonar, Fabio. "A Christian Democratization of Politics? The New Influence of Catholicism on Italian Politics since the Demise of the Democrazia Cristiana." *Journal of Modern Italian Studies* 21, no. 3 (2016).

Bondanella, Peter. *The Films of Federico Fellini*. Cambridge: Cambridge University Press, 2002.

———. *A History of Italian Cinema*. New York: Continuum, 2009.

———, ed. *The Italian Cinema Book*. London: Palgrave Macmillan, 2014.

Boneschi, Marta. *Poveri ma belli: I nostri anni Cinquanta*. Milan: Mondadori, 1995.

———. *Santa pazienza: La Storia delle donne italiane dal dopoguerra a oggi*. Milan: Mondadori, 1998.

Bonsaver, Guido. *Censorship and Literature in Fascist Italy*. Toronto: University of Toronto Press, 2007.

Bonsaver, Guido, and Robert S. C. Gordon. *Culture, Censorship and the State in Twentieth-Century Italy*. London: Legenda, 2005.

Boralevi, Antonella. *Capri*. Bologna: Il Mulino, 2000.

Borzomati, Pietro. *Chiesa e società meridionale: Dalla Restaurazione al secondo dopoguerra*. Rome: Studium, 1982.

Bosworth, R. J. B. *Italy, Least of the Great Powers: Italian Foreign Policy before the First World War*. London: Cambridge University Press, 1979.

———. *Whispering City: Rome and Its Histories*. New Haven, Conn.: Yale University Press, 2011.

———. *Italian Venice: A History*. New Haven, Conn.: Yale University Press, 2014.

Bowen, Edward. "'Take Notice of the Red Light!' A History of Adult Cinemas in Rome." *Journal of Italian Cinema and Media Studies* 5, no. 1 (2017).

Bozzo, Carlo. *La chiesa e la cultura radicale*. Brescia: Queriniana, 1978.

Braghin, Paolo, ed. *Inchiesta sulla miseria in Italia*. Turin: Giulio Einaudi, 1978.

Brancati, Vitaliano. *Ritorno alla censura*. Bari: Laterza, 1952.

Brienza, Giuseppe. *Identità cattolica e anticomunismo nell'Italia del dopoguerra: La figura e l'opera di mons. Roberto Ronca*. Crotone: D'Ettoris Editori, 2008.

Broers, Michael. *The Politics of Religion in Napoleonic Italy: The War against God, 1801–1814*. New York: Routledge, 2002.

Brogi, Alessandro. *Confronting America: The Cold War between the United States and the Communists in France and Italy*. Chapel Hill, N.C.: University of North Carolina Press, 2011.

Brook, Clodagh. "Post-Secular Identity in Contemporary Italian Cinema: Catholic 'Cement,' the Suppression of History and the lost Islamic Other." *Modern Italy* 22, no. 2 (2017).

Broughton, David, and Hans-Martien ten Napel, eds. *Religion and Mass Electoral Behavior in Europe*. London: Routledge, 2000.

Brown, Callum G. *The Death of Christian Britain: Understanding Secularization 1800–2000*. New York: Routledge, 2009.

Bruce, Steve, ed. *Religion and Modernization: Sociologists and Historians Debate the Secularization Thesis*. Oxford: Oxford University Press, 1992.

———. *God Is Dead: Secularization in the West*. Malden, Mass.: Blackwell, 2002.

———. "Secularization and the Impotence of Individualized Religion." *Hedgehog Review* 8, nos. 1 and 2 (Spring–Summer 2006): 35–45.

Brunetta, Gian Piero. *The History of Italian Cinema: A Guide to Italian Film from Its Origins to the Twenty-first Century*. Translated by Jeremy Parzen. Princeton, N.J.: Princeton University Press, 2003.

Brunetta, Giuseppe. "Il Clero in Italia dal 1888 al 1989." *Polis* 5, no. 3 (December 1991).

Bucci, P. Vincent. *Chiesa e Stato: Church-State Relations in Italy within the Contemporary Constitutional Framework*. The Hague: Martinus Nijhoff, 1969.

Bull, Anna Cento, and Giorgio Adalgisa, eds. *Speaking Out and Silencing: Culture: Society and Politics in Italy in the 1970s*. London: Legenda, 2006.

Buonasorte, Nicla. *Siri: Tradizione e novecento*. Bologna: Il Mulino, 2006.

Burleigh, Michael. *Earthly Powers: The Clash of Religion and Politics in Europe: From the French Revolution to the Great War*. New York: Harper Collins, 2007.

Buttiglione, Rocco. "Politica e cultura nell'area cattolica." *Studium* 77, no. 3 (1981).

Calandrone, Giacomo. *Gli anni di Scelba*. Milan: Vangelista editore, 1975.

Calcara, Aniello. *Il problema morale nei tempi moderni*. Alba: Edizioni Paoline, 1957.

Caldwell, Leslie. *Italian Family Matters: Women, Politics, Legal Reform*. Blasingstoke: Macmillan, 1990.

Callahan, William. *The Catholic Church in Spain, 1875–1998*. Washington, D.C.: The Catholic University of America Press, 2000.

Camaiani, Bocchini Bruna, and Ernesto Balducci. *La Chiesa e la modernità*. Rome and Bari: Laterza, 2002.

Camera dei deputati, Segretariato Generale. *Orientamenti giurisprudenziali in tema di buon costume*. Rome: Servizio studi legislazione e inchieste parlamentari, 1972.

Campanini, Giorgio, and Paolo Nepi. *Cristianità e modernità: Religione e società civile nell'epoca della secolarizzazione*. Rome: AVE, 1992.

Canals, Salvatore. *Problemi morali e giuridici del cinema*. Rome: I quaderni della rivista del cinematografo, 1957.

———. *La Chiesa e il cinema*. Rome: Ente dello spettacolo, 1961.

Candeloro, Giorgio. *Il Movimento cattolico in Italia*. Rome: Riuniti, 1982.

———. *Storia dell'Italia moderna*. Vol. 11, *La Fondazione della Repubblica e la ricostruzione: Considerazioni finali*. Milan: Feltrinelli, 1986.

Capperucci, Vera. *Il Partito dei cattolici: dall'Italia Degasperiana alle corenti democristiane*. Soveria Mannelli: Rubbettino, 2010.

Capperucci, Vera, and Sara Lorenzini, eds. *Alcide De Gasperi: Scritti e discorsi politici; Edizione critica*. Vol. 3, *Alcide De Gasperi e la fondazione della democrazia italiana, 1943–1948*. Part 1. Bologna: il Mulino, 2008.

Capussotti, Enrica. *Gioventù perduta: Gli anni Cinquanta dei giovani e del cinema in Italia*. Milan: Giunti, 2004.

Capuzzo, Paolo. "Youth Cultures and Consumption in Contemporary Europe." *Contemporary European History* 10, no. 1 (2001).

Cardini, Antonio. *Tempo di ferro: "Il Mondo" e L'Italia del dopoguerra*. Bologna: Il Mulino, 1992.

———, ed. *Il Miracolo economico italiano (1958–1963)*. Bologna: Il Mulino, 2006.

Caretti, Paolo. *Intervento pubblico e libertà di espressione nel cinema nel teatro e nelle attività musicali*. Milan: Dott. A. Giuffrè Editore, n.d.

Carlen, Claudia, IHM. *The Papal Encyclicals*. Wilmington, N.C.: McGrath, 1981.

Caroli, Menico. *Proibitissimo! Censori e censurati della radiotelevisione italiana*. Milan: Garzanti, 2003.

Carnemolla, Piero Antonio. *Un Cristiano siciliano: Rassegna degli studi su Giorgio La Pira (1978–1998)*. Caltanissetta and Rome: Salvatore Sciascia Editore, 1999.

Carrera, Alessandro. *Fellini's Eternal Rome: Paganism and Christianity in the Films of Federico Fellini*. London and New York: Bloomsbury Academic, 2019.

Carroll, Michael. *Veiled Threats: The Logic of Popular Catholicism in Italy*. Baltimore: Johns Hopkins University Press, 1996.

Casanova, José. *Public Religions in the Modern World*. Chicago: University of Chicago Press, 1994.

———. "Rethinking Secularization: A Global Comparative Perspective." *Hedgehog Review* 8, nos. 1 and 2 (Spring and Summer 2006).

Casella, Mario. *L'Azione cattolica alla caduta del fascismo: Attività e progetti per il dopoguerra (1942–'45)*. Rome: Studium, 1984.

———. *Cattolici e costituente: Orientamenti e iniziative del cattolicesimo organizzato*. Perugia: Edizioni Scientifiche Italiane, 1987.

———. *18 Aprile 1948: La mobilitazione delle organizzazioni cattoliche*. Galatina: Congedo, 1992.

———. *L'Azione cattolica nell'Italia contemporanea (1919–1969)*. Rome: AVE, 1992.

———. *Giornali cattolici e società italiana: Religione politica democratica nelle pagine de "L'Osservatore romano" e de "Il Quotidiano" (1944–1950)*. Naples: Edizioni scientifiche italiane, 1994.

———. *Clero e politica in Italia (1942–1948)*. Galatina: Congedo, 1999.

———, ed. *L'Azione cattolica del Novecento: Aspetti, momenti, interpretazioni, personaggi*. Rome: Ave, 2003.

———. *Anticlericali in Italia, 1944–1947*. Bologna: Il Mulino, 2009.

Castronovo, Valerio, ed. *L'Italia Contemporanea, 1945–1975*. Turin: Einaudi, 1976.

Catolfi, Antonio. *Televisione e politica negli anni Sessanta*. Urbino: QuattroVenti, 2006.

Cavallera, Hervé A. *Storia dell'idea di famiglia in italia: Dall'avvento della Repubblica ai giorni nostri*. Brescia: Editrice La Scuola, 2006.

Cavaterra, Emilio. *Il prefetto del Sant'Offizio: Le opere e i giorni del cardinale Ottaviani*. Milan: Mursia Editore, 1990.

Ceci, Lucia. *L'interesse superiore: Il Vaticano e l'Italia di Mussolini*. Rome and Bari: Laterza, 2013.

Ceci, Lucia, and Demofonti, Laura, eds. *Chiesa, laicità e vita civile: Studi in onore di Guido Verucci*. Rome: Carocci, 2005.

Centro Cattolico cinematografico. *Guida Cinematografica, 1934–1962*. Rome: CCC, 1962.

Centro Studi Economico Sociali. *La Radiotelevisione in Italia: Legislazione, Documenti Parlamentari dal 1958 al 1963*. Milan: Studium, 1963.

Cereda, Giuseppe, and Franco Iseppi. *Cinema e cattolici in Italia*. Milan: Editrice Massimo, 1974.

Cervone, Vittorio, and Giacomo Cesaro. *La Formazione politica*. Naples: Società Editrice Napolitana, 1980.

Cesari, Maurizio. *La censura in Italia oggi (1944–1980)*. Naples: Liguori editore, 1982.

Chadwick, Owen. *The Secularization of the European Mind in the 19th Century*. Cambridge: Cambridge University Press, 1975.

———. *The Popes and European Revolution*. New York: Oxford University Press, 1981.

———. *The Reformation*. New York: Penguin, 1985.

———. *The Christian Church in the Cold War*. London: Penguin, 1993.

Cheles, Luciano, and Lucio Sponza, eds. *The Art of Persuasion: Political Communication in Italy from 1945 to the 1990s*. Manchester: Manchester University Press, 2001.

Cherchi, Augusto, ed. *Guida all'Italia contemporanea 1961–1997*. Milan: Garzanti, 1998.

Chiarante, Giuseppe. *Considerazioni sul partito cattolico*. Florence: Giunti, 1957.

Chiarenza, Franco. *Il Cavallo morente: Trent'anni di Radiotelevisone italiana*. Milan: Bompiani, 1978.

Chierici, Arnaldo. *Una Speranza per la Chiesa: Padre Lombardi ed il Movimento Mondo Migliore*. Rome: Rogate, 1984.

Chimenti, Anna. *Storia dei Referendum: Dal divorzio alla riforma elettorale*. Rome and Bari: Editori Laterza, 1993.

Chinnici, Giuseppe. *Cinema: Chiesa e movimento cattolico italiano*. Rome: Aracne Editrice, 2003.

Christian, Linda. *Linda: My Own Story*. New York: Crown, 1962.

Civardi, Luigi. *Manuale di Azione Cattolica*. Rome: Coletti, 1961.

Clark, Christopher, and Wolfram Kaiser, eds. *Culture Wars: Secular-Catholic Conflict in Nineteenth-Century Europe*. Cambridge: Cambridge University Press, 2003.

Clark, J. C. D. "Secularization and Modernization: The Failure of a 'Grand Narrative.'" *Historical Journal* 55, no. 1 (2012): 161–94.

Clark, Martin. *Modern Italy: 1871 to the Present*. Harlow, Essex: Pearson Longman, 2008.

Clark, Martin, David Hine, and R. E. M. Irving. "Divorce—Italian Style." *Parliamentary Affairs* 27 (1974).

Clericuzio, Alessandro. *Tennesee Williams in Italy: A Transcultural Perspective*. Switzerland: Palgrave Macmillan, 2016.

Colasio, Andrea. "Forme del conflitto politico nel Veneto degli anni '50: Il processo ai 'Pionieri di Pozzonovo.'" *Venetica*, no. 2 (1984).

Coleman, Peter. *The Liberal Conspiracy: The Congress for Cultural Freedom and the Struggle for the Mind of Postwar Europe*. New York: Free Press, 1989.

Coletti, Alessandro. *Il divorzio in Italia: Storia di una battaglia civile e democratica*. Rome: Giulio Savelli editore, 1974.

Comitato Centrale Anno Santo, ed. *L'Anno santo 1950: Cronistoria del grande giubileo*. 2 vols. Vatican City: Tipografia poliglotta vaticana, 1952.

Conferenza Episcopale Italiana. *Atti della III assemblea generale: I laici nella Chiesa in Italia dopo il Concilio*. Milan: Àncora, 1968.

Congresso eucaristico nazionale. *XV Congresso eucaristico nazionale: L'eucaristia; "Sacramentum unitatis, vinculum caritatis."* Rome: Società Anonima Poligrafica Italiana, 1957.

Coppa, Frank J. *Pope Pius IX: Crusader in a Secular Age*. Boston: Twayne Publishers, 1979.

———, ed. *Controversial Concordats: The Vatican's Relations with Napoleon, Mussolini and Hitler*. Washington, D.C.: The Catholic University of America Press, 1999.

———. *The Life and Pontificate of Pope Pius XII*. Washington, D.C.: The Catholic University of America Press, 2013.

Cordovani, Rinaldo. *Padre Mariano: Il parroco di tutti gli italiani*. Padua: Edizioni Messagero Padova, 2011.

Corti, Antonio, et. al. *La famiglia nella società di oggi*. Milan: Vita E Pensiero, 1971.

Cragg, Gerald R. *The Church and the Age of Reason, 1648–1789*. New York: Penguin, 1985.

Crainz, Guido. *Storia del miracolo italiano: Culture identità, trasformazioni fra anni cinquanta e sessanta*. Rome: Donzelli, 1998.

———. *Il Paese mancato: Dal miracolo economico agli anni ottanta*. Rome: Donzelli, 2005.

———. *Autobiografia di una repubblica: Le radici dell'Italia attuale*. Rome: Donzelli, 2009.

———. *Il paese reale: Dall'assassinio di Moro all'Italia di oggi*. Rome: Donzelli, 2012.

Crapis, Giandomenico. *Il frigorifero del cervello: Il PCI e la televisione da "Lascia o raddoppia?" alla battaglia contro gli spot*. Rome: Riuniti, 2002.

Craveri, Piero. *De Gasperi*. Bologna: Il Mulino, 2006.

Cullen, Niamh. "Morals, Modern Identities and the Catholic Woman: Fashion in Famiglia Cristiana, 1954–1968." *Journal of Modern Italian Studies* 18, no. 1 (2013).

Cuminetti, Mario. *Il dissenso cattolico in Italia: (1965–1980)*. Milan: Rizzoli, 1983.

Dabhoiwala, Faramerz. *The Origins of Sex: A History of the First Sexual Revolution*. Oxford: Oxford University Press, 2012.

Damilano, Andrea, ed. *Atti e Documenti della Democrazia Cristiana 1943–1967*. Rome: Cinque Lune, 1968.

D'Angelo, Augusto. *De Gasperi, Le destre e L'"Operazione Sturzo": Voto amministrativo del 1952 e progetti do riforma elettorale*. Rome: Studium, 2002.

———. *Moro: I vescovi e l'apertura a sinistra*. Rome: Studium, 2005.

D'Angelo, Augusto, Paolo Trionfini, and Roberto P. Violi, eds. *Democrazia e coscienza religiosa nella storia del Novecento: Studi in onore di Francesco Malgeri*. Rome: Ave, 2010.

Dau Novelli, Cecelia. *De Gasperi nell'età del centrismo*. Edited by G. Rossini. Rome: Cinque Lune, 1984.

———. *Donne del nostro tempo: Il centro italiano femminile (1945–1995)*. Rome: Studium, 1995.

———. *Politica e nuove identità nell'Italia del "Miracolo."* Rome: Studium, 1999.

Davie, Grace. *Religion in Modern Europe in the 21st Century: The Factors to Take into Account; A Memory Mutates*. New York: Oxford University Press, 2000.

———. *Europe: The Exceptional Case; Parameters of Faith in the Modern World*. London: Darton, Longman and Todd, 2002.

de Antonellis, Giacomo. *Storia dell' Azione Cattolica dal 1867 a oggi*. Milan: Rizzoli, 1987.

De Berti, Raffaele. *Il cinema a Milano: Dal secondo dopoguerra ai primi anni sessanta*. Milan: Vita e Pensiero, 1991.

De Donno, Fabrizio, and Simon Gilson, eds. *Beyond Catholicism: Heresy, Mysticism, and Apocalypse in Italian Culture*. New York: Palgrave, 2014.

De Felice, Franco. *De Gasperi e la Questione Democristiana*. Milan: Publikompass, 1975.

De Felice, Renzo. *Mussolini il fascista: L'organizazzione dello Stato fascista 1925–1929*. Turin: Einaudi, 1995.

———. *Mussolini l'alleato: I. L'Italia in Guerra, 1940–1943*. Vol. 2, *Crisi e agonia del regime*. Turin: Einaudi, 1996.

———. *Mussolini il duce: Gli anni del consenso 1929–1936*. Turin: Einaudi, 1996.

de Franciscis, Maria Elisabetta. *Italy and the Vatican: The 1984 Concordat between Church and State*. New York: Peter Lang, 1989.

De Gasperi, Alcide. *Scritti politici di Alcide De Gasperi*. Edited by Pier Giorgio Zunino. Milan: Feltrinelli, 1979.

Degli Innocenti, Maurizio. "La villeggiatura: un diritto per tutti." *Il Risorgimento* 45, no. 2 (1993).

De Grazia, Victoria. *How Fascism Ruled Women, Italy 1922–1945*. Berkeley: University of California Press, 1992.

———. *Irresistible Empire: America's Advance through Twentieth-Century Europe*. Cambridge, Mass.: Harvard University Press, 2005.

Delumeau, Jean. *Catholicism between Luther and Voltaire: A New View of the Counter-Reformation*. London: Burns and Oates, 1977.

De Marco, Vittorio. *Le Barricate invisibili: La Chiesa in Italia tra politica e società (1945–1978)*. Lecce: Congedo, 1994.

———. *Storia dell'Azione Cattolica negli anni settanta*. Rome: Città Nuova, 2007.

Democrazia cristiana. *La società italiana: Atti del secondo convegno nazionale di studio della democrazia cristiana*. Rome: Cinque Lune, 1963.

De Rosa, Gabriele. *Da Luigi Sturzo ad Aldo Moro*. Brescia: Morcelliana, 1988.

———. *Il Movimento cattolico in Italia dalla restaurazione all'età giolittiana*. Rome and Bari: Laterza, 1988.

——-. *Il Partito Popolare Italiano*. Rome and Bari: Laterza, 1974.

———. *Storia dell'Italia religiosa I Dalla Restaurazione all'età giolittiana*. Rome and Bari: Laterza, 1988.

De Rosa, Gabriele, et. al. *Fanfani e la casa: Gli anni Cinquanta e il modello italiano di welfare state; Il piano INA-Casa*. Rome and Soveria Mannelli: Istituto Luigi Sturzo-Rubbettino, 2002.

De Vigili, Diana. *La battaglia sul divorzio: Dalla Costituente al Referendum*. Milan: Franco Angeli, 2000.

Di Bella, Maria Pia. *Dire o tacere in Sicilia: Viaggio alle radici dell'omertà*. Rome: Armando editore, 2011.

Di Biagi, Paola, ed. *La grande ricostruzione: Il piano Ina-Casa e l'Italia degli anni '50*. Rome: Donzelli Editore, 2001.

Di Lorenzo, Maria. *Blessed Pier Giorgio Frassati: An Ordinary Christian*. Translated by Robert Ventresca. Boston: Pauline, 2004.

Di Stefano, Carlo. *La Censura teatrale in Italia (1600–1962)*. Rocca San Casciano: Cappelli, 1964.

Diotallevi, Luca. *Religione, chiesa e modernizzazione: Il caso italiano; Aggiornamenti agli anni '90 sugli approdi del progetto cattolico di modernizzazione religiosa: Un contributo di sociologia della religione*. Rome: Borla, 1999.

———. "The Territorial Articulation of Secularization: Social Modernization, Religious Modernization in Italy." *Archives de Sciences Sociales des Religions*, 1999.

———. *Il rompicapo della secolarizzazione italiana: Caso italiano, teorie americane e revisione del paradigma della secolarizzazione*. Soveria Mannelli: Rubbettino, 2001.

———. "Internal Competition in a National Religious Monopoly: The Catholic Effect and the Italian Case." *Sociology of Religion* 63, no. 2 (2002).

Domenico, Roy. "'For the Cause of Christ Here in Italy': Evangelical America's Holy Mission in Italy and the Cultural Ambiguities of the Cold War." *Diplomatic History* 29, no. 4 (September 2005): 630–31.

———. "Gedda, il laicato e la cultura cattolica negli anni Cinquanta." In *Luigi Gedda nella storia della chiesa e del paese*, edited by Ernesto Preziosi. Rome: A.V.E., 2013.

———. "Sex, Scandal and Catholic Politics during Italy's Dolce Vita." In *Scandal! An Interdisciplinary Approach to the Consequences, Outcomes, and Significance of Political Scandals*, edited by Alison Dagnes and Mark Sachleben. New York: Bloomsbury Press, 2014.

Donovan, Mark. "Italy: A Dramatic Case of Secularization?" In *Religion and Mass Election Behavior in Europe*, edited by David Broughton and Hans-Marten ten Napel. London: Routledge, 2000.

Drake, Richard. "Catholics and the Italian Revolutionary Left of the 1960s." *Catholic Historical Review* 94, no. 3 (July 2008).

Eco, Umberto. *Il costume di casa: Evidenze e misteri dell'ideologia italiana*. Milan: Bompiani, 1973.

Eder, Franz X., Leslie Hall, and Gert Hekma, eds. *Sexual Cultures in Europe: National Histories*. Manchester: Manchester University Press, 1999.

Eilers, Franz-Josef. *Church and Social Communication: Basic Documents*. 2nd ed. Manila: Logos, 1997.

Ellis, John. *Seeing Things: Television in the Age of Uncertainty*. London: I. B. Tauris, 2000.

Ellwood, David W. *Hollywood in Europa: Industria, politica, pubblico del cinema 1945–1960*. Firenze: La Casa Usher, 1991.

———. "The 1948 Elections in Italy: A Cold War Propaganda Battle." *Historical Journal of Film, Radio and Television* 13, no. 1 (1993).

———. *The Shock of America: Europe and the Challenge of the Century*. New York: Oxford University Press, 2012.

Emiliani, Vittorio. *L'Italia mangiata: Lo scandalo degli enti inutile*. Turin: Einaudi, 1977.

Esposito, Rosario F., SSP. *La Massoneria e L'Italia dal 1800 ai nostri giorni*. Rome: Paoline, 1979.

Eugeni, Ruggero, and Dario E. Viganò, eds. *Attraverso lo schermo: Cinema e cultura cattolica in Italia*. Vol. 2, *Dagli anni trenta agli anni sessanta*. Rome: Ente dello spettacolo, 2006.

———. *Attraverso lo schermo: Cinema e cultura cattolica in Italia*. Vol. 3, *Dagli anni settanta ai nostri giorni*. Rome: Ente dello spettacolo, 2006.

Faggioli, Massimo. "Tra referendum sul divorzio e revisione del Concordato: Enrico Bartoletti segretario della CEI (1972–1976)." *Contemporanea* 4, no. 2 (April 2001).

———. "The New Elites of Italian Catholicism: 1968 and the New Catholic Movements." *Catholic Historical Review* 98, no. 1 (Winter 2012): 25–26.

Falconi, Carlo. *La Chiesa e le organizzazioni cattoliche in Italia 1945–55*. Turin: Giulio Einaudi, 1956.

———. *Gedda e L'azione cattolica*. Florence: Parenti editore, 1958.

Fanfani, Amintore. *Una pieve in Italia*. Milan: Mondadori, 1964.

———. *Anni difficili ma non sterili*. Rocca San Casciano, Capelli, 1968.
———. *Giorgio La Pira: Un profilo e 24 lettere inedite*. Milan: Rusconi, 1978.
———. *Diari*. 4 vols. Soveria Mannelli: Rubbettino, 2012.
Farinelli, Pietro. *Il Vescovo di Prato alla sbarra del tribunale penale, ossia il suo "famoso caso" alla luce dei fatti e del diritto*. Pistoia: Tipografia Pistoiese, 1958.
Farrell, Joseph. *Dario Fo and Franca Rame: Harlequins of the Revolution*. London: Methuen, 2001.
Farrell, Joseph, and Paolo Puppa, eds. *A History of Italian Theatre*. New York: Cambridge University Press, 2006.
Favilli, Lorenzo. *Lo stato e il cinema*. Rome: Favilli, 1961.
Fazzari, Giuseppe M. *L'Esercizio della giurisdizione ecclesiastica in Italia: Riflessioni sulla motivazione delle sentenza contro il Vescovo di Prato*. Naples: M. D'Auria, 1958.
Fehrenbach, Heide. *Cinema in Democratizing Germany: Reconstructing National Identity after Hitler*. Chapel Hill: University of North Carolina Press, 1995.
Fellini, Federico. *Fellini on Fellini*. Translated by Isabel Quigley. New York: Delacorte Press and Seymour Lawrence, 1976.
Ferluga, Gabriele. *Il processo Braibanti*. Turin: Silvio Zamorani editore, 2003.
Ferrara, Patrizia, ed. *Censura teatrale e fascismo (1931–1944): La storia, l'archivio, l'inventario*. 2 vols. Rome: Ministero per i beni e le attività culturali, Direzione generale per gli archivi, 2004.
Ferrari, Ada. *La cultura riformatrice: Uomini, tecniche, filosofie di fronte allo sviluppo (1945–1968)*. Rome: Studium, 1995.
———. *Milano e La RAI un Incontro Mancato? Luci e ombre di una capitale di transizione(1945–1977)*. Milan: FrancoAngeli, 2002.
Ferrer Benimeli, José, and Giovanni Caprile. *Massoneria e Chiesa Cattolica: Ieri, oggi e domani*. Rome: Edizioni Paoline, 1979.
Ferretti, Claudio, Umberto Broccoli, and Barbara Scaramucci. *Mamma RAI: Storia e storie del servizio pubblico radiotelevisivo*. Florence: La Monnier, 1997.
Ferris, Kate. *Everyday Life in Fascist Venice, 1929–1940*. New York: Palgrave Macmillan, 2012.
Festa, Federica. *Teatro proibito: In scena i tabù di una nazione*. Spoleto: Editoria and Spettacolo, 2011.
Filzzola, Renato. *Amintore Fanfani: Quaresime e resurrezioni*. Rome: Editalia-Edizioni d'Italia, 1988.
Fiore, Tommaso. *Gabriele Pepe e la sua protesta laica*. Edited by Francesco D'Episcopo. Maduria: Laicata, 2001.
Fisicaro, Emanuele. *Diritto cinematografico*. Milan: Dott. A. Giuffrè Editore, 2006.
Fo, Dario. *Il Fanfani rapito*. Verona: Bertani editore, 1975.
Fogarty, Michael. *Christian Democracy in Western Europe 1820–1953*. Notre Dame, Ind.: University of Notre Dame Press, 1957.
Follini, Marco. *L'Arcipelago democristiano*. Rome and -Bari: Laterza, 1990.
———. *La DC*. Bologna: Il Mulino, 2000.
Fondi, Enzo Maria, and Michele Zanzucchi. *Un popolo nato dal vangelo: Chiara Lubich e i Focolari*. Milan: Edizioni San Paolo, 2003.
Foot, John. *Milan Since the Miracle: City, Culture, and Identity*. New York: Berg, 2001.
Forgacs, David. *Italian Culture in the Industrial Era 1880–1980: Cultural Industries, Politics, and the Public*. Manchester: Manchester University Press, 1990.

Forgacs, David, and Stephen Gundle. *Mass Culture and Italian Society: From Fascism to the Cold War*. Bloomington: Indiana University Press, 2007.

Forlenza, Rosario. *Le elezioni amministrative della Prima repubblica: Politica e propaganda locale nell'Italia repubblicana*. Rome: Donzelli, 2008.

———. *On the Edge of Democracy: Italy, 1943–1948*. New York: Oxford University Press, 2019.

Formigoni, Guido. *La Democrazia cristiana e l'alleanza occidentale (1943–1953)*. Bologna: Il Mulino, 1996.

———. *L'Italia dei cattolici: Fede e nazione dal Risorgimento alla Repubblica*. Bologna: Il Mulino, 1998.

———. *Alla prova della democrazia: Chiesa, cattolici e modernità nell'Italia del '900*. Trent: Il Margine, 2008.

Formigoni, Guido, and Giorgio Vecchio. *L'Azione cattolica nella Milano del novecento*. Milan: Rusconi, 1989.

Fortuna, Pietro, Luciana Jorio, and Attilio Pandini. *Rapporto sul divorzio in italia*. Milan: Longanesi, 1968.

Fragnito, Gigliola, ed. *Church, Censorship and Culture in Early Modern Italy*. Cambridge: Cambridge University Press, 2001.

Frajese, Vittorio. *Nascita dell'indice: La censura ecclesiastica dal Rinascimento alla Controriforma*. Brescia: Morcelliana, 2006.

Francese, Joseph. *Cultura e politica negli anni cinquanta: Salinari, Pasolini, Calvino*. Rome: Lithos, 2000.

Franchini, Silvia. *Diventare grandi con il "Pioniere" (1950–1962) Política: Progetti di vita e identità di genere nella piccola posta di un giornalino di sinistra*. Florence: Firenze University Press, 2006.

Franco, Massimo, and Arnaldo Mondadori. *Andreotti: La vita di un uomo politico, la storia di un'epoca*. Milan: Mondadori, 2008.

Furlong, Paul. "The Italian Christian Democrats: From Catholic Movement to Conservative Party." Hull Papers in Politics, no. 25. Hull: University of Hull, February 1982.

Gaiotti de Biase, Paola. *Passare la mano: Memorie di una donna dal Novecento incompiuto*. Rome: Viella, 2010.

Gallagher, Tag. *The Adventures of Roberto Rossellini*. New York: Da Capo, 1998.

Galli, Diego. *Pannella: La vita e l'eredità*. Rome: Castelvecchi, 2016.

Galli, Giorgio. *Fanfani*. Milan: Feltrinelli, 1975.

———. *Storia della Democrazia Cristiana*. Rome and Bari: Laterza, 1978.

———. *Mezzo secolo di DC*. Milan: Rizzoli, 1993.

Galli, Giorgio, and Paolo Facchi. *La Sinistra democristiana: Storia e ideologia*. Milan: Feltrinelli, 1962.

Gambetti, Giacomo. *Cinema e censura in Italia*. Rome: Bianco e nero, 1972.

García Márquez, Gabriel. *The Scandal of the Century and Other Writings*. Edited by Cristóbal Pera. Translated by Anne McLean. New York: Alfred A. Knopf, 2019.

Garelli, Franco. *Religione e la chiesa in Italia*. Bologna: il Mulino, 1991.

———. *Forza della religione e debolezza della fede*. Bologna: il Mulino, 1996.

———. "Introduction: The Church and Catholicism in Contemporary Italy" and "Public Relevance of the Church and Catholicism in Italy." Special issue edited by Franco Garelli. *Journal of Modern Italian Studies* 12, no. 1 (2007).

Garofalo, Damiano. *Political Audiences: A Reception History of Early Italian Television.* Translated by Michael Sarnoff-Wood. Milan: Mimesis International, 2016.

Garrone, Alessandro Galante. *Calamandrei.* Milan: Garzanti, 1987.

Gauchet, Maurice. *The Disenchantment of the World.* Princeton, N.J.: Princeton University Press, 1997.

Gaudio, Angelo. *La politica scolastica dei cattolici, 1943–1953: Dai programmi all'azione di governo.* Brescia: Editrice La Scuola, 1991.

Gavuzzo, Gino. *Guida per la difesa della moralità: Indicazioni, legislazione, giurisprudenza.* Rome: Segretariato centrale per la moralità, 1952.

Gedda, Luigi. *Studio dei gemelli.* Rome: Edizioni orrizonte medico, 1951.

———. *Dieci anni al servizio dello sport.* Rome: Atena, 1954.

———. *18 aprile 1948: Memorie inedite dell'artefice della sconfitta del Fronte Popolare.* Milan: Mondadori, 1998.

Gellner, Ernest. *Postmodernism, Reason and Religion.* London: Routledge, 1992.

Germi, Pietro, and Giorgio Moscon. *Divorzio all'italiana.* Rome: Edizioni FM, 1961.

Gheda, Paolo. *Siri: La chiesa; L'Italia.* Genoa and Milan: Marrietti, 2009.

Giasanti, Alberto. *La confroriforma universitaria: Da Gonella a Malfatti.* Milan: Gabriele Mazzotta, 1977.

Gibson, Ian. *The Shameful Life of Salvador Dalí.* New York: W. W. Norton, 1998.

Ginsborg, Paul. *A History of Contemporary Italy: Society and Politics 1943–1988.* London: Penguin, 1990. Reprint: New York: Palgrave Macmillan, 2003.

———. *Silvio Berlusconi: Television, Power and Patrimony.* London: Verso, 2004.

Giovagnoli, Agostino. *Le premesse della ricostruzione: Tradizione e modernità nella classe dirigente cattolica del dopoguerra.* Milan: Nuovo istituto editoriale italiano, 1982.

———. *La Cultura democristiana: Tra Chiesa Cattolica e Identità Italiana, 1918–1948.* Rome and Bari: Laterza, 1991.

———. *Il Partito italiano: La Democrazia cristiana dal 1942 al 1994.* Rome and Bari: Laterza, 1996.

———. "Dal partito del 18 aprile 1948 al 'partito pesante' La Democrazia cristiana nel 1951." *Italia contemporanea*, no. 227, June 2002.

———. *Chiesa e democrazia: La lezione di Pietro Scoppola.* Bologna: il Mulino, 2011.

Giovagnoli, Agostino, and Luciano Tosi, eds. *Amintore Fanfani e la politica estera italiana: Atti del convegno di studi tenuto a Roma il 3 e 4 febbraio 2009.* Venice: Marsilio, 2010.

Gismondi, Arturo. *La Radiotelevisione in Italia.* Rome: Editori Riuniti, 1958.

GLBTQ: An Encyclopedia of Gay, Lesbian, Bisexual, Transgender and Queer Culture. http://www.glbtqarchive.com/literature/peyrefitte_r_L.pdf. Accessed November 13, 2019.

Godman, Peter. *The Saint as Censor: Robert Bellarmine between Inquisition and Index.* Leiden: Brill, 2000.

Gonella, Guido. *Cinque anni al Ministerio della pubblica istruzione.* Vol. 1, *La riniascita della Scuola dopo la seconda guerra mondiale*; Vol. 2, *Libertà della Scuola e nuovi ordinamenti scolastici*; Vol. 3, *Arte Cultura Storia.* Milan: Dott. A. Giuffrè Editore: 1981.

———. *Guido Gonella discorsi parlamentari (1946–1973)*. Edited by Giuseppe Ignesti. Rome: Camera dei deputati, 2005.

Gonella, Guido. *Il programma della democrazia cristiana per la nuova costituzione*. Rome: BUR, 1946.

Gonella, Guido, and Flaminio Piccoli. *Il codice di comportamento della DC*. Rome: Edizioni Logos, 1982.

Gori, Gianfranco, and Stefano Pivato, eds. *Bianco e nero: Gli anni del cinema di parrocchia*. Rimini: Maggioli Editore, 1981.

Gorresio, Vittorio. *Il Papa e il diavolo*. Milan: Rizzoli, 1973.

Grasso, Aldo, ed. *Storia e culture della televisione italiana*. Milan: Mondadori, 2013.

Greene, Graham. *Monsignor Quixote*. New York: Simon and Schuster, 1982.

Graziani, Ermanno. *Il Carattere sacro di Roma: Contributo all'interpretazione dell'Art.1, CPV., Conc*. Milan: Dott. A. Giuffré editore, 1961.

Grendler, Paul. *Culture and Censorship in Late Renaissance Italy and France*. London: Variorum, 1981.

Grignetti, Francesco. *Il caso Montesi: Sesso, potere e morte nell'Italia degli anni '50*. Venice: Marsiglio, 2006.

Gualtieri, Roberto, ed. *Il PCI nell'Italia repubblicana, 1943–1991*. Rome: Carocci editore, 2001.

Guasco, Alberto. *Cattolici e fascisti: La Santa sede e la politica italiana all'alba del regime (1919–1925)*. Bologna: Il Mulino, 2013.

Guasco, Maurilio. "La vita religiosa nell'Italia repubblicana." *Italia contemporanea*, no. 181, December 1990.

———. *Storia del clero in Italia dall'ottocento a oggi*. Rome and Bari: Laterza, 1997.

———. *Chiesa e cattolicesimo in Italia (1945–2000)*. Bologna: EDB, 2001.

Guasco, Maurilio, and Paolo Trionfini, eds. *Don Zeno e Nomadelfia: Tra società civile e società religiosa*. Brescia: Morcelliana, 2001.

Guazzaloca, Giulia. "The 'Revolution That Never Was': Rai-TV and the Launch of *Tribuna politica*." *Modern Italy* 14, no. 3 (2009).

———. *Una e divisibile: La RAI e i partiti negli anni del monopolio pubblico (1954–1975)*. Florence: Le Monnier, 2011.

Gubert, Renzo, ed. *La via italiana alla postmodernità: Verso una nuova architettura dei valori*. Milan: FrancoAngeli, 2000.

Gundle, Stephen. "Sophia Loren, Italian Icon." *Journal of Film, Radio, and Television* 15, no. 3 (1995).

———. "Feminine Beauty, National Identity and Political Conflict in Postwar Italy, 1945–1954." *Contemporary European History* 8, no. 3 (1999).

———. *Between Hollywood and Moscow: The Italian Communists and the Challenge of Mass Culture, 1943–1991*. Durham, N.C.: Duke University Press, 2000.

———. "The 'Civic Religion' of the Resistance in Postwar Italy." *Modern Italy* 5, no. 2 (2000).

———. "*La Dolce Vita*." *History Today*, January 2000.

———. "Hollywood Glamour and Mass Consumption in Postwar Italy." *Journal of Cold War Studies* 4, no. 3 (2002).

———. *Bellissima: Feminine Beauty and the Idea of Italy*. New Haven, Conn.: Yale University Press, 2007.

———. *Death and the Dolce Vita: The Dark Side of Rome in the 1950s*. Edinburgh: Canongate, 2011.

Gundle, Stephen, and Lucia Rinaldi, eds. *Assassinations and Murder in Modern Italy: Transformations in Society and Culture*. New York: Palgrave, 2007.

Hales, E. E. Y. *Pio Nono: A Study in European Politics and Religion in the Nineteenth Century*. London: Eyre and Spottiswoode, 1954.

———. *Revolution and the Papacy, 1769–1846*. Notre Dame, Ind.: University of Notre Dame Press, 1966.

Halperin, S. William. "Italian Anticlercalism, 1871–1914." *Journal of Modern History*, no. 1 (March 1947): 23.

Hanley, David, ed. *Christian Democracy in Europe: A Comparative Perspective*. London: Pinter, 1996.

Harrison, Lieta. *Le svergognate*. Rome: Edizioni di Novissima, 1963.

Haworth, Rachel. "Scandal, Motherhood and Mina in 1960s Italy." *Modern Italy* 22, no. 3 (2017).

Headley, John M., and John B. Tomaro, eds. *San Carlo Borromeo: Catholic Reform and Ecclesiastical Politics in the Second Half of the Sixteenth Century*. Cranbury, N.J.: Associated University Presses, 1988.

Hebblethwaite, Peter. *Pope John XXIII: Shepherd of the Modern World*. New York: Doubleday, 1985.

———. *The Runaway Church*. Glasgow: Collins, 1989.

———. *Paul VI: The First Modern Pope*. New York and Mahwah, N.J.: Paulist Press, 1993.

Higgins, Patrick. *Heterosexual Dictatorship: Male Homosexuality in Postwar Britain*. London: Fourth Estate, 1996.

Hilwig, Stuart. *Italy and 1968: Youthful Unrest and Democratic Culture*. New York: Palgrave Macmillan, 2009.

Ignazi, Piero, et. al. *Democristiani: Contributi*. Bologna: il Mulino: 1979.

Ignesti, Giuseppe. *Laici cristiani fra chiesa e stato nel novecento: Profili e problemi*. Rome: Euroma, 1988.

Imbriani, Angelo Michele. *Vento del Sud, Moderati, Reazionari, Qualunquisti: 1943–1948*. Bologna: il Mulino, 1996.

Impagliazzo, Marco, ed. *La Nazione cattolica: Chiesa e società in Italia, 1958–oggi*. Milan: Guerini, 2004.

———. *La diocesi del Papa: La Chiesa di Roma e gli anni di Paolo VI (1963–1978)*. Milan: Guerini, 2006.

Ipsen, Carl. *Italy in the Age of Pinocchio: Children and Danger in the Liberal Era*. New York: Palgrave, 2006.

Isastia, Anna Maria, and Alessandro Visani. *L'Idea laica tra Chiesa e massoneria: La questione della scuola*. Rome: Atanòr, 2008.

Jahec, Nancy. "Anti-Communism at Home, Europeanism Abroad: Italian Cultural Policy at the Venice Biennale." *Contemporary European History* 14, no. 2 (May 2005).

———. *Politics and Painting at the Venice Biennale, 1948–1964: Italy and the Idea of Europe*. Manchester: Manchester University Press, 2007.

Jemolo, Arturo Carlo. *Church and State in Italy, 1850–1950*. Translated by David Moore. Philadelphia: Dufour Editions, 1961.

———. *Scritti vari di storia religiosa e civile*. Edited by Francesco Margiotta Broglio. Milan: Dott. A. Giuffrè Editore, 1965.

———. *Gli occhiali del giurista*. Padova: Cedam—Casa Editrice dott. Antonio Milani, 1970.

Johnson, William Bruce. *Miracles and Sacrilege: Roberto Rossellini, the Church and Film Censorship in Hollywood*. Toronto: University of Toronto Press, 2008.

Katznelson, Ira, and Gareth Stedman Jones, eds. *Religion and the Political Imagination*. Cambridge: Cambridge University Press, 2010.

Kent, Peter. *The Lonely Cold War of Pope Pius XII: The Roman Catholic Church and the Division of Europe, 1943–1950*. Montreal and Kingston: McGill-Queens University Press, 2002.

Kertzer, David I. Ritual, *Politics and Power*. New Haven, Conn.: Yale University Press, 1988.

———. *The Pope and Mussolini: The Secret History of Pius XI and the Rise of Fascism in Europe*. New York: Random House, 2014.

Kezich, Tulio. *Federico: Fellini, la vita e i film*. Milan: Felrinelli, 2002.

———. *Federico Fellini: His Life and Work*. New York: Faber and Faber, 2006.

Kogan, Norman. *A Political History of Italy: The Postwar Years*. New York: Praeger, 1966.

Kornberg, Jacques. *The Pope's Dilemma: Pius XII Faces Atrocities and Genocide in the Second World War*. Toronto: University of Toronto Press, 2015.

Kselman, Thomas, and Joseph A. Buttigieg, eds. *European Christian Democracy: Historical Legacies and Comparative Perspectives*. Notre Dame, Ind.: University of Notre Dame Press, 2003.

La base missionaria. Rome: Ediroma, 1952.

Lai, Benny. *Il Papa non eletto: Giuseppe Siri, cardinale della Santa Romana Chiesa*. Rome: Laterza, 1993.

Lanaro, Silvio. *Storia dell'Italia repubblicana: L'economia, la politica, la cultura, la società, dal dopoguerra agli anni '90*. Venice: Marsilio, 1992.

La Francesca, Sofia. *La linea riformista: La testimonianza dei diari di Amintore Fanfani (1943–1959)*. Florence: Le Monnier, 2007.

LaPalombara, Joseph. *Interest Groups in Italian Politics*. Princeton, N.J.: Princeton University Press, 1964.

———. *Democracy Italian Style*. New Haven, Conn.: Yale University Press, 1987.

La Pira, Giorgio. *Premesse della politica*. Florence: Libreria Editrice Fiorentina, 1945.

La Russa, Vincenzo. *Amintore Fanfani*. Soveria Mannelli: Rubbettino, 2006.

Laura, Ernesto G., ed. *La censura cinematografica: Idee, esperienze, documenti*. Rome: Bianco e nero, 1961.

———, ed. *Tutti i Film di Venezia: 1932–1984*. Venice: La Biennale, Settore cinema e spettacolo televisivo, 1985.

Leonardi, Robert, and Douglas Wertman. *Italian Christian Democracy: The Politics of Dominance*. London: Macmillan, 1989.

Levi, Carlo. *Fleeting Rome: In Search of La Dolce Vita*. Chichester, West Sussex: John Wiley and Sons.

Levy, Shawn. *Dolce Vita Confidential: Fellini, Loren, Pucci, Paparazzi, and the Swinging High Life of 1950s Rome*. New York: W. W. Norton, 2016.

Liggeri, Domenico. *Mani di forbice: La censura cinematografica in Italia*. Alessandria: Falsopiano, Maggio 1997.

Lipari, Nicolò, Alberto Monticone, and Pietro Scoppola. *Cattolici e la riforma della vita pubblica*. Padua: Gregoriana, 1988.

Livi-Bacci, Massimo. *A History of Italian Fertility during the Last Two Centuries*. Princeton, N.J.: Princeton University Press, 1977.

Logan, Oliver. "Pius XII: Romanità, Prophesy and Charisma." *Modern Italy* 3, no. 2 (1998): 237–47.

Lombardi, Riccardo. *Per una mobilitazione generale dei cattolici*. Rome: Edizioni Civiltà Cattolica, 1948.

Lonero, Emilio, and Aldo Anziano. *La Storia della Orbis-Universalia: Cattolici e neorealismo*. Turin: Effatà, 2004.

Lugaro, Natal Mario. *Raimondo Manzini: Giornalista cattolico*. Milan: NED, 1988.

Lumley, Robert. *States of Emergency: Cultures of Revolt in Italy from 1968 to 1978*. London: Verso, 1990.

Lumley, Robert, and Jonathan Morris, eds. *The New History of the Italian South: The Mezzogiorno Revisited*. Exeter: University of Exeter Press, 1997.

Lupi, Maria. "Clero italiano e cura pastorale in età contemporanea: Fonti e dibattito storiografico." *Rivista di storia della chiesa in Italia* 60, no. 1 (January–June 2006).

Lussana, Fiamma. *Il movimento femminista in Italia: Esperienze, storie, memorie (1965–1980)*. Rome: Carocci editore, 2012.

———. *L'Italia del divorzio: La battaglia fra Stato, Chiesa e gente comune; Con lettere dei "fuorilegge del matrimonio."* Rome: Carocci, 2014.

Lussana, Fiamma, and Giacomo Marramao, eds. *L'Italia Repubblicana nella crisi degli anni settanta: Culture, nuovi soggetti, identità*. Soveria Mannelli: Rubattino, 2003.

Luzzati, Mario. *Il matrimonio in italia*. Milan: L. Dig. Pirola, 1967.

Luzzatto-Fegiz, Pierpaolo. *Il Volto sconosciuto dell'Italia: Dieci anni di sondaggi DOXA*. Milan: Dott. A. Giuffrè Editore, 1956.

Madeo, Liliana. *Donne cattive: Cinquant'anni di vita italiana*. Milan: Tartaruga, 1999.

Mafai, Miriam, ed. *Le donne italiane: Le chi è del '900*. Milan: Rizzoli, 1993.

Magister, Sandro. *La politica vaticana e l'Italia 1943–1978*. Rome: Editori Riuniti, 1979.

Majo, Angelo. *Storia della stampa cattolica in Italia: Con orientamenti bibliografiche*. Milan: NED, 1987.

Malgeri, Francesco. *La Chiesa italiana e la Guerra, 1940–1945*. Rome: Studium, 1980.

———, ed. *Storia della democrazia cristiana*. 5 vols. Rome: Cinque Lune, 1987–89.

———. *Chiesa cattolica e democrazia da Don Sturzo a De Gasperi*. Brescia: Morcelliana, 1990.

———. "La Democrazia cristiana nella crisi degli anni settanta." *Italia contemporanea*, no. 227 (June 2002).

———. *La Stagione del centrismo: Politica e società nell'Italia del secondo dopoguerra (1945–1960)*. Soveria Mannelli: Rubbettino, 2002.

———. *L'Italia Democristiana: Uomini e idee del cattolicesimo democratico nell'Italia repubblicana 1943–1993*. Rome: Gangemi Editore, 2005.

Malgeri, Francesco, and Leonardo Paggi, eds. *L'Italia Repubblicana nella crisi degli anni settanta*. Vol. 3, *Partiti e organizzazioni di massa*. Rome: Rubbettino, 2001.

Mannheimer, Renato, Giuseppe Micheli, and Francesca Zajczyk. *Mutamento sociale e comportamento elettorale: Il caso del referendum sul divorzio*. Milan: Franco Angeli Editore, 1978.

Marazziti, Mario. *I Papi di carta: Nascita e svolta dell'informazione religiosa da Pio XII a Giovanni XXIII*. Genoa: Marietti, 1990.

Marchesini, Daniele. *Coppi e Bartali*. Bologna: Il Mulino, 1998.

Marcus, Millicent. *Filmmaking by the Book: Italian Cinema and Literary Adaption*. Baltimore and London: Johns Hopkins University Press, 1993.

Margiotta Broglio, Francesco, et. al. *La successione: Cattolici, Stato e potere negli anni della ricostruzione*. Rome: Lavoro, 1980.

Marino, Giuseppe Carlo. *Guerra fredda e conflitto sociale in Italia: 1947–1953*. Rome: Salvatore Sciascia Editore, 1991.

———. *La Repubblica della forza: Mario Scelba e le passioni del suo tempo*. Milan: Francoangeli, 1995.

Marino, John A., ed. *Early Modern Italy, 1550–1796*. New York: Oxford University Press, 2002.

Mariuzzo, Andrea. *Divergenze parallele: Comunismo e anticomunismo alle origini del linguaggio politico dell'Italia repubblicana (1945–1953)*. Soveria Manelli: Rubettino, 2010.

Marrone, Gaetana. *The Gaze and the Labyrinth: The Cinema of Liliana Cavani*. Princeton, N.J.: Princeton University Press, 2000.

Martin, John. *Venice's Hidden Enemies: Italian Heretics in a Renaissance City*. Berkeley: University of California Press, 1993.

Martin, Simon. "From Cycling Priests to the 'Sportsman's Pope': Italy, Sport and the Catholic Church." *European Review* 19, no. 4 (2011): 548.

———. *Sport Italia: The Italian Love Affair with Sport*. London: I. B. Tauris, 2011.

Martina, Giacomo. *La Chiesa in Italia negli ultimi trent'anni*. Rome: Studium, 1977.

Martinetto, Giulo D. *Attenti ai contadini! . . . Idee di pastorale rurale*. Turin: Berruti & C., 1953.

Marwick, Arthur. *The Sixties: Cultural Revolution in Britain, France, Italy, and the United States, c. 1958–c. 1974*. Oxford: Oxford University Press, 1999.

Marzano, Marco. *Il cattolico e il suo doppio: Organizzazioni religiose e la Democrazia Cristiana nell'Italia del dopoguerra*. Milan: Franco Angeli, 1996.

Mazzanti, Manlio. *L'Osceno e il diritto penale*. Milan: Dott. A. Giuffrè Editore, 1962. Originally published in 1956.

McCarthy, Patrick, ed. *Italy since 1945*. Oxford: Oxford University Press, 2000.

McCraw, William Troy. "Political Sponsorship of the Arts: Subsidization and Censorship of Motion Pictures and the Performing Arts by the Italian National Government, 1943–1962." Ph.D. diss., Stanford University, 1966.

McLeod, Hugh. *Religion and the People of Western Europe, 1789–1989*. Oxford: Oxford University Press, 1997.

———. *Secularization in Western Europe, 1848–1914*. London: Macmillan, 2000.

———. *The Religious Crisis of the 1960s*. Oxford: Oxford University Press, 2007.

McLeod, Hugh, and Werner Ustorf, eds. *The Decline of Christendom in Western Europe, 1750–2000*. Cambridge: Cambridge University Press, 2003.

Melan, Amandine. "Pasolini e la Chiesa nell'Italia del Concilio e della Dolce Vita." *Forum romanum belgicum* (2013). http://kadoc.kuleuven.be/bhir-ihbr/doc/3_artikel_melan.pdf. Accessed December 11, 2019.

Mellini, Mauro. *Così annulla la sacra rota: Divorzio di classe nell'Italia clericale*. Rome: Edizioni Samonà e Savelli, 1969.

Melloni, Alberto, ed. *Cristiani d'Italia*. Rome: Istituto della Encyclopedia Treccani, 2011.

Melloni, Alberto, and Maurilio Guasco. *Un diplomatico vaticano fra dopoguerra e dialogo: Mons. Mario Cagna (1911–1986)*. Bologna: Società Editrice Il Mulino, 2003.

Menduni, Enrico. *L'Autostrada del sole*. Bologna: Il Mulino, 1999.

Menozzi, Daniele. *La chiesa cattolica e la secolarizzazione*. Turin: Einaudi, 1993.

Meucci, Gian Paolo. "La Pira e le istituzioni." *Testimonianze* 21 (April–July1978): 203–6.

Miccoli, Giovanni. *Fra mito della cristianità e la secolarizzazione*. Casale Monferrato: Marietti, 1985.

Miller, James. "Taking off the Gloves: The United States and the Italian Elections of 1948." *Diplomatic History* 9, no. 1 (Winter 1983).

———. *The United States and Italy, 1940–1950: The Politics and Diplomacy of Stabilization*. Chapel Hill: University of North Carolina Press, 1986.

———. *Politics in a Museum: Governing Postwar Florence*. Westport, Conn.: Praeger: 2002.

Minesso, Michela, ed. *Stato e infanzia nell'Italia contemporánea: Origini, sviluppo e fine dell'Onmi 1925–1975*. Bologna: Il Mulino, 2007.

Mitchell, Tony. *Dario Fo: People's Court Jester*. London: Methuen, 1999.

Monaco, Eitel. *L'Anica per l'industria cinematografica*. Rome: Stampa GEC, 1971.

Monteleone, Franco. *Storia della RAI dagli Alleati alla DC (1944–1954)*. Rome and Bari: Laterza, 1980.

———. *Storia della radio e della televisione in Italia*. Venice: Marsilio Editore, 1992.

Monticone, Alberto. "Religiosità popolare e coscienza civile da Pio XII a Giovanni XXIII." *Sociologia, rivista di scienze sociali* 18 (1984).

Moravia, Alberto. *Two Women*. Translated by Angus Dawson. New York: Farrar, Straus and Cudahy, 1958.

Morlion, Félix A. *The Apostolate of Public Opinion*. Montreal: Fides, 1944.

Moro, Alfredo Carlo. *Crisi nella famiglia?* Rome: Studium, 1958.

Moro, Renato. "Il 'modernizzazione buono' la 'modernizzazione cattolica tra fascismo e postfascismo come problema storiografico." *Storia contemporanea* 19, no. 4 (1988).

Morris, Penelope. "'Let's Not Talk about Italian Sex': The Reception of the Kinsey Reports in Italy." *Journal of Modern Italian Studies* 18, no. 1 (2013).

Morris, Penelope, ed. *Women in Italy, 1945–1960: An Interdisciplinary Study*. New York: Palgrave, 2006.

Mosse, George. *The Culture of Western Europe: The Nineteenth and Twentieth Centuries*. Boulder, Colo.: Westview, 1988.

Murialdi, Paolo. *La Stampa Italiana del dopoguerra*. 2 vols. Rome and Bari: Laterza, 1978.

Murphy, Francis X. "Vatican Politics: Structure and Function." *World Politics* 26, no. 4 (July 1974).

Musselli, Luciano. "Chiesa e stato all'Assemblea Costituente: L'Articolo 7 della Costituzione Italiana. *Il Politico* 53, no.1 (1988).

Mussolini, Benito. *My Rise and Fall*. Vol. 2, *History of a Year*. New York: Da Capo, 1998.

Naccarato, Alessandro. *Angeli o demoni i nostri bimbi? Storia di una montatura anticomunista; Il processo ai pionieri di Pozzonovo*. Verona: Cierre edizioni, 2011.

Nanetti, Raffaella T., Robert Leonardi, and Piergiorgio Corbetta. *Italian Politics: A Review*. Vol 2. London: Pinter, 1987.

Naro, Massimo, ed. *Società: Chiesa e ricerca storica; Studi di storia moderna e contemporanea in onore di Pietro Borzomati*. Caltanissetta and Rome: Salvatore Sciascia, 2002.

Negrello, Dolores. *A pugno chiuso: Il Partito comunista padovano dal biennio rosso alla stagione dei movimenti*. Milan: Franco Angeli, 2000.

Nenni, Pietro, *Tempo di Guerra fredda: Diari 1943-1956*. Giuliana Nenni and Domenico Zucàro, eds. Milan: SugarCo, 1981.

Nichols, Peter. *The Politics of the Vatican*. New York: Praeger, 1968.

Noll, Mark. "What Happened to Christian Canada?" *Church History* 75, no. 2 (June 2006).

Novelli, Edoardo. *Dalla TV di partito al partito della TV: Televisione e Politica in Italia*. Florence: La Nuova Italia, 1995.

Nowell-Smith, Geoffrey, and Steven Ricci, eds. *Hollywood and Europe: Economics, Culture, National Identity: 1945–95*. London: British Film Institute, 1998.

O'Malley, John W. *What Happened at Vatican II?* Cambridge, Mass.: Harvard University Press, 2008.

Onelli, Onello. *Mario Scelba: Oltre il socialismo e il capitalismo*. Rome: Al pescatore di luna, 1955.

Orfei, Ruggero. *Andreotti*. Milan: Feltrinelli, 1975.

———. *L'Occupazione del potere: I democristiani '45–'75*. Milan: Longanesi, 1976.

Orlando, Federico. *18 aprile: Così ci salvammo*. Rome: Cinque Lune, 1988.

Ottaviani, Alfredo. *Doveri dello stato cattolico verso la religione*. Rome: Benedettine di Priscilla, 1953.

———. *Il Baluardo*. Rome: Edizioni Ares, 1961.

Overbey, David, trans., ed. *Springtime in Italy: A Reader on Neo-Realism*. Hamden, Conn.: Archon, 1978.

Pace, Enzo. "A Peculiar Pluralism." *Journal of Modern Italian Studies* 12, no. 1 (2007).

Padovani, Umberto A. *Cultura e Cristianesimo*. Milan: Marzorati, 1964.

Pagnotta, Grazia. *Sindaci a Roma: Il governo della Capitale dal dopoguerra a oggi*. Rome: Donzelli editore, 2006.

Paiano, Maria. *Liturgia e società nel novecento: Percorsi del movimento liturgico di fronte ai processi di secolarizzazione*. Rome: Edizioni di storia e letteratura, 2000.

———. *Cattolici e unità d'Italia: Tappe, esperienze, problem di un discusso percorso*. Assisi: Cittadella, 2012.

Palagi, Paola. *Giorgio La Pira: Politica e opzione per i poveri*. Bologna: Edizioni Dehoniane Bologna, 1996.

Pandolfi, Vito. *Teatro italiano contemporaneo, 1945–1959*. Milan: Schwarz, 1959.

Pannain, Remo. *Delitti contro la moralità pubblica e il buon costume*. Turin: Unione tipografico-editrice torinese, 1952.

Papini, Roberto. *L'Internazionale DC: La cooperazione tra I partiti democratici cristiani dal 1925 al 1985*. Milan: Franco Angeli, 1986.

Parisella, Antonio. *Cultura cattolica e Resistenza nell'Italia reppubblicana*. Rome: AVE, 2005.

Parisi, Arturo, ed. *Democristiani*. Bologna: Il Mulino: 1979.

Pasi, Antonia, and Paolo Sorcinelli. *Amori e trasgressioni: Rapporti di coppia tra '800 e '900*. Bari: edizioni Dedalo, 1995.

Pasolini, Pier Paolo. *Scritti corsari*. Milan: Garzanti Editore, 1975.

———. *L'Usignolo della Chiesa Cattolica*. Turin: Einaudi, 1976.

Patriarca, Silvana. *Italian Vices: Nation and Character from the Risorgimento to the Republic*. Cambridge: Cambridge University Press, 2010.

Pavone, Claudio. *Una guerra civile: Saggio storico sulla moralità nella Resistenza*. Turin: Bollati Boringhieri, 1994.

Pempel, T. J., ed. *Uncommon Democracies: The One-Party Dominant Regimes*. Ithaca, N.Y.: Cornell University Press, 1990.

Pepe, Gabriele. *La Protesta laica*. Manduria: Laicata Editore, 1949.

Perenna, Roberto, ed. *Innovazioni o rinnovamento della Parrocchia? Ragioni di allarme, Motivi di speranza, Impegni di responsabilità*. Como: Cavalleri, 1950.

Perin, Raffaella. *Chiesa cattolica e minoranze in Italia nella prima metà del Novecento: Il caso veneto a confronto*. Venezia: Viella, 2011.

Peretti Griva, Domenico Ricardo. *Esperienza di un magistrato*. Bologna: Einaudi, 1956.

———. *La famiglia e il divorzio*. Bari: Laterza, 1956.

Perry, Alan R. *The don Camillo Stories of Giovannino Guareschi: A Humorist Portrays the Sacred*. Toronto: University of Toronto Press, 2007.

Perry, Nicholas, and Loreto Echeverria. *Under the Heel of Mary*. London and New York: Routledge, 1988.

Peyrefitte, Roger. *The Keys to Saint Peter: A Novel*. New York: Criterion, 1957.

Piccardi, Leopoldo, ed. *Processo al Vescovo di Prato: La requisitoria del procuratore generale, la sentenza di rinvio a giudizio . . . la sentenza*. Florence: Parenti Editore 1958.

———. *Il divorzio in italia*. Florence: La Nuova Italia, 1969.

Piccone Stella, Simonetta. *La prima generazione: Ragazze e ragazzi nel miracolo economico italiano*. Milan: FrancoAngeli, 1993.

Piersanti, Andrea, ed. *Cento Anni di Biennale di Cinema: La Presenza della Chiesa*. Rome: Ente dello Spettacolo, 1996.

Pinkus, Karen. *The Montesi Scandal: The Death of Wilma Montesi and the Birth of the Paparazzi in Fellini's Rome*. Chicago: University of Chicago Press, 2003.

Piva, Francesco. *La Gioventù cattolica in camino . . . Memoria e storia del gruppo dirigente (1946–1954)*. Milan: Francoangeli, 2003.

Pivato, Stefano. "Movimento cattolico e questione dello sport." In *Dizionario storico del movimento cattolico in Italia (1860–1980)*, edited by Francesco Tranielo and Giorgio Campanini. I fatti e le idee. Turin: Marietti, 1980–1984.

———. *Clericalismo e laicismo nella cultura popolare italiana*. Milan: Franco Angeli, 1990.

———. *I comunisti mangiano i bambini: Storia di una leggenda*. Bologna: il Mulino, 2013.

———. *Il Touring Club Italiano*. Bologna: Il Mulino, 2006.
Pivato, Stefano, and Anna Tonelli. *Italia vagabonda: Il tempo libero degli italiani dal melodramma alla pay-tv*. Rome: Carocci, 2001.
Pizzinelli, Corrado. *Moro*. Milan: Longanesi, 1969.
———. *Scelba*. Milan: Longanesi, 1982.
Poggi, Gianfranco. *Catholic Action in Italy: The Sociology of a Sponsored Organizaton*. Stanford, Calif.: Stanford University Press, 1967.
Pojmann, Wendy. *Italian Women and International Cold War Politics, 1944–1968*. New York: Fordham University Press, 2013.
Polidoro, Massimo. *Cronaca nera: Indagini sui delitti che hanno sconvolto l'Italia*. Farigliano: Edizioni Piemme, 2005.
Pollard, John. *The Vatican and Italian Fascism, 1929–1932: A Study in Conflict*. New York: Cambridge University Press, 1985.
———. *Catholicism in Modern Italy: Religion, Society and Politics since 1861*. New York: Routledge, 2008.
———. *The Papacy in the Age of Totalitarianism, 1914–1958*. Oxford: Oxford University Press, 2014.
Pombeni, Paolo. *Le Cronache Sociali di Dossetti, 1947–1951: Geografia di un movimento di opinione*. Florence: Vallecchi, 1976.
Pompei, Gian Franco. *Un ambasciatore in Vaticano: Diario 1967–1977*. Bologna: Il Mulino, 1994.
Popkin, Richard H. *The History of Scepticism from Erasmus to Descartes*. Assen, Netherlands: Royal Van Gorcum, 1964.
Pratt, Jeff C. *The Walled City: A Study of Social Change and Conservative Ideologies in Tuscany*. Aachen: Rader Verlag, 1986.
Preziosi, Ernesto, ed. *Storia dell'Azione Cattolica: La presenza nella Chiesa e nella società italiana*. Soveria Mannelli: Rubbettino, 2008.
———, ed. *Luigi Gedda nella storia della Chiesa e del Paese*. Rome: AVE, 2013.
Puma, Pascale Budillon. *La Biennale di Venezia: Dalla guerra alla crisi 1948–1968*. Bari: Casa Editrice Palomar, 1995.
Puppa, Paolo. *Teatro e spettacolo nel secondo novecento*. Rome-Bari: Laterza, 1990.
Quaglietti, Lorenzo. *Storia economico-politica del cinema italiano, 1945–1990*. Rome: Riuniti, 1980.
Rapela Heidt, Mari. "Development, Nations, and 'The Signs of the Times': The Historical Context of *Populorum Progressio*." *Journal of Moral Theology* 6, no. 1 (2017).
Rascaroli, Laura, and John David Rhodes. *Antonioni Centenary Essays*. London: BFI Palgrave Macmillan, 2011.
Riall, Lucy. *Risorgimento: The History of Italy from Napoleon to Nation State*. London and New York: Palgrave Macmillan, 2009.
Ribera, Daniela. "Maria Pia Dal Canton e la riforma di assistenza familiare in Italia negli anni Cinquanta." *Vita e pensiero* (2004): 267–84.
Riccardi, Andrea. *Roma "città sacra"? Dalla Conciliazione all'operazione Sturzo*. Milan: Vita e Pensiero, 1979.
———. *Il "Partito Romano" nel secondo dopoguerra*. Brescia: Morcelliana, 1983.
———, ed. *Pio XII*. Rome and Bari: Laterza, 1984.

———, ed. *Le Chiese di Pio XII*. Rome and Bari: Laterza, 1986.

———. *Il Potere del papa da Pio XII a Paolo VI*. Rome and Bari: Laterza, 1988.

———. *Il Vaticano e mosca*. Rome and Bari: Laterza, 1992.

———. *Vescovi d'Italia: Storia e profili del Novecento*. Milan: Edizioni San Paolo, 2000.

———. *Pio XII e Alcide De Gasperi: Una Storia segreta*. Rome-Bari: Laterza, 2003.

———. "Roma 1974 terra di missione: Anniversario del convegno voluto 40 anni fa dal cardinal Poletti." February 14, 2014. https://andreariccardi.it/roma-1974-terra-di-missione-anniversario-del-convegno-voluto-40-anni-fa-dal-cardinal-poletti/. Accessed December 19, 2019.

Riccardo, Domenico. *La familia e il divozio*. Bari: Laterza, 1956.

Richards, Peter G. *Parliament and Conscience*. London: George Allen and Unwin, 1970.

Risso, Linda. "'How She Died We Will Never Know': The Montesi Affair and the Christian Democratic Party." In *Laboratorio di nuova ricerca: Investigating Gender, Translation and Culture in Italian Studies*, edited by Monica Boria and Linda Risso. Leicester: Troubador, 2007.

Robinson, W. Sydney. *The Last Victorians: A Daring Reassessment of Four Twentieth-Century Eccentrics—Sir William Joynson Hicks; Dean Inge; Lord Reith; and Sir Arthur Bryant*. London: Robson, 2014.

Rochat, Giorgio. *Regime fascista e Chiese evangeliche*. Turin: Claudiana, 1990.

Rohdie, Sam. *The Passion of Pier Paolo Pasolini*. London: British Film Institute; Bloomington: Indiana University Press, 1995.

Romano, Angelo. *Ernesto Ruffini: Cardinale arcivescovo di Palermo (1946–1967)*. Rome: Salvatore Sciascia Editore, 2002.

Rondolino, Gianni. *Luchino Visconti*. Turin: UTET Libreria, 2006.

Rosa, Mario, ed. *Clero e società nell'Italia contemporanea*. Rome and Bari: Laterza, 1992.

Rosati, Domenico. *L'Incudine e la croce: Mezzo secolo di AC*. Turin: Edizioni Sonda, 1994.

Rossi Barilli, Gianni. *Il Movimento gay in Italia*. Milan: Feltrinelli, 1999.

Rossi, Ernesto. *Conciliazione*. Florence: Parenti Editore, 1959.

Rossini, Giuseppe, ed. *I Cattolici italiani nei tempi nuovi della Cristianità: Atti del convegno di studio della democrazia cristiana, Lucca 28–30 Aprile 1967*. Rome: Cinque lune, 1967.

———. *Modernismo, Fascismo, Comunismo: Aspetti e figure della cultura e della politica dei cattolici nel '900*. Bologna: Il Mulino, 1972.

———. *Democrazia cristiana e Costituente nella società del dopoguerra: Bilancio storiografico e prospettive di ricercar; Atti del convegno di studio tenuto a Milano il 26–28 gennaio 1979*. Rome: Cinque Lune, 1980.

———. *De Gasperi nell'et à del centrismo*. Rome: Cinque Lune, 1984.

Rovea, Giuseppe. *Vi presento il C.T.G.* Rome: Tipografia della G.I.A.C. "G. De Gregorio," 1957.

Ruffini, Attilio. *La grande tentazione*. Palermo: S. F. Flaccovio Editore, 1966.

Rumble, Patrick, and Bart Testa. *Pier Paolo Pasolini: Contemporary Perspectives*. Toronto, Buffalo, and London: University of Toronto Press, 1994.

Rumor, Mariano. *La D.C. e I problemi della società italiana: Relazione di chiusura del Segretario Politico alla Assemblea Nazionale della Democrazia Cristiana. Sorrento, 3 Novembre 1965*. Rome: Cinque Lune, 1966.

———. *Memorie (1943–1970)*. Edited by Ermeneglido Reato e Francesco Malgeri. Vicenza: Neri Pozza Editore, 1991.

Ruozzi, Federico. *Il concilio in diretta: Il Vaticano II e la televisione tra informazione e partecipazione*. Bologna: il Mulino, 2012.

Rynne, Xavier. *Vatican Council II*. New York: Farrar, Straus and Giroux, 1968.

Sabbatucci, G., and V. Vidotto, eds. *Storia d'Italia*. Vol. 6, *L'Italia contemporanea*. Rome and Bari: Laterza, 1999.

Sainati, Augusto, ed. *La settimana incom: Cinegiornali informazione negli anni '50*. Turin: Lindau, 2001.

Sale, Giovanni. *Dalla Monarchia alla repubblica: Santa sede, cattolici italiani e referendum*. Milan: Jaca, 2003.

Salemi, Giancarlo, and Gianni Martinelli. *Guido Gonella il giornalista*. Trieste: Edizioni Goliardiche, 2005.

Saler, Michael. "Modernity and Enchantment: A Historiographic Review." *American Historical Review* 111, no. 3 (June 2006): 692–716.

San Biagio Monastery, ed. *Filiberto Guala: L'imprenditore di Dio*. Casale Monferrato: Piemme, 2001.

Sanguinetti, Tatti, ed. *Totò e Carolina*. Ancona: Transeuropa, 1999.

Sansone, Luigi Renato. *I fuorilegge del matrimonio*. Milan and Rome: Edizioni Avanti!, 1956.

Sani, Roberto. *Roma cattolica*. Brescia: Morcelliana, 1986.

———. *"La civiltà Cattolica" e la politica italiana nel secondo dopoguerra (1945–1958)*. Milan: Vita e Pensiero, 2004.

Santini, Alceste. *Stato e chiesa nel processo contro il Vescovo di Prato*. Rome: Editore Giovanni Semerano, 1958.

Saraceno, Chiara. "The Italian Family from the 1960s to the Present." *Modern Italy* 9, no. 1 (2004).

Saresella, Daniela. *Cattolicesimo italiano e sfida Americana*. Brescia: Morcelliana, 2001.

———. *Dal Concilio alla contestazione: Riviste cattoliche negli anni del cambiamento (1958–1968)*. Brescia: Morcelliana, 2005.

———. *David Turoldo: Camillo De Piaz e la Corsia dei Servi di Milano (1943–1963)*. Brescia: Morcelliana, 2008.

———. *Cattolici a sinistra: Dal modernismo ai giorni nostri*. Rome and Bari: Laterza, 2011.

———. "Ecclesial Dissent in Italy in the Sixties." *Catholic Historical Review* 102, no. 1 (Winter 2016).

Sartori, F. *Partiti e sistemi di partito*. Florence: Editrice universitaria, 1965.

Scarpari, Giancarlo. *La democrazia cristiana e le leggi eccezionali,1950–1953*. Milan: Feltrinelli, 1977.

Scartezzini, Ricardo, and Carlo Tullio-Altan. *Una modernizzazione difficile: Aspetti critici della società italiana*. Naples: Liguori, 1992.

Scelba, Mario. *La Democrazia Cristiana davanti all'VIII Congresso di Napoli*. Rome: Quaderni di "Centrismo Popolare," 1962.

———. *Per l'Italia e per l'Europa*. Rome: Cinque Lune, 1990.

———. *Discorsi parlamentari*. 2 vols. Rome: Senato della repubblica, 1996.

Schacherl, Bruno. *Il critico errante: Anni Sessanta e dintorni a teatro in cerca di Storia*. Florence: Le Lettere, 2005.

Schloesser, Stephen. *Jazz Age Catholicism: Mystic Modernism in Postwar Paris 1919–1933*. Toronto: University of Toronto Press, 2005.

Schultz, Kevin M. "Secularization: A Bibliographic Essay." *Hedgehog Review* 8, nos. 1 and 2 (Spring–Summer 2006): 170–77.

Schwartz, Barth David. *Pasolini Requiem*. New York: Pantheon, 1992.

Scirè, Giambattista. *La democrazia alla prova: Cattolici e laici nell'Italia repubblicana degli anni Cinquanta e Sessanta*. Rome: Carocci, 2005.

———. *Il divorzio in Italia: Partiti, chiesa, società civile dalle legge al referendum (1965–1974)*. Milan: Mondadori, 2007.

Scoppola, Pietro. *La Nuova cristianità perduta*. Rome: Studium, 1986.

———. *La Proposta politica di De Gasperi*. Bologna: Il Mulino, 1988.

———. *25 Aprile, liberazione*. Turin: Einaudi, 1995.

———. *La repubblica dei partiti: Evoluzione e crisi di un sistema politico 1945–1996*. Bologna: Il Mulino, 1997.

Scotto di Luzio, Adolfo. *Il Pci e la scuola laica alla constituente: Storia di due manifesti*. Bobst Main: Contemporanea, 2006.

Scrivano, Paolo. "Signs of Americanization in Italian Domestic Life: Italy's Postwar Conversion to Consumerism." *Journal of Contemporary History* 40, no. 2 (2005): 317–40.

Settimana sociale dei cattolici d'Italia. *Problemi della vita rurale: Atti della XXI Settimana sociale dei cattolici d'Italia, Napoli, 21–28 settembre 1947*. Rome: Edizioni dell'icas, 1948.

Seymour, Mark. *Debating Divorce in Italy: Marriage and the Making of Modern Italians, 1860–1974*. New York: Palgrave, 2006.

Sherry, Patrick. "Disenchantment, Re-enchantment and Enchantment." *Modern Theology* 25, no. 3 (July 2009).

Siri, Giuseppe. *Il primato della verità: Lettere pastorali sull'ortodossia*. Edited by Nicola Lanzi. Pisa: Giardini Editori E Stampatori, 1984.

Smith, Denis Mack. *Italy and Its Monarchy*. New Haven, Conn.: Yale University Press, 1989.

Solmi, Angelo. *Storia di Federico Fellini*. Milan: Rizzoli, 1962.

———. *Cinema, specchio del tempo: Una storia del cinema in rapporto al costume*. Brescia: La Scuola, 1963.

Sorge, Bartolomeo. *La "ricomposizione" dell'area cattolica in Italia*. Rome: Città Nuova Editrice, 1979.

Sorgi, Claudio. *Il cristianesimo di Rossellini*. Rome: Erredici, 1977.

Sorlin, Pierre. *Italian National Cinema 1896–1996*. London: Routledge, 1996.

Spadolini, Giovanni. *Il tevere più largo*. Napoli: Morano. 1967.

———. *L'Opposizione cattolica da Porta Pia al '98*. Milan: Mondadori, 1994.

Spiazzi, Raimondo. *La missione dei laici*. Rome: Edizioni la presenza, 1951.

———. *Essenza e contemporaneità della chiesa*. Turin: Società Editrice Internazionale, 1953.

———. *Il Cardinale Giuseppe Siri: Arcivescovo di Genova dal 1946 al 1987; La vita, l'insegnamento, L'ererdità spirituale, le memorie*. Bologna: Edizioni Studio Domenicano, 1990.

Sportelli, Francesco. *La Conferenza episcopale italiana (1952–1972)*. Galatina: Congedo, 1994.

Spotts, Frederic, and Theodor Wieser. *Italy: A Difficult Democracy*. New York: Cambridge University Press, 1986.

Stagno, Cristina, ed. *Censura ecclesiastica e cultura politica in Italia tra cinquecento e seicento*. Florence: Leo S. Olschki editore, 1999.

Stajano, Corrado, and Franco Angelini, eds. *La cultura italiana del Novecento*. Rome: Laterza, 1996.

Stephen, Alexander, ed. *The Americanization of Europe*. New York: Berghahn, 2006.

Stewart, Alexander Donald, and Silvia Gavuzzo Stewart. *Gavuzzo and Gavuzzi: The History of a Piedmontese Family from the Middle Ages to the Twentieth Century*. Amelia, Italy: n.p., 2010.

Stone, Marla. *The Patron State Culture and Politics in Fascist Italy*. Princeton, N.J.: Princeton University Press, 1998.

Subini, Tomaso. "La lagrimetta negata nel finale de La dolce vita." In *Federico Fellini: Analisi di film; Possibili letture*, edited by Raffaele De Berti, 49–74. Milan: McGraw–Hill, 2006. Available at https://users.unimi.it/cinema/Tomaso_Subini_-_Pubblicazioni_files/Subini_Dolce%20vita.pdf. Accessed January 13, 2015.

———. *La necessità di morire: Il cinema di Pier Paolo Pasolini e il sacro*. Rome: Ente dello spettacolo, 2007.

———. *Pier Paolo Pasolini: La ricotta*. Turin: Lindau, 2009.

———. *La Doppia vita di 'Francesco Giullare di Dio," Giulio Andreotti, Félix Morlion e Roberto Rossellini*. Milan: Lampi di stampa, 2011.

Swatos, William, and Daniel V. A. Olson, eds. *The Secularization Debate*. Lanham, Md.: Rowman and Littlefield, 2000.

Tambor, Molly. *The Lost Wave: Women and Democracy in Postwar Italy*. Oxford: Oxford University Press, 2014.

Tarantini, Domenico. *Processo allo spettacolo*. Milan: Edizioni di Comunità, 1961.

Taricone, Fiorenza. *Il centro italiano femminile: Dalle orgini agli anni Settanta*. Milan: FrancoAngeli, 2001.

Tassani, Giovanni. *La cultura politica della destra cattolica*. Rome: Coines, 1976.

Taylor, Charles. *A Secular Age*. Cambridge, Mass.: Harvard University Press, 2007.

Tedeschi, Mario. *Roma democristiana*. Milan: Longanesi, 1956.

Tentler, Leslie Woodcock, ed. *The Church Confronts Modernity: Catholicism since 1950 in the United States, Ireland and Quebec*. Washington, D.C.: The Catholic University of America Press, 2007.

Teodori, Massimo. *Storia dei laici nell'Italia clericale e comunista*. Venice: Marsilio, 2008.

———. *Contro i clericali: Dal divorzio al testamento biologico la grande sfida dei laici*. Milan: Longanesi, 2009.

———. *Pannunzio, Dal 'Mondo' al Partito radicale: Vita di un intellettuale del Novecento*. Milan: Mondadori, 2010.

Testori, Giovanni. *Opere 1943–1961*. Edited by Fulvio Panzeri. Milan: Bompiani, 1996.

Tinazzi, Giorgio, ed. *Il cinema italiano degli anni '50*. Venice: Marsilio, 1979.

Tomasi, Tina. *L'Idea laica nell'Italia contemporanea (1870–1970)*. Florence: La Nuova Italia Editrice, 1971.

Tomasino, Renato. *Abbe Lane, Mirella Freni, Valeria Moriconi, Amy Whitehouse: Quattro sirene*. Alessandria: Edizioni Falsopiano, 2014.

Tornielli, Andrea. *Pio XII: Eugenio Pacelli, Un uomo sul trono di Pietro*. Milan: Mondadori, 2007.

Toschi, Massimo. *Per la chiesa e per gli uomini: Don Giovanni Rossi 1887–1975*. Genoa: Marietti, 1990.

Toschi, Tommaso. *La maschera e il volto: Verità su l'opera antireligiosa del P.C.I.* Bologna: Editrice A.B.E.S., 1952.

Tosi, Giorgio, ed. *La Bilancia e il labarinto: Istruttorie e processi esemplari*. Padua: Il Poligrafo, 2000.

Traniello, Francesco. *Città dell'uomo: Cattolici, partito e stato nella storia d'Italia*. Bologna: Il Mulino, 1990.

———. *Cultura cattolica e vita religiosa tra ottocento e novecento*. Brescia: Morcelliana, 1991.

Traniello, Francesco, and Giorgio Campanini, eds. *Dizionario storico del movimento cattolico in Italia, 1860–1980 I fatti e le idee*. Turin: Marietti, 1981.

Treveri Gennari, Daniela, and Marco Vanelli. "Did Neorealism Start in a Church? Catholicism, Cinema and the Case of Mario Soldati's Chi è Dio." *New Review of Film and Television Studies* 8, no. 2 (June 2010).

Treveri Gennari, Daniela, and Daniel Biltereyst, eds. *Moralizing Cinema: Film, Catholicism and Power*. New York: Routlege, 2014.

Treveri Gennari, Daniela. *Post-War Italian Cinema: American Intervention, Vatican Interests*. New York: Routledge, 2010.

Unione Giuristi Cattolici Italiani, ed. *Quaderni di "Iustitia."* Rome: Giuffrè and Iustitia, 1969.

Vaccaro, Luciano. *Il cristiano laico: L'eredità dell'arcivescovo Montini*. Brescia: Morcelliana, 2004.

Valiani, Leo. *L'avvento di De Gasperi: Tre anni di política italiana*. Turin: F. de Silva, 1949.

Valli, Giuseppe. *La Donna Moderna*. Rome: Edizioni Civitas,1966.

Vecchio, Giorgio. "L'ACI nella nuova stagione del laicato: Indicazioni per una storia del ventennio 1965–1985." In *La generazione del concilio: Tra cronaca e storia*, ed. Rosy Bindy and Agostino Moscatelli. Rome: AVE, 1986.

———, ed. *L'Azione cattolica del Vaticano II: Laicità e scelta religiosa nell'Italia negli anni sessanta e settanta*. Rome: AVE, 2014.

Venditti, Rodolfo. *La Tutela penale del pudore e della pubblica decenza*. Milan: Giuffrè, 1963.

Vené, Gianfranco. *Vola colomba: Vita quotidiana degli Italiani negli anni del dopoguerra, 1945–1960*. Milan: Mondadori, 1992.

Ventresca, Robert. *From Fascism to Democracy: Culture and Politics in the Italian Elections of 1948*. Toronto: University of Toronto Press, 2004.

———. *Soldier of Christ: The Life of Pope Pius XII*. Cambridge, Mass.: Harvard University Press, 2013.

Verdone, Mario. *Gli intelletuali e il cinema: Saggi e documenti*. Rome: Bulzoni 1982.

Vertone, Saverio, ed. *La Cultura degli italiani*. Bologna: il Mulino, 1994.

Versace, Eliana. *Montini e l'aperatura a sinistra: Il falso mito del "vescovo progressista."* Milan: Guerini, 2007.

———. "Giovanni Battista Montini: Paolo VI e la questione del divorzio." *Studium* 110, no. 3 (May–June 2014).

Verucci, Guido. *La Chiesa nella società contemporanea*. Rome and Bari: Laterza, 1988.

———. *La Chiesa cattolica in Italia dall'unità a oggi*. Rome and Bari: Laterza, 1999.

Vian, Gian Maria. "Montini e il divorzio trent'anni dopo." *Vita e pensiero*, no. 3 (2003).

Vidotto, Vittorio. *Roma contemporanea*. Rome and Bari: Laterza, 2001.

Viganò, Dario. *Un Cinema ogni campanile: Chiesa e cinema nella diocesi di Milano*. Milan: Il Castoro, 1997.

———. *Cinema e Chiesa: I documenti del magistero*. Turin: Effatà, 2002.

———. *Pio XII e il cinema*. Rome: Ente dello Spettacolo, 2005.

Voulgaris, Yannis. *L'Italia del centro–sinistra, 1960–1968*. Rome: Carocci, 1998.

Wagnleitner, Reinhold. *Coca-Colonization and the Cold War: The Cultural Mission of the United States in Austria after the Second World War*. Chapel Hill: University of North Carolina Press, 1994.

Wagstaff, Christopher. *Italian Neorealist Cinema: An Aesthetic Approach*. Toronto, Buffalo, and London: University of Toronto Press, 2007.

Walsh, Frank. *Sin and Censorship: The Catholic Church and the Motion Picture Industry*. New Haven, Conn.: Yale University Press, 1996.

Wanrooij, Bruno. "Youth, Generation Conflict and Political Struggle in Twentieth-Century Italy." *European Legacy* 4, no. 1 (1999).

Warner, Rob. *Secularization and Its Discontents*. London and New York: Continuum, 2010.

Watkin, Thomas Glyn. *The Italian Legal Tradition*. Dartmouth: Ashgate, 1997.

Weber, Max. *From Max Weber: Essays in Sociology*. Edited by H. H. Gerth and C. Wright Mills. New York: Oxford University Press, 1946.

Webster, Richard. *Christian Democracy in Italy, 1860–1960*. London: Hollis and Carter, 1961.

Werbel, Amy. *Lust on Trial: Censorship and the Rise of American Obscenity in the Age of Anthony Comstock*. New York: Columbia University Press, 2018.

White, Nicola. *Reconstructing Italian Fashion: America and the Development of the Italian Fashion Industry*. New York: Berg, 2000.

Whyte, John H. *Catholics in Western Democracies: A Study in Political Behaviour*. New York: St. Martin's, 1981.

Wickersham, Jane K. *Rituals of Prosecution: The Roman Inquisition and the Prosecution of Philo-Protestants in Sixteenth-Century Italy*. Toronto: University of Toronto Press, 2012.

Willson, Perry. *Women in Twentieth-Century Italy*. New York: Palgrave Macmillan, 2010.

Wolf, E. R., ed. *Religion, Power and Protest in Local Communities*. Berlin: Mouton, 1984.

Wollenburg, Leo. *Stars, Stripes, and Tricolor*. New York: Praeger, 1990.

Young, Kathleen Z. "The Imperishable Virginity of Saint Maria Goretti." *Gender and Society* 3, no. 4 (December 1989).

Young, Wayland. *The Montesi Scandal*. New York: Doubleday, 1958.

Zanchini di Castiglionchio, Francesco. *Chiesa e potere: Studi sul potere costituente nella chiesa*. Turin: G. Giappichelli, 1992.

Zizola, Giancarlo. "I vescovi e il referendum." *Testimonianze*, April–May, 1974.

———. *Il Microfono di dio: Pio XII, Padre Lombardi e i cattolici italiani*. Milan: Mondadori, 1990.

———. *Don Giovanni Rossi: L'Utopia cristiana nell'Italia del '900*. Assisi: Citadella Editrice, 1997.

———. "Carlo Carretto nella vita della Chiesa cattolica in Italia." *Cristianesimo nella Storia* 28 (May–August 2007).

Zoppi, Sergio. *De Gasperi e la nuova Italia: Le riforme negli anni difficili e l'affermazione della vita democratica*. Soveria Mannelli: Rubbettino, 2004.

Zucchi, John. "Luigi Giussani, the Church, and Youth in the 1950s: A Judgment Born of an Experience." *Logos: A Journal of Catholic Thought and Culture* 10, no. 4 (2007).

Index

The Devil and the "Dolce Vita": Catholic Attempts to Save Italy's Soul, 1948–1974, was designed in Quadraat with Quadraat Sans, Bebas Neue, and Marvin display type and composed by Kachergis Book Design of Pittsboro, North Carolina. It was printed on 55-pound Natural Hi Bulk and bound by Data Reproductions of Auburn Hills, Michigan.